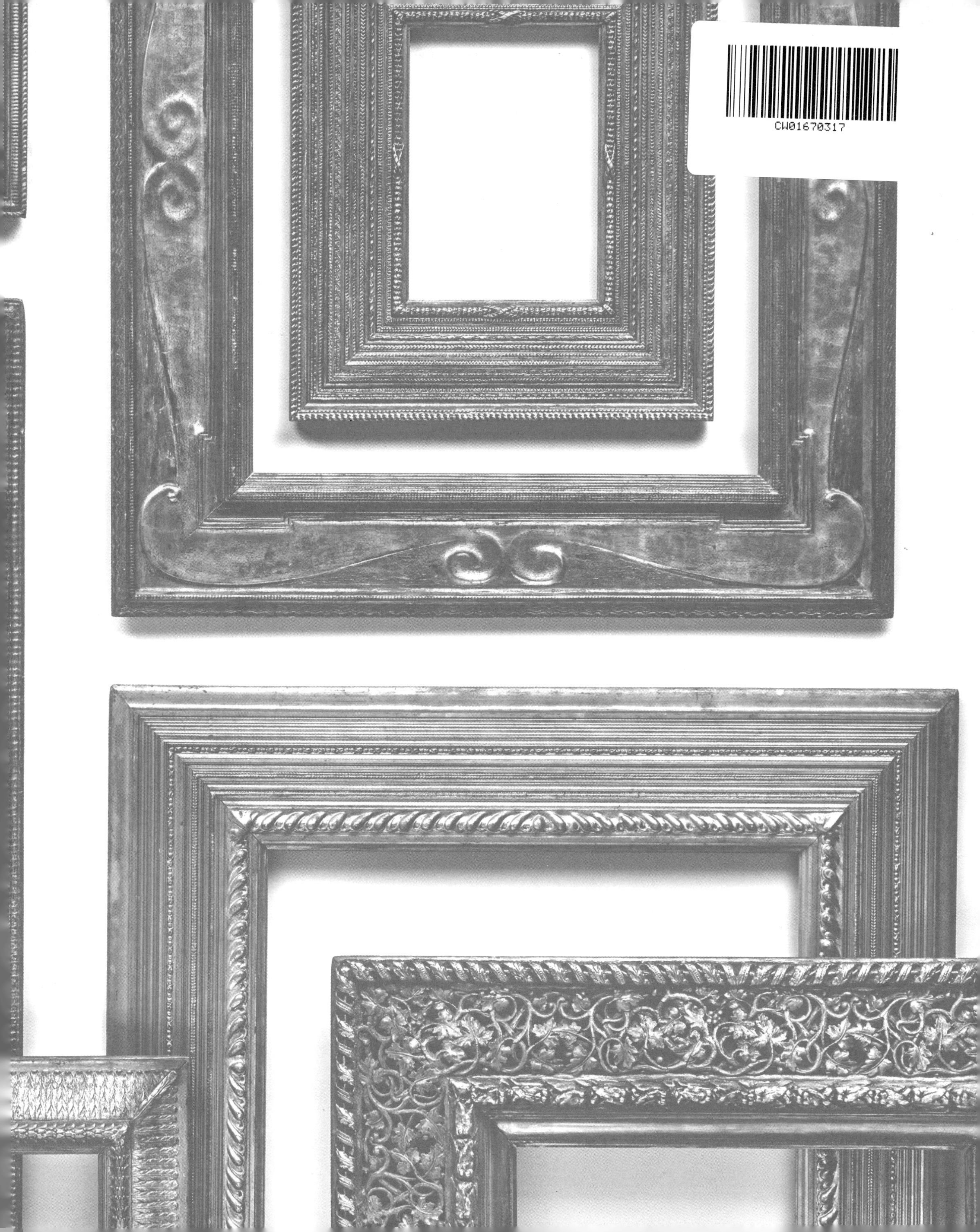

American Art
Collecting and Connoisseurship

To Linda, Alexandra, and Huntington

To present and past members of the Atlanta Art Forum

To special friends, curators, gallerists, dealers, advisors, and
so many others who have made our journey in art
so meaningful and stimulating

American Art
Collecting and Connoisseurship

General Editor
Stephen M. Sessler

Foreword by
Elizabeth Broun

MERRELL
LONDON • NEW YORK

CONTENTS

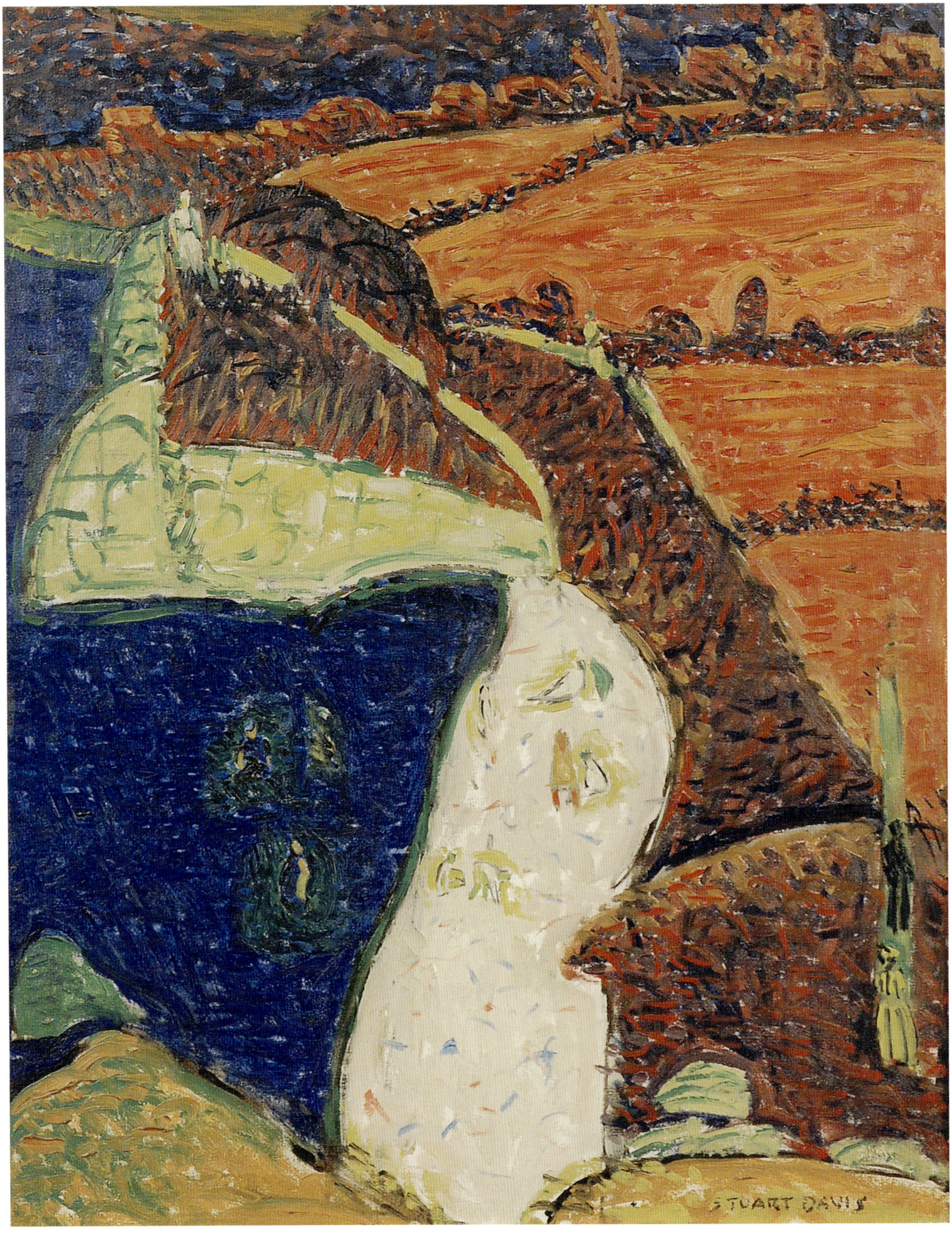
STUART DAVIS

Preface

Stephen M. Sessler

As active collectors of historical American art, my wife Linda and I became supporters of the High Museum of Art in Atlanta and joined its American art support group in the early 1990s. Membership and leadership in that group, then called the Fine Art Collectors, was a tremendously enjoyable and rewarding experience. Not only were we afforded closer access to the museum curators and staff, but the programs sponsored by the Fine Art Collectors, though limited, were always a learning experience and one of the activities that helped develop our appreciation of and "eye" for art. The highlight of each program year was always the group trip. Most frequently, we traveled to New York in early December for American Art Week to attend the auctions and to visit private collections, gallery receptions and museum exhibitions. But the Fine Art Collectors organized other memorable trips as well: to northern France to follow in the footsteps of the Impressionists, to New England to John Twachtman's home and environs, and to Boston, Philadelphia, and the Hudson River Valley. It is hard to overstate the importance of these trips for our appreciation of art and growth as collectors.

By the mid-2000s, art had become an increasingly significant part of our lives, and we seized every opportunity to see, learn, and grow in our knowledge and understanding of our chosen field. While the Fine Art Collectors group was our primary focus, we found that we wanted more information and more opportunities to meet with and discuss historical American art with experts and other collectors. With that goal in mind, I founded the Atlanta Art Forum in 2006. Completely by coincidence and unbeknownst to me at the time, the High Museum of Art had decided to scale back significantly all museum support group activities, citing the excessive burdens those activities, especially travel planning, placed on the curatorial staff. So, serendipitously, the Atlanta Art Forum came into being at a time when there was a vacuum to be filled.

The plan was relatively simple: five programs a year, each hosted in a member's home (with beverages and light hors d'oeuvres), time for socializing, and a formal program presented by an invited speaker. Drawing members into this new group went slowly at first but as the quality of the programs became known, the group quickly grew and attracted both former members of the Fine Art Collectors and new members. Speakers invited represented a virtual who's who in the art world. The programs were so insightful and stimulating that members frequently kept speakers involved in conversations long past the end of the program. In 2018, the Atlanta Art Forum consisted of roughly sixty people, including collectors, curators, art advisors,

1.
Stuart Davis (1892–1964)
Rockport Beach (A Cove)
1916
Oil on canvas
30 × 24 in. (76.2 × 60.9 cm)
Signed lower right, inscribed, signed and dated on the top stretcher
Collection of Stephen and Linda Sessler, Atlanta, Georgia

and people just interested in learning more about historical American art.

The Atlanta Art Forum is also the genesis of this book. At the end of the 2018–2019 year, I could not help but think that the information and knowledge we had been so privileged to acquire for the past twelve years should also be available to a much wider audience. Thus, many (but not all) of the chapter authors are past speakers at Atlanta Art Forum programs.

As with most worthwhile endeavors, many people have made significant contributions to this effort: the authors who gave graciously of their time and expertise with no remuneration; the extraordinarily generous sponsors; Merrell Publishing, especially Hugh Merrell, Elisabeth Ingles, Nicola Bailey, and Nick Wheldon; and Atlanta Art Forum members Jack Huber and Matt Kendall who encouraged, challenged, corrected, and supported me.

The market and the interest in historical American art have undergone a dramatic shift in the past ten to fifteen years as contemporary art has become the standard-bearer for the art market in general: auctions that used to be wholesale are now retail plus; galleries that once specialized only in historical American art have either closed, converted to private dealer status, or have changed their business model to modern and contemporary; inventory-based galleries now operate on a consignment model, and some dealers have resorted to serving as art advisors. And of course, art price databases widely available on the internet have altered the landscape dramatically, providing a useful but incomplete summary of auction sales, frequently giving potential buyers a false sense of the real market. Why incomplete? These databases contain no assessment about the uniqueness or quality of a given work within that artist's œuvre, condition (one of the primary factors in determining a painting's value), provenance, or any other detailed relevant information about a painting or an artist's market. Nor do art price databases include any information about private sales, either by galleries and dealers or by auction houses. Thus, while one can easily research the record auction price for an artist, that may or may not be an accurate reflection of the artist's best and most desirable works.

By revisiting historical American art from many different angles and perspectives, it is hoped that this collection of chapters will remind collectors, curators, and the art market as a whole of the value and intrinsic worth that still exist in this field that has stood the test of time so well.

JUNE 2019

Foreword

Elizabeth Broun, PhD
Director Emerita, Smithsonian American Art Museum and Renwick Gallery

In 2006, an Atlanta collector named Stephen Sessler decided to invite a handful of knowledgeable experts to the city to speak to friends and collectors interested in American art. At first the groups were of a size to meet in a modest living room and the members rotated homes. As word of the quality of the programs spread and more people asked to join, the number of members became more than most hosts could comfortably accommodate. So, to maintain both the social aspect of the group and a serious learning environment, the program sign-up RSVP process was modified to a first-come-first-served basis, with the host establishing the maximum number of members that could attend any given program. So began the Atlanta Art Forum, which continues to prosper after twelve years as a veritable graduate seminar in American art, with Sessler as the visionary "dean."

Over the past dozen years, Sessler maintained a schedule of five programs a year, covering an ever-widening range of topics of interest to collectors. In the first season, the subjects formed a basic primer, including "Conservation," "Assessing Quality and Value," "Buying/Selling Through Dealers/Galleries," "Frames," and "Investing in Art." But over the years the topics grew more sophisticated, exploring the nuances and purposes of art collecting generally, and of American art specifically.

Sessler brought to town guest speakers who were at the top of their fields. An equal number of twenty-one curators (from fifteen different museums) and twenty-one gallerists and auction specialists formed the core "faculty." Leavening this mix were four lawyers, three conservators, two art magazine editors, one businessman, experts on framing and lighting, and more. Topics ranged from very broad—"Directions in American Art Scholarship" and "Connecting Historical American Art to a Modern World"—to nuts-and-bolts discussions on "Fakes," "Thefts," "Donations, Gifts, and Estate Planning," and "Legal Issues for the Collector."

During the past twelve years of the Atlanta Art Forum, some of the best experts in the field of American art were showcased there, as word spread among professionals that this was a serious and sophisticated group, eager for knowledge, with a gracious host handling all arrangements, well worth the time taken from busy schedules. Soon, Atlanta, with its several important and growing collections, was "on the map" as a major site for American art.

Delving deeper into the inspiration for this unique independent collectors' group, we find motivations both general and specific. The whole field of American art experienced a Golden Age in the 1990s and 2000s, and by 2006 it had powerful momentum. Everywhere across the country there was talk of globalization, and this led curators and art collectors to reconsider the unique history of the United States, taking pride that it was the first nation ever to welcome new citizens from every country on earth, all invited to create a shared path to a future of leadership and progress. "Globalization," according to those knowledgeable about historical American art, had been the remit of the United States since the beginning.

The evidence of that evolution could be traced in America's art, especially between the mid-nineteenth and mid-twentieth centuries. Artists went to France to study after the Civil War, bringing home an Impressionist palette and a focus on fresh "found subjects" in the city and countryside, rather than tired academic studio subjects. Then the revolutionary Ashcan School artists took to the streets to paint the everyday experience of a new demographic in the cities, a rapidly changing mix of immigrants and the moneyed élite. Early Modernists followed, with their avant-garde formalist principles and dynamic abstraction, signaling a headlong rush to the future. Each wave of stylistic change testified to a newly empowered nation assuming greater leadership on the world stage, defining what would later be called "The American Century."

Inspiration for the Atlanta Art Forum came in other ways too. There was sudden generational change among collectors, as four of the most significant early figures, all of whom began collecting in the mid-twentieth century, died in quick succession, releasing to the market some of the most prized artworks in the canon. First was Arthur G. Altschul in 2002, whom Sotheby's called "one of the legendary figures in the American paintings field." In 2003, artworks from the collection of the late Meyer and Vivian Potamkin came to Sotheby's. In 2004, the doyenne of American art collecting, Rita Fraad, died, and again Sotheby's hosted a celebrated sale of the works she had amassed with her late husband, Daniel. Finally, in 2005, the passing of Ray Horowitz ended a sixty-year journey in collecting with his wife, Margaret. Each of these pioneers had served on multiple museum boards and enjoyed single-collector exhibitions in museums in New York, Washington, or Philadelphia. Each gave generously to museums, but still saved some of their greatest treasures—Childe Hassam's *The Room of Flowers* for Altschul, George Bellows's *Kids* for Fraad, among many others—for the auction block, attracting collectors and museum professionals from around the country for eagerly awaited "must-see" events. Even as museum curators grieved the loss of possible donations, the releasing of such treasures on to the market energized new collectors and led to a generational transformation and exciting ferment in the field. Mostly they were priced out of reach for museums, so they devolved into private collections; sometimes, as with Alice Walton's collection, they did eventually find their way into museums, including the breathtaking Crystal Bridges Museum of American Art in Bentonville, Arkansas.

The collegiality among collectors of American art during these decades was often recognized as dramatically different from the often secret competitive collecting in other art fields. Collectors of American art felt they were compatriots in a common cause, exploring the way this country developed through the aesthetic expressions of our best artists. Not only the "big four" collectors just cited, but more recent collectors too, often visited each other's collections, chatted openly about which auction works they intended to bid for, and traded knowledge, contacts, and expertise. Group trips, lunches and dinners, museum openings, and pilgrimages to hard-to-reach but celebrated collections (Jack Warner's vast holdings in Alabama, for instance), forged far-ranging friendships around the country, creating a commitment to public service, even as they contributed to the market buzz.

Yet, while the market for traditional American art flourished, there were early warning signs of a decisive turn among collectors and museums in the direction of contemporary art. In part, the need for the Atlanta Art Forum grew from this sharp redirection at the High Museum of Art. With museum acquisition funds and exhibition galleries increasingly devoted to contemporary artists, Atlanta's burgeoning community of traditional American art collectors felt a void. Sessler, a mechanical engineer by education and a longtime partner at a large consulting engineering firm, stepped forward to offer a new private model. Over a dozen exciting years, he spearheaded the initiative, offering exceptional leadership and extending awareness of Atlanta collections among art professionals everywhere.

Now comes this book, which is the culmination of these inspired efforts, and again we have Stephen Sessler—supported as always by Linda, his wife and colleague in collecting. Speakers from the twelve-year history of the Atlanta Art Forum were invited to contribute "chapterettes" on the collecting experience; once again they offer a wide-ranging view of the field. The assembled book is a labor of love for Sessler and for the authors, who offer their submissions without payment.

The twenty-eight chapters fall into three groups: Part I, "The Historical Overview," in which the writers discuss what American art is and how it has developed; Part II, "Connoisseurship and the Collector," covering topics that enable the collector to sharpen his or her connoisseur's eye; Part III, "Changes in the Art Market," examining how the market trends are developing and what to look out for.

Coordinating so many voices is an organizational triumph, and surely this volume captures the thrill of a movement that taught us so much about our country and ourselves, as well as our artists. Together, Stephen Sessler, the many authors here, and Merrell Publishers have made a lasting contribution to the nation.

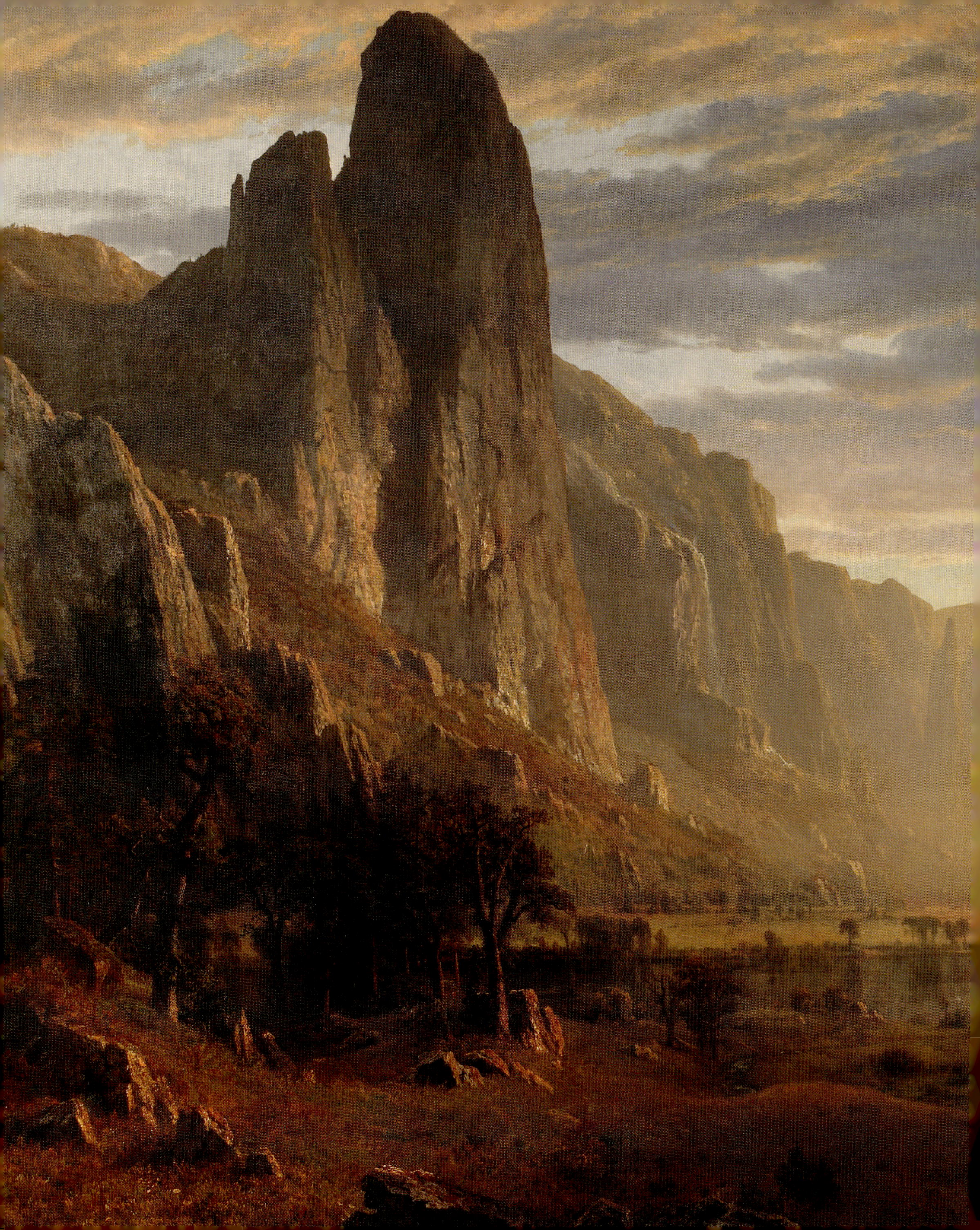

I. The Historical Overview

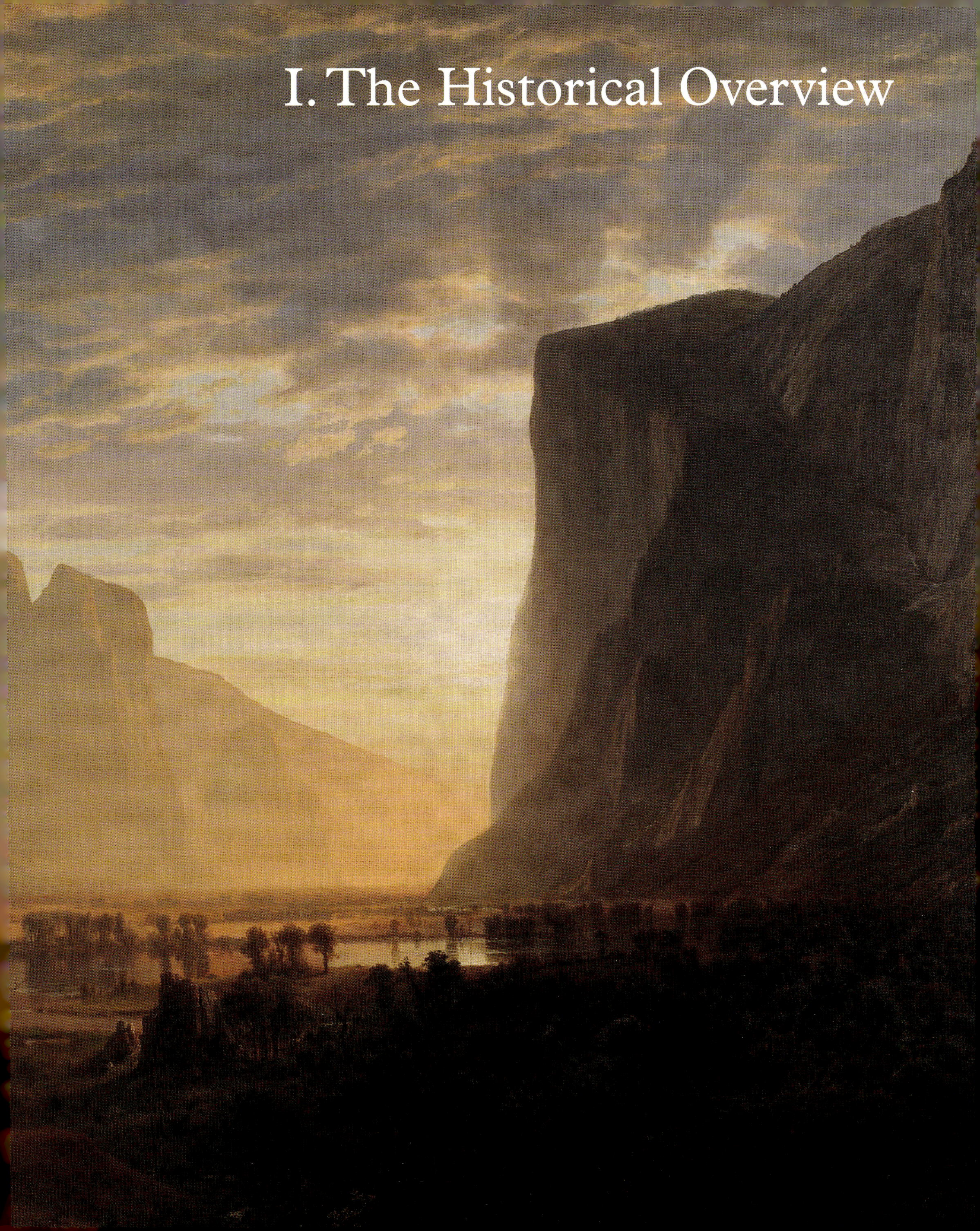

The Hudson River School
The Genesis of a Uniquely American Art

Louis M. Salerno
Owner, Questroyal Fine Art, LLC, New York

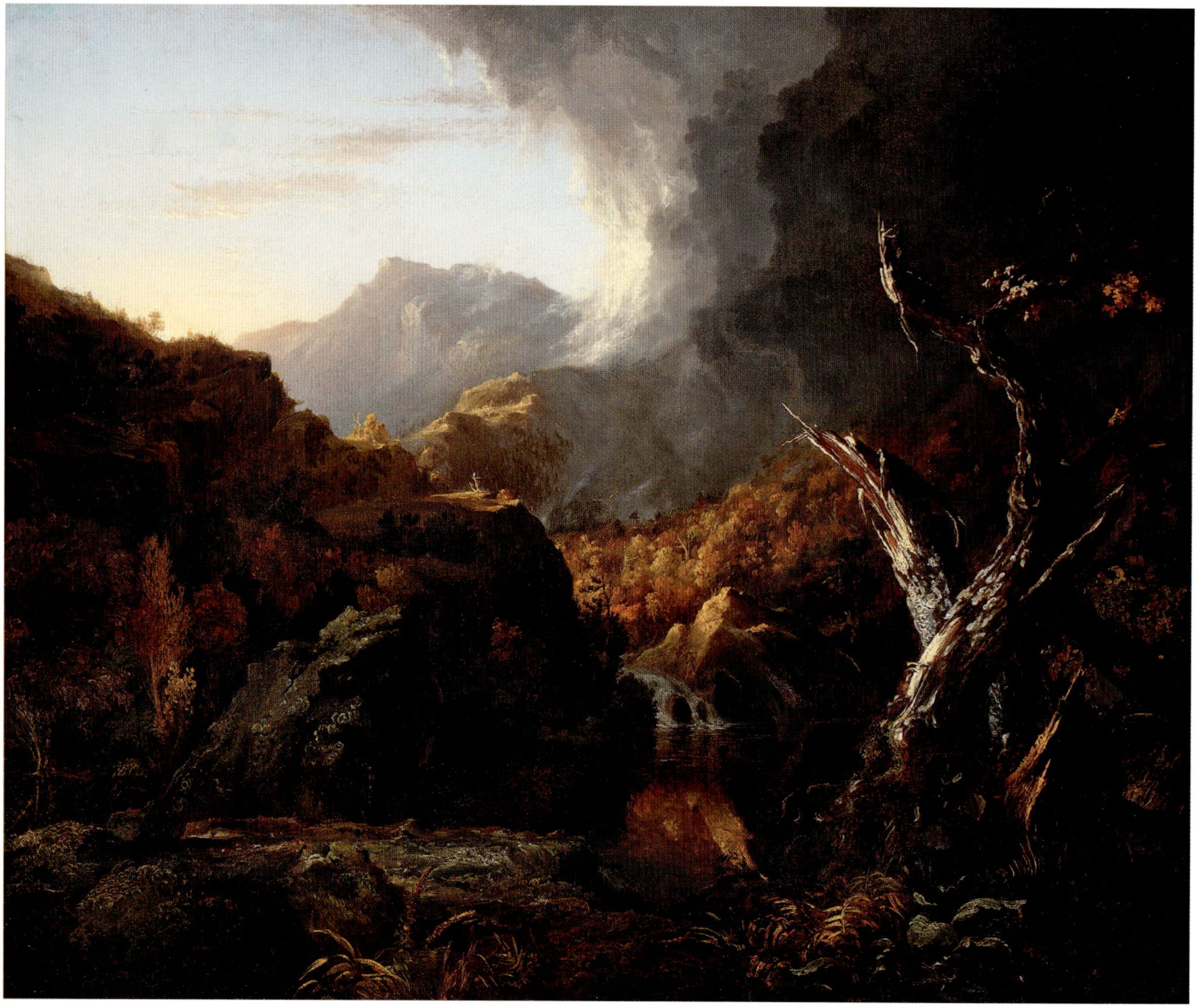

The unprecedented images conceived by the American landscape painters of the nineteenth century defied European artistic conventions. The poet William Cullen Bryant (1794–1878) recognized that the incredible wonder of the untainted American wilderness was the singular impetus of an original American art:

Pictures which carried the eye over scenes of wild grandeur peculiar to our country, over our aërial mountain-tops with their mighty growth of forest never touched by the axe, along the banks of streams never deformed by culture, and into the depth of skies bright with the hues of our own climate; … and through the transparent abysses of which it seemed that you might send an arrow out of sight.[1]

Like all innovators, these artists were doubted and criticized, thought to be too provincial and unsophisticated, ignoring and defying established practices. Sometime during the 1870s, a critic referred to their work as the "Hudson River School."[2] The term was intended to be derogatory and antagonistic, calling attention to an absence of schooling and, by implication, an art that lacked quality; however, the essence of the Hudson River School was to be found in each artist's highly personalized acquaintance with nature, which would have been hindered by formal training. Asher B. Durand (1796–1886), one of the era's most distinguished artists, cautioned young painters to avoid instruction. He urged them to go to the "Studio of Nature" first so that a personal response could be preserved.[3] Thomas Cole (1801–1848), considered to be the founder of this so-called school, advised artists not to adhere to precedents and to recognize the value of individuality.[4]

Today we marvel at the evolution of our nation's art, its astounding transitions to abstraction and beyond, often without recognizing the essential contributions arising from the free and defiant mindset of our Hudson River School painters. In their willingness to immerse themselves in nature and to allow their creativity to supersede convention, they made an indelible contribution to the art of the world.

A VISUAL POETRY

The Hudson River School painters thought that by rendering nature precisely, they might reveal its ethereal truths. This concept gave rise to a creative dilemma. The result of a strict adherence to the real would be a sterile imitation, an absence of truth. Conversely, if the ideal were overemphasized, the artist might contradict nature and obscure the truth.

In an 1826 letter, Cole was advised by a patron to paint all aspects of his landscape precisely as they appeared. He responded:

If the imagination is shackled, and nothing is described but what we see, seldom will anything truly great be produced either in Painting or Poetry…. I believe with you that it is of the greatest importance for a painter always to have his mind upon Nature…. He who would paint compositions, and not be false, must sit down amidst his sketches, make selections, and combine them, and so have nature for every object that he paints.[5]

Similarly, in a letter to the art newspaper *Crayon*, Durand directly examined the issue of the real and ideal. He wrote:

What then is Idealism?… That picture is ideal whose component parts are representative of the utmost perfection of Nature, … and also the most perfect arrangement or composition of these parts so as to form an equally perfect whole…. The artist must know what constitutes the perfection of every object employed, according to its kind, and its circumstances, so as to be able to gather from individuals the collective idea. This view of Idealism does not propose any deviation from the truth….

But the ideal of Landscape Art, does not end here; it embraces, and with even higher meaning, the application of these perfections to the expression of a particular sentiment in the subject of the picture…. In this direction we come to the action of the imaginative faculty, which perfects the high Ideal.[6]

A better understanding of the issue may be found in a musical analogy. If we consider musical notes as analogous to landscape elements, then the painter, like the composer, may rearrange these elements in the development of a composition. As the composer further

Previous page
Albert Bierstadt
Looking Down Yosemite Valley, California, 1865: detail of Fig. 2, page 25

1.
Thomas Cole
(1801–1848)
Landscape (Landscape with Tree Trunks), 1828
Oil on canvas
26 1/8 × 32 1/4 in.
(66.4 × 81.9 cm)
Signed and dated lower center: *T. Cole 1828 Boston*
RISD Museum, Providence, Rhode Island, Walter H. Kimball Fund, 30.063

perfects his work by determining melody and tone, rhythm and volume, the painter shapes and refines by mediating light and shadow, varying color and hue, and adjusting perspective and texture. The composer's nuances must remain within the chromatic scale of the instruments, and the painter's must be truthful variations of observed natural forms and phenomena. The artistic variables of both disciplines enable profound creativity without compromising a fidelity to all the defining compositional elements. The musician may not strike untrue notes, just as the landscape painter may not defile natural form.

Our painters honed an innovation that enabled the full force of their creativity to remain in harmony with the unfathomable designs of a greater power. They would sometimes add mountains that existed miles from a specific location or edit various landforms to give emphasis to the beautiful or to the unattractive. Fallen or decayed trees would be juxtaposed with pristine streams. Tranquil fields on a midsummer's afternoon could be agitated by approaching weather, or, at day's end, a blood-red sky might tint the landscape. An infinite number of variations of natural light and atmosphere could alter the perception of an image. By such selection and ordering, the artists discovered that they could present countenances of nature that would best convey profound meanings. These artists expressed truths derived from nature and resisted any inclination to infuse or apply ideas rooted only in their own imaginations.

With their novel understanding and implementation of nature's own language, the artists composed works of visual poetry and sought, as Durand imagined, the perfection of the real as a way to reach the ideal—this moment marked the genesis of a uniquely American art.

THE BEGINNING

Cole has typically been regarded as the founder of the Hudson River School, in part because of the reaction to three of his paintings that resulted from an 1825 excursion up the Hudson River to the Catskill Mountains. An older American painter, John Trumbull (1756–1843), came upon the paintings when they were on display at a New York City framemaker's shop. He told fellow artist William Dunlap (1766–1839), "This young man has done what all my life I attempted in vain to do."[7] Durand later wrote that the enthusiastic reception of these works "spread like wildfire."[8]

More recent scholarship, however, suggests that canvases by Thomas Doughty (1791–1856) of Philadelphia, executed prior to Cole's 1825 trip, may have in fact informed Cole's approach to finding the best means to express the wild American terrain.[9] With the hindsight of nearly two centuries, Doughty should be acknowledged as a forefather of the Hudson River School; however, Cole's extensive and poetic writing, documenting his ideology and artistic progression and his continued refinements as a painter, together with his untimely death at the height of his career, gave him the greater influence and fame, securing his place as the Hudson River School's founder.

Cole's widely acclaimed landscapes are known for their vigorous brushstrokes, ominous atmospheres, anthropomorphic forms, intense color, and panoramic perspectives—discrete elements that together create the most sublime imagery (Fig. 1). Twisted and dead trees, rocks poised to fall from a cliff's edge, and frightening terrain are common to many of his canvases because he believed in the congruity of nature and was unwilling to edit the imperfect. He thought that strict adherence to an established formula would yield anemic results and therefore proceeded in accord with his imagination—but not so far as to be in contradiction to nature. His art preserves the awe of discovery and an ever-prevalent sense of the unknown.

After Cole's death in 1848, Durand became the Hudson River School's de facto leader. Although Durand admired Cole's work, his own paintings were far more subtle and intimate; Cole's work shouts while Durand's whispers. This is the essential distinction between these artists. Durand thought that Cole drifted in the direction of self-expression, believing that Cole's energized brushstrokes and the intensity of his light and color deviated too far from a truthful depiction of nature. Although Durand was more restrained than Cole, he was adamant that any attempt at exact replication would be nothing more than "servile" imitation.[10] His art remained faithful to form without diminishing his ability to reveal nature's inherent mysteries.

Durand chose to give the greatest emphasis to specific detail because he thought that it would lead to "subtler truths" (Fig. 2). He wrote, "[S]imple and familiar passages … like the domestic virtues … being appreciable by all, would be more certain of just and ample reward."[11] His favored views were well defined and focused, and he would often de-emphasize or eliminate the panoramic to present intimate views—believing that this was where truth might best be revealed.

Cole's dramatic and Durand's tranquil art are at opposing points on the spectrum by which we may measure the influence of these artists on many of the Hudson River School's painters. They were the forefathers of an American art that awakened the spirit of a free people to matters beyond the province of man.

THE INFLUENCE OF THOMAS COLE

Cole's sensibilities can be seen in works by Frederic Edwin Church (1826–1900), Albert Bierstadt (1830–1902), and Thomas Moran (1837–1926). These painters, along with several others, may be considered members of Cole's branch of the Hudson River School. Common to each of them was an emphasis on the panoramic and grand. Their dramatic compositions feature bold light, intense color, and daring perspectives that provoke awe—and are at the very edge of what might be accepted as natural.

A young Church spent three years as Cole's pupil. He was gifted with extraordinary talent, especially the ability to render detail with unprecedented precision. With his combination of heroic natural phenomena and minute detail, his paintings exhibit great pictorial force. His interest in scientific discovery and advancement supplanted many of the ideologies that his predecessor and teacher imparted to him. In Church's most developed compositions, the precepts of physics, geology, and biology guided his creativity.

Church extended the boundaries of the Hudson River School with his excursions to the most remote regions of South America. The fantastic natural wonders that he encountered there amplified his creative powers and scientific curiosity. The objective understanding to be gained from his images is overshadowed by the greater mystery they suggest. This is a fascinating and anomalous consequence of his genius.

Bierstadt adopted a style similar to that of Church. He had both a great affinity with and an aptitude for expansive views and found his greatest source of inspiration in the American West. Bierstadt created his most powerful compositions by de-emphasizing certain elements of his subject matter. The effect was an exaggerated focus on the most dominant and grandest forms, which critics thought too theatrical.[12] But such intensification had a great impact on viewers, effectively evoking the

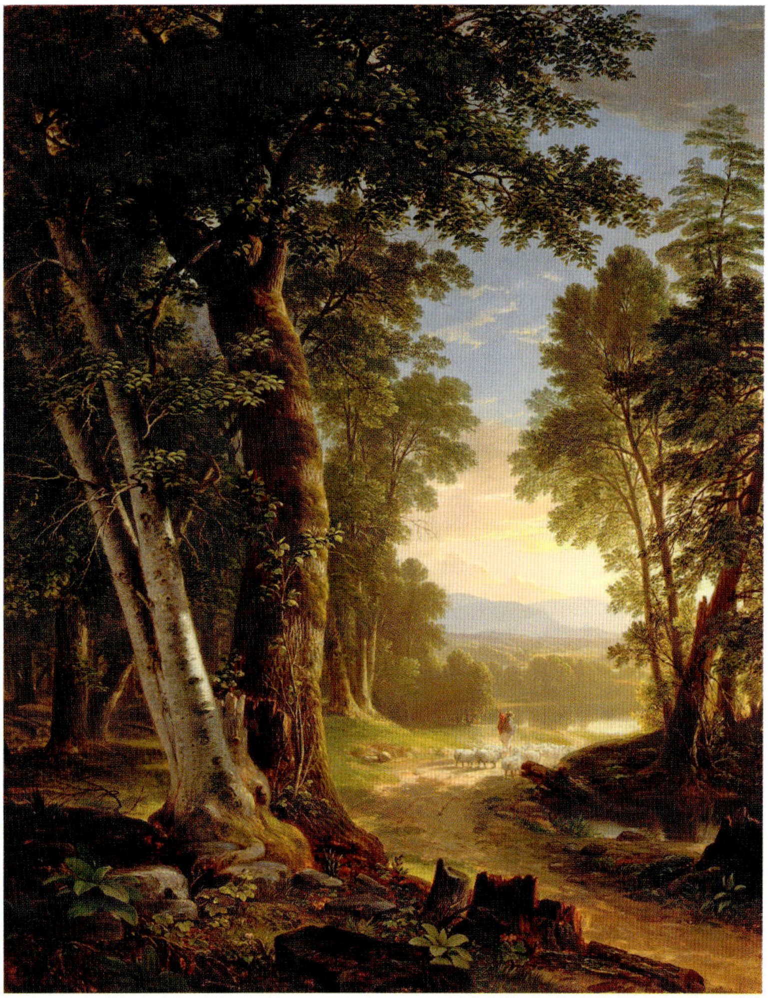

2.
Asher B. Durand
(1796–1886)
The Beeches, 1845
Oil on canvas
60 3/8 × 48 1/8 in.
(153.4 × 122.2 cm)
Signed and dated lower left:
A.B. DURAND / 1845
The Metropolitan Museum of Art, New York, Bequest of Maria DeWitt Jesup, from the collection of her husband, Morris K. Jesup, 1914, 15.30.59

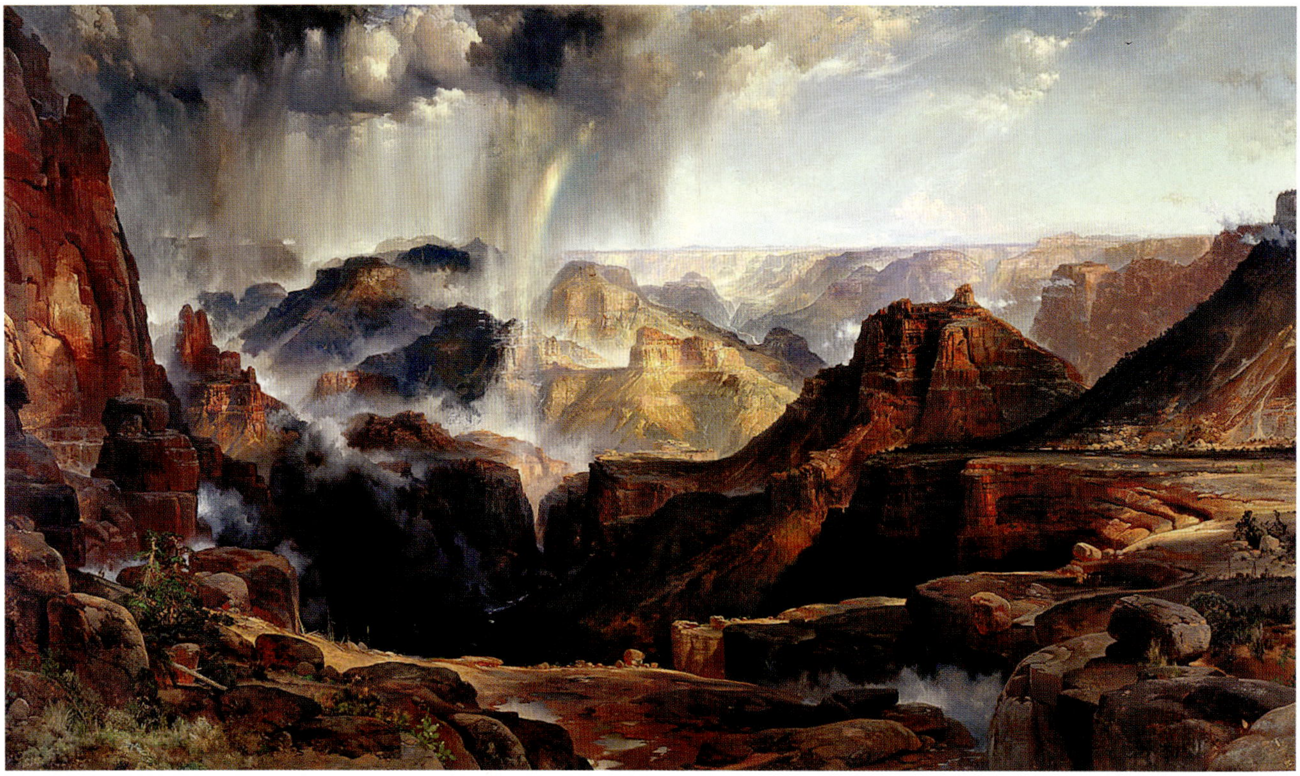

3.
Thomas Moran
(1837–1926)
The Chasm of the Colorado
1873–74
Oil on canvas mounted
on aluminum
84 ⅜ × 144 ¾ in.
(214.3 × 367.6 cm)
Smithsonian American Art Museum, Washington, DC, Lent by the Department of the Interior Museum, L.1968.84.2

majesty of the Western landscape for a popular audience. These compelling canvases, along with those of Moran, motivated the United States Congress to establish the first National Park in 1872 and fostered a sensitivity that would encourage the inception of conservationism.

Moran's primary focus was also the American West. Two of his paintings, *The Grand Canyon of the Yellowstone* (1872, Smithsonian American Art Museum) and *The Chasm of the Colorado* (Fig. 3), were purchased by Congress to display in the United States Capitol Building, and he was further honored by the naming of Mount Moran in the Teton mountain range.

During multiple excursions to Europe, Moran acquired a valuable appreciation of Joseph Mallord William Turner's (1775–1851) atmospheric mastery. But to express the majesty of the American West, Moran had to innovate. His dynamic depictions of the interplay of the Western sky's unique and variable hues, cast upon richly colored and textured mountainous façades, reveal his novel approach. Whereas the force of Bierstadt's compositions was accomplished by a command of form and space, Moran's potency was in his control of color and atmosphere.

THE INFLUENCE OF ASHER B. DURAND

The most significant divergence from Cole's aesthetic can be seen in the canvases produced by those artists influenced by Durand, the most prominent of whom were John Frederick Kensett (1816–1872), Sanford Robinson Gifford (1823–1880), and Thomas Worthington Whittredge (1820–1910).

The extremes that characterized the work of the Cole branch, especially the canvases of Church and Bierstadt, were countered by Kensett's captivating simplicity and quietude. Kensett's adoption of a Luminist manner led to increasingly more reductive compositions, culminating in the famous paintings he completed in the last summer of his life. Cast in a cool silvery light, these images are devoid of much color and detail. Most neutral space is eliminated, and the distinguishing qualities of each primary form are minimized so that land, sky, and water approach a synthesis. Because no one element stands out, the canvas imparts a sense of universal connectivity (Fig. 4). Kensett's remarkable advancement progressed toward an effective abstraction that predates the advent of the more radical twentieth-century form.

Some scholars consider such Luminist features to be a unique art form, while others see them within the scope and reference of the Hudson River School aesthetic. Whether distinct or integral, when Luminism's defining attributes were accompanied by an artist's effort to conceal creative process, especially by minimizing brushwork, the visual equivalent of transcendentalism was realized. At its best, Luminism removed the distraction of dominant forms and references to any specific time or place so that viewers were intentionally—and ingeniously—diverted from the literal aspects of an image to focus on what its aura might reveal.

Gifford's focus on atmosphere is described as an aerial Luminism. He gave substance, weight, and temperature to vacant space so that it would be seen as distinctly as any landscape form. His paintings suspend imminent atmospheric change so that a revelation seen in an expiring moment would not be lost in the progression of time. Both his presentation and command of vaporous qualities were visionary and added greater dimension to the evolution of American art.

Gifford's and Kensett's works may deviate from some of Durand's principles, but both artists maintained a belief in an egoless art form and never allowed any measure of their respective creativity to violate the integrity of nature; the very spirit of their endeavor, therefore, is consistent with that of Durand.

It was in the deepest haunts of the Catskills that Whittredge realized he would have to abandon the techniques and conventions he had adopted during his time in Düsseldorf. Those skills might allow an artist to replicate nature's countenance, but not its spirit. He immersed himself in the wild, as Durand fervently advocated, acquiring the sensibilities that would inform a genuine art. He painted compelling forest interiors that featured towering trees, pristine ponds, and other natural features, all arranged to achieve a revelation of the forest's essence, without regard to established precedent. This individualized approach—his arrangement, selection, and modulation of interior light and perspective—offered a glimpse of the ancient mysteries found in the recesses of the American wilderness.

Many artists were not fully aligned with either Cole or Durand, but this did not adversely impact the magnitude of their work. The Hudson River School painters were free-thinking mavericks who followed their own compass. But in their unambiguous reverence for nature they forged a venerable unity.

THE DIVINITY DILEMMA

Some viewers are critical of the religious connotations they perceive in paintings of the Hudson River School, believing that such

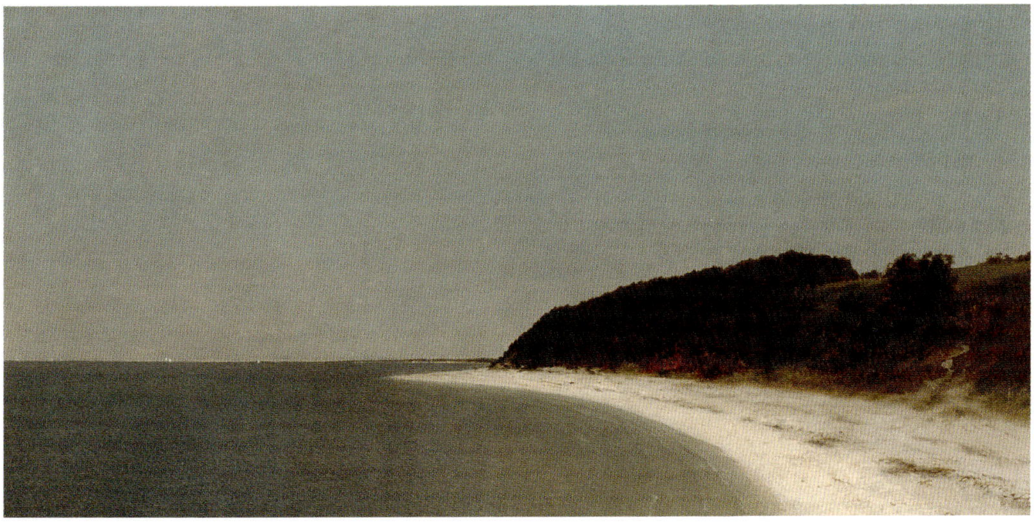

4.
John Frederick Kensett
(1816–1872)
Eaton's Neck, Long Island
1872
Oil on canvas
18 × 36 in. (45.7 × 91.4 cm)
The Metropolitan Museum of Art, New York, Gift of Thomas Kensett, 1874, 74.29

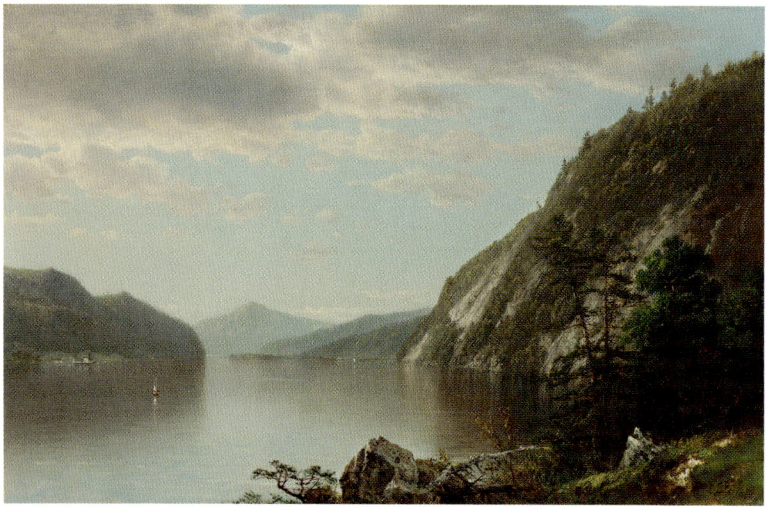

5.
David Johnson
(1827–1908)
Rogers Slide, Lake George, New York, 1870
Oil on canvas
13 3/8 × 21 3/8 in.
(34 × 54.3 cm)
Monogrammed and dated lower right: *DJ 1870.*
Collection of J. Jeffrey and Ann Marie Fox

undertones define and limit the movement's scope. However, the concept of God may also be seen in the context of transcendentalism, which was propagated concurrent with the Hudson River School by many American authors, especially Ralph Waldo Emerson (1803–1882) and Henry David Thoreau (1817–1862). Emerson's metaphor of the "transparent eye-ball" provides insight into how we may understand an artist's reaction to his experience and sense of God. Emerson wrote, "Standing on the bare ground,—my head bathed by the blithe air, and uplifted into infinite space,—all mean egotism vanishes. I become a transparent eye-ball; I am nothing; I see all; the currents of the Universal Being circulate through me; I am part or parcel of God."[13]

In the depths of the American wilderness, Hudson River School artists were close to something unknowable that has forever eluded and confounded man. Whether the mystery at the heart of this art is divine or scientific is something that every viewer must ponder.

OTHER IMPORTANT HUDSON RIVER SCHOOL PAINTERS

Jervis McEntee (1828–1891) was briefly a student of Church, but he was essentially self-taught. He preferred to paint the scenery surrounding his home in Rondout, New York, and most of his works depict quiet moments set in nondescript landscapes in the fall or winter, when nature's countenance most reflected his own moods. His lifelong melancholy and angst, extensively described in his diaries,[14] allowed him to recognize nature as both temporal and eternal: it dies, and it lives again in the unbroken cycle of the seasons. McEntee focused mainly on the moments before expiration, the solemn acceptance of a finite existence, which he expressed by his command of tone and hue, constraint of perspective, and thoughtful selection.

Jasper Francis Cropsey (1823–1900) also favored autumn landscapes. On the whole, his views were more panoramic than those of McEntee, with bolder topography and more dramatic perspective consistent with an art that did not show the season of fall as a culmination, but rather as a fruition and celebration. He presented nature at its symphonic climax, with all its varied elements calibrated to remain poised at the very peak of expression. A celestial light emanates from somewhere beyond the dome of the sky, and the scene's ethereal qualities are poignant and provoking. Like Cole, Cropsey portrayed an omnipotent nature but, it appears, without the inherent threat often associated with such sublime views.

David Johnson's (1827–1908) technique presented a structure and a level of detail not usually present in Luminism. He included specificity in what were otherwise essentially Luminist compositions, and a visual dynamic emerged that contributed a novel dimension to his work. An especially compelling example is seen in *Rogers Slide, Lake George, New York* (Fig. 5). An imposing mountainside on the right edge of the canvas acts as a backdrop that enhances the sharply focused details at the extreme front edge of the composition. The interplay between the fragile Luminist qualities visible throughout the painting and the prominent realist detail is a unique feature in some of Johnson's best work.

In one of Samuel Colman's (1832–1920) most seminal paintings, *Storm King on the Hudson* (1866, Smithsonian American Art Museum), the scene is violated by two smokestacks that spew exhaust, beginning to taint part of the pristine sky and threatening to consume all of it. The visible effects of impending industrialization portend ever greater risks to come, exemplifying the conservationist concerns shared by American artists of the period.

William Hart (1823–1894), a prolific painter, talented teacher, and skillful orator, created and promoted interest in American landscapes.[15] Several of his paintings feature portals into a pristine forest, where nature's most redemptive powers may be found. His agrarian scenes envisioned man's harmonious relationship with nature, as exemplified in his pre-eminent work *Along the Winding Way* (Fig. 6), with cows grazing at the water's edge, a grandfather helping a child over a fallen tree, and the tranquil haze of a late afternoon sun. In its abundant optimism and innocence, an inherent fragility is palpable. Hart was intuitive enough to recognize that the realization of a utopian vision depended upon man's relationship with his environment—one that would inevitably become more perilous as the population grew and man's needs and ambitions were prioritized.

Although William Trost Richards (1833–1905) is best known as one of the foremost painters of the sea, in the early 1860s he began to paint landscapes with an extreme focus on minute details. These paintings were so precise and overtly real that they risked invoking Durand's warning that art too strictly bound to the real might be inferior. Most scholars associate these works with the Pre-Raphaelite movement, founded in London in 1848. While some aspects of Richards's canvases, particularly his botanical accuracy, may relate to that movement's style, his works do not reference the themes of social injustice, piety, or moral imperatives most common in Pre-Raphaelite works. Richards's precision was not intended to scrutinize specific form. By presenting a multitude of carefully rendered details, he visualized the absolute perfection of the interrelationship and dependency of natural elements, revealing the dynamics of an ecological system that was, and will forever be, superior to the designs or engineering of man.

THE HUDSON RIVER SCHOOL IN THE TWENTY-FIRST CENTURY

The population of the New World surged as people from nearly every nation sought the opportunities and the freedoms it promised.

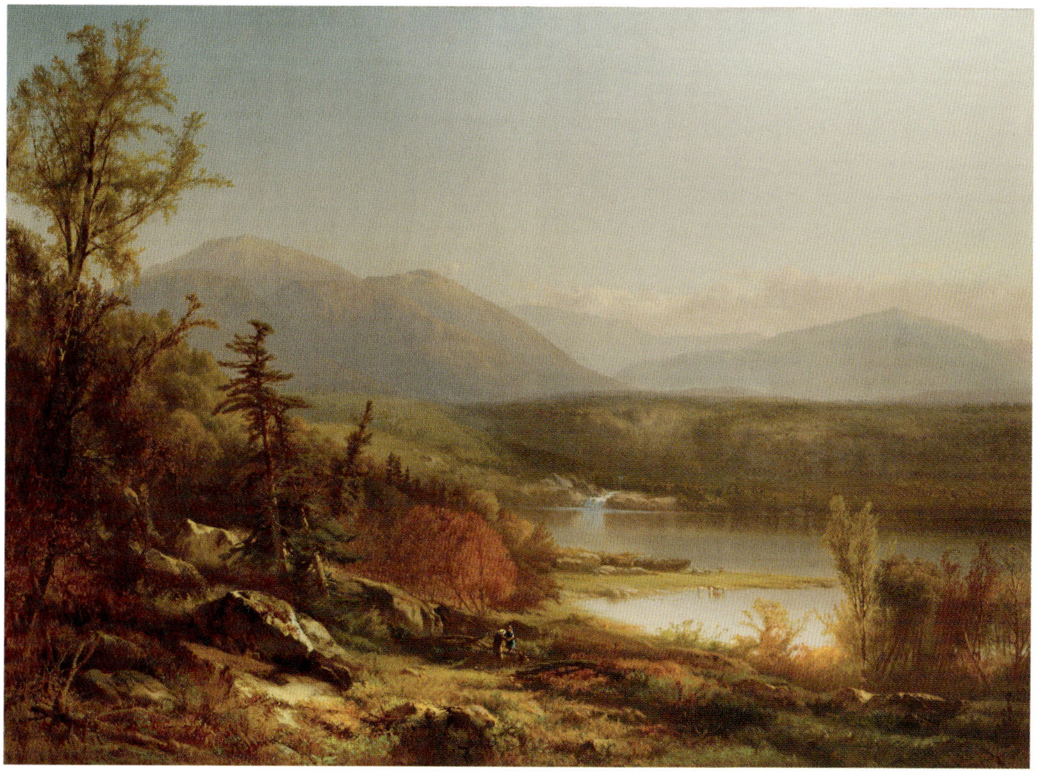

6.
William Hart
(1823–1894)
Along the Winding Way, 1864
Oil on canvas
39 ½ × 54 ¼ in.
(100.3 × 137.8 cm)
Signed and dated lower left: *WM. HART 64*
Questroyal Fine Art, LLC, New York

Over time, the American wilderness faded and today it is a remnant of what it once was. Gradually, hikes into the wild became less appealing than what might be broadcast on a box within the home. It seems the entire world has been reduced to pixels transmitted on to ubiquitous monitors that have morphed into tiny handheld devices, permanently accompanying their owners and persistently disrupting their consciousness. Most of society has become so ravenous for the unceasing innovations of a surging technology that its people's connection to the land has diminished in direct proportion to the rise of all that detracts from intimacy with it. Any awareness of the impending threats to the earth's ecology is subverted by a fascination with both artificial device and social media. In this context, we may wonder how an art conceived in the nineteenth century could be relevant and influence the mindset of a modern society. But from my own experience, and in my interactions with collectors, I recognize the potential of these paintings.

PERSONAL EXPERIENCE

I was raised in the suburbs and rode my bicycle on concrete streets all intersecting in an unending succession of ninety-degree angles. I walked on sidewalks lined by manicured hedgerows and past homes of uniform design. Trees were planted by specification and pruned to conform without distinction. My childhood friends and I played ball within the confines of plot lines, and few of our imaginations could escape the impotency of our surroundings.

I escaped.

In my grandmother's home, there was a small painting that I often admired: a dirt trail led to the edge of a vast woodland under a summer sky, with rays of soft light seeping through the canopy of foliage. My imagination soared. I wanted to follow that dirt path and wander into those woods. I never forgot that image, but, most of all, I have come to realize that my appreciation of nature was not a consequence of any real acquaintance with it; rather, it was the result of my exposure to that one small painting. Within my experience, a nearly 200-year-old art still has the potential to influence and effect change.

And I am not alone.

As an American art dealer (a career I also attribute to that very same painting), I have come upon collectors who have recounted similar experiences. Recently, a man showed me a picture that once hung in his mother's home. When he wasn't yet tall enough, he would climb on to the sofa to look at it. As a child and then as a young man, he was mesmerized by a stream that meandered through rocks and burst out of a forest; as an adult, he was determined to find that stream—and for fifty years he hiked across New England, through the Adirondacks, the Catskills, and the White Mountains. He realized early on that he didn't care whether he actually discovered the stream, because as he journeyed within the woods and mountains, he felt euphoric and connected, thrilled by the sights and sounds surrounding him, as if in the midst of a magical opera. A thousand various interactions and experiences did not affect his life, or mine, as much as did one old American canvas.

AN ORIGINAL AMERICAN ART

European landscape painters of the mid-nineteenth century endured the criticism of an academic community that viewed them as inferior because they did not reference man's historical achievements. These critics would sanction landscapes only if they were presented as a motif subservient to a greater idea. But in the New World, nature was paramount and dominated the creative consciousness of American artists. The vast wilderness was a primordial domain that possessed eternal truths. In their pursuit of these truths, and in their determination to find an innovative way to express them, these American painters created an art equal in importance to any art that preceded it.

The term "Hudson River School" lost its disparaging connotation long ago. Today it is an honorable title that acknowledges a seminal journey on the Hudson River into the soul of the American wilderness, where, upon a precipice, no remnant of man's folly was visible and a vital and enduring American art was born.

Where is the West in American Art?

Seth Hopkins
Executive Director, Booth Western Art Museum, Cartersville, Georgia

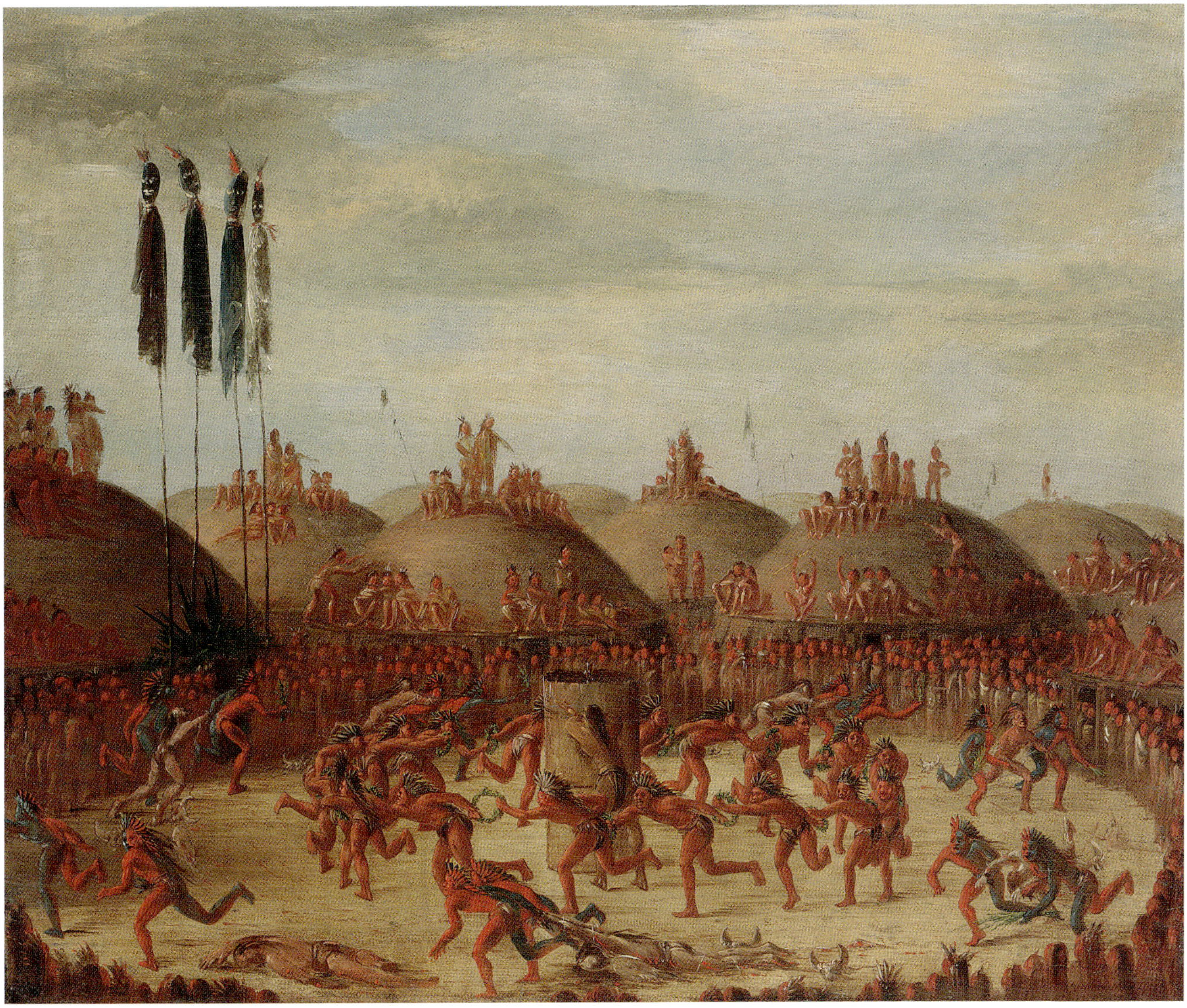

1. *(previous page)*
George Catlin (1796–1872)
The Last Race, Mandan O-kee-pa Ceremony, 1832
Oil on canvas
22 7/8 × 28 1/8 in.
(58.4 × 71.4 cm)
Smithsonian American Art Museum, Washington, DC. Gift of Mrs. Joseph Harrison, Jr., 1985.66.507

American art collections without representations of people, places and things west of the Mississippi River, or more accurately the 100th meridian, are literally excluding well over half the country in terms of land area and nearly half the population. This is not to mention the exclusion of references to the historic developments on the frontier that helped create the nation now stretching from sea to shining sea and beyond, to Alaska and Hawaii. While representations of the American West are few and far between in many important public and private collections in the eastern zones of the United States, surprisingly this is sometimes also true for collections in the West. While Western art fans may demonize Eastern scholars and curators for marginalizing Western art and not celebrating its merits, in some ways Western art connoisseurs have helped create the current separate but unequal status for art of the American West. In fact, the term Western art itself, herein referring to art of the American West that depicts typical subjects and landscapes west of the 100th meridian within the continental United States, needs definition so as not to be mistaken for the art of Western civilization.

Collectors and museums building and holding significant Western-oriented collections, reacting to real or perceived snubs, have not helped by expanding what may have once been a small fissure into a larger divide, driving a wedge between Western art and images depicting the rest of the country. This has thus created a relatively small but very passionate and resolute collector base for Western art, and a supporting cast of perhaps two dozen important museums with significant portions of their collections focusing exclusively on Western art. Understanding some basic Western history, and the artistic players witnessing the unfolding events, would therefore seem appropriate here.

At one time the West was merely the far side of Plymouth Rock, from the narrow view of the Pilgrims. Meanwhile Spanish explorers and missionaries were roaming the South and Southwest, French trappers were working in the northern Midwest and downriver to New Orleans, the British were still in North America, and Russian explorers were investigating the Pacific coast. It was far from uniform, but incursions into the interior of what would eventually become the contiguous United States came from nearly all sides.

When Thomas Jefferson issued his instructions to Meriwether Lewis and William Clark to find an all-water route across the continent, he also placed significant emphasis on surveying the flora and fauna of the newly purchased Louisiana Territory. Lewis was sent to study with many learned individuals in Philadelphia so that he might be able to make scientific notes, create maps, and determine local geology. Perhaps the greatest oversight and lament from that heroic expedition was the absence of an artist among the Corps of Discovery. An indication of that regret is evident from the fact that an artist accompanied nearly every subsequent exploring party sent west.[1]

The work of Thomas Cole and others in establishing the landscape art tradition in America, known as the Hudson River School, would open doors that artists venturing further afield would charge through as they rushed to document the seemingly exotic people and terrain of the West. Much of the earliest art depicting Native Americans or landscapes of the interior could be more accurately classified as frontier art rather than Western, owing to the relatively short distances from the eastern seaboard to where it was created.

The earliest art generally classified as Western is made up almost entirely of images of Native Americans, with limited landscapes in the mix. For our purposes, the first significant body of Western art began to be produced in 1832 when George Catlin made his trip up the Missouri River to paint portraits and scenes of everyday life among Native American tribes in the West. Catlin had painted pictures of Indians on the eastern seaboard and hoped to add many Western tribes to his gallery before their lifestyle was destroyed by America's westward expansion (Fig. 1). It may have been Catlin who first suggested the idea of creating national parks in the West, although he was more interested in fencing in Indians and wildlife to be seen by later generations than in preserving scenic areas. His sentiments, while not in line with today's thinking, were more sympathetic than those of many of his peers, who subscribed to the theory that the only good Indian was a dead Indian. He would spend the majority of his remaining years recording the lives of many Indian tribes throughout the West.[2]

Another painter who sought to record images of the American Indian for posterity was Karl Bodmer, a Swiss artist who accompanied the German Prince Maximilian on an exploration of the West in 1833. Bodmer was a better artist and more observant than Catlin, rendering greater detail in most of his paintings, although he lacked the former artist's enthusiasm for his project. John Mix Stanley and Alfred Jacob Miller would also contribute to this visual documentation, with Miller providing first-hand artistic accounts of the annual gathering of fur trappers known as "rendezvous."[3]

Catlin would eventually assemble a gallery of over 500 paintings that he hoped to sell to the United States government, but when they refused he took the show on the road, setting up viewings in England and Europe where people paid admission, and he tried to sell the collection to a foreign government. Luckily this did not come to pass, partly because the French Revolution broke out on the eve of a possible sale to the French government. Eventually these works were donated to the Smithsonian, again luckily, after the great fire that destroyed much of the early collections in 1865. Bodmer's work would be published in a major set of books penned by Maximilian; much of the original artwork would eventually find its way to the Joslyn Art Museum in Omaha, Nebraska, donated by the Enron Corporation.

Catlin and Bodmer generally portrayed Native Americans as peaceful and noble beings, in marked contrast to images showing them as bloodthirsty savages. As tensions between

2.
Albert Bierstadt (1830–1902)
Looking Down Yosemite Valley, California, 1865
Oil on canvas
64 ½ × 96 ½ in.
(163.8 × 245 cm)
Birmingham Museum of Art, Gift of the Birmingham Public Library, 1991.879

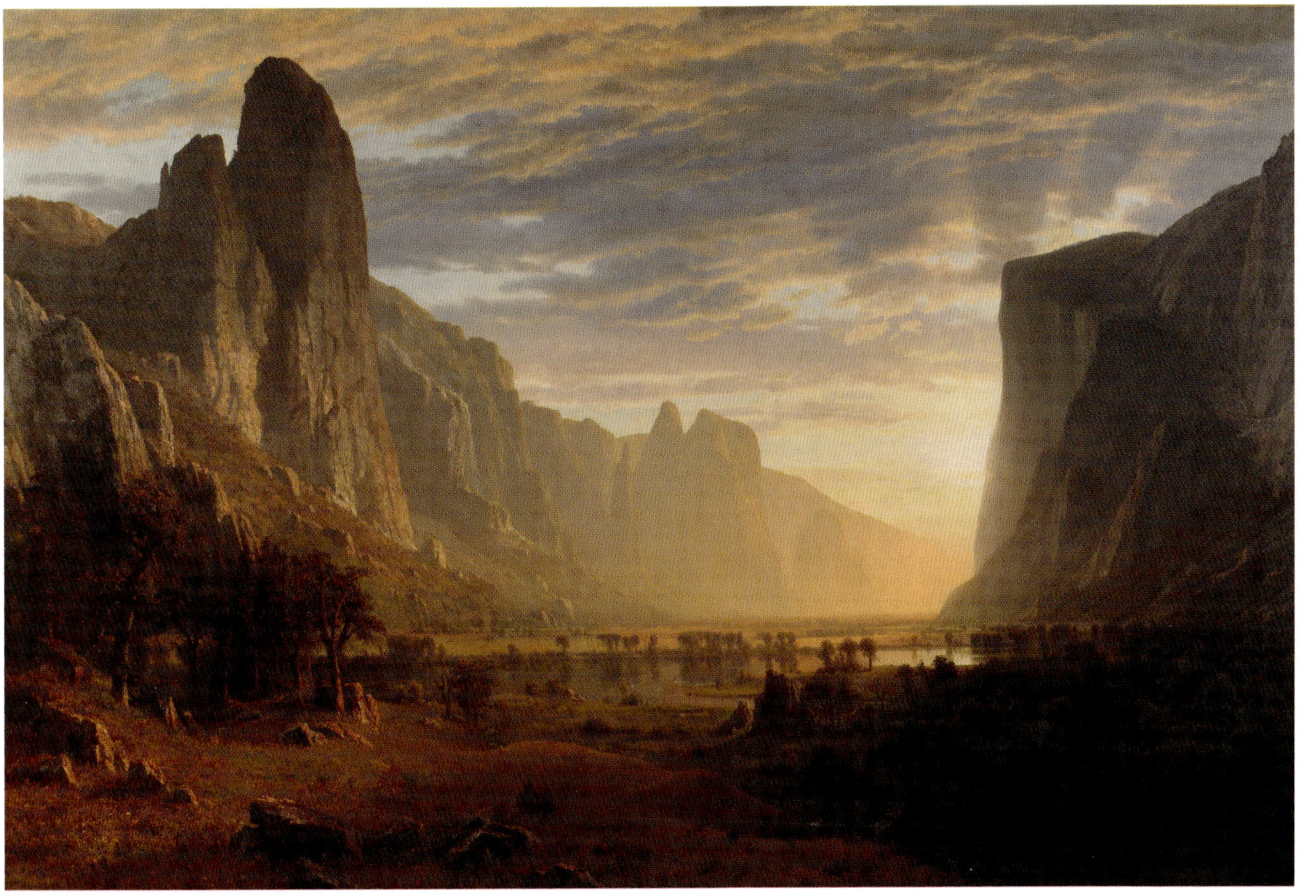

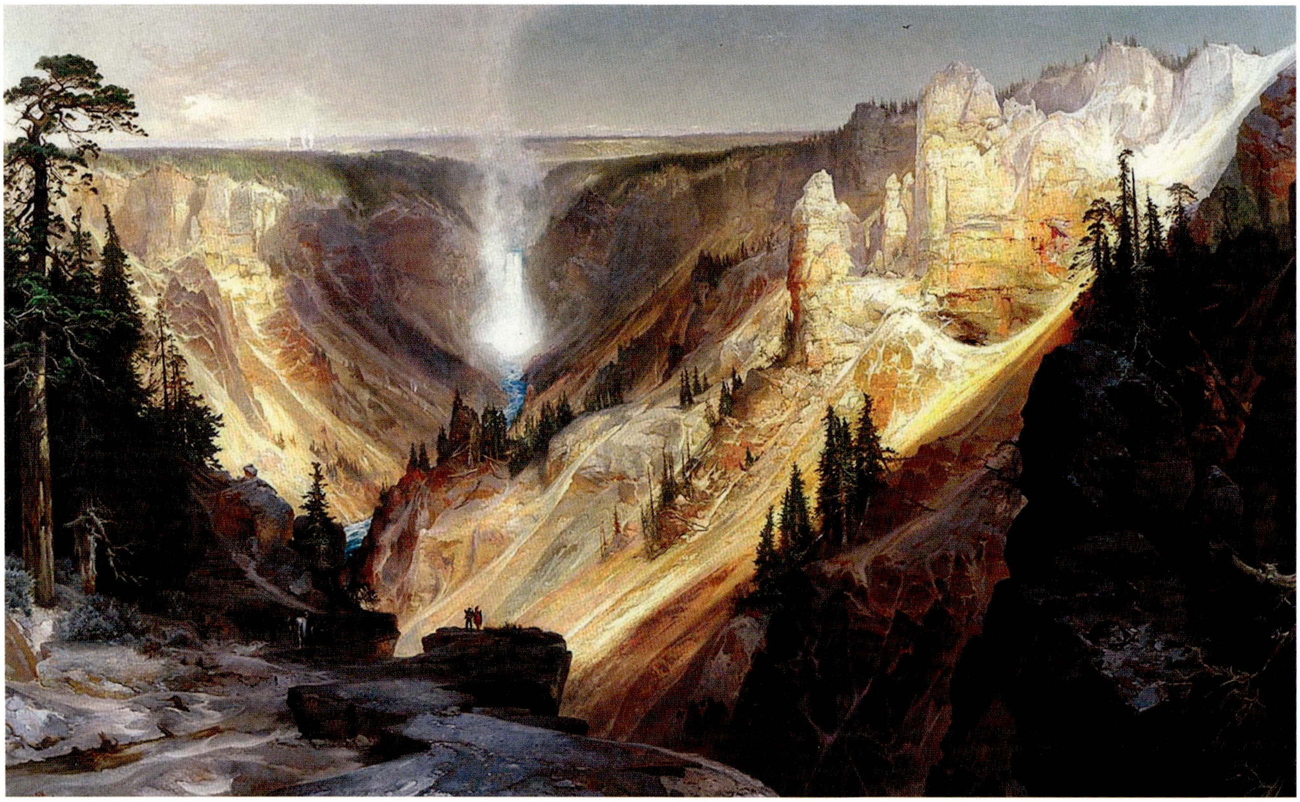

3.
Thomas Moran (1837–1926)
The Grand Canyon of the Yellowstone, 1872
Oil on canvas mounted on aluminum
84 × 144 ¼ in.
(213.4 × 366.4 cm)
Smithsonian American Art Museum, Washington, DC. Lent by the Department of the Interior Museum, L.1968.84.1

Indians and settlers increased, conflict on the plains became inevitable and art documenting these battles ensued. As the similarly inevitable conflict between North and South loomed on the figurative horizon, master landscape artists such as Thomas Moran, Albert Bierstadt and others were facing west, painting large dramatic canvases featuring literal horizons. In contrast to the Indian Wars, artists rarely painted Civil War battle scenes, preferring to paint allegorical art that shielded viewers from graphic details, leaving that to the emerging medium of photography. Post-war artists turned their attention squarely to the West, and a healthy rivalry blossomed between Bierstadt and Moran. Bierstadt claimed credit for helping to get the Yosemite Valley set aside as a nature reserve, while Moran could claim much of the credit for Yellowstone becoming our first National Park[4] (Figs. 2 and 3).

The armed conflicts with the Plains Indians provided American artists with their first hero figure, the US cavalryman in his famous blue uniform. The cavalry of the 1860s through 1880s was made up of a wide array of men, former Civil War soldiers, farm boys, immigrants, former slaves, and those on the run from the law. They were generally forgotten, ill-fed, underpaid and underappreciated, until their worst defeat made them popular martyrs in the collective American mind. This was at the Battle of the Little Bighorn, where Custer and most of his command were wiped out. There have been hundreds of paintings of this battle, most lacking historical detail but still adding to its legend.

Distributed in magazines and as prints, Western art depicting the fabulous and dangerous West became the leading subject in the popular culture of the day. The romanticized West, helped along by writers, singers, Wild West shows, and stage actors (later in TV and movies), would become standard fare for nearly 100 years. While the majority of the artists mentioned up to this point do not have enough original work entering the art market to be significantly collectible, vintage prints in a variety of media, including chromolithographs or images specifically printed for books or portfolios, and in some cases hand-colored, are readily available at relatively reasonable prices. Charles Russell and Frederic Remington are the two artists acknowledged as most readily identified with the West. Each had his own style—with its strengths and weaknesses—yet they sought to achieve similar results. They believed that the West of their mature years was not the same as the West of their youth, and they sought to preserve that earlier West through the images they created in paintings and sculpture.

Despite Remington's death before the age of fifty, he and Russell both produced large bodies of work in painting and sculpture (Figs. 4 and 5). While many of their most important works are certainly in museums, there is plenty of material coming to market each year to generate significant collector interest. There are even a few works that have trickled out of museum collections, often where the leadership has decided to focus on more general American art collecting than a concentration on the West.

Among the strongest performers over the most recent decades within the Western art market have been works by the members of the Taos Society of Artists, particularly the six founding members – J.H. Sharp, E.I. Couse, Bert Phillips, Ernest Blumenschein, Oscar Berninghaus, and Herbert Dunton. All from or with ties to the Midwest and having studied in Europe, these artists came to New Mexico in hopes of establishing an American art tradition separate from that of Europe, based on uniquely American subjects—Native Americans of the Taos Pueblo living much as they had for centuries, the organically folded landforms in the area, and the quality of the light some artists compared to that of Giverny, France.[5] Eventually the Taos art colony would attract artists from all over the world including influential Russians like Nicolai Fechin and Leon Gaspard.

The society would have roughly twenty members over its history, whether regular, associate or honorary. With the support of significant patrons and the railroad the group mounted exhibitions of their work in major Eastern and Midwestern museums, while members were also winning important

4. *(below)*
Frederic Remington
(1861–1909)
My Wounded Bunkie, 1896
Cast A, Henry Bonnard
Bronze Company, bronze
20 ¾ × 11 × 31 in.
(52.7 × 27.9 × 78.7 cm)
Birmingham Museum of Art, Gift of Dr. and Mrs. Harold E. Simon, 1973.148

5. *(bottom)*
Charles M. Russell
(1864–1926)
Bronc to Breakfast, 1908
Watercolor on paper
19 × 25 ¼ in.
(48 × 64 cm)
Montana Historical Society, Mackay Collection, X1952.01.06

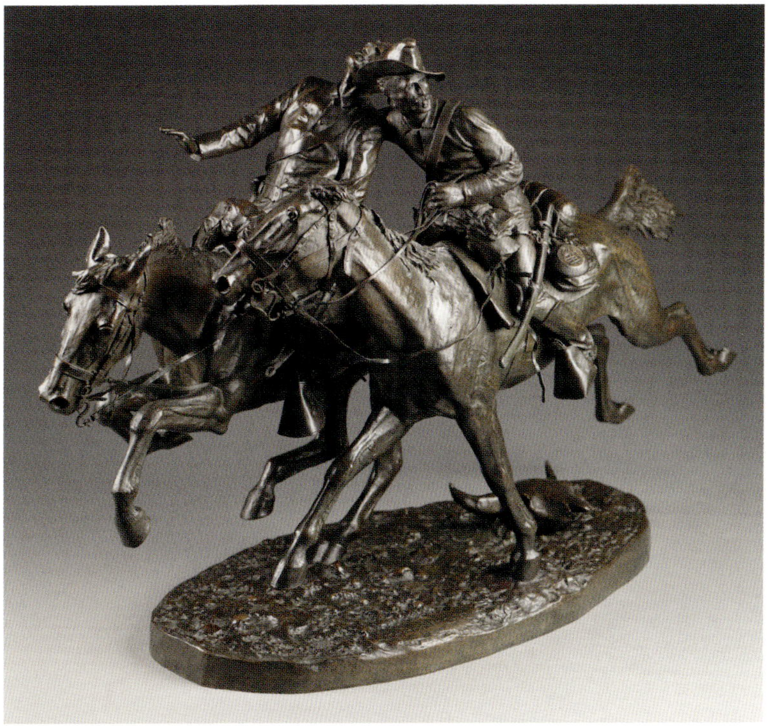

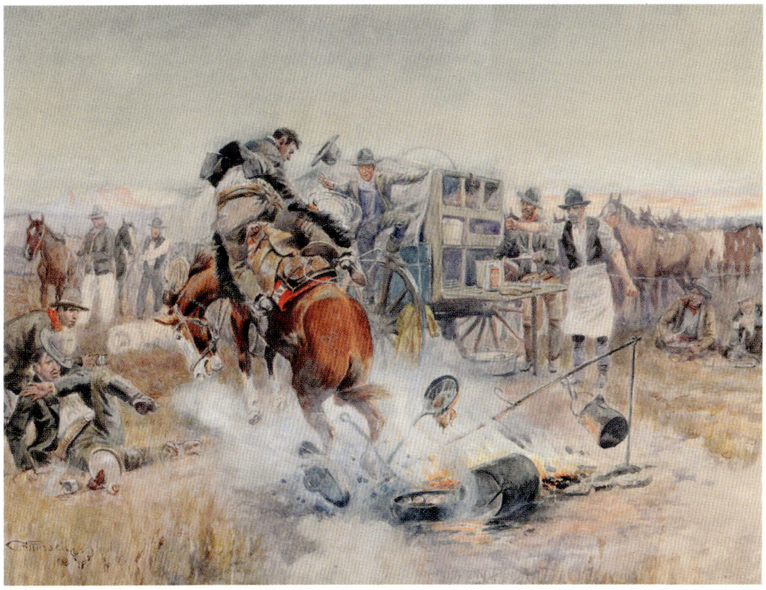

national art contests back East. Just prior to the beginning of the Great Depression the group fell apart, as many artists had achieved significant individual success and to continue the association seemed rather pointless.[6]

Just down the road in Santa Fe, New Mexico, artists were also flocking to town. However, no organization resembling the Taos Society of Artists was ever attempted. Instead Edgar Hewett, head of the New Mexico Art Museum, allowed artists to use its space to show their work and created a strong art tradition for the community. Hewett and the museum also supported a small group of young artists, the Cinco Pintores, that in some ways did emulate the Taos Society: it consisted of Will Shuster, Fremont Ellis, Walter Mruk, Jozef Bakos, and Willard Nash, although this group, sometimes derisively described as the "five nuts in the five mud huts," never attained the status of their Taos brethren. In today's market, the works of similarly trained, similarly competent artists painting similar subjects associated with the Taos Society bring two to four times the hammer price at auction compared with artists based in Santa Fe. Conversely, Santa Fe has become a dominant city and art market on the American landscape. With a total population of only about 70,000 people, the city supports nearly 250 art galleries, making it America's third largest art market behind New York and Los Angeles.[7]

In attempting to construct a neat and tidy timeline for Western art history, the period bookended by 1930 and the early 1960s proves difficult to define. Despite a profusion of Western movies, and later television programs, surprisingly little fine art of note depicting Western subjects was produced in those years. Because Western American art was generally representational in nature, it was largely ignored while Abstract Expressionism dominated, especially in the New York art circles following World War II. As the 1960s dawned John F. Kennedy used the phrase "New Frontier" in an election speech, perhaps foreshadowing a renewed interest in both historic and contemporary Western art. In the midst of the Cold War Americans may have identified with the spirit of the Old West and romantically remembered the simpler times depicted in the movies of their youth. The founding of several Western-focused museums and new scholarship in the 1950s fueled new interest in Western art of earlier periods.

However, it was the founding of two very dissimilar organizations in the 1960s that spurred a rebirth in the production, and equally importantly the collecting, of contemporary art depicting Western subjects. While there is sufficient material from a fairly limited number of earlier artists to sustain a healthy secondary market, including many galleries and several major annual auctions, it is in the field of contemporary Western art (meaning art by living artists, or at least artwork produced within the last fifty years) that I believe the best opportunity lies for enjoyment in the process of collecting.

In 1962, the Institute of American Indian Arts (IAIA) was founded in Santa Fe under the jurisdiction of the Federal Bureau of Indian Affairs. In 1965, four artists founded the Cowboy Artists of America (CAA) dedicated to perpetuating the type of art created by Frederic Remington and Charles M. Russell and with the hope of creating a market for their work.

Initially set up as a high school, IAIA is now a four-year college granting degrees in arts disciplines and several other areas. The Institute provides an opportunity for young Native Americans with artistic talent to leave their homes, often on reservations, and live on the Santa Fe campus while attempting to develop a career in art. Instruction in drawing, painting, sculpture, jewelry-making, and other specialties is offered along with liberal studies, art history, and encouragement for students to investigate their own family and tribal history. Previous attempts to provide young Native artists with art training were often led by non-Natives who usually had preconceived ideas about what Indian art should be and what subjects were appropriate.

IAIA is primarily led by Natives who have arts and/or business backgrounds. They provide ample art supplies, studio time and reassurance that experimentation is essential in moving art forward. Within a remarkably short period a number of students and faculty members became important leaders in establishing a whole new framework for Indian art, often merging Indian motifs, symbols, or spirituality with modern art sensibilities.

Indicators of the impact the Institute has had on American art include a Smithsonian-organized exhibition of work by former instructor Fritz Scholder and former student T.C. Cannon in 1972. The show opened in Washington, DC, then traveled throughout Europe (Fig. 6). In 1992, former instructor Allan Houser received the National Medal of Arts from President George H.W. Bush.[8]

It seems appropriate that artists Charlie Dye, John Hampton, Joe Beeler, and George Phippen met in an Arizona saloon to found the CAA. Their intention was to create a social club offering mutual support for artists attempting to make a living creating traditional Western art. Their stated desire was to perpetuate the memory and culture of the Old West as typified by the late Frederic Remington, Charles Russell, and others. Members of the Cowboy Artists of America were united in their traditional realism style and their focus primarily on historic Western subjects such as cowboys, Indians, or horses. At a time when most gallery walls were filled with minimalism, the Cowboy Artists consciously chose to override conceptualism in favor of traditional depictions of the Old West.

They organized an annual trail ride where they could live the life they painted and sculpted. More importantly, they partnered with the National Cowboy Museum in Oklahoma City to present an annual show where their work was offered for sale. Within a few years the event became a land rush, with patrons jostling to purchase art.

A squabble with the hosting museum led the CAA to move its show to Phoenix, while the Oklahoma museum began a new show and sale, known today as the Prix de West, loosely based on the historic art competitions known as the Rome Prize and the Prix de Rome. In the 1980s through the mid-2000s these two exhibitions/sales, along with other museum and charity sales, annually produced upward of ten million dollars in sales for the artists who participated.[9]

The trails blazed by the artists related to these two now venerable institutions have helped create a healthy contemporary Western art market. Dozens of museums have collected examples by living artists, several regular publications are dedicated to the genre, stand-alone auctions of Western art regularly include contemporary work, and numerous galleries exist in Western art meccas like Scottsdale, Jackson Hole, Santa Fe, and beyond. These latter-day trailblazers, particularly the Native artists, have also created a much wider niche for Western art.

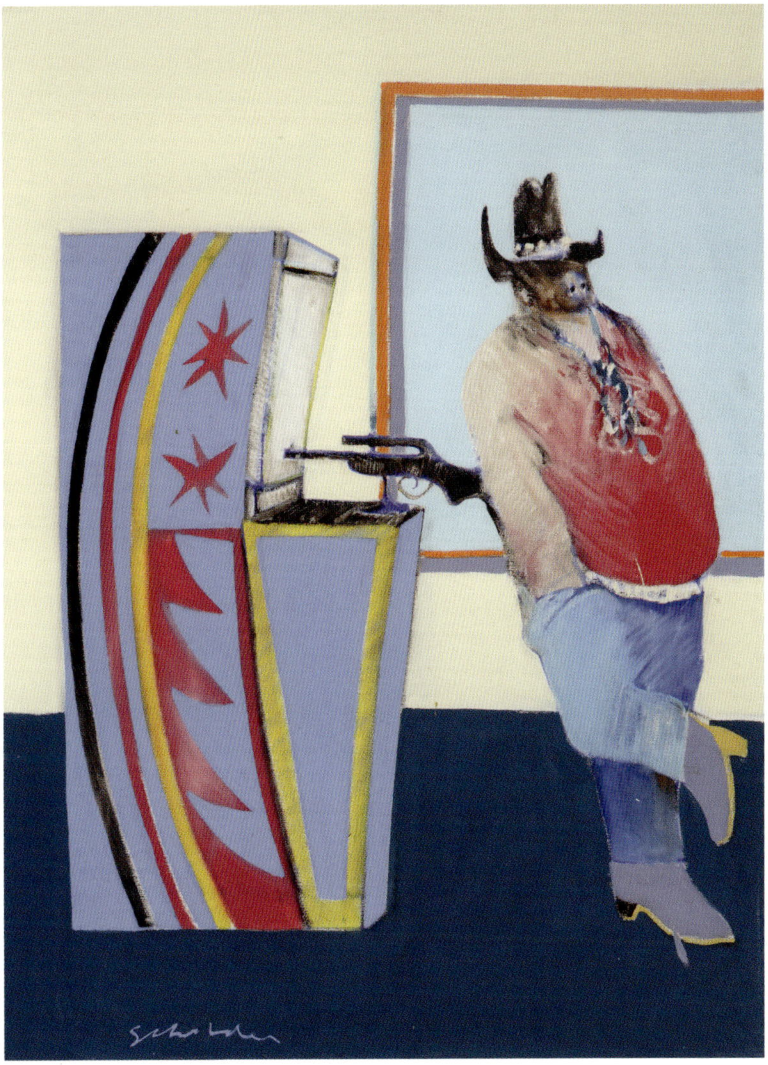

6.
Fritz Scholder (1937–2005)
Indian at a Gallup Bus Depot
1969
Oil on canvas
40 × 30 in.
(101.6 × 76.2 cm)
Booth Western Art Museum permanent collection, Cartersville, GA, 2013.011.001

Today artists who create abstract forms, infuse social commentary, appropriate from earlier artists or pop culture, practice photo-realism, and experiment with new materials can all have their work considered Western art, although some might reject the Western art label as passé or limiting. Among those pushing the envelope of the genre are Tom Palmore, Paul Pletka, Thom Ross, Donna Howell-Sickles, Bill Schenck, and Theodore Waddell.

While early Western artists were generally not a diverse group, today there is a more representative mix of artists working and receiving recognition in the field. While a significant number of Native artists have achieved status in the past fifty years, it is only in more recent times that large numbers of women, Asian American or African American artists have been seen in major galleries and entering museum collections.

Modern and Post-Modern art movements from the 1960s such as Abstract Expressionism and Pop Art have had a lasting effect on art of the West. Theodore Waddell applies the loose, gestural brushwork of the Abstract Expressionist painters to subjects close to home on his Montana ranch or at home in Idaho. Bill Schenck started using spaghetti Western publicity photos as sources for his Pop Art style while living and working in New York in the 1970s. Schenck's flattened, almost paint-by-number works blur the lines between high and low art, presenting the cowboy and others as commercial objects.[10]

The artistic responses created between 1830 and 1930 to the vastness, scenic beauty, wildlife, and varied peoples of the American West leave a daunting legacy for today's Western artists to deal with. Mainly narrative, illustrative, and meant to be perceived as documentary, the earlier art enlightened and entertained audiences eager to visualize the wonders of the West. In the simplest terms, the enduring traditions established by artists working in the first century of Western art leave today's artists two basic choices. They can generally follow the durable customs and produce art visually similar to that of preceding generations, or they may reject portions of the convention and infuse aspects of modern or contemporary art in their work. While the treatments may have changed, the Western landscape, cowboys, Native Americans, and wildlife are subjects that still inspire artists.

Some artists, going against the traditional narrative grain in Western art, have responded with social commentary embedded in their art. Works by many Native artists ask questions about America's perceived history versus reality that may not be comfortable for many to answer. Many more women artists have become prominent in the field at this time as well. Anne Coe, for example, portrays the West of today and addresses issues such as land management and urban sprawl. Montana artist Clyde Aspevig has also been involved with the environmental movements developing in the West over recent years, attracting and inspiring artists of the West who are interested in wilderness preservation. As such, he seeks out some of the last truly wild places in the West as subjects in his art. Chuck Forsman takes a clearly critical view of the landscape and its place in today's modern West by often choosing subjects such as a strip mine.

Some artists also seek out contemporary Westerners as subjects. Before his eyesight deteriorated James Bama painted people he encountered at parades, pow-wows, rodeos, or in daily life in the West. One of his most famous paintings depicts a young man in full regalia posed in front of a wall of peeling paint with the faint message "no parking violators towed away" barely visible, asking an important question about the status of Native Americans even today.[11]

The contemporary Western art world is fairly small at the top. While there might be thousands attempting to make at least a portion of their living from creating Western images, the community on top of the figurative mesa numbers less than a few hundred artists. The supporting community includes a few thousand serious collectors, several trade magazines and a shrinking number of major galleries, certainly now well under a hundred. Many of the older members of this community continue to fret about the future of the genre, wondering if those under fifty today will eventually become enamored with Western art as their parents once did after they had raised their kids and become somewhat financially stable. I tend to believe they will, although it will not be through the movies and television shows that lured the previous generations—it will be the sheer power, magnitude and beauty of the West, along with the powerful mythos that still remains.

Whether backpacking through the National Parks, learning to ride at a dude ranch, or marveling at landscapes both vast and desolate as well as verdant and breathtaking, the experiences available in the American West are life-changing. I firmly believe younger generations will continue to want vacation homes in the West and to travel the scenic byways to see the sights. For a percentage of those, although who knows how large, these experiences will trigger a latent desire to collect paintings, sculpture and photography relating to these experiences. Thus, the collecting bug will have bitten a new crop. Theoretically these younger collectors will be more attracted to the more stylized or contemporary (meaning modern leaning) artwork available in the field.

While traditional Western art, commonly representational and narrative in nature, may long remain the mainstream of the genre, artists impacted by Modern and Post-Modern trends in American art have created a significant and growing tributary. In my research I have run across articles from as early as the 1980s predicting that the more contemporary images, like those produced by Donna Howell-Sickles, Ed Mell, Kim Wiggins, Thom Ross and others, would come to dominate the field within a relatively few years. Nearly forty years have passed since some of those articles were written, and traditional-style Western art is still the mainstream, with more contemporary imagery important but still the smaller tributary, at least for now. Regardless of whether it is traditional or contemporary, imagery of the American West belongs in any significant collection of American art in some form or fashion.

Our collective thoughts about the West, the real place with real history, or the West we construct from our minds, still provide powerful stimuli for new generations of artists. The American West is a unique place; yet it also exists for many as an ideal, fantasy, myth, symbol, or a time past. Those willing to confront the enduring traditions are empowered to pick and choose those they wish to align with or reject. Their output provides a constructive framework for us to contemplate the American West anew: its turbulent past, vibrant present, and uncertain future.

Sojourns and Salons
American Artists in Europe, from the Grand Tour to Giverny

Graham C. Boettcher, PhD
The R. Hugh Daniel Director, Birmingham Museum of Art, Birmingham, Alabama

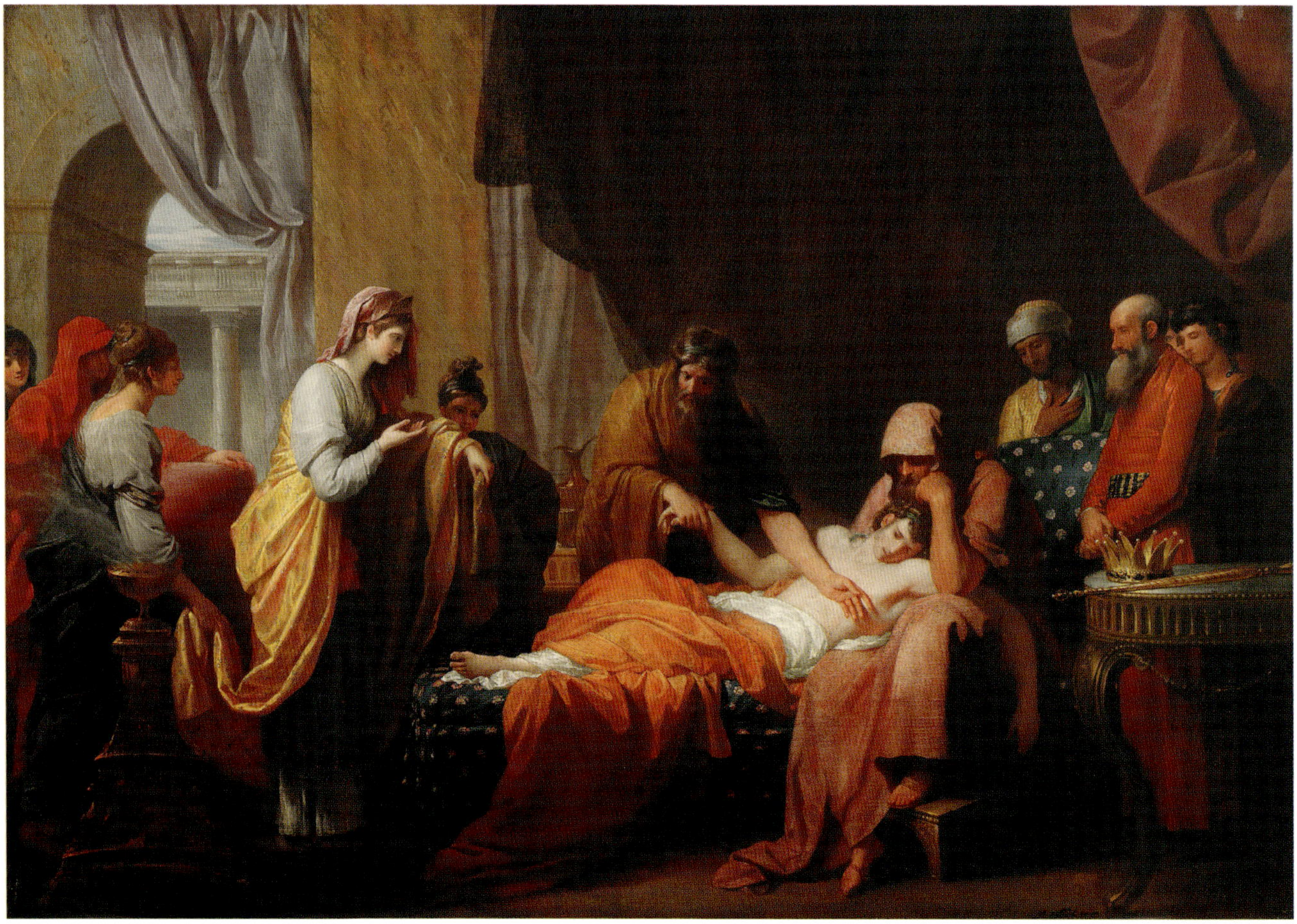

From colonial times through the early twentieth century, travel to Europe was considered essential to the artistic development of American artists. With its ancient history, unique landscapes, and superabundance of art and architecture, Europe offered American artists visual delights and opportunities for study that simply were not available at home. While some artists honed their skills by copying the Old Masters during a "Grand Tour" that included London, Paris, Rome, and Venice, among other destinations, others sojourned abroad for years, engaging in formal education in academies and exhibiting their work alongside their European contemporaries. Looking at examples from the collection of the Birmingham Museum of Art, in Birmingham, Alabama, the chapter that follows will explore how and where American artists honed their skills in Europe, and discuss opportunities for developing distinguished collections by focusing on European subjects by major American artists.

While the itineraries for Grand Tourists occasionally changed as various destinations fell in and out of fashion with the times, Italy remained a constant throughout the eighteenth and nineteenth centuries. The art historian Henry Tuckerman summed up the importance of Italy to American artists, writing:

> *A visit to Italy is perhaps more of an epoch in the life of an American artist than in that of any other. The contrast between the new and old civilization, the diversity in modes of life, and especially the more kindling association which the enchantment of distance and long anticipation occasion, make his sojourn there an episode of life.*[1]

In 1760, Benjamin West (1738–1820) became the first American artist to undertake such an "episode." He sailed to Italy and embarked on a three-year journey that developed and refined his artistic skills, connecting him to a circle of literati that ultimately propelled him to serve at the court of King George III. In Rome, West studied the human form through antique statuary (ancient Roman copies after the Greek originals) and reveled in the work of Renaissance painters. In 1774, when his contemporary John Singleton Copley (1738–1815) traveled to Italy, West advised that he "pursue the higher Exalances in the Art," through "the works of the *Antient Statuarys*, *Raphael*, *Michal Angilo*, *Corragio*, and *Titian*, as the Sorce from whance true tast in the arts have flow'd."[2] West's own adherence to this course of study is evident in his 1772 painting *Erasistratus the Physician Discovers the Love of Antiochus for Stratonice* (Fig. 1), painted the same year George III appointed him "History Painter to the King." The painting derives its subject from a legend loosely based on Greek history, telling the story of Seleucus, King of Syria, who summoned the eminent Greek physician Erasistratus to diagnose his afflicted and bedridden son Antiochus. West's painting depicts the very moment in which the doctor discovers that Antiochus' heart races at the sight of his stepmother Stratonice. According to legend, the king gave his wife to his beloved son, curing his lovesickness. West's Grand Tour influences are revealed not only through the sculptural nature of the figures and the nods to classical antiquity in the surroundings, but also through the painting's rich coloration, which earned West the nickname "the American Raphael."

Italy's pre-eminence as a destination for American artists only gained in popularity in the nineteenth century, when the advent of faster, less expensive modes of travel such as steamships and railways democratized the Grand Tour, making it affordable to the middle class.[3] Among the many American artists who made their way to Italy at this time was the Cincinnati painter Robert S. Duncanson (1821–1872). The descendant of former slaves from Virginia, Duncanson was raised in Monroe, Michigan, where he worked in his family's house-painting business. Around 1840, Duncanson relocated to Cincinnati to pursue his ambition of becoming an artist. After a slow start, he began to enjoy modest success as a portraitist, but seemed to find his true calling when he took up landscape painting. In 1853, with the support of his patron Nicholas Longworth (1783–1863), a wealthy banker and vintner, Duncanson journeyed to Europe with fellow Cincinnati landscape painters William Louis Sonntag (1822–1900) and John

1.
Benjamin West (1738–1820)
Erasistratus the Physician Discovers the Love of Antiochus for Stratonice, 1772
Oil on canvas
50 × 72 in. (127 × 182.9 cm)
Collection of the Birmingham Museum of Art; Museum purchase with funds provided by Mr. and Mrs. Houston Blount, Mr. and Mrs. Michael Bodnar, John Bohorfoush, Mr. and Mrs. Percy W. Brower, Jr., Mr. and Mrs. Thomas N. Carruthers, Jr., Catherine Collins, Mr. and Mrs. Henry C. Goodrich, Mr. and Mrs. Hugh Kaul, Harold and Regina Simon Fund, Mr. and Mrs. William M. Spencer III, Mr. and Mrs. Lee Styslinger, and other donors, 1987.4

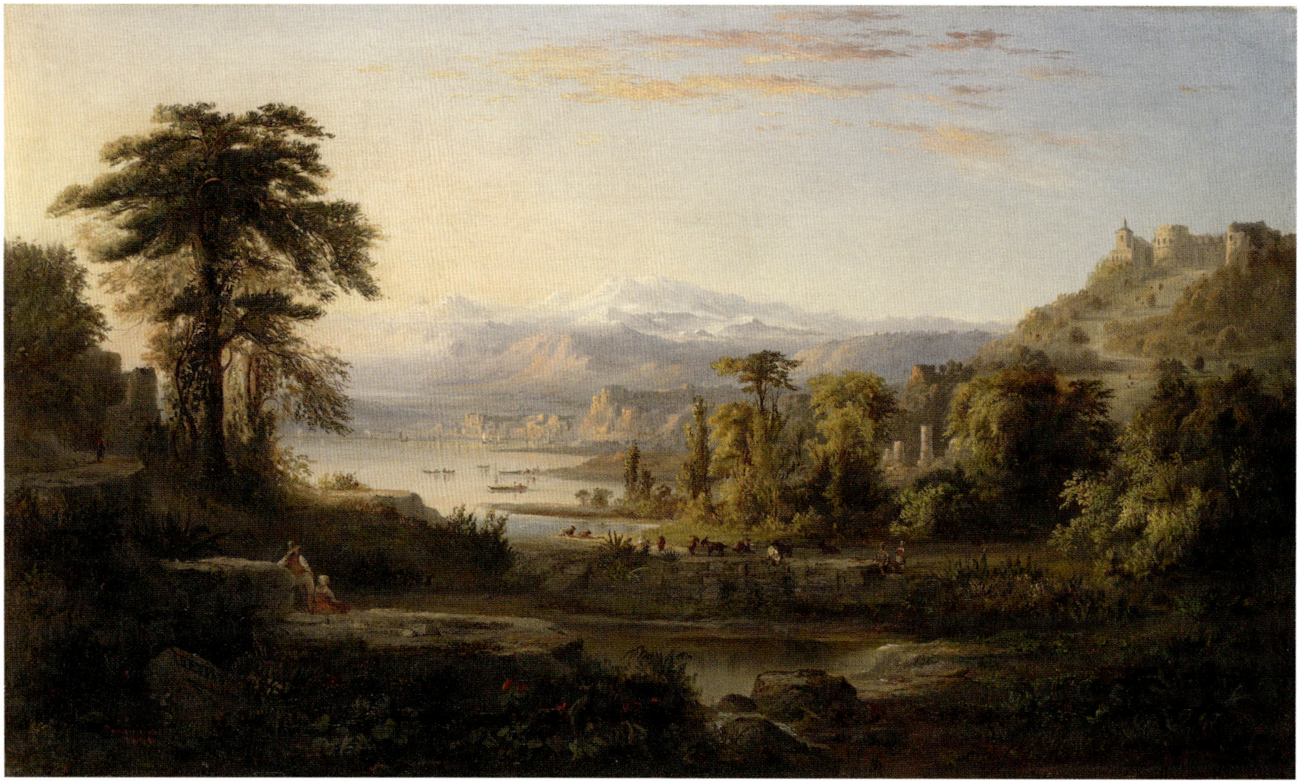

2.
Robert S. Duncanson
(1821–1872)
A Dream of Italy, 1865
Oil on canvas
20 ⅝ × 35 in.
(52.4 × 88.9 cm)
Collection of the Art Fund, Inc. at the Birmingham Museum of Art
AFI.10.2009

Robinson Tait (1834–1909). They began their Grand Tour in England, where they studied the English landscape and visited museums and private collections in London. After a brief stay in Paris, the group traveled overland to Italy, where they joined the circle of American artists centered around the Florence studio of the sculptor Hiram Powers (1805–1873), a prescribed destination for Americans passing through the Tuscan capital. Italy's rich, history-steeped landscapes had a profound effect on Duncanson, and upon returning home the following year he began a series of idealized classical landscapes based on his travels, which garnered critical acclaim.

In 1861, one critic hailed Duncanson as "the best landscape painter in the West."[4] Two years later, however, the artist's thriving career was interrupted by the Civil War, when—to escape the growing racial strife stirred by the conflict—he moved to Montreal, Canada, remaining there until after the war. *A Dream of Italy* (Fig. 2), a pastiche of scenery from the artist's travels, is among the most significant works he painted during his exile. With its central body of water and snow-capped mountains in the distance, the composition resembles Duncanson's 1863 painting of Lago Maggiore, Italy's second largest lake, located on the southern edge of the Alps, divided between the Piedmont and Lombardy regions. A romantic mood permeates the landscape, created in no small part by the warm, pale pink light washed over the scene. This, along with the couple in the foreground quietly peering out across the lake, conveys a calm and restful quality. Given the turmoil in Duncanson's native land at the time he painted this, it is difficult not to read the dreamlike landscape as evidence of his longing for a place of peace and serenity, further underscoring the important place Italy occupied in the artist's psyche.

While Duncanson's Italian sojourn lasted less than a year, the artist Elihu Vedder (1836–1923) made Italy his permanent home. Vedder first visited Italy in 1857, stopping off in Rome and Venice, but ultimately settling in Florence until 1860, when he returned to the United States. In 1866 he went back to Italy, this time establishing himself in Rome, where he remained until his death.[5] Italy provided such a wellspring of inspiration for the young artist that of his first visit, he later recalled, "at that time so much Art burst into my unprepared mind that the resulting confusion has lasted me for the rest of my life…."[6] During Vedder's first residence in Italy, he made frequent sketching trips throughout Tuscany, often in the company of the painter Giovanni Costa (1826–1903), a painter associated with the Macchiaioli, a group of Italian artists devoted to *plein-air* painting and the depiction of everyday life. It was Costa who encouraged Vedder to find his subjects in the surrounding landscape, prompting Vedder to quip, "I don't think he [Costa] saw more Nature than I did; but he saw more in Nature to paint than I did."[7] While Vedder embraced the Macchiaioli's penchant for direct observation, he did not share in their rejection of historical and mythological subjects, both genres comprising a large portion of his œuvre.

Occasionally, Vedder combined aspects of narrative and landscape painting, such as his 1867 canvas *The End of a Misspent Life* (Fig. 3) painted shortly after his return to Italy, in which an old man sits before the gate of a walled graveyard, head in hands, contemplating his life and eventual mortality. The poignant scene is set against a dramatic sunset into which a lonely path, punctuated with Mediterranean cypress trees, recedes into the distance. The sole traveler upon the byway is the man's dog, who turns to take one last look at his master before leaving him to mourn his squandered life in solitude. The setting for the work likely derives from one of Vedder's earlier sketching trips; in 1860, he visited the mountaintop walled city of Volterra in Tuscany, where he painted one of its ancient Etruscan gates.[8] Reminiscing about his own life, Vedder underscored the important role the *bel paese* (Italian, "beautiful country") played in his life, writing, "had I lived at home I doubtless should have lived more strenuously, but I know that my dreams would always have been of Italy."[9]

Whereas Florence and Rome remained ever-popular destinations, during the second half of the nineteenth century many American artists—inspired by the literary and artistic works of Lord Byron, J.M.W. Turner, and John Ruskin among others—added Venice to their itineraries. Positing the reasons for this, Nancy Anderson has noted, "Nostalgia for a non-industrial past certainly played a role, as did the dreamlike, otherworldly quality of a city floating on water. Travel literature, eagerly read, and often of high quality, also contributed to widespread interest in the city."[10] One artist who answered the call of the Queen of the Adriatic was Thomas Moran (1837–1926), the English-born American painter best known for his monumental canvases depicting the American West, particularly the Yellowstone. Although Moran didn't discover the charms of Venice until 1886, at the age of forty-nine, the city dominated his œuvre for the remaining thirty-five years of his long career. Upon arriving, Moran wrote to his wife, declaring, "Venice is all, and more, than travelers have reported of it. It is wonderful. I shall make no attempt at description but will tell you all when I get back."[11] Although little written evidence remains of Moran's activities during his first trip to Venice, it is likely that he visited Katharine de Kay Bronson (1834–1901), the sister-in-law of Moran's close friend, poet Richard Watson Gilder. Bronson, who had settled in Venice in 1876, was the doyenne of the city's Anglo-American expatriate society, hosting James McNeill Whistler, John Singer Sargent, Henry James, and Robert Browning, among

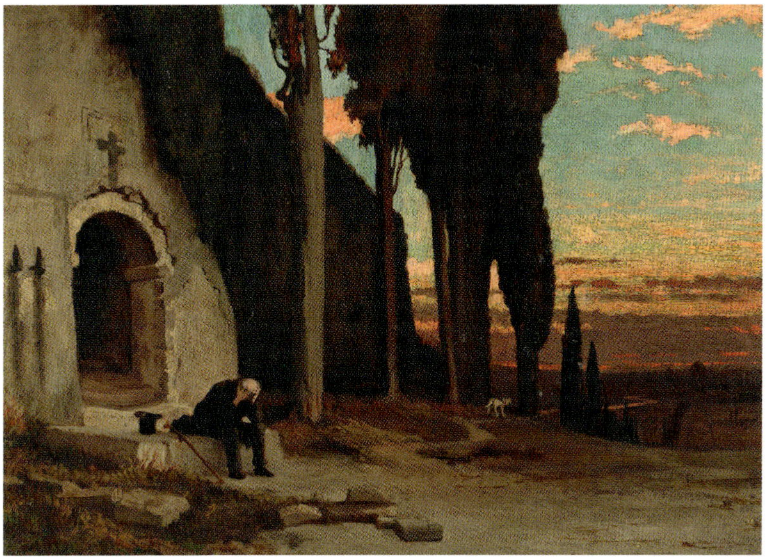

3.
Elihu Vedder (1836–1923)
The End of a Misspent Life
1867
Oil on canvas
9 ¼ × 13 in.
(23.5 × 33 cm)
Courtesy of the Birmingham Museum of Art; Promised gift of Dr. and Mrs. Frederick Baekeland in honor of Margaret Livingston
24.2005

others, in the Casa Alvisi, a palazzo at the mouth of the Grand Canal.[12] Moran also resided in the same area during his two-month sojourn, staying in the Grand Hotel.[13]

The extensive sketches and watercolors made by Moran during this trip provided the basis for a number of oil paintings completed over several years following his return. Time and distance did not diminish the artist's regard for the city or its influence on his work. In a letter of 1888, Moran wrote, "Venice is an inexhaustible mine of pictorial treasures for the artist and of dreamy remembrance to those who have been fortunate enough to visit it."[14] In 1890, Moran returned to Venice with his family, this second trip providing an even greater wellspring of inspiration than the first. The Grand Canal, the city's main aquatic thoroughfare, became the setting for many of Moran's Venetian scenes, offering the artist the chance to showcase his skills fully as a landscape painter since the locale possessed at once the opportunity for dramatic skies, reflective water effects, and rocky edifices, albeit Renaissance and Baroque structures instead of the geological wonders of the American West. In his 1906 canvas *Venice: Grand Canal at Sunset* (Fig. 4), Moran takes full advantage of each of these possibilities to dazzling result, even manipulating the composition so that two of the city's most prominent landmarks—the Campanile of St. Mark's Basilica and the domes of Santa Maria della Salute—can be seen in a single view.

While Italy may have been the earliest destination for American artists abroad, France, too, quickly rose in popularity. John Vanderlyn (1775–1852)—best remembered for his colossal history painting *Landing of Columbus* (12 × 18 ft, completed 1847) in the United States Capitol Rotunda—is regarded as the first American artist to train in France, undertaking studies in Paris from 1796 to 1801. Other American artists soon followed, treating the French capital either as their primary destination or viewing it as one among many prescribed stops on the Grand Tour. Indeed, West, Duncanson, Vedder, and Moran all spent varying amounts of time in Paris. West briefly stopped in France on his way to England in 1763, returning to Paris in 1802, where he exhibited at the Salon and met with Napoleon.[15] Duncanson's time in France was also quite short. He and his travel companions stopped in Paris in August 1853, en route to

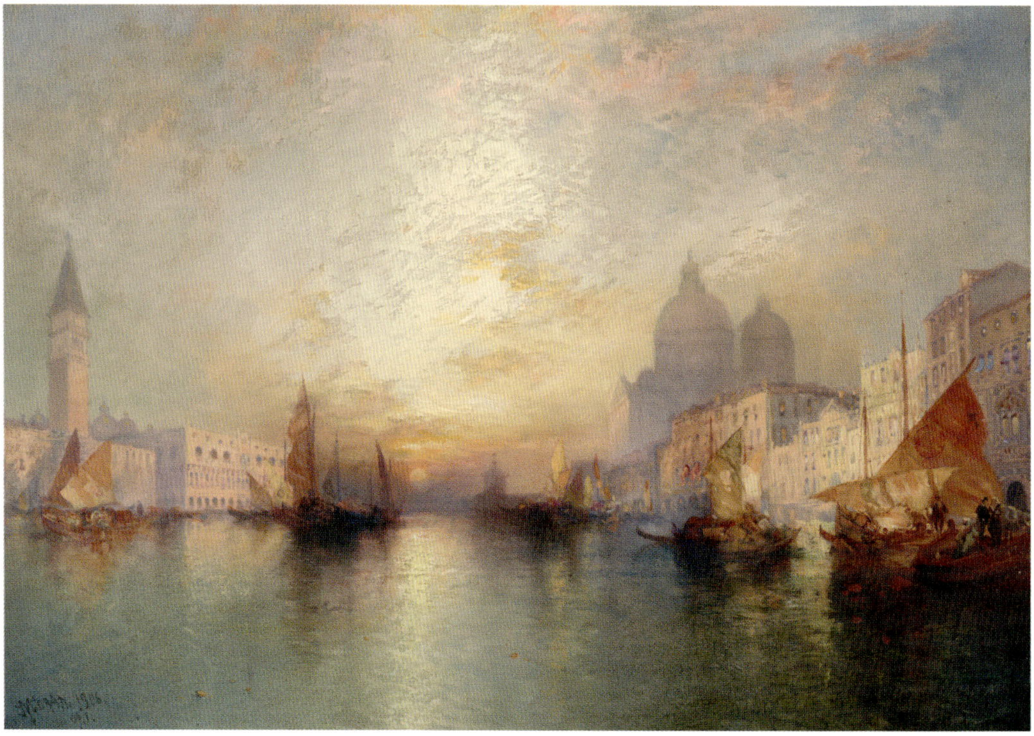

4.
Thomas Moran (1837–1926)
Venice: Grand Canal at Sunset
1906
Oil on canvas
13 ½ × 19 ½ in.
(34.3 × 49.5 cm)
Collection of the Art Fund, Inc. at the Birmingham Museum of Art; Bequest of Virginia Bissell Spencer, AFI. 79.2011

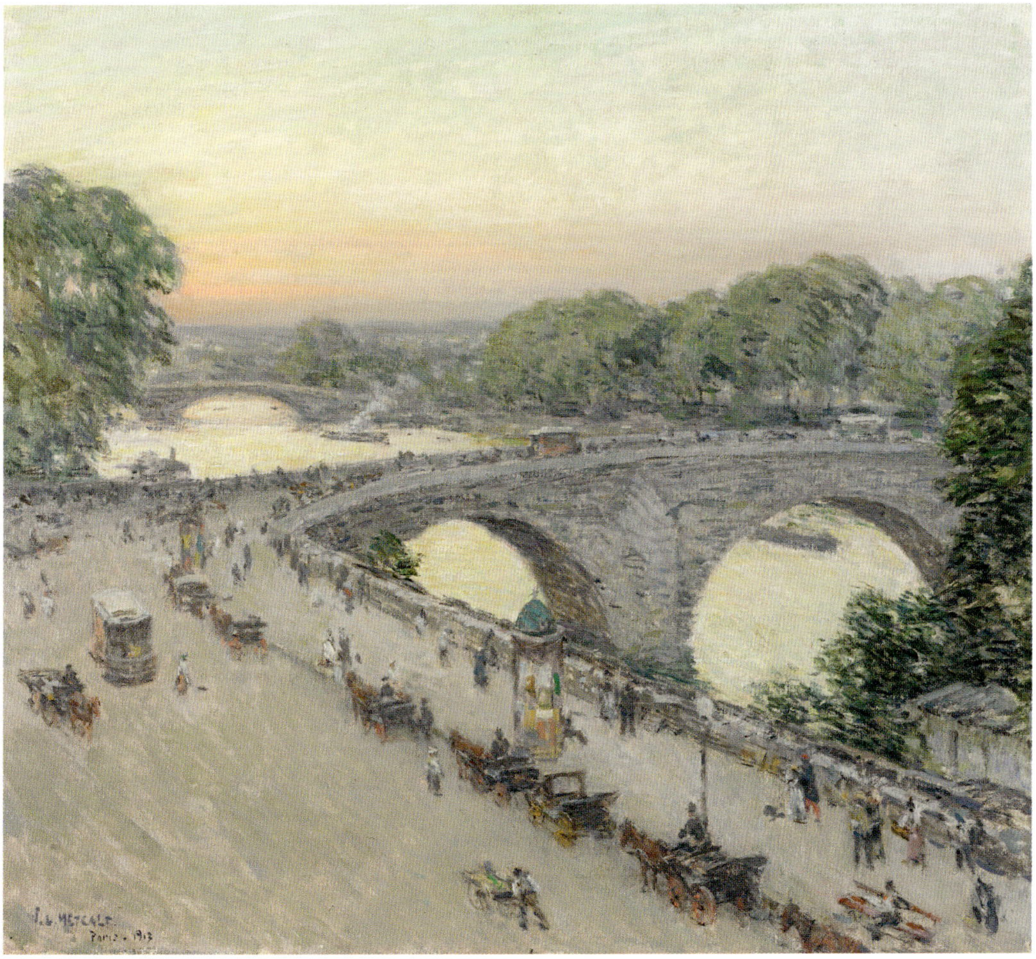

5.
Willard LeRoy Metcalf
(1858–1925)
Pont Royal, 1913
Oil on canvas
26 × 29 in. (66 × 73.7 cm)
Collection of the Art Fund, Inc. at the Birmingham Museum of Art; Partial and promised gift of Mr. and Mrs. Donald L. Cook
AFI.288.2010

Italy via France and the Swiss Alps. According to Joseph Ketner, "French art apparently did not make much of an impression on them, and they moved on to Italy within weeks."[16] Vedder, on the other hand, arrived in Paris in March 1856 and spent eight months in the studio of the narrative painter François-Edouard Picot (1786–1868) before leaving for Florence. Similarly, Moran spent five months in Paris in early 1867. There he exhibited at both the Exposition Universelle and the Salon, and had the chance to spend the afternoon with the painter Jean-Baptiste-Camille Corot (1796–1875), whose Tonalist style greatly influenced his own.[17]

As the nineteenth century progressed, Paris's popularity grew as a destination for American artists. In 1904, Clive Holland wrote, "Paris has for many years been the Mecca of Art students of both sexes."[18] Indeed, Americans were flocking to Paris as if on a pilgrimage. As Kathleen Adler observed, "It was the centre of the art world and, especially after the end of the American Civil War in 1865, thousands of American artists were attracted to Paris to study, to visit exhibitions (particularly the huge annual Salons) and to show their own work."[19] Among the thousands was the American Impressionist Willard Metcalf (1858–1925), who made his first trip to Paris in 1883, where he studied at the Académie Julian with the figure painters Gustave Boulanger (1824–1888) and Jules Lefebvre (1836–1911).[20] Founded in 1868 by Rodolphe Julian, the private art school was "probably the most famous independent atelier in the city." As Richard Boyle explains, "There, an artist could work freely and without restriction, yet also obtain disciplined instruction from well-known artists."[21] Metcalf's time in the city had a profound impact on his artistic

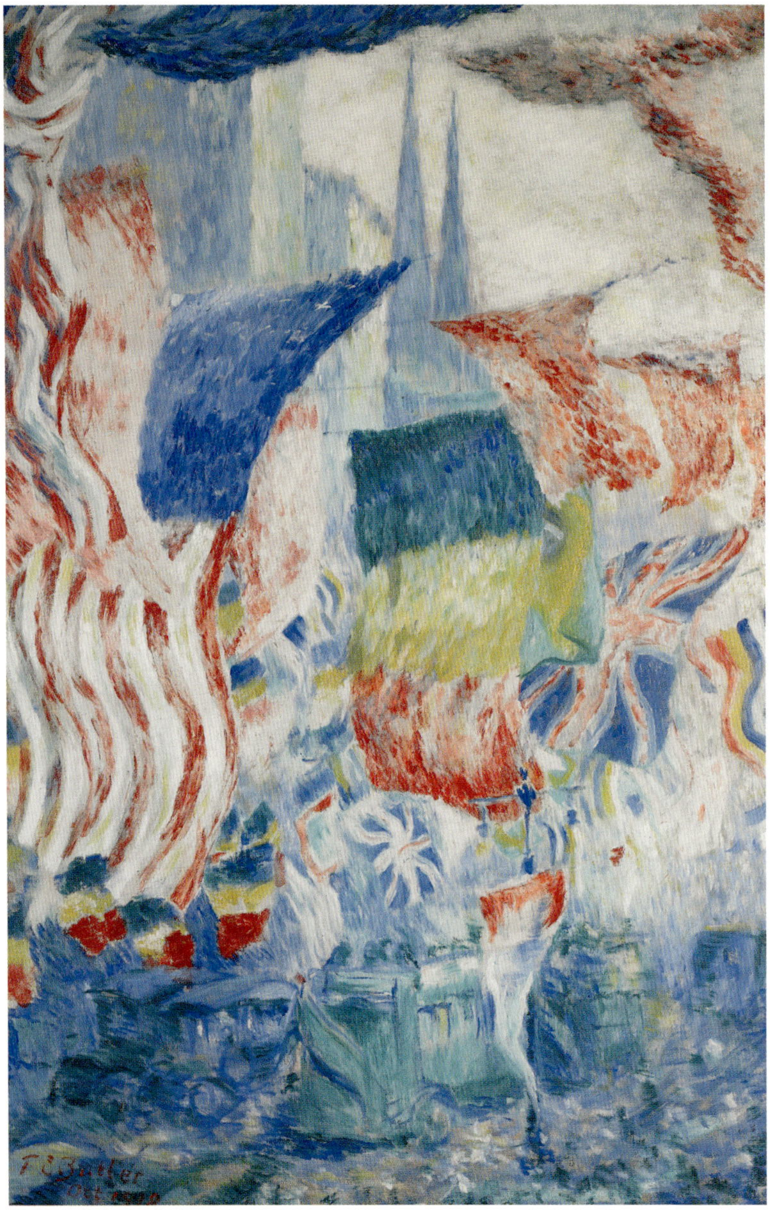

6.
Theodore Earl Butler
(1861–1936)
Flags, 1918
Oil on canvas
42 ¼ × 27 ¼ in.
(107.3 × 69.2 cm)
Collection of the Art Fund, Inc. at the Birmingham Museum of Art; Gift of Marlene and Crawford Taylor in honor of Margaret G. Livingston, Thomas N. Carruthers, Jr., and William M. Spencer, III for their long years of service to this Museum, our community at large, and for their personal examples of servant leadership at its best, AFI.20.2005

upbringing. Equally if not more important were his three trips to Giverny—home to the French Impressionist Claude Monet—between 1883 and 1887, as a result of which "he gradually adopted a lighter, high-keyed palette."[22]

Metcalf returned to Paris in August 1913, in the company of his wife and daughter. Remaining for a month and a half, he painted just a single work, *Pont Royal* (Fig. 5), which depicts Paris's third oldest bridge in the center of the composition, as seen from the Left Bank of the Seine. The thoroughfare at the lower left is the Quai Voltaire, and it is highly likely that Metcalf painted the scene from a room in Hôtel du Quai Voltaire, the same vantage point used by fellow American Impressionist Childe Hassam (1859–1935) for a similar view painted sixteen years earlier, now in the collection of the Cincinnati Art Museum.[23] Across the river, the Jardin des Tuileries is visible, while in the distance, Metcalf includes the old Pont de Solférino. During his brief stay, Metcalf returned to Giverny, but found the changes that had occurred during the long interlude since his last visit to be depressing, which might have hastened his departure from France.[24]

Among the many American Impressionists to visit Giverny, none was closer to the place and its most famous resident than the Ohio-born painter Theodore Earl Butler (1861–1936), who first visited the village in the summer of 1888, returning for nearly a year in October 1891. There, he developed an intense friendship with Monet, becoming so close to his family that in 1892 he wed Monet's stepdaughter Suzanne Hoschedé. The year after Suzanne died in 1899, Butler married her sister Marthe, who helped raise the couple's two children.[25] In 1912, Butler and his family left for America to install murals he had completed for artist James Wall Finn, which had been commissioned by the financier William A. Paine, co-founder of the brokerage firm Paine, Webber & Company.[26] While in the United States, Butler contributed three paintings to the landmark 1913 Armory Show, and visited family in Ohio.[27] Just as the Butlers were about to return to France, World War I broke out, preventing them from going. Although the fighting came to an end on November 11, 1918, when Germany signed the Armistice, lack of funds prevented the Butlers from returning to Giverny until May 1921.[28] Barely a month before the war's end, Butler painted a lively canvas depicting an Allied flag celebration on New York's Fifth Avenue, simply entitled *Flags* (Fig. 6). Like the flag paintings of his contemporary and fellow Impressionist Childe Hassam, the scene is filled with bright color, effusive light, and exuberant brushwork. Although not painted in Giverny, *Flags* incorporates all the techniques that Butler had learned from his famous father-in-law and typically employed throughout the countryside of Normandy.

The aforementioned artists are just some of the many Americans who worked in Europe during the nineteenth and early twentieth centuries. For collectors—both individuals and institutions alike—being open to collecting European subjects by American artists can provide excellent opportunities to acquire first-rate examples of an artist's work without paying top dollar. As a general rule the American art market prefers American subjects by American artists. For example, around 2010, a modest (6 × 12 in.) view of the Roman Campagna showing the ruins of the Claudian Aqueduct by the Hudson River School painter Jervis McEntee (1828–1891) could be purchased for as little as $14,000, while a nearly identically-sized canvas, depicting the Catskill Mountains, might sell for as much as $40,000. Similarly, Moran's views of Venice typically sell for between $100,000 and $200,000 at auction, depending upon the size and nuances of the composition (fiery sunsets usually sell for more than blue skies). By contrast, his paintings of the American West start in the high six figures and routinely sell for several million dollars. Of course there are notable exceptions. For example, John Singer Sargent's watercolors of Venice are among his most prized works, and major works by Duncanson are so scarce that one might pay just as dearly for an Italian subject as for an American or Canadian landscape.

Another opportunity for collectors is to purchase the work of artists who catered to Grand Tourists, such as John Gadsby Chapman (1808–1889), who arrived in Rome in 1850, remaining there for thirty-four years, selling colorful scenes of the Roman Campagna and peasants in traditional costume to American tourists.[29] Because Chapman was prolific and often repeated his most successful subjects, quintessential examples of his work can be had for anywhere between $1000 and $5000, and sometimes for less than $1000 in a regional auction house or even on eBay. The paintings of Chapman's son, John Linton Chapman (1839–1905), which resemble his father's in style and subject, sell for about the same, and are sometimes indistinguishable from the elder Chapman's work by the untrained eye.

One of the unique aspects of collecting the work of American artists abroad is the energy and immediacy of what they produced there. Because the majority of artists were traveling and had to worry about the burden and expense of excessive baggage, they tended to work on a small scale, making drawings and small oil and watercolor sketches. The Ashcan School artist Robert Henri (1865–1929), for example, used to paint on tiny wooden panels known as *pochades* (from French *poche*, pocket), which easily fit in his coat pocket along with a small painting kit. Describing the artist as a "sketch hunter," Henri wrote:

He moves through life as he finds it, not passing negligently the things he loves, but stopping to know them, and to note them down in the shorthand of his sketch-book, a box of oils with a few small panels, the fit of his pocket, or on his drawing pad. Like any hunter, he hits or misses. He is looking for what he loves, he tries to capture it. It's found anywhere, everywhere. Those who are not hunters do not see these things. The hunter is learning to see and to understand—to enjoy. [30]

Henri's pocket paintings, often depictions of places and moments encountered during his travels in France and the Netherlands, were rapidly painted and therefore capture fleeting atmospheric effects with great accuracy. These are perfect Henris in miniature and typically sell for between $5000 and $20,000, depending upon the popularity of the subject.

As Robert Frost taught us, taking "the road less traveled" can make all the difference. Collectors willing to deviate from the standard canon and tastes dominating the market can typically enjoy a much greater supply of superb pictures without stiff competition from others. In many cases this will mean acquiring a solid "A" painting of a European subject instead of having to settle for a B- or C-grade American scene. By taking a grand *détour* of their own, collectors can make their dollars stretch further without sacrificing quality or variety.

American Impressionism and the Discourse of Connoisseurship

Lisa N. Peters, PhD
St. Joseph's College, Brooklyn; Visiting Assistant Professor, Pratt Institute, Brooklyn, New York

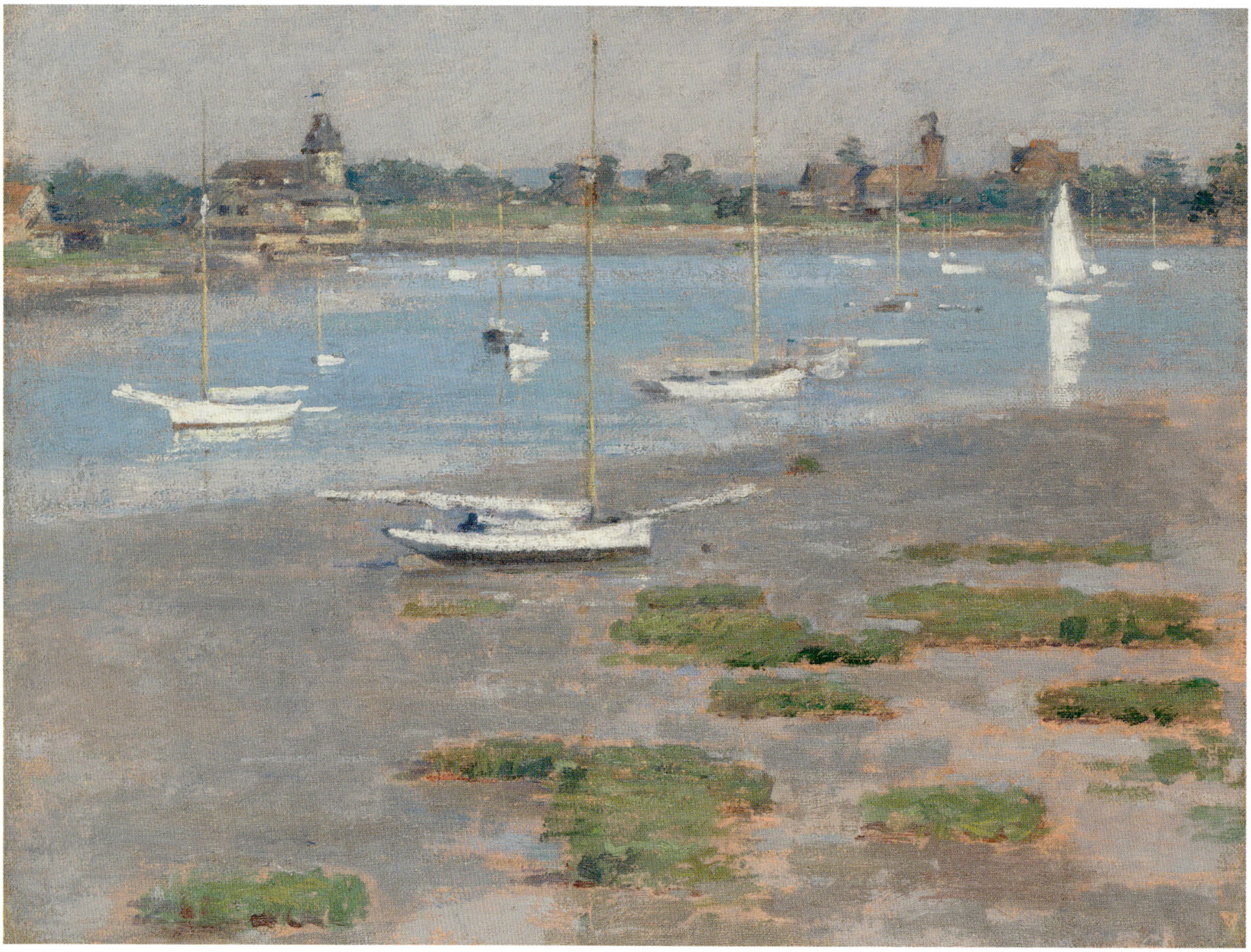

Once considered well down the scale in the evaluation of art-historical relevance, and much-maligned, American Impressionism became a subject considered worthy of study and interest only in the 1960s. This occurred through an interaction among art dealers, collectors, and scholars, whose pursuit of knowledge—constituting a discourse of connoisseurship—brought questions and inquiries to the surface and facilitated scholarship that is ongoing today.

In the context of the American art world, American Impressionism fell out of favor long before many of its leading exponents had ended their careers. The art historian and museum curator John I.H. Baur acknowledged this phenomenon in the foreword to the catalogue for the 1937 Brooklyn Museum exhibition, *Leaders of American Impressionism*, stating:

With the death of Childe Hassam two years ago, the last of America's pioneer Impressionists passed from the scene. In a sense the movement is dead, for Hassam outlived it in this country just as Monet [did] in France. It has gone through its vital stages—its radical youth, its assured maturity, and an old age marked by conservatism on the one hand and on the other by an inevitable popularization.[1]

Baur felt the time was "an auspicious one to review a current of American painting which mixed its waters with the art of this country for nearly five decades." However, he chose to include only four artists in the exhibition—Mary Cassatt, Childe Hassam, John Twachtman, and J. Alden Weir—indicating that "it is in the work of more independent and creative artists that the guiding spirit of the movement is to be found," while other artists, such as Theodore Robinson, Robert Reid, and Theodore Wendel, "had become minor."[2] When Baur organized an exhibition of Robinson's work in 1946 (also at the Brooklyn Museum), he felt the artist's achievements hinted at being "masterpieces," while noting that Robinson's art had fallen into obscurity since his death in 1896. Baur stated as well that "Impressionism, never a very robust or influential movement in American art, [had been] rapidly eclipsed by more revolutionary developments in the early century, particularly by the advent of The Eight and the impact of the Armory Show."[3]

Baur's comments reflect the discrediting of the movement and its legacy that occurred for various reasons from the 1910s through the 1950s. By contrast with the art produced in the early twentieth century by the Urban Realists—who became known as the Ashcan School in the 1930s—American Impressionism seemed blemished by European gentility and an overemphasis on aestheticism. Women in white dresses and sunlit landscapes were deemed unworthy of the nation's uniqueness and vitality in an age of technological progress and dramatic social change.

American Impressionism was pushed further into the shadows by the spread of European Modernist influence in American art in the wake of the 1913 Armory Show. The perception of art as an autonomous language freed from illusionism made paintings capturing glimpses of shifting effects of outdoor light seem overly dependent on both naturalism and realism. In a time when art was viewed as a vehicle of self-realization and individual expression, the high aesthetic standards and the view of art as a means of refining society implicit in American Impressionist art were no longer plausible or relevant. A gendered rhetoric also served to devalue American Impressionism, as its decorative and refined aspects were associated with a "feminine" conformity that contrasted with the virility and assertiveness of the "masculine" individualism of the Modernist ideology.

The 1930s initiated a period of repatriation in American art, when critics such as Thomas Craven and Edward Alden Jewell celebrated the American Regionalists—Thomas Hart Benton, Grant Wood, and John Steuart Curry—for freeing themselves from the shackles of European Modernism, devoting their attention to particular localities along with their popular legends and histories. Responding to the era's nationalism, cultural critics, such as Van Wyck Brooks, Paul Rosenfeld, Waldo Frank, and Lewis Mumford, posed questions as to what was essentially "American" in American art and literature.

1.
Theodore Robinson
(1852–1896)
Low Tide, Riverside Yacht Club
1894
Oil on canvas
18 × 24 in. (45.7 × 61 cm)
The Metropolitan Museum of Art, New York. Gift of Margaret and Raymond J. Horowitz, 2007.281.3

However, this reassessment did not revive interest in American Impressionism. In 1931, Mumford described the eclecticism and stylistic disunity of the period from the end of the Civil War to 1895 as "the Brown Decades."[4] From it, he culled the figures in the arts who, he felt, rose above the foreign trappings, the excess, and the spiritual torpor of the Gilded Age to represent an authentic and coherent American culture on which the future could be built. In his chapter "Images—Sacred and Profane," he devoted his attention to artists in the romantic tradition—George Fuller and Albert Pinkham Ryder—and to realists, Winslow Homer and Thomas Eakins. Among the Impressionists, he commended Mary Cassatt for "escaping [dark] colors and tones in her painting by living in Paris" and stated that Twachtman had continued in the nostalgic tone and autumnal palette of Fuller with "the benefit of a bath in Monet."[5] Otherwise he noted: "colour [*sic*] was to be discovered in the eighties, seized on as a thing in itself, and reduced to superficial formulas in the work of the American impressionists."[6] He felt that French influence, in general, had turned American artists into "minor copyists, who acquired all the tricks of current French art, but had missed its original content."[7]

The view that American Impressionism constituted an insignificant or aberrant part of the trajectory of American art was perpetuated in other sources in the decades that followed. For example, in his 1962 *History of American Painting*, James Thomas Flexner described Homer as "one truly major artist," whose creative force matched that of "French Impressionist colleagues," while observing that it was a misfortune that others "buried rather than refined the native tradition."[8] In his 1963 *American Tradition in Painting*, John McCoubrey stated: "Weir, Twachtman, Robinson, and Hassam brought to America a pale, belated impressionism which gave their pictures—despite a supposed devotion to particularity—only a vague, unlocalized prettiness."[9]

American Impressionism was hastened even further into obscurity when Abstract Expressionism burst into existence after World War II and its powerful, epic-scaled new art took hold of the New York art world. In 1949, *Life Magazine* asked rhetorically if Jackson Pollock was the greatest living painter in the United States.[10] To claim a national identity for the first American art of worldwide significance, scholars uprooted nineteenth-century American art from its own time and posited that its importance lay in its anticipation of what was to come. This was the premise of *The Natural Paradise: Painting in America, 1800–1950*, an exhibition held at the Museum of Modern Art in 1976, in which the European lineage of Abstract Expressionism was downplayed in favor of connections to earlier American art that seemed to prefigure it. Robert Rosenblum wrote in the show's catalogue that it was high time to join two worlds, "and to find out whether Rothko and Pollock, for instance, are not as compatible with O'Keeffe and Ryder, or even Heade and Homer, as they are with Matisse and Masson."[11] Among the links made were those between Luminist paintings and the fusion of color, atmosphere, and silence in the work of Mark Rothko. Despite the many ways that works by American Impressionists could be related to those of mid-twentieth-century abstract painters, this topic was not considered in the catalogue.

Pride in New York's art-world dominance over Paris created a kind of amnesia in relation to art that could not be aligned with the primal and gestural aspects of action painting or the uncanny silence of more romantic manifestations. Looking back, Ira Spanierman, who opened a New York gallery in 1961, recalled that "in the 1960s, Pollock and de Kooning were international celebrities but no one knew who the Ten American Painters were. Few people were familiar with Childe Hassam or William Merritt Chase, let alone John Twachtman, Thomas Dewing, or Edmund Tarbell."[12] However, in the early 1960s, interest in a body of work, then unfashionable, began to draw the attention of a small group of New York dealers and collectors. The dealers included Spanierman, Abe Adler, Norman Hirschl, and Roy Davis, and the most prominent collectors were Margaret and Ray Horowitz, Vivian and Meyer Potamkin, Rita and Daniel Fraad, and

Florence and Ralph Spencer. The interchange between the two groups initiated a process of rediscovery and reconsideration that was soon shared with the first generation of American art historians, including Baur, Lloyd Goodrich, William H. Gerdts, and William Innes Homer. What emerged was a dialogue involving the gathering of knowledge through library research and observation. In 1999, Ray Horowitz recalled that he and Margaret "visited the Metropolitan Museum virtually every Sunday and roamed through all the painting galleries." There the two were attracted to Robinson's *Bird's Eye View, Giverny*, 1889, and "realized it could hold its own with the French Impressionists and that Theodore Robinson was a magnificent painter."[13] The Horowitzes gave their Robinson painting, *Low Tide, Riverside Yacht Club*, 1894, to The Metropolitan in 2007 (Fig. 1). Other American Impressionist works collected in the 1960s have been given or bequeathed to museums, such as Twachtman's *Snow*, late 1890s (Fig. 2), and Hassam's *The Hovel and the Skyscraper*, 1904, which are part of the 2003 bequest of Vivian Potamkin to the Pennsylvania Academy of the Fine Arts.

As dealers added American Impressionist works to their inventories—often purchased from collections where they had languished without appreciation for generations—these became conduits for understanding works of art free of the biases of the past. The dealers made the rounds of auctions of American art that were filled with works undifferentiated by quality or

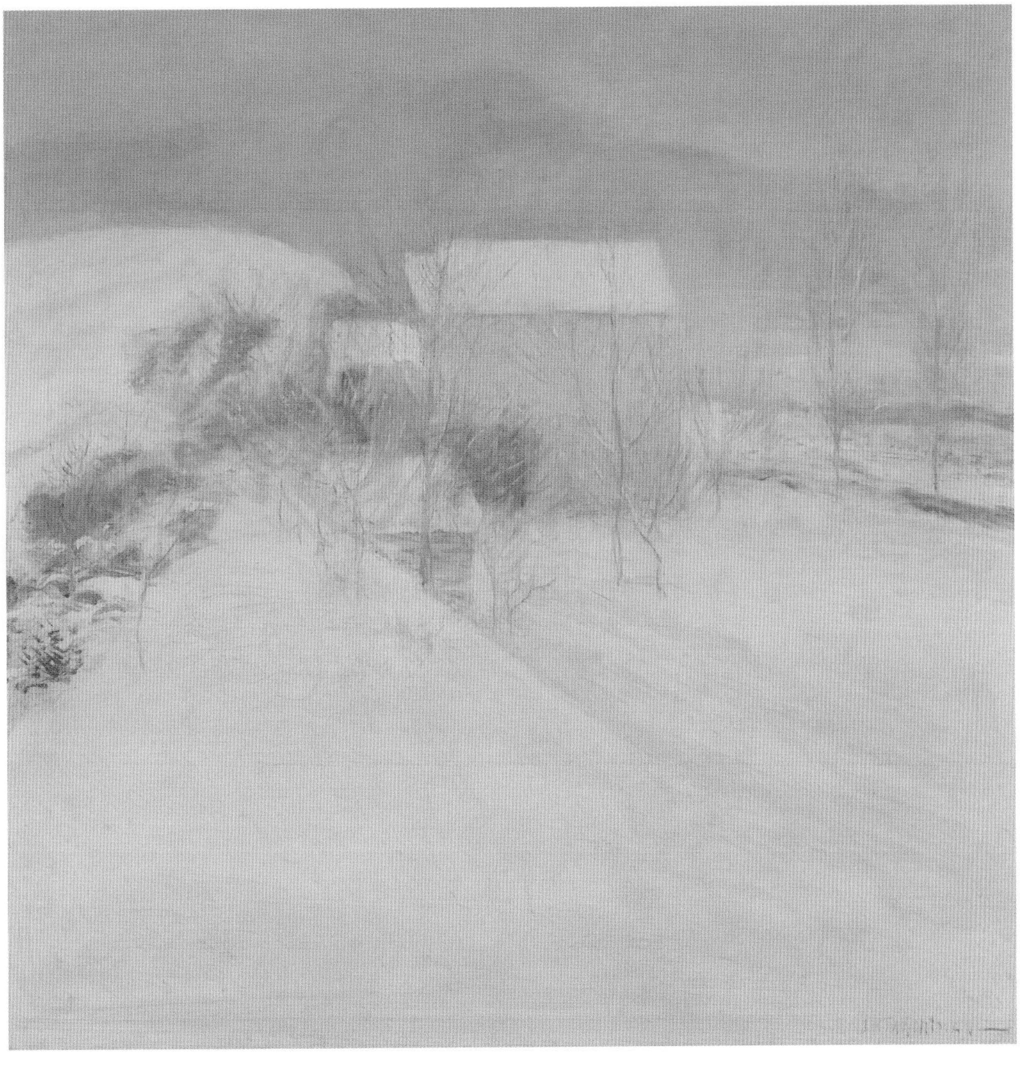

2.
John H. Twachtman
(1853–1902)
Snow, late 1890s
Oil on canvas
30 × 30 in. (76.2 × 76.2 cm)
Pennsylvania Academy of the Fine Arts, Philadelphia, The Vivian O. and Meyer P. Potamkin Collection, Bequest of Vivian O. Potamkin
2003.1.10

3. *(right)*
Cover
William H. Gerdts
American Impressionism
Exh. cat., New York: Abbeville
First edition 1984

4. *(far right)*
Cover
H. Barbara Weinberg, Doreen Bolger, and David Park Curry
American Impressionism and Realism: The Painting of Modern Life, 1885–1915
Exh. cat., New York: The Metropolitan Museum of Art, 1994

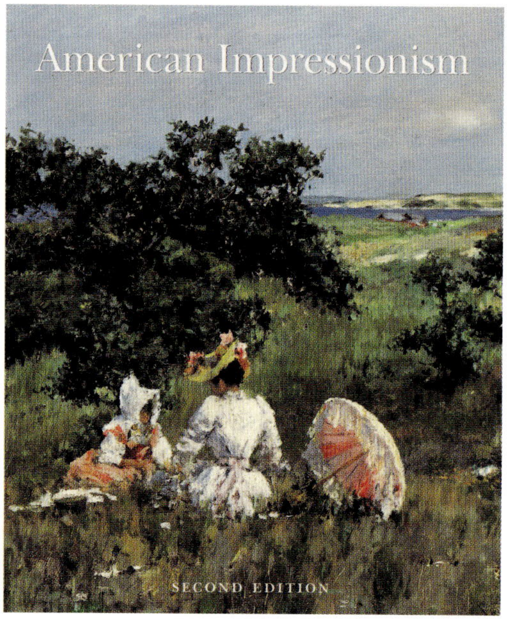

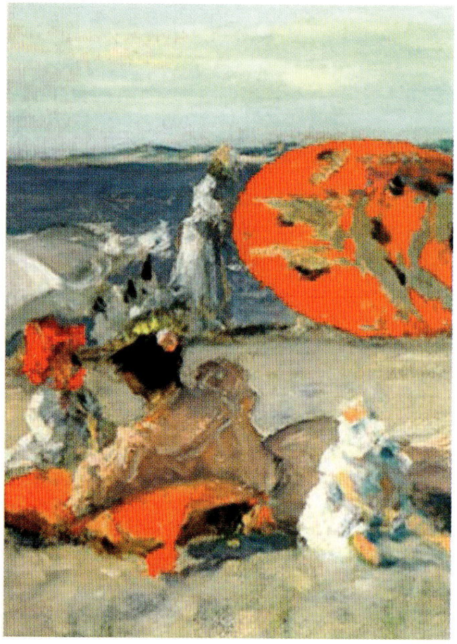

importance, and on the basis of their new acuities selected art that deserved greater attention.

The era was one in which becoming a connoisseur was valued. Deriving from the French verb *connaître* (to know), connoisseurship means being deeply acquainted with a subject. In art, a connoisseur is viewed as someone with the expertise to judge quality, but the ability to do so has been questioned in recent decades. In a 1990 article, Hal Opperman described a crisis in art-historical connoisseurship linked to the "popularity of hermeneutics on the one hand, coupled with a fall from favor of formalist aesthetics."[14] Recently, the globalization of art-historical practices and an attention more to the reception of works of art than to their contextual grounding have led to the view that connoisseurship is an elitist practice based in cultural prejudice and a hierarchical set of values.[15] However, attitudes about connoisseurship in the 1960s were less fraught, consisting of the view that being a connoisseur necessitated the counterbalancing of two types of knowledge: the development of "a good eye" through observation, and understanding the circumstances in which a work of art was made.[16] To be a connoisseur involved more of a process of discovery than of pronouncing value judgments based in subjectivity. Ray Horowitz stated:

For Margaret and me, collecting, and the development of connoisseurship were serious matters. We constantly talked to other collectors, art historians, museum curators, and dealers, trying to learn as much as possible. We traveled to museums, large and small, to look at works we had seen in reproduction, and we read everything that remotely bordered on the field.[17]

Collectors also recognized rather than hid their personal preferences. Ray Horowitz came to realize that he and Margaret "were attracted to lyrical, representational, but not academic painting; painting that expressed a definite sensibility and certain moods and feelings—warmth, tenderness, intimacy, optimism." They were interested in pictures that had "more than surface appeal," revealing "a strong structural aesthetic underpinning."[18]

Dealers were also engaged in probing the historical factors of works of art that had been lost to time, and they engaged gallery visitors in conversations about their holdings and the questions they raised. Looking back, Jay E. Cantor observed that the dealers of the 1960s acted as "casual tutors for an emerging generation of collectors in what was still a modest collecting category."[19] These open-ended discussions might be called the discourse of connoisseurship. They resulted in exhibitions and scholarship, in questioning what American artists derived from Impressionism, and in seeing their work for its own intrinsic qualities rather than judging it against that of French Impressionist counterparts. Hassam was featured in a retrospective at the Corcoran Gallery of Art in 1965; Twachtman was the subject of a large exhibition at the Cincinnati Art Museum in 1966; and a show of Cassatt's work was held at the National Gallery of Art in 1970.

Scholarship on American Impressionism and individual artists expanded in the 1970s. Museum curators Donelson Hoopes and Richard Boyle, who both had painting backgrounds, published surveys of American Impressionism, in 1972 and 1974 respectively.[20] In 1980, William H. Gerdts curated an American Impressionist exhibition for the Henry Art Gallery at the University of Washington, Seattle.[21] His catalogue, addressing regional Impressionist distinctions, provided the basis for his landmark book, *American Impressionism*, published by Abbeville Press in 1984 and dedicated to Margaret and Ray Horowitz, as well as to his wife, Abigail Gerdts (Fig. 3).[22] William Merritt Chase's *The Fairy Tale*, 1892, in the Horowitzes' collection, was featured on the cover. Gerdts's revisionism consisted in focusing on the historical context of American Impressionism rather than on the movement's "Americanism." Organized chronologically, the book assessed the precedents in American art that led to the adoption of Impressionist methodologies by American artists abroad and at home, the stylistic character of regional schools, and Impressionist influences up to and through the work of Marsden Hartley. Gerdts's equanimity is reflected in his focus on Impressionism as primarily a stylistic motive rather than one based in a particular ideology. This approach makes designating a work as an example of American Impressionism to be primarily a matter of style—such as vibrant, complementary color, broken brushwork, and compositional devices of flattening and asymmetry.[23]

In a 1988 article Wanda Corn observed that American art scholarship had come into its own largely because of the ways that the issue of "Americanness" had triggered debates about the subject, leading students to enter the field and museums to hire American art curators.[24] She also observed that a change was occurring in American art history, away from the documentary monograph, consisting of "the description of styles and the delineating of paths of influence" to a new consideration of iconography, involving new interdisciplinary considerations, issues of social history, and interpretive approaches—often linking American painting and sculpture with material culture, and American studies in general.[25] Corn felt this change was taking place primarily in the academic arena, but that museums had also begun to explore ways to address broader issues of cultural history—she acknowledged this was a difficult endeavor given the "traditional concerns of the art museum for objects of the highest quality."[26]

This challenge was taken up in 1994, when The Metropolitan Museum of Art organized *American Impressionism and Realism: The Painting of Modern Life, 1885–1915* (Fig. 4).[27] The exhibition's curators and catalogue authors, H. Barbara Weinberg, Doreen Bolger, and David Park Curry, sought to assess ways in which works of art reflected their socio-cultural milieu, and they included examples by both American Impressionists and the Urban Realists associated with the Ashcan School.[28] Their aim was to demonstrate that the two—often contrasted with each other—were more alike than they had been perceived to be in the past. As a corrective to the descriptive and monographic approach of publications such as that of Gerdts, they argued that differentiating groups on the basis of style often resulted in false dichotomies. They illustrated this by pointing out how comparisons such as those between "the lightly brushed, high-key works that Chase and Hassam executed in the late 1800s and the darker-toned urban scenes that [Robert] Henri, [John] Sloan, and colleagues produced from about 1905" were essentially superficial.[29]

Organized thematically, the show's catalogue was divided into sections on the city, the country, and the home. The authors followed the model of Robert L. Herbert's *Impressionism: Art, Leisure, and Parisian Society* (1988) in discussions that interweave fastidious historical research, contemporary literature, the artist's own statements, and close readings of the works themselves. The approach entices viewers to look closely and to see paintings through both a historical lens and one that seems transportive into a time in the past.[30]

The catalogue's close readings, effort to understand the social meaning of works of art, and its juxtapositions bring many intriguing points and questions to the surface. However, the decision to link the two groups, along with other aspects of the show and its catalogue, were heavily criticized in reviews.[31] Of most contention was the view that in their effort to see works of art objectively rather than through the lens of patriotic Americanness, the authors focused too much on how American artists backed away from modern life. They often zeroed in on the lack of candor in their work by contrast with that of European peers. They brought out how Americans avoided the "most unpleasant" aspects of their surroundings, creating cheerful and evasive images that hid rather than exposed actualities. They stated: "As we tested the visual record—the works of art—against written accounts, we found almost inevitably that both the American Impressionists and Realists tempered a commitment to portraying turn-of-the-century life with a tendency toward euphemism, optimism, nationalism, and nostalgia."[32]

That the exhibition's wall labels focused on what artists omitted rather than what they depicted led to the most disparaging commentaries.[33] One reviewer went so far as to say that "whatever pleasure [visitors] derived from the paintings was dulled by the annoyance of the wall-labels. They felt manipulated and deceived.... A great many of them felt that the exhibition was an intellectual insult."[34] Presuming that visitors would not read the catalogue, its dense discussions were reduced to a few sentences in the wall labels, resulting in an approach that was too compressed and thereby ineffective.

On the other hand, critics such as Trevor Fairbrother felt the authors had not gone far enough. He credited them with wanting to "confront such topics as class struggle, sexism, and progressivism in the arts," but noted they had essentially grafted "ideas culled from revisionist art history onto a display of paintings that followed visual conventions of 'masterpiece' exhibitions," in order to satisfy the show's corporate sponsor, Alamo-Rent-A-Car.[35] Fairbrother argued that the authors had reduced the issue of Americanness to generalizations, belying the fact that "the nativist question was a complicated stew of conflicting ambitions and impulses."[36]

Fairbrother also pointed out a problem inherent in Impressionism in general, namely the term's elasticity. Even art historians addressing French Impressionism have wrestled with the definition of Impressionism and where the line between it, realism, and other modes of representation in the late nineteenth century can be drawn. In his 1988 *Impressionism*, Herbert adhered to what he described as a pragmatic definition of French Impressionism, one "essentially of convenience." He chose to refer "to a group of avant-garde painters who made common cause and who were associated together by their contemporaries" and he narrowed his discussion to the artists who he felt demonstrated the "most meaningful innovations in pictorial language." He included Edouard Manet, even though Manet did not participate in the exhibitions of the *indépendants*—known even during their own time as the Impressionists.[37] Herbert was unconcerned with justifying whether or not a work was Impressionist, based on its stylistic features. The authors of the Metropolitan catalogue likewise narrowed their selections to those they felt demonstrated the highest degree of attention to modern life in the body of an artist's work. However, they did not acknowledge that this was their method, to the detriment of the catalogue. Their cherry-picking left out the range of modes and subjects to which American artists applied Impressionist means, leading to some glaring omissions, such as the

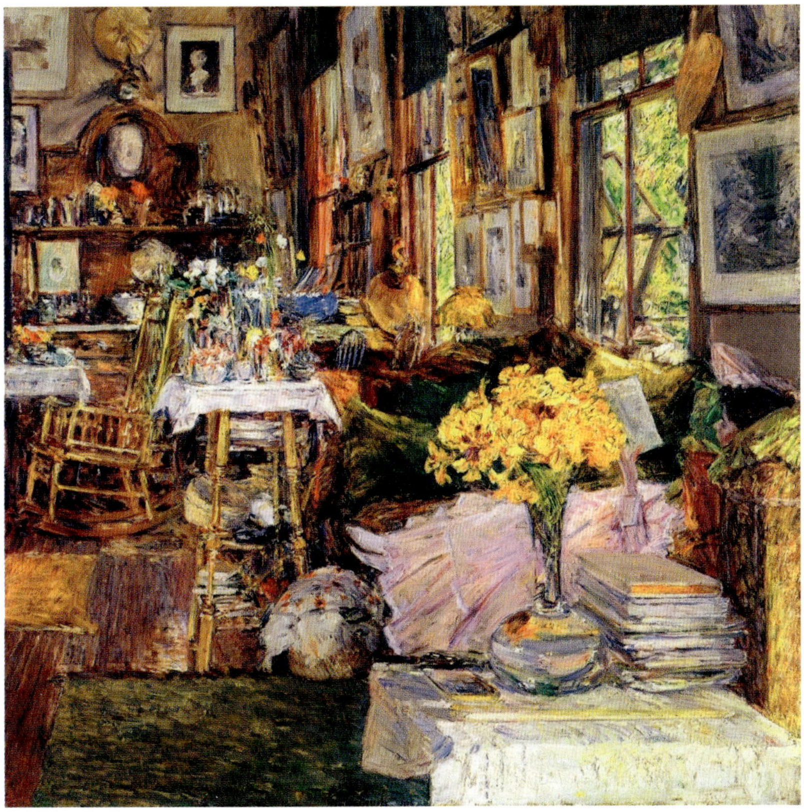

5.
Childe Hassam (1859–1935)
The Room of Flowers, 1894
Oil on canvas
34 × 34 in. (86.3 × 86.3 cm)
Sotheby's, New York,
May 27, 1993, lot 21

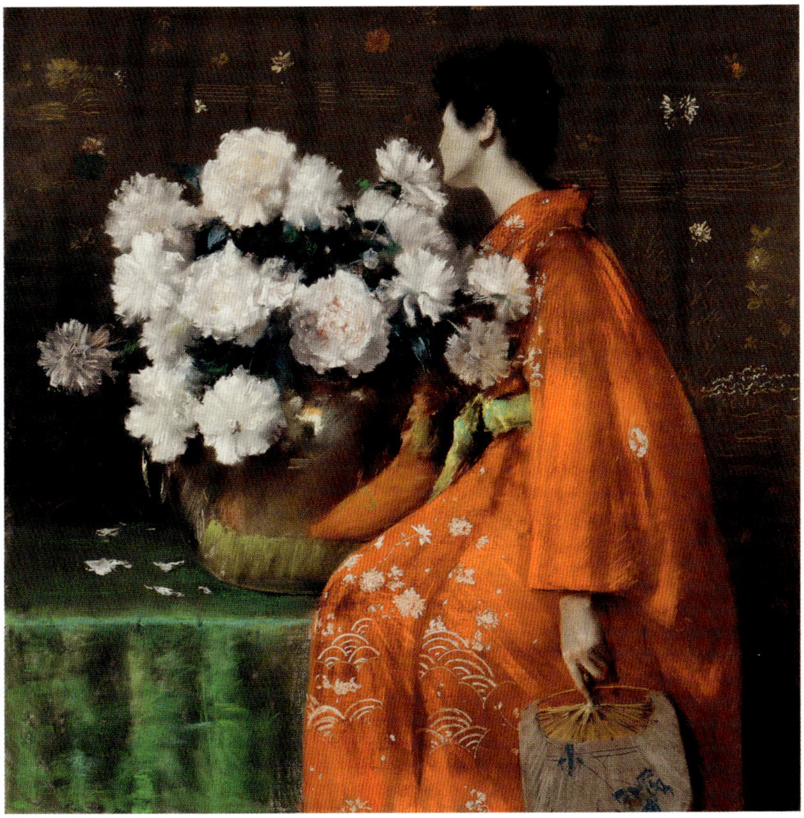

6.
William Merritt Chase
(1849–1916)
Spring Flowers (Peonies)
By 1889
Pastel on paper, prepared
with a tan ground, and
wrapped with canvas around
a wooden strainer
48 × 48 in. (121.9 × 121.9 cm)
Chicago, Terra Foundation for
American Art, Daniel J. Terra
Collection, 1999.32

7.
Dennis Miller Bunker
(1861–1890)
Wild Asters, 1889
$25^{1}/_{4}$ × $30^{1}/_{4}$ in.
(64.1 × 76.8 cm)
Sotheby's, New York, December 1, 1999, lot 31

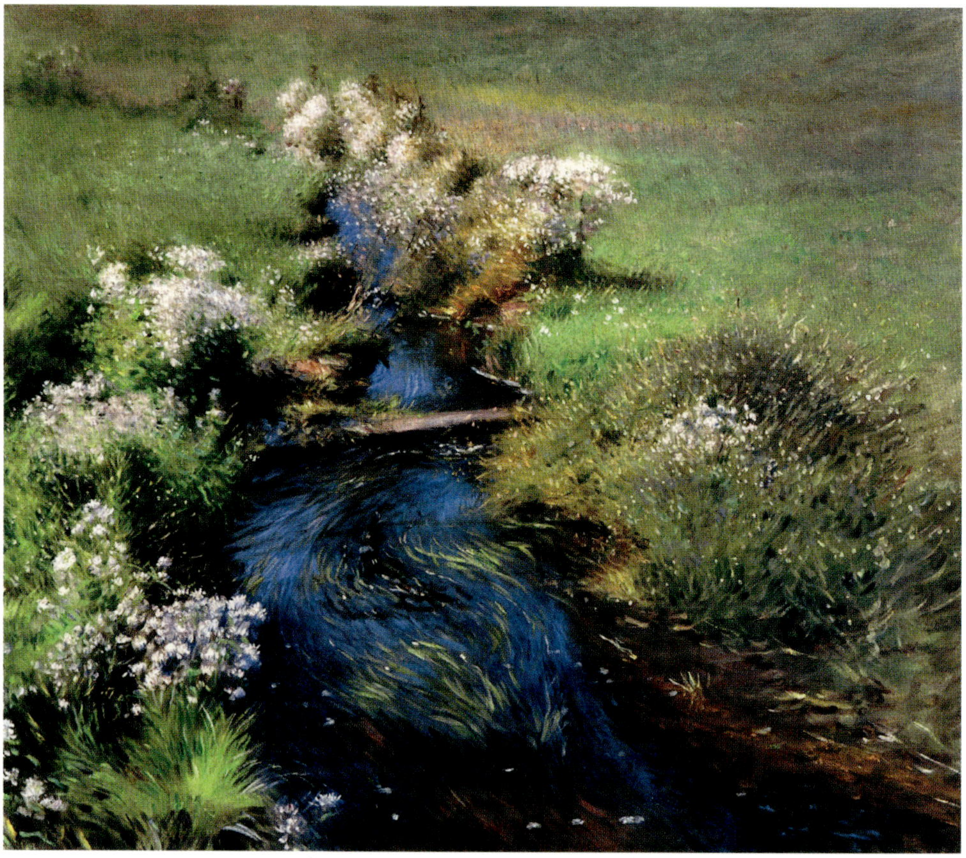

8.
Childe Hassam (1859–1935)
Spring in Central Park, 1908
Oil on canvas
$29^{1}/_{4}$ × $37^{1}/_{4}$ in.
(74.3 × 94.6 cm)
Christie's, New York, May 21, 2008, lot 74

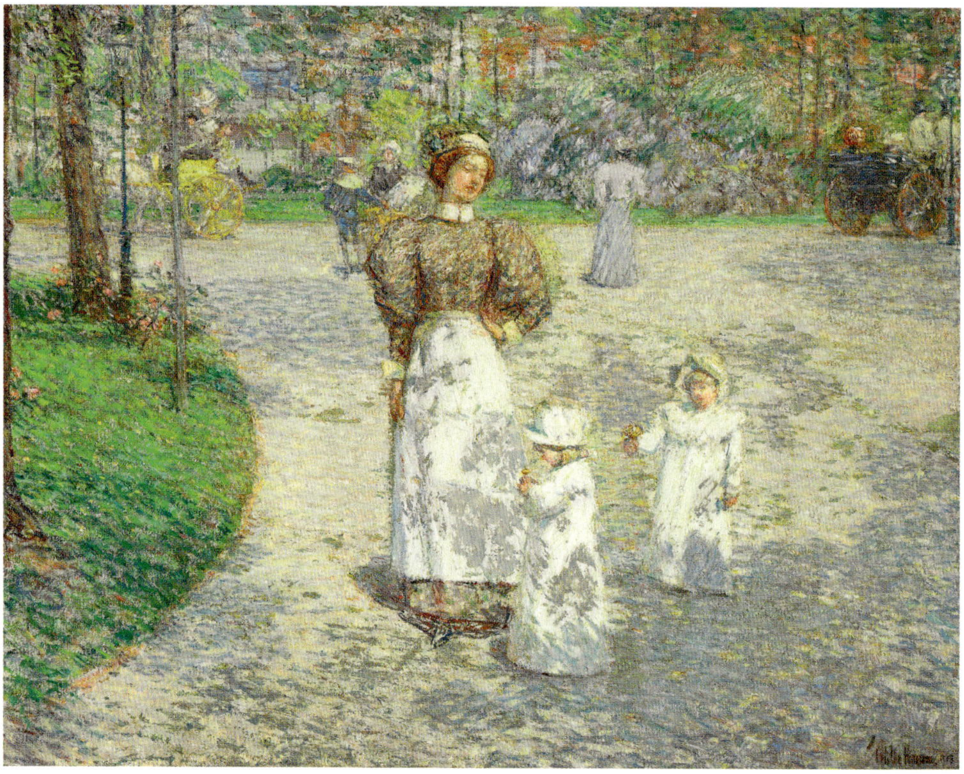

Impressionistically rendered images of idealized women by Robert Reid.

Nonetheless, thanks to scholarship, debate, and more exposure to the public, by the late 1980s American Impressionism had not only lost its former reputation as a weak and insignificant chapter in American art but had become the subject of many monographs and studies of regional groups, in which both style and iconography were taken into consideration. The previous need defensively to justify the validity of Impressionist works by American artists had mostly ceased. At the same time, American Impressionism had become fashionable and popular. The dedication of the early collectors and dealers in bringing artists and their work into the light had turned into a kind of monster, with prices for works by major artists escalating far beyond the reach of even collectors with more resources than those of the 1960s. Minor artists were being dredged up and labeled "Impressionist," with little regard for much else about their work. In response to the Metropolitan's show, James Hall wrote an article in *The Guardian* in which he expressed his dread of "the prospect of [another summer] of wall-to-wall Impressionism," and asked whether it was "time to pull the plug" on the subject.[38]

American Impressionist works brought some of the record auction prices for American art in the 1990s and early 2000s, including Childe Hassam's *The Room of Flowers*, 1894 (Fig. 5), which sold in 1993 for $5,500,000. In the same year, William Merritt Chase's pastel, *Spring Flowers (Peonies)*, 1889 (Fig. 6), sold for $3,962,500. In 1998, Hassam's *Flags, Afternoon on the Avenue*, 1917, brought almost $8,000,000. In 1999, Dennis Miller Bunker's *Wild Asters*, 1889 (Fig. 7), sold for $3,082,500. The sales frenzy continued into 2008, when, in May, Hassam's *Spring in Central Park*, 1908 (Fig. 8), went for $5,641,000.

However, by the end of the year in the wake of the demise of Lehman Brothers, the subprime mortgage crisis, and the fall of the stock market, the entire American art market went into a tailspin. What at first seemed like a correction soon turned into a downward dive, and prices for American Impressionist work plummeted, while it also soon became apparent that there were now very few opportunities to acquire premium paintings, given the purchases by individuals and museums over the years. By early in the new century, most of the dealers—including some who had seen the rise of American Impressionism from the beginning, in the early 1960s—had shifted their focus to selling American art of the mid-twentieth century, which had come to be perceived through a historical lens.

In the new millennium, to some degree a split has occurred between museums and universities in the consideration of American art. In museums, it seems that the discourse of connoisseurship has been continued. For example, curators have increasingly involved conservators in aspects of exhibitions and have developed strategies of looking beyond assumptions, often taking the challenge of thinking globally rather than with Americanness in mind.[39] Academics have become more invested in hermeneutics, issues of perception and reception, and understanding works of art as part of systems—not always timebound—reflective of aspects of material culture, politics, and art history. These pursuits promise new paradigms in the scholarship of American art in an Impressionist context, seeing it not as monolithic or in comparison with French Impressionism or the art of the Ashcan School. The engagement in the discourse of connoisseurship among dealers, collectors, and art historians belonged to its own time, but in asking questions, it raised the need to keep the door always open to new avenues of exploration.

Last of The Eight
John Sloan and Everett Shinn as Living History

Heather Campbell Coyle
Chief Curator and Curator of American Art at the Delaware Art Museum, Wilmington, Delaware

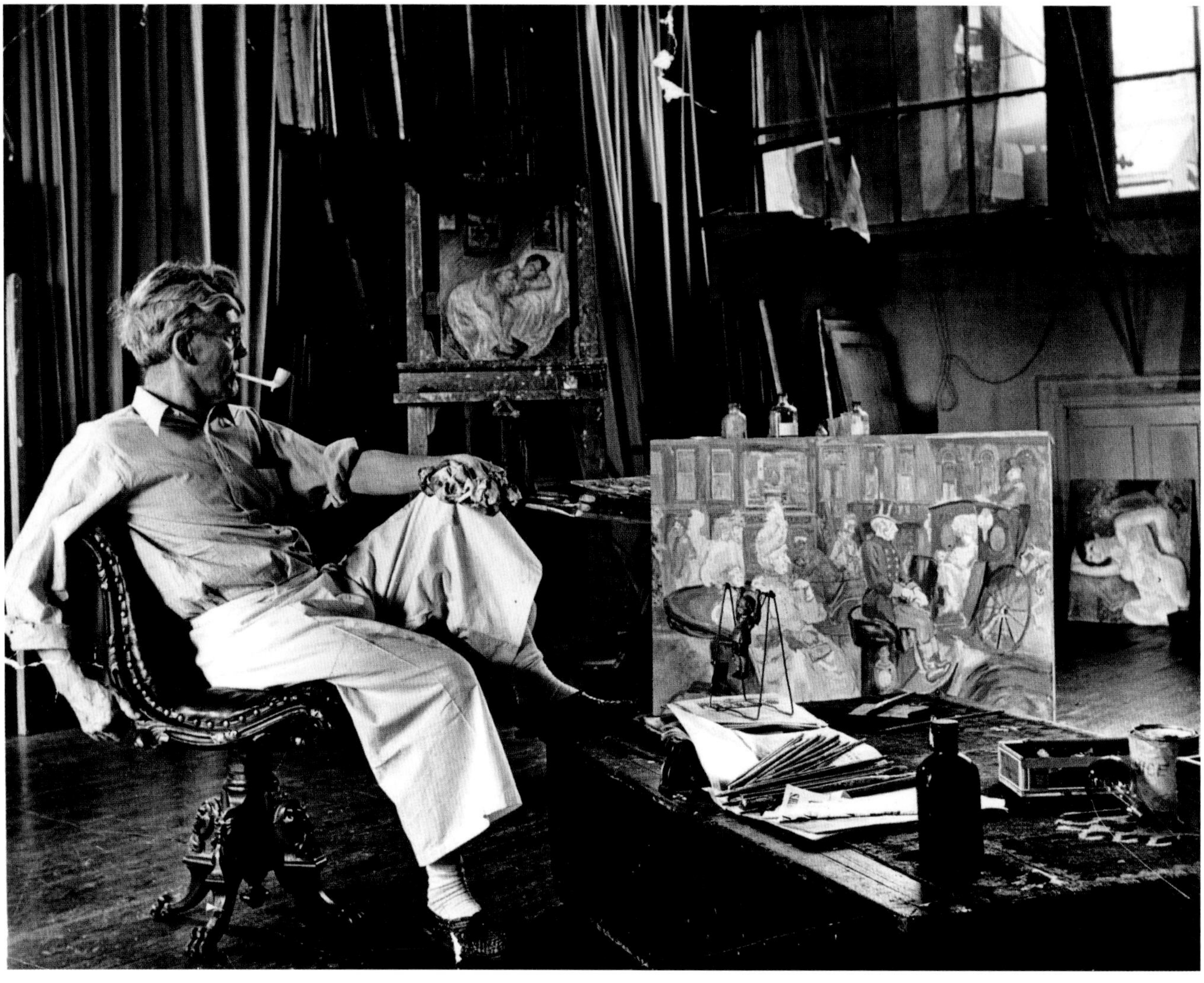

In 1937, the early work of the group of American artists known as The Eight was officially enshrined in history with the *New York Realists* exhibition at the Whitney Museum of American Art. The show featured the work of Robert Henri (1865–1929), George Luks (1867–1933), John Sloan (1871–1951), Everett Shinn (1876–1953), William Glackens (1870–1938), and Ernest Lawson (1873–1939)—six of the original Eight—as well as George Bellows (1882–1925), Glenn O. Coleman (1887–1932), and Guy Pène du Bois (1884–1958), who had been students of Henri. Despite embracing this corps of younger artists, the exhibition was limited to works produced between 1900 and 1914, focusing on this moment in American art as particularly worthy of interest. The catalogue for the *New York Realists* show explained the rationale for its focus: "As time gives perspective to our judgments, it becomes increasingly evident that the moderns of the first Roosevelt era represented an historic chapter in American art to which we owe a great debt."[1]

At the center of the Whitney's show stood The Eight and their groundbreaking 1908 exhibition. There was a sense that this group of artists, particularly Henri, Sloan, Shinn, Glackens, and Luks, were particularly important to the art being produced in the United States in 1937—to artistic movements like American scene painting, regionalism, and Social Realism. And it was decidedly the early work of these artists and their activity in organizing a protest exhibition almost thirty years previously that the show's organizers deemed pertinent to the development of American art.

New York Realists arrived after more than a decade of the collecting of these artists' early paintings by New York art museums. The show expanded interest in The Eight among collectors and museums. The exhibition defined these artists, half of whom were still living, through images of New York made decades earlier. With this show and others that would follow, John Sloan and Everett Shinn, the longest-lived of The Eight, saw themselves becoming history. Their distinct reactions—what they painted, where they exhibited, and how they managed their bodies of work late in their careers—influence scholarship and collecting to this day.

THE EXHIBITION OF THE EIGHT IN 1908

On February 3, 1908, an exhibition opened to great fanfare at Macbeth Gallery in New York. The day before the opening, the *New York Herald* trumpeted "Secession in Art," and the *World* published a full-page article on the front of their Sunday magazine. The *World*'s lengthy headline announced "New York's Art War and the Eight Rebels Who Dared to Paint Pictures of New York Life (instead of Europe) and are Holding Their Rebellious Exhibition All by Themselves."[2] In the subsequent weeks,

1. *(opposite)*
John Sloan Seated in his Studio, c. 1939
Gelatin silver print
11 × 14 in. (27.9 × 35.6 cm)
John Sloan Manuscript Collection, Delaware Art Museum

2. *(below)*
Everett Shinn in his Westport Studio, c. 1938
Gelatin silver print
6 × 4 in. (15.2 × 10.2 cm)
Everett Shinn Papers, Delaware Art Museum

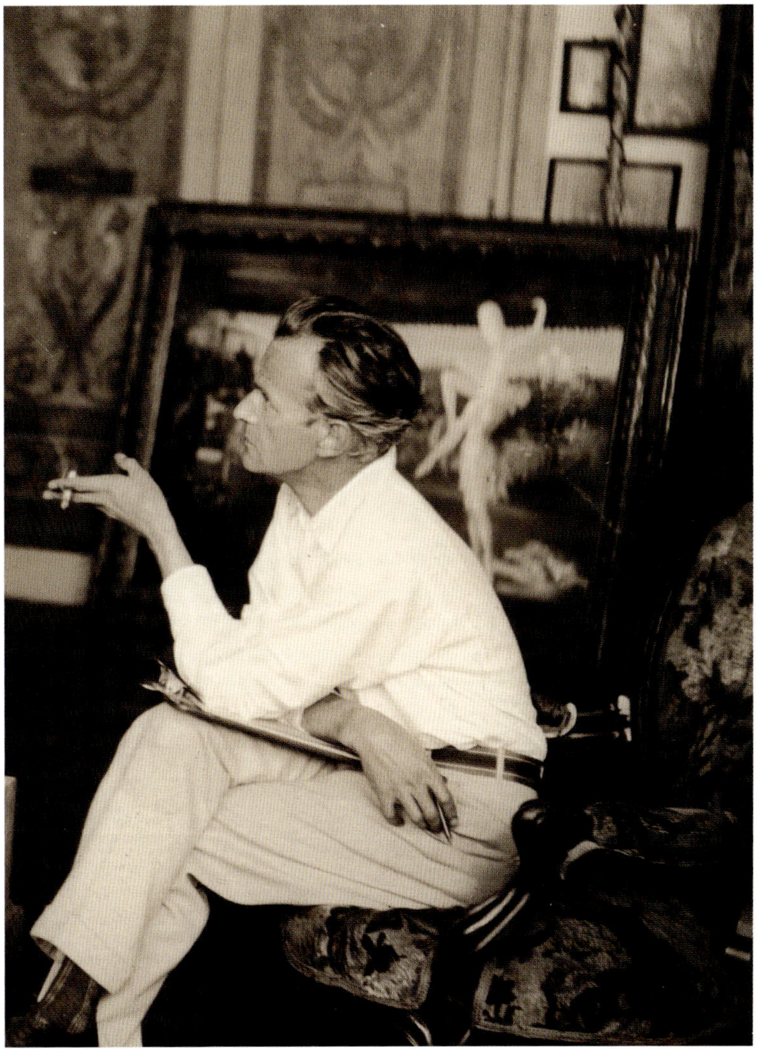

the *Philadelphia Press* and the *New York Times* covered the exhibition in detail. Articles appeared in national magazines, including *American Art News*, *Current Literature*, and *The Craftsman*. It was an impressive outpouring of interest for a thirteen-day exhibition of sixty-three paintings by artists who regularly exhibited in the city.

The enthusiastic press coverage was the result of a year-long campaign orchestrated by the artists to promote their work and their ideas about modern American art. The participants in this exhibition—Henri, Sloan, Glackens, Luks, Shinn, Lawson, Arthur B. Davies (1862–1928), and Maurice Prendergast (1858–1924)—became known as "The Eight" months before the show opened. These eight painters were not an organized group or school, and the 1908 exhibition was the only occasion when they showed together. What they shared was a sense of frustration with academic art and the institutions that served it, particularly the National Academy of Design in New York, where their work was often rejected or poorly hung in juried shows. Led by Henri and Sloan, the painters stirred up controversy almost a year before the exhibition opened, when their works were rejected (or not hung) at the Academy's annual show. In the press, the story developed into a familiar narrative of artistic rebellion, with The Eight cast as upstarts taking on the old guard at the Academy.

The Eight's publicity campaign attracted visitors as well as critical attention. A writer for the *Evening Mail* reported that "Macbeth's gallery scarcely opens in the morning before the crowd begins to arrive."[3] More surprising than the attendance and the volume of reviews was the number of sales. Seven works were sold, earning nearly $4000. Four went to a newly minted collector of art: Gertrude Vanderbilt Whitney, a sculptor and socialite. She purchased works by Henri, Shinn, Lawson, and Luks.

THE EIGHT AND THE WHITNEY MUSEUM OF AMERICAN ART

Because of Whitney's purchases from the 1908 Macbeth show, the Whitney Museum was probably the only institution that could or would have organized a show celebrating The Eight in 1937. Between 1908 and 1929, Whitney expanded her support of American artists with purchases and exhibitions hosted in her Greenwich Village studio. She imagined that her collection of modern American art would go to a major museum and offered 500 works to The Metropolitan Museum of Art in 1929. When they refused the offer, she set out to organize her own museum, opening the Whitney Museum of American Art in 1931. By that time, the collection contained major examples of works by each of The Eight, including Glackens's *Parade Washington Square*, 1912; Henri's *Storm Tide*, 1903; Luks's *Rosie*, 1919; and Lawson's *Fishermen*, 1911. After opening the museum, Whitney continued to patronize the group, adding major paintings by Sloan in 1936, including *Backyards, Greenwich Village*, 1914, to the collection. In 1937 the young museum was ideally situated to explore the artistic contributions of The Eight.

The *New York Realists* catalogue portrayed its subjects as men of historic importance, without forgetting that some were living artists: "Although five of the group continue to be active participants in the art world, the work exhibited is confined to the pre-war decade when to be a realist and paint the American scene was to be regarded as an iconoclastic radical."[4] By 1937, four of the artists in the exhibition had died: Bellows, Henri, Coleman, and Luks. By that time half of the original Eight had passed too: Henri and Luks, as well as Prendergast in 1924 and Davies in 1928. The surviving artists were becoming grand old men of American art, a trajectory this show would intensify.

New York Realists featured the Whitney's works alongside loans from the artists and their dealers, as well as paintings from other museums. Indeed, the exhibition's retrospective veneration of The Eight reflected what was becoming the status quo in museums across the nation. Paintings by Sloan, Shinn, and their circle began entering museum collections in the 1920s. Most of these works were created in

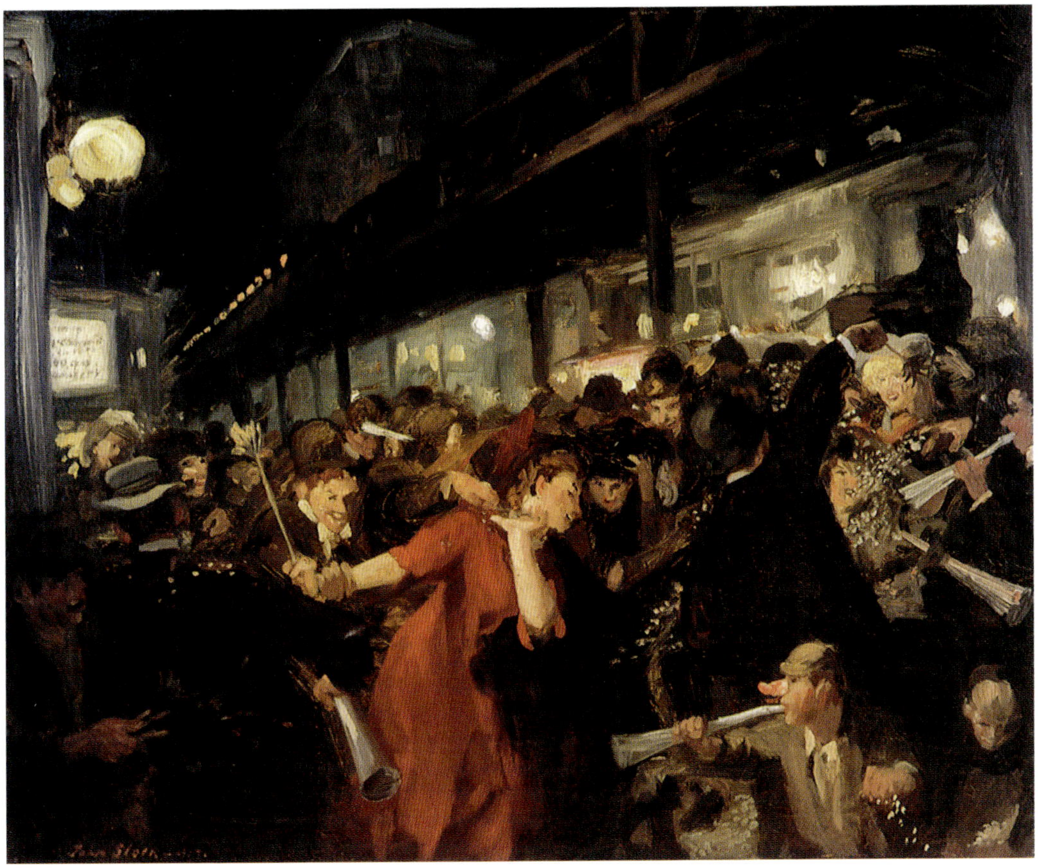

3.
John Sloan (1871–1951)
Election Night, 1907
Oil on canvas
26 ⅜ × 32 ¼ in.
(67 × 81.9 cm)
Memorial Art Gallery of the University of Rochester, Marion Stratton Gould Fund, 41.33

the early twentieth century. American museums began to acquire Henri's paintings around 1910, and key works by the rest of The Eight entered major museums a decade later. In 1921, through the George A. Hearn fund, The Metropolitan Museum of Art acquired Sloan's *Dust Storm, Fifth Avenue*, 1906; Glackens's *Central Park, Winter*, 1905; Luks's *The Old Duchess*, 1905; and Shinn's *London Music Hall*, 1918. (The Met already owned a major painting by Henri, *The Spanish Gypsy*, 1912, acquired in 1914.) This purchase seems to have gotten the ball rolling for the group. By the end of the decade, several museums had added key paintings by The Eight to their collections. In 1923, Gertrude Vanderbilt Whitney donated Sloan's *The Haymarket*, 1907, to the Brooklyn Museum. Two years later Glackens's *At Mouquin's*, 1905, was purchased for the Art Institute of Chicago by the Friends of American Art, and in 1928, the same group bought Shinn's *The Hippodrome, London*, 1902. Expanding interest in the eight New York Realists attracted positive reviews and "an unusually large number of visitors," and quickly became a model for other exhibitions.[5] In 1938, Macbeth Gallery—host to the original exhibition of The Eight—held a thirtieth-anniversary show, where, among dozens of works, three paintings from the original show were on offer. One, a critic noted drily, had been available for $500 in 1908, but was now priced at $3000, reflecting its newly burnished historical importance.[6]

In 1943 the Brooklyn Museum organized a major exhibition honoring the thirty-fifth anniversary of The Eight. The Brooklyn show featured eighty-six paintings, a gallery of drawings, and a final room dedicated to the later work of the group—a layout one reviewer described as "wisely segregated from the main showing." "Generally," he continued, "these are much brighter in color, but lack the impact of those of the 'outlaw' days."[7] Even Sloan's good friend and fellow modern artist Walter Pach, who made a passionate case for the importance of "The Eight Then and Now," saw in the later works "a failure to live up to the great promise of thirty-five years ago."[8] The preferences of the art world were clear. Brooklyn's show was so popular that the Museum of Modern Art developed a traveling version, which went to Cleveland, Columbus, Worcester, Pittsburgh, Baltimore, Toledo, and Rochester.

By this time, only Sloan and Shinn remained of The Eight, and they would hang on until 1951 and 1953 respectively. The aging artists became living historical specimens, interviewed about their early careers by reporters, curators, and scholars. Shinn and Sloan were prodded to revisit their past while they continued to produce and exhibit new work in New York galleries.

Gallerists were interested, in part, because the high-profile museum exhibitions accelerated the pace of acquisitions by American museums and collectors. Nearly every year through the late 1930s, 1940s, and 1950s, a widening group of museums acquired early paintings by members of The Eight.[9] Historically, the museum acquisitions of the 1920s through the 1950s became the artists' most published paintings—the city scenes that define The Eight in the history of American art.

When museum interest in The Eight escalated in the 1920s, Sloan and Shinn had both moved away from painting the New York subjects that museums were seeking. The two artists were at different places professionally and they reacted to the attention in distinct ways that still impact on scholars and collectors of their work.

THE STEADY, STUBBORN RISE OF JOHN SLOAN

Sloan began his career as a newspaper illustrator in Philadelphia, where he befriended Glackens, Henri, Luks, and Shinn. He studied at the Pennsylvania Academy of the Fine Arts, and by 1900 he was painting and exhibiting scenes of his neighborhood. In 1904 he relocated to New York to make his way as a freelance magazine illustrator and artist. In paintings and etchings, Sloan captured the city's parks and sidewalks

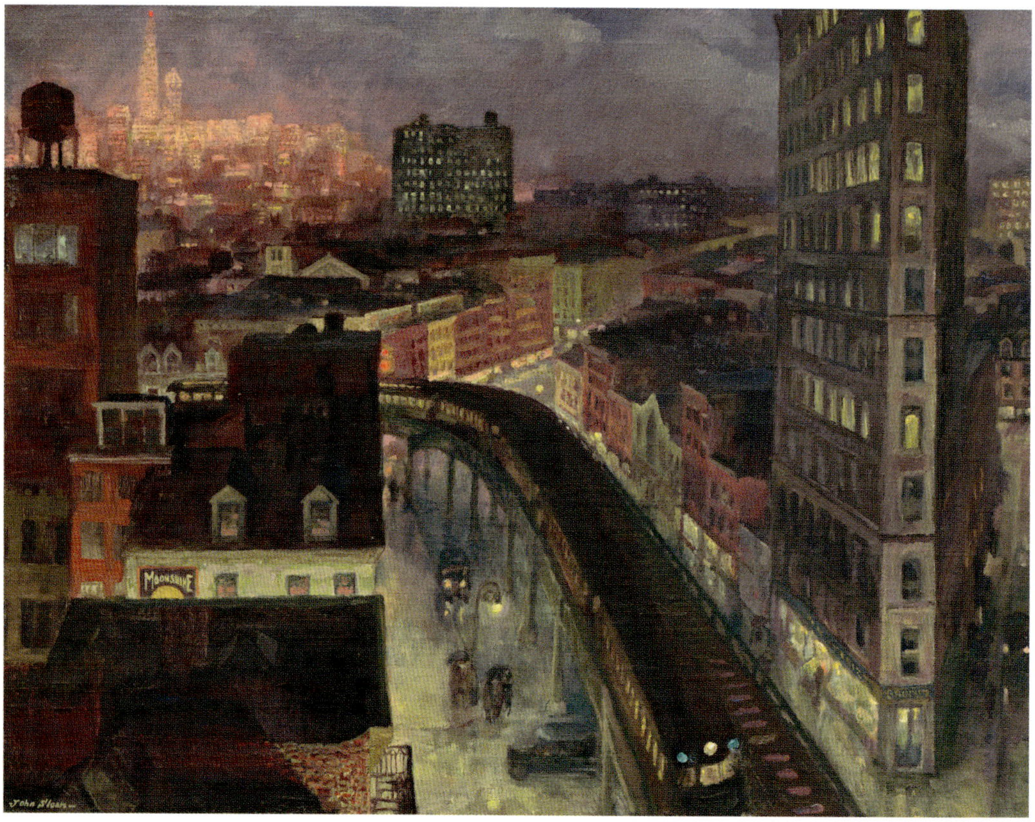

4.
John Sloan (1871–1951)
The City from Greenwich Village, 1922
Oil on canvas
26 × 33 ¾ in. (66 × 85.7 cm)
National Gallery of Art, Washington, DC, Gift of Helen Farr Sloan, 1970.1.1

from a pedestrian point of view. While his urban scenes charmed a handful of critics, genteel factions of the art establishment found his working-class subject matter coarse. In the exhibition of The Eight, Sloan showed a cohesive selection of city pictures, but he also painted vibrant landscapes and lively portraits. He exhibited widely in New York and around the country, but he sold very little work. He supported himself through illustration and, after 1916, as an instructor at the Art Students League. It was not until 1916, at age forty-five, that he finally found representation at Kraushaar Galleries.

Sloan never completely ceased painting New York, but landscapes and figure paintings were dominating his production by 1916.[10] His handful of city pictures from the late teens—such as *Jefferson Market, Sixth Avenue*, and *Bleecker Street, Saturday Night*—show a shift in his approach, as the artist's point of view zoomed out, giving more attention to architecture and less to pedestrian life. He completed only one New York painting between 1919 and 1921.[11]

In 1922, the year after his work first entered The Metropolitan Museum of Art, Sloan returned to city painting with *The City from Greenwich Village* (Fig. 4), his most sweeping view of the metropolis to date. The painting's subject encompasses the whole of New York—seen from Sloan's perspective as an artist downtown—and the effect is unabashedly romantic. As one of his paintings entered the most important museum in New York, Sloan celebrated the scope of the city and his role as its chronicler.

His renewed romance with the city continued through the mid-1920s. In 1924, Sloan made three major city paintings, including the masterful *Grand Central Station*. The following year, he started *Buses in the Square*, and in 1928 he painted *Sixth Avenue Elevated at Third Street* and *The White Way*, which landed at the Whitney Museum and the Philadelphia Museum of Art within his lifetime. In 1927 he painted *The Lafayette*, which inspired his friends to gather funds to purchase and present the work to The Metropolitan Museum in 1928. Sloan's New York paintings from the 1920s documented landmarks of Lower Manhattan with romance, drama, and a touch of nostalgia. Museums and collectors embraced these iconic vistas of their metropolis.

Having made so few sales in his career, in the 1920s Sloan cannot have failed to notice (and his gallery to point out) that his city pictures were finally finding buyers. It is impossible to say if his picturesque city subjects of the 1920s were painted in reaction to the growing market for his early work, but institutional interest may have invigorated his flagging enthusiasm for urban scenes.

After his most successful decade as an exhibiting artist, Sloan did something surprising. In 1929 he essentially abandoned city subjects and dedicated himself to painting nudes. Neither critics nor buyers supported these pictures, but he stubbornly kept making them. Without selling many paintings, Sloan had become a respected artist and teacher, and he had managed—through illustration, teaching, and the sale of his etchings—to make a living. As he approached sixty, he chose not to cater to the taste of the art establishment. He refused to paint what buyers and critics wanted, or to fade quietly into the background. A leader at the Art Students League and an inveterate organizer of exhibitions, Sloan was frequently interviewed by reporters in the 1930s and 1940s. He seemed to enjoy saying outrageous, controversial things. His cantankerous persona fit perfectly into the narrative that the Whitney and the Brooklyn Museum created around their celebrations of The Eight—a story of rebellious artists that challenge authority.

Even as Sloan drifted from his early subject matter, he endeavored to organize and document his work for posterity. He started cataloguing systematically in 1916, when he began to consign works for sale at Kraushaar Galleries. He recorded titles, dates, and media on index cards as he made new work and when he pulled out early paintings for exhibitions. His catalogue cards often feature

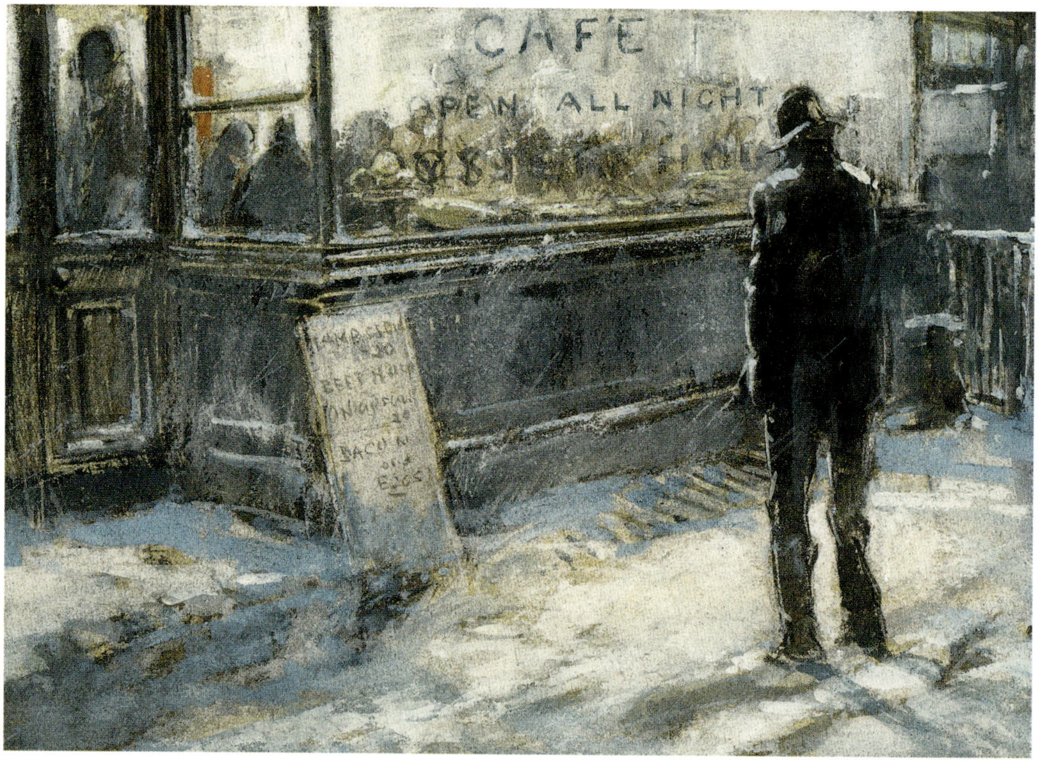

5.
Everett Shinn (1876–1953)
All Night Café, *c.* 1900
Charcoal, watercolor, and gouache
8 ¼ × 11 ⅞ in.
(20.9 × 30.2 cm)
The Huber Family Collection

thumbnail sketches and details about the making, exhibition, sale, and consignment of works. Sloan's retroactive cataloguing was probably assisted by his own diaries, where he recorded, from 1906 through early 1913, what he was working on almost daily. In this habit of keeping a diary and cataloguing his work with thumbnail sketches, he followed the precedent of his friend and mentor Robert Henri, who had kept a regular diary since his art-student days and had begun incorporating an illustrated list of his paintings by 1902.

Over time, Sloan's records proved useful for exhibition catalogues and his collaboration with his former student Helen Farr on the manuscript for a book of his teachings, *Gist of Art*, published in 1939. The original edition included a section dedicated to Sloan's commentary on specific works of art, as well as a summary of his teachings based on Farr's notes taken in Sloan's classes. Farr would marry Sloan in 1944 after the death of his first wife. During their life together, she encouraged and assisted him in cataloguing his art. She also typed and annotated his diaries and made hundreds of pages of notes when he reminisced about his youth to visiting reporters. Forty years younger than her husband, Helen Farr Sloan grasped his significance. To her generation, he was history.

After Sloan's death in 1951, Helen Farr Sloan dedicated her life to preserving and disseminating her husband's art and the information related to it. As a result, most major museums that collect American art own work by John Sloan, and there are excellent catalogues raisonnés for Sloan's prints, paintings, and illustrations in books and magazines. Helen Farr Sloan maintained an extraordinary amount of Sloan's art and archival material, which she donated to the Delaware Art Museum, creating a resource for the study of his art.

THE DAZZLING AND DISORGANIZED EVERETT SHINN

Shinn also started his career as a newspaper illustrator, and he and Sloan crossed paths at the *Philadelphia Press* in the 1890s. Shinn moved to New York to work as a freelance illustrator in 1897, and his dashing style found him work for mainstream magazines almost immediately. The following year his work was featured as the center spread in *Harper's Weekly*, announcing his arrival as an illustrator. In 1899 he had a one-man show of his pastel drawings at Boussod-Valadon in New York. He had several solo exhibitions over the next few years, at Boussod-Valadon, at Knoedler, and at Durand-Ruel, and even a museum show at the Pennsylvania Academy of the Fine Arts. In art and illustration, success came quickly for him.

All the while, he was working on one of his most ambitious undertakings, which he called *New York by Night*. First conceived around 1899, *New York by Night* was to be a richly illustrated book that paired Shinn's images of New York nightlife with text by William Dean Howells. The book was intended to be seventy-five pages of "alternate gaiety and drabness," which followed "every activity of the night until it finished its cycle of comedy and drama." [12] Shinn made a mock-up, took out a copyright in 1900, and offered the project to Harper Brothers, but they decided it would be too expensive to produce. He tried other publishers and continued to make drawings for the project, setting it aside by 1908.

Shinn's failure to publish *New York by Night* was not a huge blow to his career. By 1900 his work was being collected in fashionable circles of New York society. His fans included the architect and designer Stanford White, the decorator Elsie de Wolfe, and the actress Julia Marlowe. His elegant friends hired him to make portraits and produce decorative paintings in private homes. In 1907 he painted the decorations for David Belasco's Stuyvesant Theatre. Busy with this work, he was largely isolated from his old friends by the time the exhibition of The Eight started to come together.

As an emerging artist, Shinn established his exhibiting pattern. He exhibited widely, preferred solo shows, and demonstrated no loyalty to individual dealers.[13] He exhibited his work in private venues, including the apartments of his rich and famous friends, as well as in hotels and theaters. Shinn accepted invitations to show in exhibitions organized by

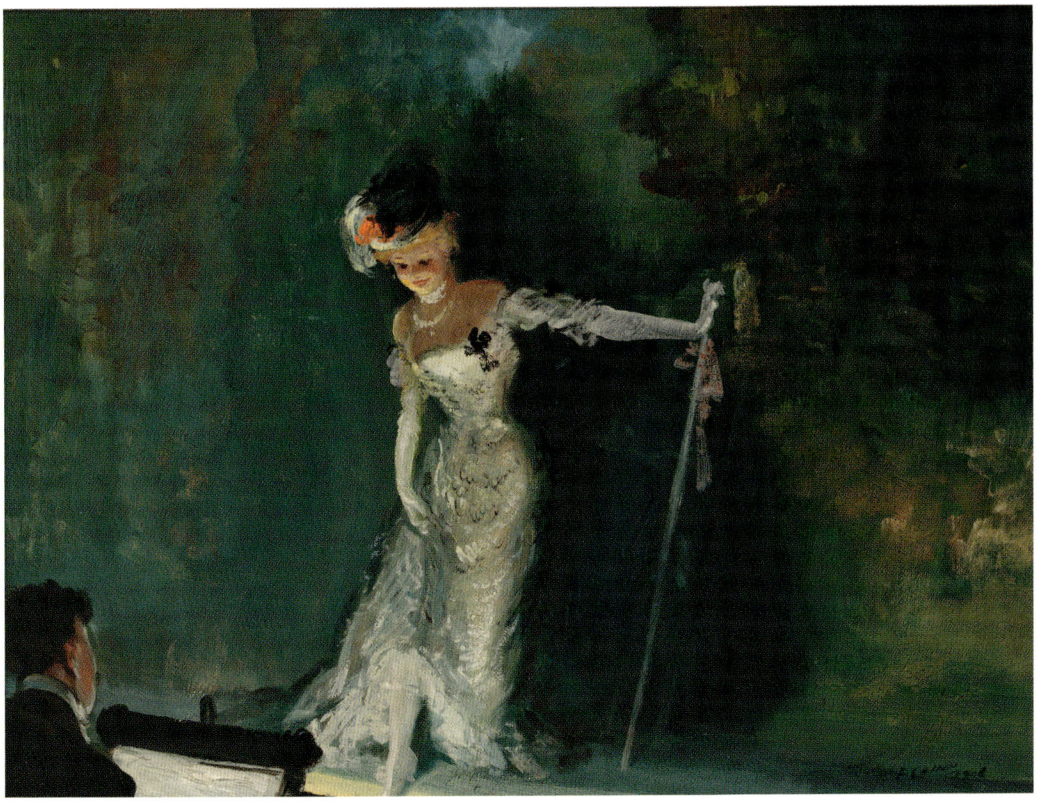

6.
Everett Shinn (1876–1953)
Revue, 1908
Oil on canvas
18 ⅛ x 24 ¼ in.
(46 x 61.6 cm)
Gift of Gertrude Vanderbilt Whitney, Whitney Museum of American Art, 31.346

John Marin and the Emergence of American Modernism

Meredith Ward
President, Meredith Ward Fine Art, New York

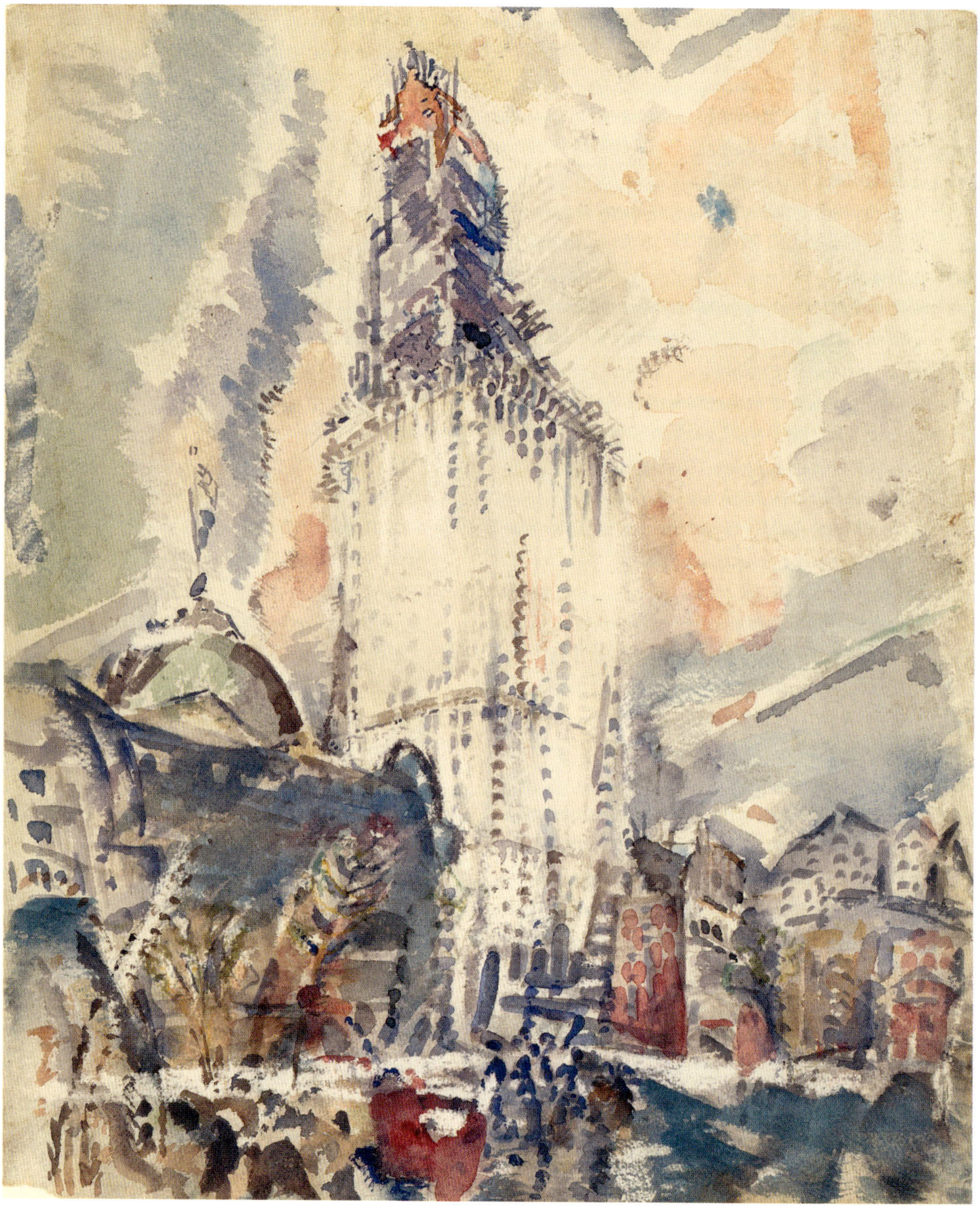

In 1948, at the age of seventy-eight, John Marin was at the pinnacle of an artistic career that spanned almost fifty years. That year, *Look* magazine named him America's "Artist No. 1."[1] The great critic of the New York School, Clement Greenberg, wrote that "if it is not beyond all doubt that [Marin] is the best painter alive in America at this moment, he assuredly has to be taken into consideration when we ask who is."[2]

National pride and recognition of Marin's genius were so great at mid-century that in 1950, the American committee for the Venice Biennale submitted a major retrospective of his work as their entry that year along with selected paintings by Arshile Gorky, Jackson Pollock, and Willem de Kooning.

Marin's art was greatly admired by people of all different artistic persuasions, from the mavens of Modernism like Clement Greenberg to ordinary American art lovers, and the next generation of artists including Rothko, Pollock, and de Kooning admired him and were influenced by him. To understand how this happened, how Marin achieved such broad recognition and success, we will have to look back to the beginning of his career as he worked to develop the language of Modernism in America.

John Marin was born in Rutherford, New Jersey, in 1870. His mother died in childbirth and his father, unable to raise the boy on his own, left him with two maiden aunts. By all accounts, young John was doted on by his loving aunts, while his relationship with his father, who was often away on business, remained distant. Marin was educated in the Cliffside public schools and then went on to Stevens Institute of Technology in Hoboken, where his father intended him to study engineering and learn a trade. Early on, Marin had shown a proclivity for drawing, sketching animals and landscapes wherever he went. The impulse rapidly to record his impressions on a sheet of paper never left him, and greatly influenced the way he approached his later work.

Marin quit Stevens after just four months of study. He found work as a draftsman in an architect's office and eventually set up his own architectural firm. Although his foray into architecture lasted only two years, this early training stayed with him. His interest in and understanding of architecture were key, as he began to explore urban subjects in and around Lower Manhattan.

In 1899, he entered the Pennsylvania Academy of the Fine Arts, Philadelphia, where he studied with Thomas Anshutz and Hugh Breckenridge. A brief stint with Frank Vincent DuMond at the Art Students League in New York followed, but Paris was the ultimate goal of all the artists of Marin's generation, and in 1905, he headed there.

Marin arrived in Paris at a unique and transitional moment, when works by Cézanne and Matisse were uprooting familiar nineteenth-century aesthetics, and his paintings of the period show how he responded. Working in oil, watercolor, and etching, and following in the footsteps of James McNeill Whistler, Marin began experimenting with new ideas in color and form. While his debt to Whistler is clear in some of Marin's French subjects, he also began exploring Post-Impressionism.

Paris before the war was rife with artistic possibilities. The bohemian milieu that Marin inhabited is wonderfully portrayed in a caricature by Marius de Zayas (Fig. 2) depicting some of the American artists who frequented Le Dôme Café in Paris. It shows Marin playing poker with

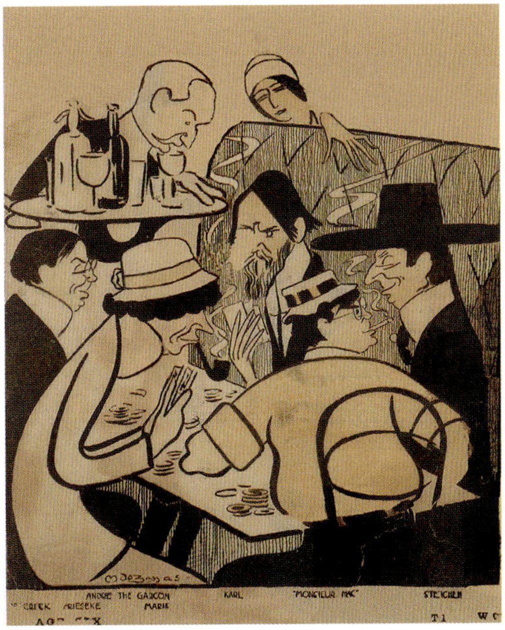

1. *(opposite)*
John Marin (1870–1953)
Woolworth Building, No. 28
1912
Watercolor over graphite
18 ½ × 15 ½ in.
(47 × 39.6 cm)
Gift of Eugene and Agnes E. Meyer, National Gallery of Art, Washington, DC, 1967.13.8

2. *(left)*
Marius de Zayas (1880–1961)
Illustration for "Where the Latin Quarter Trilbies Gather; the Domeless Dome of Paris," *The World Magazine*, November 27, 1910

Edward Steichen and Arthur B. Carles, two artists connected to Alfred Stieglitz with whom Marin would always be closely associated. Also at the poker table are the Impressionist Frederick Frieseke and the society portrait painter Robert MacCameron, artists who would never be thought of in connection with Marin today, and who would hardly be considered among the early twentieth-century vanguard. However, what these artists have in common is that virtually all were students or disciples of Whistler, and many were also members of the New Society of American Painters in Paris, formed by Steichen to challenge the conservatism of the old guard.

By the time of de Zayas's drawing in 1910, Marin had already completed an entirely new and exciting body of work and was beginning to make his mark in New York with his dealer Alfred Stieglitz. Thanks to Steichen's introduction, Stieglitz had given Marin a two-man show with Alfred Maurer in 1909, and in 1910 gave him his first one-man show and included him in a group show. Emboldened by that support, Marin produced an extraordinary series of watercolors during several weeks in the Austrian Tyrol, his most groundbreaking work to date (Fig. 3). The Tyrol watercolors display vitality, energy, and brightness, and push the limits of form and abstraction to new levels. Marin was clearly reveling in a new sense of freedom and the confidence he felt, allowing his full artistic expression to come through. The Tyrol paintings formed the basis of his next exhibition with Stieglitz in 1911.

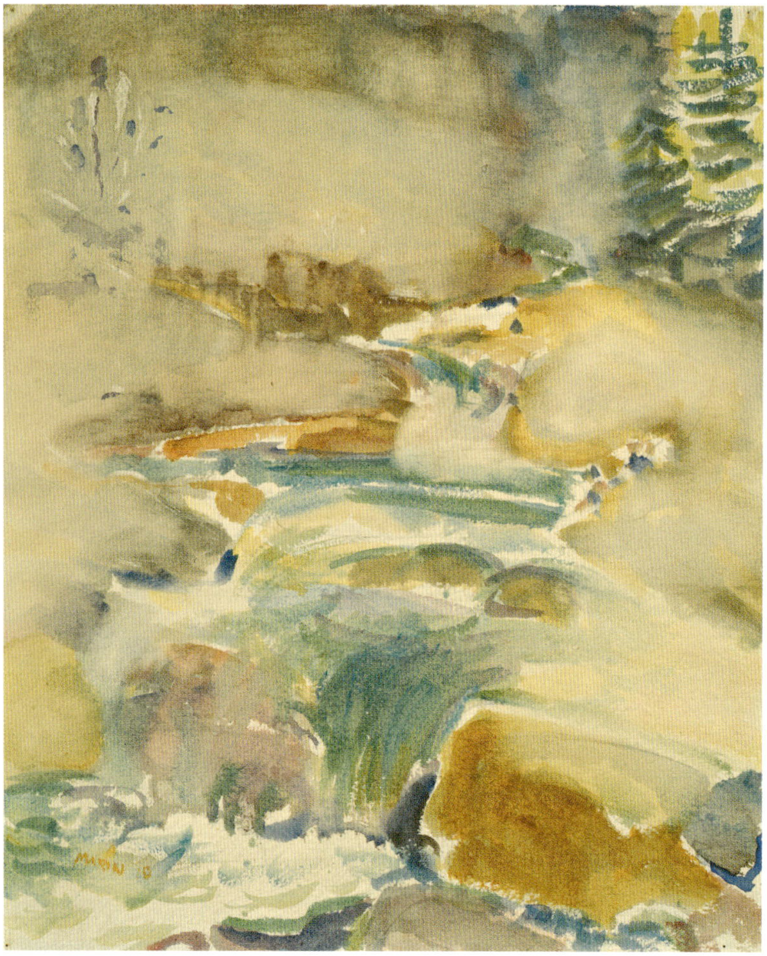

3.
John Marin (1870–1953)
The Brook, 1910
Watercolor on paper
18 ½ × 15 ⅜ in.
(47 × 39.1 cm)
Helen Birch Bartlett Memorial Collection, Art Institute of Chicago, 1926.218

Marin returned to America for good in the fall of 1910, and it was around this time that he began a series of extraordinary small oil paintings that have come to be known as the Weehawken Sequence (Fig. 4). These are among the earliest Modernist expressions produced in this country by an American artist. They depict scenes in and around Weehawken, New Jersey, where Marin grew up and whose environs he knew very well. They focus on both natural imagery and urban/industrial imagery, and their palettes vary, ranging from muted earthy tones to vibrant hues. Most astonishing about these small oils is the degree of abstraction Marin was able to achieve at this early date, conveying in quick, gestural strokes the essence of the scene in front of him. We can see in these works how thoroughly and masterfully Marin had assimilated the lessons of Paris and was applying them to his native landscape.

Another breakthrough in his stylistic development came just two years later, when the full impact of his European experience became apparent. Watercolors done in the Adirondacks and the Berkshires reveal his complete mastery of the medium, and show that he had internalized Modernist ideas and made them his own. With these works, we begin to see Marin's signature style emerging—an entirely new and distinct visual language that was perfectly suited to the American landscape. These expressive, expansive, and colorful watercolors demonstrate a new spirit, an ability to communicate perfectly the feeling—the essence—of a particular place at

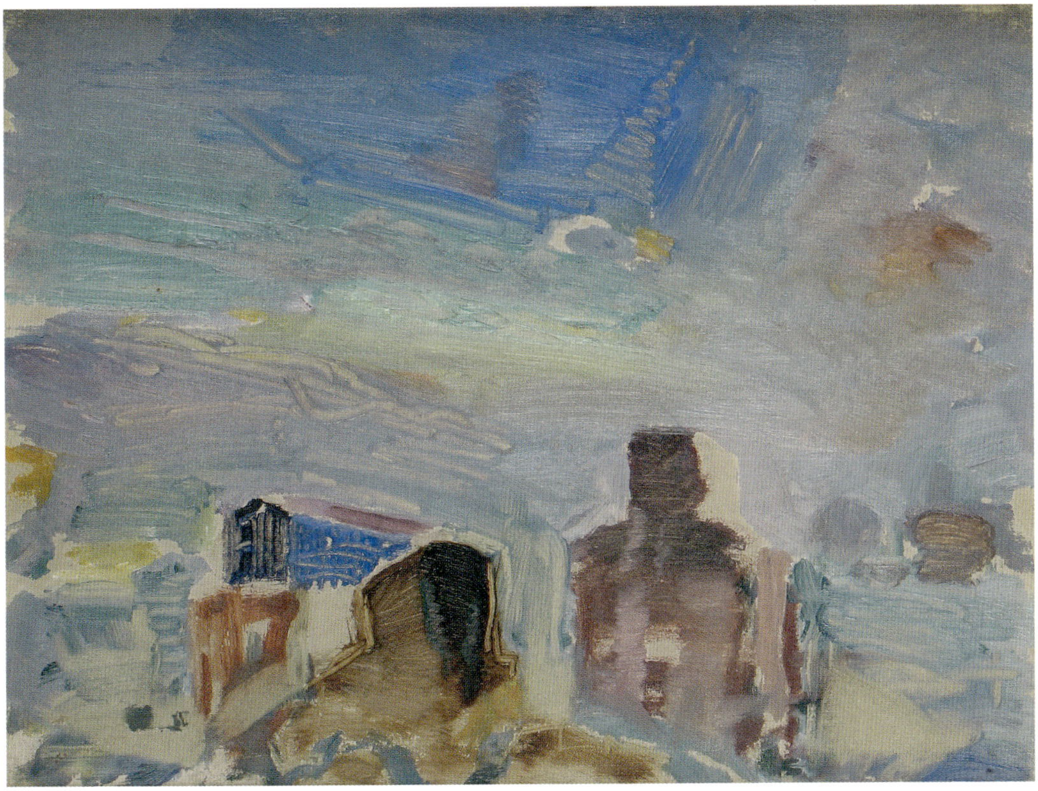

4.
John Marin (1870–1953)
Weehawken Sequence
c. 1910–16
Oil on canvas board
9 × 12 in. (22.8 × 30.4 cm)
Private collection

a particular time, whether the deep woods of the Adirondacks or a breezy summer day in the Berkshires. For Marin, form, color, and technique were not just about making the painting; they were about making the painting speak to the viewer.

Throughout this period, Marin's dealer Alfred Stieglitz was a huge supporter of his work—giving him annual exhibitions, promoting his work, and providing him with a regular stipend by buying work. But not even Stieglitz's support could match the impact and the audience of the International Exhibition of Modern Art—known as the Armory Show. The exhibition was on view in New York, Chicago, and Boston during the winter and spring of 1913, and nearly 100,000 people visited it, drawn by sensational press accounts of the bizarre art on view. Marin was invited to submit works to the show and he sent a group of Adirondacks, Berkshires, and Tyrol paintings.

Marin also exhibited his latest series of watercolors depicting the Woolworth Building (Fig. 1), which were singled out for critical ridicule. They were described as "suffering from severe indigestion," and "in the ultimate stages of vertigo." Despite these comments, or perhaps because of them, Marin carried on in 1914 with this startling new style in his paintings of New York. With these groundbreaking city views, we can see him pushing further into a Cubist-inspired abstraction that emphasizes the energy of the rapidly changing urban environment.

This was an important year for Marin for another reason: it was his first summer in Maine. Maine was becoming a popular spot for artists at this time—Marsden Hartley, Gaston Lachaise, and William Zorach spent summers there too—and so Marin and his wife Marie trundled up to a little cabin near the town of West Point, just north of Portland.

The accommodation was anything but luxurious. The two-room cabin was located fifteen feet from the water's edge at high tide, on a little island just across the harbor from West Point. There was no running water or electricity—Marin drew water for drinking and cooking from a distant well and a fireplace

5.
John Marin (1870–1953)
The Red Sun, Brooklyn Bridge
1922
Watercolor on paper
21 3/8 × 26 1/4 in.
(54.2 × 66.5 cm)
Alfred Stieglitz Collection, Art Institute of Chicago, 1949.561R

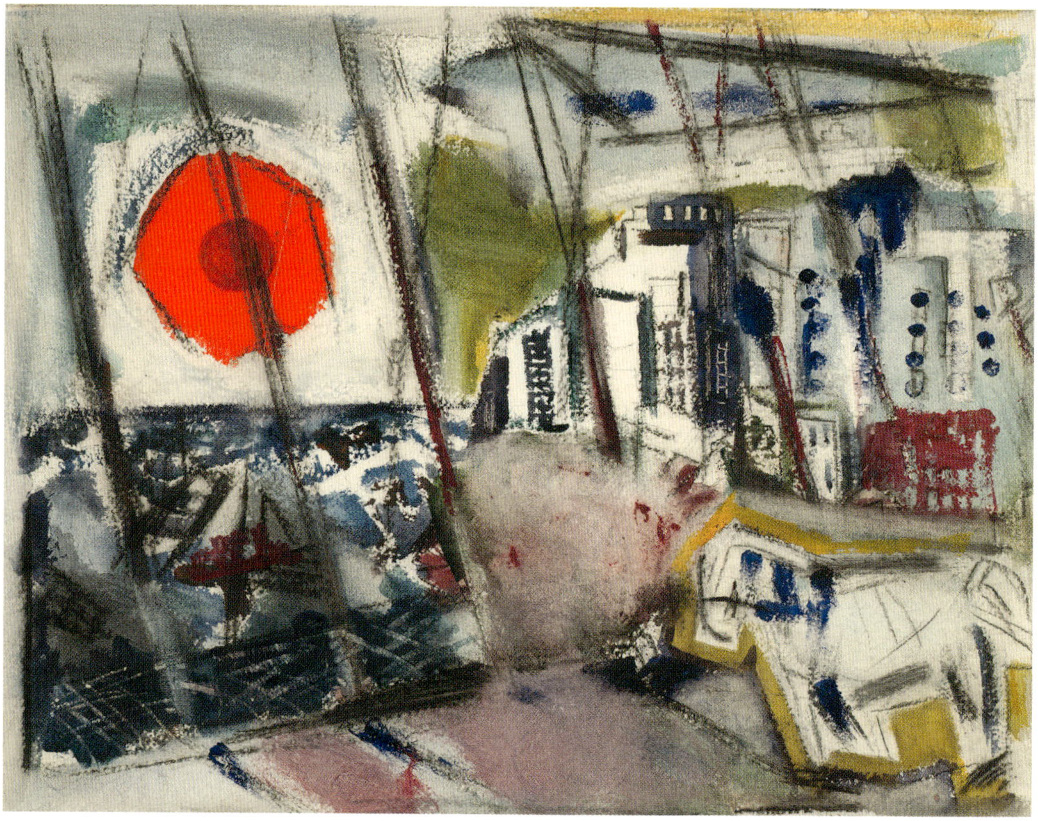

provided light and heat for cooking. He had to row to the mainland regularly for provisions.

A few days after arriving in early August, Marin wrote to Stieglitz about the place:

This is one fierce, relentless, cruel, beautiful, fascinating, hellish, and all the other ish'es, place. To go anywheres I have to row, row, row. Pretty soon I expect the well will give out and I'll then be even obliged to row for water, and as I have to make water colors—to Hell with water for cooking, washing and drinking. Don't cook—eat berries. Don't wash—you are wet all the time so what's the use. Don't drink, for surely some of this wetness must sink in.[3]

In another letter to Stieglitz in September he wrote:

You can never know what a boat means until you are stranded on an island. But it is a beautiful island and is constantly offering surprises. How tame an Estate seems as compared with it. But then I don't like tame places. I have from time to time in a vague sort of way planned out work ahead. But I find this wayward temper of mine will not allow me to … and I find things cropping up I never intentionally intended. Well, maybe this keeps me from a certain set mannerism, and this is a something I detect and what forces a dislike, an unconscious dislike, of most of the modern work I have seen. Oh, it is dangerous ever, ever to work in a studio.… Nature's arrangements are much finer.…[4]

Marin's first summer in Maine had an enormous impact on his work as he confronted the ruggedness of the landscape and the ever-changing character of the sea and sky. He returned to Maine almost every summer from that point on, and in 1934 he bought a house at Cape Split. Way "downeast," far away from the hustle and bustle of the city, the house at Cape Split became a haven for him for longer and longer periods each year.

How did Marin get from that two-room shack on the coast of Maine to being a major international artist exhibiting at the Venice Biennale? One reason was the steadfast support of his dealer, Stieglitz, who gave him annual exhibitions at his gallery and placed his work

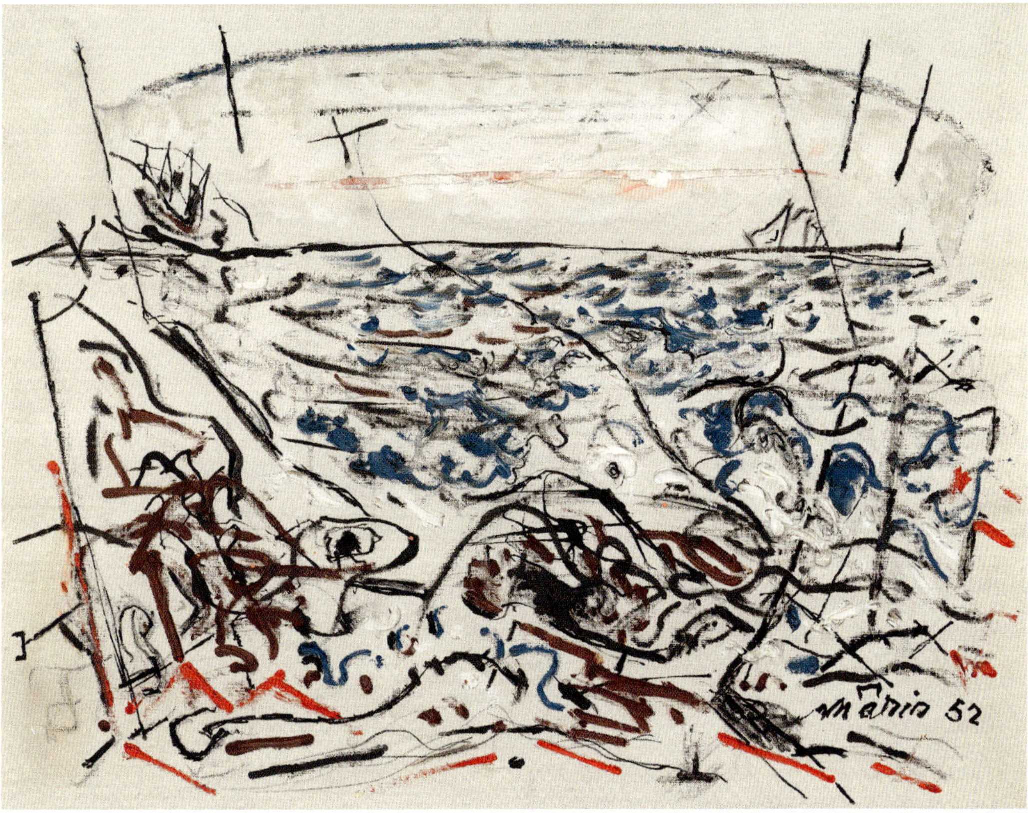

6.
John Marin (1870–1953)
The Written Sea, 1952
Oil on canvas
22 × 28 in. (55.8 × 71.1 cm)
Gift of Deborah and Ed Shein, National Gallery of Art, Washington, DC, 2009.12.1

with important collectors like Duncan Phillips and Ferdinand Howald. Marin was also given several important museum exhibitions, including a 1936 retrospective at the Museum of Modern Art, all of which were acclaimed by the critics.

And then there is the work itself. What makes Marin's work so engaging and why it is so important to the emergence of American Modernism is the balance he strikes between realism and abstraction. He never lost touch with painting directly from nature. He always has his two feet on the ground and you always know where you stand in relation to the painting's subject, so that his radical artistic innovations sneak up on you. His subjects are appealing and recognizable, and when he starts to break them up, or deconstruct them with a burst of color and swirling line, you don't mind because that is what gives the paintings their life and vitality and joy. This was his unique contribution and the secret to his success. Marin described this process himself in another letter to Stieglitz written in 1923:

If you have an intense love and feeling towards [all things seen], you'll try your damdest to put on paper or canvas, that thing. You can transpose, you can play with and on your material, but when you are finished that's got to have the roots of that thing in it and no other thing.... And an inner vision of your own has got to be transposed onto your medium, a picture of that vision.[5]

Over the next several decades he continued to evolve and innovate. Throughout the 1920s and 1930s he produced more extraordinary paintings, such as *The Red Sun, Brooklyn Bridge*, 1922 (Fig. 5), in which he mixed watercolor, opaque watercolor, and charcoal, and employed a variety of techniques such as scraping and wiping to create a *tour de force* on paper. In 1929 and 1930 he traveled west to Taos, New Mexico, where Georgia O'Keeffe was living and his good friend, the photographer Paul Strand, was also visiting. The Western landscape was completely new to him, and he loved it and tackled it with the same gutsy vision, adapting his palette and technique to the dry high desert mountains.

By this time, Marin was becoming an important role model and source of inspiration for the next generation of American artists. We know, for example, that Mark Rothko was looking at him early on. There is also an ongoing question about the relationship between Marin's late calligraphic works and the work of Jackson Pollock. By the late 1940s, Marin's Cubist-inspired style had evolved to become more calligraphic and linear. These are his great, late oils such as *The Written Sea*, 1952 (Fig. 6), painted the year before he died. This bears a striking relationship to Jackson Pollock's black paintings, exhibited in New York in 1951, in which we see Pollock returning to some kind of figuration with these mysterious forms emerging from the calligraphic lines.

Had Marin seen Pollock's work or was Pollock aware of Marin's? It isn't clear, but Marin had been working with this lyrical line since the 1940s. His calligraphic technique simply reached its apotheosis here.

Some critics noted the relationship between Marin and the Abstract Expressionists at the time. As early as 1950, Louis Finkelstein, for example, recognized an affinity between Marin's late oils and Willem de Kooning's work.[6] That connection was lost, though—either forgotten or intentionally ignored—in the ensuing decades as the creation myth of the New York School was invented in the post-war period and their supremacy reached its zenith. However, over the last few years, scholars and curators are again turning their attention to this fascinating and fertile relationship.

This is not to suggest that Marin was similar to these younger artists in mood, purpose, or personality. On the contrary, their focus on the inner life of the artist, on Jungian psychology and excavating the subconscious, was completely antithetical to Marin's insistence on inspiration directly from nature. What these comparisons do show is that the landscape of American art at mid-century was far more complex than we might imagine. There was no definitive split between pre-war and post-war American art and the boundaries were very permeable, with older and younger artists mixing together. John Marin was not only a key participant in that mix, he provided a foundation that launched American art into the twentieth century—the bridge between the era of Whistler and the era of Pollock.

From our perspective a century later, it may be difficult to imagine how radical Marin's early works appeared to audiences back then. With all the "-isms" that have shocked viewers in the last hundred years, and particularly in this age of high-impact, super-sized works of art, it is hard to believe that Marin's joyful, jazzy, human-scale paintings would have caused any upset. But groundbreaking they were, and they led American art in an entirely new direction. Marin found his path to a new way of painting, a new way of seeing the world that was unlike anything that had been done before. It was painting that allowed for invention, freedom, and personal expression, while honoring the thing being painted. That is Marin's great contribution to American art, and his ongoing gift to us.

Marsden Hartley at Auction

Elizabeth Broun, PhD
Director Emerita of the Smithsonian American Art Museum, Washington, DC, and the Renwick Gallery, Washington, DC

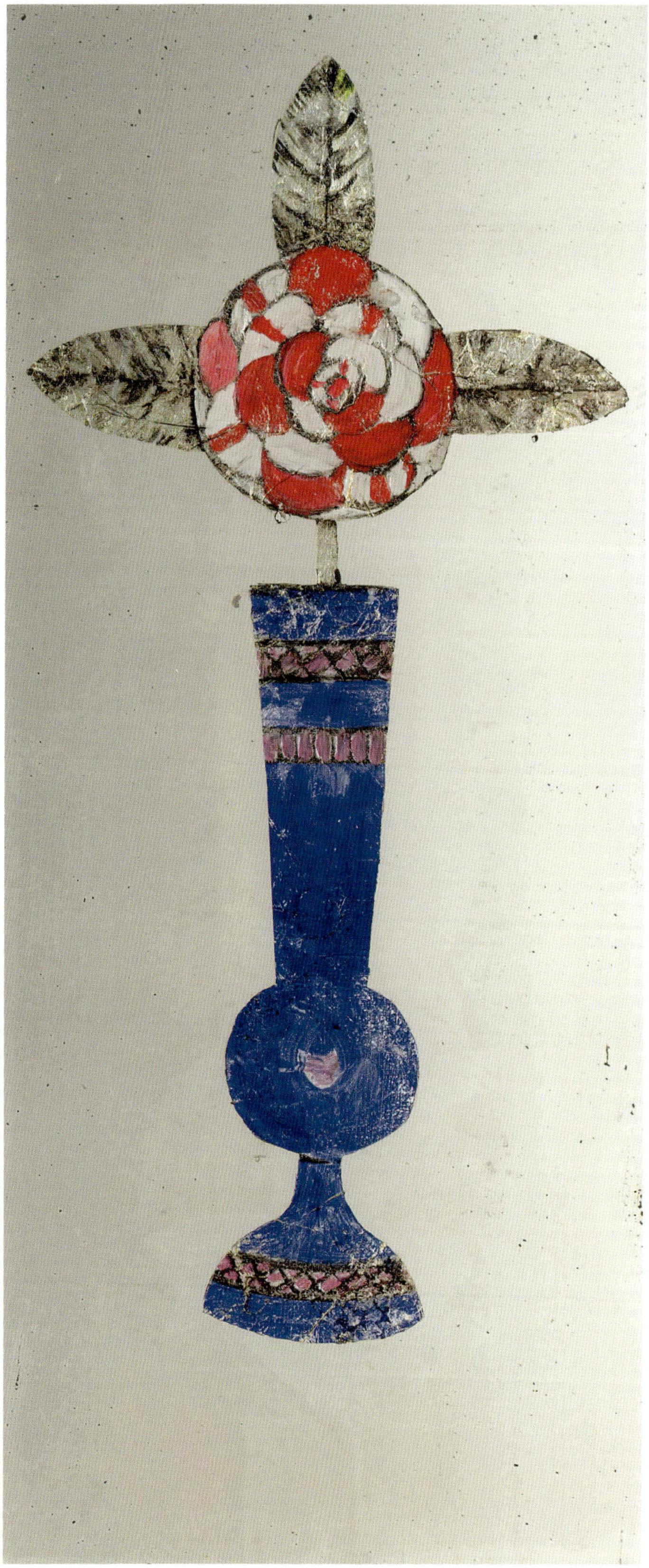

1. *(previous page)*
Marsden Hartley
(1877–1943)
Still Life, 1917
Reverse painting with oil
and foil on glass
13 ¼ × 6 in.
(33.7 × 15.2 cm),
Christie's, New York, December 2, 2004, lot 114

Wonderful artworks by one of America's first great Modernist painters can be purchased for affordable prices. Marsden Hartley is widely ranked among our most creative and accomplished artists, and he was also among the most prolific. His works are offered regularly at auction, but their fate is wildly unpredictable. An extremely large 1915 abstraction called *Lighthouse* that he painted in Berlin brought more than $6 million in May 2008, just months before the recession tamped down prices, but this was an outlier. Hartley had sold it to private collectors in Weimar within weeks of completing it, and it was later confiscated by the Soviets in 1945 and "lost" for decades before it re-emerged as an exciting and fresh-to-the-market offering. But routinely, significant and beautiful works by Hartley fail to sell at all, or sell for low prices. Of four Hartley oils offered by Sotheby's in 2017, all sold at or below their low estimates.

Surprisingly, one of the works that has twice failed at auction, in 2010 and 2011, also dates to that seminal early period in Berlin when Hartley, inspired by his recent reading of Wassily Kandinsky's *On the Spiritual in Art*, was forging an energetic abstract vocabulary of form. This artwork, *Painting No. 8* (Fig. 2), bursts with urgency and intensity, reflecting Hartley's excitement at the new ideas about the liberation of color and form that he is just encountering in Kandinsky's writings. In January 1913, Hartley made a special trip to Munich to meet Kandinsky, and the two remained in touch for several months. *Painting No. 8* shows Hartley just starting to experiment with Kandinsky's style, while adding motifs that were personal to him. Several mountain shapes are stacked one behind another, with the tallest reaching to the very top of the image. Small dark lines along the right-hand "ridge" of some contours evoke trees. The mountain silhouettes are reinforced with darker brushed tracings, adding volume to the forms. In the upper right corner is an eight-pointed star, an early appearance of this emblem of transformation that was to become

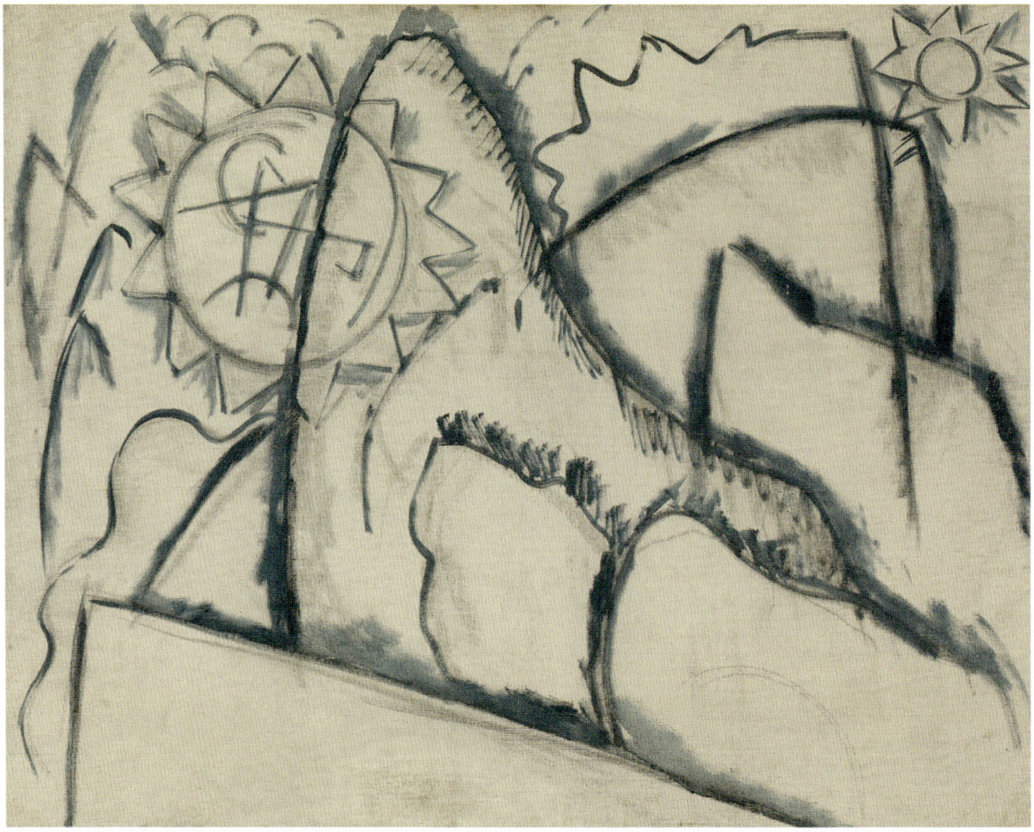

2.
Marsden Hartley
(1877–1943)
Painting No. 8, 1913
Oil on canvas mounted
on masonite
24 × 31 in. (61 × 78.7 cm)
Sotheby's, New York, May 19, 2010, lot 18, and Sotheby's, New York, May 19, 2011, lot 120

one of Hartley's favorite mystical symbols. A larger circle framed by thirteen points contains enigmatic markings, suggestive of similar "medallions" that Hartley used in his *German Officer* paintings just a year later. Dynamic zig-zag lines angle across the work; these also appear in other works ranging from the early *Amerika* series (1914) based on Native American motifs to his last self-portrait (*Sustained Comedy—Portrait of an Object*, 1939), where these zig-zag "lines of inspiration" pierce his eyes.

Painting No. 8 shows Hartley coming to grips with the sheer force of Kandinsky's radical new compositions. The better to explore the structural aspects of his work, Hartley restricted himself to shades of black, giving the work a diagrammatic quality. Around the same time, he also made a quick compositional sketch in ink as a memory aid after seeing a Picasso artwork in Gertrude Stein's collection, thus enabling him to absorb the new Cubist idiom.[1]

Painting No. 8 is a similarly urgent jotting of forms with rough brushwork. He is trying out new modes of abstraction, mentally absorbing the shapes and forms found in Kandinsky's art and Picasso's Cubism, and then personalizing them through his use of symbols and heavy brushwork. In effect, *Painting No. 8* is a rare glimpse of a great artist encountering wholly new expressions, working at fever pitch through the messy process of devouring and digesting the novel aesthetics to make them over as his own, an almost direct transmission of his mental process. This is as close to the creative moment as can be experienced.

Why then did *Painting No. 8* twice fail at auction? In 2010, the estimate was a healthy $200–300,000; a year later, it had slipped to $80–120,000, but even at this reduced price, it found no buyer. To be sure, the lack of color made it less appealing for a residential living room; maybe its sketchy quality felt somehow unresolved or incomplete rather than urgently experimental. But, more likely, prospective bidders were unaware that this work is a crucial early milestone along the development of Modernism. By integrating Kandinsky's vocabulary, Picasso's Cubism, and his own occult references, Hartley took a leap forward that would lead to the brilliant symbolic abstractions of the *Amerika* and *German Officer* series in 1914–15, often considered his career masterworks.

Another striking group of artworks grew out of this same first visit to Germany. While visiting Kandinsky and Gabriele Münter in Munich, he saw their collection of more than 100 Bavarian folk paintings on glass, and he too began to collect these inexpensive items. He wrote to Alfred Stieglitz about "… a few Bavarian glass *Bilder* which I own and which are wonderful expressions of religious symbolism. I bought them for 50c each at the *Dult* in Munchen—but they are 100 yrs old and are part of the art expression of Europe. I think it would be fine to show them among my own…."[2] Hartley, like European Modernists, admired folk art for its naïvety, simplified forms, and direct expression; Kandinsky, Münter, and Hartley not only collected these glass paintings but also experimented with the technique. In 1917, Hartley created a small but important body of work in this medium. The reverse painting technique used to paint on the back of the glass is challenging to master, for it requires upending the usual practice of painting "dark to light," where dense forms and background are laid in first and highlights added last. When painting on the verso of a glass panel, the artist must first lay in the highlights, and then add darker forms and, finally, the background. Often metal foils were laid over glazes, so that when viewed from the front, portions of the painting would glimmer with reflected light.

One of Hartley's finest examples in this technique sold for $77,675 (against estimates of $60–80,000) in 2004. *Still Life* from 1917 (Fig. 1) shows a single rose in a tall blue vase, in a dramatic format that is more than twice as tall as it is wide, 13 ¼ × 6 in. In classic folk manner, Hartley idealizes the arrangement of rose petals in tidy concentric circles and arranges the three green leaves as strict vertical and horizontals, as if indicating directions on a compass. Foils on the rose, leaves, and vase add visual delight.

Hartley had a deep love of flowers, recalling his walks through Franklin Pasture on his way to grammar school as a "vast place full of wonder." He wrote in his autobiography, "The flowers in this wooded piece [place?] I have spoken of, on my way to school, were magical and I owe I think nearly everything to them...."[3] So it is small surprise that he made a great many floral still lifes throughout his career, and few are more delightful than this one. The iconic format of the tall vase and single flower centered in a blank field gives it exceptional presence; the extraordinary elongation of the vase leads the eye up to the perfect circle of the rose and schematically arranged leaves. Hartley, though not religious in any doctrinal sense, frequently borrowed Christian symbols to deepen the associations of his works, and he explicitly characterized the Bavarian glass paintings as "wonderful expressions of religious symbolism." Christian allusions and inspirations abound in this work, without ever coalescing as a religious image: the blue of the vase summons the Virgin's traditional blue drapery;[4] the vertical and horizontal arrangement of leaves evokes a cross; the orb of the rose is a numinous halo; the shimmering foil recalls liturgical objects.

Even the elongated format of the glass support echoes the neo-gothic stained-glass Ascension of Christ in the Episcopal church that Hartley attended as a child, where he "sang magnificats and epiphanies" in the choir.[5] This "ascension" format is one he used over and over for completely different subjects, where rising vertical forms—a teepee, a lighthouse, a vase, a mountain, even an abstract triangle—surge upward to terminate in a circle. The ascendant motif implies transcendence, or regeneration; it is another of Hartley's several ways of evoking his favorite idea of "matter transformed into spirit," along with his use of the figure 8. Hartley acknowledged his interest in the subject, writing to Stieglitz, "If I had been an ardent Christian in early times I suppose I should be painting vivid ascensions and crucifixions—as I am not I am simply painting vivid sensations of finite and tangible things."[6] This is not to imply that Hartley meant this *Still Life* as a religious image, but his genius is to borrow hallowed motifs from Christian iconography and embed them in secular subjects, lending them deeper resonance and iconic status. It is this penchant for seeing nature and all creation as a manifestation of the spirit that links Hartley to the Transcendentalists.

In his early twenties, Hartley turned more intensely toward religion, and he briefly considered entering the priesthood as a higher alternative to art.[7] More than a decade later, art and religion had almost merged in his mind; he wrote to Stieglitz in October 1912, "... art is like religion, one must be faithful and devoted if one would express something real.... I find growing in me and I think to more purpose—a recurrence of former religious aspirations—taking a finer form in personal expression...."[8] Hartley's well-known devotion to occult authors—Jacob Boehme, Meister Eckhardt, Paracelsus, and many more—has obscured his more frequent use of traditional Christian imagery and references in his art and poetry. But whether he appeals to traditional ritual or to an occult mysticism, he imbues his subject with deeper associations. So, this rose-in-vase is imprinted in our minds as something significant and symbolic, not just a secular folk-inspired still life, but a distillation of the spiritual that should be cherished, even venerated. The lucky bidder who won this work at auction secured a bargain.

Hartley also made innumerable table-top fruit arrangements, each in some sense a homage to Cézanne, who was such an inspiration that Hartley even went to live in his hometown of Aix-en-Provence for several months in late 1926 and summer–fall 1927. As with every subject, Hartley moved beyond his immediate inspiration to make the still lifes personal, even private, with his own concealed meanings. Paul Rosenfeld, a discerning critic, wrote about how "a cold and ferocious sensuality seeks to satisfy itself in the still-lifes, with their heavy stiff golden bananas, their dark luscious figs, their erectile pears and enormous breast-like peaches."[9] He locates in these arrangements the tension Hartley always felt between Cézanne's pure intellectual idealism and his visceral emotional response to his own desires.

Rosenfeld might have been writing about a lovely undated pastel on paper called *Still Life with Pears* (Fig. 3) that sold in 2012:

And so, in the paintings of Hartley, these great dark pears, for instance, bedded upon hospital white linen on a background of severe dry black, are both the magnificent fruits shown against ascetic noble stuffs, and the entire world as a certain grim experience of life has shown it to the painter. In their doubleness, they satisfy the whole organism.... There is grim and tragic resignation in the great dark pears among their magnificent white.[10]

The "grim experience" and "tragic resignation" in this description surely allude to the artist's frustrations on returning from the more sexually tolerant Europe, where he associated freely with other gay men, to the disapproving puritanism of the United States in the early 1920s.

Hartley entrusted this private portrayal of "erectile" and "bedded" fruits to his good friend Adelaide Kuntz, who had grown close to him when she and her artist husband lived in Aix-en-Provence when he was there. Kuntz held on to the work throughout her lifetime, and it stayed with her family after her death until a descendant offered it for sale more than eight decades later, finally making this intimate artwork public. The price realized at auction was $15,000 (against estimates of $10–15,000), which feels low for a densely worked and richly colored image that is 15 × 19 ¼ in., sizeable enough to hold a wall. The modest sale price suggests that the confidential nature of this artwork still remains a privileged understanding; the image was perhaps accepted at its most obvious face value as a simple arrangement of pears. Interestingly, a very similar pastel—same palette, very slightly larger—sold for $64,625, well above the high estimate of $35,000, in 2000. Did this healthy price result from a competition between two discerning collectors, or does it reflect more generally the greater popularity of American Modernism at the turn of the millennium and the ebbing of interest over the past two decades, as contemporary art sweeps the field?

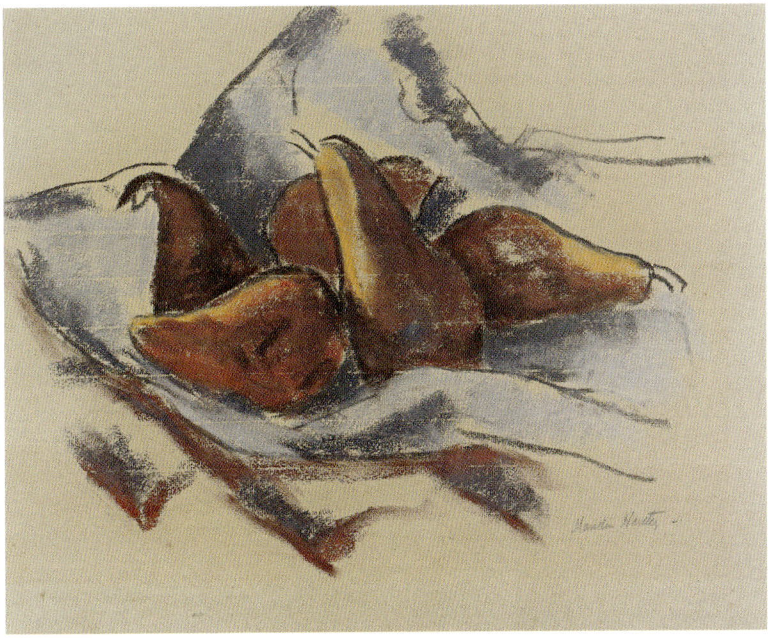

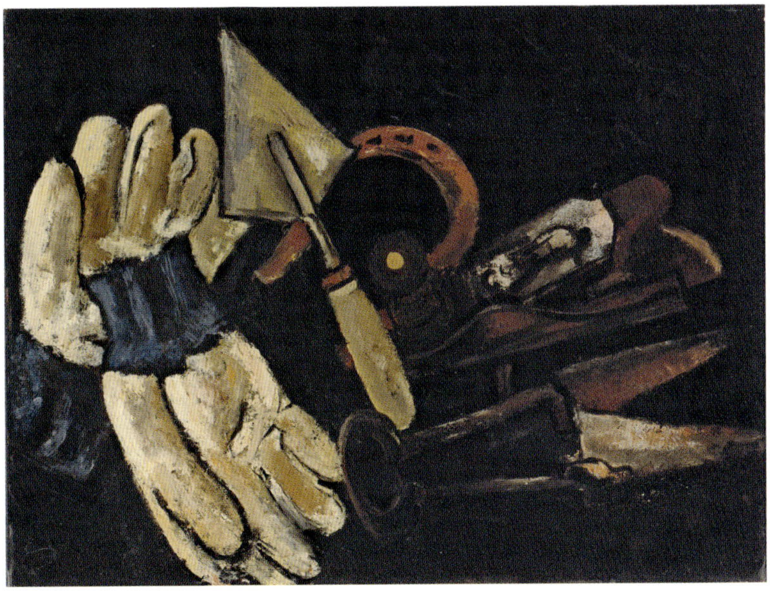

A very different kind of still life failed to sell in 2013. *Gardener's Gloves and Field Implements* of 1937–38 (Fig. 4) is an unusually complex composition and of good size, supporting a pre-auction estimate of $150–250,000. It is a powerful image: two rough white cotton gloves with blue cuffs lie together limply in a "recumbent" position at left, while a bricklayer's trowel, horseshoe, carpenter's plane, and gardening shears cascade across the right half of the painting. The contrast between the empty

3. *(top)*
Marsden Hartley (1877–1943)
Still Life with Pears, c. 1920
Pastel on paper
15 × 19 ¼ in. (38.1 × 48.9 cm)
Sotheby's, New York, April 5, 2012, lot 5

4. *(above)*
Marsden Hartley (1877–1943)
Gardener's Gloves and Field Implements, 1937–8
Oil on canvas board
17 ⁷/₈ × 24 in. (45.4 × 61 cm)
Sotheby's, New York, May 22, 2013, lot 26

cloth gloves and the sharp metal implements once used by absent hands creates a *frisson* of tactile sensations, making this a sensory memory painting of workers and the tools they handled. Hartley was personally averse to manual labor, and his assorted tools are not all "field implements" as the title implies, suggesting an unfamiliarity with their use. But he liked hanging around the local blacksmith's shop with its "coils and coils of rope, lovely smell of tar and shavings ... carpenter's tools and odd objects and bottles," and surely the shop's masculine environment of lumberjacks and laborers attracted him, as did the beach, with its lifeguards and fishermen. More than just a homage to labor, the painting contains a significant subtext about vulnerability and aggression, with its juxtaposition of soft and hard, pliable and sharp, rounded and pointed. Duncan Phillips, the prescient collector in Washington who founded America's first Gallery of Modern Art in 1921, purchased a slightly smaller but similar image in 1939, soon after Hartley made it; this *Gardener's Gloves and Shears* more directly features the threat of open shears on the vulnerable fingers of a glove, poised to snip.

One might claim that finding vulnerability in a pair of gloves and aggression in gardener's shears is over-reading the image, and of course it may be, since there is no written statement of Hartley's intention to guide us. But he again and again asserted the symbolic aspect of his art, starting with his early abstractions in Paris and Berlin, and continuing through his life. If Hartley's art often underperforms at auction, perhaps it is because he was too successful at concealing his private meanings, and we are too busy or literal-minded to probe below surface appearance, leading to a consistent under-reading of his art.

Fish in the Sky (Fig. 5) belongs to a group of large (22 × 28 in.) paintings that Hartley made in the early 1940s, when he was living in Maine's coastal villages. In his mid-sixties, he experienced increasing frailty and debilitating

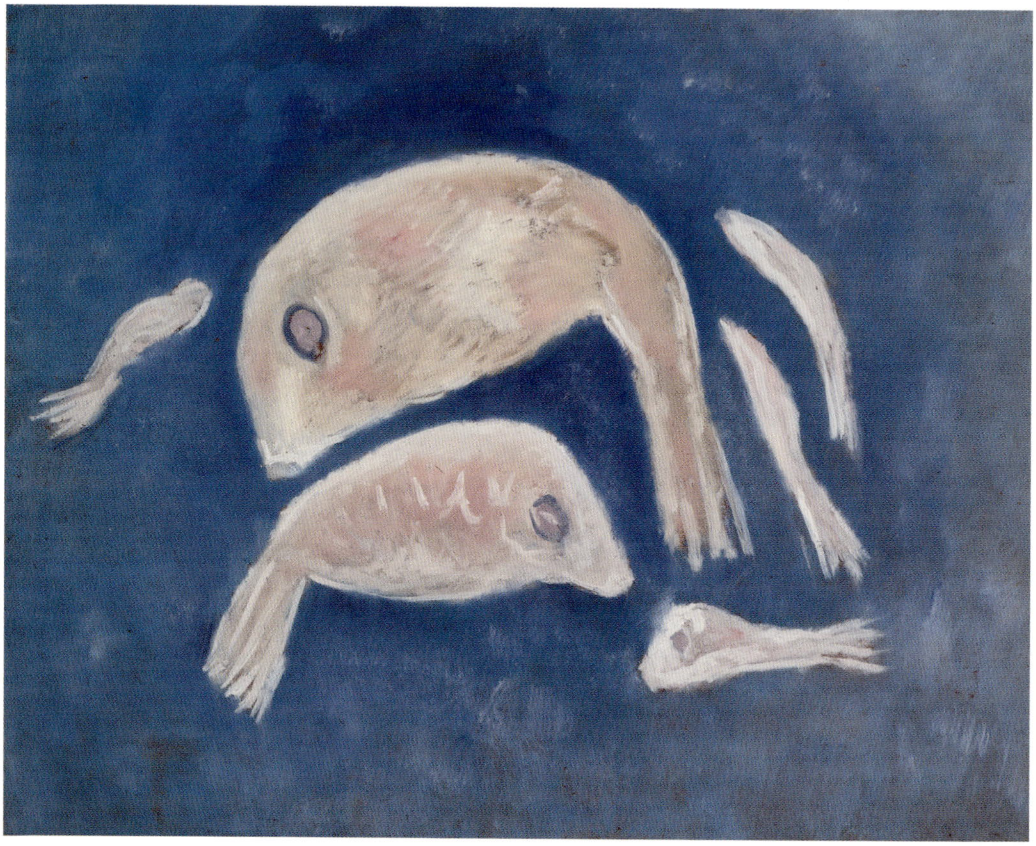

5.
Marsden Hartley
(1877–1943)
Fish in the Sky, 1942
Oil on masonite
22 × 28 in. (55.9 × 71.1 cm)
Sotheby's, New York, May 21, 2014, lot 21, now Alexandre Gallery, New York

health problems, and he sometimes gave in to bitterness, having failed to achieve the recognition he felt he deserved, and having endured painful years of concealment in homophobic America. His childhood loneliness returned in full force, born of feelings of abandonment after the death of his mother when he was just eight; increasingly in later life he craved friends, even a semblance of family and home, having lived his entire adult life in rented rooms, in more than thirty towns. The group of works that grew from this despair focuses on birds and sea creatures against mostly blank backgrounds, each an analogue for the artist himself. *Gull* (Brooklyn Museum) is shown *in memoriam*, evoking the poignant small *Dead Bird* (The Phillips Collection) by his hero, Albert Pinkham Ryder, an aesthetic connection with his early mentor that strengthened as Hartley aged. *Lobster on Black Background* (Smithsonian American Art Museum) is a recumbent *odalisque*. Fish appear, often singly or in opposed pairs, in a blank field.

Among this group, *Fish in the Sky* occupies a curious place. The unidentified fish have downward-curved tails resembling those of shrimp, but there are no antennae or swimmerets to confirm that identification. The most prominent pair, arranged head-to-tail, appear too plump to be shrimp; they most resemble the two opposed fish in a painting titled *White Cod* (Brooklyn Museum). In both these paintings, the opposed arrangement and "pairing" remind us of Hartley's persistent longing for intimacy and tenderness; it has been suggested that *White Cod* recalls the deaths of his close friends Donny and Alty Mason in 1936, which haunted Hartley until his own death.[11]

Fish in the Sky is an unusually lyrical work, with two featured fish and four smaller ones surrounding them. Where most of Hartley's fish appear dead, these six beauties circle each other in a graceful choreography, evoking *The Dance* by Matisse, one of the Modernists Hartley most admired. The delicate coral and pink bodies of the two principal "dancers" evoke flesh-tones, and their prominent eyes reinforce the human association. Spatial references vanish in the flattened composition, but the larger fish seems to hover over and protect the smaller one. This ballet is set in a brilliant cerulean field that would surely be considered water in any normal interpretation, but Hartley's title tells us that it is not water, but sky. And with that poetic displacement, we move into the other-worldly realm of the imagination, which was Hartley's spiritual home. Once again, in this magical image, he creatively transforms matter into spirit; it is yet another "ascension into heaven," transcending a troubled earthbound reality.

Yet *Fish in the Sky* failed to sell when offered at auction in 2014, with an estimate of $150–250,000, despite its "track record" of being selected for major Hartley exhibitions in 1946, 1964, and 1967. This failure at auction is all the more surprising, as another similarly sized painting from this 1942 group, titled *White Sea Horse*, sailed past its $400–600,000 estimate to reach $965,000 less than six months earlier, in 2013. How can we account for two such similar artworks having such disparate auction experiences? Was the brushwork of *Fish in the Sky* too summary, or was the very idea of fish in the sky just too weird? Likely, the rich personal associations underlying this simple image—Christian sacrifice and ascension, lovers and friends, longing for transcendence—simply went unrecognized, or, more prosaically, there were too many Hartleys on offer in a short period. It could have been purchased for the low estimate of $150,000 or perhaps even less, making it a bargain compared to nearly a million dollars for *White Sea Horse*. So, here was another missed opportunity to own a deeply affecting work by a profound and tragic artist. As Paul Rosenfeld wrote, "One returns always to the Hartleys. One returns not once, but over and over again. They are the most charming of companions.... They delight with their distinguished presence."[12] Perhaps, if prices for Hartley's works continue to swing so erratically, one day these marvelous Hartley paintings will be affordable for art historians.

Modern Appearances

Jane Bianco
Curator, The Farnsworth Art Museum, Rockland, Maine

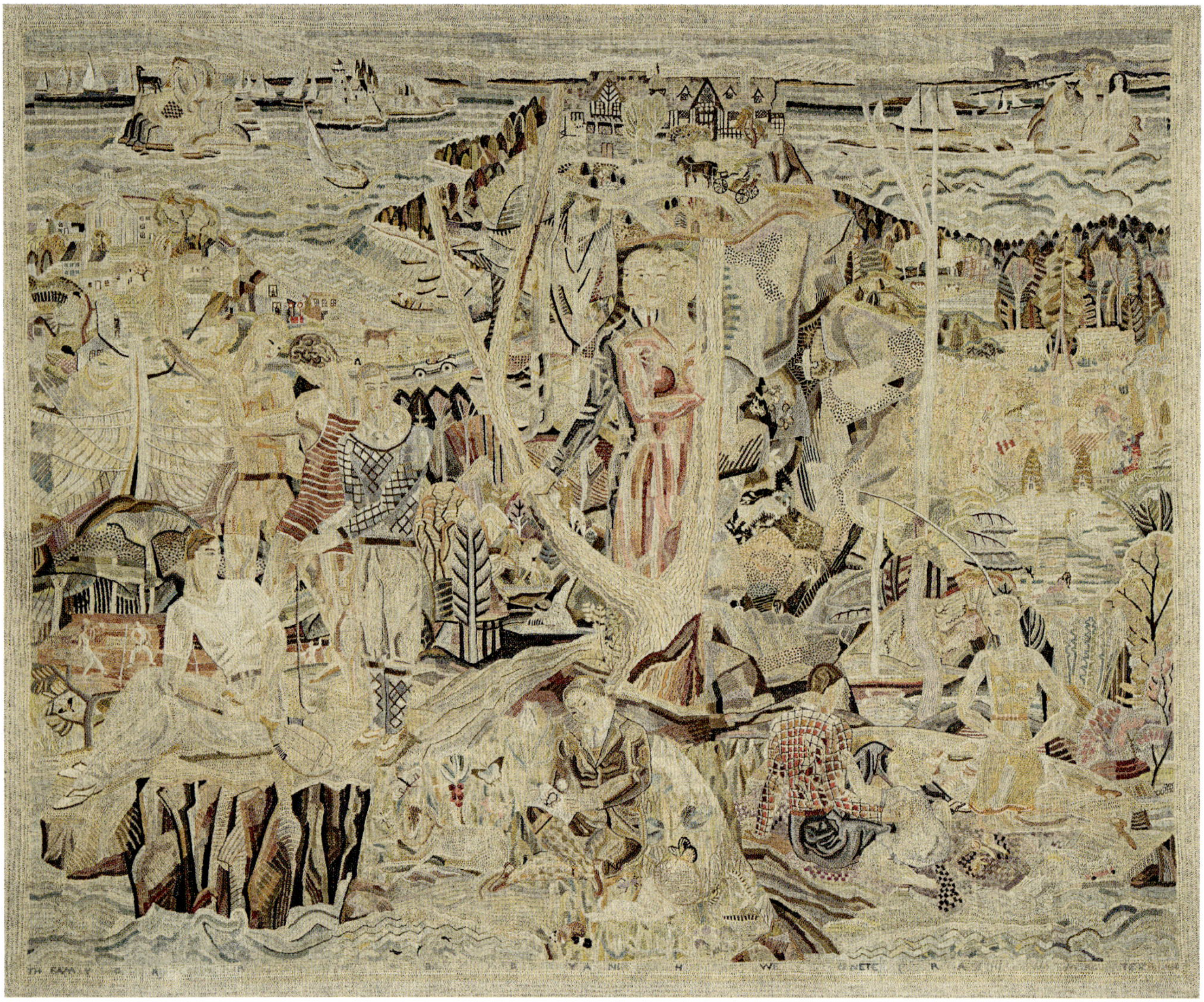

Dearest boys, I am sitting at my desk and I have just been making out a list of the chief interests and characteristics of each of you children. Mrs. Zorach is going to make an embroidered picture of our life here at Seal Harbor and I am going to hang it in the playhouse at Tarrytown. Mrs. Z is coming up here next week to make sketches of the place and the boats, etc. If either of you have any special hobby of yours that you want in it, just write it to me. The picture will be about 6 by 10 feet and will be correct with small figures, flowers, water, boats, horses, buildings, etc., something like a 13th century tapestry, only very modern....[1]

With those words from her patron, Abby Aldrich Rockefeller, the artist Marguerite Thompson Zorach (1887–1968) was launched into one of her most ambitious projects. Zorach's commission for a portrait of one of America's best-known families was over three years in its making, at a monumental scale, and in intricate detail through an uncommon medium.

The recent Marguerite Zorach retrospective at the Farnsworth Art Museum in Rockland, Maine, has prompted consideration of the nature of Zorach's portraiture, prevalent in her paintings and her more rare and unusual needlework.[2] This chapter examines the artist's career and a range of her production through the 1940s in order to emphasize the importance of two factors in appreciating her work—content and biography. At the core of this focus, Zorach's portrait *The Family of John D. Rockefeller, Jr., at their Summer Home, Seal Harbor, Maine, 1929–1932* (Fig. 1) exemplifies her experimental approach—vital in her work—to the long-standing art tradition of portraiture. While employing the convention of depicting a prominent family within a setting they have shaped in their own vision, her daring portrayal departs from custom in medium and detail, prompted partly by the Modernist cultural climate in which she thrived, and by the creative freedom granted by her patron. Zorach's execution of the Rockefeller portrait in embroidered form is a high point of her accomplishments, surpassing even her painted portrayals of colleagues, family, and friends.

Marguerite Thompson enjoyed a comfortable upbringing in Fresno, California, as daughter of a strong mother and bookish lawyer father. Having first been propelled into the culture of European Modernism between 1908 and 1912 by way of her studies in Paris and travels with an enlightened aunt through Europe and Asia, she began the process of reinventing herself as a full-time artist upon her return to the United States.[3] This culminated in her move from her conservative home in California to New York City, and marriage to fellow artist William Zorach. Her exposure to diverse cultures and her self-sufficiency served her well as she navigated the gallery world and life in New York's Greenwich Village, a rich enclave of avant-garde artists, many with intellectual roots abroad. During her fifty-year career Marguerite Zorach lived with William Zorach, a sculptor, and their two children in the Village and later in Brooklyn, and, beginning in 1923, the family regularly summered in their coastal Maine home, seven hours north of the city. The inhabitants of Maine as well as New York were subjects of Zorach's art. Throughout her career it was her ability to recognize what was meaningful in her world that drove her to create works "built out of my life and the things that have touched my life."

PROFESSIONAL LIFE

Zorach developed as a Modernist during her student years, in classes given by the progressive Scottish painter John Duncan Fergusson (1874–1961) at the Académie de La Palette in Paris. There she explored bold brushwork and unorthodox juxtapositions of color. She came to know the work of the Fauves, and in her experiments with color and subject matter abstracted from the natural world, she synthesized form and meaning, visually and emotionally. Her early work, consistent in its emphasis upon pattern, was drawn from a wide range of design sources: Renaissance tapestries, Chinese scroll paintings, Persian and Indian miniatures, Greek red-figure vases, and from the intrinsic charm and sophistication of folk art, which she collected and lived with, as did others in her circle of friends and colleagues.

Zorach came to be identified with the 1913 International Exhibition of Modern Art,

1.
Marguerite Zorach
(1887–1968)
The Family of John D. Rockefeller, Jr., at their Summer Home, Seal Harbor, Maine, 1929–1932
Wool embroidered on linen
51 × 64 in. (129.5 × 162.5 cm)
Private collection

known as the Armory Show, the first important exhibition of works shown jointly by progressive European and American artists. Originating in New York, and traveling to Chicago and Boston, the exhibition took place during an era of cultural change described by one critic as "a groping period in intellectual and artistic development, an effort to get away from passive acceptance of things, a period of discovery, an effort to 'standoff' and look at life with fresh eyes, to grasp the magnitude and wonder of it all...."[4] In keeping with the Modernist precepts that drove the Armory Show, Zorach showed *Adam and Eve*, a portrait of spiritual and idyllic union, a motif she came to reiterate in other forms throughout her body of work.[5]

Zorach believed that "Art must change and develop just as it always has done, just as everything does. The ideas and ideals, the great impulses and movements ... must necessarily find expression in new ways." She was active in New York art organizations whose members drove the avant-garde movement in America and fostered democratic representation of artists. As vice president of the Society of Independent Artists with president John Sloan in 1922 she organized exhibitions and an imaginative costumed artists' ball, details of which were mentioned in *The New York Times*. By 1929 Zorach's work was featured among the "radicals" of *33 Moderns* at the Grand Central Galleries, the same year she was commissioned to design and embroider the highly unusual family portrait for the John D. Rockefeller, Jr. family.

New York's Downtown Gallery owner Edith Halpert was a dealer friend who organized several shows for Marguerite Zorach, and it was Halpert who introduced Abby Aldrich Rockefeller to her paintings, batik designs, and what Zorach called her "embroidered tapestries," at a time when Rockefeller was collecting folk art and works by emerging artists. Review articles of Zorach's exhibitions of textiles and paintings and interviews with the artist were published throughout the 1920s and 1930s in the New York press as interest in her work grew.

Zorach's work varied in subject matter over time and between commissions and exhibition offerings. During the Great Depression she was awarded contracts to execute large-scale US Post Office murals of a regionalist style in Iowa, Tennessee, and New Hampshire. In the 1930s and 1940s she submitted other designs for federal buildings celebrating scenes that embodied nationalistic themes of government, labor, and family, though these were not commissioned. Through the 1960s her work was represented sporadically in New York, garnering good reviews. Late in her career she focused on still life and landscape painting, prompted by travels to the American West, Canada, and Central America.

Zorach maintained relationships with major New York galleries and museums throughout her career. Significant examples of her art may be found in collections of the Art Institute of Chicago, Museum of Fine Arts, Boston, Bowdoin College Museum of Art, the Brooklyn Museum, Colby College Museum, Cooper Hewitt Museum, the Farnsworth Art Museum, The Metropolitan Museum of Art, Smithsonian American Art Museum, the National Museum of Women in the Arts, the Portland Museum of Art, the Whitney Museum of American Art, the Wichita Art Museum, Williams College Museum of Art, Worcester Art Museum, as well as in the Peterborough, New Hampshire, Monticello, Iowa, and Ripley, Tennessee, US Post Office buildings. In recent years her paintings have appeared in major exhibitions in the context of her pioneering contributions to the American Modernist movement. Occasionally, strong examples of Zorach's paintings (but very rarely her textiles) emerge in the national and international marketplace.

MARGUERITE ZORACH'S PORTRAITURE—AN ENDURING ART

An artistic genre among the earliest practiced, portraiture continues to maintain its appeal to artists and their audiences. Until the photographic medium was widely employed, of course, painted or drawn or sculpted portraits memorialized a face, a person, a personage and their particular attributes, including symbolic references to religious or political ideals, property, profession, wealth or power. From an art-historical perspective, it might seem that ancient iconography gave way to specificity; and faithful likeness since modernity has given way to suggestion and artistic concept. During Zorach's time Modernist interpretations of appearances referenced precedence but often pre-empted conventional representation by favoring the expressive vision and material, stylistic, or compositional concerns of the artist.

One of Zorach's portraits of Edith Halpert is significant for incidental detail. Although recognizable in her signature stylish attire, rather at odds with her pastoral surroundings in *The Picnic*, 1928 (Fig. 2), Halpert is crowded by secondary figures whose antics introduce distraction and anecdote into the scene. The figure next to Halpert, resembling her close friend, fellow collector Holger Cahill, awkwardly rifles through a picnic basket. Sandwiching the pair are a young girl and boy resembling the Zorach children, aiming for a bird's nest in a background tree, and in the foreground, a self-possessed Marguerite Zorach languishes like Goya's *Maja*, competing for the viewer's attention.[6] On a cliff off to the side an unidentified man with a camera surveys the distant vista, which could be rural Maine—in 1928, a rich source of folk art. The scene invites conjecture, as do many of Zorach's painted portraits.

Zorach's work was frequently autobiographical and included self-portraits, which enlivened her creative expressions. In *The Golden Orb*, 1921 (Fig. 3), whose title refers to the moon and its light animating a young girl, the work might be read as a symbolic self-portrait. Zorach has depicted a mother figure who fusses behind lace curtains before drawing the window shade, while the girl cups her hands to catch moonbeams. Her skirt flounces like the exotic red leafy plant thriving before the window. She is ebullient, in defiance of her mother's high-collared restraint. These details suggest tension between mother and free-spirited daughter, reflecting Zorach's own flight into independence as her own mother withdrew from her sphere of influence.

Though Zorach portrayed people and places she knew—dealer Edith Halpert, sculptor

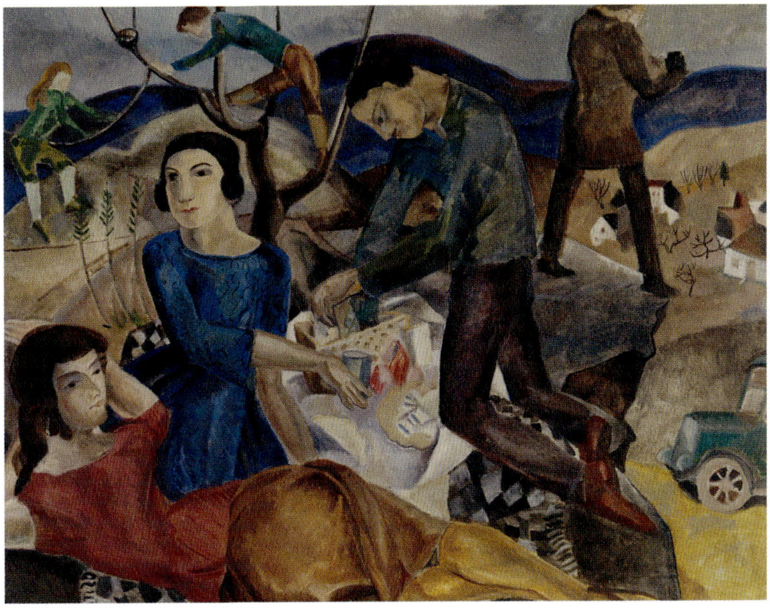

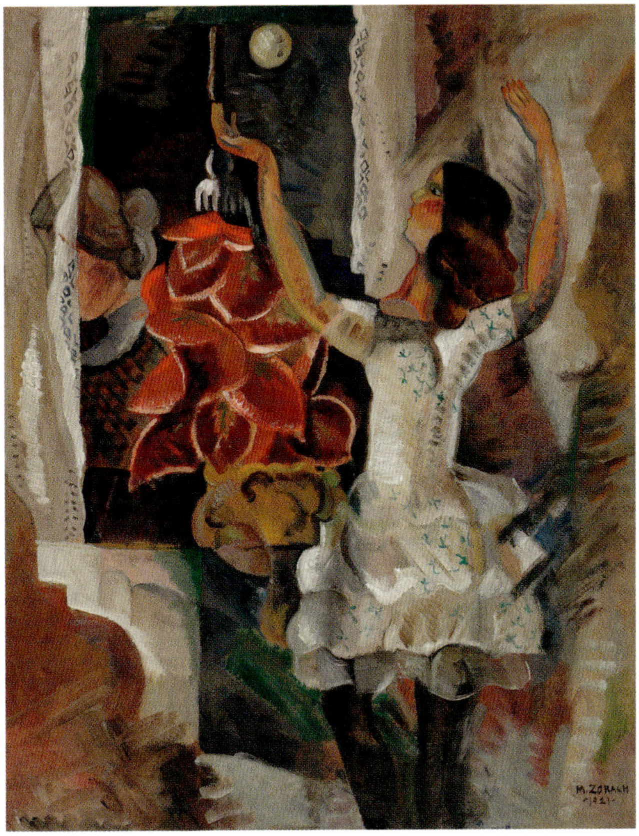

2. *(top)*
Marguerite Zorach
(1887–1968)
The Picnic, 1928
Oil on canvas
34 × 44 in. (86.4 × 111.8 cm)
Private collection

3. *(above)*
Marguerite Zorach
(1887–1968)
The Golden Orb, 1921
Oil on canvas
30 × 24 in. (76.2 × 60.9 cm)
Private collection

Gaston Lachaise, painter Lucy L'Engle or poet Marianne Moore, for instance—many of her portrayals tended to be less specific or even ambiguous expressions of character, mood or circumstance. Some of her figurative works have often been more about abstract ideas or unexpected gender roles and not readily consigned to a portraiture category. While her drawings are sensitive and spare, her painted figures often appear anatomically distorted or arbitrarily colored—"inclined to be fashionably primitive," according to one critic.[7] Like other American Modernist women struggling to achieve balance as artists, artistic and marriage partners, and mothers, she allowed professional and personal arenas to overlap and sometimes merge. She frequently portrayed her children or pets in domestic settings, but she also generalized and uplifted subjects to convey weightier themes in such paintings as *Death of a Miner* (*c.* 1930). The painting *The Family Evening* (1924) and, even more so, the embroidery *The Family Supper* (1922) are examples of portraits of family members used as compositional devices and titled to suggest the everyday but universal quality of family units or other relationships.[8]

Zorach sometimes cast her subjects into anecdotal scenes of "type" bordering on caricature. These latter works were described by Halpert as depictions of "The American Scene and the American People," and bring to mind the satirical portraits of personalities, situations or street scenes by such New York contemporaries as Peggy Bacon or John Sloan.[9] Along these lines Zorach's portraits include *Maine Sheriff*, a country official "oblivious to every immediacy,"[10] or *Cook's Holiday*, portraying a tired, middle-aged woman, seated opposite her husband, uncommunicative during a respite from work.

Early in their careers the Zorachs spent the 1915 summer in Randolph, New Hampshire, in a dilapidated farmhouse owned by artist-collector Hamilton Easter Field, lent in exchange for a painting from each of them. Marguerite Zorach made a somewhat humorous series of watercolors of visitors and neighbors, with such titles as *Leisure*, *Saturday Night in a New England Kitchen*, *The Country Sociable—New England.* Most famously, she completed an autobiographical portrait of her family on the stoop of the house within the greater natural landscape, a grouping repeated as a vignette in her later paintings and commissioned bedspread designs. Zorach's idea of home was a place beyond actual boundaries of physical space, and she elevated scenes of domesticity amid idyllic landscapes into which she incorporated self-portraits, family, and friends.

Halpert promoted the decorative nature that distinguished Zorach's work, but also underscored what she characterized as its intrinsic nativism in press releases such as this one:

Marguerite Zorach (née Thompson) was born in California, but her family was identified with the East. Her father was of Pennsylvania Quaker stock. On her mother's side she is descended from a family of New England mariners, many of whom had been masters of clippers and sailing ships. Several members of the family were painters, and one of these guided Mrs. Zorach's first steps in art....[11]

Zorach's emblematic subjects for large-scale murals were another form of portraiture during the Great Depression when the nation's attributes were celebrated through its arts. From 1935 to 1942, government-funded programs subsidized the nation's artists, who brought written, performing, and visual arts to public attention as part of a nationwide effort to celebrate America's strengths. Zorach's designs represented values celebrated through depictions of the anonymous workers and dreamers of an idealistic society. During the years that she sought federal commissions she painted *Land and Development of New England* (Fig. 4). It was an example, perhaps, of her ability to compose on a grand scale in keeping with themes of mythological proportions. Its union of mother, father, and children presents heroic imagery of a pioneer family in harmony with bountiful resources of the region known for the birth and regeneration of national identity. This symbolic family portrait celebrates potential during a period of economic decline. The visual references to lumbering, coastal communities and farming—including the detail of the L.L. Bean boots—indicate, as well, the Zorach family's personal ties to the state of Maine, which were to be long-lasting.

THE ARTIST´S VISION AND THE COLLECTOR´S VISION

The outstanding modern portrait, *The Family of John D. Rockefeller, Jr., at their Summer Home, Seal Harbor, Maine, 1929–1932* (Fig. 1), celebrates the vision of John D. Rockefeller, Jr., who helped shape what became Acadia National Park on Mt. Desert Island, Maine.[12] Monumental in concept and scale, Zorach's embroidered portrait was unique in its time, incorporating emblematic references to each member of one of the wealthiest families in America, their relationships to one another and to individual interests, in and around their beloved Maine summer estate, The Eyrie.[13]

Zorach's portrayal of this powerful family is also a portrait of the environment they shaped and held dear—one that resonates today and transcends the time of its making. It portrays lands still recognizable and draws attention to the Rockefeller legacy of both designing and preserving land in keeping with the family's altruistic leanings.[14] It describes activities and landmarks of Seal Harbor, including the Abby Aldrich Rockefeller Garden, created just a few years prior to Zorach's work by landscape designer Beatrix Farrand. The garden structure is much the same today as Zorach depicted it in 1929.

John D. Rockefeller, Jr. was heir to family businesses that included Standard Oil Company, an enterprise that thrived, as the gasoline-powered automobile became the vehicle of choice for many Americans. His wife, Abby Aldrich Rockefeller, a champion of contemporary arts and artists, commissioned the large embroidered tapestry soon after seeing Zorach's nearly-completed portrait of the Selda and Ralph Jonas family, now in the collection of Cooper Hewitt Smithsonian Design Museum. Its *millefleurs* carpet of a garden with small animals and birds is the Edenic setting for the Jonas family portrait and combines incongruously with the contemporary city view in the background. Its resemblance to a late medieval tapestry mixed with modern qualities somehow sparked attention from Mrs. Rockefeller.

She may have also been thinking of what became known as the Unicorn Tapestries which hung from 1922 in the family's New York City residence, when she envisioned a wall hanging "something like a 13th century tapestry, only very modern...." Zorach's embroidered portrait of the Rockefellers offers evidence of such appropriation: in materials and in scale, density, coloring and subject matter it recalls such textiles as the loomed Flemish tapestries commissioned for European aristocracy. And Zorach's allegorical treatment of the Rockefeller family follows a long-standing tradition of portraiture emphasizing the dynastic legacy of prominent families situated within the properties they have shaped under their dominion.

In order that the artist might prepare sketches and familiarize herself with the family, their estate, and the community where they

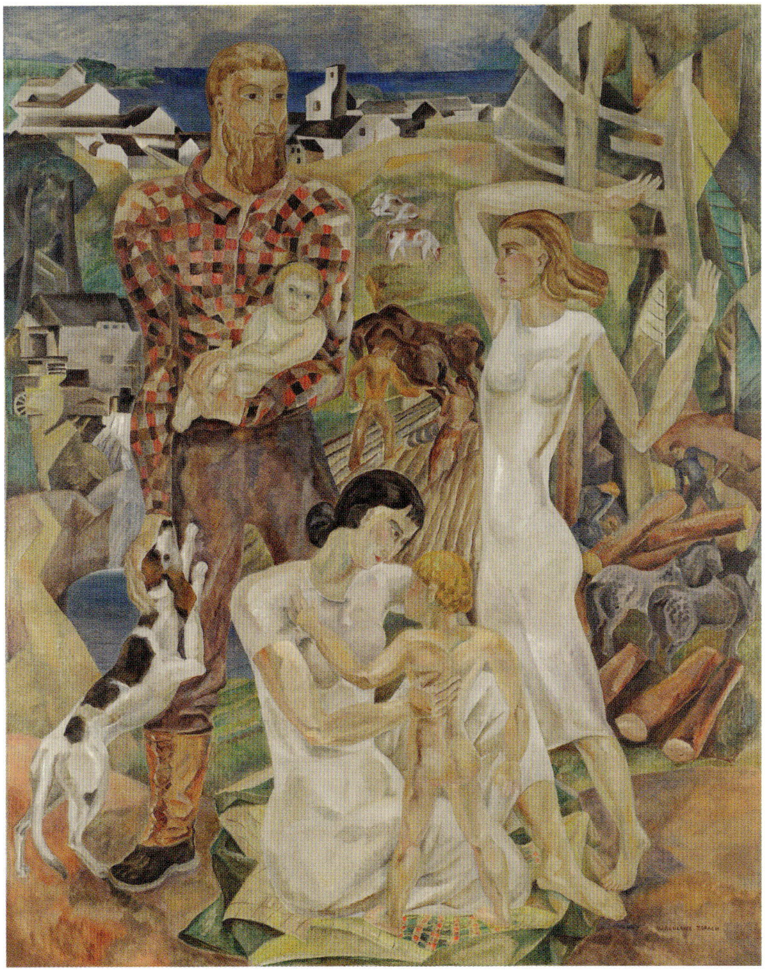

4.
Marguerite Zorach
(1887–1968)
Land and Development of New England, c. 1935
Oil on canvas
96 × 78 in. (243.8 × 198 cm)
Collection of the Farnsworth Art Museum, Rockland, Maine, Museum purchase 1991.17

summered, Marguerite and William Zorach, and their children Tessim and Dahlov, were invited in 1929 to spend a week at the Seal Harbor estate on Mount Desert Island. Between hours of sketching and painting Marguerite Zorach enjoyed sailing and horse-drawn carriage rides along miles of woodland roads established over decades by John D. Rockefeller, Jr. During this same time Abby Aldrich Rockefeller, amid planning and raising money for the opening of the Museum of Modern Art, spoke of this project with the Zorachs. One might imagine that Zorach's preparation of the embroidered portrait was influenced by this very week—her concept for the project inspired by the landscape, personalities, conversations, rides along estate carriage paths, Modernist ideals—all in a kind of heady mix.

Most importantly, the portrait celebrates the vision of Mrs. Rockefeller, who championed modern art and artists by purchasing and living with their work in her homes. She paid a sizeable stipend of $500 per month to Zorach over the three-year period that the artist took to complete the large portrait. As Zorach commenced working just before the 1929 stock market crash in October, this monthly salary constituted an enormous payment (equivalent in 2020 dollars to well over $7000 monthly), astonishing for any artist who struggled after the crash. It was this money that allowed the artist couple to continue to live and work as artists in New York through the difficult years of the Depression. Indeed, one wonders whether Marguerite Zorach would have had the freedom to direct her energies to her prodigious works of the 1930s and 1940s, such as US Post Office mural commissions or her large-scale painting, *Land and Development of New England*, had she not had this initial surge of financial security which paved the way for other critically important works.

The completed work was shown in public infrequently but was exhibited with other of Zorach's textiles; in later years it was exhibited in the context of the history of family portraiture in America. Described as a work executed "in Brueghelian detail," the portrait includes touches of humor: sly insertions of self-portraiture and reference to Rockefeller, Sr.'s empire.[15] At one with their home, their family and the land, Abby and John Rockefeller stand at center within the arms of a tree whose trunk and branches become pathways to The Eyrie above them, and toward their children within the surroundings about them. In keeping with the Edenic theme coursing throughout her body of work, Zorach has cast the Rockefeller parents like modern-day Adam and Eve entwined with a Tree of Life, within and overseeing a paradise of their own making. To the right of their parents, their sons John, Nelson, Laurance, and Winthrop wrestle and pose with tennis and golf gear. To their left their grown daughter Babs picnics with her husband and two young daughters. And below them a young David Rockefeller appears immersed in examination of butterflies and beetles with his magnifying glass—his portrait is prophetic.

In her portrayal of David Rockefeller happily engrossed in observing insects and flowers with little fishes in a pool at his feet, Zorach was especially prescient, as he practiced lifelong reverence for the natural world and was active in its preservation. Indeed, the important collection of beetles, amassed and studied over his lifetime, and his recent gift to the public of 1000 acres from the family estate in Seal Harbor are consistent with his boyhood interests depicted in the portrait.

Zorach's body of work with its dual figurative and abstract leanings repeats motifs and autobiographical elements that she incorporated in later portraits of her children. These works favor densely crowded scenes of bustling activity, making them very different from her earlier paintings such as *Block Castle*, *c.* 1920 (Fig. 5), a slightly Cubist portrait of her young daughter Dahlov that incorporates an inventive structure the child has built. Early in the 1940s Zorach created scenes of domesticity involving her grown children, their families and pets, and the setting beyond as glimpsed through windows and passageways of their homes. Two detail the chaotic home life of her two children, their own young families—and in turn, all young families.

In *The Ipcar Family at Robinhood Farm*, 1944 (Fig. 6), Zorach's hand stitchery describes a familiar red linoleum floor scattered with toys and mats, the sheen of pots and pans, the texture of drying clothes hanging on the line, her animated grandsons, and placid farm animals beyond the door. Like many of her compositions this one is generous with color and detail. The flow of threads guides the eye to the adult Dahlov as she bends over the oven in a yellow dress, or to the pet Dalmatian's graceful spotted form, defining and encircling small worlds within the cluttered scene of family life. Elements that shaped their lives are suggested by the pine-dotted hillside or watery cove seen through the kitchen window, and within a corner of the room a tiny Sears tag that dangles from the clothes basket.

When she was in her fifties, Zorach portrayed herself daydreaming in a hammock of her long-ago home in Fresno. Within that memory she depicted herself at various stages of life in a nostalgic recollection of the past.

A large white gingerbread house, light and airy and delightful in stitches, the magnolia trees and palms, the children playing hide and seek under the street lamp at night, the Chinese vegetable man—my mother, children, activities and the vacant lots of a small town.

Artist retrospectives can be of value to the collector who aims to appreciate the scope and the sequential development of artists' work. Both the preparation and presentation of the recent Zorach retrospective at the Farnsworth Art Museum afforded unexpected opportunity to review her portraiture—not intended to be the main thrust of the show. A narrower selection or arrangement of her figurative work may not otherwise have suggested that self-portraiture is so present in her body of work. And as museum teams know, bringing together borrowed objects not often seen together can set up dynamics for a perspective that extends beyond or even contradicts the originally conceived storylines and subplots. In her work-and-life blend Zorach aimed for personal style with a focus on relationships, especially those between male and female, and between parent and child. The challenge in understanding her Modernist approach to portraiture is made interesting because of these undercurrents that strongly emerge in a broader view of her work.

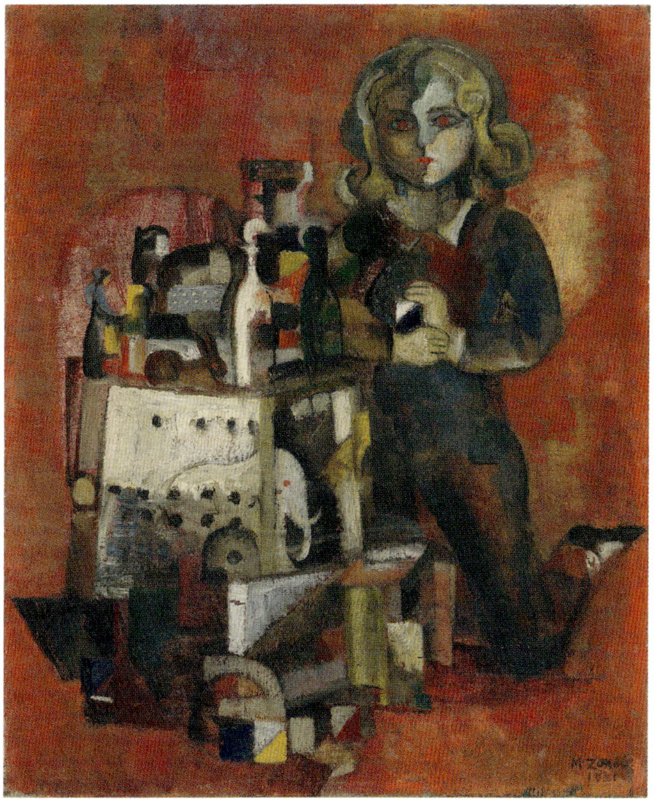

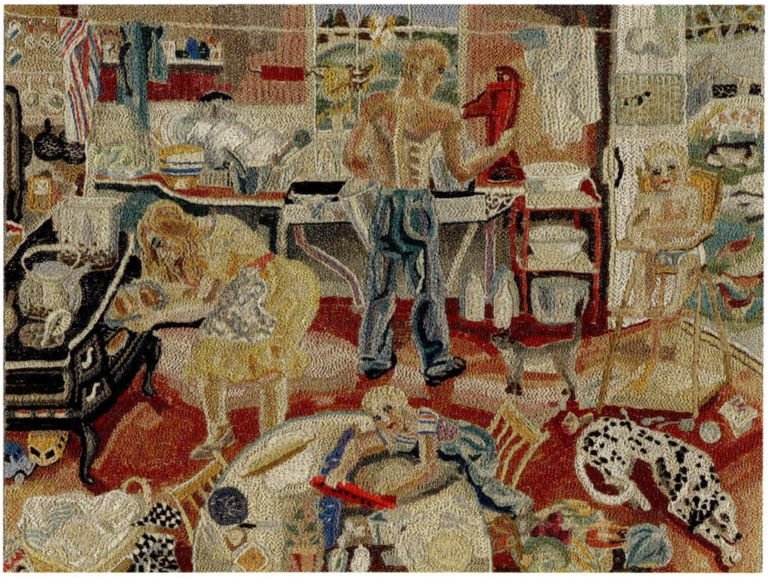

5. *(top)*
Marguerite Zorach
(1887–1968)
Block Castle, c. 1920
Oil on canvas
18 × 15 in. (45.7 × 38.1 cm)
Private collection

6. *(above)*
Marguerite Zorach
(1887–1968)
The Ipcar Family at Robinhood Farm, 1944
Wool embroidered on linen
17 ½ × 23 ½ in.
(44.5 × 59.7 cm)
Collection of Robert Ipcar and Jane Landis

Stuart Davis—Variations in Black and White

Priscilla Vail Caldwell
New York-based Independent Curator and Advisor; Board Member, SculptureCenter in Long Island City, New York; Member, Advisory Committee, Block Museum of Art, Evanston, Illinois; Northwestern University, Evanston, Illinois

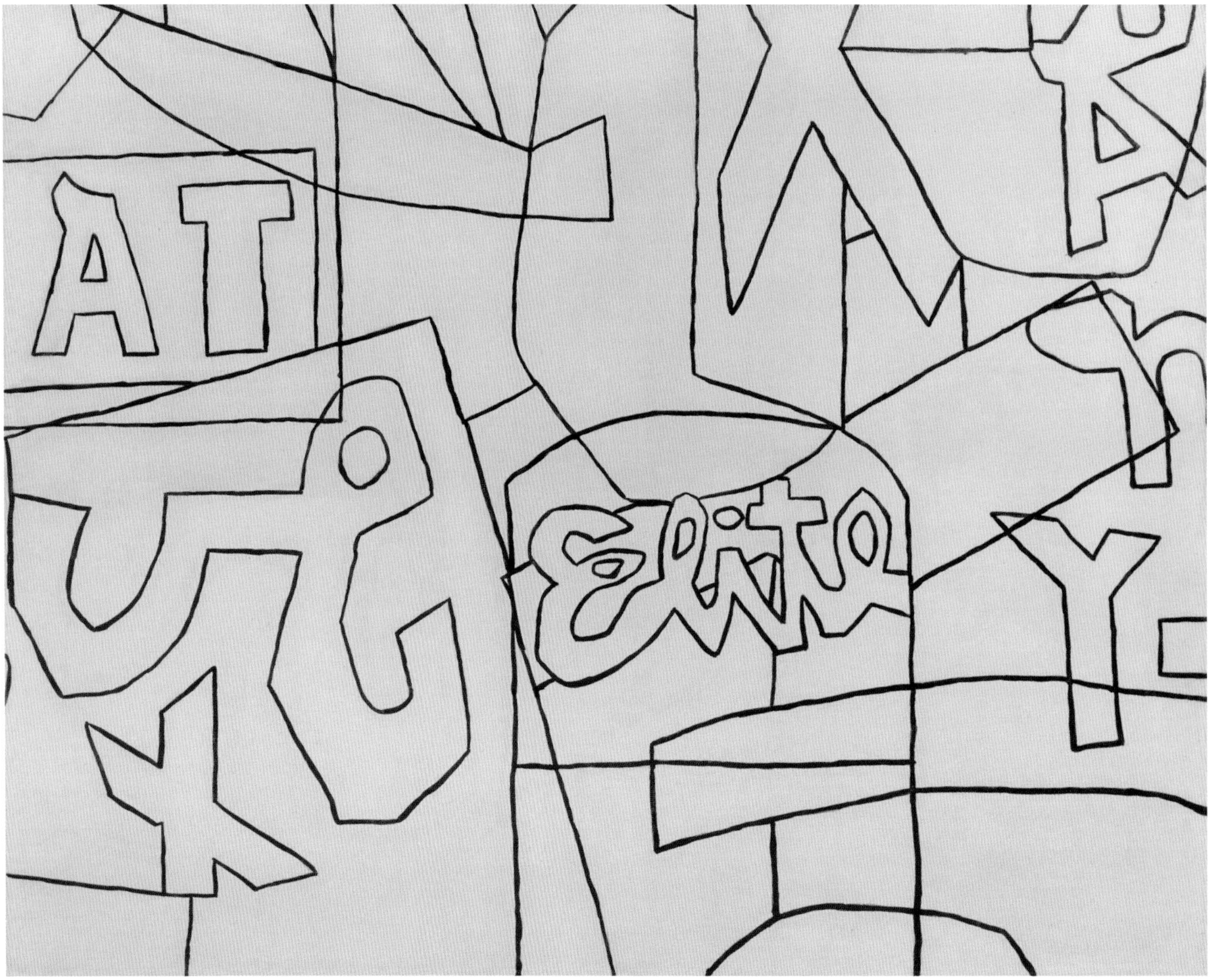

In 1962, the sculptor Donald Judd made his admiration for the painter Stuart Davis abundantly clear in an enthusiastic review of Davis's solo exhibition at Edith Halpert's Downtown Gallery. Judd wrote in his column *In the Galleries*, "The present exhibit of paintings done between 1958 and 1962 is first-rate.... The amazing continuity of Davis' work does not seem to have been kept with blinders, in fact, could not have been. Neither has Davis been startled into compromises with newer developments."[1] The paintings Judd notes in the exhibition, for instance *Unfinished Business* (Fig. 2) or *Standard Brand* (Fig. 3), number among Davis's emblematic paintings of the 1950s and early 1960s and are composed with the artist's signature planes of heavily impastoed primary color and painterly arabesques. These paintings have been the focus of most scholarship. Yet Davis's pared-down black and white variations on his colorful compositions deserve further consideration as they subtly indicate the decline of the importance of the unique aesthetic object, a hierarchy whose authority would be questioned with the advent of Minimalism, as well as the migration of painting into a third dimension.

Ruthlessly edited works such as *Untitled (Black and White Variation on "Pochade")* (Fig. 1) or *Untitled (Black and White Variation on "Quinciette")* (Fig. 5) reveal the true nature of Davis's ultimate intent.[2] Both paintings derive from earlier iterations (*Pochade* and

1. *(opposite)*
Stuart Davis (1892–1964)
Untitled (Black and White Variation on "Pochade")
c. 1956–58
Casein on canvas
28 × 36 in. (71.1 × 91.4 cm)
Estate of the artist

2. *(below)*
Stuart Davis (1892–1964)
Unfinished Business, 1962
Oil on canvas
36 × 45 in. (91.4 × 114.3 cm)
Private collection

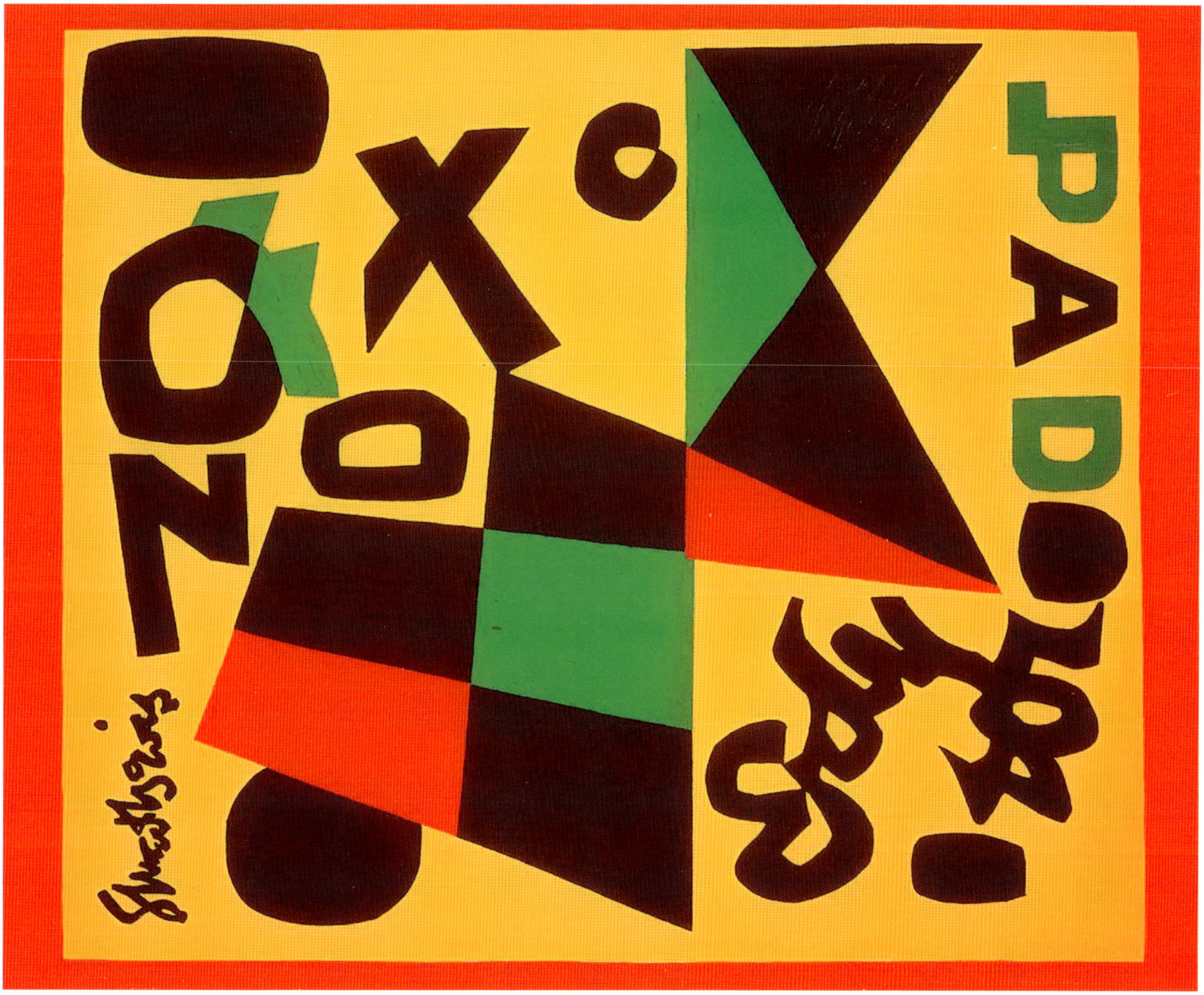

3.
Stuart Davis (1892–1964)
Standard Brand, 1961
Oil on canvas
60 × 46 in.
(152.4 × 116.8 cm)
The Detroit Institute of Arts, Founders Society purchase, General Membership fund, 63.156

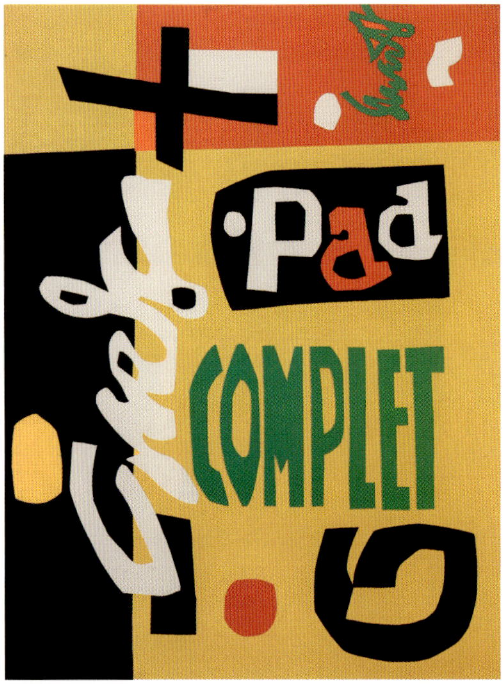

Quinciette) (Fig. 4 and Fig. 6), composed in the saturated hues of his standard palette. The formal purity of these later versions, whose origins are traced back to the conversation started in 1915 by Kazimir Malevich's *The Black Square* (Fig. 7), is the true apotheosis of Davis's rigorous experimentation and deliberate logic. Additionally, this process of elimination would surface in other seminal bodies of work including Willem de Kooning's black and white series of the late 1940s; Frank Stella's black paintings featured in Dorothy Miller's groundbreaking MoMA exhibition *16 Americans* (1959–60; Fig. 8), or Yayoi Kusama's exhibition of white paintings at the artist-run space Brata in 1959.

Davis's drawings on canvas, as the artist referred to them, were a fertile subspecies, a family of closely related images. They provided a structure, based on the mathematical equations he so meticulously mapped out in his notebooks,

4.
Stuart Davis (1892–1964)
Pochade, 1956–58
Oil on canvas
52 × 60 in. (132.1 × 152.4 cm)
Thyssen-Bornemisza National Museum, Madrid, 514 (1977.38)

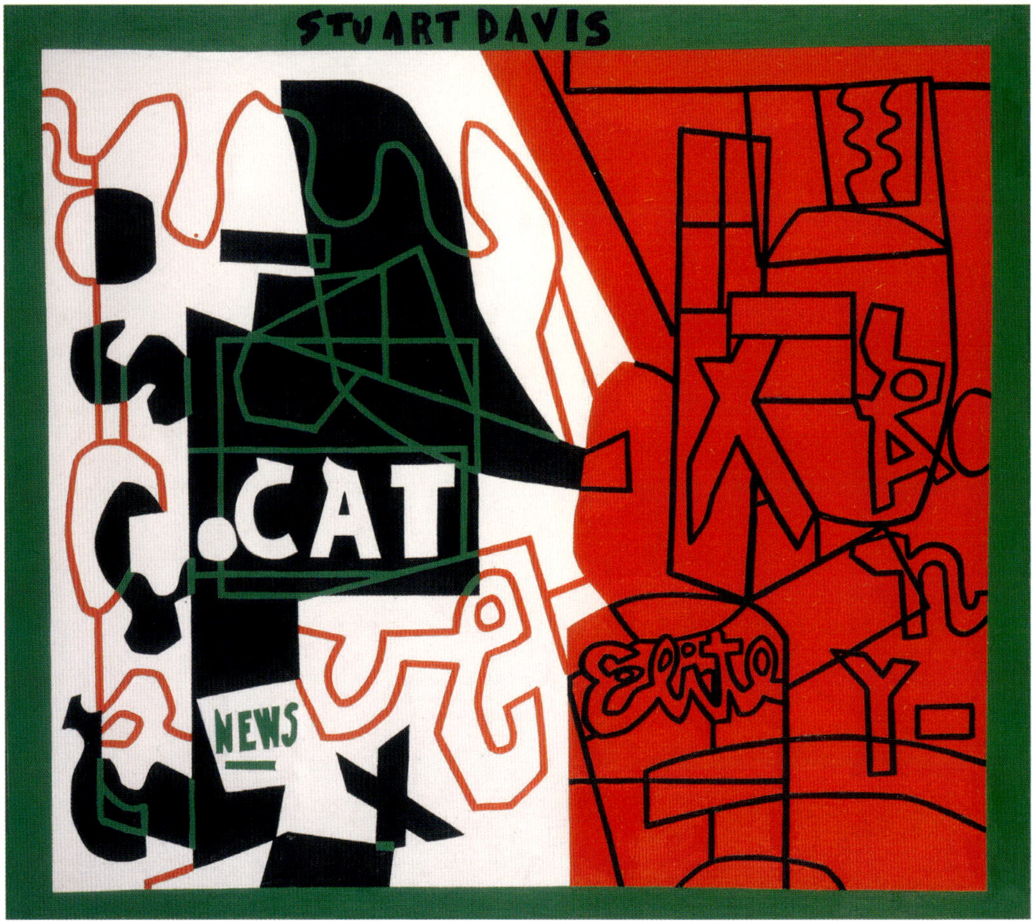

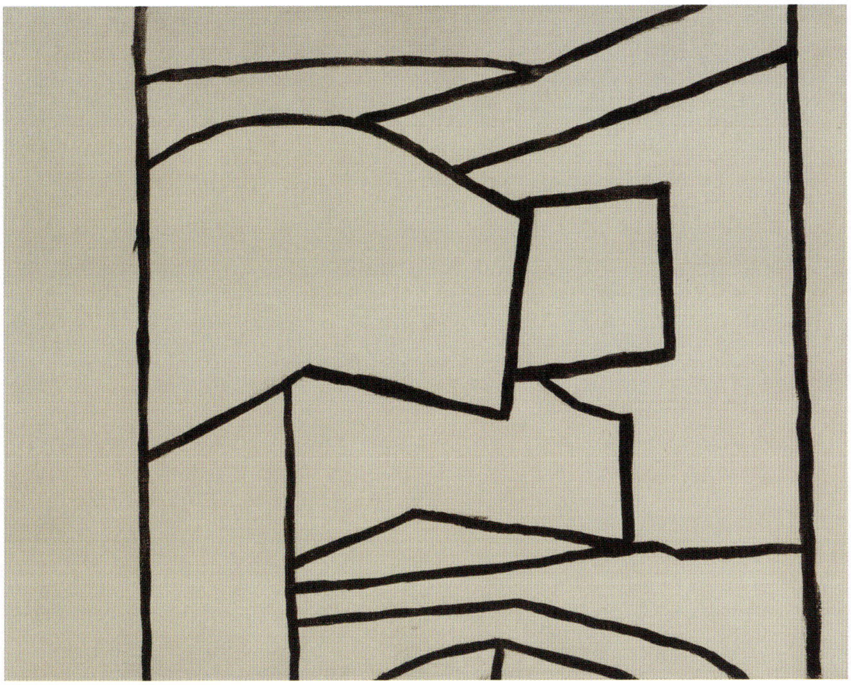

5.
Stuart Davis (1892–1964)
Untitled (Black and White Variation on "Quinciette"), 1964
Casein on canvas
14 ⅛ × 18 ⅛ in.
(35.8 × 46 cm)
Private collection

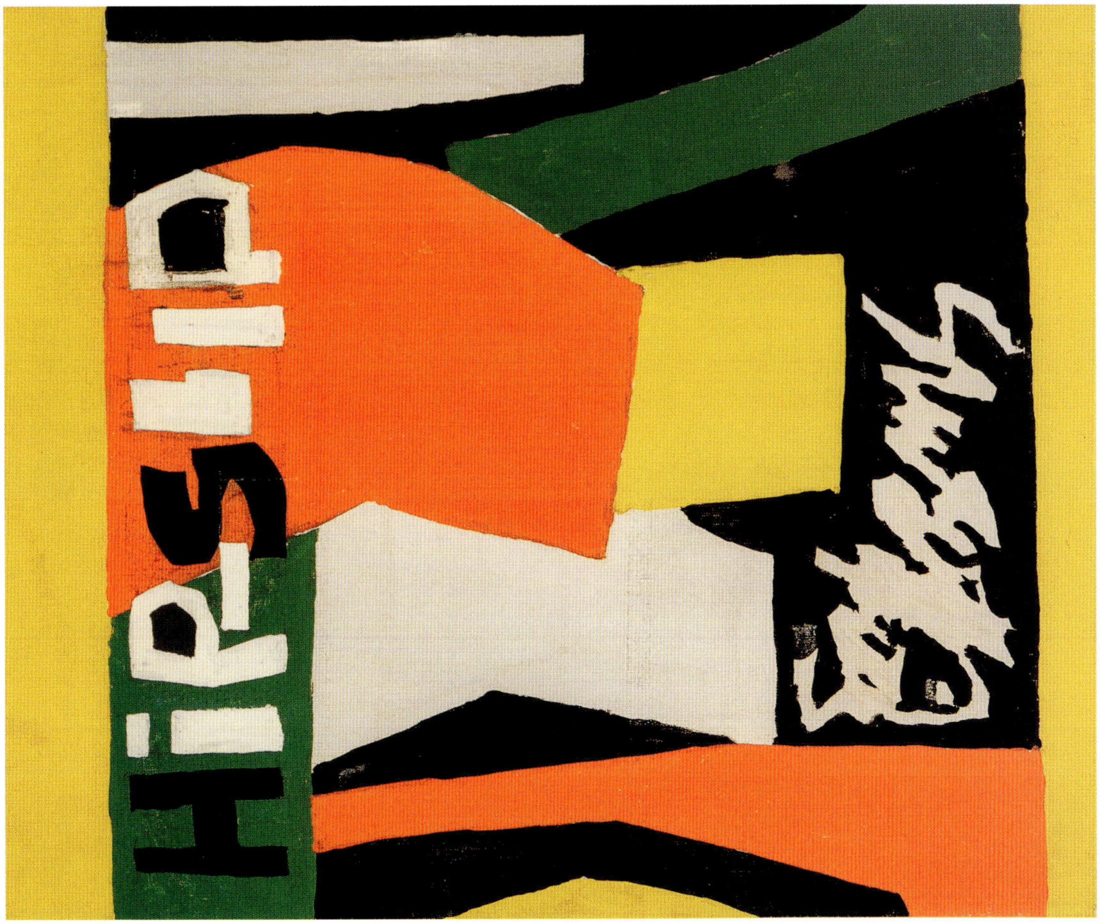

6.
Stuart Davis (1892–1964)
Quinciette, 1964
Oil on canvas
Private Collection

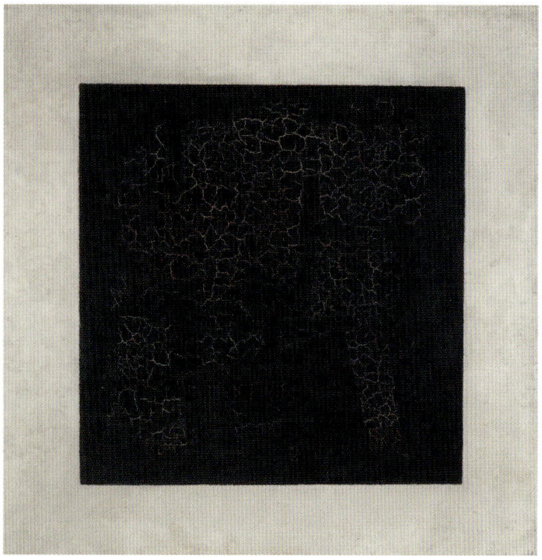

7. *(above left)*
Kazimir Malevich
(1879–1935)
The Black Square, 1915
Oil on linen
31 × 31 in. (78.7 × 78.7 cm)
The Tretyakov State Gallery, Moscow, 11925

8. *(above right)*
Frank Stella (b. 1936)
The Marriage of Reason and Squalor, II, 1959
Enamel on canvas
90 ¾ × 132 ¾ in.
(230.5 × 337.2 cm)
Larry Aldrich Foundation Fund, Museum of Modern Art, New York, 725.1959

9. *(right)*
Stuart Davis (1892–1964)
Cask in Rigging, 1932
Oil on canvas
16 ½ × 20 ½ in.
(41.9 × 52 cm)
Private collection, Washington, DC

that allowed Davis to experiment with the effects of color, a spectrum that, for him, included black and white. As early as 1932, Davis, already known for his use of a vivacious palette, started executing these crossword puzzle-like compositions such as *Cask in Rigging* (Fig. 9). Eliminating color was a bold move for the artist, a maneuver that reflected Davis's restless, ongoing synthesis and reductive process. These neutral compositions take into consideration Davis's acute interest in geometry, manipulating the flat picture plane like a polyhedron with the potential to project into three-dimensional space. Through this paring down of his work,

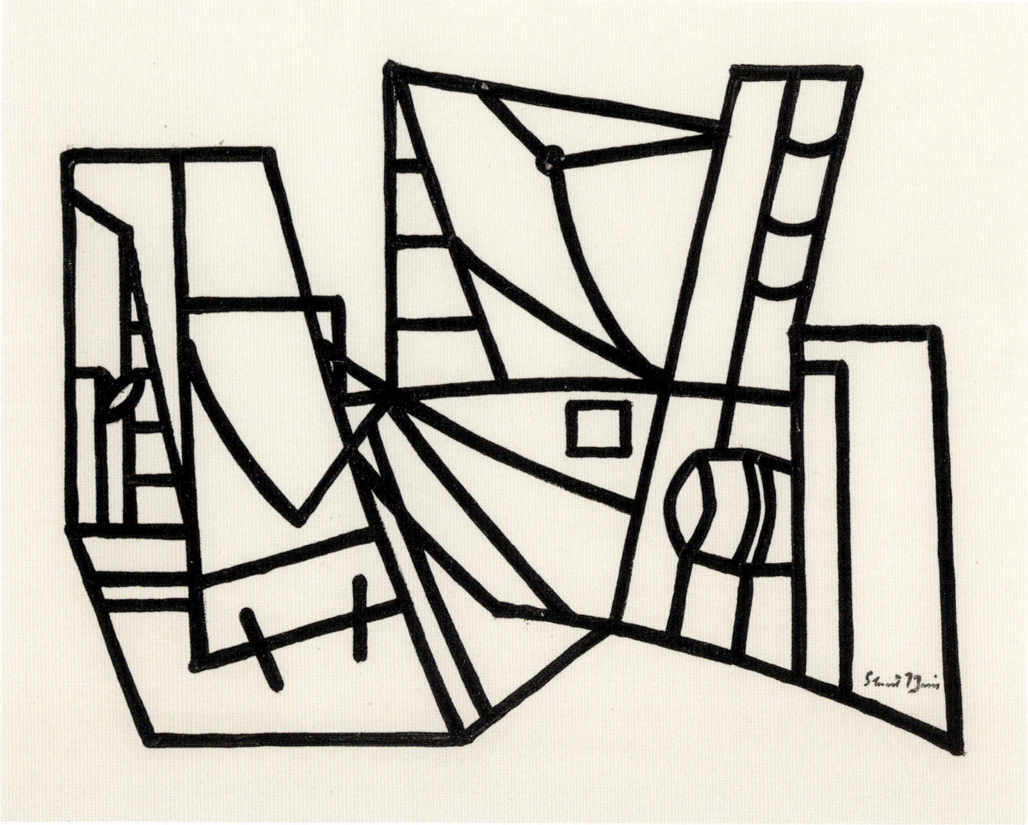

defined by seriality and a resolute adherence to a limited, meaningful vocabulary of shapes, Davis consistently aspired, however elusive that goal may have been, to reach a wider audience.

Davis tracked his theories and philosophical reflections in numerous journals dating back to the early twentieth century, many of which were gifted by the artist's widow to Harvard University's Fogg Art Museum in 1979. He consistently applied his elaborate ideas to his own practice, tasking himself with the difficult proposition of increasing the popular understanding of art. Davis's point of view contrasted with that of the Abstract Expressionists, as his priority was much broader than simple self-expression. These aspirations come through in many of his journal entries, as this one where he noted that "a work of art is created for the pleasure of the artist and automatically for that of the audience. Where it requires indoctrination, it is not art."[3] By mid-century it was important to Davis that in his paintings "You see things as a unit at the same time."[4] This concept would echo the theoretical practice of a younger generation, later classified as Minimalists, as observed in Robert Morris's Gestalt theory, the belief that one's experience with an object such as Morris's *Untitled*, 1965/71, a group of four boxes refabricated for his show at the Tate in 1971 (thus the double date) (Fig. 10), is greater than the sum of its parts, a notion reinforced in Judd's *Untitled (Stack)*, also a work based on a series of objects, in Judd's case ten identical stacked copper and red Plexiglas boxes (Fig. 11).[5]

Davis's paintings also aim to capture the impact of the American experience. Compositions such as *Rapt at Rappaport's* include passages inspired by the sonic contours of his beloved jazz, tributes to artists such as Earl Hines, George Wettling, or Duke Ellington, and popular imagery including billboards, gas pumps, mouthwash bottles, and cigarette packs. He devised clever ways to render his subjects that reflect the textured cacophony of the modern-day city while simultaneously embracing his radical political leanings. By the 1930s, due to the impact of the Great Depression, his views were conclusively

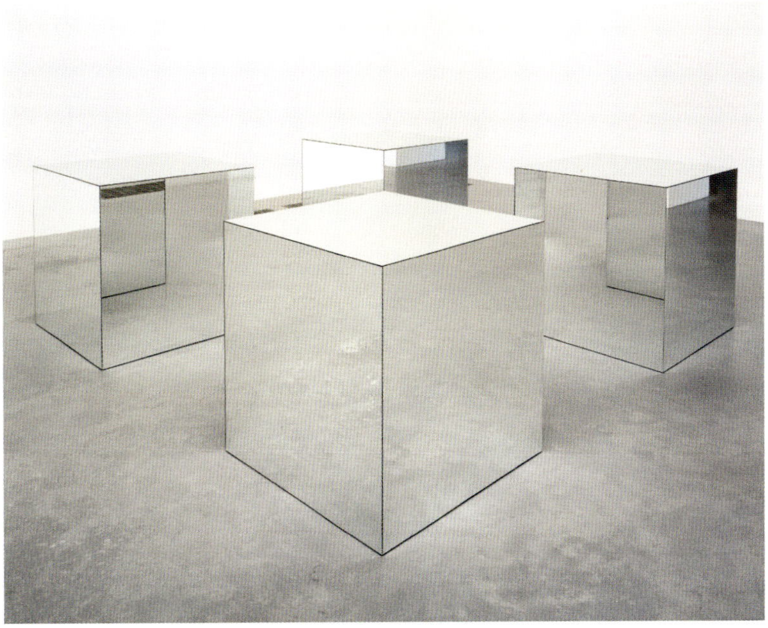

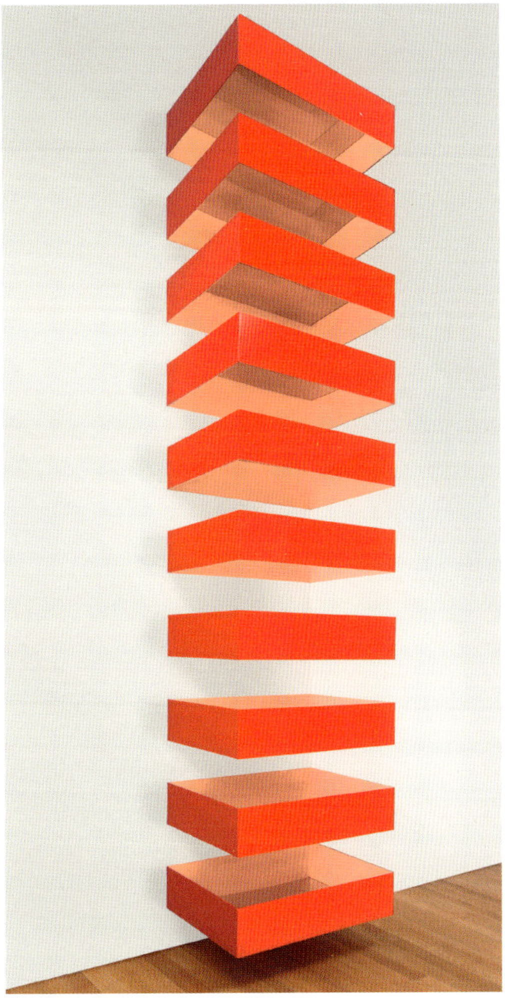

10. *(above)*
Robert Morris (1931–2018)
Untitled, 1965
(reconstructed 1971)
Mirror, glass and wood
Each cube 36 × 36 × 36 in.
(91.4 × 91.4 × 91.4 cm)
overall
Collection Tate Modern, London, T01532-1972

11. *(left)*
Donald Judd (1928–1994)
Untitled (Stack), 1989
Copper and red Plexiglas
10 elements each:
9 × 40 × 31 in.
(22.9 × 101.6 × 78.7 cm)
(Bernstein 89–24)

anti-capitalist. So, while Davis's complex compositions are frequently identified as precursors to the Pop Art Movement, his particular choice of the secular over the spiritual more closely aligns with the experimental philosophies of sculptors such as Judd or Morris than with the more free-wheeling irony of Pop. As Diane Kelder notes in her essay for The Metropolitan Museum of Art's Davis exhibition in 1991, "The emergence of Pop Art during the last years of his life accorded a contextual relevance to Davis' cool, standing dialogue with popular culture, but the artist was disdainful of this superficial linkage, which failed to recognize his very different motivations and objective."[6]

Form more than color drove Davis's compositions, as reflected in his description of the origin of the subject for his painting *Visa*, as well as the later version titled *Little Giant Still Life (Black and White Version)*, from 1952 (Fig. 12):

> *As to this particular painting, the big word in there, the word "Champion," is clearly the subject matter of the painting and that was derived quite casually and spontaneously from a book of paper matches which has this word painted on it, and the design of this matchbook was singularly uninteresting and it was the challenge of the lack of interest in this case, rather than the direct stimulus of a subject, but nevertheless the matchbook was the source.*[7]

This tendency would lead him inevitably in further search of more distilled subject matter. For Davis, firm in his regret "that I have long been 'type cast' as 'Abstract' because my interest in Abstraction is practically zero," art posed a

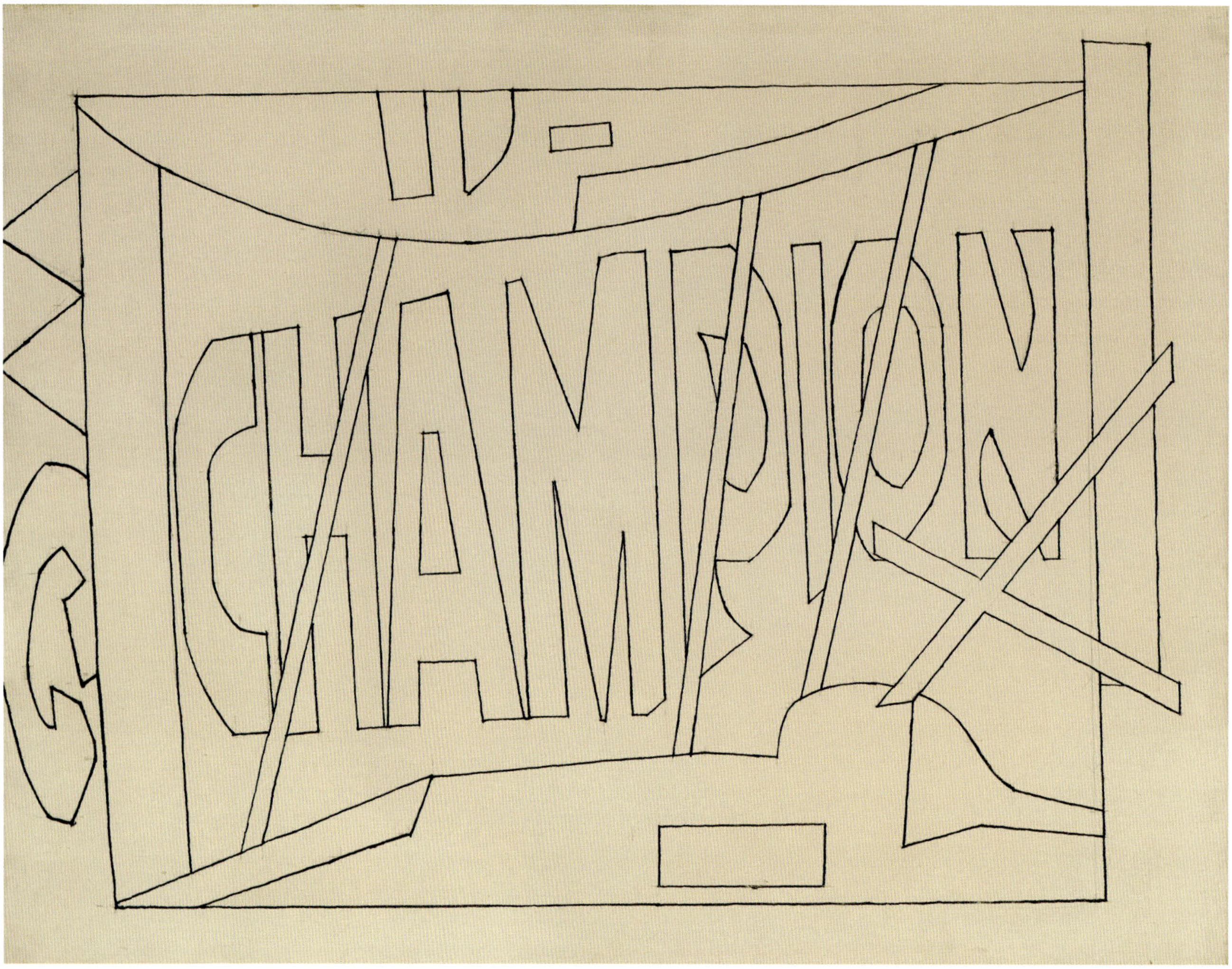

12.
Stuart Davis (1892–1964)
Little Giant Still Life (Black and White Version), 1953
Casein and pencil on canvas
32 ⅞ × 43 in.
(83.5 × 109.2 cm)
Private collection

problem he intended to solve.[8] This problem is echoed in Stella's statement, "If the painting were lean enough, accurate enough, you would just be able to look at it. All I want anyone to get out of my paintings, and all I ever get out of them, is the fact that you can see the whole idea without any confusion … what you see is what you see."[9] Davis too, above all else, wanted his work to be relatable. He, like Stella, aspired to executing that one lean, accurate painting.

Davis's recursions, his allegiance to subject matter and his practice of resurrecting compositions in order to retune and refine, are central to the artist's process and, more importantly, prescient in their resolute commitment to that process.[10] As Harry Cooper describes, "It is difficult to think of an artist who returned to his own work more persistently than Davis. While this self-cycling has never been a secret, its extent did not become clear until the publication of the catalogue raisonné of the artist's work in 2007."[11] As suggested by the historian Barbara Haskell, Davis's use of repetition as a means to an end would be further advanced and echoed in the practice of the great artists of the 1960s and 1970s. His approach can be seen as predicting the principles of Minimalism as they were set forth by this future generation of artists whose careers marked the beginning of an era. Additionally, like fellow truth-seeker Judd, he observed that execution, rather than subject, was most important to any given discipline. Davis's practice has been compared to many icons of the past, but while reaching back, he moved art forward to foreshadow radical innovation just on the horizon. What Davis shares with Judd is an interest in "the modernist imperative toward the purification of media."[12] Where Davis leaves off Judd picks up and it may therefore be no coincidence how closely Judd's paintings from the late 1950s resemble those of Davis's final compositions (Fig. 13), just as it may be no coincidence that Davis is the only American painter of his generation that Judd curated into his own personal collection. A print by Davis, *Detail Study for Cliché*, 1957, color lithograph, 21/20, hung in the nursery of Judd's building,

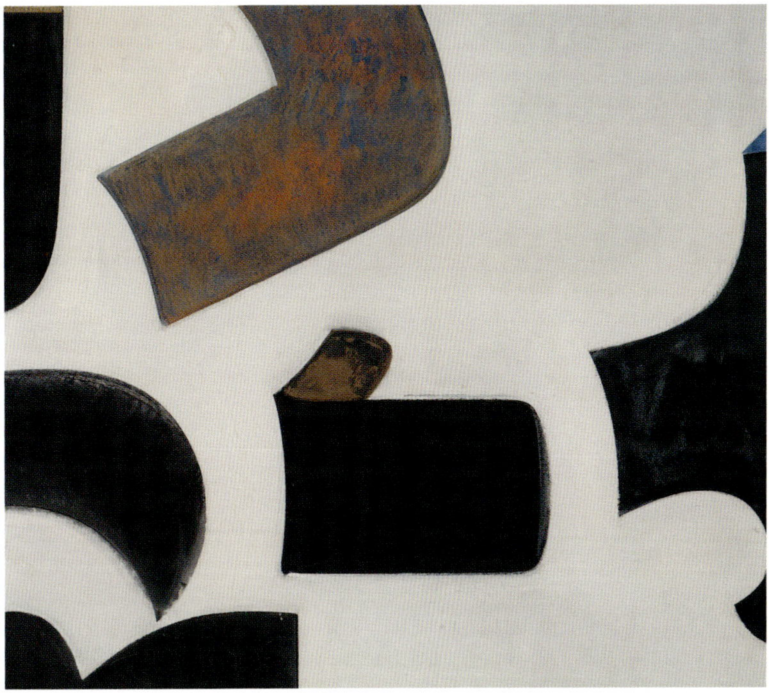

13.
Donald Judd (1928–1994)
Untitled, 1958
Oil on canvas
51 ½ × 56 in.
(130.8 × 142.2 cm)
Collection of the Foundation

now home to the Judd Foundation, at 101 Spring Street. For both painter and sculptor, it was the process and choices underpinning their work that counted. As Judd would describe the method in his own spare prose, "one thing after another."[13]

Davis's late black and white compositions, the apotheosis of his theories, deserve reconsideration. Relying upon nothing more than form and shape, they confirm the objective world and stand in strident opposition to the subjective nature of Abstract Expressionism. As it was for his admirer Donald Judd, it was crucial for Davis that something "known" be at the heart of the making process. This position would be adopted by some of the most important artists to follow and is made clear in an enfilade of objects that includes Judd's stacks, Jasper Johns's flags and numbers, or the "one shot painter" Kenneth Noland's targets. In his late black and white compositions, Davis made significant strides toward creating what he too described as a "Universal Style."

The Four Musketeers of American Modernism

Stuart Davis, Arshile Gorky, John Graham, and Willem de Kooning

Karen Wilkin
Curator and Advisor, Teaching in the New York Studio School's MFA Program

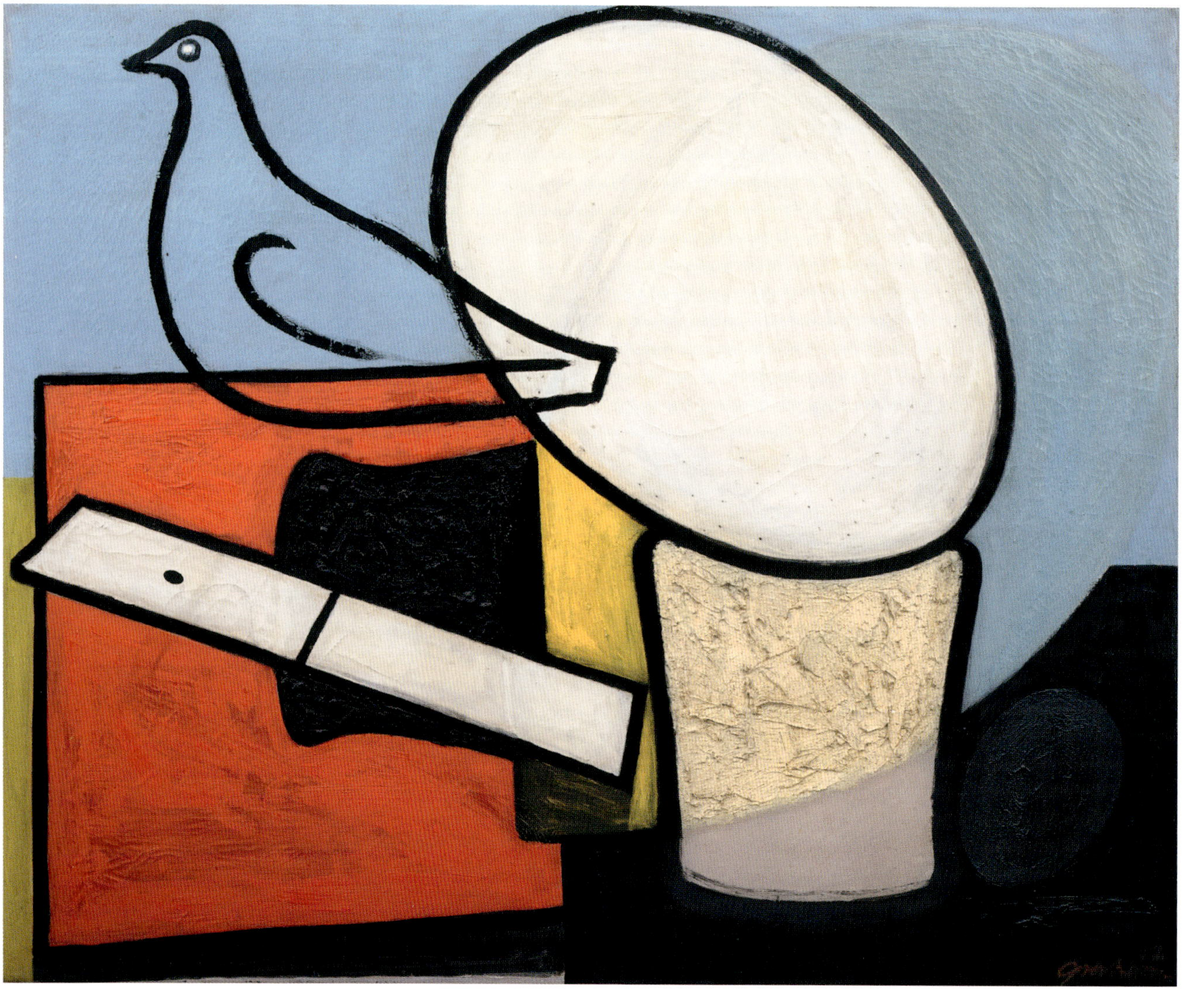

The late 1920s to 1940 were formative years for some of America's most inventive and important Modernist painters and sculptors, then beginning their professional lives. Their work expanded the possibilities for American art, changing forever the definitions of painting and sculpture. Together, they laid the foundations for ideas that would be ardently debated in the 1950s, sometimes by their older selves, at the legendary Abstract Expressionist haunts, the Club and the Cedar Tavern. At the core of this pioneering group were such now iconic figures as Stuart Davis, Arshile Gorky, Willem de Kooning, and their older friend John Graham. They were linked by friendship, common aspirations, proximity as neighbors, shared aesthetic assumptions, progressive politics, and, often, poverty.

During this period, this small, diverse group forged their identities as artists, assimilating the lessons of adventurous Europeans such as Pablo Picasso, Georges Braque, and Joan Miró, but also paying attention to each other's efforts and finding their own voices. Universally rejecting the sentimental, conservative Social Realism of the American Scene painters, they embraced Cubism's geometry and spatial inventions, along with Surrealism's biomorphism and ambiguity. They embraced, too, the conviction that a work of art's material presence was part of its meaning and that the artist's role was to reveal the invisible, not to report on the seen. The result was a brash, uniquely American idiom based on generous scale, openness, and an emphasis on physicality.

Despite their strong commonalities, the backgrounds and formations of these forward-looking New York artists varied dramatically. Davis (1892–1964), born in Philadelphia and raised in New Jersey, had lived in New York since enrolling at Robert Henri's art school, at age sixteen. De Kooning (1904–1997), Gorky (1904–1948), and Graham (1886–1961) were European immigrants, de Kooning from the Netherlands and Gorky from Armenia—although he claimed to be Russian—while Graham, originally Ivan Gratianovitch Dombrowski, came from Russia. Davis had studied with the most progressive teacher in New York. Gorky had one semester of drawing classes before becoming a drawing instructor himself. De Kooning had been trained in both commercial art and traditional painting techniques, at the Rotterdam Academy of Fine Arts and Technical Sciences. Graham was essentially self-taught.

A fervent commitment to Modernism drew this otherwise disparate group together, but Graham, described by his friend, the artist Dorothy Dehner, as a "brilliant, contrary, witty, insightful and sometimes exasperating personality,"[1] was the glue that held things together. Born in Ukraine to minor Polish nobility, he spent his early life in Russia, was trained as a czarist lawyer and served in the Czar's army. He said he was imprisoned by the Bolsheviks, as a counter-revolutionary, but escaped and made his way to the United States in 1920. (Graham's account of his history, however, is notably unreliable.[2]) From then on, he devoted himself to art, a hobby in Europe, but an obsession in America. Graham was an accomplished, if quirky painter, connoisseur, aesthete, theorist, collector, and advisor to collectors. He was also a sometime poet and full-time mystic, with a wide-ranging, idiosyncratic command of the history of art, surprising depths of knowledge about Eastern as well as Western art, and real expertise in African sculpture. Because he traveled often to Paris and seemed to know everyone, he was specially informed about vanguard European painting and sculpture.

Graham's direct knowledge of advanced European art was invaluable for his New York artist friends—many of whom had been introduced by him, in the first place—as a source of timely, inspirational, first-hand information. His young friend David Smith, for example, began constructing with welded metal—the first such sculptures made in the United States—after seeing Graham's issue of *Cahiers d'Art* dedicated to Picasso and Juli González's pioneering collaborations in steel. Smith's mature constructed works transformed the language of three-dimensionality, even the very nature of sculpture (Fig. 2). Graham's importance could be even more diverse. When Smith and his wife,

1.
John Graham (1886–1961)
Table Top Still Life with Bird
1929
Oil on canvas
32 × 39 in. (81.2 × 99 cm)
Collection of Tommy and Gill LiPuma, New York

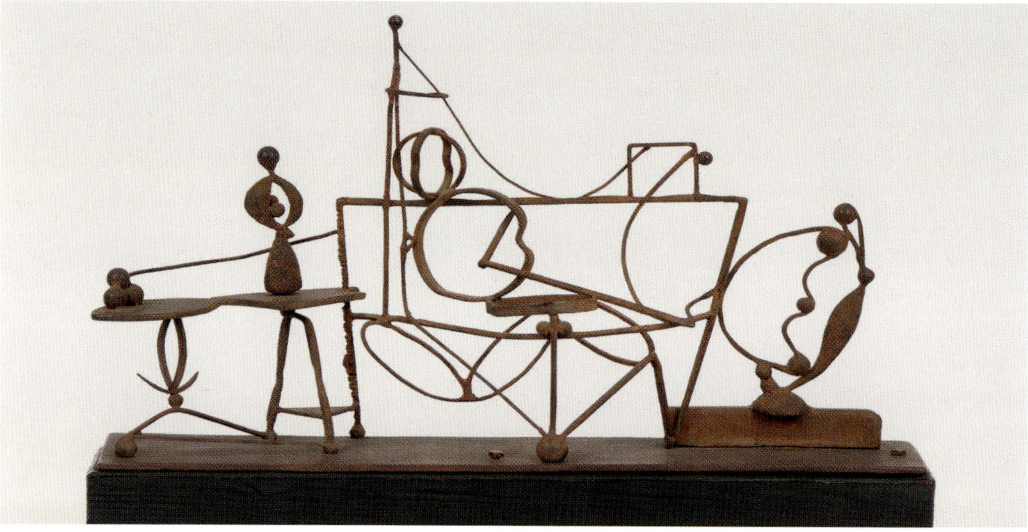

2.
David Smith (1906–1965)
Interior, 1937
Welded steel with cast-iron balls
15 ⅝ × 26 × 6 in.
(39.7 × 66 × 15.2 cm)
Weatherspoon Art Museum, University of North Carolina at Greensboro. Museum purchase with funds from anonymous donors, 1979. 1979.2668

Dorothy Dehner, traveled to Paris, Graham met them and introduced them to vanguard artists, writers, and collectors—and more.

Graham's cranky volume, *System and Dialectics of Art*, published in 1937, provides a glimpse of the passionate discussions held among his circle. A Socratic dialogue of questions and answers, the book reflects the truths agreed upon within Graham's milieu, dissecting ideas about creativity, the collective unconscious, primitivism, and abstraction, along with such problems as the relationship between art and crime: "two things apart."[3] Graham catalogues fundamental Modernist beliefs of the period: art is a kind of communication, independent of mimesis, that reveals the unknown; the unconscious is the source of creativity. "What is art?" is answered by "*a creative process of abstracting*" (italics Graham's). "Art in particular is a systematic confession of personality." Yet it is also "a social manifestation."[4] There are allusions to Freudian concepts of the self and Jungian ideas about shared cultural memory, echoes of Wassily Kandinsky's spiritually charged writings and of *The Golden Bough*, Sir James Frazer's pioneering account of how religion and rituals transcend time and place.

"The purpose of art in *particular*," Graham wrote, "is to reestablish a lost contact with the unconscious,… with the primordial racial past and to keep and develop this contact in order to bring to the conscious mind the throbbing events of the unconscious mind."[5] This connection is crucial, since "Our unconscious mind contains the record of all our past experiences—individual and racial, from the first cell germination to the present day.… The unconscious mind is the powerhouse, the creative agent."[6] Even Graham's later mysticism is prefigured. "The origin of art lies in the human longing for enigma, for the miraculous … for communication and consequently—life eternal."[7] *System and Dialectics of Art* makes us privy to the topics Graham and his friends talked about—or listened to him talk about.

Graham said that he drew and wanted to be an artist, "from earliest childhood,"[8] but received no formal art instruction, since "artist" was an unacceptable calling for anyone of his class. But if, in Russia, drawing and looking at art were avocations for the aristocratic military man with legal training, in the United States, making art, theorizing and writing about art, advocating Modernism, and bringing like-minded artists together became his main preoccupations. In New York, Ivan Dombrowski became "John Graham,"[9] and began to study art seriously. He enrolled at the Art Students League in 1922, most importantly in John Sloan's drawing class, where his fellow students included Adolph Gottlieb and Alexander Calder. It was the beginning of Graham's web of connections with the progressive American art world, a web that became more complex after 1924, when he married a fellow student at the League and moved to her native Baltimore. He began to exhibit, with some success, and soon met the region's leading collectors of Modernism, Dr. Claribel Cone and her sister Etta, in Baltimore, and Duncan Phillips, in Washington. Warm friendships developed and the Cone sisters and Phillips began to acquire Graham's work. The network expanded after 1926, when Graham began spending time in Paris, exhibiting at Leopold Zborowski's gallery, seen by French critics as an "American painter," a gifted foreign-born member of the School of Paris (Fig. 1). After re-establishing himself in New York in 1928, Graham returned annually to Paris, continuing to show there until 1930. His fluent French, the residue of his upper-class Russian upbringing, facilitated his entrée into the French vanguard, as did his role as a connoisseur/dealer who acquired work for American collectors.

Graham's New York artist friends were avid for information about new European art. In the mid-1920s, European art less than a hundred years old could enter the United States duty-free (which was not permitted at the time of the 1913 Armory Show) but advanced recent art was shown at only a few commercial galleries and a handful of institutions, such as The Société Anonyme, founded in 1920, a forerunner of the Museum of Modern Art, or the Whitney Studio Club, founded in 1918, an ancestor of the Whitney Museum of American Art. Things had improved by the late 1920s. The Gallery of Living Art—Albert Gallatin's collection, which emphasized French Cubism—opened in December 1927, at New York University; the Museum of Modern Art opened in 1929; and over the following decade, a number of commercial galleries began to provide New Yorkers with first-hand, but very modest exposure to radical European ideas.[10] Yet most American artists had not been to Europe. Stuart Davis's fifteen months in Paris, in 1928/29, conferred lasting authority on him, enhancing his reputation as a well-informed, uncompromising Modernist. Dehner described Graham as bringing "the excitement of the French art world to us,"[11] showing his artist friends "copies of *Cahiers d'Art* and other French art publications of which we had been unaware,"[12] supplemented by news of exhibitions, gossip, and works of art brought for the collectors he advised—a more complete and vivid account of current innovations than anything available in New York.

Graham seems ubiquitous within the small progressive art world of the period, the center of an ever-enlarging constellation of artist-colleagues. He had an instinct for bringing together artists with significant common ground, with lasting effect. The center of his multivalent, wide-reaching reticulum was his close relationship with Stuart Davis and Arshile Gorky. Davis and Graham are thought to have met in 1928, before Davis left New York for Paris; they were probably introduced by John Sloan, whom Graham knew from the League, and to whom Davis had been close since boyhood, when Sloan did newspaper illustrations for Davis's art editor father. Gorky and Graham also seem to have met in 1928. Gorky and Davis were introduced by Graham after Davis's return to the United States in 1929. By then, when de Kooning had gotten to know all of them, Graham, Davis, and Gorky were so close that the admiring young Dutch painter dubbed them "the Three Musketeers"[13] and joined them as d'Artagnan did Dumas's fictional heroes. They were an impressive, if unlikely trio: two tall, rather exotic immigrants, distinguished by mustachioed good looks, and one irreducibly American, rather short, native son, all revered by fellow artists for their knowledge of and commitment to Modernism. Recalling his early years in New York, de Kooning often spoke of the Musketeers as crucial to his understanding of Modernism. "I was lucky enough when I came to this country," he told Harold Rosenberg in 1974, "to meet the three smartest guys on the scene: Gorky, Stuart Davis and John Graham."[14]

Graham's and Davis's friendship solidified while Davis was in Paris, in 1928. Funded by the sale, in New York, of two paintings to Gertrude Vanderbilt Whitney, Davis rented a studio in Montparnasse; Graham soon arrived for an extended sojourn and moved into a nearby studio. The two painters almost certainly worked at the same print studio, while Davis's letters and recollections suggest other connections. Graham arranged for Fernand Léger and Davis to exchange studio visits, for example, and as Davis noted in his informal autobiography, "The prevalence of the sidewalk café was an important factor. It gave easy access to one's friends...."[15]

Graham's and Davis's paintings of the period attest to their friendship. They both explored recognizably "French" subject matter, such as Parisian streets, and aggressive surfaces, sometimes roughened with sand, perhaps inspired by Braque's methods. Even before Graham and Davis met, their work suggests a shared predilection for compressed space and crisply delineated shapes, similarities that speak to their common awareness of European Modernist precedents, although Davis's stylized improvisations are generally the more structurally and chromatically audacious. Yet some of Graham's canvases of the late 1920s, unlike Davis's, reveal his interest in the recently launched Surrealist movement. While he originally dismissed Surrealism as appropriate only to literature, he seems to have changed his mind, adopting its underlying faith in the potency of the unconscious. Graham's insistence on the importance of our interior life to making art, stated explicitly in his provocative book and implicitly by some of his imagery, makes his close friendship with the pragmatic, ironic Davis more surprising.

Davis always stressed his independence from the literal but also adamantly refused to be called an "abstract" painter, insisting that his art of what he called "color space logic" derived solely from his experience of actuality—sights, sounds, textures, moods, and temperatures—translated into linear "configurations" and animated spatially with color. While some of Davis's strongest paintings of the early 1930s, made after his return to New York from Paris, seem indebted to Miró and Picasso, they are also about observation, filtered through a uniquely American version of Cubist construction. Davis wholly rejected a conception of art based on internal sources. "Surrealism," he wrote, "denies the objective world and is escapist. It denies the classic function of art—bold assimilation of the environment."[16] In 1922, Davis had declared that a work of art should be "first of all impersonal in execution, that is to say it should not be a seismographic chart of the nervous system."[17] Twenty years later, he had not changed his mind. "Emotion, Sensibility, Stimulation does not produce Art except when it is integrated with an emotionally conscious theory of dimensional structure,"[18] he wrote—a typically convoluted verbal equivalent of his firmly constructed paintings, which distill perception into syncopated patterns and rhythmic, hard-edge color planes.

Yet we draw conclusions about the chameleon Graham's position at our peril. In *System and Dialectics*, he may have emphasized the central role of enigma but he also stated that "*Art is a subjective point of view expressed in objective terms*"[19]—italics his. He asserted, too, that "The only legitimate abstract painting is the painting based on and departing from hard reality and not from the imagination"[20] and that "A painting is a *self-sufficient* phenomenon and does not have to rely upon nature."[21] He wrote, as well: "Art has nothing to do with representation, impersonation, interpretation, decoration, compromise, character or psychological problems. It contains psychological problems but deals with them in terms of form and not subject matter."[22] These are sentiments worthy of Davis, reflections, perhaps, of the two artists' friendship.

Unlike Davis, who never wavered in his cool-headed dedication to "color space logic," Graham seems to have been equally drawn to internal and external reality as his starting point. He could, as Davis did, derive his imagery from the visible world, in Cubist-inflected works, but he could also produce highly charged mythological images, conjuring up imagined events with interlocking shapes that pay homage both to the Surrealists' biomorphic dreamscapes and to Picasso's paintings of the 1930s—themselves a response to Surrealist notions. By the early 1940s, Graham's work, while still wide-ranging, seems more driven by what he called "the human longing for enigma, for the miraculous" than by "departing from hard reality."

Yet the Three Musketeers had broader aims for their art, independent of existing European-

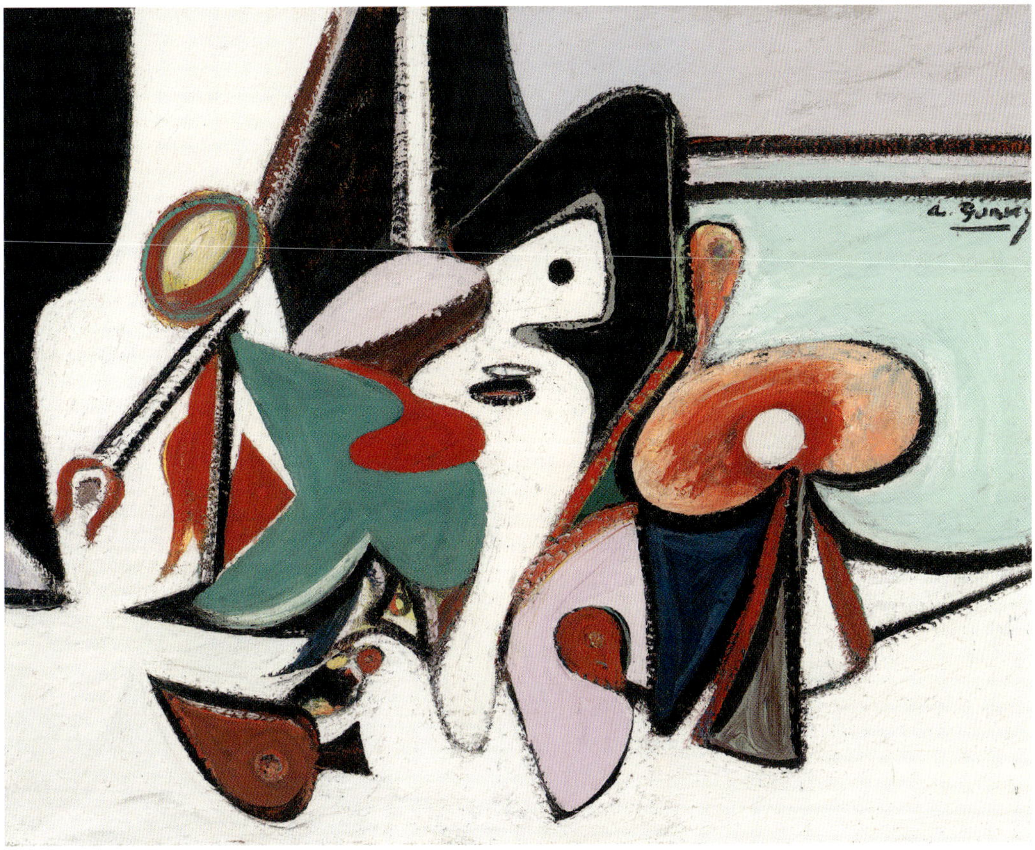

3.
Arshile Gorky (1904–1948)
Painting, 1936–37
Oil on canvas
37 15/16 × 47 7/8 in.
(96.4 × 121.6 cm)
Whitney Museum of American Art, Inv. N.: 37.39

inspired approaches. In December 1930, Graham wrote to Duncan Phillips, in Washington, that "Stuart Davis, Gorky, and myself have formed a group and something original, purely American is coming out from under our brushes."[23] Despite his desire to identify himself as an "original, purely American" artist and significant as his friendship was with the American-born Davis, Graham in many ways had more in common with his fellow immigrant, Gorky. Gorky, too, had reinvented himself in the United States, disguising his identity as Vosdanig Adoian, a survivor of the horrific persecution of Armenians by Turks, by becoming "Arshile"—a version of "Achilles," and "Gorky"—a Russian, related, he said, to the writer Maxim Gorky—itself a pseudonym. (Gorky's close friends knew his real origins; the fiction could not be sustained with the Russian-born Graham and Davis even visited Gorky's Armenian relatives near Boston with his friend.[24]) Like Graham, Gorky was sure of his aesthetic convictions and ready to lecture anyone about art, at any time. He was deeply informed about the art of the past, the recent past, and the present, a result of his passionate study of works of art and his self-imposed apprenticeship to his artist heroes, as he systematically absorbed the aesthetic lessons of Paul Cézanne, Picasso, Matisse, Braque, and Miró. By 1930, Gorky's own voice had emerged clearly, without obscuring his earlier obsessions or his ongoing conversation with his fellow Musketeers. Gorky's voracious study of Picasso and Miró is visible in his works of the mid-1930s, such as *Painting*, 1936–37 (Fig. 3), as well as his connections with Davis's *Egg Beater* series, such as *Egg Beater No. 1*, 1927 (Fig. 5), made a decade earlier. The dense surfaces of Gorky's works of the late 1920s and 1930s—evidence of prolonged reworkings and overpaintings—may owe something to Braque's sand-thickened expanses but may also reflect Graham's insistence on the importance of edges. Dehner recalled that "the quality of the 'edge' was something that Graham spoke about constantly," recalling, too, that he "stressed the necessity of keeping the paint alive."[25]

Gorky's work offers suggestive evidence of fruitful cross-fertilization among the Musketeers. A drawing from his surrealizing series, *Nighttime, Enigma, and Nostalgia*, *c.* 1931–32, seems to pay homage to Picasso with its over-scaled silhouetted profile and to Graham with its title, yet a brash street sign arrow could have come straight from one of Davis's urban improvisations. The American and the Armenian were close at the time and there are signs of reciprocal influence. The eerie, atypically biomorphic shapes in Davis's paintings made in 1931, when the Musketeers were inseparable, provocatively recall Gorky's explorations at that time. Similarly, the stylized airplane imagery and bold shapes of Gorky's Aviation murals for the Newark Airport Administration Building, which he worked on between 1934 and 1937, suggest that he was especially attentive to Davis, who had already completed a major mural project for the Men's Smoking Lounge of the new Radio City Music Hall. That the two artists deeply appreciated each other's work is well documented. In September 1931, Gorky wrote an enthusiastic appraisal of Davis for the magazine *Creative Art*, praising him—surprisingly, given the simmering intensity of Gorky's own work—for his Apollonian detachment. "…The silent consequences of Stuart Davis move us to the cool and intellectual world where all human emotions are disciplined by rectangular proportions," a place "…where all dreams evaporate and logic plays its greatest victory."[26] Twenty years later, after Gorky's death, Davis wrote a wry, affectionate, admiring tribute for the *Magazine of Art*.[27] But there is never a simple—or a single—pattern for the relationship of the works of the Musketeers and their friends. Ideas triggered by the European vanguard were tossed back and forth among them and transformed along the way.

4.
Willem de Kooning
(1904–1997)
Untitled (Still Life with Eggs and Potato Masher) c. 1928–29
Oil and sand on canvas
18 × 24 in. (45.7 × 60.9 cm)
Collection of the Honorable. Joseph P. Carroll and Dr. Roberta Carroll, MD, New York

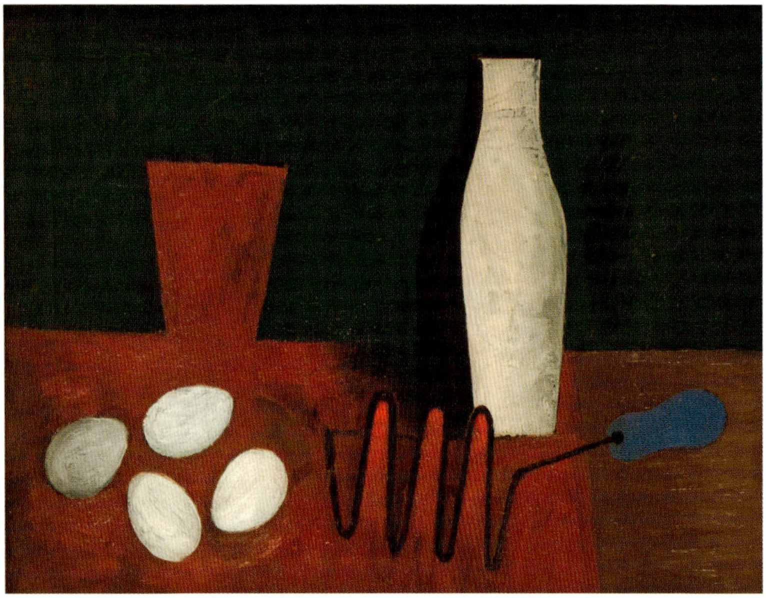

If, as de Kooning teasingly claimed, Graham, Davis, and Gorky were the Athos, Porthos, and Aramis of the New York art world before World War II, he himself quickly assumed the role of d'Artagnan. Accounts differ and dates vary, but it seems fairly certain that in the spring of 1929, de Kooning encountered Graham, who was holding forth at an exhibition of his paintings at Dudensing Gallery, and introduced himself. Later that year, according to de Kooning, he and Gorky met at the Russian artist Misha Reznikoff's studio and nearly came to blows, but when the young Dutchman visited Gorky's studio about a year later, after a chance meeting, an intense friendship began.[28] Each of the Musketeers was significant to de Kooning's evolution as an artist, but Gorky was the most important. He was de Kooning's contemporary and fellow immigrant, but a less recent one, and a far more sophisticated Modernist. De Kooning always acknowledged his debt to Gorky, cryptically giving the address of the latter's studio on Union Square as the place he "came from."[29] The studio itself provided a model of professionalism and dedication, while Gorky's "interpretations" of Picasso and Miró, in the 1930s, provided an education in Modernism.

De Kooning, in turn, introduced Gorky to the sign painter's liner brush, which permitted him to paint the thin, supple, whiplash lines that became such a crucial aspect of his mature work.[30] Although many works provide ample evidence of the two men's shared interest in highly charged, biomorphic abstraction, the clearest evidence of their closeness can be found in their exquisitely crafted figure paintings, which both continued to make in the 1930s and into the 1940s, while also exploring other possibilities—mysterious works that aspire to a fusion of abstraction and reference, delicacy and robustness. These qualities are present in both artists' ravishing later abstractions, but it is nonetheless tempting to speculate about what the evolution of Modernist painting in New York might have been, had these two virtuosi of the enigmatic portrait not abandoned figuration.

Both Gorky and de Kooning shifted back and forth from economical abstractions to hypersensitive interpretations of the seen, as each searched for his identity as a painter. But if there are close connections between their figurative works at this time, it is also conceivable that the clean shapes, limited palette, and assertive drawing of some of de Kooning's near-geometric abstractions of these years reflect Davis's influence. During the mid-1930s, Davis was so involved with social activism that he had little time to paint and concentrated on drawings constructed with bold, even-handed lines, punctuated with sharply defined planes of color. A much earlier de Kooning, *Untitled (Still Life with Eggs and Potato Masher)* (Fig. 4), suggests that he may have been paying attention to Davis's work even before Graham introduced them. The utilitarian wire gadget irresistibly suggests a connection with Davis's *Egg Beater* series, such as *Egg Beater No. 1* (Fig. 5), with its eponymous kitchen tool, electric fan, and rubber glove, or with his even earlier still lifes incorporating a saw, a lightbulb, a giant eggbeater, or a percolator—banal trophies from the hardware store or the kitchen chosen, perhaps, as much for their ordinariness as for their forms.

Whether or not de Kooning was aware of Davis's "gadget still lifes" remains a matter of speculation. There is no doubt, however, about the relationship of Gorky's and de Kooning's figure paintings to Graham's intermittent experiments with the figure in the 1930s and early 1940s. In the representational work of all three artists, features and forms melt into passages of refined brushwork or detach themselves into almost autonomous shapes to create enlivening tension between suggestion and form, allusion and materiality. It is as if the artists' aim were to make their paintings solely about the act of painting itself, independent of subject matter, without ceding any of the mysterious power inherent in recognizable images. All three had complicated responses to the presumed need to choose between image and abstraction. Gorky continued to work on his two great portraits of himself as a child with his mother between 1926 and about 1942, even while he was becoming increasingly fascinated by psychologically loaded, abstracted imagery identifiable by almost no one but himself. Graham later repudiated abstraction entirely and devoted himself to eerie, carefully rendered figures. De Kooning returned regularly to figural references, most notoriously in his *Women*, beginning in 1950.

Graham's discussion of abstract art in *System and Dialectics* provides a clue to his intentions, during these pivotal years, and, by extension, to those of his friends. Early in the book, Graham defines all art as a process of abstraction, since "a painter abstracts three-dimensional phenomena on a two-dimensional plane,"[31] and later categorizes abstract art as being "based on profound knowledge of reality, knowledge of anatomy of space and bodies and

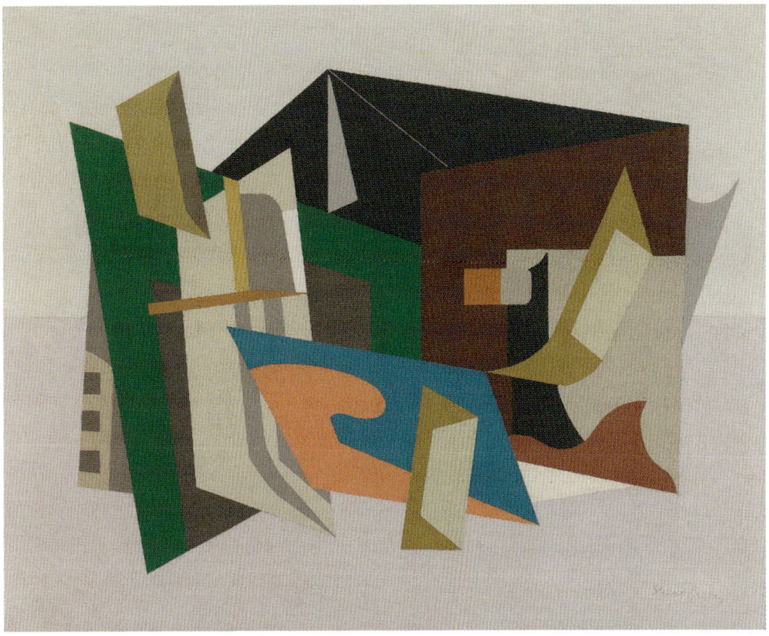

5.
Stuart Davis (1892–1964)
Egg Beater No. 1, 1927
Oil on linen
29 3/16 × 36 3/16 in.
(74.1 × 91.9 cm)
Gift of Gertrude Vanderbilt Whitney, Whitney Museum of American Art, New York, 31.169

plastic destination as well as origin of forms;" the abstract painter "uses this knowledge as a *point of departure*."[32] Abstract art "operates directly in the medium itself—paint, stone, etc.—with full understanding of their *sensuous qualities* and potentialities instead of relying on make-believe representation."[33] The eerie portraits and figures painted by Graham and his colleagues, while intensely evocative of particular individuals, also embody Graham's ideas. Rather than dissembling their medium in quest of a "make-believe representation," the most adventurous figurative works by Gorky, de Kooning, and Graham, at this time, seem poised on the brink of dissolution into incidents of "pure" painting. Only at the last minute do they resolve themselves as compelling *images*. Paint has been brought to life, made to coalesce into something we recognize, at least momentarily.

System and Dialectics of Art was published in Paris and New York in 1937. By then, although Graham went annually to France, refreshing his friendships with the Paris vanguard and acquiring work for resale, he exhibited solely in the United States, defining himself as a New York artist. Not surprisingly, Graham's book addresses the question "What is American art?" The answer: "Art made in America by American artists."[34] He presents a list of "Young, outstanding American painters: [Jan] Matulka, [Milton] Avery, Stuart Davis, Max Weber, David Smith, W. Kooning, Edgar Levy, Boardman Robinson, S. Shane and a few others. Some are just as good and some are better than the leading artists of the same generation in Europe."[35] For the renamed Ivan Gratianovitch Dombrowski, the definition of "American" was not rigid. Many on the list, such as Matulka, Weber, and de Kooning, were immigrants, as he was. ("Young" was also a flexible category. Davis was forty-five, Matulka forty-seven; Avery at fifty-two and Weber at fifty-six were older than Graham.) Weber's presence is explained by his early, Cubist-inspired paintings, made during his years in Paris. Others are immediately explicable because of their dedication to Modernist ideas. Friendship may account for others. Robinson, though he flirted with Cubism, is best known for Social Realist works. "S. Shane" remains an enigma. Gorky's name is conspicuously absent, although he is mentioned elsewhere, along with Levy and Matulka, as an "example of highly developed taste."

In 1935, two years before the publication of *System and Dialectics*, the relationship of all Four Musketeers and their friends seems to have been intact. David Smith recalled that "...we once formed a group, Graham, Edgar Levy, Resnikoff, de Kooning, Gorky, and myself, with Davis being asked to join.... Our only action was to notify the Whitney museum that we were a group and would only exhibit in the 1935 abstract show if all were asked. Some of us were, some exhibited, some didn't and that ended our group."[36] But there are indications that the Musketeers' connections were loosening by the time Graham's book came out. The friendship between Davis and Gorky, which endured despite the differing character and objectives of their work, eroded because of their disparate attitudes toward social action. Davis was deeply involved in the artists' organizations formed during the Depression, as his friend initially was. But as Davis later wrote, "Gorky was less intense about it and still wanted to play.... Our interests began to diverge and finally ceased to coincide altogether. Our friendship terminated and was never resumed."[37] Although the break was not complete, Gorky became increasingly fascinated by Surrealism by the end of the 1930s, and became part of a different group of artists.

Perhaps the clearest indication of change is found in *American and French Painters of the 20th Century*, which Graham organized for McMillen, Inc., a decorating firm that also held exhibitions,[38] in January 1942. The show combined well-known Europeans—Picasso, Matisse, Braque, Pierre Bonnard, André Derain, Georges Rouault, Amedeo Modigliani, André Dunoyer de Segonzac, and Giorgio de Chirico—with established American Modernists—Davis, Walt Kuhn, and Graham himself—and unknowns, at the time—"William Kooning," Jackson Pollock, and Lenore Krassner (not yet renamed "Lee Krasner"). Graham's close Russian friends

David Nicholas Burliuk and Nicholas Vasilieff were also represented, along with de Kooning's girlfriend, Virginia Diaz. It was not the first time progressive Americans were shown with European vanguardists; in 1928, the Société Anonyme organized an exhibition that included Davis in the company of Kandinsky, Léger, de Chirico, and Paul Klee, but Graham's show was more comprehensive. The extant checklist is tantalizingly approximate, with listings such as "Picasso—Portrait of Dora Mare [*sic*]" and "Bonnard—Large Interior," but the works that can be identified attest to the ambition of the selection. One Picasso now belongs to the Minneapolis Institute of Art, the Modigliani to the Museum of Modern Art, the Pollock to Tate Modern, London, and the de Kooning (probably) to the Wadsworth Atheneum, Hartford, Connecticut. It is difficult to imagine how Graham managed to assemble the European works in the show, which opened during World War II, less than a month after Pearl Harbor and America's entry into the conflict. He obviously had to use what was available in the United States, but the excellence of the identifiable works indicates his good relations with American collectors and dealers.

Because of the show, de Kooning always credited Graham with having discovered Pollock and, on the strength of Pollock's painting, Krasner was prompted to introduce herself to its author. The exhibition attracted some attention. A sympathetic reviewer in *The Art Digest* was particularly struck by an intense painting of a male nude. "A strange painter is William Kooning [*sic*] who does anatomical men with one visible eye, but whose work reveals a rather interesting feeling for paint surfaces and color."[39]

Among the most unexpected works at McMillen was the de Chirico, from a series of gladiators and antique soldiers made in the late 1920s and early 1930s. While Graham's circle admired de Chirico's metaphysical townscapes, the inclusion of a fairly insipid Neo-classical painting of male nudes signals a radical shift in Graham's taste, a forewarning of the meticulous, Ingres-inspired fidelity to appearances of his later work, such as the triple self-portrait, *Poussin m'instruit* (Fig. 6). Gorky's absence from the show is further evidence of change.

Yet if Graham's selection of artists for the McMillen exhibition suggests that by late 1941 the Four Musketeers were no longer a cohesive group, their work affirms their shared aspirations and the rich cross-fertilization of ideas among them. It brings to vivid life, too, the animated, now lost, exchanges among Graham and his friends when they frequented each other's studios, looked at exhibitions together, and spent time in passionate discussions, banded together like Dumas's heroes to do battle for the cause of progressive art in America.

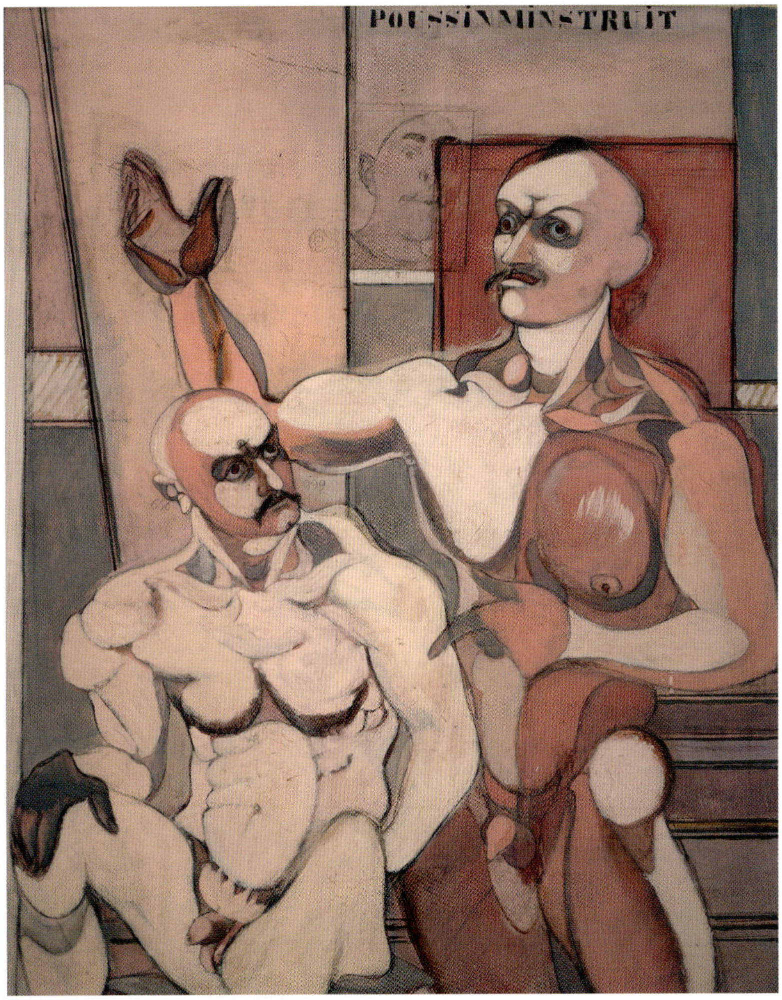

6.
John Graham (1886–1961)
Poussin m'instruit, 1944
Oil on panel
60 × 48 in. (152.4 × 122 cm)
Collection of Anthony F. Bultman IV and Family

Gertrude Vanderbilt Whitney and Guy Pène du Bois

"A True History of Eight West Eighth"

Betsy Fahlman, PhD
Professor of Art History, Arizona State University, Tempe, Arizona, and Adjunct Curator of American Art, Phoenix Art Museum, Phoenix, Arizona

Few individuals made more of an impact on American art during the first half of the twentieth century than Gertrude Vanderbilt Whitney (1875–1942).[1] As critic Henry McBride observed after her death: "It is not an exaggeration to say that there is not a contemporary artist of note in America who has not been helped by Mrs. Whitney."[2] Born into one exceptionally wealthy family and married into another, she was not satisfied with the gilded cage of a society matron and chafed against the restrictive behavioral norms for women of the period. To maintain her independence and to give herself purpose beyond the expected socialite charities and functions, as well as the typical duties of a wife and mother, she established her studio in Greenwich Village, the bohemian epicenter of cultural life in New York. Restless and ultimately unhappy in her marriage, she found that the arts enabled her to engage in multiple roles as artist, patron, gallerist, and museum founder.

A talented sculptor, she eschewed the amateur status to which artist members of her élite class were relegated. In an era when American male artists were busy with public monuments, Whitney was a member of a small group of ambitious women who actively sought major commissions and won them in competitive processes. These include the *Titanic Memorial* in Washington, DC (1916), *Buffalo Bill—The Scout* for the Buffalo Bill Center of the West in Cody, Wyoming (1923–25), the *A.E.F. (American Expeditionary Forces) Memorial* (1926) in St-Nazaire, France, and *The Founders of the Daughters of the American Revolution* (1929) in Washington, DC.[3]

Whitney began to study sculpture in 1900, but her active participation in the American art scene dates from 1907 when she established her studio in Greenwich Village at 19 MacDougal Alley, not far from Washington Square. There she began mounting informal exhibitions and organizing art-related activities. Purchasing a brownstone at 8 West 8th Street in 1914 and knocking down the adjacent wall to her MacDougal Alley space, she formally established the Whitney Studio as a place with galleries and offices for exhibitions and socializing. Four years later, in 1918, she founded the Whitney Studio Club, committed to supporting contemporary American artists. Those in Whitney's circle received encouragement, financial support, group and solo exhibitions (for many, their first, including that of Pène du Bois in 1918), and she purchased their work. In 1928, the Whitney Studio Galleries opened, closing two years later with the founding of the museum.[4]

In an era that favored European artists, the allegorical academic paintings and sculptures of the American Renaissance, and French Impressionism, Whitney became a champion of contemporary American art. Her efforts with the Whitney Studio Club gave artists a place to meet, share ideas, showcase and sell their work, and through it she was able to make additional benefactions to both individuals and institutions. By the time the Whitney Museum of American Art opened in 1931, she had amassed a collection of more than 1300 works of art (in 1929, her offer to donate her collection to The Metropolitan Museum of Art, as well as to endow and build a new wing to house it, had been speedily and disdainfully turned down by the museum's director, Edward Robinson). Whitney was part of an élite female sisterhood of philanthropy: only a year or so earlier, in 1929, Abby Aldrich Rockefeller, Mary Quinn Sullivan, and Lillie P. Bliss founded the Museum of Modern Art. But Whitney took her acts of matronage one step further by appointing a woman as her museum's first director: Juliana Force, her assistant since 1907. The museum she founded remains emblematic of the "splendid multiplicity"[5] of her many efforts on behalf of American art and artists.

This chapter considers a portfolio of seventeen witty watercolors executed by painter and critic Guy Pène du Bois (1884–1958) in 1921.[6] Grandly purporting to be "A True History of Eight West Eighth," the suite is a highly personal view by an artist who benefited in many personal and professional ways from Whitney's philanthropy, private benefactions, and friendship. Indeed, she was his most important patron. There are fifty-six works by Pène du Bois in the collection of the Whitney: that institution possesses more artworks by him than any other museum.[7]

The commission was arranged by Juliana Force, who, aware that the artist was facing one of his periodic bouts of financial challenges, alerted Whitney. The pair, who worked closely with each other for more than three decades, were an effective team, as Lloyd Goodrich observed: "Every action of either Mrs. Whitney or Mrs. Force was really the action of both, for it was taken after full consultation and in complete agreement."[8] His observation echoes that of Forbes Watson who recollected that they were women of "singularly complementary qualities."[9] Force suggested to Whitney that she offer the artist $2000 to create a series of watercolors that would comprise a gently satiric visual chronicle of the Club, as well as a portrait, *Juliana Force at the Whitney Studio Club* (1921, Whitney Museum of American Art).[10] Force and Whitney devised an imaginative way of helping an artist in need and this was a project well suited to someone who was a keen observer of contemporary art-world life. The grateful artist wrote in his diary on July 15, 1921:

A few days ago I started the making of a pictorial history of 8 West 8 which commission was given me by Mrs. Force who suggested it to Mrs. Whitney. I have, to date, done a cover design and a portrait of Mrs. Force. I am tremendously interested in the project and feel that it may in the end, contribute not a little to my success. It has, financially, already netted me $2000. It may start me doing satirical drawings of real importance.[11]

The series was described by Pène du Bois, whose humor and affection for the Whitney Studio Club would have been shared by other members:

A pictorial history of Eight West Eighth containing a complete series of portraits of important and amusing people who have contributed to the fun or to the glory of the famous studio also accurate and explicit replicas of events which in initial wisdom or ultimate folly outshine the multitude of others with which this place has been honored the whole done into pictures with the kindly strokes of the pen and brush of Guy Pène du Bois.

The artist intended it to be a distinctly idiosyncratic history, conveying the vitality of the organization, as well as the fun that its participants enjoyed and the professional camaraderie they shared.

The title page pictures Whitney, floating goddess-like above a group of six artists who are walking toward the four-story-tall building (four more are clustered at the entrance), many of them carrying portfolios, undoubtedly in hopes of securing sales and exhibitions (Fig. 1). Whitney's car is parked in the background, with two uniformed chauffeurs standing ready to do their employer's bidding promptly. Whitney, whose hair is fashionably bobbed and whose mouth is highlighted in the red lipstick she favored, is clad in a revealing, stylish, fringed pants outfit made from a thin fabric that comes to mid-leg. Pène du Bois accurately captures an individual described by Kennedy Fraser as "a tall, thin woman with very white skin and very black hair."[12] The draping on her upper shoulders is secured with small bows, and a long strand of pearls highlights the plunging *décolletage*. It is not

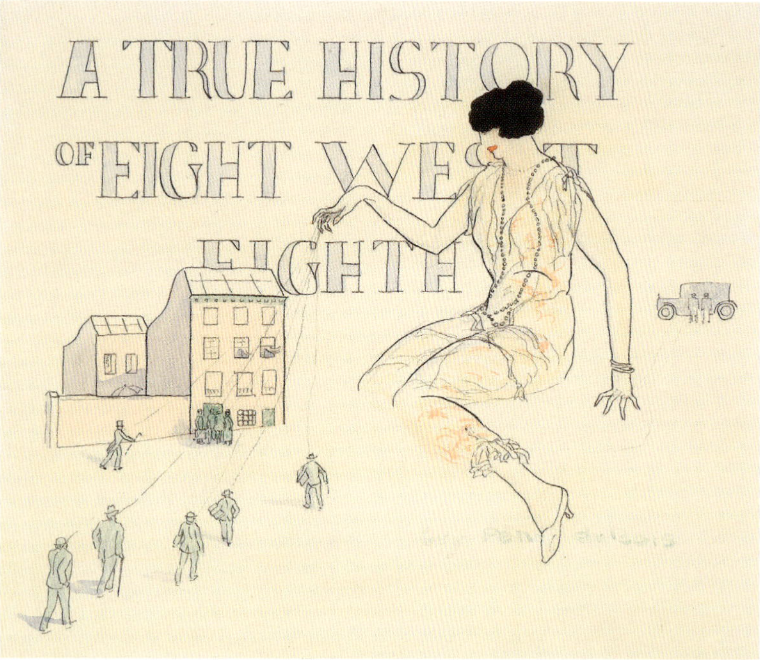

1. *(above)*
Guy Pène du Bois
(1884–1958)
Title Page, 1921
Watercolor, pen and ink, and graphite pencil on paper
Sheet (sight) 11 ¾ × 14 in.
(29.8 × 35.6 cm)
From *A True History of Eight West Eighth*, Whitney Museum of American Art, New York, Gift of Flora Miller Biddle, 2014.74.1

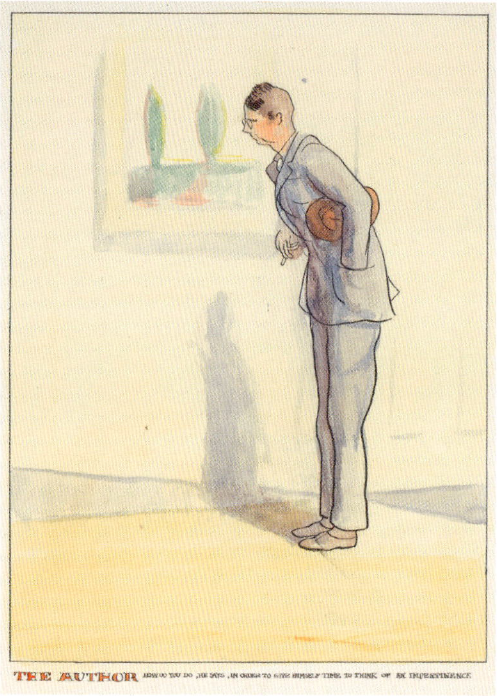

2. *(right)*
Guy Pène du Bois
(1884–1958)
The Author, 1921
Watercolor, pen and ink, and graphite pencil on paper
Sheet 26 ⅞ × 19 ⅞ in.
(68.3 × 50.5 cm)
From *A True History of Eight West Eighth*, Whitney Museum of American Art, New York, Gift of Flora Miller Biddle, 2014.74.16

an outfit she could have worn in public, and it suggests Robert Henri's 1916 portrait of Whitney lounging on a sofa in pants (she displayed it in her studio, as her husband would not allow it to be hung in their Fifth Avenue mansion). In both, she displays herself as a decidedly self-possessed New Woman. Whitney, while not a notable beauty, was striking in other ways, and Fraser notes how expressive were "her narrow, long fingered, and flexible hands."[13] With her right hand, Whitney gestures toward the scene below as if she is about to make something wonderful happen by magic. The thin filaments extending from the fingers of her right hand, attached to six of the figures making their way to the Club, suggest that while she was sympathetic to the challenging economics of many of the artists in her circle, she did not wish her efforts to assist them to seem like outright charity, and thus she modestly deflects her role.

Pène du Bois, who had been an active participant in many of Whitney's artistic ventures, has included himself in this visual history as *The Author* (Fig. 2). As he must have done many times in his years as a critic, he stands near a painting hanging in a gallery. Wearing a suit and tie, he holds a cigarette in his right hand, and with his hat tucked under his left arm, he bends forward to look closely at a landscape. To the unseen person who stands nearby, he says "How do you do," giving "himself some time to think of an impertinence." He was a smart writer whose reviews were infused with a Gallic wit, and while he chafed at the time away from his studio when he had to write reviews for a living, he was an insightful observer of the American art scene, particularly of the realist and progressive artists of his generation.

Two watercolors reference a pair of unusual exhibitions held at the Whitney Studio Club in 1918: one of painting, and another of sculpture. The first scene in the history, titled *A Meeting of the Society for the Propagation of Indigence Among Artists*, refers less to the impoverishment experienced by the Club's many artists early in their careers, a condition often alleviated by Whitney's generosity, and more to the fact that they were American artists (regardless of where they were born). Seven men are pictured (Fig. 3). Robert Winthrop Chanler stands at the left (as a member of the Astor family, he was decidedly not indigent). Beside him is Pène du Bois (like Chanler, he wears glasses), and beside him is a man with his head turned away. A stocky, black-bearded Jo Davidson stands leaning on his cane (a sartorial preference, not something to give him support as a result of injury or illness), and beside him is a dandified man with a moustache and a pointed goatee, and shiny shoes. Seated are two unidentified men, one bald and the other with his hands pressed together as if in prayer. Whitney's close friendship with Chanler and Davidson is attested by the fact that they appear in three works in the series. Davidson had met Whitney in Paris in 1908, and she became one of his earliest patrons.

The title references the Indigenous Painting Exhibition that took place at the Whitney Studio Club from February 4 to 25, 1918. About twenty artists participated, and when they arrived at the studio, they were given blank canvases of varying sizes that were distributed by lottery. The artists were provided with "all the creative tools,"[14] which included, in addition to paints and brushes, generous supplies of alcohol, cigarettes, and cigars. Not surprisingly, the atmosphere was very convivial. The artists had a week in which to produce a work for exhibition. Participants included Gifford Beal, Glenn O. Coleman, Eugene Higgins, Eugene O. Goldbeck, Leon Kroll, F. Luis Mora, John Sloan, Guy Pène du Bois, George Luks, Jo Davidson, Paul Dougherty, and Robert Winthrop Chanler. Robert Henri and George Bellows declined to take part, and Kroll left after the first day. Critical response of the results varied from "remarkably successful"[15] to "indigestible."[16] But the point was camaraderie as much as the art produced, and it did fulfill Whitney's goal of supporting contemporary American artists, who likely did not have so much fun at the stuffier National Academy of Design.

The painting show was followed in March by the sculpture exhibition, portrayed in *Indigenous Workers* (Fig. 4). The sculptors, who brought their own tools, were provided with clay, and, like

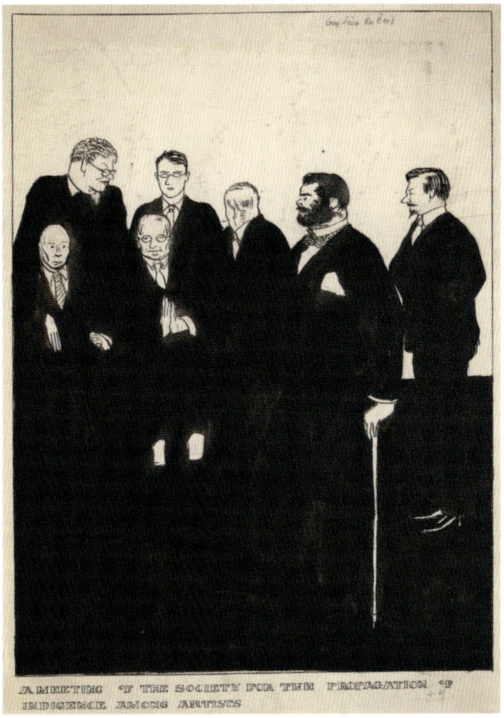

3.
Guy Pène du Bois
(1884–1958)
A Meeting of the Society for the Propagation of Indigence Among Artists, 1921
Watercolor, pen and ink, and graphite pencil on paper
Sheet 19 ½ × 14 ¼ in.
(49.5 × 36.2 cm)
From *A True History of Eight West Eighth*, Whitney Museum of American Art, New York, Gift of Flora Miller Biddle, 2014.74.3

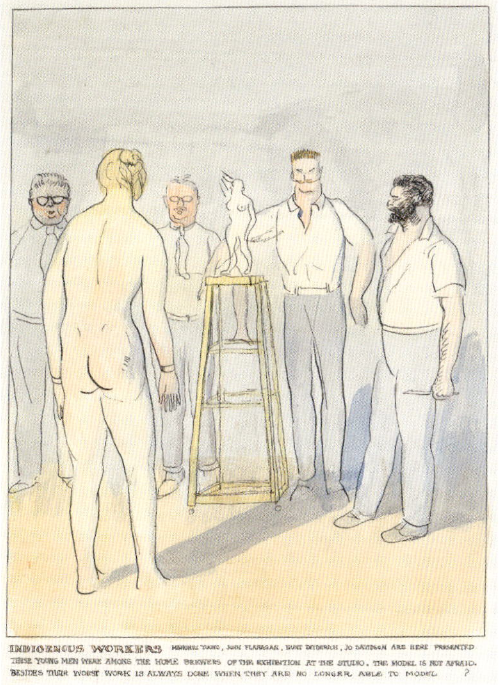

4.
Guy Pène du Bois
(1884–1958)
Indigenous Workers, 1921
Watercolor, pen and ink, and graphite pencil on paper
Sheet 22 ½ × 15 ¼ in.
(57.2 × 38.7 cm)
From *A True History of Eight West Eighth*, Whitney Museum of American Art, New York, Gift of Flora Miller Biddle, 2014.74.7

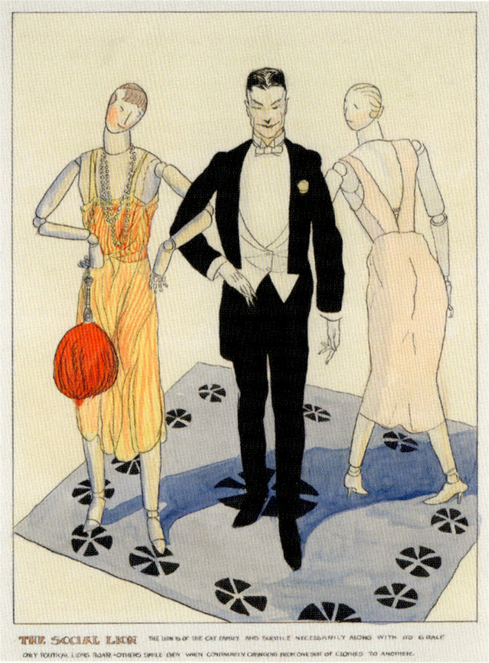

5.
Guy Pène du Bois
(1884–1958)
The Social Lion, 1921
Watercolor, pen and ink, and graphite pencil on paper
Sheet 22 ½ × 15 ½ in.
(57.2 × 39.4 cm)
From *A True History of Eight West Eighth*, Whitney Museum of American Art, New York, Gift of Flora Miller Biddle, 2014.74.5

the painters, they too received ample quantities of whiskey and cigars. They had three days in which to complete a piece. Portrayed are four of the twenty artists who were invited to participate. Standing facing the viewer are four prosperous-looking sculptors: Mahonri Young, John Flannagan, Hunt Diederich, and Jo Davidson. A nude model is seen from the back and looks at the sculpture they have created (presumably of her) which is displayed on a sculpture stand. Pène du Bois's caption is somewhat mysterious: "These young men were among the home brewers of the exhibition at the studio. The model is not afraid. Besides their worst work is always done when they are no longer able to model."

When they were done, a small piece was made in Whitney's honor: "On a pedestal, standing, is a slender figure of a woman, and strenuously attempting to storm the position are admirers, clambering up the pedestal." Inscribed on the base are these words: "Erected in admiration of the woman and sculptress who can cage twenty sculptors without bloodshed resulting therefrom." The works produced in both shows were to be sold for charity," probably "for the benefit of American artists who go to the front."[17]

Readily recognizable as a signature work by Guy Pène du Bois is *The Social Lion*, which portrays the typical interchangeable social male and female figures he favored during the 1920s (Fig. 5). "The lion is of the cat family and subtile necessarily along with its grace. Only political lions roar. Others smile even when continually changing from one suit of clothes to another." The artist chose to use the archaic form of "subtle," perhaps to convey the exclusivity of the world in which his characters could be characteristically found. The man's stylized face is exactly the type of well-groomed and formally dressed society gentleman the artist typically admired. His thinly delineated facial features and unusually slender, long fingers combine a feline grace with the feral character of a discreet, yet cunning, social predator. On his arm is one of the stylized female manikins that he favored in so many of his paintings. Her jointed arms evoke the models used by artists. She is a skinny flapper, with bobbed hair and rouged cheeks, clad in a bright yellow dress with red stripes and carrying a red bag. Walking away from the couple is another woman, her feet awkwardly askew, suggesting she has been cast off in place of a new model. The artist favored social types, often the sleek young woman, on the arm of an elderly male "rounder" who is no match for her. But in *The Social Lion*, the male figure is younger and more cunning, perhaps equally adept in the social jungle of fashionable society.

Whitney had a strong personal connection to the architect William Adams Delano (1874–1960), who, with his partner Chester Holmes Aldrich (1871–1940), designed many buildings for patrons who were part of the same social stratum as Whitney.[18] They designed the second clubhouse for the Colony Club (1914–16) in Manhattan; Whitney was an active member of this élite women's club founded in 1903. In 1913, Delano designed her Long Island studio in Old Westbury (1913–15). Pène du Bois's watercolor, *Billy the Draughtsman*, pictures the dapper architect standing with his hands in the pockets of his summer suit, his hat tucked under his left arm, and his cane tucked into his pocket.

Robert Winthrop Chanler (1872–1930) shared with Whitney a blue-blooded background, and the ability to function in bohemian and aristocratic worlds.[19] He executed commissions for both her Manhattan and Long Island studios, and she purchased several of his expensive and unusual screens. Tempestuous in nature and six feet tall, he was possessed of a commanding physical presence. He named his Gramercy Park home "The House of Fantasy," and hosted exuberant parties where prodigious amounts of alcohol were consumed. Pène du Bois, who had written a number of articles on Chanler, titled one of the images he made of his friend *God Give Me Strength*. His second portrait was titled *The Symbolical Sheriff*, referencing his election as Sheriff of Dutchess County in 1907, a position he held until 1910.

Jo Davidson is also portrayed as *The Entertainer* and stands in front of a group of busts on pedestals, of which five are visible (Fig. 6). These are part of his series of fourteen Allied military leaders and statesmen, who were among the participants in the Paris Peace Conference setting the terms for peace at the end of World War I in the 1919 Treaty of Versailles. He has lined them up as if they are watching a parade, their hands raised in salute. The first he completed was Marshal Ferdinand Foch (far right), and others included Woodrow Wilson (fourth from left), General John J. Pershing, and Georges Clemenceau. Their arrangement also suggests a production line, as Davidson later observed: "The speed with which one sitter replaced another, each being a distinct personality, taught me to simplify more and extract the essentials needed to make a portrait."[20]

Ivan the Terrible presents a fierce image of Ivan Narodny (1870–1953), a revolutionary Russian émigré who arrived in New York in 1906. The words that appear on the posters behind him summarize his various intellectual and political interests: Anarchy, Individualism, Baltic, Black Sea, Bolshevism, Mysticism, Metaphysics. He was also an art writer and critic, who published a book on Robert Winthrop Chanler in 1922.

Robert Henri (1865–1929), one of the most charismatic art instructors of the first quarter of the twentieth century (Pène du Bois was one of his many students), makes an appearance as

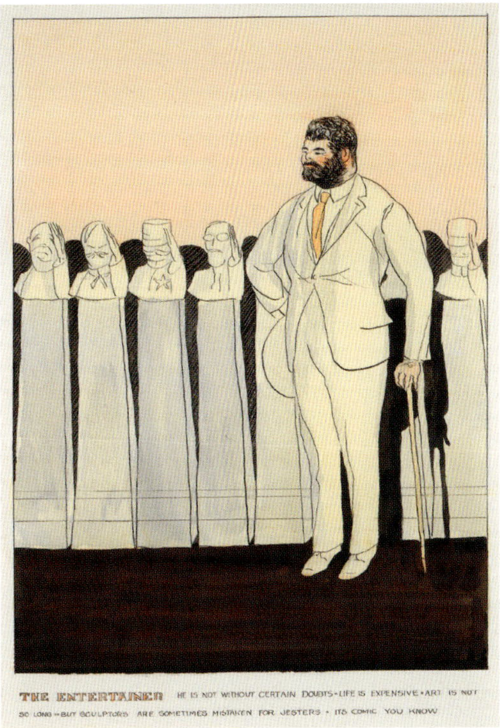

6.
Guy Pène du Bois
(1884–1958)
The Entertainer, 1921
Watercolor, pen and ink, and graphite pencil on paper
Sheet 22 9/16 × 15 1/2 in. (57.3 × 39.4 cm)
From *A True History of Eight West Eighth*, Whitney Museum of American Art, New York, Gift of Flora Miller Biddle, 2014.74.14

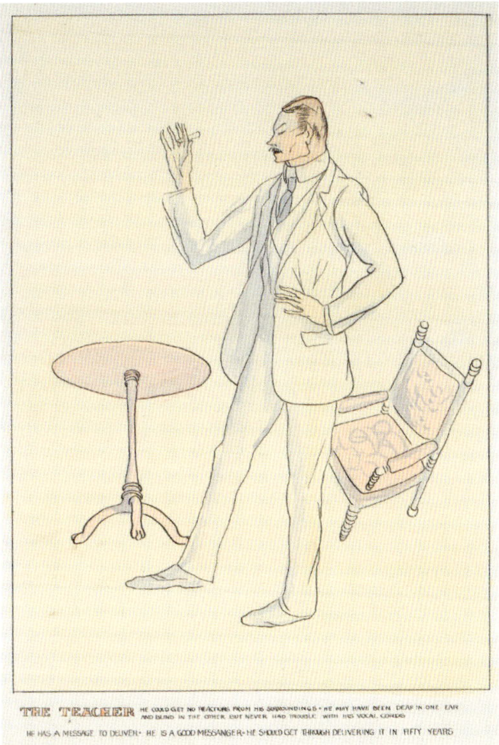

7.
Guy Pène du Bois
(1884–1958)
The Teacher, 1921
Watercolor, pen and ink, and graphite pencil on paper
Sheet 22 9/16 × 15 5/8 in. (57.3 × 39.7 cm)
From *A True History of Eight West Eighth*, Whitney Museum of American Art, New York, Gift of Flora Miller Biddle, 2014.74.11

8.
Guy Pène du Bois
(1884–1958)
The Three Hour Portrait, 1921
Watercolor, pen and ink, and graphite pencil on paper
Sheet 27 × 20 in.
(68.6 × 50.8 cm)
From *A True History of Eight West Eighth*, Whitney Museum of American Art, New York, Gift of Flora Miller Biddle, 2014.74.17

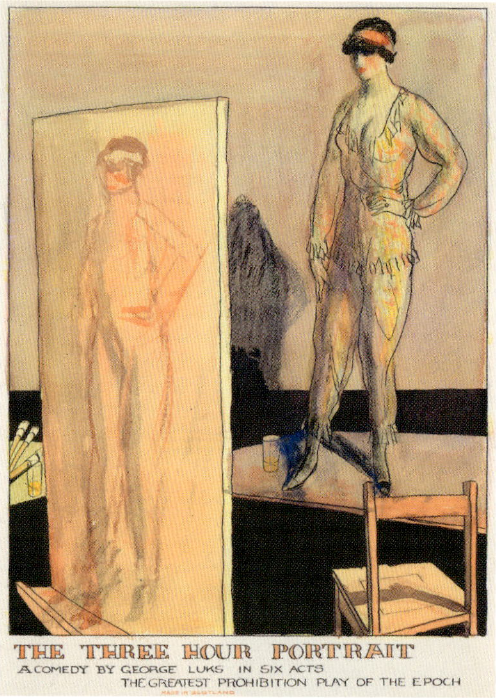

The Teacher (Fig. 7), which is captioned: "He could get no reactions from his surroundings. He may have been deaf in one ear and blind in the other but never had trouble with his vocal cords. He has a message to deliver. He is a good messenger. He should get through delivering it in fifty years." He stands to make some point, his left hand on his hip, gesturing with his right. He has stood up suddenly, knocking over a chair and table in doing so. It reminds one of Pène du Bois's memory of his experience in Henri's classroom: "Henri set the class in an uproar. Completely overturned the apple cart.... The talk was uncompromising, the approach unsubtle, the result pandemonium."[21]

Several of the watercolors portray single figures whose identities remain obscure. *The Word Carpenter* is obviously a critic, though not one Pène du Bois admired as his caption reveals: "The word carpenter is here shown leaving with his carpenterings or shavings. It is said that they will help heat a bungalow in the Catskills where there are many listeners in the shape of mountains. Ever hear of the main act? No wonder he is sad." *The General* is shown in uniform, while *Pneumonia* pictures a young man wearing a greatcoat standing facing the viewer with a cane over his right arm. *The Creation of a Veteran* pictures the sort of event in which the civic-minded Whitney participated regularly. She stands in front of members of various branches of the armed forces, with dignitaries behind her, and a press photographer off to the side. The scene appears to be an international event, likely in relation to World War I.

The series ends where it started, with Gertrude Vanderbilt Whitney in the same skimpy outfit she wore in the first watercolor of the series. *The Three Hour Portrait* (Fig. 8) is described in the caption as "A comedy by George Luks in six acts. The greatest Prohibition play of the epoch. Made in Scotland." Of the man famed for his prodigious consumption of alcohol, Pène du Bois observed: "Whiskey and painting and Luks were not a good mixture."[22]

These watercolors represent a beguiling glimpse of a moment in the American art world: a heady period when contemporary American artists found they had a champion in a wealthy woman who was also an artist, and who was willing to purchase their work, encourage them, and ultimately establish a museum in which to display her collection. Her philanthropy was not of the sort to increase her social standing (as it did for the capitalists who collected the Old Masters), but rather was rooted in her own artistic ambitions and the desire to do something concrete for the artists who were her contemporaries.

ACKNOWLEDGMENTS
For their kind assistance in the preparation of this article, the author would like to thank Avis Berman, Anita Duquette (Whitney Museum of American Art), Laurent Davidson, Laurette McCarthy, and Joel Rosenkranz (Conner•Rosenkranz).

The African American Aspect of American Art

A Brief Overview

Amalia K. Amaki, PhD
Artist, Art Historian, Curator, and Writer

Repositioning discussions of African American art from the margins toward the center of America's canon is a paradigm shift that merely requires racial blindness. Dating back to the colonial era, slaves and free African Americans created objects and images that conjoined with the intent of Caucasians to dispel European notions that Americans were under-achievers in the fine arts. African American intellectual Edward M. Thomas stated in 1862 that "where the fine arts are not reflected, there exists some fault in construction of a nation, and … the individual;" and he proceeded to endorse selected works by African Americans in an advertised exhibition mounted in the living room of his New York residence.[1] Making art was evidence of cultural revival in the face of slavery for African Americans, while serving simultaneously to proselytize the abolitionist cause. It was a noble act, as artists were considered "a credit to the race."

On the collector side, art was often a status symbol for wealthy white Americans who displayed their acquisitions (including those by African Americans) at home in ways that rendered the space, though private, a legitimate exhibition venue. Opportunities for any artist to show work elsewhere were limited by the small number of institutions like the New York Academy of Art, Boston Athenaeum, and Pennsylvania Academy of the Fine Arts; and alternative sites including entrepreneurial galleries, private galleries, public spaces and massive fairs and expositions. The dilemma was compounded by race for African Americans, with a precious few having access to these spaces—Robert Douglas, Jr. and Henry Ossawa Tanner at the Pennsylvania Academy of the Fine Arts, and Edward Mitchell Bannister at the Providence Art Club being among them. With exhibition rosters of academies compromised severely by racial bias, knowledge of the abilities, historical significance and very existence of most African American practitioners was lacking.

The artists fared best with public displays. African American photographer, abolitionist, and entrepreneur James Presley Ball, Sr. (1825–1904), for example, held shows at his Great Daguerrean Gallery of the West in Cincinnati, and organized tours of panoramas that artists like Robert S. Duncanson helped to hand-paint.[2] Paintings by Henry O. Tanner were shown at the Cotton States and International Exposition in Atlanta in 1895. Sculptor (Mary) Edmonia Lewis and painter Edward M. Bannister had pieces among the 100 artworks by Europeans and Americans on view at the Philadelphia Centennial Exposition of 1876. Another outlet was art commissions, frequently from private collectors, but initially, mostly from abolitionists capitalizing on the potential impact of first-hand accounts, and the real people and events depicted in the images—images reproduced in newspapers and other media that placed a candid picture of slavery bluntly before the general public. As illustrations portraying individual slaves were widely distributed, portraiture became an increasingly popular genre for African American artists. The effectiveness of the candid imagery, evidenced by President Andrew Jackson seeking passage of a congressional law banning their circulation in the South, underscored the inseparability of the original work from the relevance, richness, and credibility of the nation's overall creative narrative and its axiomatic art standards.

Joshua Johnston (also Johnson) (*c.* 1765–1830) was ignored by the art establishment for a century after his death, despite having been the highly regarded painter of 100 commissioned portraits for affluent residents of Baltimore. The first documented African American with a professional art career, he made a portrait of Reverend Daniel Coker, a founder of the African Methodist Episcopal Church (A.M.E.), among his paintings of African Americans. Johnston's quasi-two-dimensional, yet lifelike depictions of subjects with rigid arms and legs posed near furniture with brass studs led to him being called the "brass tack" artist. He was stylistically linked to Ralph Earl (1751–1801) and Charles Peale Polk (1767–1822), contemporaries whose work was routinely covered in national and regional exhibitions and literature about the period, including *American Paintings of the Eighteenth Century* published by the National Gallery of Art in 1995. Landscape artist Jacob Hall Pleasants (1873–1957) attempted to call attention to the oversight in "An Early Baltimore Negro Portrait Painter, Joshua Johnston," a 1939 essay in *Walpole Society Notebooks*; and "Joshua Johnson, the First American Negro Portrait Painter" in the *Maryland Historical Magazine* in 1942. The most promising attention to the merits of his work has come through auctions, including the January 19, 2019 offering at Sotheby's, where Johnston's portraits of *Dr. R. Andrew Aitkin (1757–1809)* and *Mrs. Andrew Aitkin (Elizabeth Aitkin, 1761–1811) and her Daughter, Eliza Aitkin (1798–1885)* sold for $675,000 to a Maryland collector, exceeding Sotheby's estimated value of $60–$80,000.[3]

Robert S. Duncanson (1821–1872), Edward M. Bannister (*c.* 1828–1901) and Grafton Tyler Brown (1841–1918) were among the celebrated nineteenth-century landscape artists who painted subjects that aligned with prevailing American ideals and principles. Like their white contemporaries, they referenced the native geography, new political ideology and collective ideals of individualism, freedom, opportunity and democracy through romanticized, yet realistic portrayals of the Hudson River Valley, Ohio River Valley and Pacific Northwest and West. They were each trained via self-directed paths: Duncanson meticulously studied prints of famous European paintings and subsequently traveled abroad; Bannister taught himself to sketch in childhood and studied anatomical drawing with William Rimmer through public lectures, while Brown developed strong drafting and compositional skills as the owner of a printing business and transferred the fundamentals to painting.

Robert Duncanson was the first African American artist to become well known beyond the United States. Educated in Canada and Scotland, he traveled frequently to both countries, plus England and Italy, and was considered "the best landscape painter in the West" by European curators and art connoisseurs.[4] He helped define the Ohio River Valley regional style of landscape painting along with Thomas Worthington Whittredge (1820–1910) and William Louis Sonntag (1822–1900). Recognized most for such works as *Blue Hole, Flood Waters, Little Miami River* (1851, Fig. 1) and the Alfred Tennyson-inspired painting *Land of the Lotus Eaters* (1861), his vistas embodied the concept of a national landscape. He heeded Hudson River School urgings to use photography (daguerreotypes) to record detailed references quickly, allowing more time for execution of final images in the studio. Duncanson sold paintings to the British Queen, and his most important portrait commission was of Nicholas Longworth, for whom he also painted a series of murals for the hall and reception room at Belmont, the Longworth mansion (now the Taft Museum) in Cincinnati. The museum calls the murals "evidence of Duncanson's most ambitious artistic creations.... Together, the eight paintings constitute one of the largest existing pre-Civil War domestic mural decorations in the United States."[5]

Edward Bannister was highly regarded as a painter at home and abroad without traveling to Europe. Motivated by an article in the *New York Herald* in 1867 that stated, "the Negro seems to have an appreciation of art [but was] manifestly unable to produce it," he painted

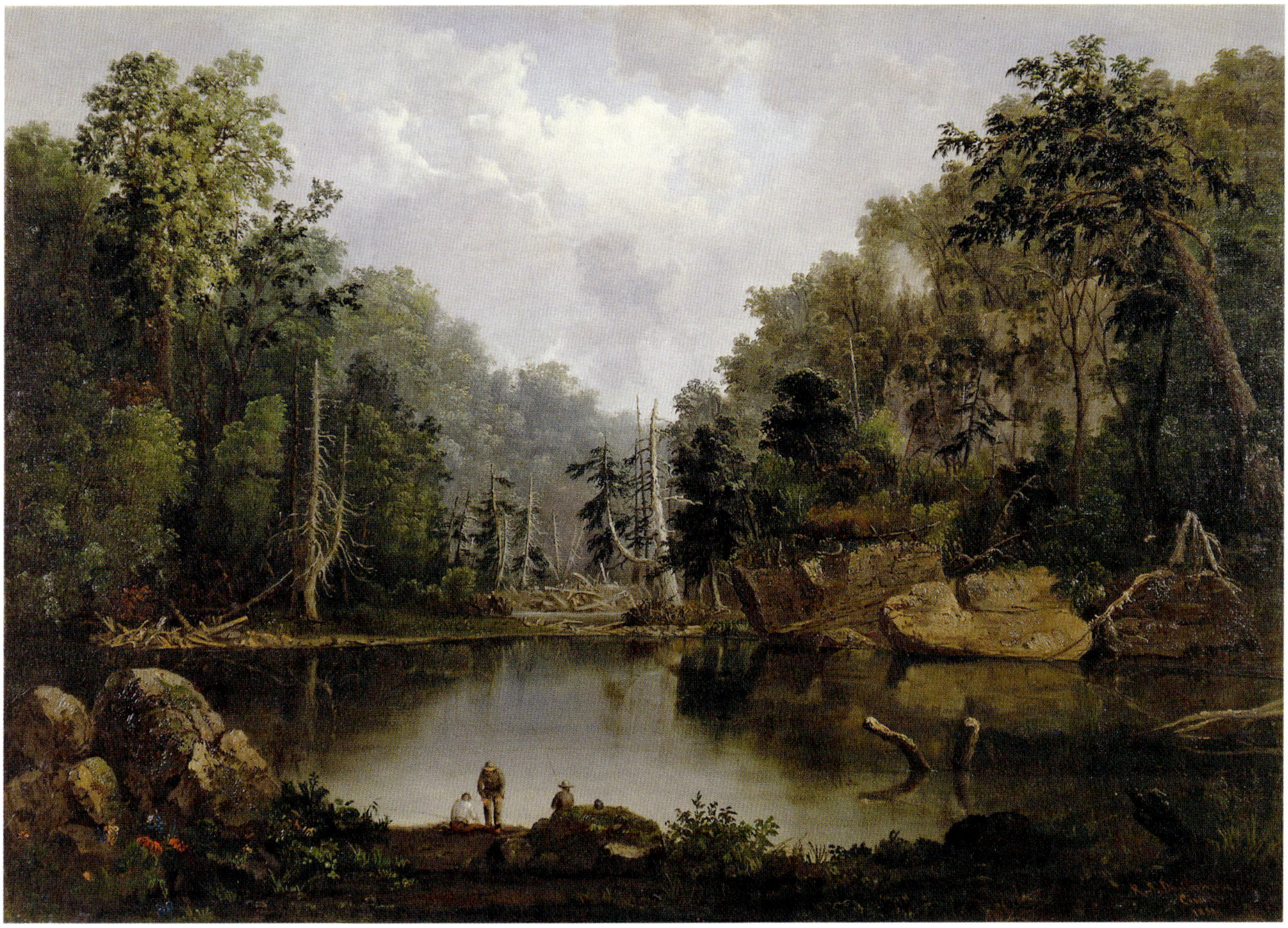

1.
Robert S. Duncanson
(1821–1872)
Blue Hole, Flood Waters, Little Miami River, 1851
Oil on canvas
29 1/5 × 42 1/4 in.
(74.2 × 107.3 cm)
Cincinnati Art Museum, Cincinnati, Gift of Norbert Heermann and Arthur Helbig, 1926.18

works such as *The Newspaper Boy* (1869) and landscapes glorifying nature, and won first prize at the Philadelphia Centennial Exhibition in 1876 for *Under the Oaks*.[6] It was the first time an African American had won a national award, and it brought him publicity and fame as an "American" artist. The flow of honors, awards, and commissions that followed allowed Bannister to paint full-time. He was a founding member of the Providence Art Club and an initial board trustee of the Rhode Island School of Design. With more than 100 landscapes in Providence collections, later works such as *Approaching Storm* (1886) showed his subtle, philosophical departure from the Hudson River style, as he became interested in intimate commentaries on the struggles of mankind and the wild beauty of the American landscape.

Grafton Tyler Brown was the first African American artist to paint extensive scenes of Wyoming, the Pacific Northwest and British Columbia. Born in Harrisburg, Pennsylvania, the longtime San Francisco resident sold his successful lithography business and began painting in 1879. Brown created dramatic, bird's eye views of Mount Rainier (1884–85), Mount Hood (1885–88), and Yosemite and Yellowstone National Parks, especially the Grand Canyon, his favorite subject between 1886 and 1891. His scenes of the Fraser, Thompson, Okanagan, and Similkameen Valleys, and southern Vancouver Island were celebrated in Victoria, British Columbia, following his inaugural exhibition in 1883. Brown painted the Cascade Mountains while on the Amos Bowman Geological Survey team and received private commissions in Montana and Oregon. Except in African American accounts, Brown was disregarded totally in applicable literature until a retrospective catalogue essay, "Grafton

Tyler Brown: Visualizing California and the Pacific Northwest," was written to support the exhibition at the Pasadena Museum of Art in 2014. Previous exhibitions at the Oakland Museum of Art in 1972, California African American Museum (San Francisco) in 2003, and Walters Art Museum in Baltimore in 2004 were mounted without publications.

The first internationally recognized African American sculptor was (Mary) Edmonia Lewis (*c.* 1844–1907). She studied at Oberlin College in Ohio with the encouragement and financial support of her older brother. Her talents were realized at Oberlin, but after being falsely accused of poisoning two white classmates and beaten by a white mob before the charges were dropped, she fled to Boston. Mentored by local abolitionists, she made busts of William Lloyd Garrison, John Brown, and Colonel Robert Gould Shaw, who would lead the all-African American 54th Regiment during the Civil War. She received considerable media attention, primarily in the abolitionist press in New York and Boston. Like many other American sculptors, Lewis spent much time in Rome, arriving in Europe in 1865. She mastered the portrayal of complicated themes, applying ideal figures to marble sculptures addressing topics such as emancipation (*Forever Free*, 1867) and Christian narratives (*Hagar in the Wilderness*, 1868). Lewis soon reached celebrity status in Europe, attracting studio visits from Frederick Douglass, tourists, and American art critic Henry T. Tuckerman, who wrote in 1866 that she had "great national genius, originality, earnestness and simple genuine taste."[7] She secured prominent clientele from both continents, Ulysses S. Grant among them, with other subjects including Abraham Lincoln (1871) and Henry Wadsworth Longfellow (1868–71), whose poem *The Song of Hiawatha* (1855) inspired a series of works produced from 1866 to 1872. Her multiracial identity, being of African American and Native American (Anishinaabe/Ojibwe) descent, and gender consistently informed her work. *The Death of Cleopatra* (1876), a ten-ton marble sculpture, was shown at the centennial celebration in Philadelphia and in Chicago two years later. Critics praised her execution of the piece for its stark, personalized realism and unique portrayal of the Egyptian ruler at the moment of death instead of the usual depictions of the subject in a pensive or reverent pre-death state. In her rendition, Lewis moved away from idealized classicism of the past toward a personal expression and realist style that was trending in American art between 1876 and 1917.

Henry Ossawa Tanner (1859–1937), the first African American artist to gain widespread international fame, decided to become an artist at thirteen. He studied two years at the Pennsylvania Academy of the Fine Arts with realist Thomas Eakins (1844–1916), who encouraged him to paint genre scenes drawn from his cultural heritage. Moving briefly to Atlanta, Tanner opened a photography gallery that proved unsuccessful, then taught one year at Clark College (now Clark Atlanta University) before moving permanently to France in 1891. He took classes at the Académie Julian, set up a studio and commenced painting landscapes, genre scenes and biblical themes, becoming best known for *The Banjo Lesson* (1893), *The Thankful Poor* (1894), and *Nicodemus Visiting Jesus* (1899). Several critically acclaimed exhibitions made him famous and triggered his receipt of numerous honors and awards. In 1899, the Philadelphia Museum of Art purchased the religious painting *Annunciation* (1898), becoming the first American museum to acquire a work of art by an African American. In 1923, Tanner was named honorary chevalier of the Order of the Legion of Honor, France's most distinguished award. Four years later, he became the first African American named full academician of the National Academy of Design. The doyen of expatriate artists in France, Tanner mentored, gave moral support and inspired most African Americans destined to play significant roles in future art developments, among them Augusta Savage, Hale Woodruff, and Romare Bearden.

The impact of Urban Realist Robert Henri and the Ashcan School painters associated with the rejection of the nation's academy, beginning in 1900, that was clarified further in The Eight exhibition in 1908, was one indicator of the advent of American Modernism. A more definitive marker was the Alfred Stieglitz-led Photo-Secession initiated in 1903, advancing fine art photography, pioneering the latest art trends in Europe, and extolling African art as a source of inspiration for many modern artists in events at the Little Galleries of the Photo-Secession (later "291") that opened in 1905. A subsequent mark was made by the International Exhibition of Modern Art in New York City in 1913 that traveled, in part, to Chicago and Boston. Called the Armory Show, the controversial blockbuster was a massive display of "colonial trophies to modernist icons" according to The Metropolitan Museum of Art. But the exhibition drew unprecedented crowds and had residual impact on galleries, collectors, museums, and general art-viewing populations across the country. Two-thirds of the paintings on view were by Americans, although Europeans Vincent van Gogh, Paul Gauguin, Paul Cézanne, Pablo Picasso, Henri Matisse, and Marcel Duchamp were the sensation. The term avant-garde was used to describe painting and sculpture for the first time, women began building modern art collections from the show in significant numbers that benefited American museums soon after, and artists, the Association of American Painters and Sculptors, were the visionaries responsible for the transformative exhibition.

In the aftermath of the Armory Show, the New Negro movement of the 1920s and 1930s forged a sensation of its own, with its centerfold, the Harlem Renaissance, reiterating that New York City was the titular headquarters of modern art in the nation, and establishing Harlem as the cultural capital of Black America. The wealth of talent that gathered in Harlem across disciplines enabled the Renaissance to spread its influence beyond America's shores. The influx of returning African American soldiers at the end of World War I to urban cities instead of their restrictive hometowns; the hundreds of thousands of African Americans from rural, mostly southern states, migrating north for improved opportunities beginning in 1913; the increasing middle class congregating in urban centers; and the broadening cultural milieu,

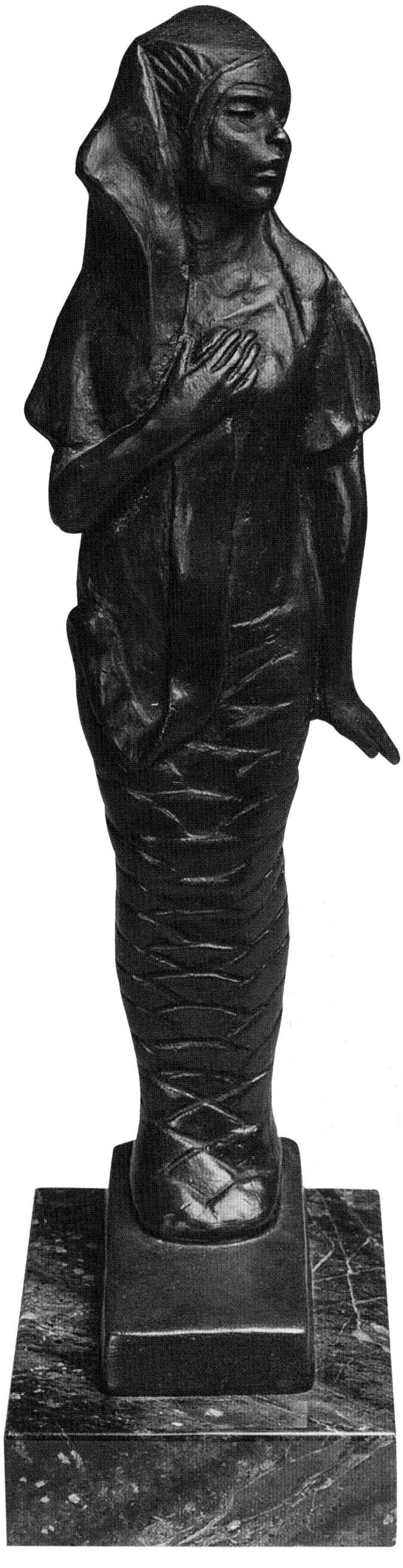

2.
Meta Vaux Warrick Fuller
(1877–1968)
Ethiopia Awakening, c. 1921
Bronze
67 × 16 × 10 in.
(170.2 × 40.6 × 25.4 cm)
Collection of Chrislan Fuller Manuel, The New York Public Library/Schomburg Center for Research in Black Culture, Jean Blackwell Hutson Research and Reference Division, The New York Public Library, New York (Astor, Lennox and Tilden Foundations)

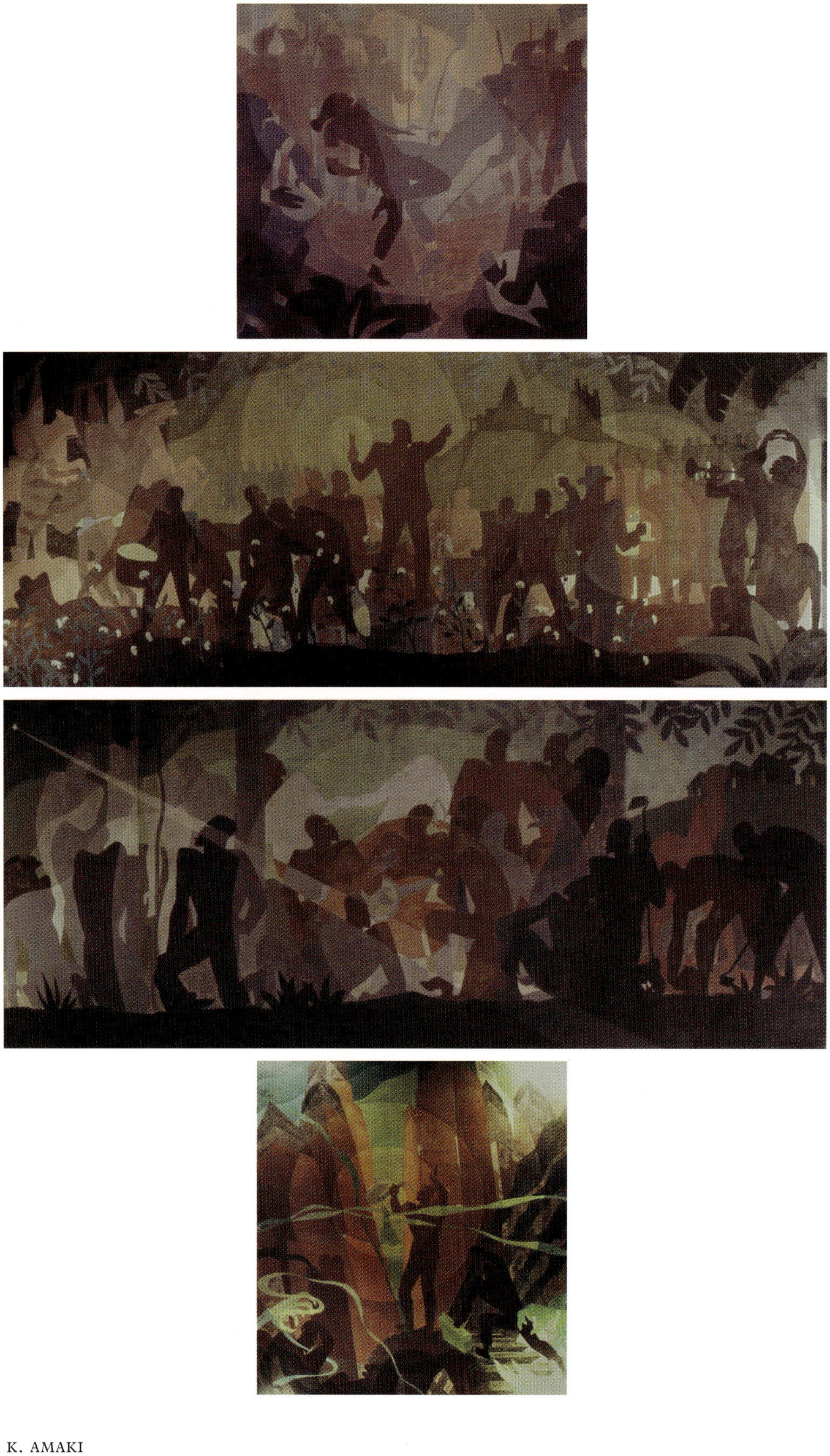

from the founding of social, professional and arts organizations, to the expanding, discursive nature of jazz, positioned African American lifestyles within the rapidly forming mass culture in America. In the visual arts, the Negro Renaissance raised points of observation and assimilation to white observers as well, such as early American Modernists Arthur G. Dove (1880–1946) and Stuart Davis (1892–1964), abstract painters influenced by African American culture, especially jazz; and writer and photographer Carl Van Vechten (1880–1964).

Sculptor Meta Vaux Warrick Fuller (1877–1968) conceptualized basic components of the movement in *Ethiopia Awakening* (1914), a bronze, standing female Pharaoh breaking free from bondage with her right hand over her heart, looking toward the future (Fig. 2). Predicting the New Negro movement in many ways, Fuller's use of Ethiopia as a metaphor for African Americans and anticolonialism, and Egypt as a symbol of cultural heritage and self-determination, aligned with the Pan-African art criteria promoted by scholar and activist W.E.B. DuBois. Considering art to be a conduit to racial equality, DuBois encouraged artists to use black subject matter and themes for social and political purposes.[8] Subsequently, when painter Aaron Douglas (1899–1979) blended influences from Art Deco, ancient Egyptian art, African sculpture and Negro spirituals in flat, figural profiles of silhouettes against geometrical patterns to depict biblical and historical narratives, he complied with philosopher Alain Leroy Locke's appeal for a Negro art derived from an African ancestral legacy.[9] Douglas solidified his art leadership role in this regard with illustrations for Locke's anthology, *The New Negro* (1925), James Weldon Johnson's book of poems, *God's Trombones* (1927), and numerous other book and journal covers including the NAACP's *Crisis* magazine and National Urban League's magazine *Opportunity*. His status was enhanced by the murals he painted in the 1930s addressing the collective history of African Americans, as in the series *Aspects of Negro Life*, 1934 (Fig. 3).

James Van Der Zee (1886–1983) compiled the most authentic, comprehensive and influential visual record of Harlem during the Renaissance period.[10] Balancing portrait studio work with prolific images of street scenes and daily life activities, Van Der Zee produced photographs that reflected the spectrum of aspirations, self-determination, and new self-image of the inhabitants of the neighborhood he knew so well. *Couple in Raccoon Coats (Harlem Couple)* (1932), depicting a self-confident couple posed in fur coats with a Cadillac on West 127th Street in Harlem, stood out among exemplary photographs taken of the growing middle class and became iconic of the movement itself. Van Der Zee photographs were central to another Harlem story of national consequence during the Civil Rights era when The Metropolitan Museum of Art presented the controversial *Harlem on My Mind* exhibition in 1969. While the exhibition was lambasted by African Americans and art critics for gross social and political errors in judgment, especially the decision to use blow-ups of Van Der Zee photographs rather than the actual works, Harlem's most famous photographer witnessed a career revival that catapulted his portfolio to the forefront—again a celebratory position he enjoyed for the remainder of his life (Fig. 4).

Another New Negro era central figure was Augusta Christine Fells Savage (1892–1962). An artist, teacher, administrator and activist, Savage graduated from Cooper Union School of Art and attended the Académie de la Grande Chaumière in Paris, where she joined poet Claude McKay, civil rights activist Walter White, painter Palmer Hayden, performer Josephine Baker, and other artists as part of the Negro Colony. A member of the Harlem artist-based 306 Group that convened at the West 141st Street studio of painter Charles Alston, she became the first African American to join the National Association of Women Painters and Sculptors. Savage founded an art school in Harlem that served the rising generation of African American artists, was the principal organizer of the Harlem Artists Guild, served as the first director of the Harlem Community Art Center, and lobbied for African American inclusion in Works Progress Administration (WPA) projects. Her best-known works, *Gamin*

3.
Aaron Douglas (1899–1979)
Aspects of Negro Life, 1934
Oil on canvas (four-panel mural)
Panel 1, *The Negro in an African Setting*: 73 × 80 in. (185.4 × 203.2 cm)
Panel 2, *From Slavery to Reconstruction*: 59 × 140 in. (149.8 × 355.6 cm)
Panel 3, *An Idyll of the Deep South*: 59 × 144 in. (149.8 × 365.7 cm)
Panel 4, *Song of the Towers*: 73 × 80 in. (185.4 × 203.2 cm)
The New York Public Library/Schomburg Center for Research in Black Culture, New York, Public Works of Art Project (Works Progress Administration) Commission

immediately after the New Negro movement.

Jacob Lawrence (1917–2000) insisted on telling American stories through the historical narratives of African Americans and used his clout as a leading artist to compel established art communities to define him as an American painter. Romare Bearden (1911–1988) combined southern matter, urban contexts, popular materials, and African icons to articulate visually the universality of everyday life, journeying, and rituals. He managed to place an "everyman" stamp on larger-than-life allegories in ways that made them relevant, yet even more mammoth simultaneously, rendering the model culturally specific and symbolic at the same time.

Richard Hunt (b. 1935), Martin Puryear (b. 1941), and Melvin Edwards (b. 1937) took different routes to manipulating materials in the formation of abstract sculptural objects: Hunt through explorations of the implications of interactive forms in nature; Edwards following African diasporic intents related to resistance, liberation, and power; and Puryear delving into ways of defining identity and culture in hand-formed sculptures made from natural materials. The methods of all three converge at angles, intersections, curves, and ambiguous planes that, at first contact, shroud cultural immediacy. Their sculptures embody a universality so succinctly that the association is not erased upon their deeper scrutiny and clearer understanding. But is the work, according to the "canon," "American" enough to be "white"? Or "white" enough to be "universal"?

Barkley L. (Leonard) Hendricks (1945–2017) and, perhaps, to a greater extent, Jean-Michel Basquiat (1960–1988) became iconic in relation to the art developments with which they are associated. Hendricks restated the African American subject in revolutionizing post-modern American portraits. Dismissing the white gaze, he depicted cool, self-aware, and self-assured figures in natural poses, and, presumably, in their own environment. Most

5.
Norman Wilfred Lewis
(1909–1979)
Untitled (Alabama), 1967
Oil on canvas
45 ¼ × 73 ½ in.
(114.9 × 186.7 cm)
National Gallery of Art, Washington, DC, Gift of the Collectors Committee, 2009.45.1

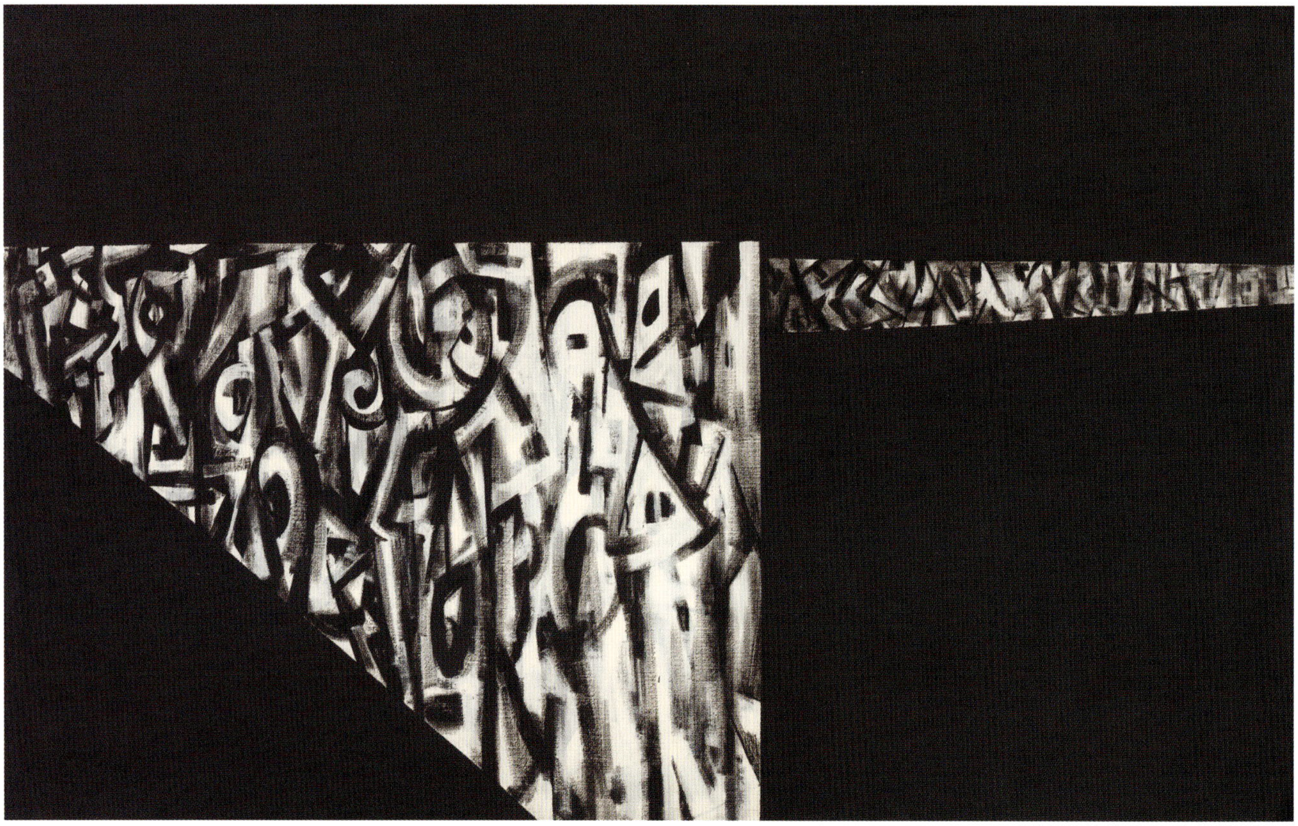

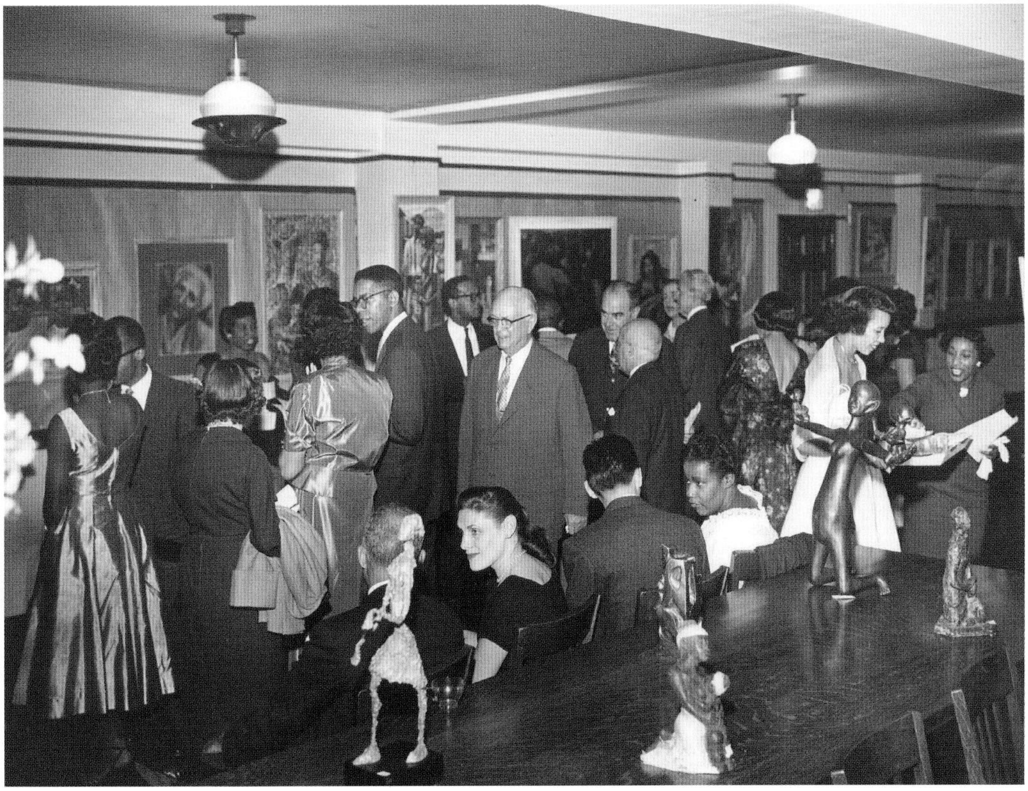

6.
Opening Reception for Trustees, 16th Exhibition of Paintings, Prints, and Sculptures by Negro Artists of America (1957)
Atlanta University Photographs, Atlanta University Center, Robert W. Woodruff Library, Atlanta, auc.001.0552

prolific between the 1960s and 1980s, the work was distinguished further by his attention to dark complexions, clothing, and accessories. The reverberating roots of the New Negro in Hendricks's portraits are hauntingly present if not initially apparent; yet the authenticity of each portrait is reconfirmed in contemporary appropriateness that has influenced some of his peers along with generations of artists that have come behind him.

Jean-Michel Basquiat exemplified the 1980s punk art movement in America. Determined to become a legitimate artist star, he recontextualized the most common materials, objects, and surfaces in terms that ignored original purpose, fragility, or grittiness; and mirrored the urban, unapologetic rap and hip-hop œuvre from which his work partly evolved. He put the "counter" in counter-culture, masked himself as a miscreant and made the art-making process itself, at times, anti-social. Yet Basquiat, in all his originality, stood, at least partially, on the rebellious shoulders of Civil Rights era artists who made body prints, watered rocks as performance pieces, made off with flaking or bullet-ridden window frames for molding to encase paintings done on mattress ticking, and constructed shack miniatures out of junkyard scraps. Nonetheless, Basquiat was an art world anomaly whose meteoric rise epitomized what was and is possible in America.

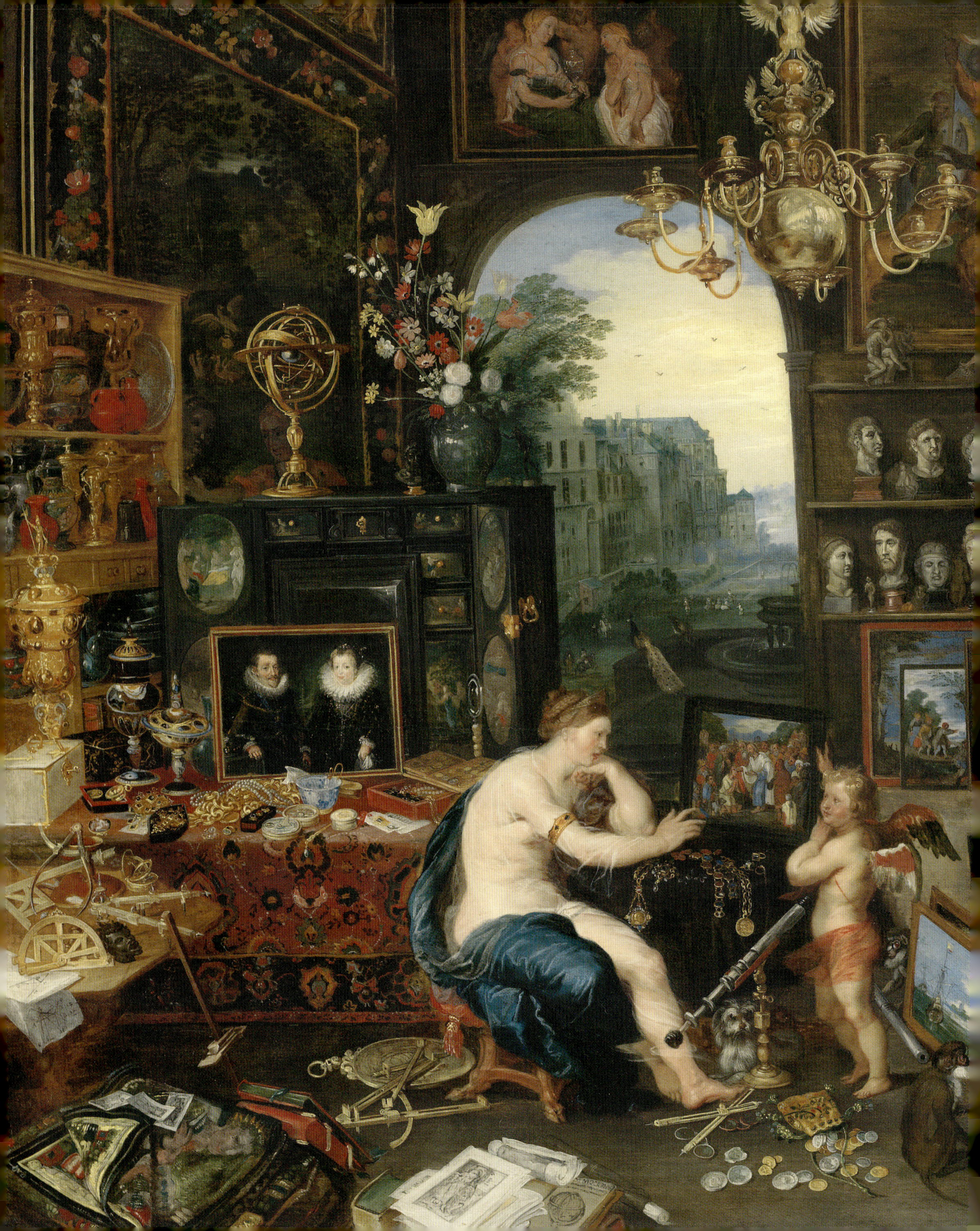

II. Connoisseurship and the Collector

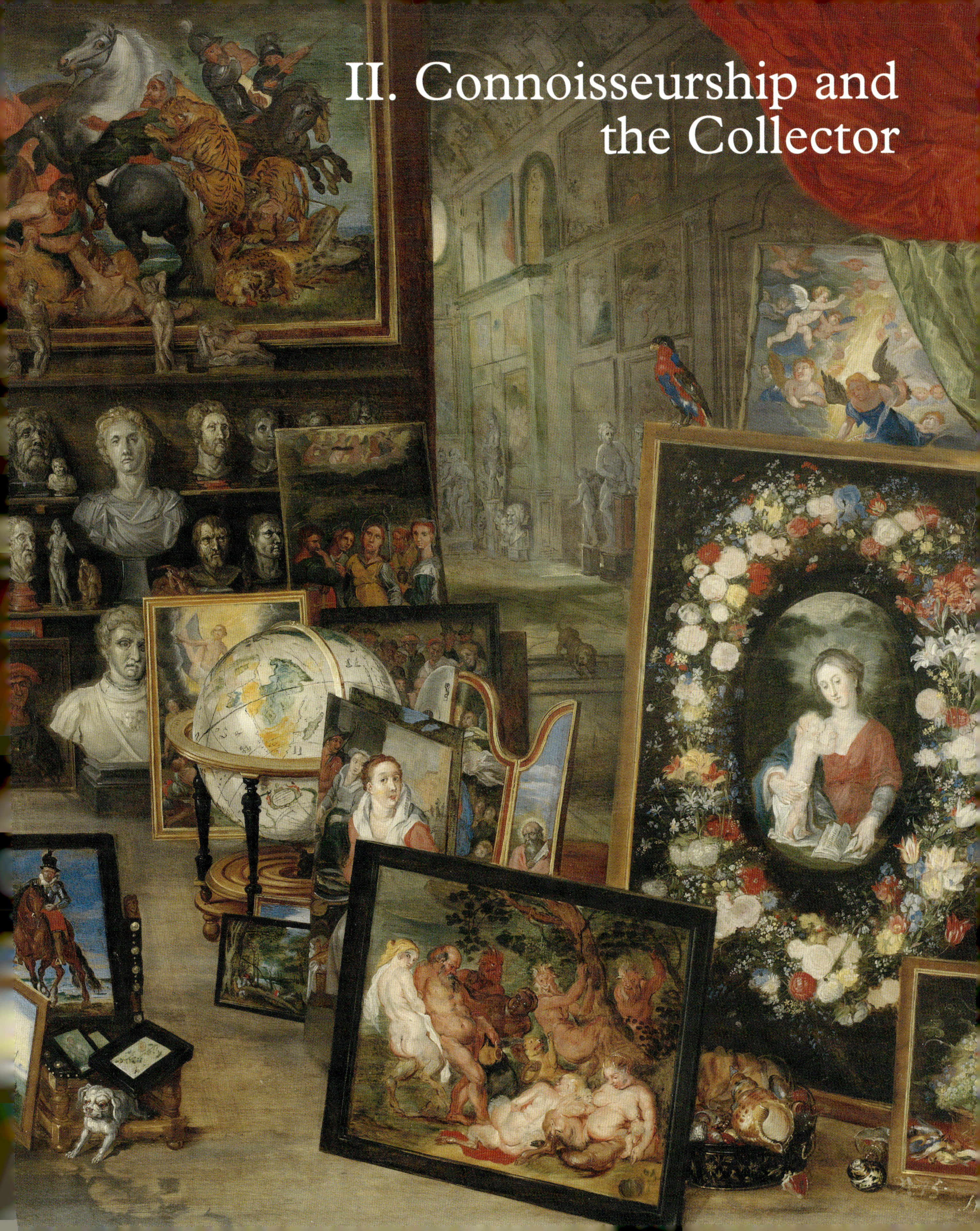

Embracing the Third Dimension
Some Guidelines on Collecting One Hundred Years of Figurative American Sculpture, 1840–1940

Joel Rosenkranz
Co-founder, Conner • Rosenkranz Gallery, New York

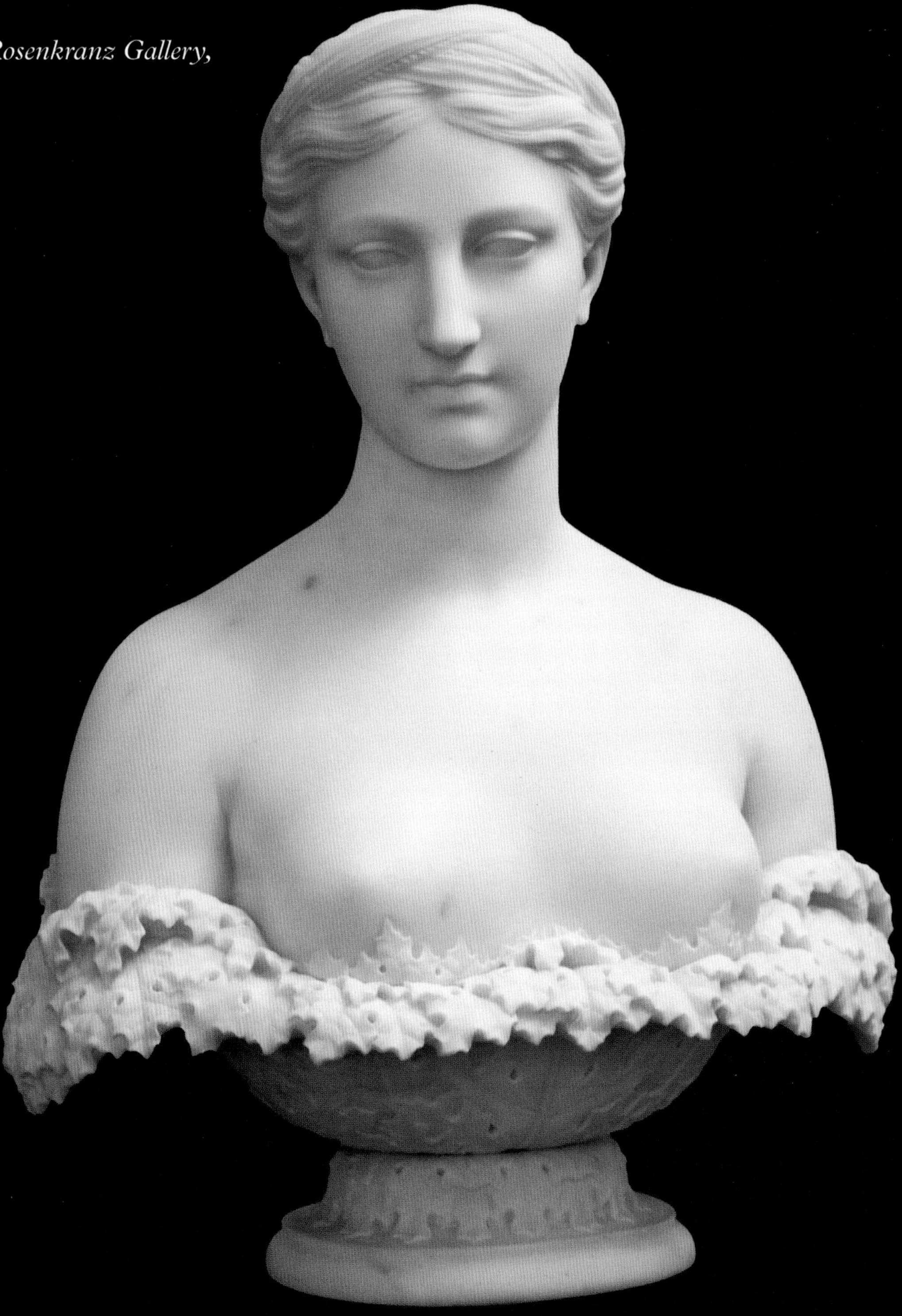

Unlike Europe, where the tradition of collecting works of sculpture for domestic display and personal pleasure is deeply rooted, richly varied, and widely accepted, in America sculpture is often viewed as a stepchild of the arts, a lesser sibling in comparison to the greater family of painting, drawing, and printmaking.

The reasons for this bias have principally to do with the relatively recent rise of a collecting population in America that barely goes back two hundred years, while in Europe the tradition has survived for closer to a thousand years. As a result, during our still-brief national history, we have had hardly a score of generations of collectors, and the habit of collecting is only recently embedded in our cultural DNA.

Moreover, the hesitation an American collector might have in focusing on sculpture may reflect the inherent challenges of embracing three-dimensional work. A primary obstacle is that a sculpture insistently occupies a physical space in a way that two-dimensional works do not. The singular object, whether displayed on a pedestal or table or standing on its own, is often heavy, intransigent, and cannot be ignored—and thus, by extension, requires a commitment on the part of the collector.

Yet sculpture by its nature rewards a collector in a way that a painting cannot. Unlike a painting, which offers only one point of view, straight on, a sculpture has multiple points of view. Indeed, it allows a 360-degree view, for it can be rotated or walked around as the impulse grabs the viewer, offering many different perspectives. For me, this is one of the great pleasures of living with sculpture: you are constantly able to see a favored but familiar object in a new way. In other words, it stays fresh. Another important aspect is the variety of materials commonly used—marble, bronze, terracotta, wood, stone, and even plaster—each of which has its own distinctive tactile and visual appeal.

While sculpture involves the same concerns for authenticity and condition that apply to all the arts, those issues become more complicated in sculpture because a work is often produced in multiples, and the history of its production may extend throughout the artist's career (and beyond). Collectors who become interested in a particular artist or period are almost obligated to do their own research—to build a reference library, visit museums and galleries to see other works by the same artist, learn from art historians and dealers, and even engage in dialogue with conservators to get a firmer grasp of relevant issues of execution and condition.

By the early 1830s, a handful of talented and ambitious American sculptors ventured to Italy to establish studios, drawn, like young artists from Europe, to Florence and Rome by the omnipresence of sculpture in public and private settings, which provided a constant source of inspiration. In addition, they benefited from inexpensive housing and the availability of studios, as well as access to skilled artisans and an endless supply of the finest marble with which to execute their models. The first generation of American Neo-classical sculptors in Italy included Thomas Crawford, Horatio Greenough, and Hiram Powers, the last becoming the pre-eminent American sculptor of the period.

Born in Vermont, Powers established a studio in Florence in 1837 that became a required stop by wealthy Americans on the Grand Tour, and he soon developed a robust business producing commissioned portraits and ideal busts and figures. In the course of his nearly forty-year career, Powers kept an atelier of carvers constantly busy producing allegorical busts such as *Proserpine* (Fig. 1), depicting the goddess of Springtime with a wreath of wheat in her hair as she rises out of the acanthus leaves (symbolizing immortality) around her waist. Unprecedentedly popular, *Proserpine* was produced in several versions, with more than 150 examples documented in studio records.[1]

Given this production scenario, how is it possible to determine the market value for a single bust of *Proserpine* when one comes on the market? The answer is that the interested collector needs to take into account the many examples that have entered public collections over the years (although on occasion de-accessioned), and also the numerous busts that, more than a century after they were carved, have suffered damage

Previous page
Jan Brueghel the Younger
The Five Senses: Sight, c.1625: detail of Fig. 1, pages 168–69

1.
Hiram Powers (1805–1873)
Proserpine, 1848–49
Marble on original socle
25 × 19 × 11 in.
(63.5 × 48.26 × 27.94 cm)
Signed H. POWERS/SCULP: (lower rear)
Conner • Rosenkranz, New York

2.
Harriet Goodhue Hosmer
(1830–1908)
Medusa, modeled 1854
Marble on original socle
27 ½ × 19 × 10 in.
(69.85 × 48.26 × 25.4 cm)
Signed HARRIET HOSMER/
ROME (rear of socle)
McGuigan Collection, Harpswell, ME

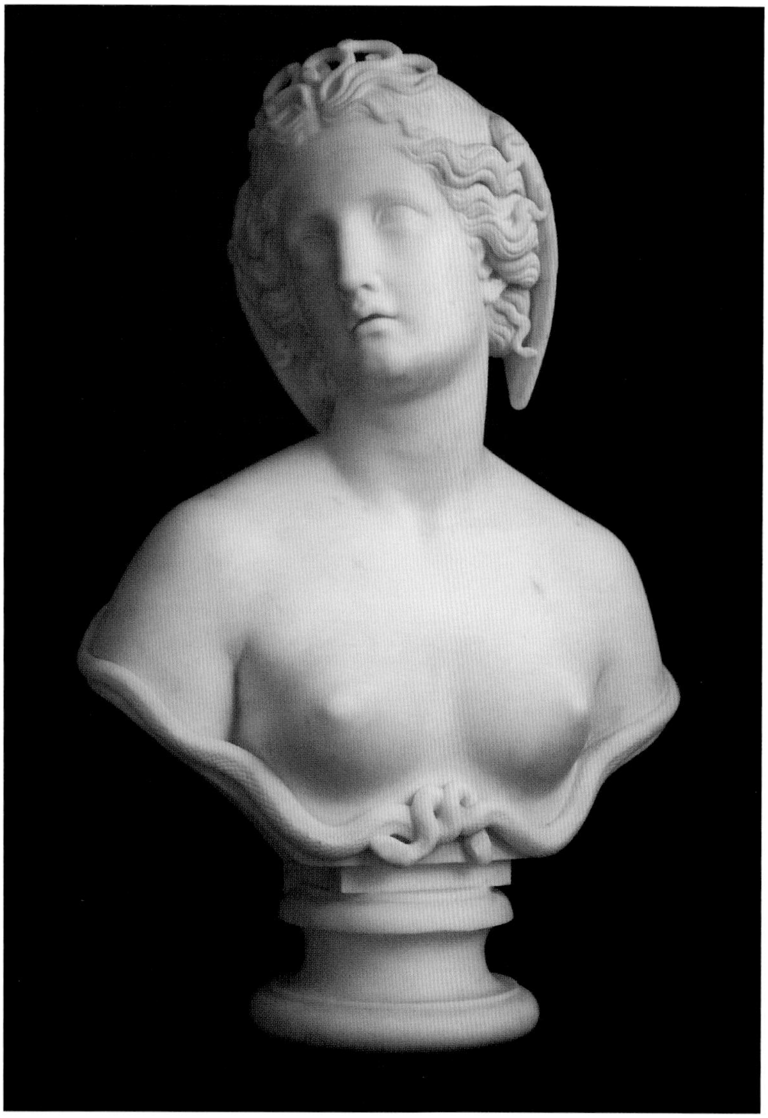

or repairs, compromising aesthetic and market value. As a result of these factors, despite the large number of marbles produced by Powers's studio, the actual number of desirable examples available today is surprisingly limited. Auction results for *Proserpine* and other ideal models by Powers are all over the place—and the wise collector should take these scattershot results with a grain of salt. If the goal is to acquire a fine example of *Proserpine* in excellent condition (and a bonus would be a good provenance linked back to the artist), then one should recognize that exceptional examples rarely come on the market—and view the cost in that context. This collecting philosophy would logically apply to all Neo-classical sculptures produced in multiples in the nineteenth century, not just Powers's marbles.

The next, and larger, wave of Americans arrived in Italy in the 1850s and included William Wetmore Story, Chauncey Bradley Ives, Randolph Rogers, William Henry Rinehart, and many others, who continued to explore mythological, biblical, literary, and other themes in their work. Concurrently, a small group of colorful, pioneering, independent-minded women sculptors congregated in Rome, such as Emma Stebbins, Harriet Hosmer, and Edmonia Lewis. Their acceptance by the artistic and critical community was not easy. Hosmer, for example, was publicly accused by a fellow American artist of not being the author of her own work, despite incontrovertibly demonstrating her competence and skill while serving an apprenticeship with leading British sculptor John Gibson before opening her own studio.[2]

More broadly, Henry James disparagingly termed this sorority of women sculptors "a white, marmorean flock,"[3] certainly not a term he would have applied to their male colleagues. Despite such challenges, many of these women created private and public works of great ambition and complexity, a prime example being Hosmer's *Medusa* (Fig. 2).

For those interested in studying examples of Neo-classical sculpture, public collections with strong holdings on the East Coast include The Metropolitan Museum of Art, the Newark Museum, the Museum of Fine Arts, Boston, the Chrysler Museum of Art in Virginia, and the Yale University Art Gallery. In the Midwest there is the Art Institute of Chicago; and on the West Coast the Huntington Library, Art Collections, and Botanical Gardens in San Marino, California, has an outstanding collection. Elsewhere, smaller selections of nineteenth-century marbles can be found in numerous museums across the country.

In contemplating Neo-classical marble sculpture, the primary consideration is always condition. Because it was common in the nineteenth century and later for marbles to be placed outdoors in gardens or other settings where they were exposed to weather and temperature changes, surviving busts and figures may show surface wear, pitting, excessive veining, missing digits, and overall loss of crisp surface detail. Often, these busts and figures may exhibit old repairs or, at the behest of a more recent owner, may have been sanded, polished, bleached, or otherwise manually treated in an attempt to recover a pristine surface. However, the resulting surface is most certainly not pristine; it does not reflect the surface intended by the artist or its original aesthetic impact. Thus, a potential purchaser should inspect the surface with great care, examining it for excessive veining (which becomes more prominent in marble that has been exposed to the weather), feeling the undercuts for evidence of polishing, and consulting with a conservator or trusted dealer before making an acquisition. The pleasure of acquiring an object of classical beauty in exemplary condition more than rewards the effort.

In the late nineteenth century there was a destination drift away from Italy and toward Paris among the next generation of talented young American sculptors, including Augustus Saint-Gaudens, Frederick MacMonnies, Edward McCartan, Janet Scudder, Harriet Frishmuth, and countless others. Paris, with its numerous training academies, salons, and foundries, was ideally suited to these eager Americans. And like Rome and Florence, it was affordable, with a plethora of inexpensive studios. One important result of this new direction was a shift away from marble as the preferred medium in favor of bronze, a material that was widely used by French artists working in the Beaux-Arts tradition. The tensile strength of bronze permitted more open compositions, providing the sculptor with greater freedom to explore a wider range of subject matter and emotional content. In addition, the play of light over the bronze surface activated the three-dimensional form and became an essential part of the visual experience. Bronze was also advantageous in terms of making replicas. Unlike the laborious process that Neo-classical sculptors such as Powers went through to have each new example of *Proserpine* carved by hand, requiring multiple specialty artisans to rough out and then carve particular details, a sculptor working in bronze could simply request that the foundry cast another example from the mold. The artist would (or should) remain involved in decisions regarding surface quality and patina, but the entire process of replication was considerably shortened.

Saint-Gaudens was among the first to recognize the potential of producing small-scale

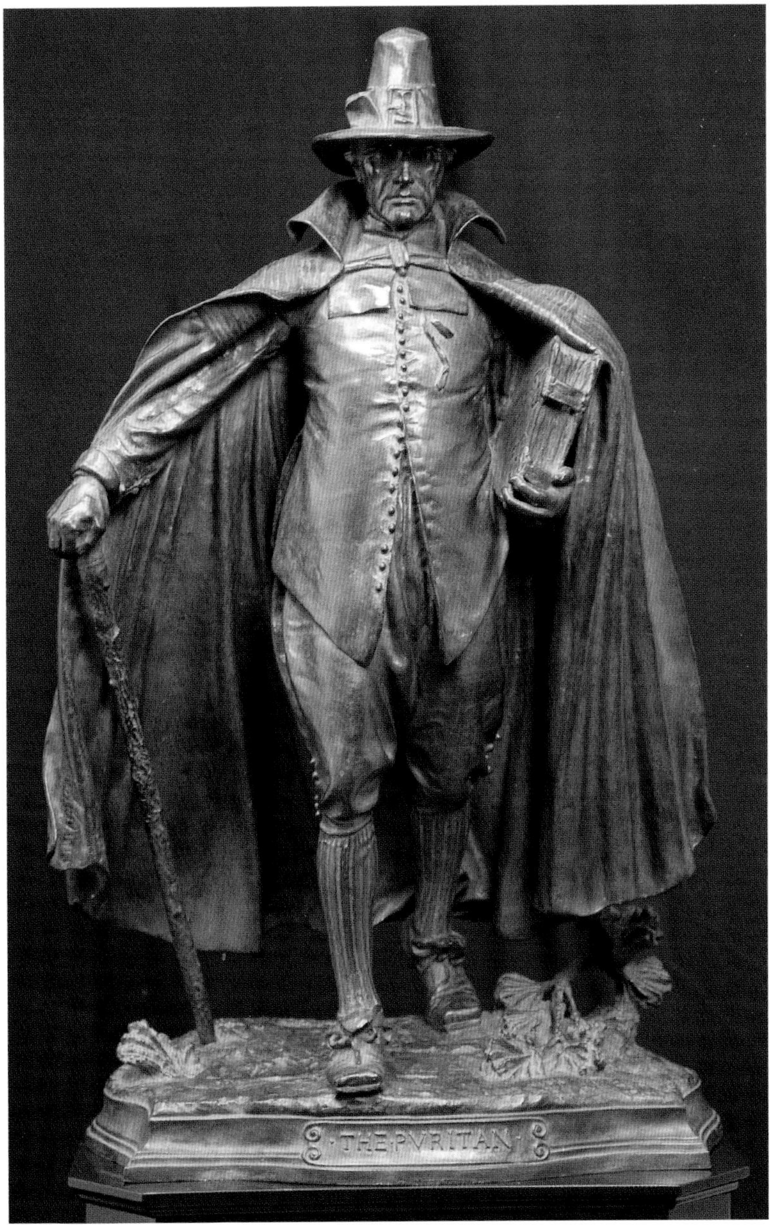

3.
Augustus Saint-Gaudens
(1848–1907)
The Puritan, 1883–86
Bronze
30 ½ × 19 ½ × 12 ¾ in.
(77.47 × 49.53 × 32.39 cm)
Signed AVGVSTVS SAINT GAVDENS (rear of self base), marked THE PVRITAN (front of self base)
Copyright by/Avgvstvs Saint Gavdens/MDCCCXCIX
(rear of self base)
Private collection

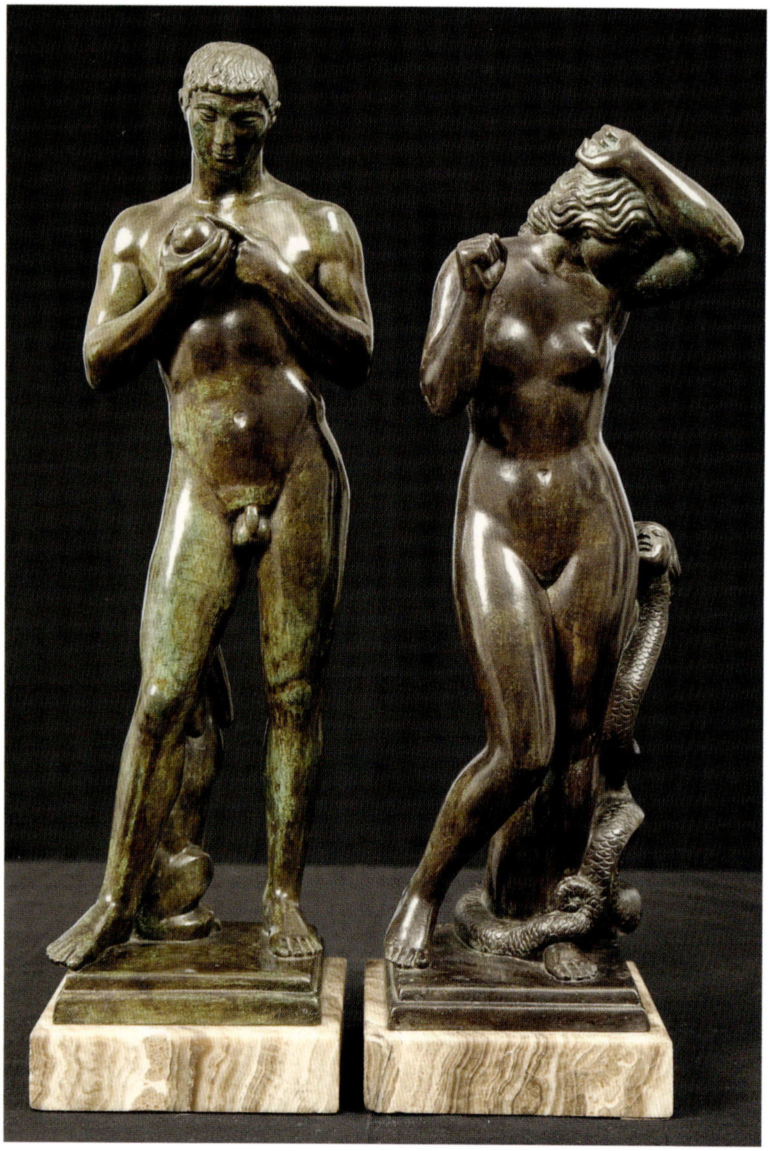

4.
Paul Howard Manship
(1885–1966)
Adam and Eve, 1924
Bronze on original marble bases
Adam: 17 ¾ × 6 × 4 ⅝ in.
(45.09 × 15.24 × 11.74 cm)
Signed P. Manship/© (rear top, self base), marked Alexis. Rudier/Fondeur Paris (rear, self base)
Eve: 16 × 6 ⅜ × 5 ¼ in.
(40.64 × 16.19 × 13.33 cm)
Signed P. Manship/© (rear top, self base), marked Alexis. Rudier/Fondeur Paris (rear, self base)
Private collection

bronzes for the home with such works as *Robert Louis Stevenson* (1887–88), *Diana* (1892–93), and *The Puritan* (Fig. 3)—of which more than forty casts were ultimately produced.[4] Supported by only four narrow points on the base, the imposing wide-caped, striding figure of Deacon Chapin succeeds in part because of the play of light on the numerous in-and-out and layered elements of his costume. His hat, cape with deep folds, semi-buttoned vest, and striped stockings all catch the light and help animate the form.

As America entered the twentieth century, it also entered a golden age of sculpture production and acquisition. Coinciding with the creation of industrial wealth, the growth of cities, and the cultural aspirations of the moneyed classes, people of means started to collect small-scale sculpture for display in their homes and businesses, and to purchase or commission larger garden and fountain sculptures for the grounds of their homes and estates. In addition, demand for sculpture to fill public plazas, parks, and other open spaces kept pace with the private appetite for sculpture, and an enormous array of commercial, civic, and educational buildings incorporated sculptural ornament.

To meet this cultural change, the National Sculpture Society (NSS) was formed in 1893 with the goal of fostering further appreciation of sculpture. By the 1920s, the NSS had organized two landmark surveys of contemporary American sculpture, in New York (1923) and San Francisco (1929). During these years numerous sculpture exhibitions mounted by museums traveled across the country, and galleries and showrooms also got into the act, cultivating a clientele with exhibitions. The Gorham Manufacturing Company, for example, included sculpture made by its bronze division in its popular showroom on Fifth Avenue in New York City. Meeting strong demand, Gorham published a sale catalogue in 1928 titled *Famous Small Bronzes* that featured works by twenty-five sculptors, ranging from bookends to fountains and varying in price from $30 to $3500.[5]

With the explosion in the number of working sculptors, different "schools" developed. Some artists were primarily interested in the theme of the Western frontier, such as Frederic Remington, Charles Russell, Alexander Phimister Proctor, and Hermon Atkins MacNeil. Others, like Edward Kemeys, Anna Hyatt Huntington, and Albert Laessle had a lifelong interest in animal subjects, and these artists continued a tradition established in France by Antoine-Louis Barye and other *animalier* sculptors in the nineteenth century. Some sculptors were actively engaged in the production of garden and fountain sculpture for private and public settings. Harriet Frishmuth dominated this market, but other notable exponents were Edith Parsons, Malvina Hoffman, and Edward McCartan.

Still others satisfied the demand for domestic imagery: Bessie Potter Vonnoh was the leading artist in this area.

At the same time, particularly after the groundbreaking Armory Show in 1913, other movements emerged, such as the Ashcan School, which, like the school of painters for whom the name was coined, celebrated quotidian life. Mahonri Young depicted the masculine world of labor while Abastenia Eberle explored the tender world of domestic life in numerous mother-and-child subjects. In addition, there was a generation of conservative-minded sculptors who went to study at the American Academy in Rome, where they embraced an archaic and classicizing style. Paul Manship, Paul Jennewein, John Gregory, and Leo Friedlander were among the most successful artists in this group, and Manship's *Adam and Eve* epitomizes this style (Fig. 4).

With the growing popularity of bronze sculpture, it became increasingly necessary to understand the capabilities of particular foundries. In the nineteenth century, the primary means of making bronzes was "sand casting," in which individual elements of a sculpture were pressed into sand molds, cast separately, and then pinned together to form the whole. John Williams Inc. and the Henry-Bonnard Company, among other firms, utilized this method. In contrast, the ancient method of "lost wax" (or *cire-perdue*), revived in modern times, utilized a wax model of the entire sculpture that was then encased in a mold. When molten bronze was poured into the mold, the wax was "lost," replaced by the bronze. This method allowed a sculptor to work on the wax model, usually leading to a bronze surface that was more refined than a sand cast.

Roman Bronze Works established a lost-wax foundry in New York in 1900 and during the next three decades was arguably the best American foundry available to sculptors. Its chief rival in quality was Gorham's foundry in Rhode Island. But there were several smaller foundries in the New York area—including the American Art Foundry, the Kunst Foundry, B. Zoppo, Griffoul and Brothers, and S. Klaber & Company—whose capabilities were mostly limited to casting smaller-scale works. The lifespan of each of these foundries was relatively brief, but knowledge of their history can be useful to a collector: for example, when you hold a bronze of *The Windy Doorstep* (Fig. 5) by Abastenia Eberle that has an S. Klaber & Co. mark, you can be assured that it is a period cast produced around the time it was modeled by the artist.

American sculptors active in Europe similarly had multiple foundry options, and all had their favorite firms. Frederick MacMonnies preferred Gruet Jeune Fondeur and Jaboeuf et Rouard in Paris, while Paul Manship's Paris foundry of choice was Alexis Rudier, best known as Auguste Rodin's foundry, and skilled in producing sharp

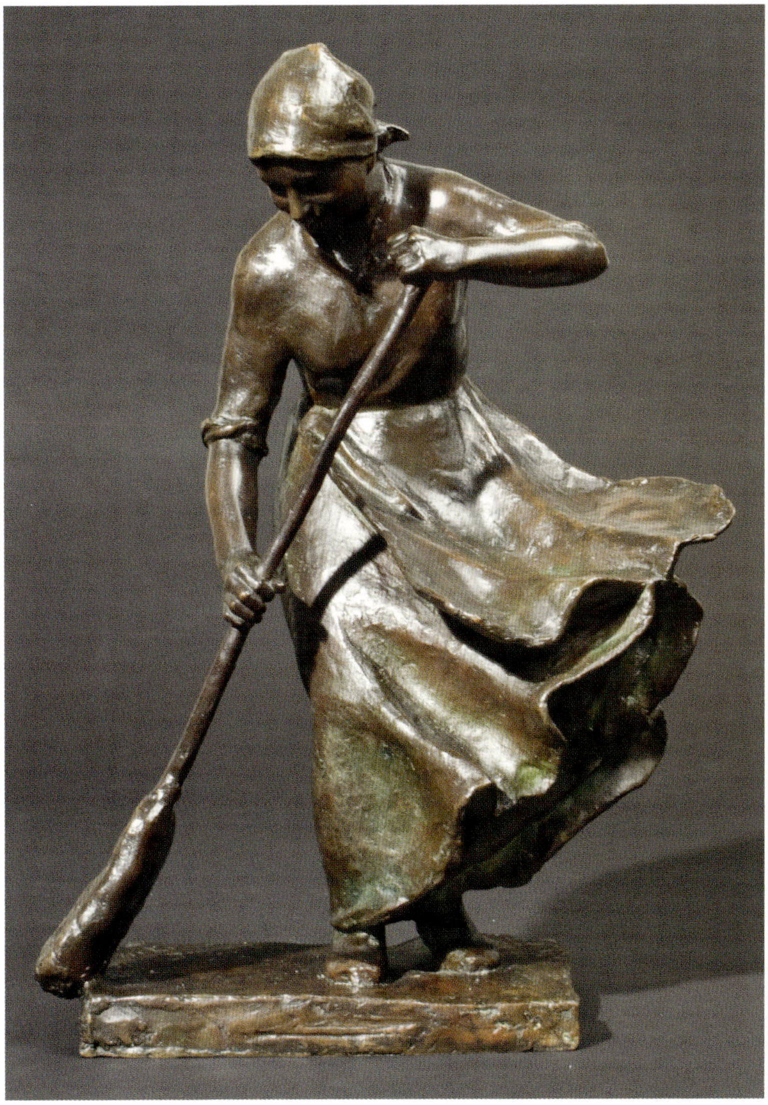

5.
Abastenia St. Leger Eberle
(1878–1942)
The Windy Doorstep, 1910
Bronze
14 × 10 ½ × 6 in.
(35.56 × 26.67 × 15.24 cm)
Signed A. StL. Eberle/1910,
marked S. KLABER & CO
(rear edge of self base)
Private collection, Washington, DC

casts with lustrous patinas. Priessmann Bauer in Munich was Paul Jennewein's preferred foundry; for Cecil Howard, who spent much of his career in Paris, C. Valsuani was his only foundry.

One important point about the casting history of a sculpture is that bronzes cast during the course of an artist's career by different foundries (or even by the same foundry but with varying degrees of artist involvement) may vary noticeably in quality. On inspection, a bronze may be light or heavy, the composition may be sharply cast or not, the surface may be thoroughly "chased" (that is, finished by hand to a certain level of refinement) or not, and the applied patina may be complex, rich, and lustrous—or not.

So while there is a certain understandable appeal for collectors in acquiring a bronze made soon after the moment of artistic inspiration and execution, it does not necessarily guarantee that it is a better cast than one produced later in a career by another foundry. Indeed, a later cast by Roman may be superior to an earlier cast by Klaber in all of these respects; but the reverse could also be true. The issue for a collector is thus really about personal choice and connoisseurship—being familiar with the range of possibilities—and deciding what suits one's individual taste.

For the collector of bronzes, nearly always the first thing to look for is the foundry mark, even ahead of the signature, because the mark of the foundry can not only provide useful information but also be an initial indicator of quality. An Alexis Rudier mark, for example, will signal what is probably a fine cast. Once the Rudier mark is identified, then it would not be a surprise to see a typical Rudier patina of black over green on a bronze— although the foundry was capable of producing a wide variety of other tonalities.[6]

Foundry marks are usually stamped on a bronze after it is cast and chased, but before it is patinated— in other words, prior to being fully finished. The foundry may use a metal stamp (e.g. "ROMAN BRONZE WORKS N.Y." or "GORHAM CO. FOUNDERS"), and an artisan hammers it on to the sculpture or base, discreetly placed where it will not distract from the image. Sometimes, if the stamp is applied unevenly, one side may be more legible than another. In rare instances, the mark may be stamped on the hollow interior of a bronze, and in some cases it may not be there at all, either at the request of the sculptor or because there is not an appropriate spot to locate it, or even because of an oversight at the foundry.

Encountering a bronze without a foundry mark is when the fun begins. Then it is up to the person considering the object to exercise a level of connoisseurship—examining the casting quality, inspecting the details to see if they are finely chased, and gauging the patina to see if it shows evidence of wear and age.

If a sculpture is small enough to hold comfortably in your hands, the first step is to assess its weight. Unlike the popular notion that more is better, when it comes to early twentieth-century bronzes, less is actually better. A light cast signifies that expert artisans made an efficient mold and used the minimal amount of bronze (which is costly) in the casting process. So, assuming the hollow underside is not filled with plaster or core material from casting, and the walls are thin, a light cast is usually a quality cast.

Next, consider wear. Evidence of handling wear is a hallmark of older bronzes. In the process of repeatedly picking up a bronze or holding it in a habitual way, contact with skin can result in a minuscule diminishment of the patina in those areas. If the action is repeated regularly over a period of years, some of the applied patina will actually be rubbed away, revealing more of the underlying warm coppery bronze; this change is known, not surprisingly, as "handling wear." For me, this surface alteration is an appealing feature because it is a visible indicator of the sculpture's history and suggests that it was treasured and handled regularly. In some instances, however, excessive or careless handling, or on occasion the misguided application of a metal cleaner, will cause the patina to become distressed to an excessive degree. When this happens, a conservator needs to "restore" the patina, which is best done with a dealer or curator providing guidance.

Bronze fountains and garden sculpture will eventually display oxidation of the surface as the copper component of the bronze chemically interacts with air and rainwater to produce copper oxides, which may streak or totally discolor the surface. The resulting green, called "verdigris," is an acceptable appearance for many owners. However, if the oxidation is excessive and unattractive or if the integrity of the metal is at risk, then it is best to consider re-patination. In that instance it is advisable to use protected areas of the original patina as a guide. Or, if none has survived, use other casts of the same sculpture in good condition to inform the conservator or patineur at a foundry.

After examining a sculpture for its casting and patination, one finally looks for a signature, which is usually found on the base, but may also be found on a lower portion of the sculptural image itself. The signature is often put into the wax model during an early stage of the casting process. An artist's signature may vary during the course of a career. For example, before marrying Robert Vonnoh in 1899, Bessie O. Potter signed with her maiden name; afterwards all her bronzes were signed "Bessie Potter Vonnoh." Mahonri Young tried several iterations before settling on "Mahonri," adjacent to his thumbprint, likely by the 1910s. Often the signature will be accompanied by a copyright symbol ©, if the artist believes the model will be popular, along with the date on which it was modeled, although not necessarily cast.

After World War I, a generation of sculptors who were either born in Europe or had trained there put a Modernist spin on the figure or, in some cases, abandoned it altogether. Key players in this group include Gaston Lachaise (once an assistant to Paul Manship), who pushed the figure to an extreme, sometimes to the point of distortion, as a means of conveying his appreciation of the female form as embodied by his wife and muse, Isabel Nagle. Elie Nadelman, who was born in Poland and rose to fame in London when Helena Rubinstein bought his entire exhibition in 1911, had his first show in New York at Alfred Stieglitz's 291 Gallery five years later. Inspired by classical Greek prototypes, Nadelman's highly polished heads with radically simplified features expanded the parameters of possibility for sculpture. Nadelman's friend Hunt Diederich was fascinated by the innate beauty, rhythm, and dynamism of animals, which he depicted with extraordinary simplicity in bronze sculptures and such metal decorative objects as chandeliers and firescreens. Alexander Archipenko, Ukrainian by birth, whose career took him to Paris and Berlin before he arrived in America in 1923, combined sculpture and painting early on and consistently experimented with deliberate distortion and fragmentation and colorist effects. Chicagoan John Storrs spent a long apprenticeship in Europe, becoming Rodin's last assistant before leaving the figure entirely for the creation of his celebrated architectural sculptures.

Given the peripatetic nature of these artists and their careers, their use of different foundries at home and abroad, and the frequent lack of foundry marks on their bronzes, it is sometimes difficult to know where or when or in what numbers and sizes a work was cast. Often no clear records exist that confirm the authenticity of a particular sculpture under consideration. In such instances, it is most helpful to have a detailed exhibition history or provenance tracing the work back to the artist. Failing that, it is necessary to locate another authentic cast of the same model and make a side-by-side inspection, comparing refinement of surface detail, similarity of patina (although there can often be a great deal of variation in patinas of the same model), aged appearance of the underside of the bronze if visible, and exact measurements of all three dimensions.

The reason for precise measurement is to determine if a bronze is a surmoulage—a bronze cast from another bronze rather than from an artist's original plaster. Although unethical and frowned on by the artistic community, it is legal to have a copy cast if a sculpture is not protected by copyright. In such cases, the copy will be a fraction smaller in all dimensions than the original and will often lack the crisp surface detail that characterizes the original. The problem of surmoulages is not widespread, but it does occur, so if a bronze is suspect, careful measurement and comparison are essential.

Generally, most American sculptors did not cast bronzes in editions or set numbers. Rather, they ordered new bronzes based on sales or exhibition needs.[7] Accordingly, the number of casts of different models might vary considerably. Bronzes ordered by the artist are called "lifetime bronzes" and include models of earlier works that the sculptor cast toward the end of a career. After an artist's death, the estate could decide to continue production of a work for various reasons: to satisfy a strong ongoing demand; to cast work that was not previously produced in a permanent material; to complete an edition number that is deemed appropriate; to fund research and scholarship; or simply to benefit the heirs financially.

The families of Elie Nadelman, Gaston Lachaise, Alexander Archipenko, and William Zorach, among others, are examples of heirs who at one time or another authorized the casting of bronzes to be sold with the imprimatur of the artist's estate. Although casting decisions regarding the quality and appearance of the bronzes are obviously made without the involvement of the artist, every good-faith effort is usually made by the estate to produce bronzes that are consistent with the sculptor's aesthetic and known standards. However, changing foundry technology almost guarantees that a 1970s estate bronze, say, of *Classic Torso* (1924) by Lachaise will be noticeably different from a lifetime cast from the 1920s or early 1930s. The market does distinguish between "lifetime" and "estate" casts and generally places a premium on the former.

Beginning in the 1920s, especially in New York, a generation of modern sculptors began to embrace a radically different approach toward artistic creation. Robert Laurent, John Flannagan, William Zorach, Chaim Gross, John Hovannes, José de Creeft, and Berta Margoulies were among the dozens of artists who temporarily abandoned bronze in favor of wood and stone, in part driven by economic necessity, since bronze casting was expensive while wood and stone were affordable or easily accessible as found materials or recycled objects. But the compelling reason for this shift was the desire by these artists to have a direct connection with the medium itself, to derive inspiration from the inherent qualities of the block of stone or wood (which they often attacked without a preliminary model or sketch), and with the view that the arduous task of carving it was an essential part of the creation of a work of art. In the late 1930s, many of these artists formed the Sculptors Guild to organize outdoor exhibitions in the New York area, providing a wider platform for their very personal and progressive view of sculpture-making.

One of the most influential of this group of "direct carvers" was the immensely talented but tragically short-lived John Flannagan. Early in his career, starting in 1924, he employed various kinds of wood as his primary material, but over the course of the next decade, he turned to direct carving of field stones, river stones, and other stones he found. In a somewhat mystical artist's statement, "The Image in the Rock," included in the catalogue of a memorial exhibition at the Museum of Modern Art in 1942, Flannagan wrote:

> *Often there is an occult attraction in the very shape of a rock as sheer abstract form. It fascinates with a queer atavistic nostalgia, as either a remote memory or a stirring impulse from the depth of the unconscious.... To that instrument of the subconscious, the hand of the sculptor, there exists an image within every rock. The creative act of realization merely frees it.*[8]

Flannagan's deep and spiritual connection to the beauty of stone is apparent in such works as *Sitting Figure* (Fig. 6), among many others.

By the late 1930s, when Flannagan's health began to decline, and until his death in 1942, he authorized the making of a small number of bronze casts of a handful of his carved stone models as a way of modestly expanding his output. Given the slow and arduous nature of direct carving, several other sculptors had already made the same decision to produce bronze and/or terracotta replicas of unique stone or wood carvings to increase their potential income stream. William Zorach and Chaim Gross, particularly, authorized small bronze editions. While a unique stone or wood carving is distinguished by the quality of the material and the nature of its carving, the same cannot be said of a bronze cast, the patina of which cannot, and does not try to, mimic the surface of the original carving. From a market standpoint, the original carving is usually valued more highly than a bronze or terracotta cast.

Depending on their size, wood carvings might display surface cracks, or "checks," a normal by-product of the seasonal changes in temperature: as wood expands in hot weather and contracts in cold, the internal pressure results in slight separations of the wood on the surface. Once checks appear, the wood is usually stable and does not change further. If checking was extensive, a sculptor would likely use a filler material to repair it. The extent of checking and the condition of the surface of a wood carving are thus considerations in assessing it. Some sculptors embraced the natural grain of wood, checks and all, and saw it as integral to the natural life of a carving. However, sculptors whose taste was a bit more formal sought to avoid this result by carving laminated blocks of wood—a strategy that usually prevented checking from occurring.

The hundred years between 1840 and 1940 should be considered a golden age in the production of sculpture in America, as one generation after the next explored different artistic centers at home and abroad, the changing nature of materials and their inherent possibilities, and the constantly shifting themes from the ideal to the ordinary. In the process, these successive waves of sculptors continuously expanded assumptions about the nature of sculpture—a metamorphosis that continues to this day.

6.
John B. Flannagan
(1895–1942)
Sitting Figure (also *Resting*)
1927
Brown sandstone
13 ¼ × 9 ½ × 16 ½ in.
(33.66 × 24.13 × 41.91 cm)
Collection of the Columbus Museum of Art, Columbus, Ohio: Museum Purchase with funds provided by the Greater Columbus Irish Cultural Foundation, 2018.015, acquired in honor of Michael D. Hall, Adjunct Curator of Folk and Self-Taught Art, with support from his friends and family: Bonnie and Chris Duckworth, Pat Glascock, Ken Katz, David Lusenhop, Rane Hall and Bruce McColl, George and Nannette Maciejunes, Dan Shogren, David and Ronnie Thauberger, and Gary and Donna Zych

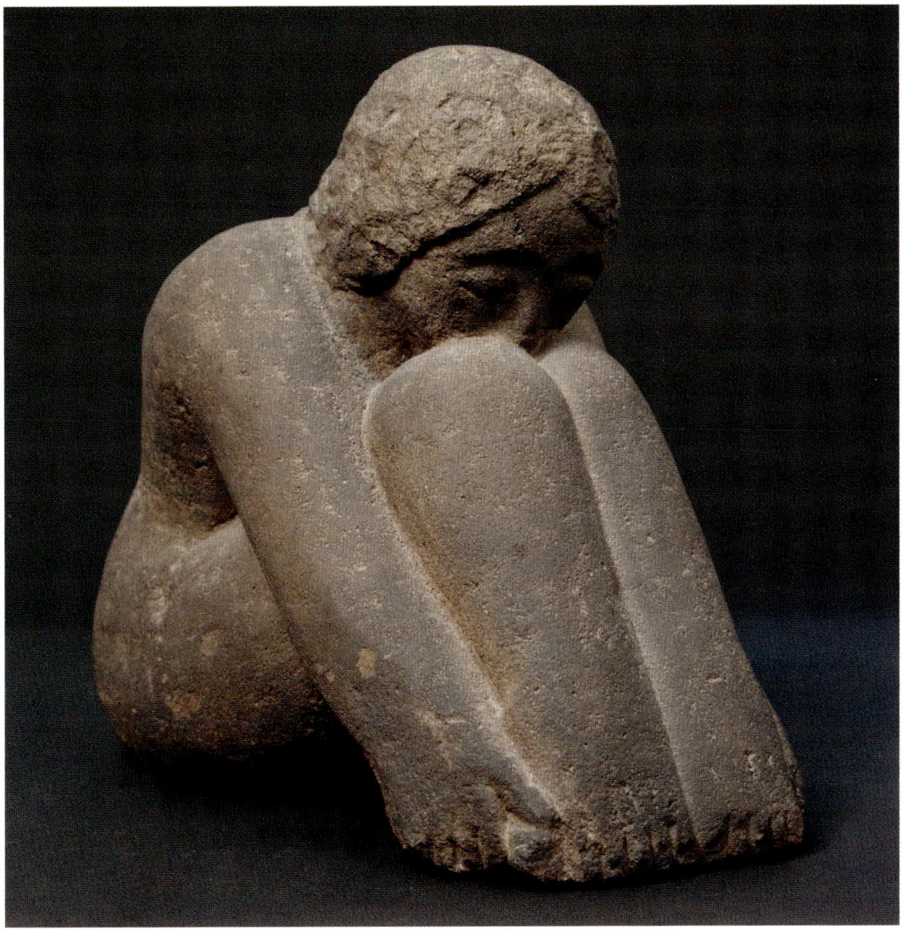

American Period Frame Connoisseurship in the Twenty-First Century

Tracy Gill and Simeon Lagodich
Frame Scholars, Consultants, and Co-founders of Gill & Lagodich Fine Period Frames, New York

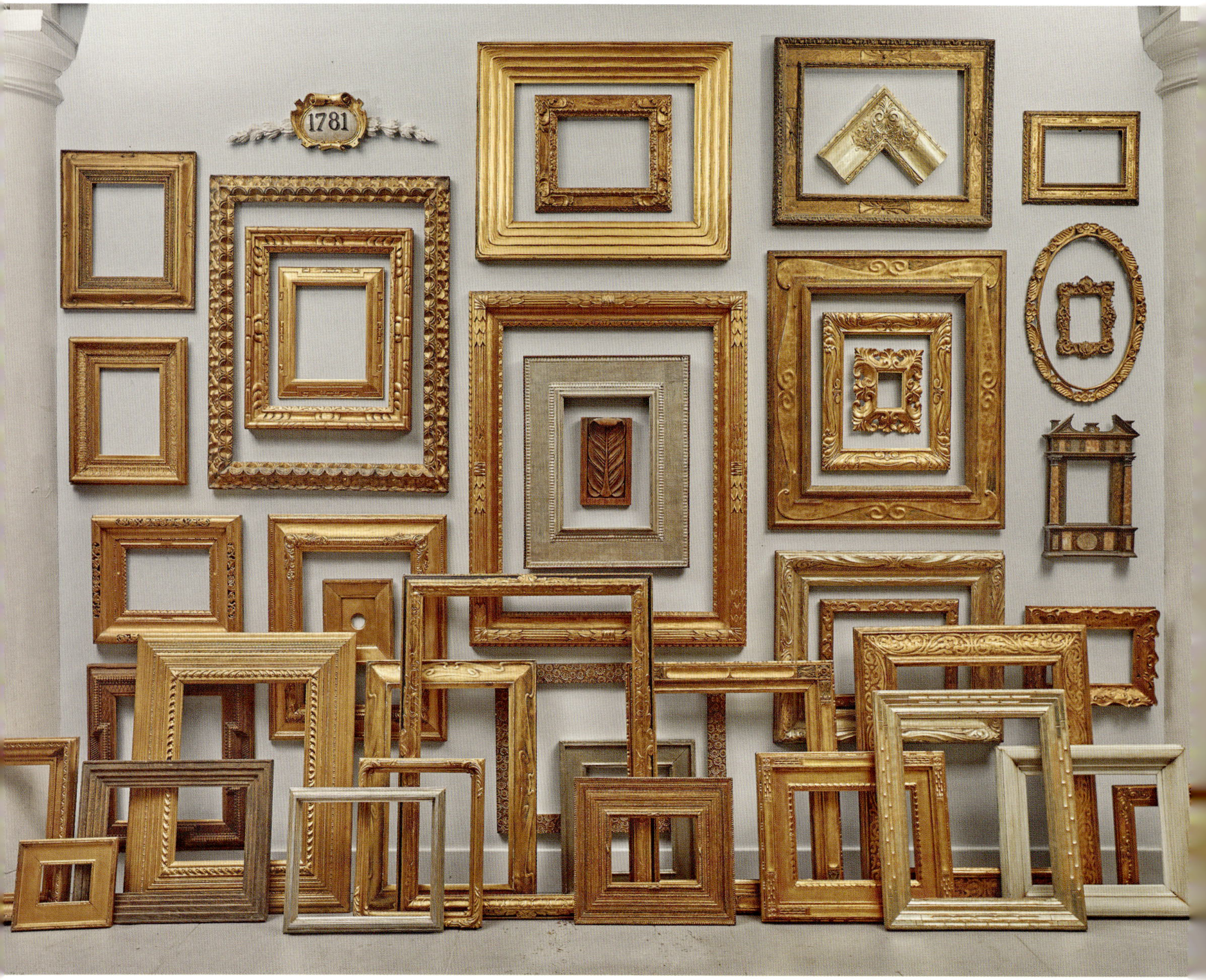

Period frame connoisseurship is, simply put, deep knowledge of the history, style, and application of frames. Displayed empty, containing a painting, built in place or as a moveable object, the frame appears consistently across the timeline of art history. To be clear, period frames are not just "antique" but are also "modern" and their scholarship incorporates many historical and contemporary styles, e.g. Old Master, Neo-classical, Arts and Crafts, Modernist, and Minimalist. A frame provides the basic function as protection for a picture, but it is not merely a utilitarian object. The picture frame hangs at the nexus of fine art and decorative art, connecting with paintings, drawings, prints, and photography, and also with furniture, interior design, and exterior architecture.

In the broadest context, the learning curve of frame scholarship is akin to that of furniture—a virtually limitless study that crosses many cultures and spans multiple centuries. A connoisseur of frames sees each frame as an individual object worthy of consideration. Ideally, each frame must be understood in the context of its time, in relation to the art it surrounded and the interior it lived in.

Frames have been integral to art since time immemorial. From cave paintings to Egyptian tombs to Pompeian frescoes, man has sought to delineate with borders a world apart from everyday reality. The earliest appearances were frames as painted borders or moldings integral to a picture and the architectural surround. The mobile or detached frame for secular paintings appeared around the thirteenth century. At first functioning as a protective surround for a portable picture, the frame developed with decidedly decorative tie-ins to interior furnishings. As pictures became more commonly moveable, separate from permanent installations or no longer painted directly on to a wall, frames became necessary furniture, designed to protect paintings and focus attention. From elaborate architectonic and ecclesiastic constructions and simple protective moldings, frames evolved to share aesthetic concerns with paintings in addition to interior environments. The marriage of decorative art and fine art lasted well into the twentieth century when painting, challenging traditional roles, often moved out of the frame to engage surroundings without an intermediary.

As frame consultants, it is our job to discriminate and determine when a period frame matters, when its separation from a painting matters, and to advise when restoration of an original or replacement with a period-appropriate frame is needed.

We are fortunate to be frame dealers as well as scholars and have therefore lived with hundreds of frames for many years. Collecting frames since the 1980s, beginning with one-of-a-kind folk art, we advanced into gilded and finer wood frames that caught our eye; the education came later. As many longtime art collectors will affirm, one learns by doing, by looking, by purchasing mistakes or masterpieces one does or does not recognize at the time. As a gallery business for three decades and counting, over ten thousand frames have crossed our threshold; better and worse, each frame has taught us something. Spanning four hundred years, the earliest example dates from fifteenth-century Italy and our inventory moves forward to unique artist-made frames of the early twentieth century. Our small personal collection of favorites and extensive gallery inventory of several thousand frames serve as a reference library of historical ornament, original patinas, gold colors, fabrication methods, framemakers, artists, and designers, from which we continually draw knowledge and make comparisons every time someone asks us to reframe a painting (Fig. 1).

In spite of centuries of rich history, the picture frame has often been an afterthought in the art world: originals lost to changing fashion, new owner's taste, damage and neglect, high restoration costs, and more. However, art buyers on all levels should understand the value and importance of good frames. In essence the serious collector is a connoisseur, collecting with deep knowledge on two levels: the art and the frame.

As the evolution of American framing is relatively short in comparison with the European tradition, it can come as a surprise to European painting and frame collectors, dealers, and connoisseurs to learn that certain

1.
A wall of empty picture frames, each freed from its original function as a surround for a work of art, reveals the frame as an art form in itself. Here, a selection of sixteenth-century European to twentieth-century American frames at the Gill & Lagodich Gallery, New York

American frames of the late nineteenth and early twentieth centuries are some of the most valuable and sought-after frames in the world today. Comparable in value to some important American paintings, stellar American frames have sold for hundreds of thousands of dollars.

We consult for museums and collectors to review and assess which frames are correct, original, unrestored, or show clues to previous alterations. Our careful assessment of a collection can run the gamut from paintings we consider well framed to those we call "frame emergencies."

Preserving the original marriage effectively invites the viewer to enter a period room for the painting. But an original frame may be lost, not to a current collector's or curator's taste, or not up to the level of the rest of a collection, and then it is time for a change.

To advise on reframing a painting, we take into consideration the palette, the medium, the date, and perhaps developmental changes throughout an artist's career that might warrant different frame styles.

The academic approach means looking for historical precedent—including photographic records of public exhibitions and private collection galleries—as essential to understanding ornament, design influences, and traditional applications of a particular model of frame in relation to specific types of art and associated artists.

The default framing solution is to place an American painting in an American frame of the same period. What we refer to as "framing by the numbers" is a somewhat rote exercise which has become the orthodoxy of the period frame gallery. For instance, an American Hudson River School painting from the mid-nineteenth century, e.g. 1860s, would be framed in a gilded Neo-classical fluted cove frame or a custom-ordered replica of the same style.

There are more than a few exceptions to the default solution. The subject and geography of the painting, as well as an artist's travels, may affect frame choice. American artists might have preferred non-American frames for certain of their paintings. As many of them painted abroad, frame styles from other countries can be appropriate for paintings of foreign subjects: for example, a French frame for an American Impressionist artist working in France, e.g. Mary Cassatt (1844–1926), Willard Metcalf (1858–1925), and Theodore Robinson (1852–1896), or Italianate frames for works by expatriate artists such as Elihu Vedder (1836–1923) or Charles Caryl Coleman (1840–1928). A well-traveled artist like John Singer Sargent (1856–1925) might be appropriately framed in American, French, or Italian frames. Artists who traveled to the Middle East, e.g. Sanford Robinson Gifford (1823–1880), Frederic Edwin Church (1826–1900), and Edwin Lord Weeks (1849–1903), might have chosen "Orientalist" frames, sometimes inventive variations of the artist's own design.

When an artist is not known to have designed or commissioned frames himself or to have preferred a particular frame style, then we will recommend an exemplary model of the same period, and, perhaps, geographical origin, as the painting. We cannot emphasize enough that every painting deserves individual consideration, even when framing multiple works by the same artist.

For example, Gill & Lagodich has reframed eight paintings by George Inness (1825–1894) for the Art Institute of Chicago.[1] The paintings date across many decades from 1848 (not long after the artist's first showing at the National Academy) to 1894 (the year of his death), and show the development of his style and subject matter. For years, most of the paintings were displayed adjacently in the same frame style—a collector's or dealer's frame of French Louis XIII-derived bunched floral design, gilded and finished with a chalky pinkish patina—not the ideal choice for a nineteenth-century American landscape painting. While the original collector might have preferred a uniform look in his home, when an artist's body of work spans years, such uniformity is not the best framing choice for a museum. We have been working on the Inness project for over two decades, reframing one by one in period-correct models. Approaching the project academically, the curators chose replacement frames contemporaneous with the dates of each painting in styles the artist himself might have chosen. The result is that, whether one "knows" period frames or not, one can get a sense of which paintings date to the earlier and later decades of the nineteenth century, simply by looking at the properly married canvases and frames. Thus the visitor can really absorb the development of a single artist over his lifetime; the difference in viewing is remarkable.

When framing works by an artist who bridges the nineteenth and twentieth centuries, generally one would select a frame close to the true date the painting was made, although sometimes a painting dealer or collector might frame a later work in an earlier style, from the height of an artist's popularity. Thomas Moran (1837–1926) comes to mind, as nineteenth-century frames seem to be preferred for this painter.

Artists themselves used different frame designs at different points in their careers. For example, framing paintings by Childe Hassam (1859–1935) requires some study of what the artist wanted, as the artist himself chose very different frame designs over the years. It is common for painting dealers to reframe many Hassam paintings in an early twentieth-century so-called "Hassam-style" cassetta frame, as the artist did commission variations of these after 1904. We maintain it is a mistake to frame an 1890s Hassam painting in an Arts and Crafts model when the artist was selecting more traditional European frames at that time. The same applies to the Hassam flag paintings that retain their original narrow rippled 1918 exhibition frames, which, to the contemporary eye, might not seem important enough for these significant works.[2]

A collector who does not learn about period frames when studying period art is only learning half of the equation. If you do not trust your own eye or frame knowledge then it might be a good idea to consult with a frame expert. This can be as simple as visiting a reputable painting or frame dealer (or several) for advice, gathering different framing ideas, examining period styles with varying decorations, and, yes, comparing prices. Ideally, a frame dealer will offer a range of options, and can explain the reason for every different price. The serious art collector should be able to discern the difference in frame choices: that includes not just design patterns but also quality and original gilded surfaces, period patina, and so on. On a deeper level, known framemakers or period galleries may be discussed, particularly if an artist was known to have exhibited at a certain gallery or favored a particular frame style or dealer in his lifetime.

To select the frame that best suits the art, a painting should be brought to the framer (or a selection of frames brought to the painting) so one can see the nuances of color, weight (i.e. width and depth of molding), and proximity of ornament to the painting. If a personal visit is not possible, a photomontage supplied by the framer of several appropriate frame options allows time to mull over the choices.

When there is more than one "best" frame equally representing different aesthetics from the same period, it becomes a subjective decision and perhaps requires deeper consideration of the contexts of the artist, date, subject, or locale.

If the original frame is missing and no appropriate period model is accessible, we might advise recreating a period frame facsimile, effectively putting the painting in a time machine back to its original setting. Reproductions or replicas are certainly required for very rare, large, or difficult-to-find frames or to meet a restricted budget. The best quality replicas should compare with extant period frames with correct color, crisply defined ornament, and aged patina. A copy frame almost always costs less than an original.

Museums and art auctions are excellent public venues to see how similar works of art are framed. As we have discovered, however, not all museum frames are correct to the period or artist, and paintings consigned to auction may retain previous outdated framing from a collector or be overdressed with an inappropriate model by a dealer seeking to attract a buyer. If you like a painting on view it would not hurt to ask the auction house if they have any information on the frame—while it may not be described in the catalogue entry, department specialists may have insight on originality of style, material, or frame provenance. (We often answer informal queries from auction representatives asking for aid in frame identification.)

A museum painting that has retained the original frame (or been thoughtfully reframed) can be a valuable learning tool. However, museums—although this is changing—do not often describe the frames on didactic wall labels or websites, even when they are original to the painting. Therefore, to determine if the frame is original, one has to learn to see anomalies. Has a frame been changed in size (are there any visible cut marks across a molding, or cracks and seams where there should not be? Is the decoration evenly spaced on all four sides; do the corner ornaments match?) Is the gilding original (is it the right color for the period? Are there any flaking areas that show previously gilded layers?) Do the frame style and origin (e.g. American versus European) relate to the date and origin of the painting and artist? If you have determined that the museum frame is original or period-appropriate you can revisit and use it as a basis for comparison with other frames you encounter and for ideas in reframing works in your own collection.

As period paintings changed hands, original frames were replaced as style and fashion dictated, perhaps as a statement of ownership, to simplify or aggrandize, or to blend with a new décor. When painting and frame have been separated, a replacement frame must be located. How should those divorced paintings be reframed today? Looking back from the twenty-first century, how can a collector, curator, or painting dealer be sure of making the best choice for framing a specific work of art? Taken on a case-by-case basis, considerations might include: conventional versus creative framing (popular versus individual taste); matching the date of a painting to a frame of the same period (or not); preferences of the original artist; and new frames custom-designed for a specific painting. The display preferences of a collector or curator desiring cohesiveness in a collection or gallery as a whole and preferences for a painting to complement an interior design may also be important.

What to look for when choosing a period frame? Foremost: original condition. We look for good gilding and patina, preferably *unrestored.* We would pay more for a period frame with some broken ornament and a dirty surface than one that was incorrectly restored. Regilding, over-restorations, and alterations of frame design should be avoided. Many good period examples will need some restoration and that is OK. If a frame surface is original it can be judiciously cleaned, touched up, or in-gilded in damaged areas to suit the taste of the new owners. In our shop we rarely restore a period frame before it has been chosen for a painting; it is thus apparent how the frame came down in history. Ideally, a restoration studio will use traditional methods—our gilders follow traditional recipes to cast composition for missing ornament and keep many karats of gold leaf on hand to match to original frames.

Tantamount to connoisseurship of historical American frames is understanding gilding materials and methods and whether period moldings retain their original surface. Identifying correct period gold color is a must when ordering a custom replica or restoring an original frame. Unfortunately, much regilding, restoration, and reproduction work made by those unfamiliar with period frames is done with a uniform "frame shop 22-karat" gold leaf with a standard darkening toner over it, a combination that may not reference the original gilding of the period in which the frame was made, and ignores the changed appearance of a gilded surface over time.

The trained eye can learn to spot fabrication subtleties at a glance: it can tell if the ornament on a frame is cast plaster or composition, or wood carved by hand; notes color of the clay substrate; discerns methods of gilding or finishing (including identification of genuine gold or silver leaf, Dutch metal or aluminum leaf, Roman gilding, stippled gesso, or paint); and is able to distinguish a wide range of gold leaf colors (Fig. 2).

Genuine gold leaf used for frame gilding is an alloy of any combination of gold, copper, silver, platinum, or palladium, which is beaten by hand or machine to an extreme thinness (1/250,000 of an inch) and cut into 3 ⅜-inch squares. The karat of gold is a measure of its purity, with 24k being the purest number of parts of gold. Copper

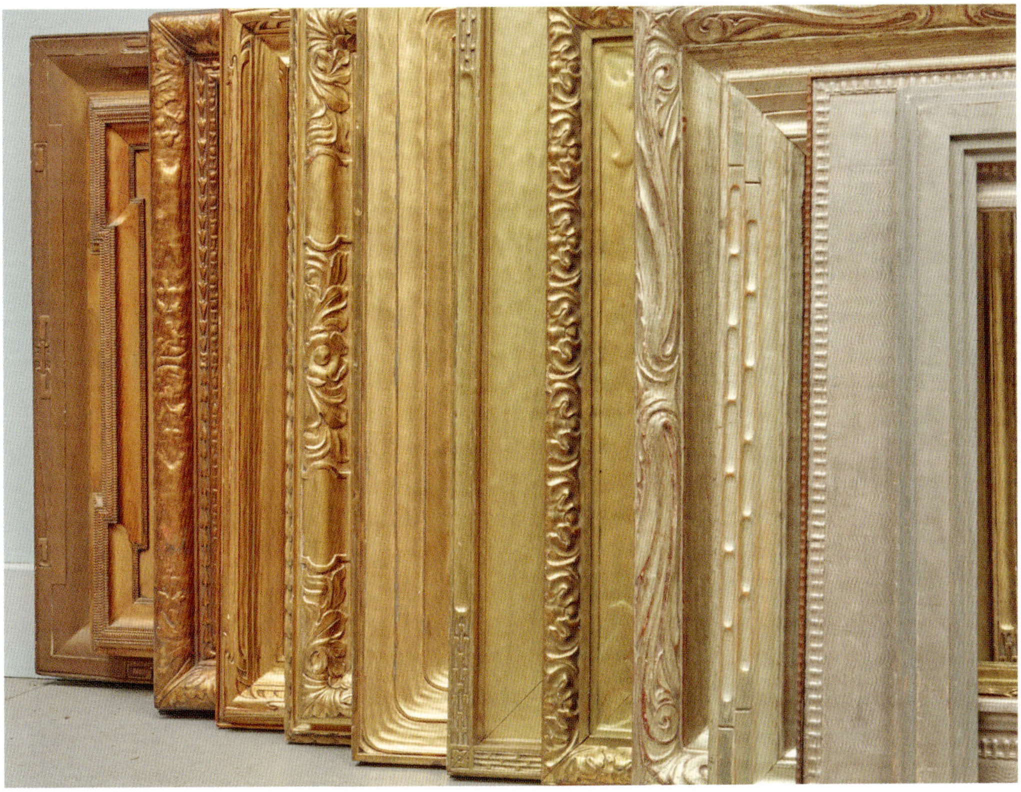

2.
Frames dating from the late 1890s through the 1920s depict a range of gilding techniques and tonalities. From left, Roman gilded Taos-style and *c.* 1900 eared-corner frame; patinated metal-leafed Western-style frames; brightly burnished water-gilded rich gold and lighter lemon karats of genuine gold leaf on hand-carved Arts and Crafts frames; early twentieth-century silver leaf; and aluminum-leafed modernist frame, all illustrate the range of artistic options during the most innovative period of American framemaking.

is added to gold leaf to add a redder tone, and silver to lighten it; white gold is a 50–50 alloy of gold and silver.

Gilding is the application of metallic leaf or powder. Traditionally, frames are either water gilded: adhesion using a mixture of water, alcohol, and animal glue over layers of gesso (gilder's whiting and animal glue) and colored bole (fine-grained clay and animal glue); or oil gilded: adhesion with a mordant or oil-based varnish or size. Water-gilded objects can be burnished to a mirror-like sheen; oil-gilded objects remain matte. On nineteenth-century American frames, alternating rows of decorative elements were oil- and water-gilded to create subtle contrasts in light reflectivity and tonality.[3] That certain parts of a frame may be gilded differently is crucial knowledge for the frame conservator as well, so that attempts to clean a period surface do not dissolve the gilding beneath. Knowing the traditions helps one see deviations from the norm.

In general, one good clue to determining if a frame is American is the bole color. Gold leaf is transparent and clay adds a rich color from beneath: a red bole will warm up the gold, and gray or black will result in a cooler appearance. A frame from the nineteenth century or earlier with red bole is almost certainly European, likely French, Italian, or Spanish. There are exceptions, but, until the early twentieth century, American gilders primarily used shades of black, pinkish gray, and ochre bole, which gave their frames a cooler appearance. This is useful knowledge for dating frames from the 1800s. At first glance, an early nineteenth-century frame with Empire-style rosettes or Neo-classical fluting might appear French but a gray (versus red) bole color will indicate American manufacture. The rule changes in the early twentieth century when American Arts and Crafts framemakers used red bole for their hand-carved reinterpretations of traditional European designs.

Bole color can also expose incorrect restoration on a frame. An American frame has been badly regilded if the bole color is wrong for the period and design. The gold leaf on a period frame may wear thin in areas where it has been handled; the clay color becomes apparent, and solid gold stripes become visible at regular intervals. These "lay lines" occur where two leaves of gold overlapped in the original gilding process. Lay lines spaced every three inches or so indicate genuine gold leaf. When a frame is first gilded these overlaps are not obvious—they appear only if the gilding has been rubbed in some way, either naturally over time or purposely by a gilder wanting to make a new frame or new gilding look old. A common mistake with reproduction frames is visible lay lines all the way around a frame or on the liner; if that is not done as an aesthetic choice (as on some Modernist frames, for example), then it illustrates a misconception that a period frame would wear evenly on every edge.

Metal leaf, sometimes called Dutch metal, varies in color depending on the percentage of copper or zinc alloy it contains. Sheets of metal leaf, much thicker and larger than genuine gold leaf (5 ¼ inches), are traditionally applied with oil gilding and darken over time through oxidation. Metal leaf cannot be burnished to a reflective shine as gold can, so it was not used on frames that needed glinting highlights. Unlike gold leaf, which has a softer look, a metal-gilded frame has a solid cast appearance.

Learning which frames might have originally been gilded with metal leaf is important; nowadays frames may be metal-leafed as a cost-saving measure, but it was not always about cost. Some forward-looking frames designed by American Renaissance architect Stanford White (1853–1906), and some early twentieth-century "Ashcan" or modern frames used by Social Realist artists such as Robert Henri (1865–1929), George Bellows (1882–1925), and John Sloan (1871–1951) were purposely gilded in metal leaf as an "antidote" to gold.

Roman gilding, another alternative to genuine gold, first appeared on manufactured Aesthetic print frames after the Civil War; it is not gilding with leaf at all but a painted-on solution of colored bronze powders suspended in animal glue to create the look of solid cast metal.

Regional differences in frames are important to learn. Paintings by early twentieth-century artists of the American West and Southwest, e.g. Charles Marion Russell (1864–1926), Joseph Henry Sharp (1859–1953), and Eanger Irving Couse (1866–1936), are often framed in metal-leafed or Roman-gilded models, usually deeper tonalities to complement their subjects. The ultimate value of a frame is not necessarily determined by materials. Metal-gilded and Roman-gilded frames are more widely understood and appreciated in recent years. As their surfaces tarnish and darken over time, not long ago they might have been routinely regilded in gold leaf; these days, original surfaces are desirable, even if all that glisters is not gold. An original Couse frame is a rare and valuable artifact (Fig. 3).

Composition ("compo" in framers' vernacular) is a clay-like casting material used for centuries as architectural decoration where carved wood was not practical or just too costly. From the early nineteenth century into the early twentieth, most American frames were ornamented with applied castings glued over wood moldings that were later gilded, painted, or shellacked to look like carved wood. Compo is made of whiting (calcium carbonate), Venice turpentine, linseed oil, rosin, and animal-hide glue; it is pressed into molds, cut into lengths and wrapped around curved moldings, or seamlessly joined as several lengths of patterned castings to adorn a larger frame. Compo has the color of wood but once dry becomes hard as a rock. One trick of the trade to tell if a frame is cast or carved is to poke it with a fingernail; compo will not budge, but wood should give a little. Another clue is that antique wood frames will naturally separate or crack along the length of a molding in the direction of the wood grain as the frame ages, whereas frames with applied ornament will crack and separate *across* the ornament, usually *against* the grain of the wood substrate (Fig. 4).

Frame books with glossy pictures show frames in their best light and help to educate on styles, dates, and motifs, but do not allow one to examine up close the gilding, the wood, the joinery, or hand-carved signatures, order numbers, or other marks on the verso. Ask to look at the back of a frame. When we consult on museum frame collections, the curator usually asks a gloved art handler or two to accompany us on a walk-through, to take a painting off the wall so we can photograph the back of the frame, and examine it for inscriptions or labels that may help identify the maker. We also look for original hangers and nail holes to determine if the same painting has been in the frame its entire life.

Removing an original frame from a significant painting requires careful consideration by the caretaker of the painting, i.e. a collector, curator, or dealer. If the frame on a painting was selected by the artist or possibly the artist's dealer during the artist's lifetime, and is still in good condition, then one would probably consider leaving that original frame in place. If a collector wants to remove that original frame we advise keeping it in storage and including the frame documentation with the painting data.

However, sometimes the original frame is not the best choice, for any number of reasons. Often artists could not afford the frames they might have wanted, or they may have been at a point in their career where they did not frame up to today's value level of the painting; occasionally very simple generic frames were used as a placeholder or out of economy, considered a temporary solution, perhaps for exhibition or sale, and not the personal preference of the artist; and some artists had little interest in framing so the "original" frame may not have an important relation to the artwork.

Other reasons why one might decide to remove the original would be when the frame is in bad condition, represents the taste of a zealous art dealer who wanted to augment a canvas for exhibition or sale, or if a previous collector chose a frame that worked better with his interior décor than with the painting.

For example, early Modernists, such as John Marin (1870–1953) or his dealer Alfred Stieglitz (1864–1946), may have specified a subtle white flat or stepped frame from New York framemaker George F. Of, Jr. (1876–1954), but today's collector might decide that a narrow white frame belies the importance of the work and seek a gilded model with greater wall presence.

We have owned three original John Marin frames: one polished white George Of molding, and two wood bolection profiles with hand-painted and carved modifications by the artist. From gallery labels on the verso, we identified the paintings original to each frame. We offered an original to the current owner of one "divorced" painting, but he did not want an empty Marin frame just to store it. (He had already reframed the painting in a model he preferred to display in his home and apparently did not care for Marin's more rustic artistry.) That original artist-made frame will likely find new life as an exhibit or loan to a museum study center; or perhaps it will be married to a different Marin painting down the road. We discovered that our white George Of frame was originally married to a Marin watercolor now at the Birmingham Museum of Art and decided to donate it; today the frame and art are reunited, with the frame properly identified on the didactic label.[4]

The whimsical frames of Charles and Maurice Prendergast are also examples where the taste of the artist may vastly differ from that of a future collector. Our first important frame acquisition was a rare original Charles Prendergast frame that had surrounded a Maurice Prendergast *c.* 1909 watercolor of Saint-Malo. In this case the collector wanted to put a mat around his watercolor to make the art look bigger on the wall; years earlier he had had another framer make a larger copy of his frame and had put a mirror in the original. We advised him to keep the original frame as it was artist-made, unique, and valuable, but he preferred to sell the now mirror frame. We explained that Maurice mostly did not use mats; the active interaction of frame and painting right next to each other was purposeful. To the contemporary eye, that juxtaposition can be a visually busy combination and this collector definitely preferred the broad neutral space of a mat between the watercolor and the frame. While sadly divorced from its original mate, Charles's gilded hand-carved masterpiece has had an

3.
Selected objects from the collection of connoisseur Edgar O. Smith: *c.* 1903 Edward S. Curtis (1868–1952), platinum print, "Chief Joseph," tribal leader of the Nez Perce (1840–1904); *c.* 1906 Roycroft Shops, personal bookcase of Dard Hunter (1883–1966), quarter-sawn oak; *c.* 1855–60 Navajo weaving, two-piece woman's dress; *c.* 1906 Roycroft Shops pedestal, quarter-sawn oak; *c.* 1916–18 Louis Vigdor frame for E.I. Couse, metal-gilded hand-carved wood; *c.*1904 Teco Pottery, jardiniere, earthenware. Photograph from *Beaux Arts & Crafts*, *op.cit.*, p. 4, plate 2.

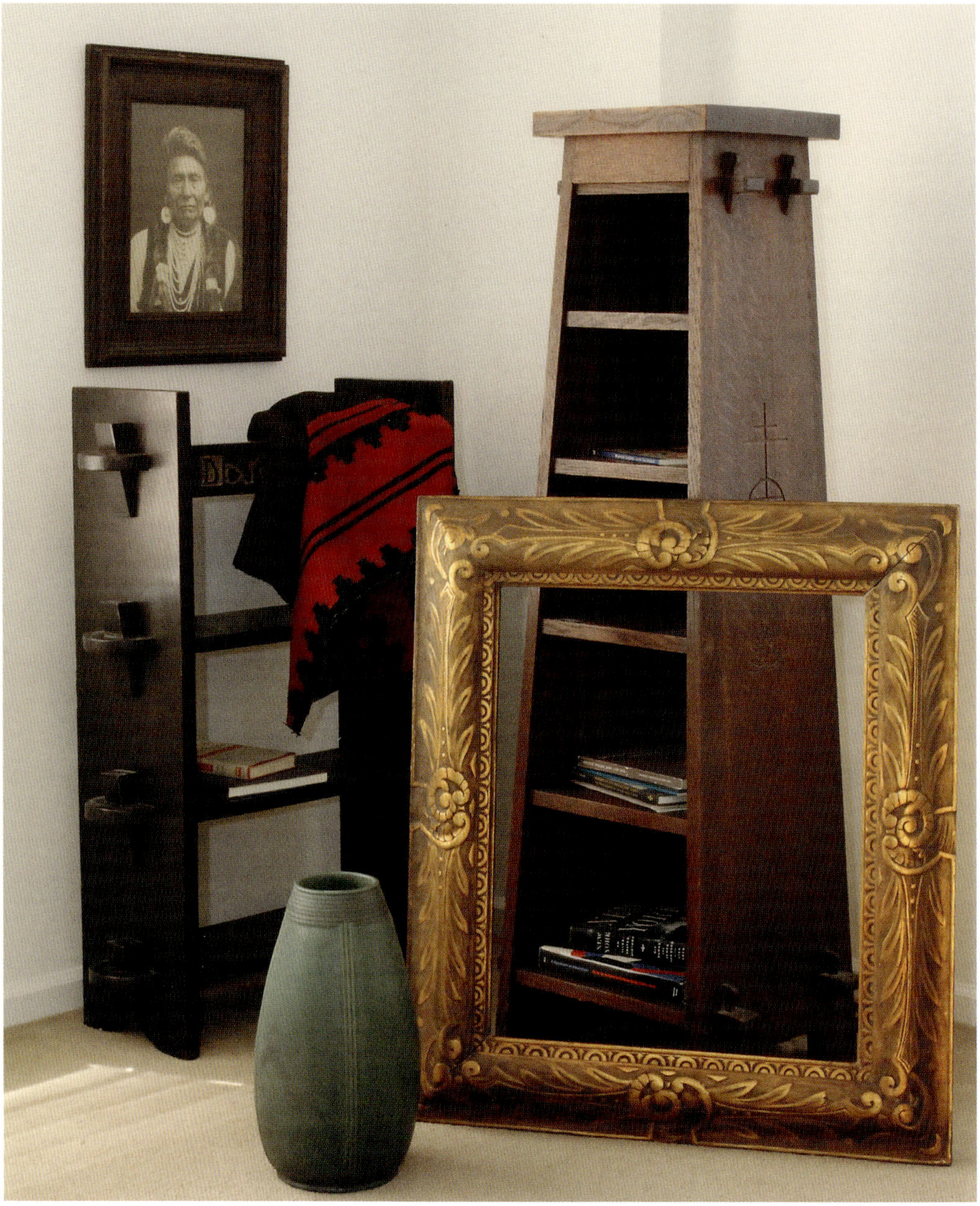

active life *sans* original watercolor partner; we have replicated it for museum exhibitions where it was paired with other Maurice watercolors, and it has been displayed empty in several frame exhibitions. The original frame remains in the Gill & Lagodich Collection, a quintessential example of Charles's methodology—it appears that he "drew" the lyrical design with his chisel as it moved around the frame molding; no sides are exactly alike. This is what distinguishes the hand of the artist from the manufactured or made-to-order frames of the previous century: quirky variations of traditional polychrome, punchwork, and hand-drawn adaptations of European styles. We have reframed other Maurice works with Charles frames originally made for different paintings. Charles himself, and later his wife, Eugénie, repurposed his frames often, so for us, it is a fine goal to find new homes for these divorced originals. A dozen or so Prendergast frames currently reside in the Gill & Lagodich Collection; while they may someday unite with a painting, to us, each is a stand-alone masterwork.

Frame collections—once the sole province of frame and painting dealers—are emerging. More museums and collectors appreciate and advance the importance of the empty picture frame freed from its original function as a surround for a work of art and displayed as a separate sculptural art form.

Since 1996, Gill & Lagodich has curated four exhibitions of empty period frames at venues across the country, each accompanied by a scholarly catalogue.[5] Other notable exhibitions of American frames were organized first by William Adair, Washington, DC (1983), and, later, by Eli Wilner & Company, and the venerable Julius Lowy Frame & Restoring Company, New York. Frame dealers, recognized experts with excellent collections, have organized the majority of American exhibitions, but dealers are not the only ones to laud the art of the frame; significant exhibitions have been hosted by museums.

In 2011, the High Museum of Art, Atlanta, exhibited the most important private collection of American frames, *Beaux Arts & Crafts: Masterpieces of American Frame Design 1890–1920*.[6] The collector, Edgar O. Smith, embodies connoisseurship at the highest level. His scholarship and several significant collections embrace the best of the best of American arts and handcraftsmanship, from Native American textiles to Arts and Crafts pottery and furniture, and, most recently, exemplary picture frames that are displayed on the walls of his home as individual works of art (Fig. 3).

In the accompanying High Museum of Art exhibition catalogue, Mr. Smith described the evolution of his collections and the process of connoisseurship. We quote at length to underline that exceptional dedication to *really* looking at objects, and deep investigation into specific arts, is rare in today's speed-of-sound-bite world.

In the early 1980s I was a pioneering collector of decorative arts of the American Arts and Crafts period (1901 to 1910). I was attracted to the straightforward designs, celebration of nature, and the philosophical and historical basis of the movement. As my collection grew it came to include furniture, pottery, metalwork, woodcuts, and also Navaho blankets and American photographs. I always sought the finest examples in original condition. Two decades later I became aware of the related frames of the period and also those frames designed by Stanford White during the preceding decade. Seeing this new (to me) art form of frame making—sculptural forms of carved or ornamented wood, gilded in varied colors of gold or patinated in warm bronze tones—I was at once attracted to the distinctly American adaptations/translations of traditional forms.

In 2002, collecting empty frames—particularly American frames—and documenting them was a relatively new phenomenon. These were decorative art objects rarely mentioned in the pages of Arts and Crafts books or pictured in exhibition catalogues. I recognized that artistic American frame making was an embryonic yet emergent field of scholarship and I set out to learn as much as I could. Certain frames shared an aesthetic with the furniture I had been collecting. This aesthetic, which emphasized the process of tasteful creation, i.e. handcraftsmanship steeped in appreciation of beauty, nature, and art, came to the fore in the last decade of the 19th century and the beginning of the 20th. As with American Arts and Crafts furniture, the models for these frames were partly derived from earlier European and Medieval and Renaissance designs. However, the emergent furniture and frame designs of this period also bore the new robust stamp of American artists. . . .

In assembling my Beaux Arts and Crafts frame collection I have gathered those frames that best capture the creative and sincere American spirit. Frames whose designs evolved from the innovative Beaux Arts ideas of Stanford White into the hands-on artistry of the American Arts and Crafts. Thus I have been able to add another important aspect of American decorative art to my collecting experience.[7]

As a true connoisseur, Edgar Smith has embraced the highest level of collecting; to this day, his American frame collection remains unsurpassed.

The finest period frames are arguably masterpieces of craftsmanship, examples of traditional methods and dedicated hand-making that are rapidly being lost in the age of twenty-first-century technology. We predict that over the next fifty to one hundred years the relative values of the best frames will only appreciate. Respected as art objects on their own, examined as finely crafted pieces of furniture or original sculpture, superior frames will undoubtedly become more precious as time passes.

European frames have been valued for hundreds of years, but the study of American frames really began in the last quarter of the twentieth century. In recent decades, collectors and curators of American art have begun seriously re-evaluating the relevance of American frames and recognized them as historically important artifacts.

Most people who go to museums and galleries look first at the art. We encourage visitors to look at a painting, and take a closer look at the art *around* the art—the art of the frame. American frames are historical objects representative of a specific time in our nation's history, necessary for the proper presentation of a period painting. Hopefully, to the attentive viewer, the two will not seem disparate, but instead will seem joined in a picture-perfect marriage.

AMERICAN FRAME STYLE CHRONOLOGY

Following is a brief summary of American frame chronology—a broad overview of fabrication methods and style changes of American frames from the late eighteenth to the mid-twentieth century. We include this as a guide to help determine if a frame might be original to a painting and offer clues to identifying period-appropriate models when considering reframing.

Initially a derivation of European traditions brought to the New World, the American frame developed stylistically in close parallel with the evolution of American art. Generally, throughout the nineteenth century, American frame styles changed almost decade by decade. By memorizing a dozen or so types of ornament, some basic construction methods, and learning how to distinguish basic types of gilding, one can identify and date an American frame pretty well. Collectors and caretakers of nineteenth-century American paintings can therefore choose from identifiable models of good quality from a particular decade and find themselves mostly correct in framing choices.

The development of decorated homes in America began around 1700. However, with the exception of more elaborate rococo confections or trophy frames designed and commissioned for formal portraits of the American gentry later in the century, most American frames were primarily simple unadorned profiles, gilded or decorated with paint, sometimes in a *faux bois* pattern to imitate more exotic and unavailable woods, perhaps crafted by the same talented cabinetmaker or local carpenter who was making the door and window moldings.

As the country entered the nineteenth century, European influences and designs were still highly desired, and American craftsmen continued to consult English pattern books or imported examples to create frames on this side of the pond.

In the post-Revolutionary Federal Period, frame design elements were adapted in the regional vernacular of early American furniture, with straight profiles, perhaps embellished with twisted wood spindles, and a small leaf or shell in the corners.

From about 1810 more American frames began to be decorated with cast ornament that, in the early decades, appeared softer, almost mushy, with less crisp delineation than European counterparts; American moldings were generally straighter and heavier, lacking delicacy or finesse in profiles. "Sully" frames, named for artist Thomas Sully (1783–1872), were simple, unsophisticated American gilded models, beveled or scooped, sometimes with cast or carved ornament to cover the corner miters. After 1820, French Empire-inspired Neo-classical furniture was in vogue, expressed in America with regional interpretations in frames as well.

The "Cole" frame, popular in the 1830s and 1840s, was named for Thomas Cole (1801–1848), so-called father of American landscape painting and the Hudson River School. In 1837, Cole wrote to fellow painter Asher B. Durand (1796–1886), "The frame I desire to be massy, covered with small ornament." These were American variations of British "Lawrence" and of finer eighteenth-century hand-carved French

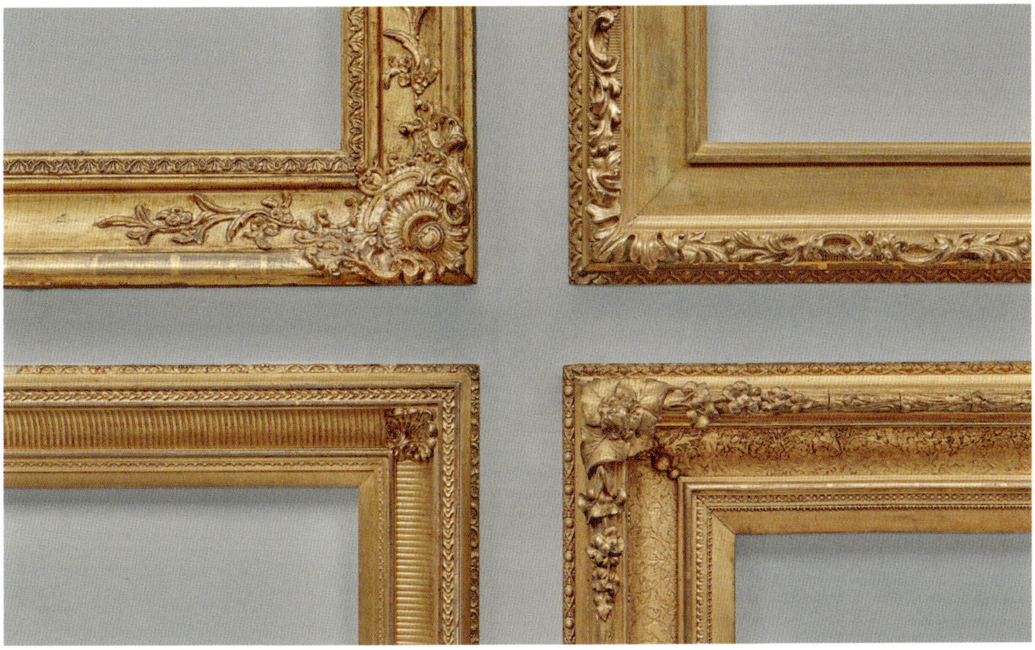

4.
Four nineteenth-century American frames illustrate how cast plaster and applied composition ornament emulated the decorative effects that carved wood had in previous centuries. Clockwise from upper left: *c.* 1840s scotia profile with French-influenced design motifs of prominent shell cartouche and scrolling foliate corners—this frame shows a natural wearing of the gold leaf on one rail exposing the original gray bole substrate and lay lines in the gold, both clues to the originality of the gilded surface; *c.* 1890s frame exemplifies how busy foliate ornament moved away from the heavy Barbizon style of the previous decade, relegating it to the outer edges with wider undecorated panels closer to the canvas; typical motifs of the 1850s include a gilded twig top edge, overgrown flower corners (often local flora instead of a traditional European acanthus), and a stenciled sand cove (here with scrolling foliate pattern, but most often seen with a scattered rock pattern that resembles giraffe spots); 1860s Neo-classical fluted cove frame, the "little black dress" of American nineteenth-century frames, here accessorized with a shell replacing the typical corner leaf, perhaps designed for a marine painting.

Régence frames. Placed side by side with the European, the American versions are clunkier and clearly less sophisticated. Adorned with applied composition ornament glued to wood moldings, these twining filigreed frames are found on paintings by Cole, Durand, and early works of Frederic E. Church. Other frames of the 1840s are simple coved or ogee wood profiles with large cartouche or foliate corners, with, most often, applied composition (Fig. 4).

Artists of the 1850s embraced American interest in nature and cultivated landscape. Frame decoration incorporated new techniques such as gilded embossed paper; fine sand stenciled in patterns resembling scattered rocks or scrolling vines; diamond-shaped quilted patterns (medieval diapering); and neo-gothic forms. A gilded twig top edge overgrown with blooming foliate corners also dates to this decade (Fig. 4).

American art and frames developed rapidly as a more cosmopolitan sensibility came of age in the newly prosperous post-Civil War era, with emerging industrial production, exposure to motifs from more foreign cultures, and a burgeoning urban population eager for home furnishings.

By the mid-nineteenth century the fluted Neo-classical-revival frame had become the first international frame style. American Neo-classical frames are variations on the European, with classical motifs: a laurel leaf-and-berry or inset guilloche-pattern top edge and a wide central cove with parallel recessed channels derived from the fluting on Ionic columns. The American versions often have narrow corner leaves, are gilded over gray bole, and made in several attached molding parts (European versions are more often one-piece moldings with wider fluting, broader acanthus, and a red bole substrate.) The fluted cove—what we call the "little black dress" of American frames—is a model that basically looks good on every nineteenth-century painting. These are frames most clearly associated with Hudson River School artists, although when framing a work by one of these painters one might parse the selections further, and choose a frame closest to the date of the painting to better complement an artist's development at a certain point in time (Fig. 4).

The predominant motif of the 1870s was the spade-shaped anthemion, sometimes combined with an incised Greek key or fret pattern frieze. These were classical motifs taken directly from pattern books, most popularly Owen Jones's *Grammar of Ornament*, first published in London,

1856. As with earlier and later nineteenth-century American frames, these were manufactured with stock molding profiles and a selection of popular decorations. An artist or collector could go to his framemaker and specify motifs; there would be a set order of placement for each pattern, often alternating rows of matte oil-gilded and burnished water-gilded composition ornament. Frames of this decade introduced liners, an extra plain strip of molding at the frame's sight edge, to allow more breathing room for Luminist vistas and open landscapes of second-generation Hudson River School painters.

The 1880s were the height of America's "Age of Opulence." Frames of this decade may appear over-decorated, but they were appropriate to the ornate interiors they lived in, and also exemplify the rapid growth of American commerce. At this time, reproductions of famous oil paintings in ostentatious gilded frames were being sold in American department stores; the frame was a sales tool, the bigger and golder the better. The frame style *du jour* was American Barbizon, gilded cast plaster over wood, bunched-leaf-and-flower variations a few steps removed from French Barbizon and earlier Louis XIII origins. Though today's tastes lean toward minimalist, when framing an 1880s American painting one would still appropriately choose an American Barbizon style.

Later in the decade, American artists recognized a new sensibility with a rejection of ornament and what it historically represented. New surface treatments emerged, such as gilded oak, where gold leaf is applied to the surface of a frame without intermediary gesso or bole layers. Oak's beautiful striations are enhanced by gilding and become an overall pattern in lieu of applied ornament on broader panels. First popularized by the British Pre-Raphaelite Brotherhood beginning in the 1860s, gilded oak frames appeared in America in the 1880s and continued into the early twentieth century.

Other innovations introduced in Europe by artists such as Edgar Degas (1834–1917) and expatriate American James McNeill Whistler (1834–1903) (who drew inspiration from his Pre-Raphaelite contemporaries), were frames with little or no reference to organic motifs in ornament, instead allowing color and finish to be in harmony with the painting. Degas designed simple reeded bolection profiles and flat white panels bordered with straight gilded lines, and Whistler, also preferring bundled reeds and alternating them with flats, would specify different gold karats to complement his paintings, and he sometimes painted decorations or signed the faces with his butterfly cipher. With the appearance of modern designs, linear motifs, and wider flattened profiles, artists' choices and perceptions of frames were forever changed.

Up until the 1890s American frames had been mostly a commercial product, manufactured by tradesmen. Toward the end of the nineteenth century the influence of the artist-framemaker or *couture-auteur* rose to prominence with American designers and makers such as Stanford White, Charles Prendergast, Hermann Dudley Murphy (1867–1945) and others, who extended the artistic sensibility of the canvas on to the frame. Some savvy New York framemakers used this newfound sensibility as a sales tool, putting words like "Artistic Framing" or "Artists Framing Company" or "Frames … toned to harmonize with paintings" on their labels, as they sought to become known for custom-designed one-of-a-kind frames for artists.

In America, from about 1880 to 1920, the academic Neo-classical Beaux Arts was a style of the Gilded Age metropolis, expressed in grand buildings and highly decorated interiors. Stanford White, infamous New York-based architect and interior designer, realized original concepts for picture frames that are unrivaled to this day. His sensitivity to individual artists such as Thomas Wilmer Dewing (1851–1938), Dwight Tryon (1849–1925), Abbott Handerson Thayer (1849–1921), and Augustus Saint-Gaudens (1848–1907) led to exceptional frame designs that contain a sense of both tradition and modernity (Fig. 5).

Although often covered with ornament, Stanford White-designed frames are generally flat to the wall; even if copiously decorated or sloping back, the frame is often on the same plane as the picture. By designing frames destined to be inseparable from paintings, White's own form of

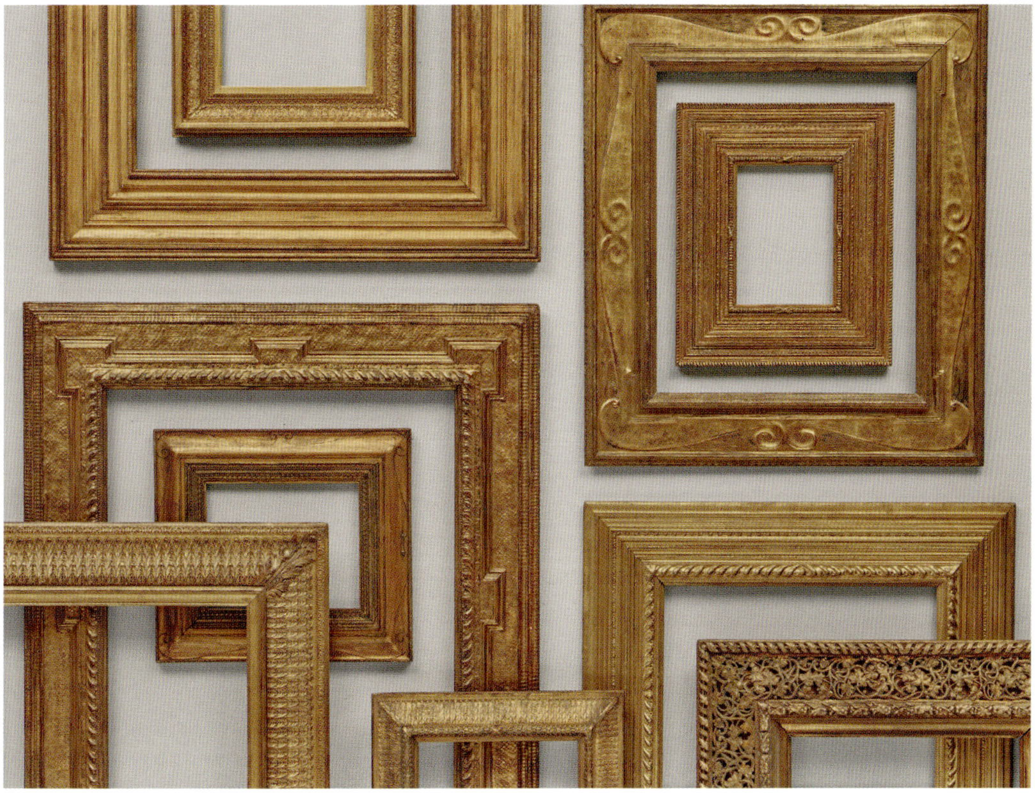

5.
Stanford White was a champion frame designer. For adaptation of classical elements into new works of art, White's frame designs for American artists remain unsurpassed. He embraced, experimented, and transformed traditional patterns. Architectonic tabernacle styles, frames with pierced foliate and arabesque patterns, basket weaves, fish-scales, twining leaves, and fence-like grilles with different tonalities of gold and metal leaf were specifically created to harmonize with each individual painting.

artistry becomes part of a greater work of art as a whole: painting and frame. Indeed, many of his artist friends declared that their work would be incomplete without a White frame. His designs revisited the centuries-old notion of an attached frame, growing organically from the interior architecture.

The name "Stanford White" tends to connote an automatic assumption of higher value. With the exception of the limited original frames produced during his lifetime this is not necessarily true. Later diluted reproductions of White's designs evolved into a manufactured product of lesser value. It is important to differentiate date and quality; and when commissioning a White replica, it is best that the molds and measurements are taken from an early model.

By 1900 America was the world's leading industrial power. Interestingly, this was also the time when American artists revived hand-craftsmanship in framemaking. From the late nineteenth century into the twentieth, practical reassessment of how paintings and frames interacted meant a rejection and reinterpretation of earlier European models. Taking hold from the 1890s, the Arts and Crafts movement had represented America's search for a new design vernacular and a return to old-world traditions paired with consideration of each frame as an individual creation for a specific painting. Inspired artist-framemakers played with tonality and decorative variations, now created with hand-carving elaborate designs in wood; the age-old art of gilding was reconsidered as artists selected from a range of gold leaf karats and experimented with colored glazes and opaque polychrome over the gilding.

The Boston firms of Carrig-Rohane (founded 1903, with principals Hermann Dudley Murphy and Charles Prendergast making frames for fellow artists from the mid-1890s), and Foster Brothers (founded 1875) have gained renown for their intimate connection with American Impressionist painters such as Frank Weston Benson (1862–1951) and Edmund Tarbell (1862–1938), who commissioned their frames with specific colors of gold to complement the palette of their canvases. Many of these frames show visible

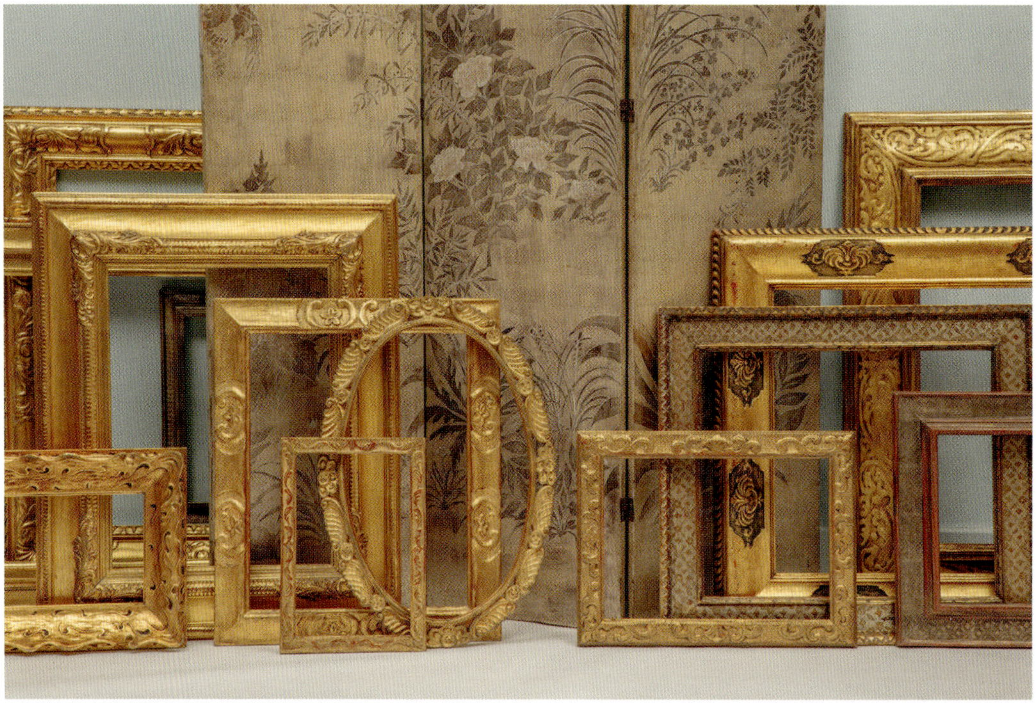

6.
Gilded, hand-carved, artist-made frames *c.* 1890s–1930s illustrate the originality of American design in this period. Counterclockwise from top left: Foster Brothers, Carrig-Rohane, J.H. Miller, Frederick Harer (1879–1949), Charles Prendergast (four), Max Kuehne (1880–1968), Prendergast, Harer, Kuehne; *c.* 1930s three-panel screen by Max Kuehne, silver leaf on wood, with incised and polychrome decoration.

carve marks under the gilding, echoing the artist's brushstrokes. As further testament to the framemaker as artist, every Carrig-Rohane frame is signed, numbered, and dated on the back; an inspired collector can go to the Archives of American Art and look up the original order books. A signed frame married to its original painting may significantly increase the value of both (Fig. 6).

Painted or silver- or metal-leafed Modernist frames with simple steps or broad profiles devoid of ornament and color represent nearly the last vestige of design and hand-craftsmanship. As the new century progressed, artists moved away from the coloration and symbolism of traditional gold-leafed frames toward a wider use of metal-gilded and bronzy Roman-gilded frames. Dark-toned or muted painted surfaces created the effect gold leaf had in previous centuries: a neutral surround for a work of art. Artists of this period wanted to be freed of associations, disentangled from the history of painting and the history of frames; they wanted the frame to be as modern as the art. This was achieved with new approaches to surface treatment and, when traditional forms were referenced, the profiles were pared down to their barest bones. As the rejection of ornament progressed, more modern forms emerged; minimal borders, strip frames, and other reductionist profiles were chosen by artists such as John Marin, Stuart Davis (1892–1964), Charles Sheeler (1883–1965), and Georgia O'Keeffe (1887–1986).

American Social Realist painters such as Edward Hopper (1882–1967), John Sloan, and his fellow Ashcan painter George Bellows, specified frames that would not interfere with their depictions of urban modernity. Gilded frames were darker and simpler—mostly without excess decoration, perhaps just a stippled or combed gesso substrate—to augment their unvarnished views and oft-times gritty realistic subjects.

Continuing the trend, manufactured frames of the 1920s to the 1940s and into the 1950s, though not always made by or for specific artists, had surfaces mitigated with paint, and gilding might be relegated to the inner liner or outer edges of the molding. Sometimes texture was combed or stippled into the gesso substrate in lieu of ornament, and, instead of traditional gilding, these modern frames were sometimes finished in chalky white or gray washes over polychrome, gold, silver, aluminum, or metal leaf; over distressed or worm-eaten wood, or lightly rubbed with pigment to enhance the natural wood grain[8] (Fig. 7).

Artist-framemaker Robert Kulicke (1924–2007) is credited with inventing the welded aluminum frame for the Museum of Modern Art in 1956, as well as the Plexiglas box frame (1960), and was an early manufacturer of the new metal-section frame. By this time the frame had been reduced to a synthesis of form and function; decoration had ceased to exist.

Ultimately, twentieth-century frames and paintings became literally and conceptually distinct. Frames no longer had to be connected to the design of interiors or specific styles of a period in time. As succinctly stated by Gertrude Stein, "A picture remaining in its frame was a thing that always had existed and now pictures commenced to want to leave their frames…."[9]

Historically, an unframed canvas would rarely have been shown outside the artist's studio. Today, many works of art never marry with a frame. In fact, the entire concept of a frame may be rejected altogether. Thus it can be difficult to discern the place of the historical or period frame in a post-modern landscape, or even to imagine the importance of the relationship of frame and painting over centuries, when resources might have been spent equally on the creation of the gilded hand-carved frame and on the commissioned painting.

One cannot predict the future popularity of any particular model or style, in part because the value of some frames may be tied to the fluctuating art market. We continue to track shifting frame trends. Although collectors, dealers, art institutions, and auction houses may seek a more creative solution to re-energize a period-correct aesthetic and to create appeal to the starker modern tastes of a contemporary audience, we conclude that the most significant works of art will continue to be framed period-appropriately. In a time of changing tastes, whether choosing frames in a purely academic context, or more creatively, collectors today have the freedom to explore and adapt their choices from transformative designs across the American frame canon.

7.
A selection of American Modernist frames, including original frames designed, made by, or associated with, the following artists or framemakers (listed alphabetically): Bernard "Ben" Badura (1896–1986), Stuart Davis, Frederick Harer, Henry Heydenryk, Jr., Max Kuehne, Yasuo Kuniyoshi (1889–1953), John Marin (frame original to *Spring No. 2*, 1953), and Charles Sheeler. Notable are the lack of ornament, and combined uses of white, polychrome, and scumbled gesso with gilding (gold, aluminum, silver, and metal leaf), and natural or distressed wood.

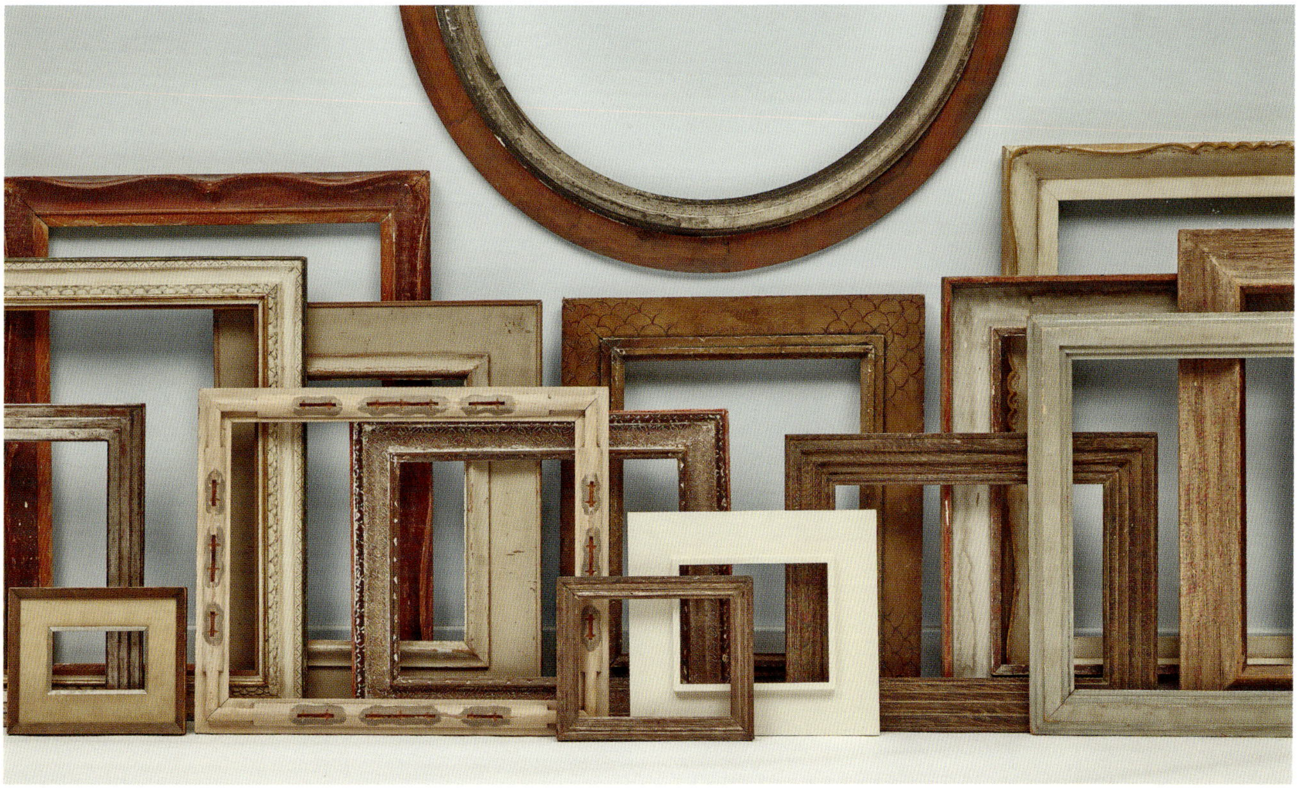

Connoisseurship and Quality in American Art

Eric Widing
Deputy Chairman, Christie's Americas, New York

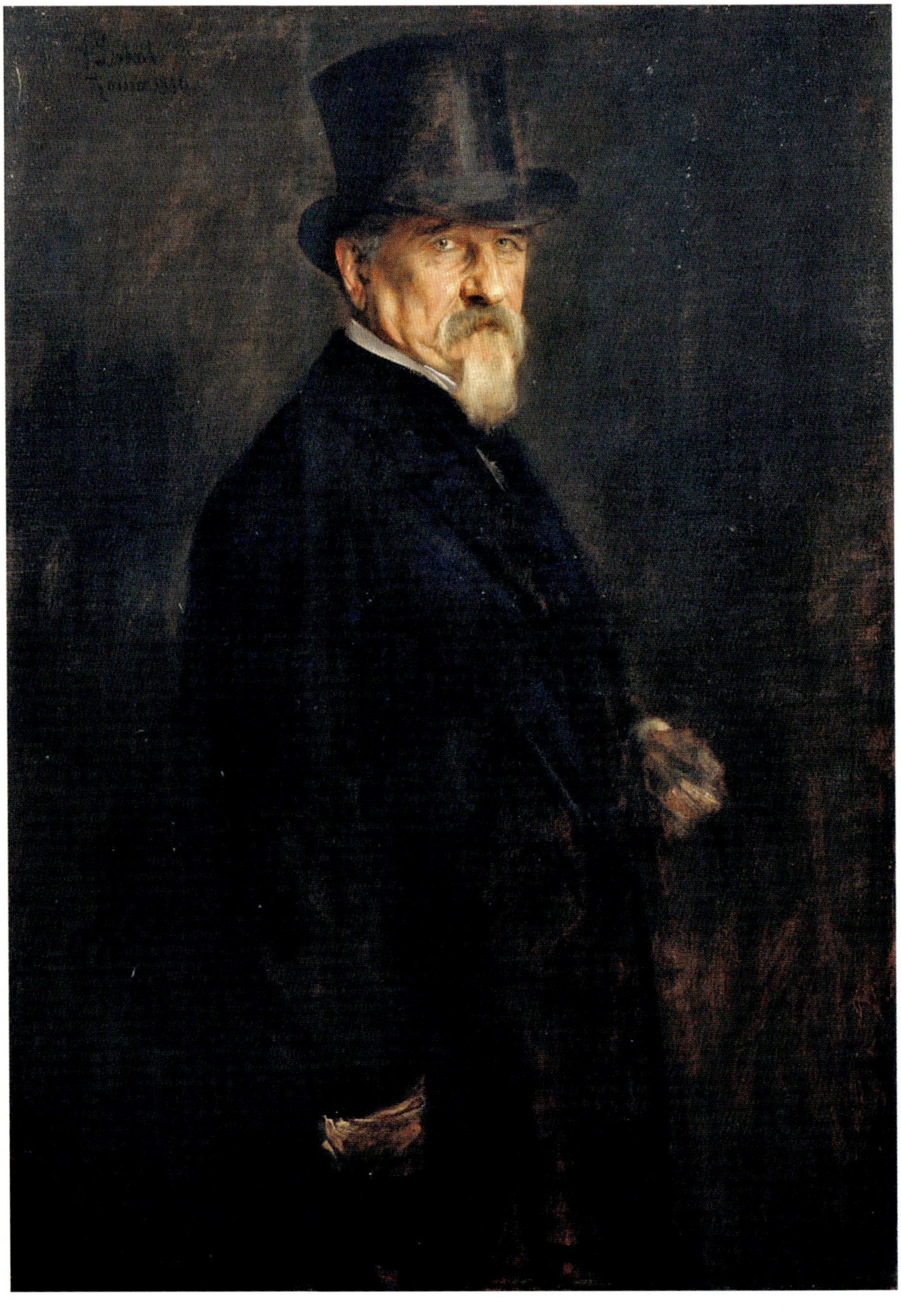

In the auction business, the two most frequently asked questions about an art object are, "Who created it?" and, "How good is it?" Simple as these questions may seem, they can be challenging to answer, and touch on two of the most fundamental aspects of art history: connoisseurship and quality.

In formal art history, connoisseurship is defined as the determination of authorship, and, if possible, the date of creation of an art object. The common assumption that the words "connoisseurship" and "expertise" are interchangeable is not quite accurate, because true connoisseurship is expertise of a very particular kind. It is applied in the study of a painting, a drawing, or a sculpture to answer the specific question, "Who made this?"

It almost goes without saying that our efforts to understand the vast canon of art must rest on the firm foundation of correct attribution. All other aspects of art history are built upon it. The study of patronage, the history of taste, the impact of religion, politics, economics, military history, and virtually every other aspect of human culture applied to the understanding of artworks—all of it starts with connoisseurship. So, too, with the study of symbols and meaning, which in art history is viewed from the lofty heights of iconography and iconology. These aspects of art can be assessed only when the fact of an object's authenticity has been established. Accurate connoisseurship also frees the viewer to look deeper, both to the broader aspects of art, and to look within, to their personal reaction, which creates meaning in the viewing of an object. Connoisseurship also allows us, at the outset, to address the second question posed above, that of quality.

Today, the obvious assumption for any museum-goer is that the art and objects in every museum are authentic and as described on the wall text. While this is overwhelmingly the case, there have been some famous disputes about certain works and artists. In recent years, for example, the Rembrandt Research Project debunked many famous works attributed to the master. Later, some debunked works were "re-bunked," accepted back into the canon of Rembrandt's works after all. Connoisseurship can be messy.

Presently, connoisseurs of American art are greatly aided by a multitude of books, nearly all of them published since 1980. In the United States, a small number of scholars have labored to produce catalogues raisonnés, which are systematic catalogues that aim to record every work of art produced by a given artist. Some of these scholarly achievements fill single volumes (Maurice and Charles Prendergast), while others require multiple volumes (William Merritt Chase, Winslow Homer, and John Singer Sargent). They all contribute to an elevated level of scholarship, based on connoisseurship, allowing a clearer understanding of our own cultural heritage. That said, most artists do not have a catalogue raisonné of their work, and connoisseurs must rely on their own eye and experience to determine an attribution for a work of art to a specific artist. They are also helped by the fact that most American art is no more than two centuries old, and is in generally good condition. This is less common with Old Masters and ancient art, for instance. It is easier to establish an attribution for an artwork in good condition, which more closely represents the artist's original intentions.

In American art, we also have well-documented exhibition histories and provenance (the history of ownership), which can help verify attributions. For example, thirty years ago, while touring a private collection, the owner off-handedly pointed to a small landscape in a hallway and said, "There's my fake Kensett." I looked and declared somewhat boldly that the painting was right—it was the signature that was fake. The next day, in the library of the American Wing at The Metropolitan Museum of Art, I pulled an ancient, oversized tome from the shelves. It was a beautifully bound book from 1873, filled with photographic plates of every wall of the John F. Kensett memorial exhibition at the National Academy of Design. Painstakingly, I looked at the plates, which showed hundreds of paintings. The works were depicted in surprisingly sharp detail, and sometimes I could see lot numbers on white cards stuck into the

1.
Giovanni Morelli (1816–1891) by Franz von Lenbach, 1886
125 ½ × 90 ⅕ in.
(318.8 × 229 cm)
Accademia Carrara di Belle Arti di Bergamo

frames. Eventually, I found an image of the Kensett in the hallway, thus confirming that it was in the 1873 Kensett sale and therefore authentic. How did it get the fake signature? Kensett died unexpectedly in 1872, and since he did not usually sign his paintings until they were leaving his studio, most of the works in the 1873 sale had no signatures. At a later date, many of them acquired the artist's initials, added by other hands.

A relatively modern discipline, connoisseurship originated in the nineteenth century with an Italian professor of comparative anatomy, Giovanni Morelli (1816–1891), who applied his training to the analysis of art (Fig. 1). The problem he sought to solve was that of authorship in Renaissance art. Most Renaissance paintings are unsigned. Most depict similar subjects—commonly a short list of saints, angels, the Madonna and Child, and the adult Christ. All the artists used essentially the same paints and supports, since little variety in the way of art materials was then available. Many worked in outwardly similar styles.

To figure out which artists painted which artworks, Morelli began to systematically study minor details, seeking patterns and repetitions. He soon reduced his analysis to three details common to nearly all of these paintings: fingernails, earlobes, and nostrils. He posited that Renaissance artists, directed by their patrons to depict certain subjects in a more-or-less conventional style, would express themselves in the details, and would do so in a personalized and consistent way. He was right. Using this method to compare anatomical details in varied artworks, in 1880 he famously reattributed an odalisque in Dresden from Titian to Giorgione, which attribution is still widely accepted nearly a century and a half later.

How does this method work in modern practice, or in the field of American art? Having spent decades in the American field, I have looked closely at tens of thousands of American paintings. In addition, as an auction specialist, one of my daily tasks is to confirm authorship and the date of execution for artworks. This close scrutiny is an essential part of our appraisals, and is the basis for assessing artistic importance as well as value.

When examining an object, the first impression is often reliable. It is the gut instinct on which professional connoisseurs rely—along with training. Long study is required, and it can take years to reach proficiency.

As an undergraduate at Williams College, I sometimes attended lectures by Julius S. Held, the renowned professor, collector, and connoisseur of Old Master art and drawings (Fig. 2). He emphasized the need for constant looking to have a high level of mastery. He even insisted that his art students have a magnifying glass with them at all times when studying art. I remember him saying that he had to constantly train his eye, and that a two-week vacation could throw off his connoisseurship. But, by looking at vast numbers of artworks, he also became finely attuned to the differences between artists and their methods. This laborious study allowed him to be instantly alert in matters of attribution. In short, with training, connoisseurship can become almost instinctual.

At Williams, art history students were taught to respect the primacy of the object. Before putting forward any conclusions, we were expected to analyze art closely, even obsessively. This may seem obvious, but forty years ago, as today, there were many art historians who would begin with a premise, and then seek out artworks to support their thesis. The shortcomings of this process are clear: by looking only for what you want to find, an art historian is not likely to discover a new idea, or a surprising, unexpected truth. In contrast, close study might lead you someplace you never expected to go.

A few years ago at Christie's, we were tasked with the appraisal of a museum's entire collection of American art. This required many visits over a year, the last of which led to the basement to look at their works in storage, a windowless room outfitted with rolling racks, many of them large enough to hang a dozen works of art on each side. On this particular day, we pulled out each rack in succession until one revealed, high above, a large landscape with cows by a river. "What a nice Bierstadt," I said. The museum professional nearby said, "Umm, it's an Inness." So I climbed a ladder and studied the details. "No," I said, "it's a Bierstadt." "It's signed Inness," came the reply. How did I know almost instantly that this work was by Albert Bierstadt? At first glance, the work as much as said to me, "I am a Bierstadt."

Such impressions need to be supported, however, by closer study. A good start is a technical analysis of the paint layer, size and support. Often these details are consistent within the body of an artist's work, and this is the case with Bierstadt. I could see that the painting was an oil on paper (though the registrar had it noted on an inventory card as an oil on canvas, upon unframing we could see that it was an oil on paper mounted on canvas). Bierstadt often painted oils on paper, especially in the field, where manhandling a canvas in a wind would have been challenging. Later, in his studio, he might use these works on paper as the basis for larger compositions painted on canvas. With paper, the artist tended to work in two sizes: a full sheet, 20 by 28 inches (50.8 × 71 cm), or a half sheet, 20 by 14 inches (50.8 × 35.5 cm). This work was 18 by 28 inches (45.7 × 71 cm). I began to wonder why it was not quite as large as Bierstadt's usual full sheet.

The composition depicted likely shows a location somewhere in New Hampshire, a less common subject for Bierstadt, who is better known for his views of the West, particularly California. In its rendition of cows in a mountain landscape in summer, the composition superficially resembles a pastoral landscape by George Inness, and indeed it does bear a signature at lower left: G. Inness. However, that signature looked to my eye a bit stiff and awkward and was, in my opinion, probably added at a later date (and not by the artist).

The question remained, why was the work 18 by 28 inches? With the landscape unframed and looking at the edges of the paper, I could see that the left, top and right edges had oxidized to a brownish tone. The bottom edge was cleaner, closer to white. The fair supposition is that the work may once indeed have been about 20 by 28 inches. At some point in its existence the bottom two inches were removed, most likely to eliminate the original signature, which I believe would have been Bierstadt's. Why would someone do such a thing? It's a guess, but years ago, perhaps in the early twentieth century, someone decided to "upgrade" the work from the then less-fashionable Albert Bierstadt to the more fashionable George Inness. Bierstadt's signature was cut off, and Inness's added, thus making the work more marketable.

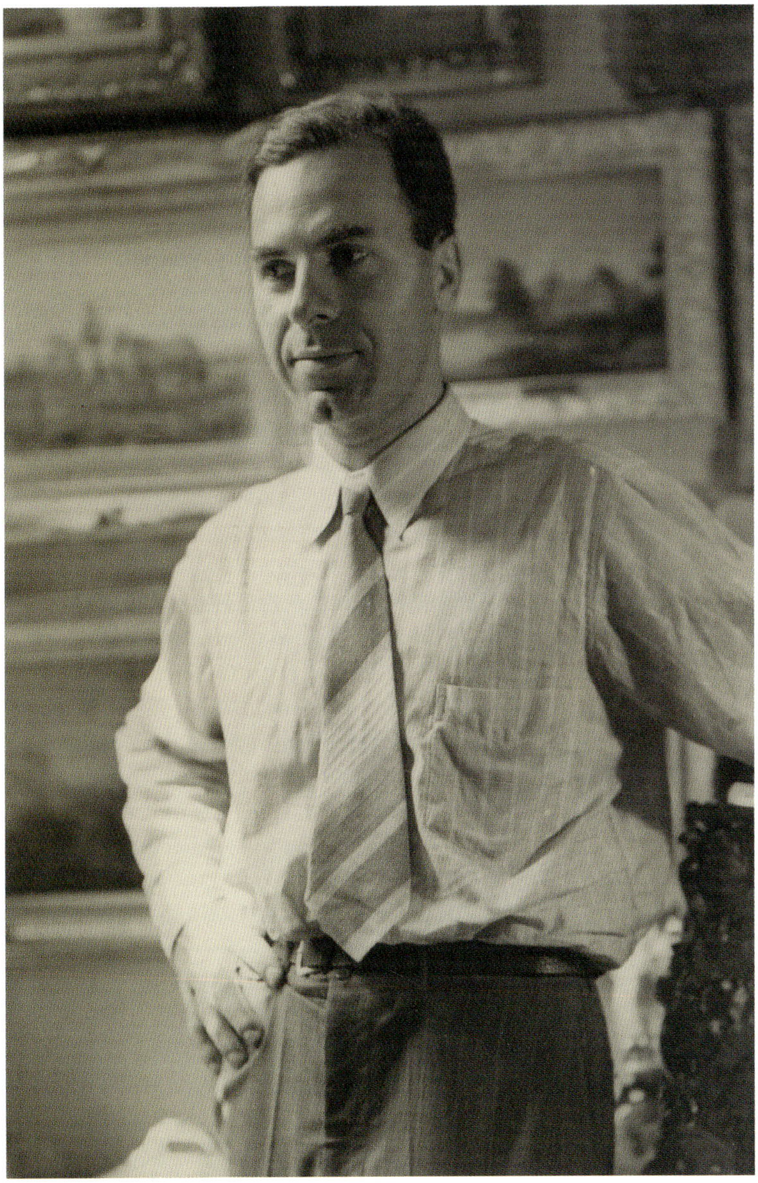

2.
Julius S. Held (1905–2002), *c.* 1940

As noted above, my first impression was that the painting was by Albert Bierstadt. While I trusted my gut instinct and my review of the

Confessions of an Art Collector Turned Dealer

Richard Rossello
Avery Galleries, Bryn Mawr, Pennsylvania

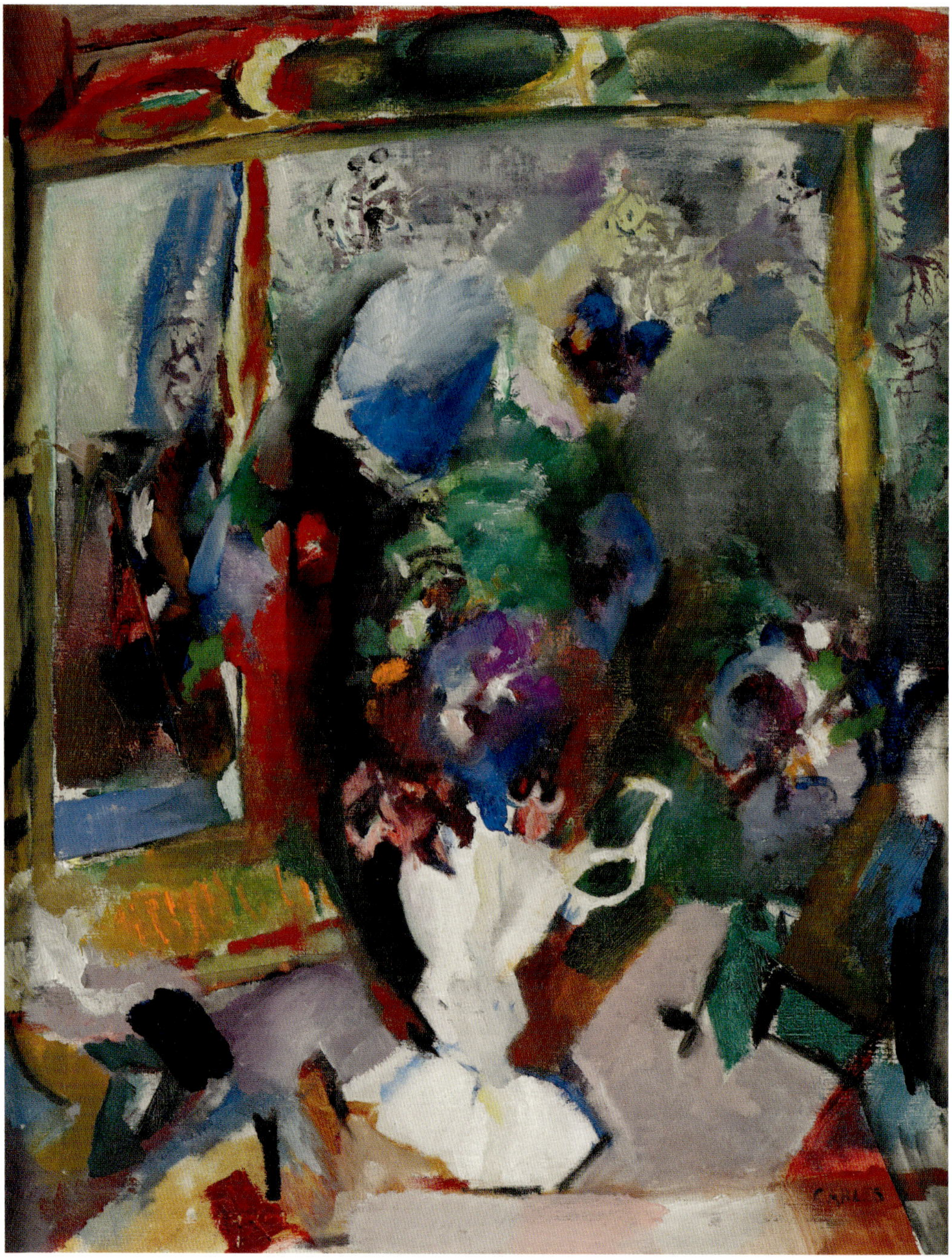

My career as a collector has a clear beginning and it had nothing to do with actually buying art. I was an economics student in London in the fall of 1974. The Royal Academy had just opened an exhibition of J.M.W. Turner's paintings and I asked an attractive young woman if she would like to go take a look. As one might suspect, I was more motivated by the aesthetics of the young woman than I was by those of Mr. Turner. Of course, the irony is that Turner's paintings, not my date, made the indelible impression that changed my life. As I stood before Turner's works, I had two thoughts. First, how could his paintings be imbued with such emotional power and energy, and, second, how could someone from the early 1800s depict the world so abstractly and yet so profoundly? Turner's *Snow Storm: Steam-Boat off a Harbour's Mouth* is a whirlwind of paint. Its swirling imagery connects us to the storm in a way that no literal interpretation could ever achieve. *Death on a Pale Horse* is as haunting a vision of mortality as I ever want to experience. As we wandered through the halls of the Academy, we came upon glassed cases of the artist's sketchbooks. Looking closely at the way he worked on the problems of composition, color, and perspective, it was almost as if we could feel him at the other end of his brush. His art did not look anything like the paintings of his contemporaries. His vision was uniquely and defiantly his own. It was then that I knew, with certainty, that a fulfilling life for me would have to include works of art—not just decorative pictures, but art that intensified and expanded one's perception of the world.

My formal education was focused on economics and finance, but my personal education was a journey into the history of art. When I graduated with a Master's degree from Wharton, my first celebratory acquisition was a painting. Mundane things like cars, clothes, and gadgets came a distant second. Visiting galleries on weekends became something of a hobby for me and although I had a minuscule budget, I fell in love often—too often. Perhaps this chapter will serve as a cautionary tale for beginning collectors!

Since looking directly at paintings is completely different and much more fulfilling than looking at photographs of paintings, I made it a habit early in my collecting career to frequent local galleries and befriend the owners. It was a pleasant surprise to learn how willing most gallery owners were to share their knowledge about the art they owned and the artists they represented. Many Saturday mornings were spent in galleries soaking up the information that they shared so freely. I would attend local auctions, patiently sitting through sales that lasted for hours, even when I knew that I had neither the intention nor the means to buy the paintings I liked. Before the actual sale date, I would pore through the print catalogue, noting the paintings that caught my eye and then taking some time to learn about the artist who created them. I would circle the lots that I wished I could own and track them during the sale to see whether or not they performed better or worse than the estimates listed in the auction house's catalogue. It built my confidence to see that most of the time I was selecting paintings that sold well. In retrospect, I believe that my lack of funds at this time was a blessing in disguise. The beginner mistakes I made during these "dry runs" cost me nothing, but taught me a great deal.

Eventually our family finances improved to the point where I could start bringing pictures home, and I did so with great enthusiasm—probably far too much, in my wife's view. "One's eye needs to harden" is a phrase I have heard that sounds quite painful, but is, in fact, an apt description of the maturing process we collectors go through. What we are initially drawn to is almost invariably different from what we wind up with. There are two common starting points for collectors—strong, vibrant color that catches us the way sparkling objects attract crows, and/or pictures that represent an important aspect of our lives. What we hang on our walls is a way of telling our own stories. This is not an original thought. Just look at the cave drawings from tens of thousands of years ago in which hunters boasted of their kills on the cave walls. Or, better yet, look into a typical teenager's room, hung

1.
Arthur B. Carles (1882–1952)
Flowers (Abstract Still Life)
c. 1932
Oil on canvas
26 × 20 ¼ in. (66 × 51.4 cm)
Signed lower right: *Carles.*
Avery Galleries, Bryn Mawr, PA

with posters of sports stars or rock musicians or whatever reflects their passion. Why should it be different for adults? During the early years of my art-buying career, having grown up on Cape Cod my passion was seascapes and sailboats. Eventually, my wife put her foot down, telling me that if I brought one more painting of the ocean or boats into the house, she hoped I would enjoy living with them all by myself! As I learned more and more about art, I was increasingly willing to step outside of that narrow focus I began with and, more importantly, I did not feel the need to buy everything I saw that looked like a good buy. You know your "eye" is hardening when you say to yourself, "That's nice, but it doesn't really add to my collection."

One of the earliest pieces we ever acquired (back in the early 1980s) is a William Trost Richards oil. We deliberated over it for two weeks because we had never spent so much on a painting before. The price was $14,500, and even though we have been offered much more for it on several occasions over the years, we can't bring ourselves to part with it. It is a piece of our family lore. Over time, of course, we ran into the problem that all collectors face—the lack of wall space. Other than a few sentimental favorites, the solution was to sell some of our paintings to friends, freeing up wall space and, just as importantly, cash with which to buy more art. I did not go out and solicit buyers, but over the years, friends would visit for dinner or cocktails and occasionally admire the art. When they asked if I would consider selling something, I usually said yes. In the back of my mind, I hoped that the sale would allow me to find something I liked even better. These transactions were tricky and required total transparency. It would be a poor trade to sell a painting, only to lose a friend who felt that you had taken advantage of them. The practice of selling to friends was a good, early lesson on why fair and open deals are, in the long run, good business.

Once, when I had brought yet another painting home, my wife asked me how much money I intended to spend on art. Since we had children to educate, she was more than a little concerned about my priorities. I took the time to add up all of the paintings that we had purchased over the years and then I added up all of the paintings I had, in turn, sold to friends. I was as surprised as she was to learn that almost our entire collection had been paid for through the sale of other paintings. It was at that moment that the idea of making my passion a real business started to take shape.

My wife and I were both fully committed businesspeople. She was a vice president at a major pharmaceutical firm, and I was an entrepreneur who developed and operated a number of restaurants in Pennsylvania and Delaware. Stress was our daily accompaniment. With such busy calendars, the thought of adding another business venture to the mix did not seem feasible, so I decided to take a half step and create and run an "art club." The American Art League was organized as a partnership with a number of limited partners. The idea, which, I found out much later, was not entirely original, was to pool funds from a number of investors. A local dealer and I would act as general partners and buy art on behalf of the League. Once we had amassed a certain number of paintings, we would have a big evening cocktail party for all the partners where we would hold a silent auction for them. Works that were not sold that evening would then be sold to the general public. All profits from the auctions and the general sales were distributed evenly among the partners. For a couple of years it was great fun and the investors all made a good return on their investment, but there was one big drawback. It was a lot of work! Despite a small commission that I earned from my role as general partner, I was devoting time I did not have to a pursuit that paid substantially less than the minimum wage. Of course, I had only myself to blame, since it was my bright idea! After winding down this fun but unprofitable experiment, things might have gone back to the status quo, but fate intervened. In 2001, on my forty-eighth birthday, the cosmos decided to reward my hard work with a heart attack. It was a relatively minor myocardial infarction, but along with the ensuing quintuple bypass operation, it got my attention. It was time for a complete lifestyle overhaul, beginning with

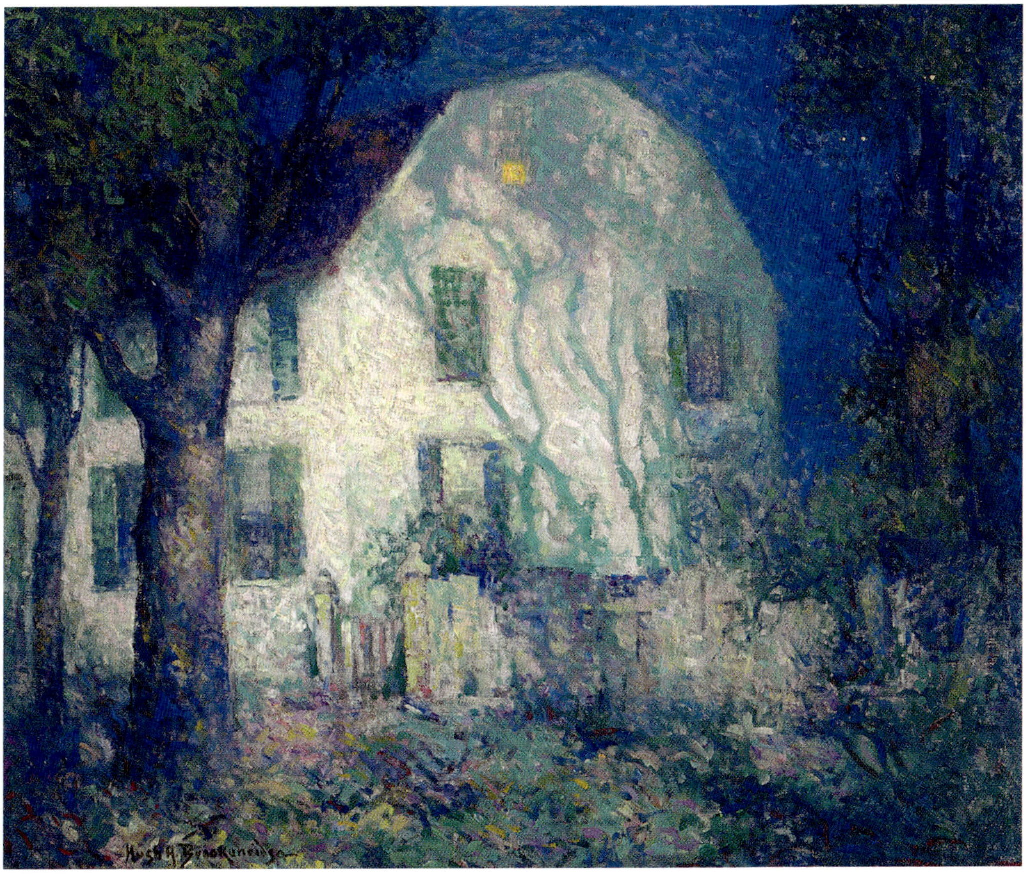

2.
Hugh Henry Breckenridge
(1870–1937)
Moon Shadows, c. 1910s
Oil on canvas
24 × 30 in. (61 × 76.2 cm)
Signed lower left: *Hugh H. Breckenridge*
Avery Galleries, Bryn Mawr, PA

a major reduction in stress. That involved giving up my role running the restaurant company. Realizing how fragile life can be, I decided to spend whatever time I had left in doing something I love. Art was the obvious choice. As soon as I was up and about, I worked with a longtime friend to start Avery Galleries.

We were complete neophytes in the gallery business when we started Avery, so we felt that it was best to keep things simple. We began with a few ground rules. First, we decided that rather than solicit consignments we would purchase our art outright, enabling us to pick and choose the works in our collection. We were fortunate to have the funds available to do so, knowing that it would be impossible for most start-ups to invest the several million dollars required. Secondly, we decided that we would never go into debt to fund our business. That may have cost us a few opportunities, but it has kept stress to a minimum and I have no desire to revisit the cardiac care unit. Thirdly, we vowed never to buy art just because it would be profitable to do so. Any painting we bought would have to be a painting that we would be pleased to hang in our own collection. Now, twenty years later, Avery still operates in accordance with those simple tenets.

In the early years we quickly learned how different the art world is from other businesses. When I was in the restaurant business, competition was fierce. In the art world, for the most part, it was collegial. Many gallery owners around the country generously answered our naïve questions and shared their own start-up experiences with us. This sharing attitude underlined some realities about the business. First, being a competent dealer means that you must be, at heart, a teacher. It is obviously an obligation to pass on basic information about the paintings you sell—provenance, condition, exhibition records, etc. These hard, objective facts are an important element in making a decision about whether or not to buy a painting, but a good dealer will also share their subjective and visceral reaction to the painting. What moves a work of art from competent to magical? This deeply personal response to art will always vary from person to person, but dealers can and should share their own subjective judgments. We look at so many paintings that we have a broad context to draw on. Knowing that not everyone will respond to a painting the same way does not mean we shouldn't share our perspective. For example, some collectors look at the early Modernist paintings like the Carles (Fig. 1) or Breckenridge (Fig. 2) pictured here and say, "I don't get it!" It may or may not help when we explain that the artists, who were in the forefront of American Modernism, used strong, vibrant colors to create paintings that were beautiful in their own right rather than being realistic representations of other beautiful objects. That said, if it cannot be said in clear, simple English, then skip it! There is enough art-speak gobbledygook out there already. Secondly, the art business is incredibly "old school." Transactions are based on trust and, as in Lloyd's of London's famous motto, "Your word is your bond." Dealers routinely allow paintings worth hundreds of thousands of dollars to go out on approval to clients' homes or other galleries with nothing more than a signed slip of paper. In most other businesses, smaller transactions require attorneys, notaries, and title insurers. It is gratifying to say that in almost twenty years there have been only a handful of instances in which that trust has been violated, which brings me to the next segment.

The biggest mistakes I have made as a dealer are still in the racks of my gallery storage space. They sit there as silent reproof of my naïvety. I speak, of course, of the paintings that I bought thinking they were fine originals, only to discover after it was too late that they were forgeries. How can this happen to an experienced, knowledgeable dealer? It is a fair question. The simple explanation is that, at the time, I didn't know what I didn't know. The world of art is vast and if anyone tells you they know every facet of it, they are not telling the truth. My narrow area of expertise is limited to American art created in the nineteenth and early twentieth centuries. Someone I believed to be reliable offered me two post-World War II paintings related to the Abstract Expressionist school. I did not let the fact that I had never studied Abstract Expressionism get in the way of making a deal. My hubris was duly rewarded when I discovered that the works could not be authenticated and, to add salt to my wounds, the private dealer who sold them to me could not refund my money. All told, the "tuition" paid for rushing ahead without due diligence was almost $100,000. Just retelling the story causes pain! Lessons learned: admit to yourself that you cannot know everything and when you are not sure if you have enough information, do not pull the trigger.

Another instance of misplaced confidence happened soon after we opened the gallery. We owned a small George Luks painting that was executed on paper card stock. It was unframed and stored flat in a drawer. One day, in a cavalier, "I know what I'm doing" manner, I pulled it out of the drawer by grabbing a corner with two fingers. When the paper, made brittle by the dried paint and age, snapped off in my hand, I found myself holding Luks's signature on a two-inch triangular piece of paper, while the body of the painting remained in the drawer. Of course, I was sickened by what I had done and arranged to take it directly to a conservator. Since it was a clean break, my hope was to piece it back together without any significant losses. Compounding my mistake, I rushed the painting and the signature to my car without packing it properly. As I took it out at the conservator's office, a gust of wind caught the picture and, while it was in my hands, broke it into two more pieces! I didn't know whether to laugh or cry, so I did both. Remarkably, the expert was able to get everything back together, but the value of the little painting was severely diminished. More importantly, my negligence had caused damage to a work of art that had survived intact for a hundred years before, literally, falling into my hands. Lesson learned: a version of "measure twice, cut once." Never take short cuts when handling art—especially works on paper.

When buying art, we are often looking at pictures that have been left untouched for many years. There are layers of soot, dirt, and old, discolored varnish that can obscure the artist's work, and we must make a judgment or best guess regarding how the painting will look after cleaning and restoration. This is our favorite way to find paintings—like diamonds in the rough. Watching the grime fall away to reveal the beautiful colors underneath is thrilling. That said, on a few occasions there have been severe disappointments. One particular instance comes to mind when I bought a large William Trost Richards oil and there were streaks of black gunk running through the small interstices in the painting. These marks were quite distracting, but I convinced myself that the restoration process would address the problem. Unfortunately, the streaks would not budge even with the most aggressive treatment. It turned out that Richards had mixed linseed oil into his paint and over time that oil had darkened. Since the oil was literally part of the paint surface, the only way to remove it would be to erase the painting. Lesson learned: whenever possible, test an area of the painting to determine whether or not it will clean as expected. Failing that, at least get an expert opinion on condition prior to writing the check.

One mistake had a happy ending. I spotted a lovely picture at a trade show. The Japanese artist Leonard Foujita worked primarily in Paris and had no association with America. There was no reasonable argument I could make for why adding it to the gallery inventory made sense. I just thought it was beautiful and wanted it. As one might expect, given the fact that our clients are collectors of American art, the small watercolor was admired, but no one wanted to take it home. I displayed the painting at more than a half dozen shows and two or three years passed without success. I finally decided that it had to be shown to a more appropriate audience, and consigned it to an auction in New York. When the auction house representative called me, I braced for the worst—an unsold lot. However, what she said was, "I'm about to be your favorite person of the day!" The painting brought three times what I had been asking for it at the gallery. First lesson learned: make sure that the art you offer is in alignment with the clientele you serve. Second lesson learned: every now and then take a leap of faith when you find something extraordinary. Just keep the first lesson in mind when you do.

I wonder how many art dealers are born under the sign of Gemini? Being a successful dealer, I believe, requires juggling twin skills that can, occasionally, conflict with one another. The first is the genuine love of art and an in-depth knowledge that can only be acquired through patient research and hard-won experience. Second is an addiction to the adrenalin rush of treasure-hunting. Somehow, we have to walk the line between aesthete and prospector. As a dealer, I look at hundreds of paintings for each one that I acquire. The yardstick that I bring to bear has two scales. The first and most important measurement is: "Would I want this for my own collection?" The answer has to take into account the beauty of the painting, its condition, its provenance, the importance of the artist and the importance of the work in the context of that artist's œuvre. If it passes those hurdles, the next question is, "Can it be purchased for an amount that will allow me to resell it at a fair price?" Since the art market is one of the last of the imperfect markets (meaning that the difference in people's knowledge can make a big difference in recognizing value), making the right decision is the difference between success and failure. The reputation of any gallery over the long term relies on how often we get it right. Having been born in June, I suppose the requisite dual focus comes naturally to me.

I am grateful that I started as a collector. Knowing what it is like to walk into a gallery understanding almost nothing about art has helped me to appreciate the importance of teaching. First, sharing knowledge with our clients is one of the most important functions we have. Not only does it help them to make wise choices about what to buy, it helps them appreciate the works they own at a deeper level. Secondly, it was clear from the beginning that dealer–client relationships should be long-term and not rely on a single or a few transactions. Most serious collectors are in it for the long haul and helping build collections is not only good business, it makes for long-lasting and satisfying friendships. To accomplish this, there has to be an inherent fairness and transparency in the relationship. If a dealer counts a transaction as a success because he or she has been able to extract top dollar for a painting, or if a collector is happy only if they know that the dealer made no profit on a deal, that relationship will not flourish. The overcharged collector will find someone else they can trust to treat them fairly. The dealer who was beaten up over the last few dollars on a sale will place that collector at the bottom of the list the next time a desirable painting comes their way.

Starting as a collector has also helped keep the "love of art" above the "love of the deal." There are many instances when we bought beautiful paintings by artists who are virtually unknown. Two of them, Elizabeth Sparhawk-Jones and William Bliss Baker, are represented here (Figs. 3 and 4). Tragically, Baker died at only twenty-seven years old, cutting short what would have been a spectacular career. Sparhawk-Jones fell ill in her early twenties and for many years never lifted a brush. These two artists prove that buying paintings trumps buying signatures. Avery was founded on one central idea: "We love people who love art." Some folks cannot afford to build collections and may never buy a single painting from us, but if they love the art, they are welcome to visit us anytime. We have learned amazing things from some of the unlikeliest people. On one occasion at a show in Boston, an elderly man came to our booth and, seeing a chair, asked if he could sit and rest for a bit. Of course, we

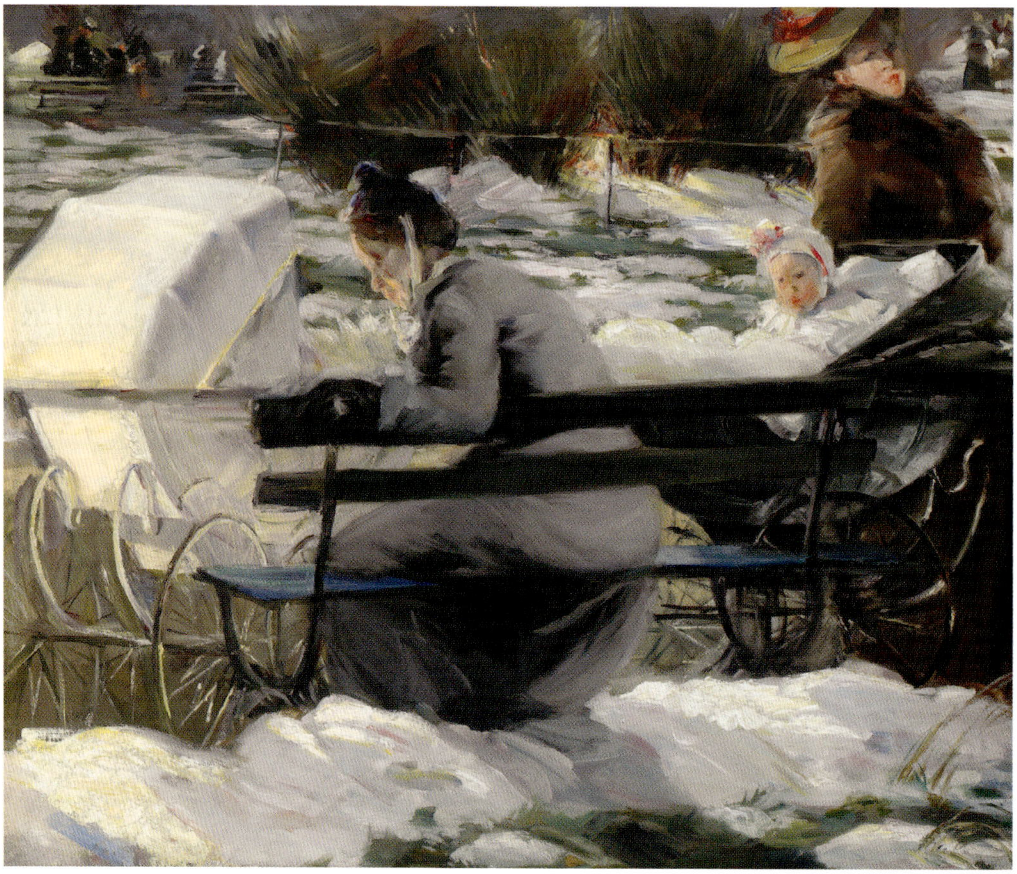

3.
Elizabeth Sparhawk-Jones
(1885–1968)
In Rittenhouse Square, c. 1908
Oil on canvas
30 × 36 in. (76.2 × 91.4 cm)
Richard Rossello, Haverford, PA

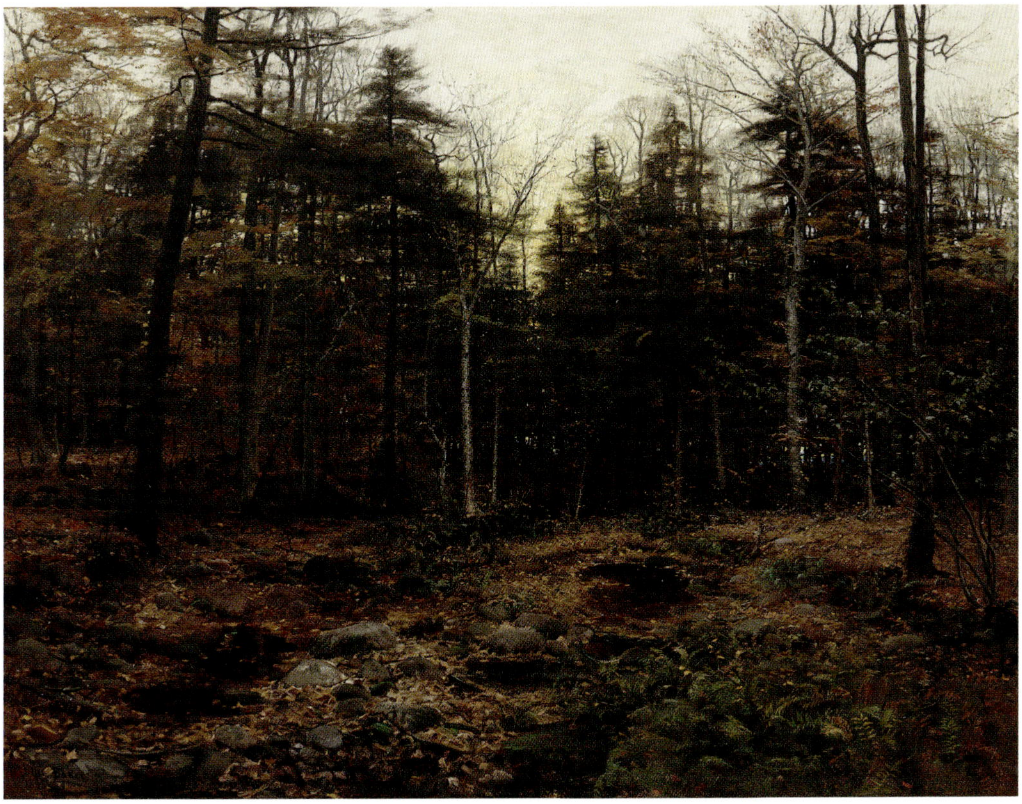

4.
William Bliss Baker
(1859–1886)
Woodland Scene, 1885
Oil on canvas
38 × 50 in. (96.5 × 127 cm)
Signed lower left: *W Bliss Baker 1885*
Avery Galleries, Bryn Mawr, PA

told him to make himself comfortable. While he was sitting and resting his feet, he looked around the booth and his attention was caught by a wall of Modernist works. He pointed to one in particular and said, "I love that one, how much is it?" The picture was a small, but magnificent Georgia O'Keeffe pastel. I apologetically told him that it was almost one million dollars and acknowledged that it was an awful lot of money. His response floored me. He said, "Well, you know, that's not too much to pay for a piece of our civilization's DNA." Before he wandered off, I let him know that I had every intention of retelling the story and promised to give him credit. This is proof that not all wonderful and worthwhile interactions are sales.

The greatest rewards I have received from the years spent in the art world have been the friendships formed along the way. The many dealers who helped us start the gallery with no intention of profiting from their kindness; the innumerable clients who have become long-time friends and have allowed us to partner with them as unofficial curators on their behalf; the museum administrators and curators who have been unfailingly generous with their in-depth knowledge and enthusiasm—I am deeply grateful to them all. Our favorite memories are of helping clients find just the right spots in their homes for special paintings, knowing that they will enhance their lives for years to come. I love to revisit the paintings we have sold whenever possible and I like to remind their owners that, despite the financial and legal realities, a little part of each picture will always be mine!

The Painting Conservator and Connoisseurship in American Art

Joyce Hill Stoner, PhD
Edward F. and Elizabeth Goodman Rosenberg Professor of Material Culture Studies; Director, Preservation Studies Doctoral Program, University of Delaware

Why should curators, collectors, art historians, and dealers consult with conservators? If "connoisseurship" relates to "knowing," would it not be best to know more about the techniques and materials of a particular work? It is possible that the painting you are about to purchase at auction has been more than 50% overpainted (and the image by the original artist is something quite different), or perhaps the painting is a clever forgery. You might be authoring an essay on a painting, and it turns out—when the painting is x-rayed—that what appears to be a blank background was once an architectural setting. Wouldn't you like to have this information before going forward? Many curators realize that working with paintings conservators is a win-win situation. The two professions, with their particular approaches to "close looking," can be enriched by collaboration, and both sides can avoid situations of embarrassment by working together.

Over the last several decades, our faculty and students at the Winterthur/University of Delaware Program in Art Conservation have examined paintings that had been cleverly overpainted by restorers, transforming the original artists' compositions below. A painting of Cleopatra holding an asp to her breast had been "restored" to become a Mary Magdalene looking heavenward. A "St. Margaret of Cortona" with her hand on a little fluffy dog was actually a *memento mori*—the saint had originally been painted with her hand on a skull. An x-radiograph and an ultraviolet photograph taken of an African American sitter revealed a Caucasian sitter underneath. In all three cases the paintings had probably been repainted to increase the likelihood of a sale.

"Technical Art History" and "Technical Connoisseurship" are two phrases that have embodied collaboration between conservators and art historians/curators (and often conservation scientists), especially in the last quarter of the twentieth century and increasingly in the twenty-first, as new tools and techniques for technical examination have become accessible. We try to teach both approaches to our University of Delaware Painting Conservation students in all three levels: undergraduate majors, Master's-level students studying to become practicing conservators, and doctoral students carrying out intensive research in order to write interdisciplinary dissertations (their committee members usually include art historians or historians, scientists, and conservators). This chapter will discuss insights and discoveries made about American paintings due to the interweaving of the documentary and visual evidence typically revealed by art-historical inquiry with the results of conservators' in-depth examination of the physical material and structures of works of art and how they are prepared, used, combined, and manipulated, and how an artist arrived at finished or unfinished works; many of these studies involved our graduates.

Marc Simpson, independent art historian, notes:

Time I have spent with conservators at the Fine Arts Museums of San Francisco and the Williamstown Art Conservation Center has enriched the fashion in which I look at pictures, expanded the questions I am prepared to ask about a work's presentation, and has deepened my knowledge/appreciation of the works I was able to study in those contexts (and, I hope, has helped me to bring that knowledge/appreciation to bear elsewhere).

Exhibitions, too, have been an important arena for me to learn from conservators. Traveling with Kristin Hoermann Lister (WUDPAC [Winterthur/UD Program in Art Conservation] 1981) for Winslow Homer: Paintings of the Civil War*—studying works from other collections as we prepared our loan requests—was an education all in itself. Her essay in the catalogue of that show established a basis for the study of Homer's early oil technique. At the Clark Art Institute, working with Jamie Martin (WUDPAC 1989) in considering Sargent's early Venetian genre scenes, too, was of great value for me and other scholars of Sargent's works in understanding the grounds for varying opinions about certain of them and in weighing the merits of those views.*

I learned things of immense value in 2008 discussions with you [the present author] concerning "Materials for Immateriality" as we prepared the Like Breath on Glass *exhibition catalogue, which gave me the means to understand both how certain effects were achieved as well as the weighty, conscious choices artists made to attain them.*[1]

Technical examination tools have been available to art historians since 1896 when paintings were first x-rayed to detect hidden damages, changes by the artists, or entirely different paintings beneath the surface. Ultraviolet light has been used since the 1910s and 1920s to detect overzealous retouching or partial cleanings, and infrared photography has been used to reveal underdrawings since the 1930s. Infrared reflectography (with video cameras and television screens) has been available since 1969, and cross-section fluorescent staining has helped to determine paint stratigraphy (media and pigments) since the 1980s. American art symposia involving curators, conservators, and scientists have taken place since at least 1971 when the conference "American Painting to 1776: A Reappraisal" was held at Winterthur Museum. At this meeting, Eleanor Quandt, a curator from the Corcoran Gallery of Art in Washington, DC, emerged as a founding mother of technical American art history. The first female curator at the Corcoran, Quandt was married to a conservator, Russell Quandt, and together they developed an approach to American art that was grounded in close examination of the material components of a painting.[2] Subsequent collaborative studies have revealed key findings about the connoisseurship and understanding of the components and subsequent look of paintings by Ralph Blakelock, Thomas Cole, Thomas Wilmer Dewing, Willem de Kooning, Thomas Eakins, Ralph Earl, Hans Hofmann, George Inness, John Frederick Kensett, Georgia O'Keeffe, Rembrandt Peale, Albert Pinkham Ryder, John Singer Sargent, Henry Ossawa Tanner, and James McNeill Whistler, among many others.[3]

We encourage the graduates of our program to participate in joint research projects with their collaborating curators whenever possible. Shelley Svoboda (WUDPAC 1990), Paintings Conservator of Colonial Williamsburg, consults regularly with her curator, Laura Pass Barry (Fig. 1), before a painting is purchased or loaned. In the case of the anonymous *Child with Hoop* (Fig. 2), during her pre-loan condition assessment, Svoboda noticed what appeared to be the ridged impasto of an architectural setting present below the flat green paint of the background surrounding the figure of the child. An x-radiograph (Fig. 3) revealed the architectural scheme, costume changes, a bowl of fruit at the child's feet, and a carpet typical of the American Fancy period. Was this the work of the artist or additions from a later hand? The answer came from Svoboda's careful examination of the painting's surface under the microscope. Her examination revealed wet-on-wet paint mixing of many compositional elements; the upper and lower paint layers had been worked concurrently and were essentially locked together in time. Also, still-wet paint had flowed up from the lower layers in the composition through breaks in the upper paint layers where it had dried. This physical evidence shows that all the paint layers were applied in quick succession by the artist as s/he worked to create the composition; this was not by a later hand. Of this finding, Barry noted:

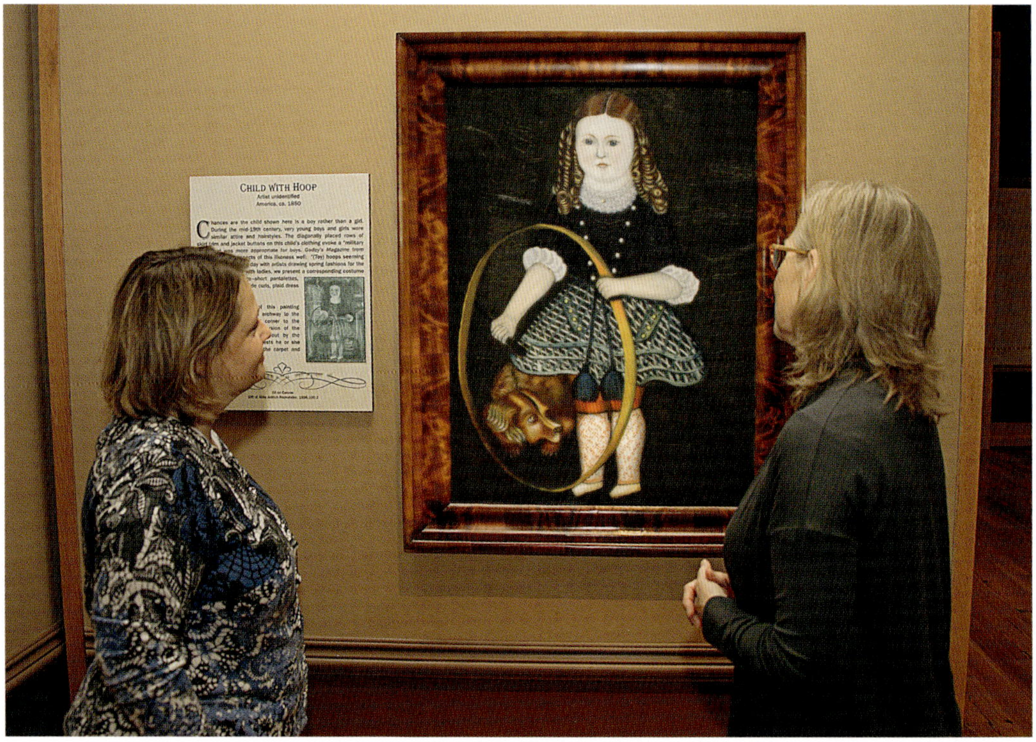

1. *(top)*
Shelley Svoboda (WUDPAC 1990), Senior Paintings Conservator of Colonial Williamsburg (CW), consults regularly with her curator, Laura Pass Barry.

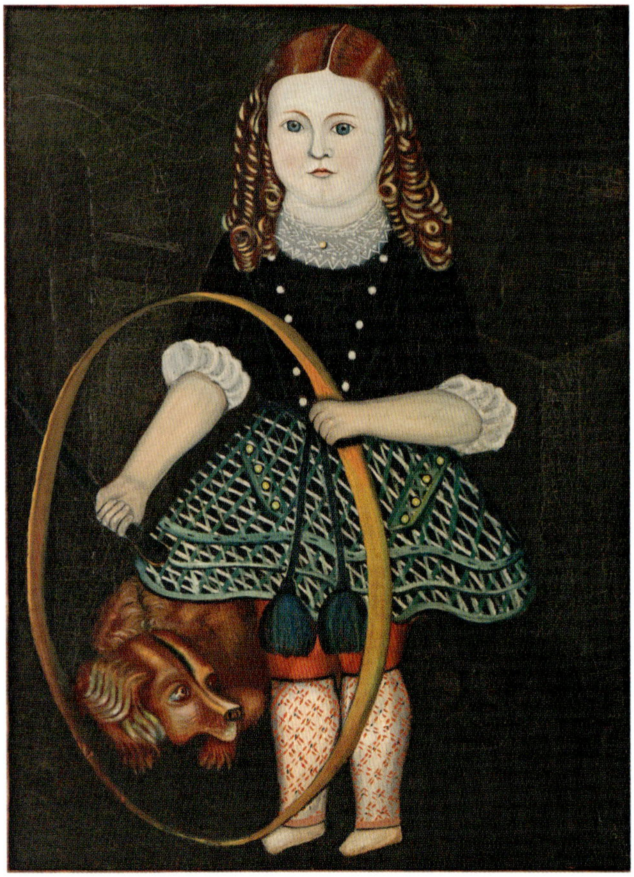

2. *(below left)*
Artist unknown
Child with Hoop, c. 1850
Oil on canvas
36 × 26½ in. (91.4 × 67.3 cm)
Colonial Williamsburg Foundation

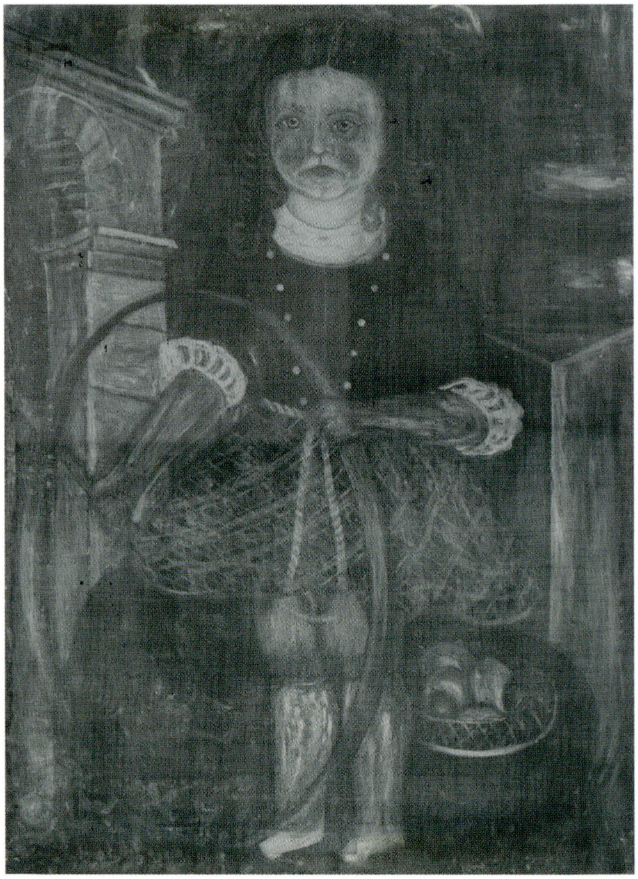

3. *(below right)*
An x-radiograph revealed the architectural scheme, costume changes, a bowl of fruit at the child's feet, and a carpet typical of the American Fancy period.

Without period documentation, we often know very little about an artist's intent. Here, we have tangible evidence that shows us the conscious choices this artist made in developing his/her composition. We now have confirmation that the artist worked in a very dynamic way, systematically editing his/her work as s/he went along.

In this case, the collaboration between a curator and a conservator provided invaluable insight into the working methods of this yet-unidentified nineteenth-century artist. Barry went on to say, "Our work is all the richer because of our strong working relationship. We build off each other in virtually every instance."[4]

Another interdisciplinary team, Anna O. Marley, the curator of historical American art at the Pennsylvania Academy of the Fine Arts (PAFA), and Amber Kerr (WUDPAC 2008), now head conservator of the Lunder Conservation Center at the Smithsonian American Art Museum, worked together and discovered a long-lost painting by Henry Ossawa Tanner (1859–1937). They traveled together to the Musée d'Orsay in Paris in September 2009 to look at Tanner paintings to prepare for an upcoming PAFA exhibition. Kerr set up a raking light, routinely used by conservators to aid in the detection of lifting paint or unusual paint topography. While looking at *The Pilgrims of Emmaus*, 1905, Amber exclaimed that she could see the outline of what looked like a woman playing a cello. Marley, with her mental compendium of Tanner's works, recalled a missing painting by him from 1902 of his wife, Jessie, playing the cello: *The Cello Lesson*, and pulled up an image of an old photograph of the missing painting from the Archives of American Art. The photo matched exactly what they had seen in raking light; a lost painting was discovered using a very simple technique.[5]

Dorothy Mahon, Conservator in the Department of Paintings Conservation at The Metropolitan Museum of Art, working with Elizabeth Mankin Kornhauser, Alice Pratt Brown Curator of American Paintings and Sculpture, used paint cross-sections and an infrared reflectogram to examine the famous *Oxbow* painting by Thomas Cole (1801–1848) in connection with a 2018 Cole exhibition. Infrared reflectography (IRR) penetrates the surface of a painting and can reveal artists' changes and preliminary drawings carried out in carbon-based materials. They discovered that it was likely that Cole had prepared a large canvas support for *The Oxbow* but had first used that support to try out ideas for *The Consummation of Empire*; Cole mentioned this in a letter to Luman Reed.[6]

We have regularly escorted our graduate students to the nearby Philadelphia Museum of Art (PMA) and have been treated to a chronological survey of American paintings in the galleries by Kathleen A. Foster, The Robert L. McNeil, Jr. Senior Curator of American Art, and Director, Center for American Art. Sponsoring this field trip is *de rigueur* for me as a professor of paintings conservation; Foster embodies multiple approaches to connoisseurship: social art history, gender studies, quality of execution, originality in materials, and full awareness of discoveries made by her PMA colleagues, past and present, in the Conservation Department. One of our regular stops is in front of the painting known informally as *Rachel Weeping* (dated 1772–1818) by Charles Willson Peale (1741–1827).[7] After studying the x-radiograph of the painting (Fig. 4) Foster determined that the original painting was only the lower section, depicting just the artist's baby daughter Margaret after her death from fever in 1772. However, Peale later attached an additional piece of canvas above the child, adding his first wife Rachel (1744–1790) behind the baby, looking heavenward and dabbing her tears with a handkerchief. The enlarged canvas demonstrated to Foster:

... the quality of experimentation and ambition in Peale's work, as he cast his wife in the Biblical role of Mary (or Rachel), enacting all the classic attributes of grief. The enlarged painting became a demonstration of the artist's command of historical figure painting, and a theatrical addition to Peale's new Philadelphia museum. With characteristic showmanship, he covered the painting with a curtain carrying a sign warning visitors (particularly young parents) that the picture beneath might be

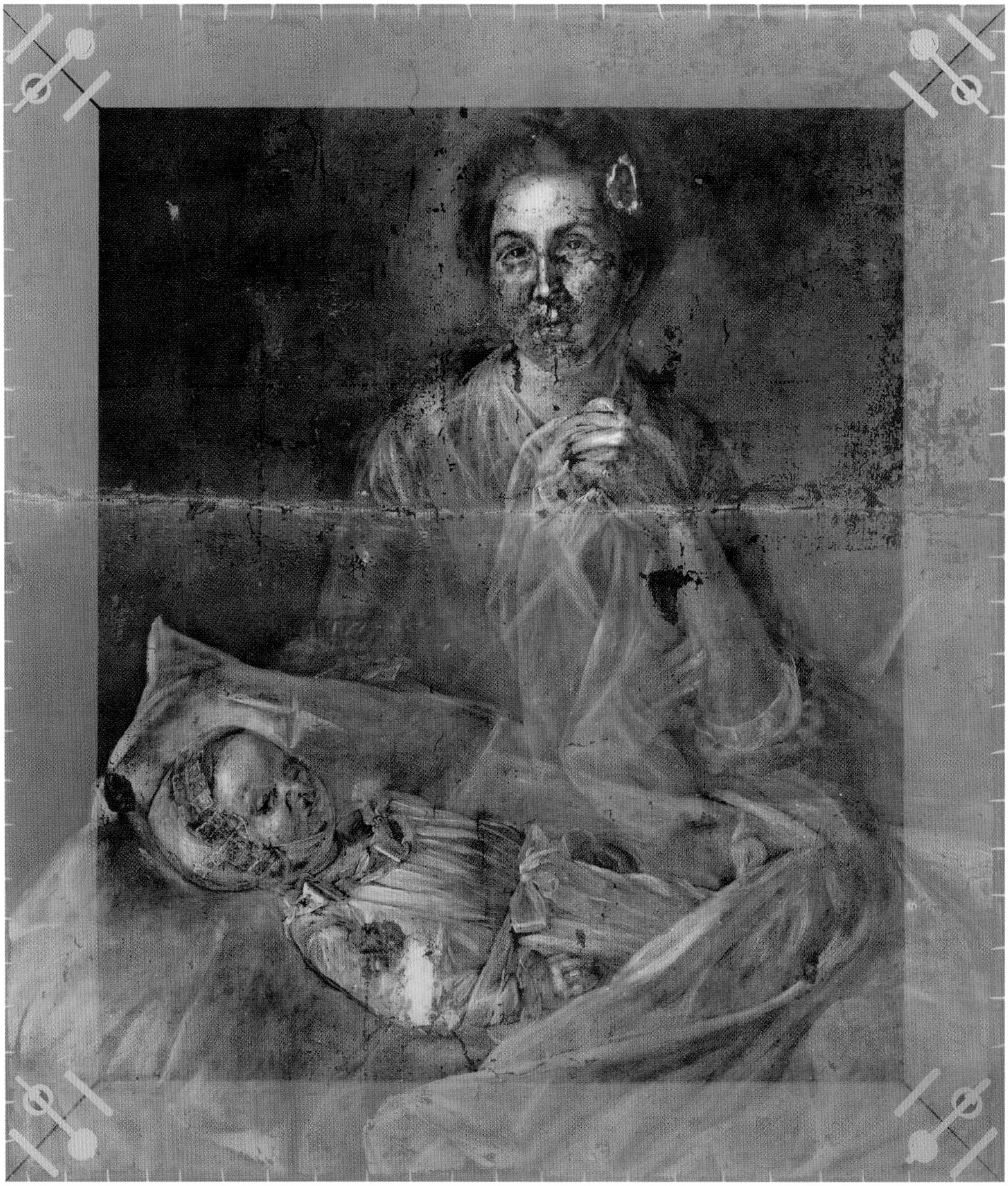

4.
X-radiograph of *Rachel Weeping* (1772–1818).

Charles Willson Peale (1741–1827)
Mrs. Peale Lamenting the Death of Her Child (Rachel Weeping), 1772, enlarged 1776, retouched 1818
Oil on canvas
36 13/16 × 32 1/16 in.
(93.5 × 81.4 cm)
Philadelphia Museum of Art, Gift of The Barra Foundation, Inc., 1977 (1977-34-1)

upsetting—a message at once compassionate and totally enticing. From this complexity, we learn that Peale was an imaginative and original painter, and an entrepreneur not above using a family tragedy to bring audiences to his museum.[8]

Foster also worked with conservator Mark S. Tucker (now The Neubauer Family Director of Conservation at the PMA) in 2007–08 to determine how Thomas Eakins's 1875 masterpiece *The Gross Clinic* had been altered significantly by aggressive early cleanings. The team posted on the museum's website their key findings, and why they decided to remove the 1961 restoration and carry out a new restoration in 2010. The result, "far more consistent with the painting's original appearance," turned out to be "very different from the way it had been known since the early 1920s." The past cleanings had "disrupted Eakins's carefully crafted tonal balances" and damaged paint and glazes. A documentary was made by the paintings conservator and filmmaker Suzanne Penn. Tucker noted that many visitors expressed a new appreciation "for ways that an awareness of links between craft, aesthetics, individual artistic vision, and condition might be applied more broadly to consideration of other works of art."[9]

Collaboration can be crucial for investigating the authenticity of replications of twentieth-century artists' works. Jeffrey Weiss, former Senior Curator at the Guggenheim Museum, noted:

Guggenheim conservator Francesca Esmay and I co-organized the long-running Panza Collection Initiative, an intensive study of works in the collection by Donald Judd, Dan Flavin, Robert Morris, Bruce Nauman, and others. Conservators tend to focus on material analysis, while art historians devote their time to the historical and conceptual issues at stake in a given body of work. Our feeling—and that of more and more people in the field—is that the two disciplines are often wrongly kept apart. What Francesca and I valued most in our working relationship was that we were able to challenge each other, and thereby avoid the limitations of what is so often a one-sided approach to the material versus the historical side. One area in which the relation between the two is so important, we found, is that of the problem of authenticity with regard to re-fabrication of works—a common practice for art of the 1960s and 1970s. It is crucial, in a case like that, to bring technical, material, historical, and theoretical considerations together.[10]

Forgeries abound of the works of Albert Pinkham Ryder (1847–1917) and Ralph Blakelock (1847–1919). As witnessed in the evolution of the Rembrandt Research Project (1968 to the present), authentication studies are most often successful when carried out by an interdisciplinary team. Technical studies of paintings by Blakelock were carried out in the early 1970s by conservators and conservation scientists at the Smithsonian Institution using neutron activation autoradiography in coordination with the Brookhaven Medical Research Reactor. For this procedure, in which paintings are exposed nondestructively to a beam of thermal neutrons for a short time, a series of photographic films is placed in contact with the surface of each painting, showing distribution of pigments that contain radioactive elements. Important information can be revealed by autoradiography that would be blocked by white lead grounds in traditional x-radiography. Six Blakelock paintings were analyzed; two were found to have signatures other than Blakelock's which had been overpainted, had stylistic differences, and one used substantially different pigments.[11] In 2017, another interdisciplinary team at Yale (a conservator, curator, and conservation scientist) returned to the study of a single painting: Blakelock's *Moonlight* of *c.* 1888. They used x-ray fluorescence spectroscopy, Fourier-transform infrared spectroscopy, Raman spectroscopy, scanning electron microscopy-energy dispersive x-ray spectroscopy, and pyrolysis gas chromatography-mass spectrometry. Between ten and thirty-eight paint layers were identified in each of the seven sites tested; Blakelock was interested in capturing and refracting light in the depths of his paint. (One should be suspicious of Blakelock paintings with minimal paint layering, something forgers were not likely to realize, as will be mentioned again below with regard to Ryder forgeries.) However, like many artists, Blakelock often reused his prepared canvases; there appears to be a woman below the moonlit landscape, providing additional explanation for the extraordinary number of paint layers in this case.[12]

Pioneer interdisciplinary neutron activation autoradiography studies in American art at the Smithsonian continued with a focus on Thomas Wilmer Dewing, published in 1990. In addition to autoradiographs, curator Susan Hobbs studied infrared reflectographs and x-radiographs. The autoradiographs especially revealed alterations made by Dewing to his painting *Tobias and the Angel*, 1887, including eliminating two trees, lowering the horizon line, and changing Tobias' arm, which had been reaching toward the angel.[13] (Another exciting autoradiography project, *Insights into the Genesis of Paintings by Rembrandt, Van Dyck, and Vermeer*, was published in 1982 by The Metropolitan Museum of Art in collaboration with Brookhaven National Laboratory; this study revealed, for instance, how Rembrandt sometimes changed the profile of hats in his paintings up to seven times.[14])

Emmett Carl Grimm, one of our University of Delaware doctoral program graduates, studied both attributed and forged works by Albert Pinkham Ryder.[15] Ryder's working methods included continuous reworking of many of his paintings, sometimes while the paint was still wet, or many years later; he varnished works in progress, putting them away horizontally in drawers to dry. He sometimes mixed in candlewax for translucent effects. Minor technical defects did not disturb the artist; the late nineteenth-century art critic Sadakichi Hartmann noted that some of Ryder's paintings had "not only extensive crackings but regular varnish slides, moving lava-like through the surface."[16] Lloyd Goodrich believed there to be about a thousand Ryder forgeries.[17] The Lloyd Goodrich–Albert Pinkham Ryder Archive at the University of Delaware Library contains a number of forgeries detected by art-historical analysis in conjunction with radiography. Grimm sampled these paintings and compared the layered paint application with samples from three of the accepted works at The Metropolitan Museum of Art. Paint cross-sections from the accepted works show clear evidence of reworking and "whipping up" of the paint films and underlayers into convoluted wave forms. In addition, accepted works contain unusual inclusions such as proteins and non-drying oils. The forgeries may superficially have convincing discolored, cracked, and golden surfaces, but under the microscope the cross-sections from such forgeries reveal tidy horizontal bands of layered paint films with no sign of Ryder's typical "whipping up" or odd inclusions (Fig. 5). Forgers may have successfully imitated the surfaces of Ryder's works, but apparently were not aware enough of his true techniques (similar to Blakelock studies, mentioned above); these artists' "fingerprints" would be immediately evident to an informed conservator.

Three important twenty-first-century publications demonstrate the in-depth understanding possible through technical art history. Many conservators who teach art history undergraduates have been pleased to recommend reading *Seeing Through Paintings: Physical Examination in Art Historical Studies* by Andrea Kirsh (art historian) and Rustin S. Levenson (paintings conservator). Kirsh and Levenson worked together on the book, first published in 2000, to demonstrate their collaborative findings in an accessible format, copiously illustrated and including many fascinating case studies. For American art history especially, a married team of conservators, Lance Mayer and Gay Myers, have published a two-part study, *American Painters on Technique*, and have been reaching out to art historians and curators, lecturing at the College Art Association, and holding study days and seminars at museums. The first book covers the Colonial period to 1860 (published in 2011) and the second covers 1860 to 1945 (William Page to Isabel Bishop, published in 2013).

How can independent curators, art historians, and collectors arrange to investigate the materials and techniques of paintings that have come to their attention? There are now at least two accessible avenues established by or in connection with paintings conservators who have businesses in Florida, New York, and London. Emily MacDonald-Korth (WUDPAC 2011) operates Longevity Art Preservation (Miami and worldwide) (Fig. 6). Her company can provide condition assessment and reports; technical photography, including high-resolution imaging under visible, ultraviolet, and infrared light; paint and paint stratigraphy analysis using pigment and binding media identification and

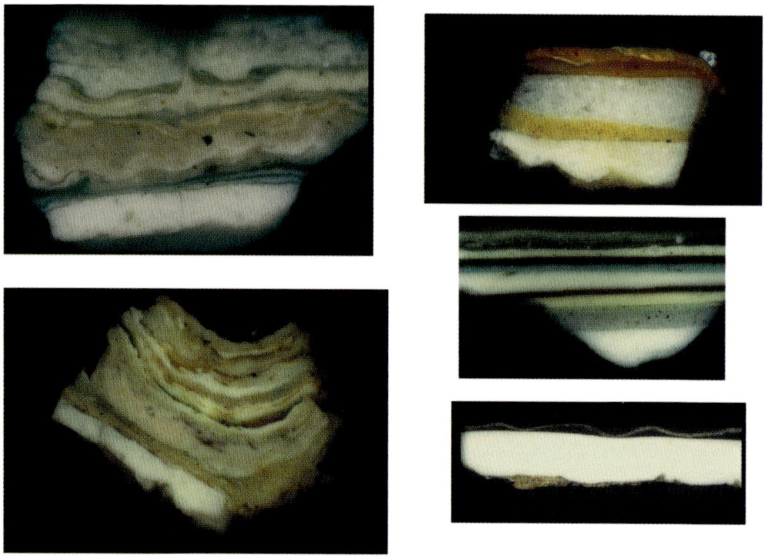

5.
Composite collage of paint cross-section samples taken from accepted (left side) and forged (right side) examples of paintings by Albert Pinkham Ryder. A dissertation submitted to the Faculty of the University of Delaware in partial fulfillment of the requirements for the degree of Doctor of Philosophy in Art.

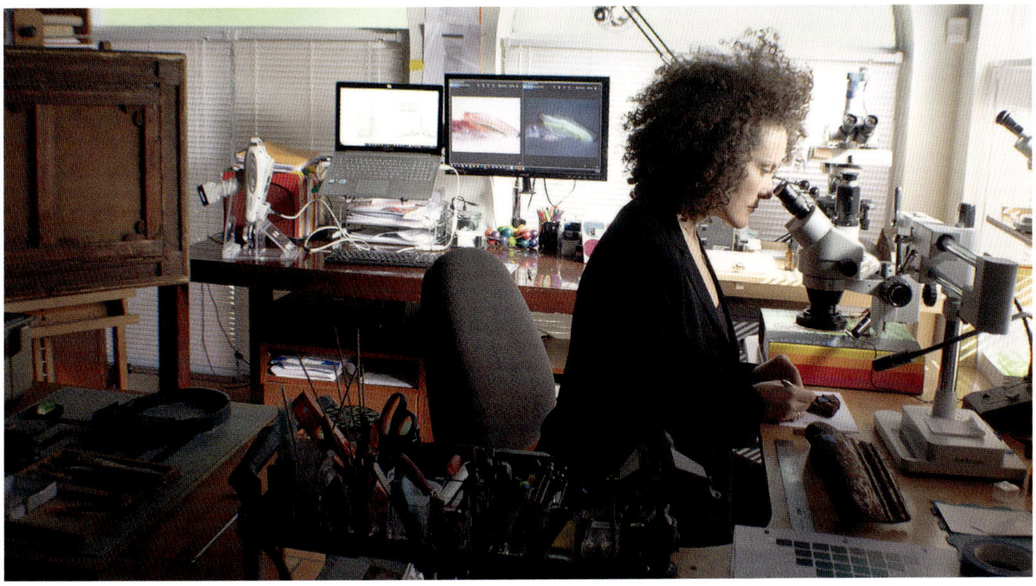

6.
Emily MacDonald-Korth of Longevity Art Preservation (Miami, FL and worldwide) at work carrying out paint analysis under the microscope.

cross-sectional optical microscopy; wood and fiber identification; and analysis of historical paint samples with *in situ* excavations, sampling, microscopy, material documentation, color matching, and color measurement (info@artlongevity.com, 917-684-1065). Suppose you are wondering if the "seventeenth-century Italian landscape" a dealer is offering for sale is truly as old as advertised. You have a sneaking suspicion that it might be a nineteenth-century copy, typically made by art students in major museums two centuries ago. (For instance, the young James McNeill Whistler copied an Ingres in the Louvre.) You could send a sample of the blue sky (blue is a particularly "telling" pigment) to Longevity Art Preservation and possibly learn that the blue pigment is Prussian blue, a pigment not available to artists until the eighteenth century or later. MacDonald-Korth's detective work was recently cited in *Smithsonian Magazine* and artnet; using ultraviolet light she found hidden images in a 1981 Basquiat painting: https://www.smithsonianmag.com/smart-news/basquiat-painting-has-hidden-blacklight-images-180971167/; https://news.artnet.com/art-world/basquiat-hid-secret-images-in-work-1422499.

Nica Gutman Rieppi and Jilleen Nadolny, both graduates of the Conservation Center of the Institute of Fine Arts of New York University, work with Art Analysis & Research, which has offices in New York City and in London (http://www.artanalysisresearch.com/about/). The New York office email is nyoffice@artanalysisresearch.com 917-539-6120. Art Analysis & Research (AA&R) offers pigment and binding media analysis of historical paint; dendrochronology, paper history, wood identification; high-resolution digital imaging in the visible, infrared, x-ray and with ultraviolet fluorescence; and interpretation of technical imaging.

As illustrated above, collaborative technical studies of paintings have often provided insights into artists' processes and approaches, detected forgeries, and revealed unexpected histories and later changes. Many conservators and art historians have established partnerships to work in tandem for catalogues raisonnés about entire œuvres or for monographs about a single important work. Another recent trend among museums has been "public-view treatments" with didactics encouraging all passersby to learn what can be discovered about beloved artworks through our typical arsenal of x-radiography, microscopy, and multi-spectral imaging (including ultraviolet and infrared techniques, with even more exciting techniques on the horizon). This author hopes sincerely this trend will continue; everyone's "connoisseurship" can be truly enhanced as a result.

Meditations on Art Collecting
The Wise Choice of Many Alternatives

Carol Strone MA, JD
Founder of Carol Strone, Advisory, Inc., New York

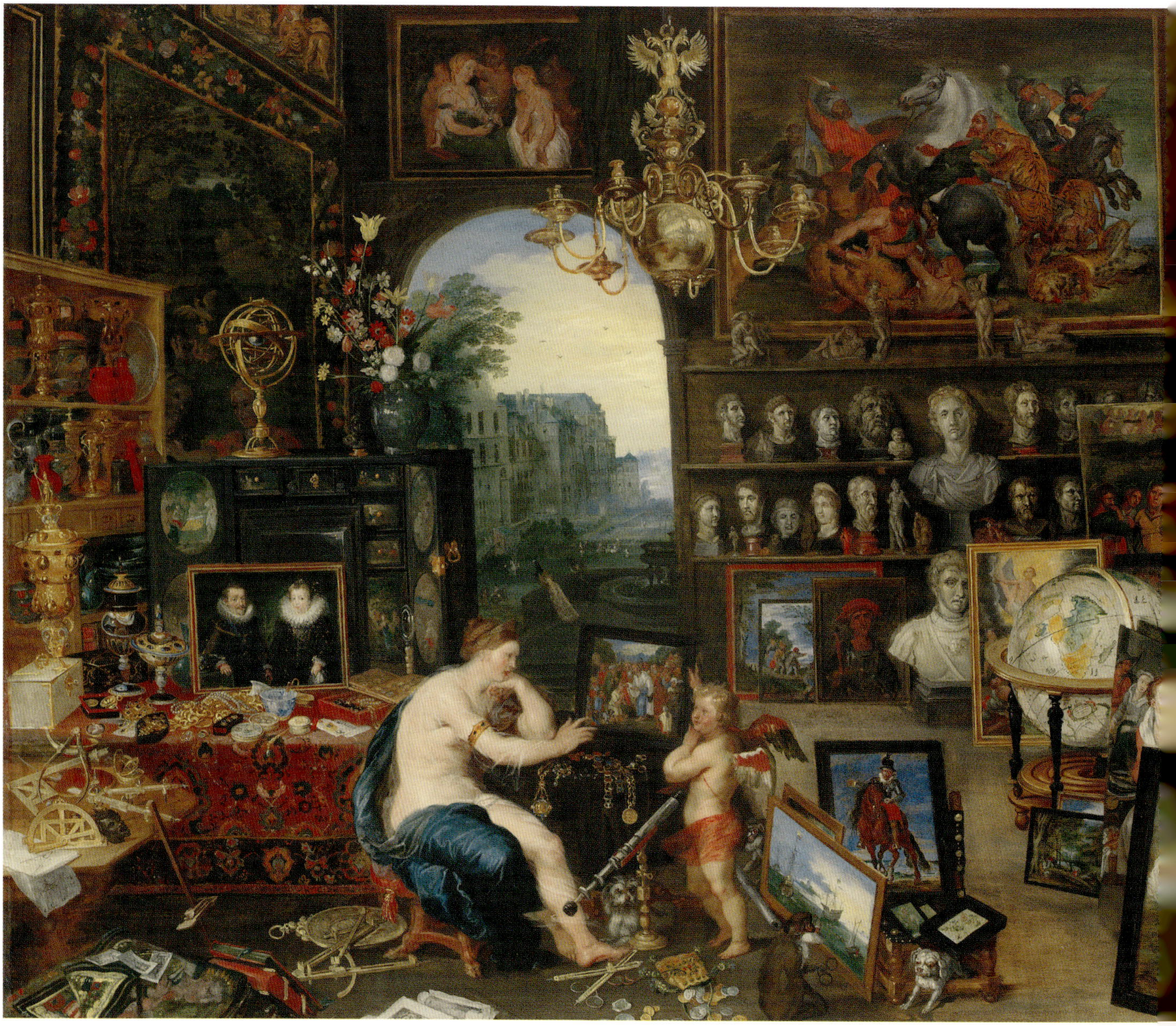

Quality is never an accident; it is always the result of high intention, sincere effort, intelligent direction and skillful execution; it represents the wise choice of many alternatives.

John Ruskin (1819–1900), English author, poet, artist, polymath

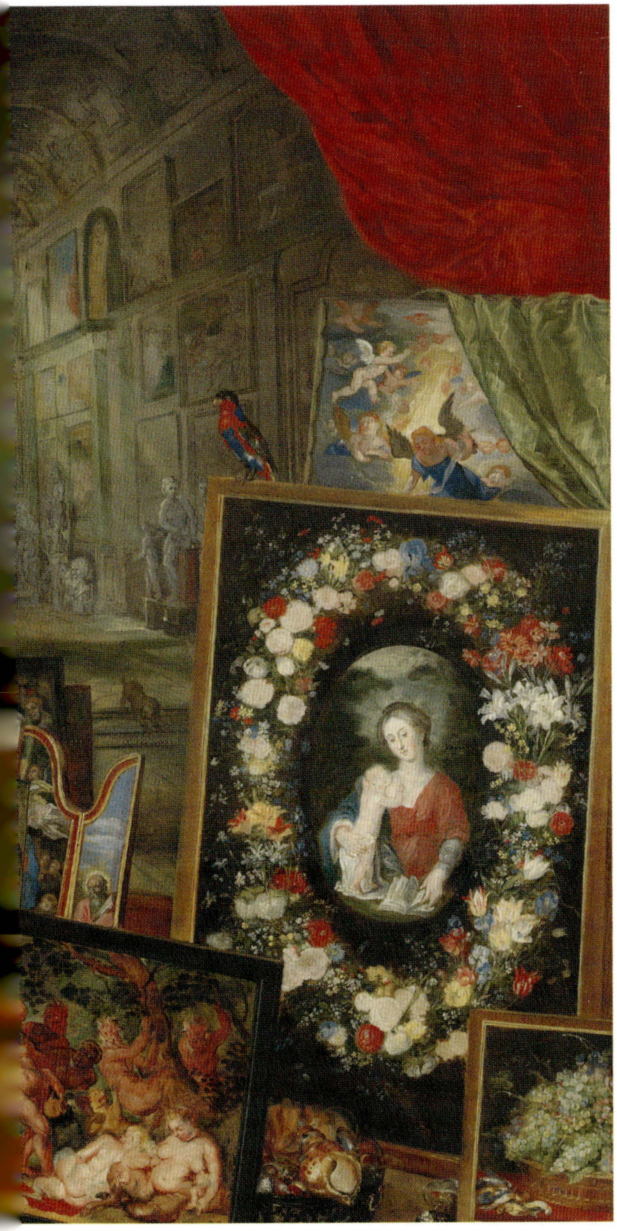

THE COLLECTOR'S DILEMMA: MASTER OF MANY OR MASTER OF ONE?

In contemplating the vast potentialities of their material worlds-in-the-making, collectors often ask a simple two-tiered question: focus on one area of interest or on many? Go deep or go wide? Invariably, the asking furthers the iterative process of framing individual collecting goals, be they aesthetic, intellectual, financial, social, or otherwise.

The question, however, belies the fact that visual art is a complex stimulus involving physiology, psychology, cognition, and emotion. And that collecting is a sophisticated pursuit involving the selection, interpretation, and organization of sensory information, which extends far beyond consumerism and accumulation to something greater.

To reframe and enlarge the question: what are the implications of being a specialist, generalist, or polymath? Why choose one approach over another? What influences choices? A focused approach might suit one personality type, but not another. At times, it might be more valuable to cross-pollinate, at others to concentrate.

For every collector, there are forks in the road. Markets shift, supplies dwindle, finances fluctuate, tastes evolve, knowledge deepens, perspectives change, new opportunities arise. Collecting is a prolonged and adaptive process of looking, learning, and choosing. If the goal is to be an engaged hunter-gatherer and a reflective choice-maker of Ruskinian high intention, then it pays to take stock early and often.

Choices for trophy hunters may be limited, but most collectors enjoy an abundance of choice in an over-networked marketplace. As the conception of "Art" has dilated in a Post-Duchampian world to include 2D-digitized, 3D-printed, and AI-generated objects, so too has the universe of collecting alternatives. The greater the number of alternatives, the greater the need to justify one's choices among them.

Everyone fears making bad choices. No collector escapes making at least one regrettable purchase. And those who hesitate regret at least one that got away. Buyer's Remorse and

1.
Jan Brueghel the Younger
(1601–1678)
The Five Senses: Sight, c. 1625
Oil on panel
27 ⅝ × 44 ⅝ in.
(70.2 × 113.3 cm)
Allen Family Collection

Hesitator's Remorse: they are the Scylla and Charybdis of every collector's Odyssey.

THE WHY, WHAT, AND HOW OF COLLECTING: HIDDEN FORCES AT WORK

When people begin purchasing art, most focus on filling empty spaces, not on why they choose a particular work, or where it will lead. Few set out to be collectors. For most, becoming a collector is gradual, part conscious, part subconscious. Moving beyond mere art lover, a collector feels compelled to possess, and then becomes possessed.

Collectors give considerable thought to how their choices shape their collections; less to what shapes their choices. Although the visible "what" and "how" of collecting hinge on the invisible "why" of collecting, art historians rarely address the "why." Neuroscientists and psychoanalysts have taken the lead in this area.

For every collector, the objective "why" of collecting begins with the "high" of collecting. Right before acquiring an object of desire, every collector experiences a dopamine "high." The anticipation of receiving a reward stimulates the pleasure center of the brain (the *nucleus accumbens*). Any subsequent positive emotional reinforcement of that physiological high increases the likelihood of acquiring again, in order to re-experience it. Such is the genesis of an art habit that Boston collector Isabella Stewart Gardner famously characterized as being "as bad as the morphine or whisky one."

The subjective "why" of collecting has to do with the fact that habit-forming emotional "reinforcers" of that universal high differ for every collector. They are as varied as feeling a sense of security in the quest for wealth, genius in the quest for knowledge, control in the quest for order, belonging in the quest for community, immortality in the quest for legacy, and awe in the quest for emotional responses to art.

Personality traits can further account for divergent choices among the same alternatives. Psychologists have linked the "Big Five" to aesthetic preferences. For example, higher degrees of Openness, Extraversion, and Neuroticism have been found to correlate with preferences for non-traditional art and emotion-driven collecting (i.e. concern for how art makes people feel and how it expresses their identity). Higher degrees of Agreeableness and Conscientiousness have been found to correlate with preferences for traditional art and reason-driven collecting (i.e. concern for how art enhances living spaces, personal relationships, and material well-being).

Choices can be influenced as well by cognitive abilities, such as "attentional focus" and pattern recognition, and by life experiences, such as childhood memories and art education. Collectors may rarely ponder the hidden "whys" of collecting, but if wise choices are about being true to oneself, then self-knowledge is key to aligning what hangs on the wall with what lies within. To interpret Art is to interpret Self.

HISTORICAL PARADIGMS: *THEATRA MUNDI* AND WORLDS IN MICROCOSM

Beyond the Self, there is Society. Call it *Zeitgeist*, ethos, fad, fashion, or trend, socio-cultural forces can affect how people collect. As social creatures, people want to connect with something greater than themselves. Collecting offers myriad ways to do so. The art world is more social than ever, thanks to the power of social media to connect people to art and to enhance their brands as collectors via digital avatars.

At the same time, the art world is tribal, stratified, clubby. If the desire is for recognition and belonging, then choose the right pond and stay in it. Or choose multiple ponds if you are a cultural chameleon. One of the most consequential aspects of collecting is the world that a collector gradually ends up inhabiting through the objects they collect. Each microcosm has its own distinct population and power dynamics.

History offers some visually indelible paradigms for how individual collecting intersects with larger social constructs. Two in particular capture the imagination—the proliferation of Greco-Roman statuary in antiquity and of cabinets of curiosities in the Renaissance. For present-day collectors, these historical antecedents illustrate some of the timeless ways in which art and ambition can become entwined. Lest they hit too close to home, a safe distance in time and place affords a comfortable vantage point.

Never before or since has there been such a prolonged collective consuming passion for a single art form as there was for statuary among the populace of Imperial Rome. The immense quantity of statues on public and private display has been likened to a second population rivaling the city's living population, in both number and vivacity, with many featuring realistic color effects. By the mid-second century AD, an estimated half a million free-standing figures, busts, and reliefs of humans, animals, deities, and mythological creatures adorned Rome's temples, shrines, mausolea, arches, porticoes, fountains, baths, theaters, fora, stadia, and villas—roughly one for every two persons.

Among the more ambitious public displays according to Pliny the Elder's *Naturalis Historia* was Marcus Aemilius Scaurus' three-story-high theater built in 58 BC, populated by an astounding 3000 bronze statues. Elite dwellings housed further extravaganzas where displays of art were considered essential to making good first impressions for status-seeking socializing. One spectacular feat of one-upmanship: the summer palace of Tiberius at Sperlonga featured an outdoor dining cave with a tableau of life-size statues re-enacting scenes from Homer's *Odyssey* in 3D.

For much of their conspicuous consumption, Romans emulated the cultural achievements of Greece to lay claim to a legitimizing lineage. Short of plundering original Greek statues, they commissioned near-copies or variants according to Roman taste, in order to perform as model-citizen patrons of the arts in forging their own cultural identity. Art as such served, first, to provoke reactions in others, secondly to provide aesthetic pleasure to its owners. There is no more striking example of an outward-looking approach to collecting than Imperial Rome, where each generation added to the *theatrum mundi* of statuary, seeking eternal recognition through sculpted avatars. It makes a compelling visual metaphor for the human desire to matter in the world and for what Pliny characterized as *humanissima ambitione* (a most civilized form of rivalry).

So much of collecting seeks to quell existential anxieties. There is a fear of what the Romans called *damnatio memoriae* ("condemnation of memory"). Affluent ancients erected effigies

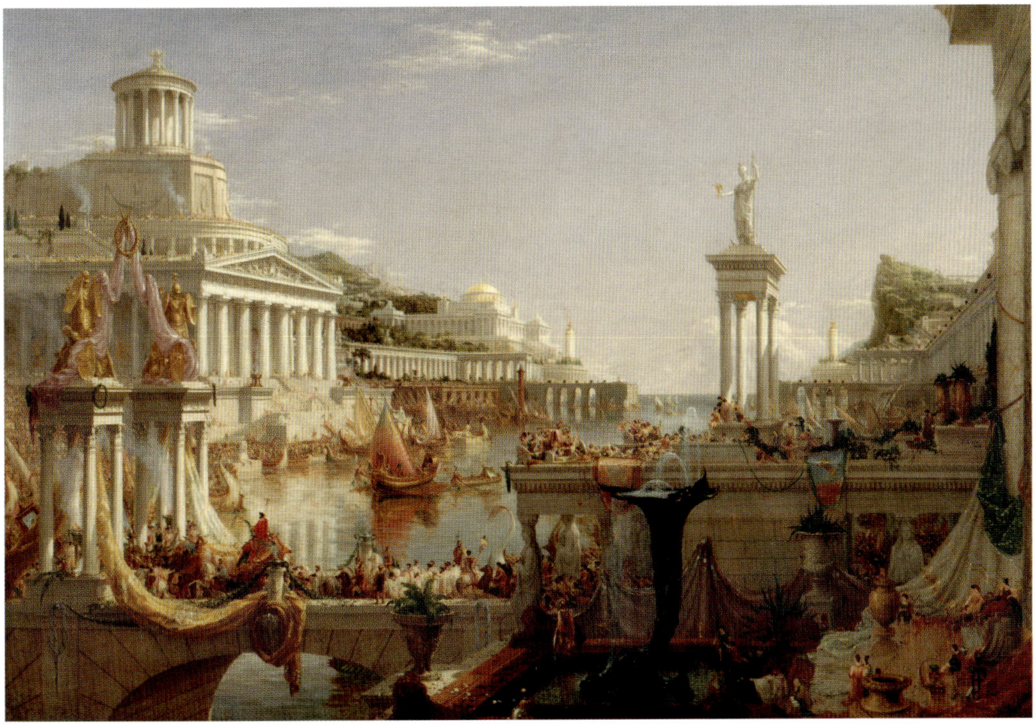

2.
Thomas Cole (1801–1848)
The Course of Empire: The Consummation of Empire
1835–36
Oil on canvas
51 ¼ × 76 in. (130.2 × 193 cm)
New-York Historical Society Museum & Library, New York, Gift of The New-York Gallery of the Fine Arts, 1858.3

in public venues. Today's élites enshrine art collections in public museums—grand gestures chasing grandeur beyond the grave. The Roman ideal was for *all* art—even privately held art—to have a public benefit. The consequences of art ownership and display preoccupied Roman thought. Many worried that ostentatious luxury (*magnificentia*), especially private displays of art, would corrode the Empire.

For how Imperial Roman luxury looked in its mature stages of accumulation, there are contemporaneous accounts. For a visual allegory of the negative consequences thereof, there is Thomas Cole's *The Consummation of Empire* (Fig. 2), third in a series of five paintings titled *The Course of Empire* inspired by the artist's 1832 visit to Rome. Dwarfed by prodigious architecture and statuary, civilization has reached the overripe stage at which glory declines into greed, vice, and corruption. Enthralled by a red-robed demagogue, throngs ignore Minerva, goddess of Wisdom, crowning a distant pediment.

What lessons apply for today's collectors? If concern is for legacy in an age of great wealth, income disparity, and grand gesture-making, then collecting choices carry all the more weight. Is the primary motivation to draw attention to the art, one's community, or the collector? Private collections have public consequences.

In the Renaissance, a different quest for cultural identity through collecting spawned unprecedented zeal for the "cabinet of curiosities," known in German-speaking regions as a *Kabinett der Kuriositäten* or *Wunderkammer* (chamber of wonders), and on the Italian peninsula as a *studiolo*, *museo*, or *galleria*. These "cabinets" often consisted of entire rooms in dwellings of all manner of *curiosi* from emperors to naturalists who indulged in being curious about everything. Within them, deliberately heterogeneous arrays of rare and exotic *mirabilia* (marvels)—*naturalia* (natural specimens), *artificialia* (human-made objects), and *scientifica* (scientific inventions)—were ascribed mystical powers of unlocking the secrets of the universe. Collecting was interactive knowledge production.

In these microcosmic worlds-made-private, antiquities mingled with modern marvels to offer a God's-eye view of the world. There was nothing new about this combinatorial approach. Emperor Augustus was among many Roman élites who exhibited a plethora of curiosities alongside their vaunted sculptures. But cabinets of curiosities took encyclopedic collecting to an extreme in the Renaissance and Baroque periods.

The cumulative potency of these assemblages was to elicit wonder at both the marvels and their owners. The greater the knowledge on display, the greater was one's social status. Knowledge was power; collecting was power-brokering. One *curioso* to achieve global renown was seventeenth-century Jesuit scholar and polymath Athanasius Kircher. His Museo Kircheriano in Rome united a mind-boggling variety of antiquities, ethnological artifacts, natural specimens, and technological wonders. In the thirty-six lavishly illustrated large-format books that Kircher produced on everything from Noah's Ark to the Tower of Babel, he moved freely among bodies of knowledge to formulate inventive ideas such as a talking statue (*statua citofonica*) connected to a speaking tube inspired by his exploration of acoustical science. For today's collectors, Kircherian syncretism offers a tantalizing paradigm for broad synergistic collecting.

Among the earliest American collections to evoke Old World cabinets of curiosities was that of Philadelphia-based Swiss-American painter Pierre Eugène du Simitière, first in his home in the 1770s, and then in his museum opened in 1782. Simitière is also credited with the motto for the Great Seal of the United States, *E Pluribus Unum* ("Out of Many, One"). It is fitting that this aphorism applies equally as well to uniting diverse objects as it does to uniting diverse peoples, in order to form a whole greater than the sum of its parts. When Charles Willson Peale opened his "Repository for Natural Curiosities" in 1786, he had just such a mission in mind. His 1822 self-portrait, *The Artist in His Museum* (Fig. 3), depicts rows of American portraiture and natural specimens symbolizing how interdependent species had collectively formed a New World republic.

Flash forward to the present. These two historical paradigms—the collectivity of a single class of objects (Greco-Roman statuary) and

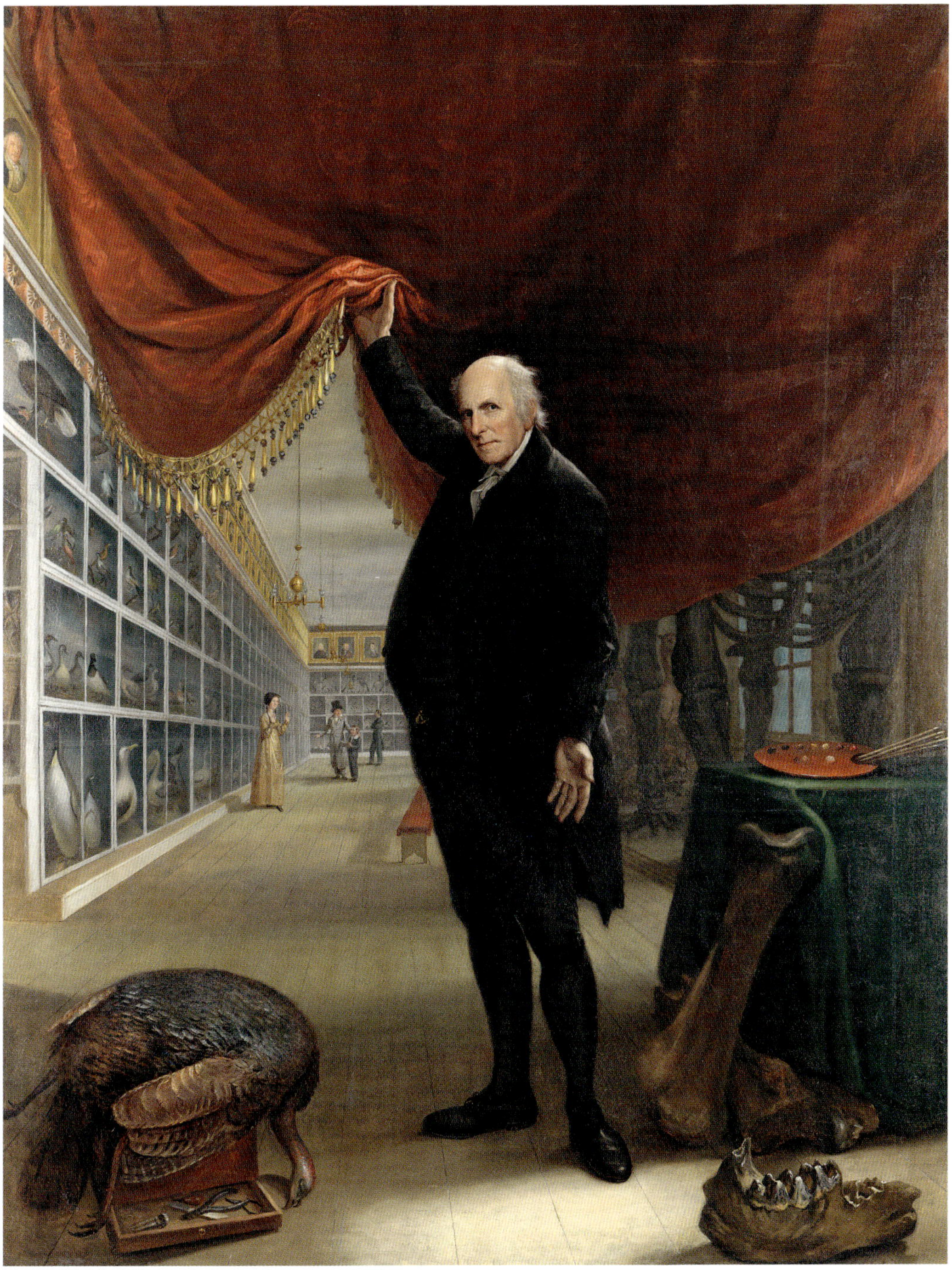

3.
Charles Willson Peale
(1741–1827)
The Artist in His Museum
1822
Oil on canvas
103 ¾ × 79 ⅞ in.
(263.5 × 202.9 cm)
Pennsylvania Academy of the Fine Arts, Philadelphia, Gift of Mrs. Sarah Harrison (The Joseph Harrison, Jr. Collection), 1878.1.2

the collectivity of multiple classes of objects (cabinets of curiosities)—offer reference points for how much or little changes across millennia. Different modes of collecting, from the hyper-focused to the hyper-generalized, may wax and wane, but societal motivations for collecting remain eternal.

An ethos of conformity exists in every era and the "lemming effect" is alive and well today, yet there are fewer culturally normative strangleholds on collecting than ever before. As *axes mundi* of their own domesticated worlds, collectors can mine historical paradigms as they see fit, with an ultra-liberated post-modern way of thinking about art and society. Knowledge in all its forms has its virtues.

COLLECTING TAXONOMIES: HEDGEHOGS AND FOXES

What exactly does it mean for today's collector to "focus" or not? Erasmus's *Adagia* of 1500 offers some instructive wisdom in quoting the Ancient Greek poet Archilochus: *Multa novit vulpes, verum echinus unum magnum* ("the fox knows many things, the hedgehog one big thing"). Many have adopted this aphorism to differentiate between great thinkers who tie everything to one organizing principle (i.e. Plato), and those who explore many avenues untethered to any one organizing principle (i.e. Aristotle). One path is centripetal, the other centrifugal. The same goes for collectors.

Some have an astonishing compulsion to concentrate on a single interest with the laser-focused eye of a specialist. Call him or her *Homo specialitus.* Others feel compelled to graze on many interests with the omnivorous eye of a generalist, *Homo universalis*. Then there are the rare polymaths who, with an extraordinary abundance of intellect, time, and resources, succeed in collecting broadly and deeply across multiple areas of interest as generalist-specialists: *Homo univeralis-specialitus*.

A collection of visual art is characterized more easily by recognition upon seeing it than by description. Some would argue that to characterize one as "focused" and another as "unfocused" risks making false distinctions and qualitative judgments between two equally worthy pursuits. Nevertheless, when weighing the well-suitedness of different collecting methodologies and outcomes to individual personalities and needs, it helps to envision the alternatives in one's mind's eye.

Any number of flattering or pejorative adjectives can be used to describe the specialist collection: focused, in-depth, disciplined, single-minded, obsessive, orderly, structured, thematic, taxonomic, methodological, coherent, unified. A flawed attempt at a succinct definition might be: a cohesive assemblage of works with a unifying thread, such as a certain artist, school, movement, period, place, style, subject, or medium. An analogy would be a vertical wine tasting of one varietal from one vintner over multiple vintages; or the highly systematic musical thinking and fluent composition of Wolfgang Amadeus Mozart.

For many who view the world in terms of categories, set completion is the goal, "wish lists" in hand. As restaurateur-collector Michael Chow told *Surface* magazine in 2014, "The way I collect is I have boundaries. You create a boundary and then you become the king of the boundary, like Leonard Lauder with Cubist paintings. You will it and do whatever you have to do. You're very patient." Collectors thus seek to fill "gaps" over time in assembling a set to illustrate the expressive range of an artist, or to tell a story with a beginning, middle, and end, or to demonstrate some other point.

The "point" among collectors like Hollywood filmmakers Steven Spielberg and George Lucas whose focus is Norman Rockwell—and Rockwell's vision for America—is one of cultural idealism. They are drawn to works that explore the ideals and myths of American culture—collecting to tell a human story. "All the things that were in Rockwell's paintings were part of my life," reminisced Lucas in a short film that accompanied the 2010–11 exhibition *Telling Stories: Norman Rockwell from the Collections of George Lucas and Steven Spielberg* at the Smithsonian American Art Museum in Washington, DC. "What he did was document what life was like then, and that's what I tried to do in *American Graffiti* … and that [film] is a direct descendant of Rockwell."

Similarly, the focus is national narrative for civic-minded individuals like Atlantans Margaret and Terry Stent, who have appeared often on the annual list of the world's top 200 collectors in *ARTnews* for their collection of nineteenth- and twentieth-century American art. "What's interesting to us," Mr. Stent explained to the *Atlanta Journal-Constitution* in 2005, "is that American art can tell the history of our country. These are not just pretty pictures. They tell a story." The Stents' personal story of collecting for nearly forty years has been one of giving back, in supporting exhibitions, endowing

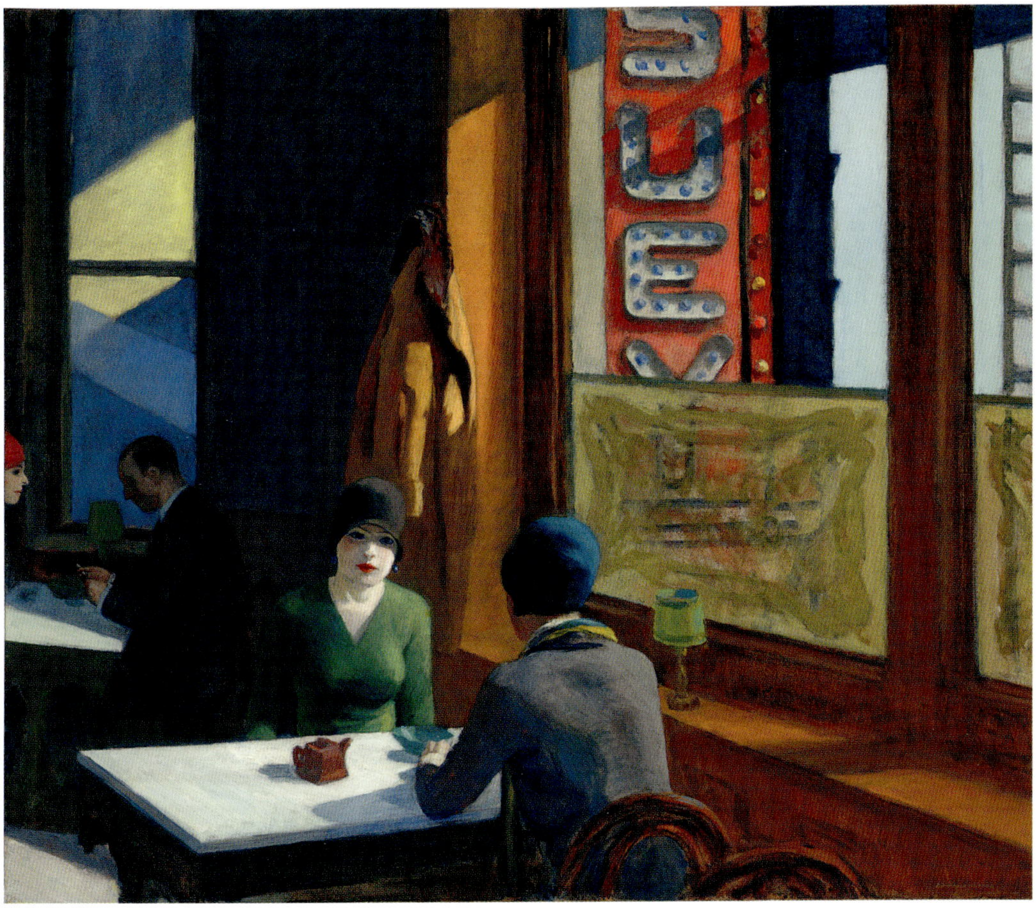

4.
Edward Hopper (1882–1967)
Chop Suey, 1929
Oil on canvas
32 × 38 in. (81.3 × 96.5 cm)
Private Collection

curatorships and in helping to position Atlanta's High Museum of Art as a leading national museum and a local community gathering place. Strikingly symbolic of the ties that bind patron and museum is how one iconic example of Andrew Wyeth's metaphorical storytelling, *The Quaker* of 1975, resides with the Stents, while the watercolor study for the painting resides with the High, perhaps to be reunited one day.

Sometimes "focus" means only the best money can buy. Seattle-based luxury travel magnate Barney Ebsworth took this "billionaire's ballgame" approach toward early American Modernism until he could no longer find "A-plus" pictures by "A-plus" artists, and then moved on to Abstract Expressionism and Pop Art. Another Ebsworth ground rule: only dead artists, to see their full range and to buy their best period. In a 2017 oral history for the Smithsonian Institution Archives of American Art, Ebsworth described his process as "focus rather than collection." Sustained looking at a single period equipped him to zero in on acquiring museum-quality works, which toured museums in 1987 and 2000. His connoisseurship and pragmatism paid off for his heirs when the crown jewels of his collection were auctioned at Christie's in 2018, including Edward Hopper's 1929 masterwork *Chop Suey* (Fig. 4) for a record-setting $91,875,000. Ebsworth had paid $180,000 for it in 1973. His brand-name collecting helped fuel the steady ascent of an entire market sector.

Some collections abandon timeframes, while maintaining focus. One Texas-size effort, the Houston-based collection of Frank and Michelle Hevrdejs, traces American still-life painting across two centuries. When it was exhibited as "A Feast for the Eyes" at the Houston Museum of Fine Arts in 2017, some compared it to the Philadelphia Museum of Art's 2015 exhibition, "Audubon to Warhol: The Art of American Still

Life." Philadelphia's curators had culled 130 works from multiple collections to tell a more complete story, whereas the Hevrdejses told a more personal story through sixty-seven works that resonated with them emotionally. Mr. Hevrdejs explained to the *Houston Chronicle* how works like Joseph Decker's *Bough of Pears with Yellow Jacket* of 1884–85 triggered childhood memories. "When I was a kid," he said, "we had a neighbor that had a fence like that, and I used to eat their pears that grew over on our side, and I got stung by a yellowjacket. When I saw this painting, I had to have it. It reminds me of being a ten-year-old." The Hevrdejses left gaps to fill, yet after thirty years of collecting, their collection had achieved coherence and depth worthy of a rare single-owner museum exhibition.

Focus can sometimes shatter aesthetic boundaries in choosing, for instance, to collect the work of an artist and their students to show a stylistic progression in a period of transition. The work of younger generations may look entirely different from that of their predecessors. A case in point is a collection assembled over some thirty years by D. Frederick Baker and Ronald G. Pisano, consisting of works by William Merritt Chase, his peers and students, many of whom abandoned Chase's Impressionism for Modernism. As pioneering scholars, Baker and Pisano relied on keen intellect and meticulous research to compensate for finite buying power in acquiring nearly 300 works, which they donated to the Heckscher Museum of Art in Huntington, New York, in 2001, the single largest gift to the museum since its founding in 1920. This proves that significant collections can flourish without great fortunes and that private collecting can transform institutions where the need is greatest.

What these different "focused" approaches have in common is the mindful application of an editorial filter, rooted partly in Victorian collecting. Victorians felt that a collection needed to be carefully edited to exclude undesirable influences on the home as the foundation of the nation and its moral education. Nothing better illustrates this than Seymour Joseph Guy's *The Contest for the Bouquet* of 1866 (Fig. 5), depicting the family of Metropolitan Museum of Art co-founder Robert Gordon in their New York dining room. Mr. Gordon's densely hung collection of American Luminist and Hudson River School landscape paintings would have been considered at the time instructive of any number of social, moral, and political values, including purity, godliness, and patriotism. As such, art collecting was character formation.

To the extent that collecting reflects personal values, little has changed since then, though values may have. For some, the decision to focus still boils down to patriotism. In collecting for her Crystal Bridges Museum of American Art in Bentonville, Arkansas, Walmart heiress Alice Walton has constructed an evolving narrative "to celebrate the American spirit." "My parents were both very patriotic, and I just would never have considered collecting anything but American art," she professed to *The New Yorker* in 2011.

At what point does a collection cease to be "focused"? Is one spanning multiple periods of American art "unfocused"? Or is it focused simply because it contains only American art? Suffice it to say that there is a continuum from the specialist to the generalist to the polymath, with no clear points of demarcation. Where a collection stands at any given time is a matter of context, and often it will evolve from one approach to another as it matures.

In their 2017 oral history for the Smithsonian, former Dexter Shoe Company president Peter Lunder and his wife Paula described how they began collecting. As Paula recalled, "We had no restrictions or any agenda that it had to be this or that. We lived with it." Their home was not a museum. They worried though that they had no "collection" at first because their interests were unconfined to a single place or period. Once they decided they would eventually gift their collection to the Colby College Museum of Art in Waterville, Maine, their focus shifted to building "little important collections" with "a story to tell" that could be used as teaching tools. One such emphasis was nearly 350 works by James McNeill Whistler telling the artist's "story of the beautiful." The Lunders added depth in select artists, while collecting some 1500 works from

Aestheticism to Minimalism to ensure Colby's place as a great college art museum. Similar shifts can happen whenever recurring themes elicit deeper focus.

Meanwhile, the vast universe of tempting alternatives in the marketplace lures many into the realm of a "generalist" where they remain for the rest of their collecting lives. Numerous flattering or pejorative adjectives can be used to describe the generalist collection: broad-ranging, diverse, heterogeneous, catholic, eclectic, unscripted, unconstrained, intuitive, haphazard, random, incoherent. A fool's-errand attempt at a definition could be: an accumulation of visibly diverse works representing a broad range of artistic expression cutting across any number of genres, periods, and styles, undefined by any single organizing principle. Some evocative auditory analogies are the bebop jazz saxophone improvisations of Charlie Parker, and contradictory interior monologues in James Joyce's novel *Ulysses*.

Though generalists defy classification, they exhibit common tendencies. They engage in liminal thinking to find connections across multiple fields. Their promiscuous eye excites one associative leap after another. Just as "sampling" portions of music recordings creates new blended sounds, remixing visual images unlocks new protean ways of seeing. The *raison d'être* of the generalist is the remix, distinguishable from someone who builds multiple specialized collections—sequentially or simultaneously—kept segregated from one another.

"We want the works of art to have a conversation," explained *ARTnews* "Top 200" collector J. Tomilson Hill to *Sotheby's Magazine* in 2018 when describing how he and his wife Janine go about displaying their disparate collection, ranging from Renaissance and Baroque bronzes to post-war and contemporary art. "I will, for example, place a Venus figure by Giambologna in front of a Twombly blackboard

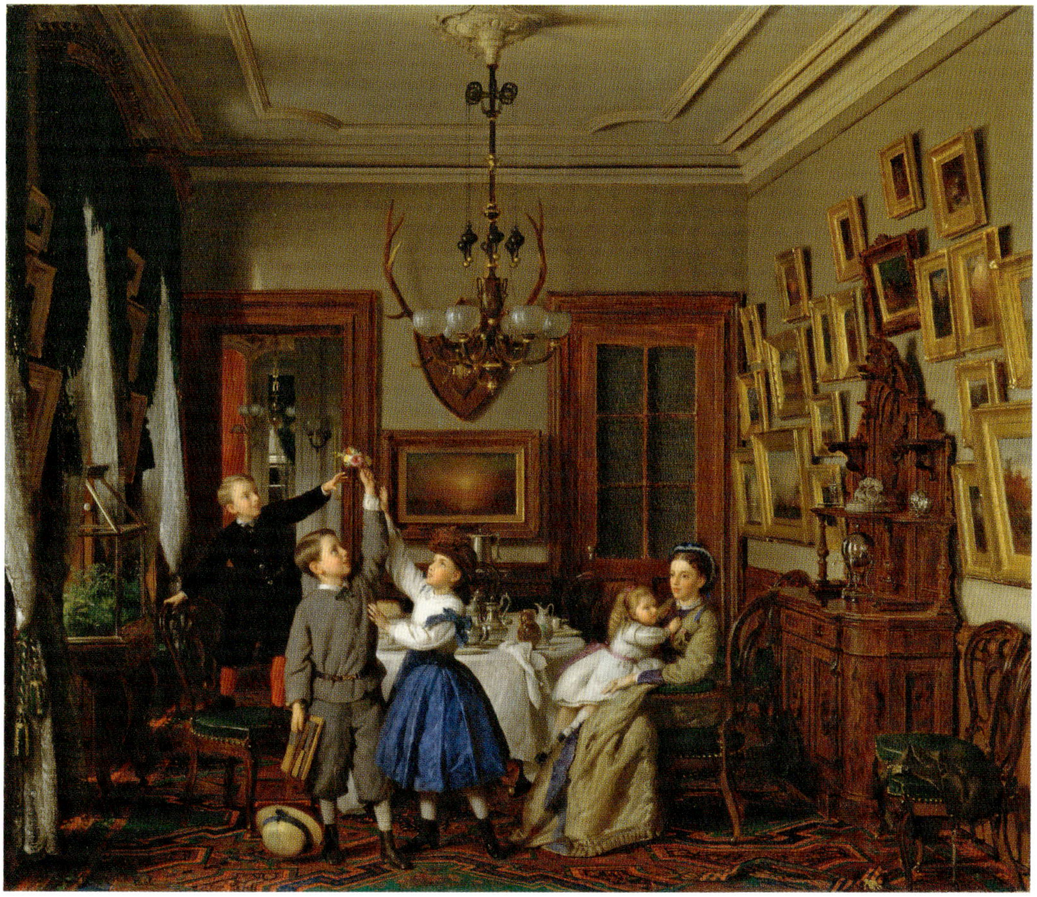

5.
Seymour Joseph Guy
(1824–1910)
The Contest for the Bouquet: The Family of Robert Gordon in Their New York Dining-Room, 1866
Oil on canvas
24 ⅝ × 29 ½ in.
(62.5 × 74.9 cm)
The Metropolitan Museum of Art, New York, Purchase, Gift of William E. Dodge, by exchange, and Lila Acheson Wallace Gift, 1992.128

piece because the curves of the Venus match the curves on the blackboard."

Grouping disparate works in close proximity to one another draws attention to their multipotentiality and to the collector's individuality. A line from Walt Whitman's poem *Song of Myself* comes to mind: "I am large, I contain multitudes." Whitman characterized the union of our nation's many different peoples, places, and things as "unrhymed poetry." So too is an art collection that unites multiple irregular visual cadences—collecting as free verse.

Some refer to themselves as "hopeless generalists." Typically, this is more of a "humble brag" than a true confession. There is this notion though that a generalist suffers from attention deficit disorder, hence the occasional labels of "dilettante" and "jack of all trades, master of none," all to suggest multiple half-baked talents. This ignores the fact that practiced generalists often possess visual fluency that transcends book learning. Collecting, after all, is not just an intellectual process, it is an aesthetic process of experiential looking. Being a generalist does not necessarily mean lack of intention. Wide-ranging exploration is the very serious intention, fueled by an abiding openness to aesthetic experiences. Generalists can take a highly educated approach to collecting, with no single path in mind.

There was no pre-ordained path for trailblazing Philadelphia-based collectors Meyer and Vivian Potamkin, who over fifty years built a renowned and varied collection that included modern European art, American Impressionism and Modernism, Native American art, and American folk art. Embracing diversity of experience with a seriousness of purpose, they "never went into a gallery looking for any particular artist," Mrs. Potamkin explained in the couple's 2001 Smithsonian oral history. "We went into a gallery to see what was there. And that's how we acquired things. So, our collection was never structured. And it's just a representation of our taste and our opportunity.... We're not filling holes. Never did we want to fill a hole."

However diverse, every collection has a point of view. To see a collection is to see its creator. Its expressive value lies in its selection and display. To fold its contents into another is to erase that value—all traces of its creator: *damnatio memoriae*. Expressionist collecting is seen as *speculum majus* ("the great mirror") and as identity preservation. Spanish philosopher José Ortega y Gasset captures this dual notion in his 1914 *Meditations on Quixote*: "I am I plus my surroundings, and if I do not preserve the latter, I do not preserve myself."

And so it was for Isabella Stewart Gardner, a rare individualist of the Gilded Age. A New York heiress who had married into a prominent Boston family and was then widowed, Gardner had a fierce collecting habit. Her Venetian palazzo-style Fenway Court, which she opened as a museum in 1903 while living on the top floor, mixes thousands of works of fine and decorative art from different times and places to form a singular monument to her collecting and to her being. After seeing it *in situ*, it is hard to imagine a work like John Singer Sargent's *El Jaleo* of 1882 out of its Isabellan context, enshrined in a Moorish-arched niche, floodlit from below, flanked by Mexican tiled walls, arranged by Isabella herself in her Spanish Cloister (Fig. 6). For her crest of a phoenix rising from the ashes above Fenway Court's 1900 entrance, Isabella chose the motto *C'est Mon Plaisir* ("It's my pleasure"), lest anyone forget they are entering *her* world.

A generation later in 1925, scientist-entrepreneur Dr. Albert C. Barnes opened his own idiosyncratic monument to recombinatory aesthetic experience. Barnes mixed European and American works of fine and decorative art of various periods with African, Greco-Roman, Egyptian, and Native American artifacts to explore the interaction of formal aesthetic elements—shape, color, texture, harmony, measure, rhythm—within unusual "ensembles" (Fig. 7). From a Barnesian egalitarian perspective, pluralism formed a more perfect union. As Barnes explained in his book *The Art in Painting*: "Coherence, in brief, means not mere sameness but sameness in difference; not the unity of grains of sand but of parts of an organism which complement each other but are not all cast in the same mold." Ever since the collection was moved in 2012 to Philadelphia from its off-the-beaten-path home in

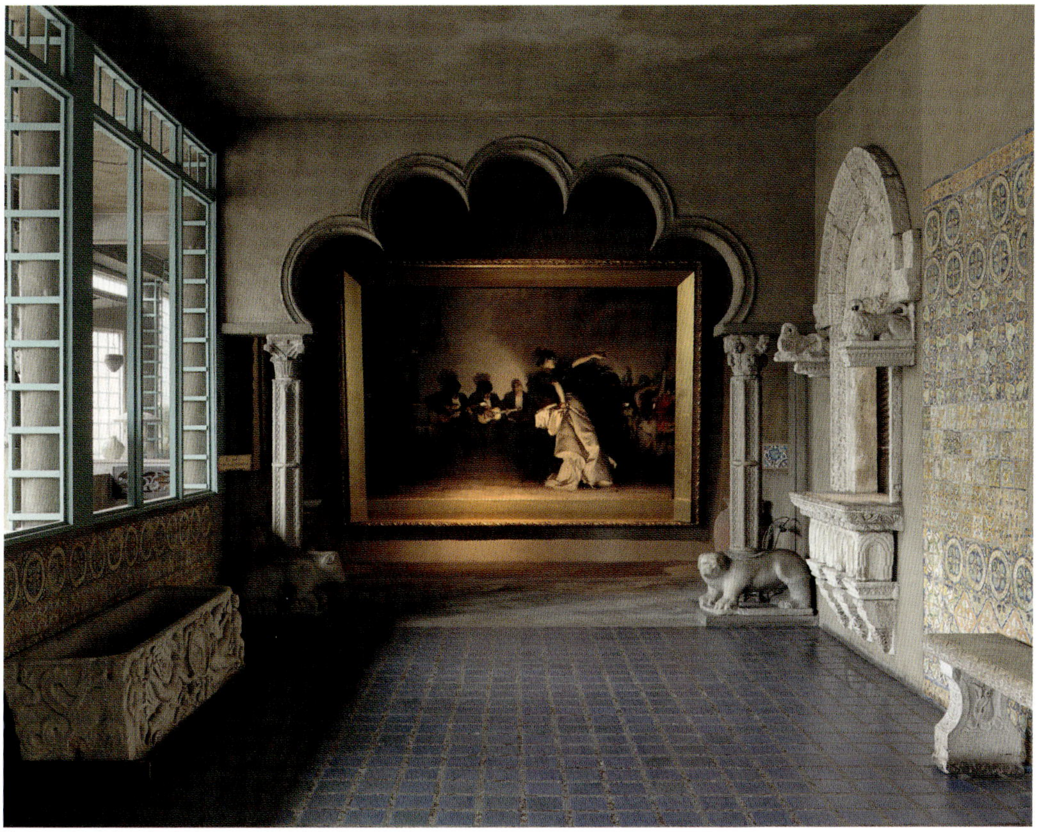

6.
View of
John Singer Sargent
(1856–1925)
El Jaleo, 1882
Oil on canvas
91 5/16 × 137 in.
(232 × 348 cm)
Gift in 1914 from T. Jefferson Coolidge, P7s1, as installed in the Spanish Cloister of the Isabella Stewart Gardner Museum, Boston

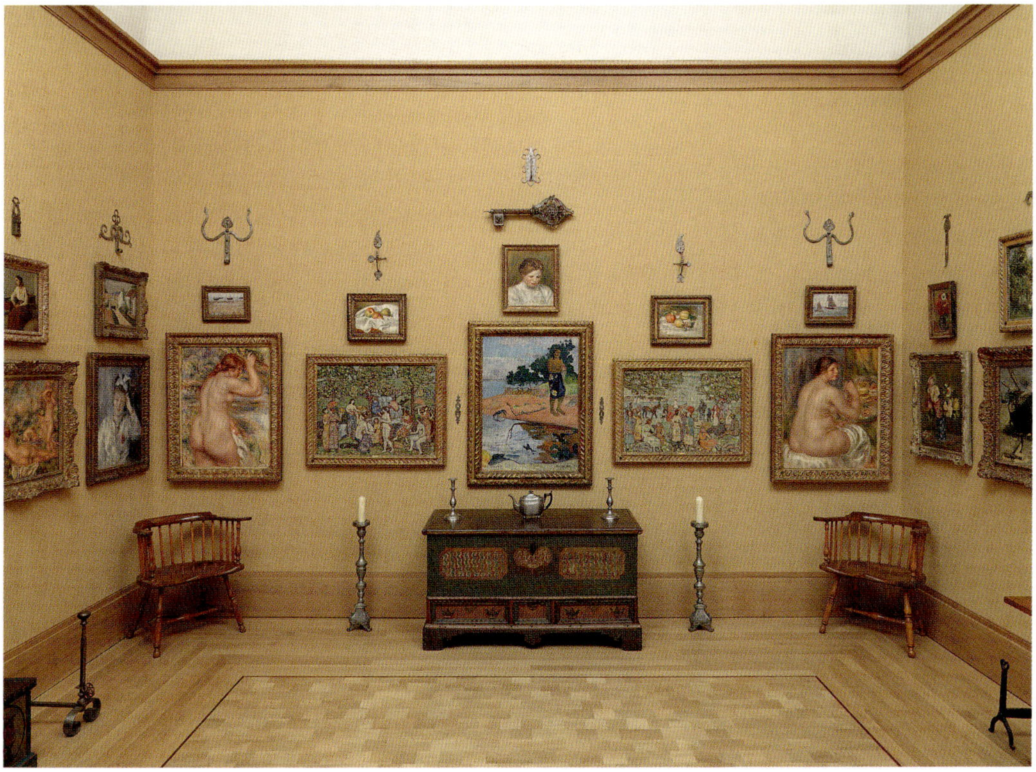

7
Ensemble view, Room 6, South Wall
The Barnes Foundation, Philadelphia, 2012

Merion, Pennsylvania, the mold has never been broken in quite the same way. Part of a collection's psychic value is the place that it inhabits.

Gardner and Barnes assembled two of the great polyglot collections in America. Yet historians stop short of classifying either one of these collector-creators as polymaths. Perhaps they were conversant in many areas, fluent in some, but not fluent in all, if that is the distinction to be made. Definitions vary, but one thing is for certain: extreme depth paired with extreme breadth is for polymaths. In this hyper-information age, however, human knowledge has expanded far beyond the wildest Baroque dreams of Athanasius Kircher. Polymaths are an endangered species, among humans at least. The future of polymathic cognition belongs to artificial intelligence. Think IBM's Watson.

Great polymaths in history whose trans-disciplinary interests encompassed the visual arts include Leonardo da Vinci, Raphael, Michelangelo, Leon Battista Alberti, Thomas Jefferson, and John Ruskin. Perhaps it should come as no surprise that none of the polymaths appearing on any Top 100 lists ever made the cut for their art collecting, though some were collectors. One polymath in recent memory who managed to build a great art collection while achieving even greater things was Microsoft co-founder Paul Allen: technologist, inventor, investor, philanthropist, humanitarian, explorer, musician, sports franchise owner, and collector.

Indeed Allen, who passed away in 2018, assembled a vast collection, reportedly worth $1 billion-plus, ranging from European and American art to antiquities, African and Aboriginal art and beyond. For Allen, on *ARTnews*'s Top 200 list since 1999, collecting was a way of challenging himself intellectually. He owned and read every publication and consulted every major expert about every artist whose work he collected, and he remembered everything. Some say quality of works in the collection ran the gamut from good to great, perhaps because the *raison d'être* of collecting for Allen was to connect with art in a deeply personal way that did not always involve trophy hunting. Interest in ancient Rome led him, for example, to acquire *Ruins in the Campagna di Roma, Morning* of 1842 by Thomas Cole, stunningly intimate in its small-scale minimalist imagery compared to Cole's more theatrical grand-scale maximalist *Empire* series.

In 2016–17, a fraction of Allen's collection toured five museums in "Seeing Nature." Unexpected groupings of thirty-nine works spanning four hundred years mirrored Allen's penchant for experimentation. Georgia O'Keeffe, for example, hung with Ed Ruscha, Gerhard Richter, David Hockney, René Magritte, and Max Ernst—quite a conversation. Jan Brueghel the Younger's *c.* 1625 series *The Five Senses* opened the exhibition with magnificent cabinet-of-curiosities-style images signaling a broad-spectrum aesthetic journey—hence, *Sight* as the opening image for this chapter (Fig. 1). Some characterized the compare-and-contrast mode of display as simplistic. It was fitting though for a man whose many talents, according to Bill Gates, included the "great ability to explain complicated subjects in a simple way." Unseen obviousness is the root of all invention. As a self-professed "idea man," Allen explained in the exhibition catalogue how he was "always trying to figure out where the future's going, looking outward in a certain way." For Allen, art was imagination and potentiality.

Allen had the luxury of traveling to see great works in person. Crucial for all collectors is the costly, time-consuming travel to do the seeing that eludes two dimensions, even in high definition: sorry, Google Arts & Culture. As one great patron of the arts, Paul Mellon, put it in his 1967 commencement address to the Carnegie Institute of Technology, "there is no substitute for the world of direct sensual experience," whether it be the sight of an original artwork or the taste of "the evening's first cold and dry martini." Those short on time and means can take solace in that first martini.

THE ELEPHANT IN THE ROOM: MONEY ON THE WALL

For many collectors, one factor too big to ignore is the investment potential of art. "It's not like eating some spaghetti Bolognese just because you want to," expounded Michael Chow to

Surface magazine in 2014. "When you spend a million dollars on an object, you want to make sure you're going to get a million back at some point. The most important thing about collecting is to follow your heart and your passion. But having said that, the rest is business, the market, and money."

Commercialization, globalization, and financialization have catapulted art into the realm of viable asset classes, despite lingering skepticism. Though it may be of secondary concern for some, there is always the hope that one's collection will appreciate in value over time, notwithstanding recessionary cycles. The hope is all the greater when global markets boom with eye-popping returns for a handful of collectors.

In times when post-war and contemporary art generate a majority of the value of the world's fine-art auction sales, many earlier periods of art suffer. Rarely if ever does consumer demand spread evenly across all collecting fields. Nevertheless, in the 1980s and 1990s it was more balanced than it has been since. The wait is on for markets to recalibrate. Nobody knows when or if this will occur. Polymorphous tastes can mutate quickly in a digital age of insta-trends chasing returns, yet that remains to be seen.

Subjectivity, opacity, illiquidity, volatility, finite quantity, insider information, price manipulation, and lack of regulation all make the question of investment potential impossible to answer. A "buy low, sell high" strategy is difficult to execute in any market, but especially so in the unchecked art market. Make no mistake about it, collecting for profit is gambling and the house almost always has the advantage.

The value of art is audience-driven. The rise and fall process of markets hinges on the powers of persuasion of experts—dealers, auctioneers, curators, advisors, and critics—to convince collectors of the lasting value of works of art. In markets for credence goods, much depends on relationships of trust among a complex network of taste-makers, market-makers, and collection-builders. The herd is malleable yet fickle, and so are markets.

Many collectors have suffered the consequences of investing in a period that has fallen out of favor. A case in point is nineteenth-century American art, which appreciated from the 1930s through the 1980s, backslid in the early 1990s, appreciated again in the late 1990s, then backslid again after 2008, with a recession, growing preference for early American Modernism, and the unwavering hegemony of post-war and contemporary art.

In the face of uncertainty, one strategy is diversification. Collect broadly to hedge against vagaries of taste. Common wisdom is that it increases the likelihood of ending up with at least some winners over time. Typically, the value of a collection is concentrated in a few artists who turn out to be the winning lottery tickets, often purchased at auction or in depressed markets where bargains can be had more easily.

A more focused strategy is to capitalize on the superstar economy of the art market. The list of top-selling instantly recognizable artists changes little year over year. Worldwide, Warhol is always on the list. In America, Edward Hopper is a perennial favorite. To the extent it is possible to collect in depth the work of a name-brand artist whose œuvre is abundant enough to sustain a market, returns can be great. This is possible with Warhol, but not with Hopper, whose finest oils are nearly all in museums. It is all the harder to do when only great works by great artists are selling well in a highly selective market, with few takers for ordinary works by the same great artists.

A long-term gamble is to ignore popular taste, often out of necessity, having arrived at the party too late. The aforementioned Peter Lunder recalled in his oral history for the Smithsonian how he and his wife Paula had collected European art early on, but that by the 1980s, "Asians and Europeans were in the auction rooms, never put down their paddles, and it was impossible to compete against them, and that's when we switched to American art, because it was plentiful, it was available, and it was affordable."

For a time, it seemed as if most were not in it for the money. Lifelong collector Raymond Horowitz lamented in 1999 about how the art world had changed: "Nowadays, these paintings are regarded as assets more than as works of art. I *must* tell you that when we first started, the idea that these would become valuable was one of *the most* distant things in our mind. Our test was could we afford to lose half the money." At the time, Mr. Horowitz and his wife Margaret had been collecting since the 1940s. The National Gallery of Art in Washington, DC, had invited them to speak on the occasion of exhibiting their pioneering collection of American Impressionist and Social Realist works, which had by then become valuable. They never did cash in, except to reap a lifetime of pleasure from aesthetic experiences and kindred spirits. Instead they gifted their collection to the National Gallery and to other fortunate beneficiaries.

In the end, psychic returns are the only sure bet. When trustee Joseph Choate christened the new Central Park home of New York's Metropolitan Museum of Art in 1880, he envisioned a different kind of investment, in the civic-minded spirit of the ancient Romans:

> *Think of it, ye millionaires of many markets—what glory may yet be yours, if you only listen to our advice, to convert pork into porcelain, grain and produce into priceless pottery, the rude ores of commerce into sculptured marble, and railroad shares and mining stocks—things which perish without the using, and which in the next financial panic shall surely shrivel like parched scrolls—into the glorified canvas of the world's masters, that shall adorn these walls for centuries.*

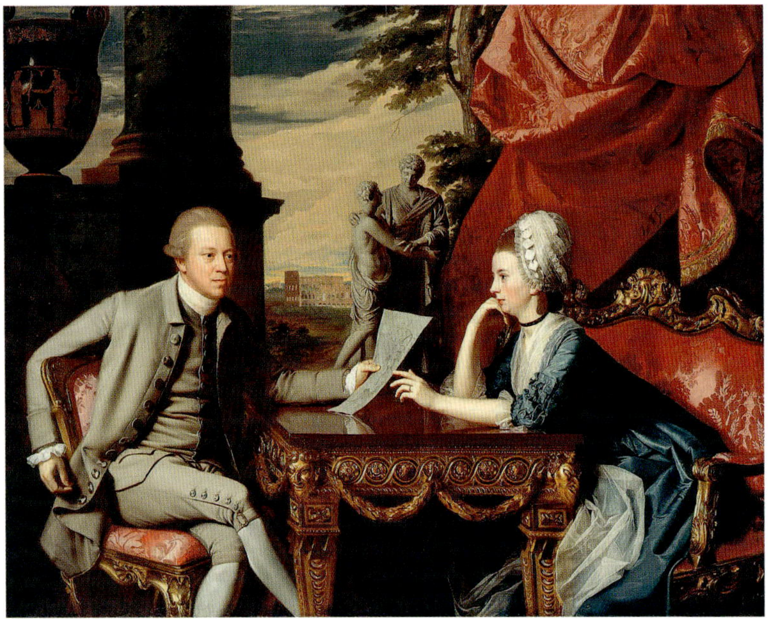

8.
John Singleton Copley (1738–1815)
Mr. and Mrs. Ralph Izard (Alice Delancey), 1775
Oil on canvas
68 ¾ × 88 in.
(174.6 × 223.5 cm)
Museum of Fine Arts, Boston, Edward Ingersoll Brown Fund, 03.1033

Far less lofty, but essential to happily converting one's riches into art, is to be clear about one's relationship with money. Some feel satisfied only when they get a bargain. They take pride in being financially acute. Conversely, others enjoy bragging rights of paying top dollar in a competitive game of one-upmanship, or, as Andy Warhol put it: "I like money on the wall." Either way, habit-forming reinforcers of the collector's high are at work, and they hold the key to making wise choices within one's comfort zone.

LOOKING BACK TO MOVE FORWARD: HISTORICAL ART IN A CONTEMPORARY WORLD

For much of their collecting history, Americans have looked back to move forward. Colonists, for instance, looked to antiquity for moral guidance and cultural legitimacy. This is deftly illustrated in John Singleton Copley's 1775 portrait of *Mr. and Mrs. Ralph Izard* (Fig. 8), portraying South Carolina Lowcountry élites as connoisseurs traveling in Rome on the Grand Tour. The Colosseum-in-ruins in the distance—symbolic at the time of imperialism gone wrong—is political subtext for the choices that colonists faced under the weight of British rule. On the ledge above, a fifth-century BC Greek volute krater vase depicting Leto and her divine twins, Artemis and Apollo, speaks to the Izards' erudition, as does the sketch Mr. Izard holds of the sculptural group *Orestes and Electra* standing directly behind—all carefully curated aspirational signifiers of status.

Americans looked back as well to their ancestral homes. It is no coincidence that the Izards, of English ancestry, chose Copley, who emulated cosmopolitan English painters in adopting the eighteenth-century Grand Tour portrait format. As nation builders, culturally insecure Americans collected European art in the face of European condescension for American art, an inferiority complex that

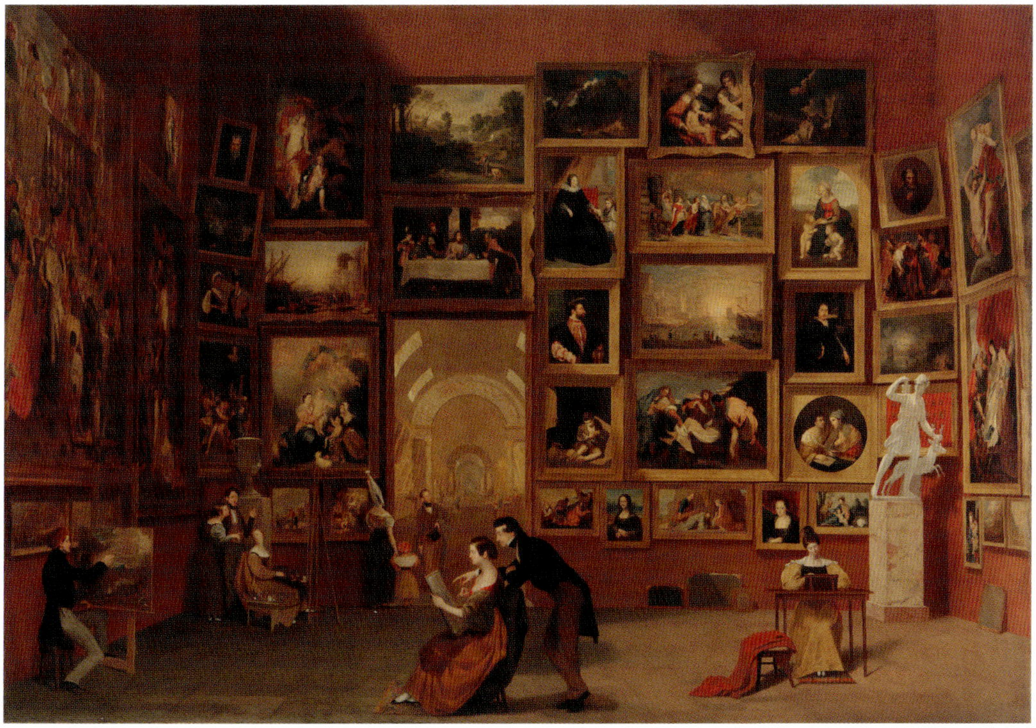

9.
Samuel F.B. Morse
(1791–1872)
Gallery of the Louvre, 1831–33
Oil on canvas
73 ¾ × 108 in.
(187.3 × 274.3 cm)
Terra Foundation for American Art, Daniel J. Terra Collection, Chicago, IL, 1992.51

persisted well into the twentieth century. When they mixed American with European works, it was to position themselves within the greater narrative of Western Culture. A minority were confident enough to focus on American art, out of national pride, if not genuine appreciation.

Artist-inventor Samuel F.B. Morse's *Gallery of the Louvre* of 1831–33 (Fig. 9) epitomizes America's desire to appropriate the best of the past and of other cultures in shaping its future. Morse's six-by-nine-feet canvas meticulously replicates forty-two European masterworks in Paris's Musée du Louvre, including Leonardo da Vinci's *Mona Lisa*, to signify the level to which nineteenth-century Americans aspired. The composition itself imitates seventeenth-century European "gallery paintings," which depicted aristocratic collectors in chock-full cabinet-of-curiosities-style settings.

It was not until Abstract Expressionism in the mid-twentieth century that American artists finally arrived at what many felt was an autonomous indigenous art form owing no debt to the past or to Europe, one that prompted the center of the art world to shift from Europe to New York. It had been a long journey of legitimizing American art in the eyes of the world and many never looked back. In forward-looking times, the unfinished job of legitimizing earlier periods of American art fell to a relatively small group.

Scholarship barely existed when the great collections of pre-1945 American art—from Colonial portraiture to Modernism—began to be formed in the shadow of Abstract Expressionism. Pioneering collectors had to do their own detective work. Navigating with few bearings required intense focus. Thus, a scholarly group of Americanists-on-a-Mission emerged. Collecting as excavation aided in constructing an entirely new body of knowledge.

Once a body of knowledge exists, markets mature and historical gaps widen, how far back will younger generations look in their collecting? Every field faces this question sooner or later. For Americanists as a case in point, how to bridge the gap between today's white-walled minimalism and yesterday's gilt-framed opulence? How to look within dated images to the timeless content that brings us face to face with ourselves? The opportunity exists for rebranding older periods of art as worthy of collecting, in tandem with three major cultural shifts taking place in critical thought, technology, and lifestyle.

First, capitalize on the fact that art-historical critical thought has evolved to incorporate material culture, social history, race, gender, and identity studies. People may think they know the story of American art. Institutions have been telling a privileged Manifest Destiny version of it since the *First Chronological Exhibition of American Art* held at the Brooklyn Art Association in 1872. Collecting has long been biased by an over-simplified narrative. Less well told are stories of American women, Native Americans, African Americans, and other marginalized groups. Previously overlooked artists are entering the canon, while stalwarts are being re-evaluated. Collecting choices are all the more consequential within a new, more complicated and more democratized *Rashomon*-style narrative.

Shifts in critical thought are also toppling temporal barriers. Even historic homes like the Isabella Stewart Gardner Museum and the Thomas Cole National Historic Site are looking forward in time with contemporary art installations looking backward in time. Similarly, cross-collecting has become fashionable among private collectors. The emergent paradigm favors a more unbounded story of art—one of coexistences, confluences, and cross-currents. For those who worry about diminishing regard for formal attributes of objects, recontextualization draws more attention to them, not less.

Secondly, take advantage of how technology is reconceiving historical art forms. Audiences are lining up to see digital displays by the likes of teamLab, a Japanese collective of artist-technologists dedicated to using 3D technology to explore multi-perspectival modes of spatial recognition originating in premodern Japanese scroll painting. Likewise, they are flocking to digital art museums like the Atelier des Lumières in Paris, whose 360-degree video productions immerse visitors in masterworks by such maestros as Vincent van Gogh set to symphonic soundtracks. Entertainment? Yes. Ways to democratize and modernize older art forms that might otherwise feel elitist and irrelevant? Yes.

The real revolution though in re-envisioning historical art is taking place in virtual reality ("VR"). At the Musée de l'Orangerie in Paris, after viewing a panorama of Claude Monet's *Water Lilies* in person, visitors can take a VR tour of Giverny's gardens, seen through Monet's deteriorated eyes, and of Monet's studio, where a virtual canvas simulates the build-up of brushstrokes. Following immersive time travel, visitors report feeling greater empathy for how an artist lived and worked, *and* they report wanting to see more real-world works. Thanks to 3D mapping and digitization, museums and collectors can also offer VR tours of entire collections, with close-up inspection of works, front, back, all around. Technology as a delivery system for art has its virtues.

Meanwhile, the internet weakens the stronghold of gatekeepers who have long regulated the canon—and economic value—of art. Though low barriers of entry admit some charlatans, more voices are an asset in the Wikipedia era of pooled knowledge. Influence is now an open-source project in which collectors exert increasing power through social media. Distributed networks of expertise enable groups of collectors to vet and value works of art in peer-to-peer online marketplaces, further shrinking the bricks-and-mortar footprint of traditional commerce. Historical works can thus find new outlets in a more inclusive open-ended art world made possible by technology.

Thirdly, adapt to post-materialist lifestyles. Minimalist Millennials are forsaking Baby Boomer materialism. They prefer experiences over possessions. Yet collecting can be a source of human connection and therapy in an era of anxious disconnectedness. It is no coincidence that a wellness app called Moodrise was launched in 2018 to deliver curated images, video, and audio as "digital nutrition" by "pairing proven science with the power of storytelling to help you feel better." The time has come to promote the health benefits of historical narrative art that tells a good story—adaptive reuse of the past for present-day needs.

Younger generations also worry about how consumerism impacts the environment, so why not some pre-owned art to minimize their carbon footprint? The future belongs to "green collecting." If you can align preservation of cultural heritage with growing public awareness of the need for sustainability, then historical art takes on added value in an at-risk consumer society.

Consider as well how hyper-consumption of information in people's professional lives prompts some to balk at having to consume even more in their private lives to master complex bodies of art-historical knowledge. An intuitive Barnesian approach that focuses on visual experience may be more palatable to overloaded minds. No doubt, scholarly connoisseurship takes a hit, but free-base collecting can be a gateway drug to art. Get people hooked emotionally, and then they will embark on the deeper learning. Eventually you have to know your art history if you wish to rewrite it and to understand where a work fits within the canon, but *coup-de-coeur* collecting has its merits.

In navigating these cultural shifts, wise choices boil down to identifying personal needs and motivations. If those can be identified, then all the alternatives in the marketplace can be filtered through the personal "why" of collecting, with a greater understanding of that "I *gotta* have it" feeling. True, choices can grow slim as the finest works get removed from circulation by museums. Yet, many collectors are content with smaller marvels that can still be had. And today's undervalued works may be tomorrow's masterworks. Proving the point in a 2009 interview for the *Seattle Met*, Barney Ebsworth recalled how he had wondered "what kind of an idiot would buy those pictures" when he first saw Andy Warhol's *Big Campbell's Soup Can with Can Opener (Vegetable)* and Wayne Thiebaud's *Bakery Counter* in 1962. Ebsworth was the "idiot" who eventually bought both, decades later.

Incidentally, 1962 was the year that Norman Rockwell's *The Connoisseur* (Fig. 10) graced the cover of *The Saturday Evening Post*—still the primary delivery system for art among many Americans at the time. The image is an iconic metaphor for opposite worlds encountering one another: traditional–modern, conservative–liberal, mainstream–iconoclastic. Rockwell himself appreciated abstract art, and even studied it. He stepped into Jackson Pollock's shoes to experience what it was like to re-enact subversive Abstract Expressionist drips on the canvas. In placing the gray-suited connoisseur's back to the audience, Rockwell leaves it to the over-the-shoulder viewers to form their own opinion of the explosive technicolor composition confronting them. He invites everyone to do the kind of immersive slow solitary looking that sparks new mind-blowing ways of seeing. In 1962, Rockwell the realist lived in an abstract world. For decades, critics denigrated his work as nostalgic illustration. Nowadays, judging from the rehabilitating sums that Rockwell's work is fetching, there is ample room for both worlds. Perhaps it is time for those who have only been looking forward to look back. And vice versa.

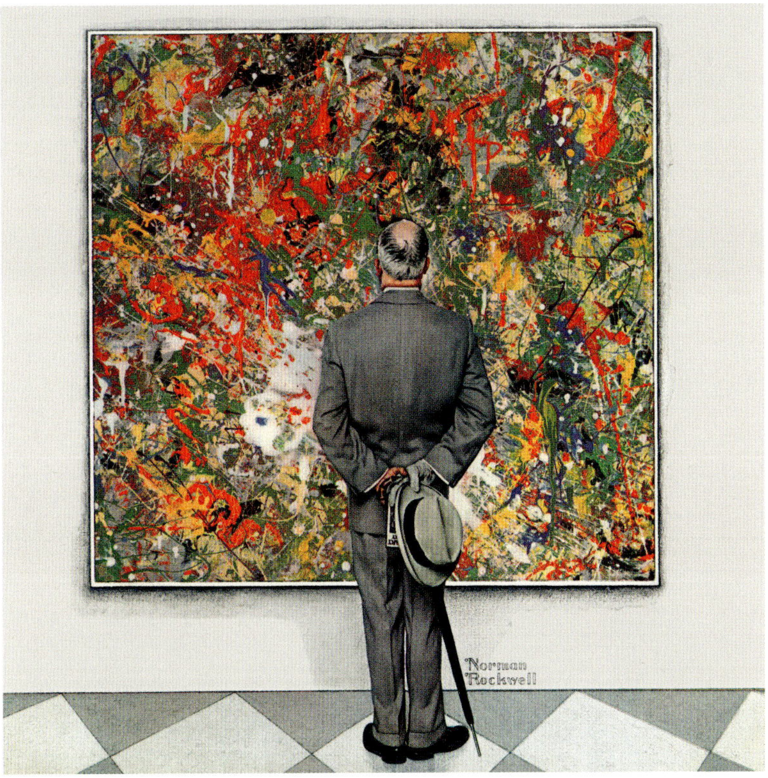

10.
Norman Rockwell
(1894–1978)
The Connoisseur, 1961
Oil on canvas
37 ¾ × 31 ½ in.
(95.9 × 80 cm)
Cover illustration for *The Saturday Evening Post*, January 13, 1962
Private Collection

You Have Nothing to Fear
Collecting American Artworks on Paper

Betty Krulik
Betty Krulik Fine Art, Ltd; Certified Member of the Appraisers Association of America and Member of the Private Art Dealers Association, New York

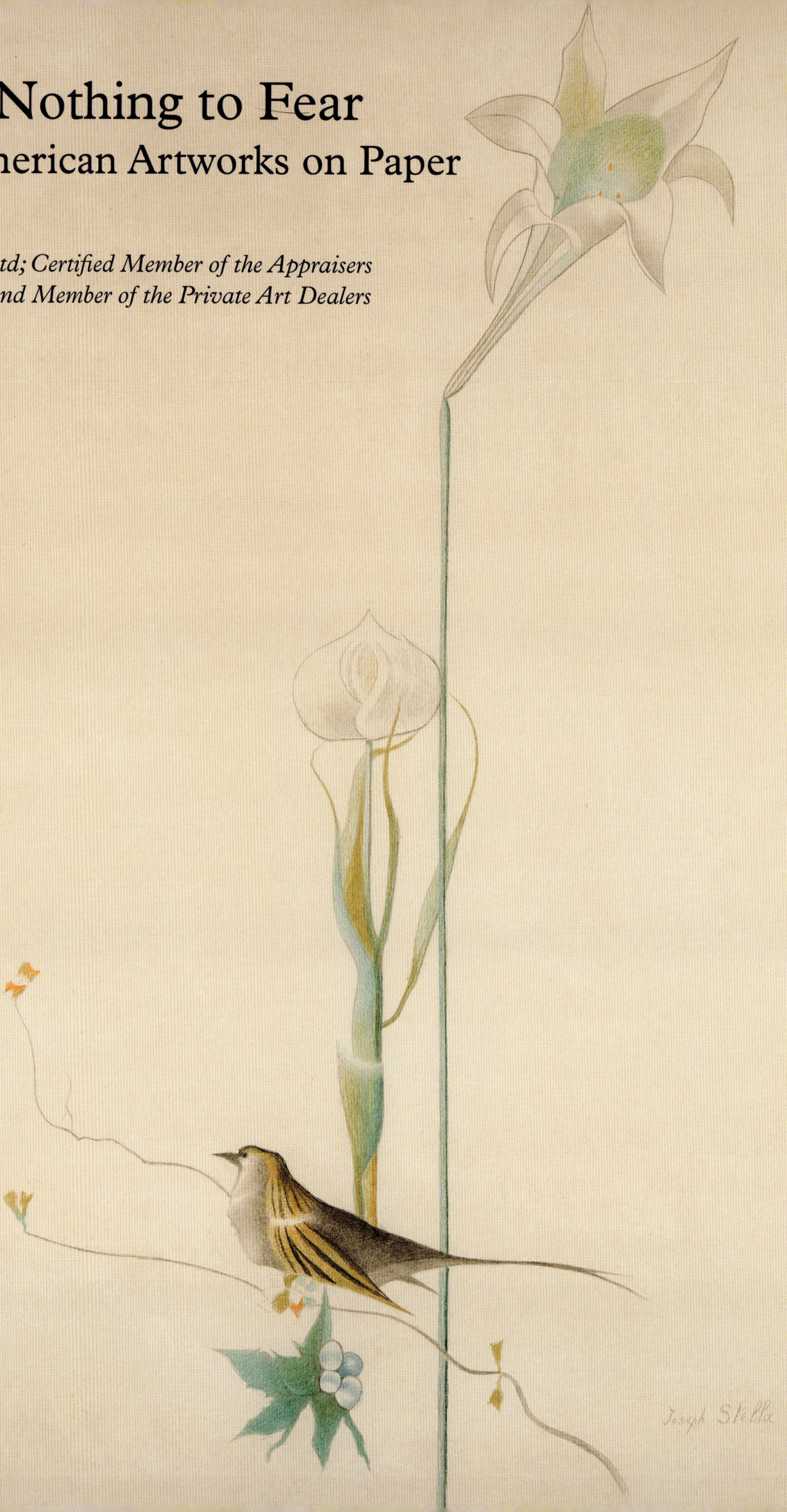

Works on paper need frighten neither the casual collector nor the seasoned collector. There is a perception that works of art on paper are fragile, and therefore to be feared. In fact, with a few precautions at the outset you will be able to enjoy your collection for many years. This chapter will address what to consider at the time of purchase: paper issues, conservation and preservation, and collection maintenance.

It is rewarding to collect works of art on paper, and it is still possible to build a museum-quality and encyclopedic collection of drawings, watercolors, and pastels with a relatively modest financial commitment, as opposed to buying comparable works in oil. There are of course exceptions, such as works by Mary Cassatt, Maurice Prendergast, Winslow Homer, and John Singer Sargent, whose works on paper can exceed the prices for comparable oils.

In history, drawings were considered studies or sketches for the artist's later projects in oil, where the artist works out their ideas. It is fascinating to see the artistic thought-process and the way the artist works out the problems of line, composition, and color. By the eighteenth to the twentieth centuries works of art on paper became accepted as full and finished works in their own right. Societies were formed of artists that worked in watercolor and in pastel, especially active in the United States in the late nineteenth and through the turn of the twentieth century. Some of them are still active today.

1. (*opposite*)
Joseph Stella (1877–1946)
Lily and Bird, c. 1919
Silverpoint and colored pencil on paper
29 × 23 in. (73.7 × 58.4 cm)
Hirschl & Adler Galleries

WORKS ON PAPER MEDIA

Black and White Media

Graphite, pencil (Fig. 2), charcoal, Conté (crayon) are dry media with varying degrees of hardness: graphite and pencil are the hardest; charcoal is soft and smudgeable; Conté waxy and dense. These media are generally stable and do not degrade over time. The support, the paper, however, must be protected.

Ink (black to sepia tones) is a wet medium that can be used either with pen to achieve hard lines or with a brush for a fluid, washy coverage. Often Chinese white is used to highlight pen and ink drawings. Chinese white is a zinc-based medium that does not turn black as does lead white. Ink is not susceptible to degeneration of color. The support may discolor (we have seen

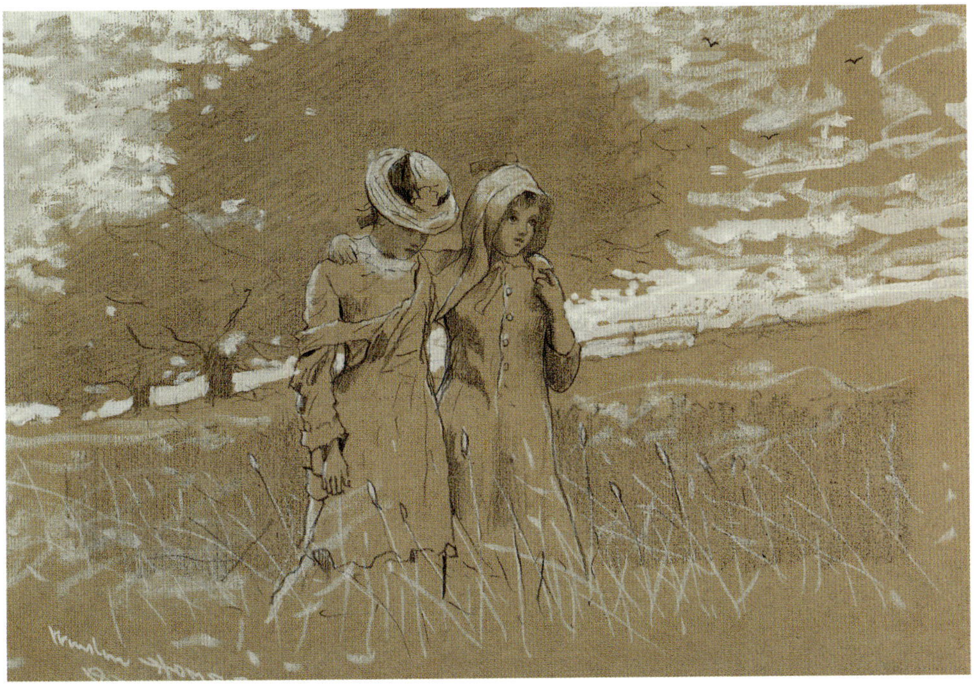

2.
Winslow Homer (1836–1910)
Through the Fields, 1879
Pencil and gouache on paper
9 ⅞ × 14 ⅞ in. (sight size) (25.7 × 38.7 cm)
Signed and dated lower left: Winslow Homer/1879
Private collection, Louisiana

paper the color of brown shoe leather, which upon treatment will return to its original buff color), as the acids contaminating the paper are "washed" out.

Silverpoint

A unique category is that of silverpoint (Fig. 1), where a very sharp stylus of silver (though sometimes gold) is drawn into a prepared paper, leaving a deposit in the incised line which over time develops as the silver "tarnishes." The draftsman must be very precise, as mistakes will show in time. The paper is prepared with a gesso medium that is susceptible to abrasion; and it is very difficult to repair if abraded.

Watercolor

Watercolor (Fig. 3) is a translucent medium, mixed with gouache or tempera for opacity or used on its own. There are numerous techniques that are revelations as you study a watercolor; the virtuoso watercolorist will use wet or dry paper, wet or dry brush to achieve the desired result. They experiment with scratching through dense watercolor with the back of the brush, blotting, and even the use of razor blades. Artists such as John Singer Sargent (1856–1925) and Winslow Homer (1836–1910) would work their watercolors with wax (also called wax resist or frisket), creating and layering areas where the watercolor is prevented from bonding with the paper. This is a highly sophisticated and modern experimental approach used by the best watercolorists of the late nineteenth and early twentieth centuries. A stellar article on the use of watercolor is "Observations on the Watercolor Techniques of Homer and Sargent" by conservator Judith C. Walsh, who wrote it for the Worcester Museum's *American Traditions in Watercolor* exhibition of 1987.

Early in the twentieth century modern artists would experiment with technique and materials; for example, Charles Demuth (1883–1935) applied salt to wet areas of some of his watercolors to create a grainy, pebbly surface.

Watercolor must be protected from the effects of light, as the pigments will fade; once faded the value of the work is significantly diminished. Once lost, color cannot be brought back.

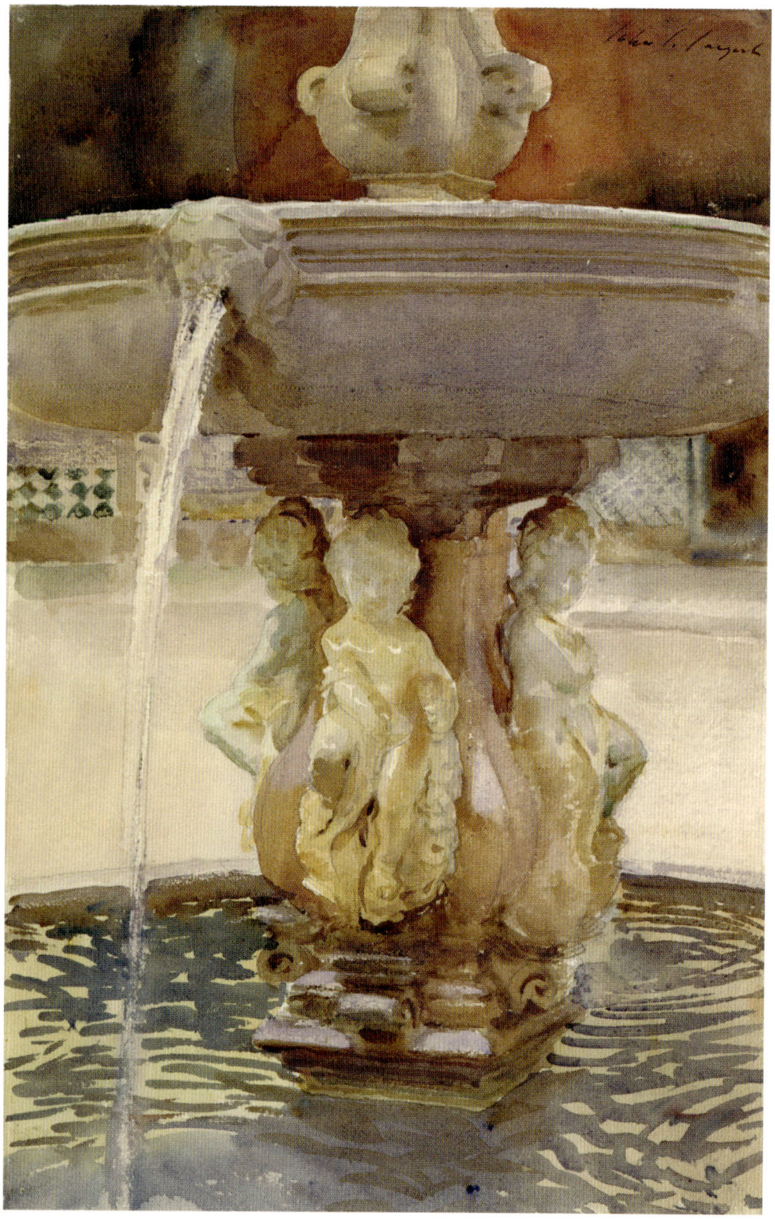

3.
John Singer Sargent
(1856–1925)
Spanish Fountain, 1912
Watercolor and graphite on
white wove paper
21 × 13 ¾ in.
(53.3 × 34.9 cm)
New York, Metropolitan Museum of
Art. American, N. inv.: 15.142.6

Pastel

Pastel came into fashion for portraits by French artists in the eighteenth century. Americans of French descent, among them Charles Balthazar Julien Févret de Saint-Mémin (1770–1852), made pastel portraits in the eighteenth century. It was also frequently used by John Singleton Copley (1738–1815) for portrait commissions. The use of pastel reached its apex in the 1880s with the Society of Painters in Pastel. Included in that group were the greatest painters of their day: William Merritt Chase (1849–1916), Robert Frederick Blum (1857–1903), Childe Hassam (1859–1935), Robert Reid (1862–1929), and John Henry Twachtman (1853–1902). The William Merritt Chase *Self-portrait* has the distinctive "Society of Painters in Pastel" stamp with its red skull-like form. That group exhibited only a handful of times in the six years they were active (1884–90) (Fig. 4).

Pastel is a pure pigment, with a binder, used in sticks. As such, it is almost incorruptible; it does not lose color. However, there have been rare instances of fading. Here, too, artists varied their technique, using wet papers and working the pastels into a rich creamy surface, or leaving them powdery and fresh. Works in pastel must be treated with great care. The powdery surface can separate from the support; therefore, they must be covered with a *non-static* glazing. Static can pull pastel particles from the surface. Because they are so fragile, such works should not be moved or jostled as the surface is so delicate; if they have to be moved, they should travel flat, and face up.

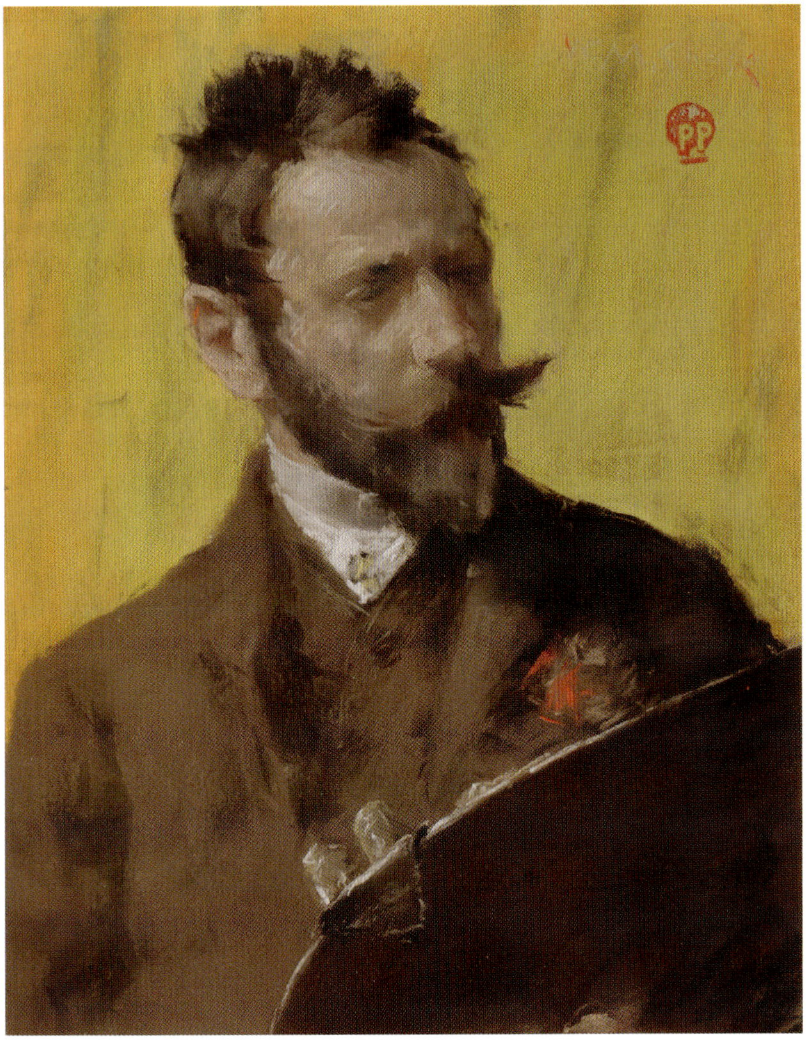

4.
William Merritt Chase
(1849–1916)
Self-portrait, *c.* 1885
Pastel on paper
17¼ × 13½ in.
(43.8 × 34.3 cm)
Private collection, Boston

A Collector's Guide to Researching Paintings

Inge Reist, PhD
Director Emerita, Center for the History of Collecting, The Frick Collection and Frick Art Reference Library, New York

Research for collectors combines the conventional approach to art history with a methodology of its own. This chapter presents some of the myriad research tools and resources that are today available to paintings collectors. They include primary and secondary resources such as personal archives, inventories, and government documents; traditional resources such as catalogues raisonnés, annotated auction catalogues, dealer exhibition catalogues and pamphlets; and an increasing number of online resources that are accessible on the internet or available through subscription databases at museum and university libraries.

When seeking a full understanding of a work of art that may already be in the hands of a collector or that he or she aspires to acquire, the starting point is, naturally, careful examination of the object itself. For this, an informed appreciation of an artist's style and technique is essential and may best be achieved by consulting monographs and exhibition catalogues on the artist. The collector can further sharpen his or her own connoisseurship skills by tracing past published opinions about authenticity and attributions as they have been recorded in photograph archives. Equally important is gaining an awareness of provenance issues and how to piece together the line of past ownership. For this, knowing how to assess archival material and art market documentation, including auction records, helps any collector make informed judgments.

EXAMINING THE OBJECT

Developing an eye for quality and authenticity is perhaps the greatest challenge for any collector. This may explain why many collectors, even very seasoned ones, rely on trusted experts—scholars, museum curators, and some dealers—whose connoisseurship skills have been honed over years if not decades. Indeed, all of the respected art fairs rely on a vetting committee of such experts as a way of reassuring potential buyers that what they see and read on label copy can be trusted. Nevertheless, looks can be deceiving, as many a duped collector would confess. A spurious signature of a great master may have been added on the surface of a work decades, even centuries earlier; or, less dramatically, and perhaps with no deliberate intention to deceive, a restorer may have so drastically repainted a work that too little of the original remains to attest to the work's original aesthetic or monetary value. The picture may display a plausible, even pleasing, composition even if it was cut down to dimensions a previous owner preferred; or elements of a picture thought by a previous owner to have been unpleasant may have been painted over.

A great many of the basics needed for a careful examination of a painting can soon become second nature to the collector/connoisseur. These include:

- Taking the picture out of its frame so as to scrutinize the edges, looking for evidence that any of them have been trimmed;
- Examining the back of the work to look for labels affixed by dealers or auctioneers and, just as importantly, to know if the canvas has been relined (not unusual for a nineteenth-century picture) and if so, was that process

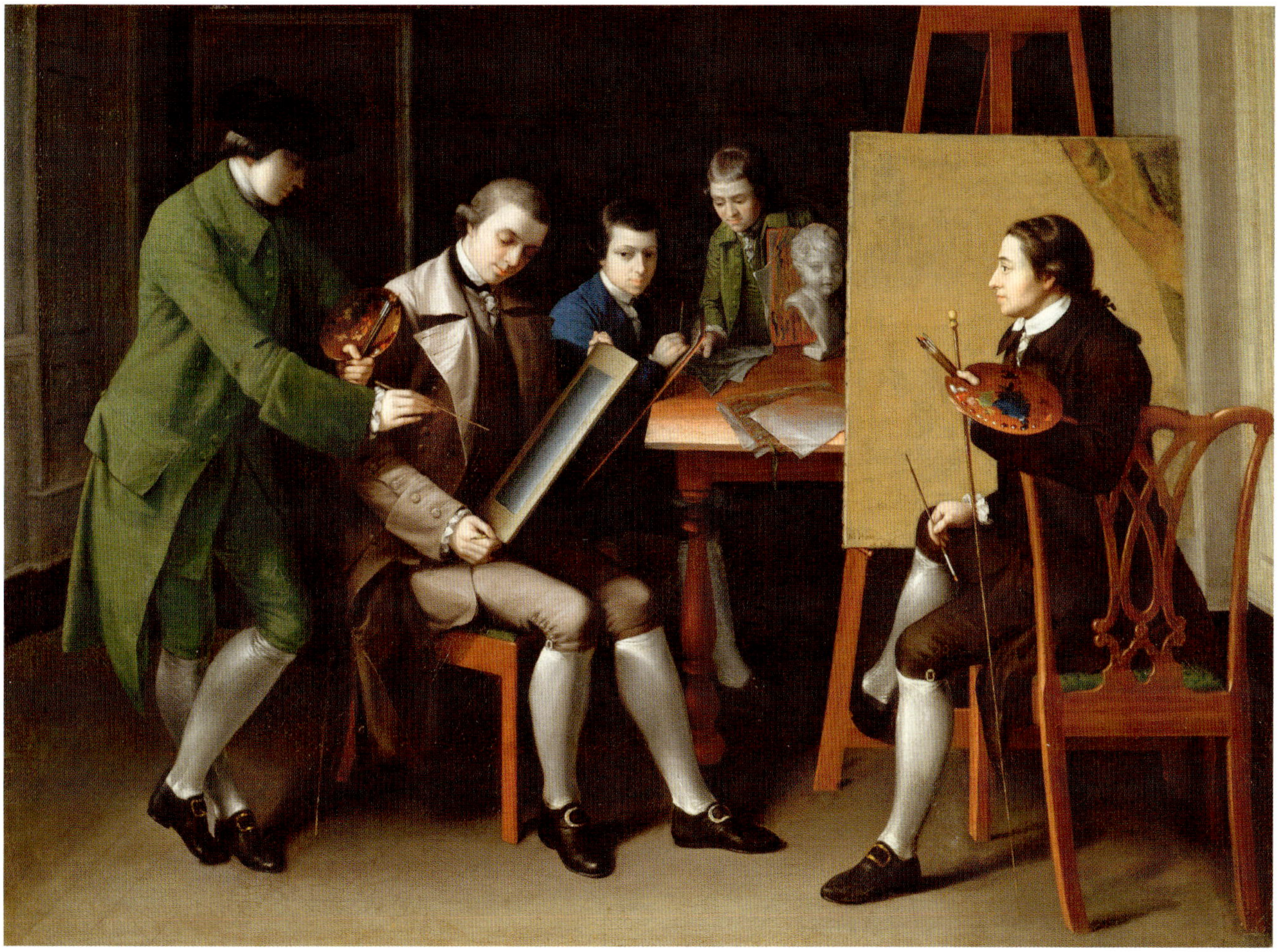

carried out gently enough to avoid flattening any heavily applied impasto passages of paint? This commonly happened when too much heat and pressure were applied to affix the lining fabric to the original canvas;

- For a painting on wood, scrutinizing the wood itself to know if the support has warped or become worm-infested;
- Examining the paint surface with an ultraviolet light or black light in order to call attention to pentimenti (whether by the artist or others) or later additions by restorers.

For any highly valued work, a request for x-rays or infrared examinations would not be unreasonable. These are costly procedures, generally carried out for museum-quality works, but they can reveal stunning information both about the creative process of the artist and about

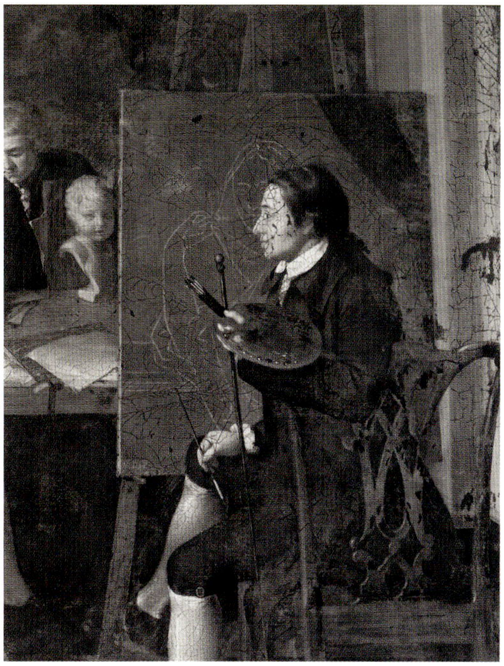

1. *(above and left)*
Ultraviolet photo of a detail of Matthew Pratt (1734–1805)
The American School, 1765 (the studio of Benjamin West)
Oil on canvas
36 × 50 ¼ in.
(91.4 × 127.6 cm)
As published in Kathleen Luhrs (ed.), *American Paintings in The Metropolitan Museum of Art*: Vol. 1, *A Catalogue of Works by Artists Born by 1815*, John Caldwell and Oswaldo Rodriguez Roque, with Dale T. Johnson (eds.), Metropolitan Museum of Art, New York, *1994*, p. 58

alterations made long after the work left the artist's easel. Recently, making headlines in 2018, x-rays of Pablo Picasso's *La Miséreuse accroupie* ("The Crouching Beggar"), from his so-called Blue Period, proved that beneath the paint surface was a landscape composition by him; and just four years earlier, the Phillips Collection announced that x-radiographs and infrared reflectography examination of *The Blue Room* revealed a portrait of a man beneath the surface of Picasso's 1901 masterpiece.

Among American works of art, examination of an ultraviolet photo of Matthew Pratt's (1734–1805) painting *The American School* of 1765 (Fig. 1) offers an intriguing example of a conservation revelation that impacts the interpretation of the composition as a whole. In this group portrait of Pratt's mentor and master Benjamin West (1738–1820) and other less securely identified individuals, the artist at the easel has been tentatively judged to be one of West's assistants working on a portrait of a woman sketched out by West. The sketch is invisible to the naked eye, so the connection to West goes unnoticed until the work is examined under ultraviolet light.[1]

To learn about the extraordinary strides made by conservation teams in the United States and abroad during the later twentieth century and in recent years can be both rewarding and confidence-building for any collector. Museum exhibitions and journals have focused increasingly on displaying and publishing the details of conservation and restoration interventions and we have all benefited greatly from this. Nowadays, for works of art as famous as Rembrandt's *The Night Watch* (Rijksmuseum, Amsterdam) and Donatello's *David* (Museo Nazionale del Bargello, Florence), museum administrators have taken the decision to have the conservators restore their masterpieces in the galleries, open to the scrutiny of the general public. Didactic exhibitions and detailed journal articles such as those that appear in the *Technical Bulletin* published by the National Gallery, London, explain in layman's terms the role x-rays, infrared reflectography, and taking pigment samples can play in assessing the state of, and restoration requirements for, a work of art. Thus, any collector can easily educate him- or herself about technical issues without necessarily taking courses in chemistry or painting conservation.

HOW LIBRARY RESOURCES CAN HELP

For library research, the collector should be aware that art libraries can vary considerably in their focus and not all can offer great depth for object-oriented research. Those that are part of an academic institution tend to acquire monographs and periodicals supporting the art history curriculum of that institution, which, more often than not, emphasizes the historical context and stylistic development of a given artist or iconographic interpretations of the works they created. These institutions may offer a good starting point for the collector's research, when looking initially for a catalogue raisonné or major monographic study on the artist; however, connoisseurship and meticulous tracking of provenance can be more difficult to research at such libraries, because they rarely collect auction or dealers' catalogues, focusing rather on monographs, major museum retrospectives, and periodicals so they cannot offer the range of comparative images that can be found in a major photograph archive.

By contrast, museum libraries and those attached to major research institutes such as the Getty Research Institute (Los Angeles), the Clark Art Institute (Williamstown, Massachusetts), the Center for Advanced Study in the Visual Arts (Washington, DC), and the Frick Art Reference Library (New York), have long championed object-oriented research, even as they also accommodate researchers seeking to learn about stylistic developments and iconographic interpretations. At these libraries, the collector can, and should, consult photo archive files on the artist, auction and dealer catalogues, and online databases for archives and auction results.

PHOTOGRAPH ARCHIVES

With the plethora of art publications available today, it would be natural to assume that works by virtually all artists have been published in some form or another, but this is hardly the case. Hundreds of thousands of works remain unpublished because they are in private collections or in the hands of dealers, yet these are the very works that a collector would want to know about. Even for very well-known artists such as Winslow Homer (1836–1910), a photo archive can provide a visual record and important documentation. For example, until 2008 a captivating Homer watercolor, *Shepherdess Among the Trees* (Fig. 2), was known only from a photograph taken in the 1950s during one of the Frick's many photography campaigns. These campaigns, carried out between 1922 and 1967, took the staff photographer to private collections and small public institutions across the United States, eventually amassing a collection of more than 55,000 negatives as well as documentation conveyed by the owners about provenance and subject matter. Thus, when the Homer scholars charged with compiling records for the multi-volume, definitive catalogue raisonné of the artist, sponsored by Spanierman Gallery, undertook their research, they knew to come to the Frick photo archive to ferret out information on unpublished works that remained in private collections. In this case, they learned that this signed watercolor had a Macbeth Gallery label on the back, indicating that the work was at one time with that dealer; that in 1951 it was owned by Mrs. Bartlett Arkell (*née* Louise Ryals) of New York who died in 1970, leaving the picture to her daughter Mrs. Orland Campbell; and that by 1976 it was owned by Mrs. Stephen A. Wilson of New York.[2]

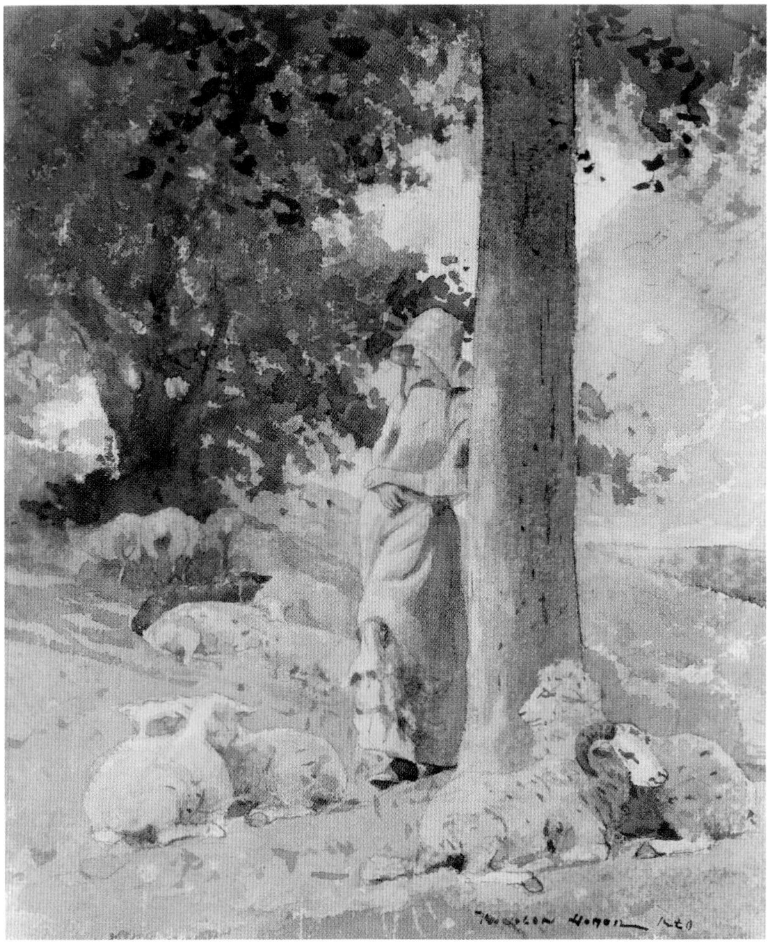

2.
Frick Art Reference Library Photo archive: Winslow Homer, *Shepherdess Among the Trees*, signed, 1880.

For little-known artists, for whom no monograph has ever been published, the photo archive files may not only be illuminating, but may be the only source of visual material and text documentation. For example, the portrait of Angelica Charlotte Thompson (Mrs. James Erwin Yeatman) in her bridal dress was captured by Frick photographer Ira W. Martin in 1929, and the physical history of the work was recorded on the back of the study mount, which also contains pre-restoration images of the work. At the time of the Frick photographer's initial visit, the owners explained that this wedding portrait had been commissioned by the subject's husband, a businessman from St. Louis who founded the Yeatman-Woods Bank of Nashville, Tennessee, to commemorate their marriage on September 11, 1838. The portrait remained in the family until 1955, when, as heirs of the picture informed the Frick, it was destroyed by fire in the family home in Glenco, Missouri. In 1929, the portrait was attributed by Mrs. Leroy Ellis to C. Mygand, a Hungarian portrait artist active in the South during the mid-nineteenth century. However, since photo archive documentation is continuously updated, we now know that an alternative attribution was proposed in 2015 in an email communication to the Frick from Jon Bernard. In his view, the portrait may be the work of Manuel Joachim de Franca (or deFranca) (1808–1865), a Portuguese artist active in Kentucky, Tennessee, and Missouri.

In other cases for which there is a degree of uncertainty about the attribution, the collector

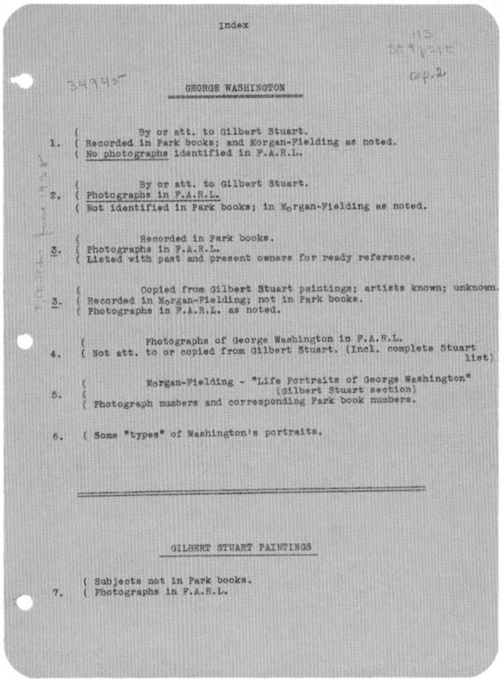
Index

GEORGE WASHINGTON

1. (By or att. to Gilbert Stuart.
(Recorded in Park books; and Morgan-Fielding as noted.
(No photographs identified in F.A.R.L.

2. (By or att. to Gilbert Stuart.
(Photographs in F.A.R.L.
(Not identified in Park books; in Morgan-Fielding as noted.

3. (Recorded in Park books.
(Photographs in F.A.R.L.
(Listed with past and present owners for ready reference.

3. (Copied from Gilbert Stuart paintings; artists known; unknown.
(Recorded in Morgan-Fielding; not in Park books.
(Photographs in F.A.R.L. as noted.

4. (Photographs of George Washington in F.A.R.L.
(Not att. to or copied from Gilbert Stuart. (Incl. complete Stuart list)

5. (Morgan-Fielding - "Life Portraits of George Washington" (Gilbert Stuart section)
(Photograph numbers and corresponding Park book numbers.

6. (Some "types" of Washington's portraits.

GILBERT STUART PAINTINGS

7. (Subjects not in Park books.
(Photographs in F.A.R.L.

3.
Jessie E. Trindle, "List of Portraits of George Washington, by Gilbert Stuart and Others" (unpublished manuscript at the Frick Art Reference Library), 1938

can consult files on all the artists whose names have been associated with the picture, judging for himself where he finds similarities and differences in composition, brushwork, subject matter, and scale. One such example, again the product of the Frick's photography campaigns, is the portrait said to represent Mrs. Richard Randolph, Sr. (Jane Bolling) attributed to John Wollaston (1710–1775). Once again, the process of continuously adding to the documentation means that, unlike a publication that is finalized at a specific date, the information on the study mounts of the photo archive grows organically over time, allowing the researcher to benefit from this constant updating. With respect to the Wollaston portrait, Swedish researcher Carl Gomer suggested in 1927 that the portrait might have been executed by a Wollaston follower and imitator, the Philadelphia artist John Hesselius (1728–1778). His opinion was recorded on the study mount, inviting researchers to make their own comparisons with similar works by both artists. After due consideration, the photo archivists decided to retain the photograph in the file for Wollaston.

Because photo archives proudly amass multiple images of a single work of art, each offering unique visual documentation of the picture at a given moment in time or as interpreted by a particular photographer, it is often possible to learn a great deal about the physical history of the object. For example, the portrait of William Stewart Halsted by an unknown New York artist of the second half of the nineteenth century could easily be taken at face value as a charming record of a young boy who, we learn from the documentation, eventually became the first professor of surgery at the Johns Hopkins Hospital, which now owns the picture. However, thanks to communications from later owners and Dr. Alfred Blalock at Johns Hopkins, we know that this single portrait was once part of a larger family portrait of Mrs. William Mills Halsted with her three children. That painting was later cut up to produce three individual portraits of the children, William, Richard, and Minnie, while the section portraying their mother was destroyed.

In another case, an early photograph of a portrait of a member of the Schuyler family by John Watson (1686–1768) shows that the picture was the victim of mischief by young family members, who used it for target practice, shooting it with arrows to inflict multiple tears in the canvas; but, as evidenced by a later photograph and updated information from the Albany Institute, it has now been sensitively restored to what must be close to its original appearance.

Copies, pastiches, and secondary autograph versions of well-known artists' works are seldom published in monographs, even if they are listed in an author's notes. This is not least because of the high cost and bulk of book illustrations. Again, photo archives come to the rescue, because copies, versions, and preliminary studies are all retained in a given artist's file, and by constant looking through the files, the collector can sharpen his eye to detect tell-tale signs of the hand of a copyist. Within the field of American art, few works were replicated more than Gilbert Stuart's (1755–1828) first portrait of George Washington, the so-called Vaughan portrait (cf. page 235). Of the more than one hundred portraits Stuart painted of the nation's first president, this one, named for its first owner, Washington's friend the London merchant Samuel Vaughan, is perhaps the most recognized. The prime version, though one now recognized as a replica Stuart himself made, is the one painted for Vaughan, in the collection of the National Gallery of Art in Washington, a gift of the Gallery's founder Andrew W. Mellon.[3] The picture and its replicas are mostly listed in John Morgan's and Mantle Fielding's exhaustive study of Stuart's life portraits of Washington, published in 1931.[4] However, during the years since that publication appeared, other copies and versions have surfaced as they passed through the hands of dealers. Many of these are documented in the Frick photo archive, which boasts thirty-one different examples of the Vaughan portrait, some by Stuart, including the one in The Frick Collection itself, and others that are obvious copies. Typical of the proactive approach to documentation that prevails at the Frick Library is a typed manuscript by Jessie E. Trindle, who in 1938 compiled a list of the portraits of Washington, analyzing in detail which ones were published in Morgan's and Fielding's book and/or in the four-volume catalogue of all of Stuart's works by Lawrence Park (see the index of Trindle's study, Fig. 3).[5] More recently, thirteen of the versions of the Vaughan portrait as well as the existence of a fourteenth unlocated version were listed and analyzed by Carrie Rebora Barratt and Ellen G. Miles for the 2004 exhibition at The Metropolitan Museum of Art.[6]

Preliminary drawings made by artists throughout the creative process are also works that are neither consistently noted nor reproduced in publications, in part because of the limitations imposed by cost and bulk mentioned above. Thus, for the collector of drawings, research in photo archive files can yield bountiful results. For example, in 2005 the Frick Art Reference Library received a generous gift of nearly 20,000 photographs of paintings and drawings from the Kennedy Galleries and within that gift was a treasure trove of mostly unpublished photographs of drawings made during the earliest years of Edward Hopper's career. Much of this juvenilia, such as his drawing *The Bicyclist* (Fig. 4), may have been known to Hopper experts, but it has hardly been published and was thus inaccessible to the layperson.

The same is true for the vast majority of drawings recorded by the Gernsheim Corpus Photographicum, an undertaking begun by Walter Gernsheim in the 1930s that continued into the 1990s. The project was dedicated to compiling a corpus of photographs of drawings held in public collections and a handful of private collections in Europe, Great Britain, and the United States. Many of these collections have published selected elements of their drawings collections, but the sheer numbers held in these museums have precluded comprehensive publication of their holdings. The Gernsheim Corpus photographs were acquired by subscription by several art libraries in the United States including the Cleveland Museum, the National Gallery of Art, the Getty, and the Frick. Each box that arrived through the subscription came with a list that documented the artist, title, medium, support, and dimensions of the drawing, and it also recorded information about proposed attributions that experts occasionally recorded in the curatorial files. By tradition, the

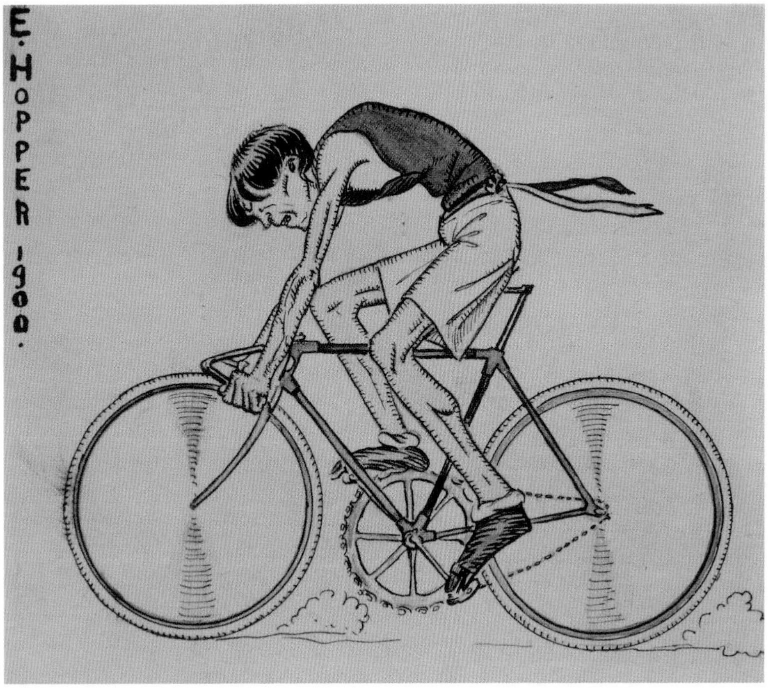

4.
Frick Art Reference Library Photoarchive: Edward Hopper (1882–1967), *The Bicyclist*, signed and dated upper left: E. Hopper 1900. Present whereabouts unknown.

Catalogue information:
At one time with Kennedy Galleries, Inc., New York (stock number A18331/2).
Current repository unlocated.
Images Photograph, unidentified photographic source, possibly Brenwasser Studios 13.946 Gift Kennedy Galleries, Inc., New York February 16, 2005.
Digital image, 20005722a_POST.jpg photograph 10/5/2007
Digital image, 20005722b.jpg photograph back 10/15/2007
Copy/Inscriptions
Signed and dated upper left: "E. HOPPER 1900.".
Sources Information from reproduction.
LC subject Hopper, Edward, 1882–1967

expert's identity was recorded with just initials, but some libraries have made every effort to construct a key to their identities. For example AEP, PP, and JG stand for the renowned British Museum experts A.E. Popham, Philip Pouncey, and John Gere, KO for the Austrian expert and later Harvard professor Konrad Oberhuber.

At the time of this publication, many of the most robust photo archives are actively engaged in digitization projects that will eventually ensure online access for researchers to multiple repositories of photographs and the documentation on the works of art they record. In 2013, PHAROS, The International Consortium of Photo Archives, was established with the ambitious goal of eventually enabling online access to the images and documentation for an estimated 25 million reproductions of works of art collectively held by the fourteen current members of the consortium located in the United States, Britain, and Europe.

PRIMARY AND QUASI-PRIMARY MATERIALS AND EPHEMERA

Some art libraries and research institutes hold collectors' and dealers' archives that may contain collection inventories, bills of sale, conservation reports, stock books, and correspondence, providing irrefutable documentation for the collector regarding market transactions and/or the condition of the work. As more and more archival material becomes available, both at the repositories themselves and through digitization projects that post the materials online, researchers can incorporate specific information about price and negotiations with unprecedented accuracy. The collector/researcher can access, for example, all of the stock books for Knoedler & Co., Goupil & Cie, Duveen Bros., and Jacques Seligmann via the websites of the Getty and the Archives of American Art, respectively, and, in doing so, can significantly enhance the information previously gathered from publications and photo archive documentation. The researcher cannot, however, be certain of the attributions listed in stock books, nor can those records necessarily provide an unbroken chain of ownership. Inventories, such as the many published and now available online via the Getty and other websites, can also be helpful, as are probate records held by the courts.

In recent years, one resource that has become invaluable for archival researchers is the *Archives Directory for the History of Collecting in America*. This online publication, authored by Samantha Deutch and hosted by the Center for the History of Collecting at the Frick Art Reference Library, is continuously augmented and updated, offering researchers a searchable database containing records for American collectors and those with whom they dealt either as advisors or dealers. The *Directory* guides the researcher to the locations of the papers pertaining to a given collector and, at the same time, offers a profile of the collector and, in most cases, an indication of the type of art he or she collected. For example, for the collector J.J. Haverty from Atlanta, the record indicates that his papers are held at the Atlanta History Center and also, more incidentally, in a photographic record at the Archives of American Art in their collection of Regional Directors and Administrative/Public Works Art Project files. The *Directory* tells us that Haverty's collection included works by Mary Cassatt (1844–1926), William Merritt Chase (1849–1916), Thomas Gainsborough (1727–1788), Childe Hassam (1859–1935), Joshua Reynolds (1723–1792), John Singer Sargent (1856–1925), J.H. Twachtman (1853–1902), J. Alden Weir (1852–1919), and Henry O. Tanner (1859–1937). We also learn that, in addition to being a collector, he was a patron, businessman, founder of Haverty Furniture Co., president of the Rhodes-Haverty Investment Company and Haverty Realty and Investment Company, and director of the First National Bank of Atlanta; he served as chairman of the Atlanta Art Commission and the board of trustees of the High Museum of Art. He was a member of the Painters and Sculptors Gallery Association, Inc., of New York; American Federation of Arts, Washington, DC; Society of Medalists, New York; Southern States Art League; Museum of Fine Arts, Houston, Texas; Telfair Academy of Arts and Sciences, Savannah; New York Southern Society and Liturgical Arts

Society; and that his clubs included the Capital City, Piedmont Driving, and The Old Guard of Atlanta.

In contrast to the very concentrated holdings of Haverty's papers, those that pertain to Arabella Huntington's collecting activities are more scattered. Indeed the *Directory* points to some rather unexpected repositories that hold the papers of this collector, who was based in California, New York, and Paris, namely Syracuse University and the Archives of American Art. Moreover, the *Directory* reminds the researcher that the records of her two Huntington husbands, Collis and Henry, as well as those of her son should also be consulted to obtain a complete picture of her activities.

Beyond the unique papers held in archives, the collector/researcher interested in knowing the full provenance of a work of art will likely have to consult what might be called "quasi-primary" materials such as annotated auction catalogues. Nowadays, results for prices paid may be available online through artnet and other resources and this can be extremely helpful, leading the researcher to past auctions and filling in gaps of past ownership. For auction results that predate the mid-1980s, the physical catalogues are often of greater value, because up to that time the auction houses tended to publish both the prices paid and the names of the buyers (although, not unusually, the buyer's name was listed as the agent acting on behalf of the collector and not the name of the collector him- or herself). For catalogues published up to the time of World War II, researchers must rely on hand-written annotations made at the time of the sale. The copy annotated by the clerk of the auction house is, not surprisingly, the most complete record and, therefore, of the greatest value, but even incomplete annotations can fill in a gap with information uniquely recorded in that catalogue.

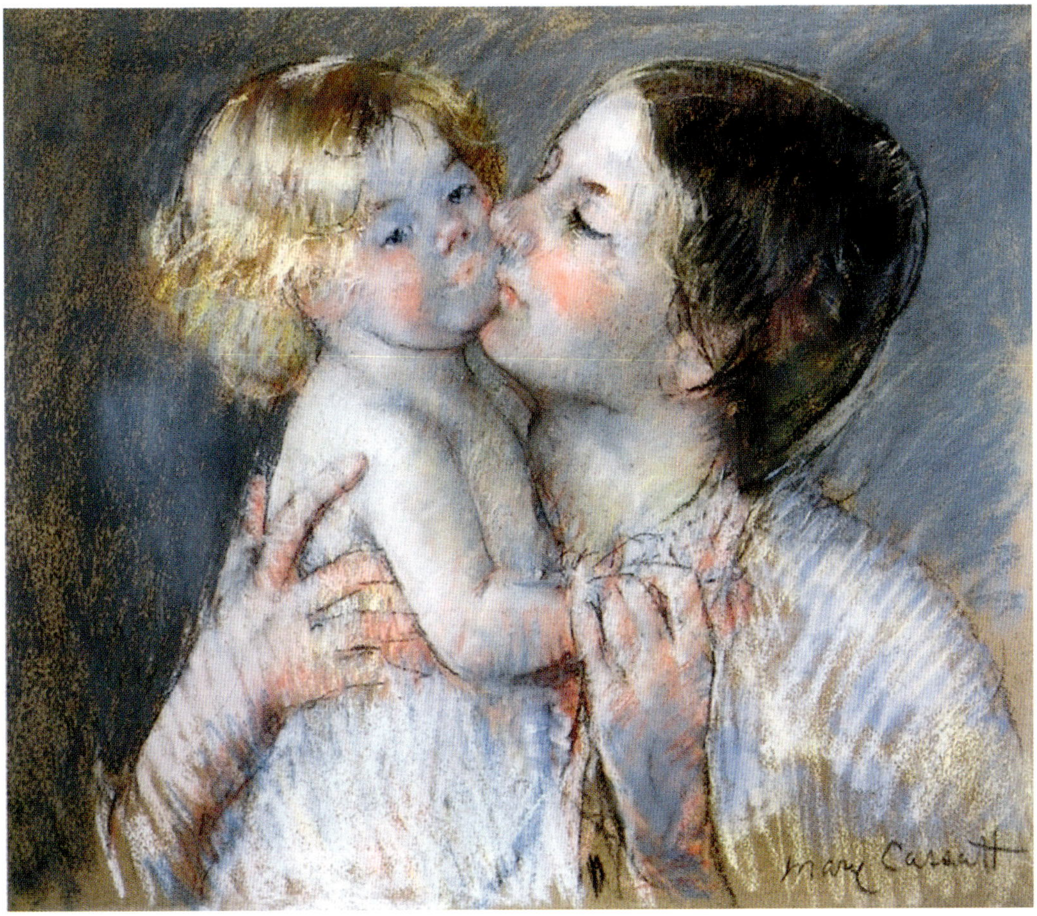

5.
Mary Cassatt (1844–1926)
A Kiss for Baby Anne (no.3), 1897
Pastel
17 × 25 ½ in. (43.2 × 64.8 cm)
Private collection, Sotheby's May 20, 1998 (sale no. 7135), lot 20

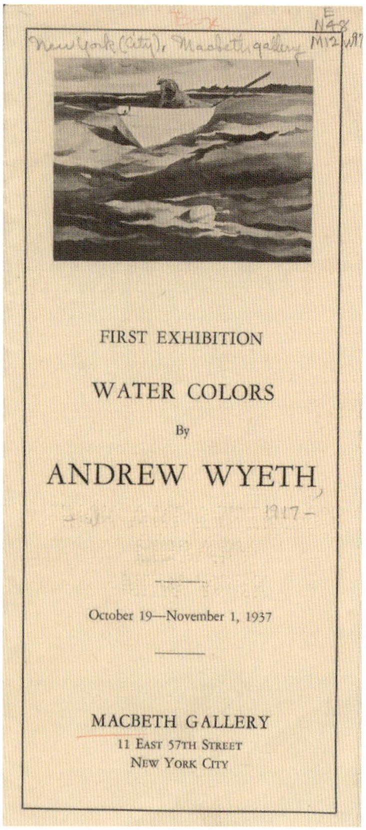
FIRST EXHIBITION

WATER COLORS

By

ANDREW WYETH

October 19—November 1, 1937

MACBETH GALLERY
11 EAST 57TH STREET
NEW YORK CITY

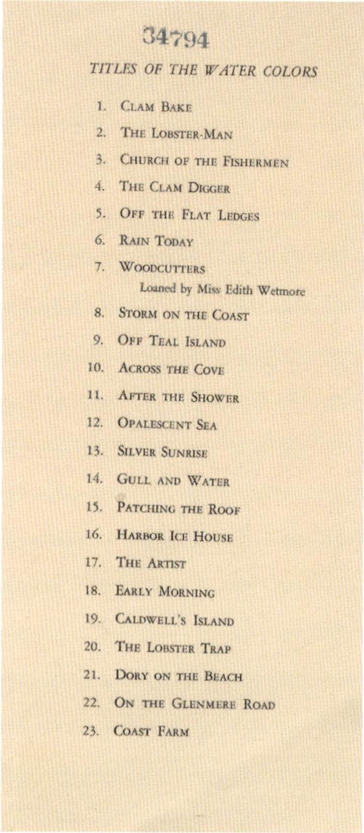
34794

TITLES OF THE WATER COLORS

1. CLAM BAKE
2. THE LOBSTER-MAN
3. CHURCH OF THE FISHERMEN
4. THE CLAM DIGGER
5. OFF THE FLAT LEDGES
6. RAIN TODAY
7. WOODCUTTERS
   Loaned by Miss Edith Wetmore
8. STORM ON THE COAST
9. OFF TEAL ISLAND
10. ACROSS THE COVE
11. AFTER THE SHOWER
12. OPALESCENT SEA
13. SILVER SUNRISE
14. GULL AND WATER
15. PATCHING THE ROOF
16. HARBOR ICE HOUSE
17. THE ARTIST
18. EARLY MORNING
19. CALDWELL'S ISLAND
20. THE LOBSTER TRAP
21. DORY ON THE BEACH
22. ON THE GLENMERE ROAD
23. COAST FARM

6.
Macbeth Gallery, New York: *First Exhibition: Watercolors by Andrew Wyeth*. October 19–November 1, 1937.

Undisputed works by well-known artists often surface at auction after years in obscurity. A case in point is the beautiful pastel *A Kiss for Baby Anne (no. 3)* by Mary Cassatt (Fig. 5). This picture was once handled by Durand-Ruel, the Paris and New York dealer for Cassatt, and is recorded as such both in the Cassatt catalogue by Adelyn Breeskin and in the photo archives files of the Frick, but it only returned for a brief moment after the death of its private owner, when it sold at a Sotheby's auction on May 20, 1998, for $1,600,000 ($1,762,500 with the premium to the house).[7] The image is now so popular that online sellers offer it not only as painted and framed reproductions, but also as shower curtains and beach towels!

Another category of "quasi-unique" research material is designated by librarians as "ephemera." For art librarians, these tend to take the form of exhibition invitations and checklists that are commonly thrown away after the event. Invitations are of little value, but the checklists can be extraordinarily useful for tracing works of art. For example, the gallery of Paul Rosenberg in Paris was the premier venue for monthly exhibitions of artists whom the Nazis labeled as "degenerate" (Picasso, Braque, and Matisse, to name just three) and was the victim of Nazi looting in 1940. Being able to review the checklists for Rosenberg's exhibitions of 1939 has been essential to researchers seeking to know specifically which works by these prolific artists were—or at least might have been—in the Rosenberg gallery just before the looting took place. Less historically wrenching, but just as significant for researchers of American art, are the checklists published by the Macbeth Gallery in New York. This was a gallery where many an American artist got his or her start. Thus, to know if a painting was in Andrew Wyeth's first one-man show, consulting the checklist for the 1937 exhibition can either confirm or disappoint (Fig. 6).[8] In recent years, all of the Macbeth Gallery catalogues and checklists were digitized and made available online through the combined efforts of the Frick Art Reference Library, the Thomas J. Watson Library at The Metropolitan Museum of Art, and the library of the Brooklyn Museum.

This brief outline of the myriad resources available to collectors who aim to learn more about works they already own, or wish to acquire, only scratches the surface of what is available both online and at research institutions across the country. What is intended here is to provide a general survey of the categories of resources that any collector can consult. Most importantly, everyone should bear in mind that even as the collector must always think of the perils of *caveat emptor* when it comes to a purchase, the opposite is true when consulting information professionals at libraries and archives, who are always there to advise and help, with no concern for their own self-interest.

Art Advisors

Barbara Guggenheim, PhD
Partner, Guggenheim Asher Associates, New York

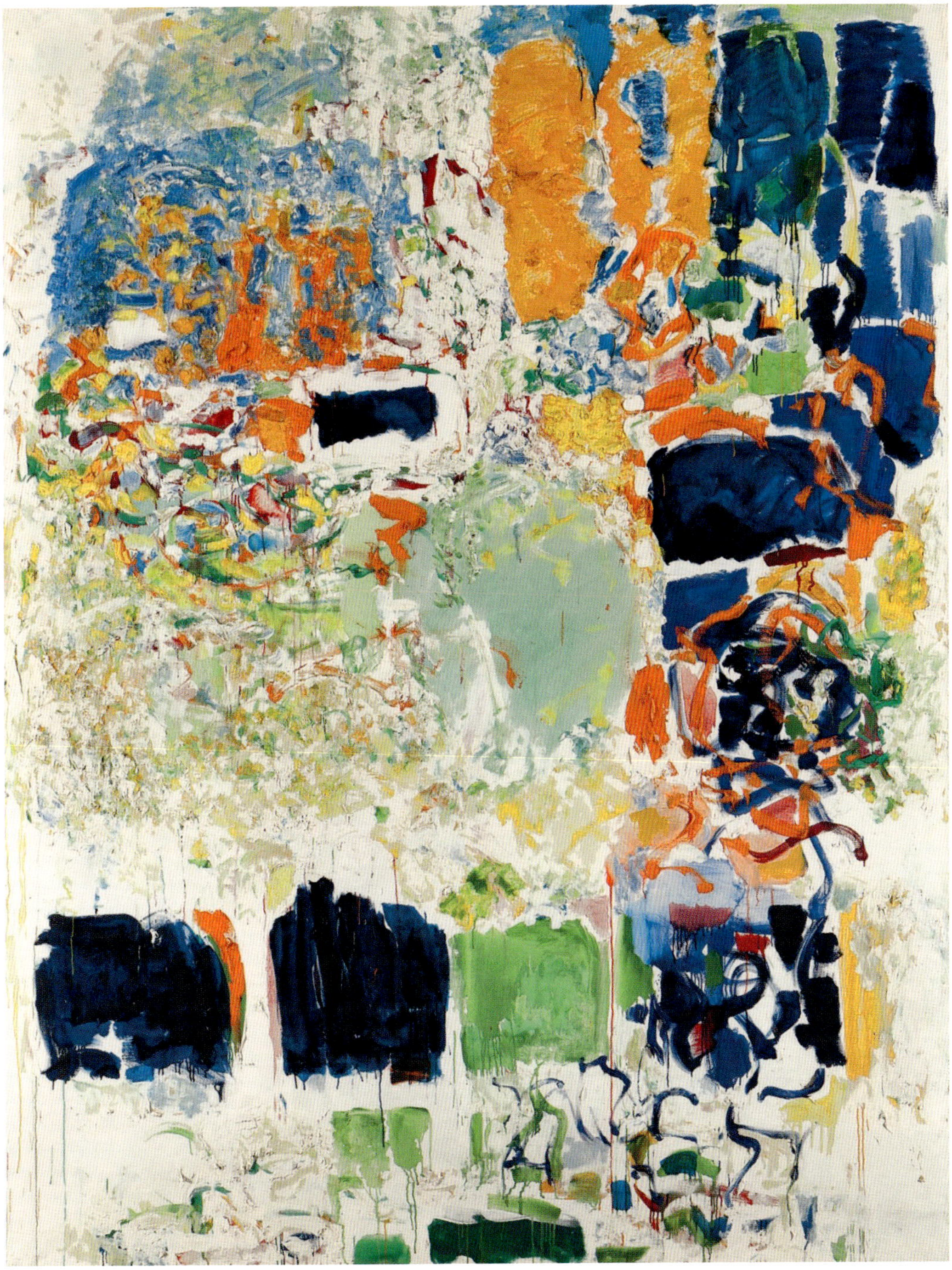

1. *(previous page)*
Joan Mitchell (1925–1992)
Noon, 1969
Oil on canvas
103 × 79 in. (262 × 200.6 cm)
Private collection

There's nothing new about art advisors. For centuries, individuals have sought the experts in building collections. They may not have been called advisors, but their job was the same. In about 1490, for example, the Duke of Milan wrote his Florentine agent asking for "hot" artists for a particular job. The advisor suggested Botticelli, Filippino Lippi, and Perugino—not a bad line-up. Later, Isabella d'Este wrote her advisor in Venice asking for a Giorgione. He answered, sadly, that she was too late: Giorgione had died, and no owners wanted to sell. *Plus ça change*.

By the turn of the twentieth century, American mega-collectors, including Albert Barnes and Henry and Louisine Havemeyer, used American artists, such as William Glackens and Mary Cassatt, respectively, to scout potential buys in Europe. Decades later, Impressionist scholar John Rewald performed the same function for a whole generation of American collectors.

In the 1980s, the art market was still pretty quiet. Prices were low, and collectors bought strictly for love. Uttering the words "money" and "art" in the same sentence was simply not done. As galleries proliferated, auction houses grew more powerful, and prices rose exponentially, buyers became less comfortable relying on "I love it!" as their guiding principle. They wanted assurance that they were not throwing their money away, and they needed guidance to make their way through an increasingly complex field. The art advisory profession came of age. Some collectors kept their advisors under wraps, along with their hair colorists and plastic surgeons. Perhaps they wanted the world to think all those brilliant collecting moves were theirs alone. Today, it's different. Serious collectors flaunt them. For many collectors, cruising galleries, auctions, and art fairs with an advisor by their side is like bringing a pit-bull lawyer to a serious business meeting. It sends a clear and powerful message, "I'm serious. Don't mess with me."

Still, many people collect without using advisors. Serious collecting is a twenty-four/seven job and takes years of experience. What you need to know about one artist may be different from what you need to know about another. For example, if a nineteenth-century Hudson River painting has a little craquelure or a tiny repair, it shouldn't stop you from buying it. But a single crack in an Ellsworth Kelly can be a career killer. And who knew that, if you're considering buying a Jean-Michel Basquiat, you need authentication from the estate or have airtight provenance even if it were coming up at an esteemed auction house? An advisor would. It's a little like being a novice picking mushrooms. What looks benign may be poisonous. Put another way, would you drill for oil without a geologist's advice? Of course not. Forming a collection without an advisor's help is no different.

I can see some of you shaking your heads, certain that advisors are not for you. Perhaps you think you're not spending enough to warrant professional help, or you don't want anyone imposing their taste on you or pushing you into buying something you don't want. Maybe you're a do-it-yourself type who relishes a challenge. Or, you just don't want to pay extra fees or commissions. I've heard it all, but please read this chapter before deciding to fly solo in the art market's sometimes not-so-friendly skies. Then, if you still want to go it alone, "Go with God."

If you're interested in American art, there are some things you need to know about the American market. The first thing is that all American art does not perform in the same way. Colonial portraiture doesn't sell the way that American nineteenth-century landscape, American Impressionism, Modernism, Social Realism, or post-war or contemporary American art does. Whereas the heat on the market is on post-war and contemporary art, fewer collectors are after traditional American art at the moment. As an art lover, I can't think of anything more transporting than a Thomas Moran painting of the Grand Canyon or a Sargent watercolor of Venice. And some Winslow Homers make me burst with pride. Although some iconic artists have always been sought after—Edward Hopper and Georgia

O'Keeffe, for instance—there may not be enough supply and demand at any given time to make an active market. Maybe paintings in big gold frames don't work in the homes most new millionaires are building. Maybe those rural scenes don't turn them on or maybe they're not coinage at a party where names like Urs Fischer and Cecily Brown are dropped, like Hermès and Vuitton. Or perhaps the heavily collected areas don't take a lot of connoisseurship and collectors want to buy only things that yield a quick profit. But all that could be changing. Instead of looking for the next hot artist, many collectors are looking back at artists who have been overlooked, particularly women and African American artists, such as Joan Mitchell, Helen Frankenthaler (Figs. 1 and 2), and Jacob Lawrence. I'm hoping this leads to a wake-up call and collectors realize that, for the cost of an average George Condo, they can have an American masterpiece.

But what do art advisors do? Essentially, as much or as little as our clients want, from helping them identify an area in which to collect to helping them sell or give works away decades later. In the beginning, we often spend time with clients exposing them to a lot of art, helping them learn art history, ways of looking, and the workings of the art world. We encourage clients to take their time and not jump in and buy. Once a client identifies areas they love and a budget, we'll direct them to works they can afford. Connecting a collector with the right collecting field is like being a great matchmaker, and when we succeed, it is enormously satisfying.

A Texas couple called with a dilemma. "We like Renoir and Monet, but we can't afford them," the husband lamented. If French Impressionism was too costly, I reasoned, they might like the American Impressionists, whose works are as colorful and light-filled as their French counterparts, but not as pricey. On our first day making the rounds of New York galleries, sensitive to price point, I showed the couple second-tier American Impressionists. They bought a beautiful Venetian scene by Jane Peterson for around $20,000. I was delighted

2.
Helen Frankenthaler
(1928–2011)
Cygnes, 1978
Acrylic on canvas
71 × 117 in. (180 × 297 cm)
Private collection

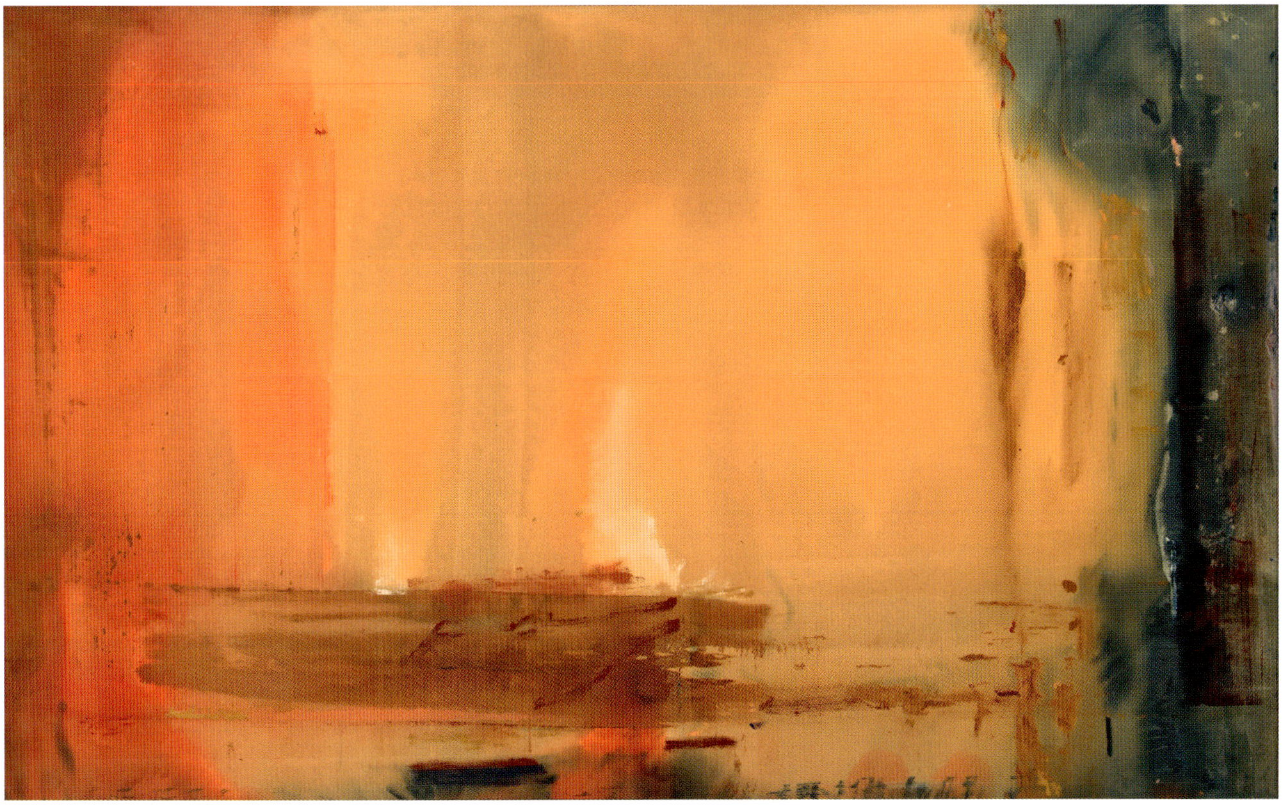

3.
John Singer Sargent
(1856–1925)
The Sulphur Match, 1882
Oil on canvas
23 × 16 ¼ in. (58.4 × 41.2 cm)
Private collection

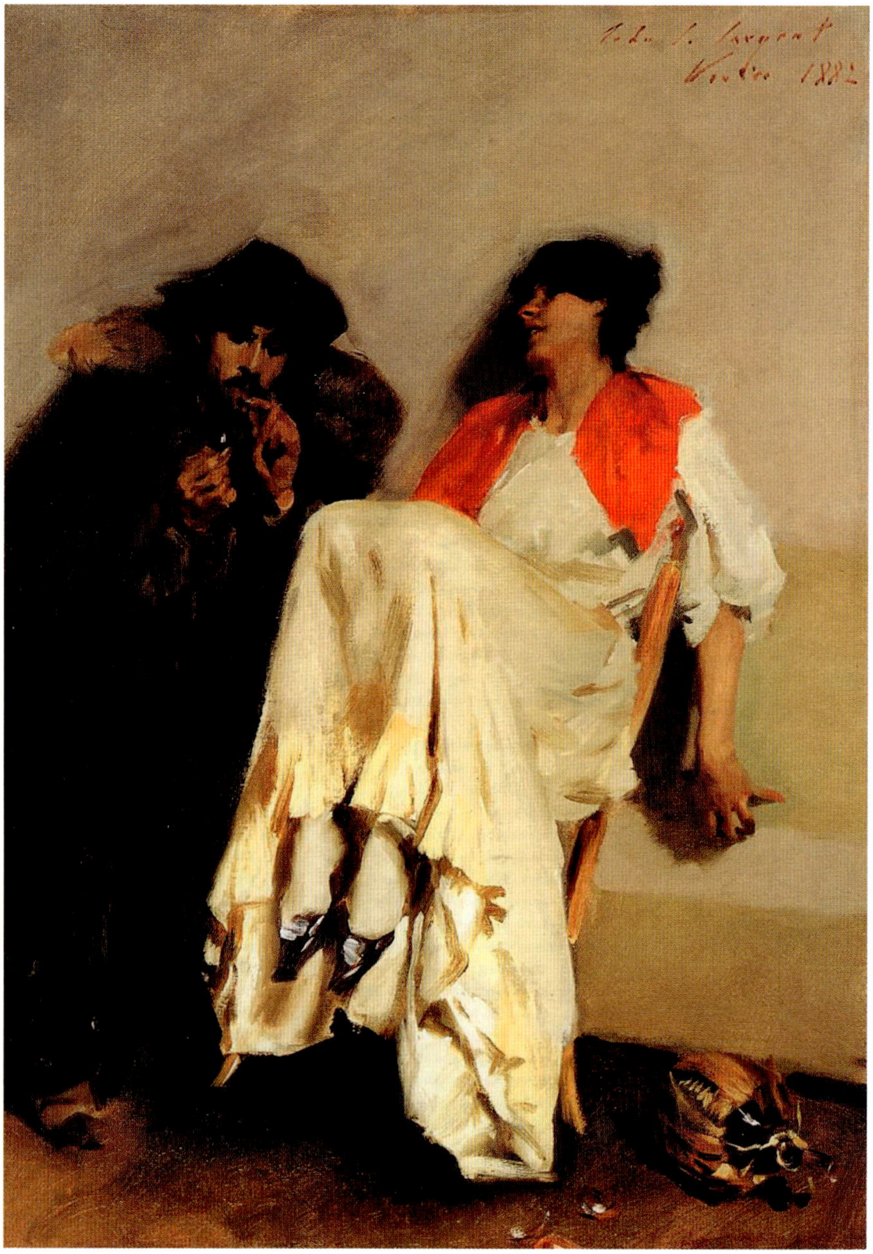

that we found a direction and went home to plan the next day's itinerary. That night, the husband called and, in a drawl, asked sheepishly, "Hon, y'all think you could show us something a little more expensive?" No problem! Over the next few days we looked at works by first-tier American artists John Singer Sargent (Fig. 3), Childe Hassam, and William Merritt Chase (Fig. 4). The couple bought the best of what they saw that week, and over the next several years their collection became one of the greatest in the field in private hands.

Years ago, a young East Coast couple came to me with a limited budget and no clear direction in mind. For the husband, a management consultant, "process" was at the core of his profession. I suggested sculptors' drawings. They loved the idea, and today they own drawings by major American twentieth-century sculptors from Elie Nadelman to Richard Serra. Their collection has been the subject of a catalogue and two museum exhibitions, and, for not a lot

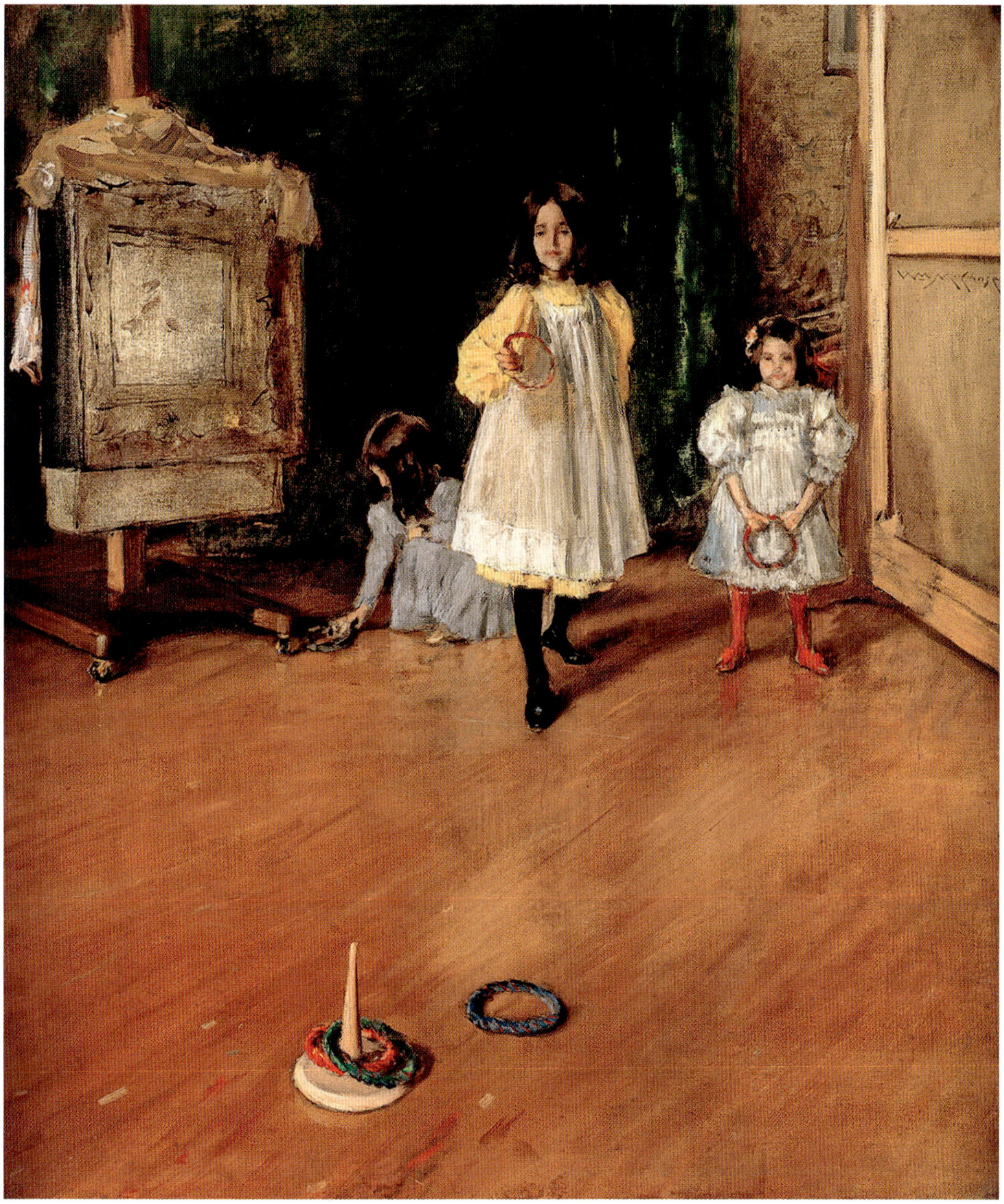

4
William Merritt Chase
(1849–1916)
Ring Toss, *c.* 1896
Oil on canvas
40 ⅜ × 35 ⅛ in.
(102.5 × 89.2 cm)
Private collection

of money, they've achieved a big bang for their buck. Over the years, as their business flourished, the couple added sculptures for which their drawings are studies.

For years, I've worked with many Hollywood producers and directors, such as Steven Spielberg and Kathy Kennedy. Among the things Steven and his wife Kate collected are Norman Rockwell paintings (Fig. 5). It fits that the greatest storyteller of the late twentieth century is drawn to the best storyteller of the early twentieth century. Kathy Kennedy and her husband, Frank Marshall, a producing-directing couple, collect Social Realist works, such as paintings of workers, done between the wars. Kathy and Frank see themselves as socially responsible storytellers and collect art that reflects that (Fig. 6). In general, I think the best collectors are those who build collections that reflect their personalities, and my job is to help a client realize that potential.

A powerful example was working with Alice Walton when she started collecting.

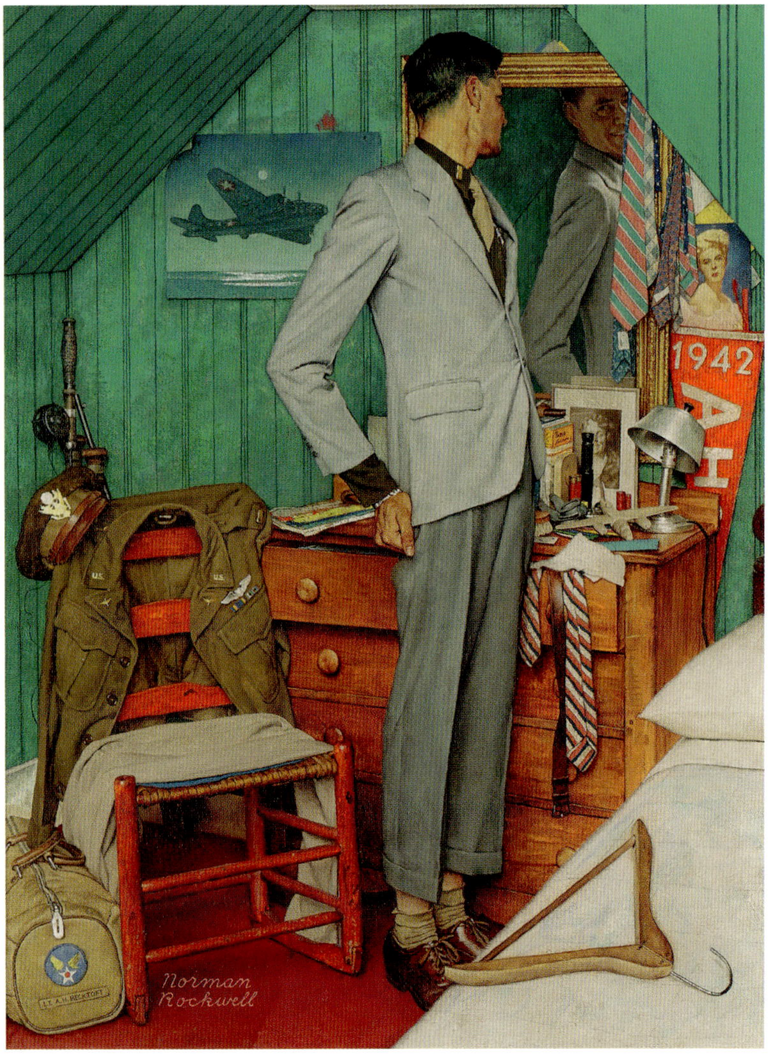

5.
Norman Rockwell
(1894–1978)
Back to Civvies (Imperfect Fit), 1945
Oil on canvas
39 × 30 in. (99 × 76.2 cm)
Private collection

No one understands nature and the American landscape as well as she does. This palpable love for America has led her to create Crystal Bridges Museum in Arkansas. Another of our clients, who loves scopic landscapes, does so with a caveat. Whenever he finds one he likes, he has to take his children to the spot where the painting was made. I've benefited, tagging along to the Grand Canyon, Monument Valley, and the like.

Once a client identifies what turns him on, I become a bird dog chasing the best examples. Since great works aren't always hanging in galleries, and the number of galleries dealing with American art is dwindling, my job is to get clients into the offices of private dealers and to collectors' homes. That's where good advisors are worth their weight in Warhols. Why? Getting in the door of a gallery is easy. Getting access to the best stuff is not so easy. Let's say that Mr. Smith walks into a gallery for the first time, alone. Any assistant or dealer could easily ignore him. If, however, Smith walks into the gallery with a well-respected art advisor, that changes. The advisor's presence signals that Smith is serious, and every dealer wants to help form an important collection. The dealer also feels confident that if he shows Smith something he wants kept under wraps, Smith and his advisor will keep quiet. So, what would have been a missed opportunity for Smith becomes a significant collecting moment. The lights come up in the private viewing room and there, on an easel, is Mr. Smith's dream painting. It doesn't always happen, but a skilled advisor makes it far more likely that it will.

Recently, a Midwestern couple came to New York, one step ahead of Mr. Smith. Armed with an introduction from their local museum director to an upscale Madison Avenue gallery, they were asked by the gallerist into the gallery's back room. On one hand they felt special, but they didn't have a clue whether anything they were shown was worth considering or priced fairly. Fortunately, mutual friends suggested they call me, and I accompanied them to the gallery the next day. Of the six works they'd been shown, only one, a small jewel of a Franz Kline, was an appropriate buy, though it was too small for any of their walls. While there, however, I asked the dealer to bring out a beautiful Edward Hopper watercolor he'd shown me the week before. He'd clearly sized up the couple and decided that the Hopper was out of their league, but he was wrong. They flipped for it and bought it. They've been clients of ours and the gallery ever since.

If advisors thrill when clients connect with a certain area, the moment I live for is when a client finds a work he can't live without. It's also the moment I switch gears. If the work is on the primary market, there's little to do; there are no condition problems, no issues on authenticity, provenance, etc., and the price is set, with, perhaps, some room for negotiating. But if the painting is on the secondary market, there's much to do. I become vigilant in looking, researching, and evaluating the information I gather. This requires an investment of time and skills that can only be developed over years, including a working knowledge of art history, an ability to identify the right objects to buy and which way taste is going, knowing the questions to ask, and figuring out the right price to pay. This reminds me of my first scuba-diving lesson in Mexico. The local instructor, non-certified to be sure, suited me up and began firing commands in Spanish I only half understood. I think he was screaming, "Hold this cord!" "Breathe in!" and "Kick this way!" while I kept protesting, "No entiendo." He then pushed me backwards off the boat into the deep. If I'd failed to do any one of the things he'd "taught" me, I'd have drowned. Luckily, I didn't, but I remember thinking I'd have been better off with a good interpreter. You see where I'm going with this? A competent art advisor will make sure you don't wind up at the bottom of the sea. Collecting is easier, safer, and more fun when you have someone at your side translating the mountains of elusive, specialized, and complicated intel that go into making a wise purchase.

In such situations, I'd ask a conservator to examine the work and explain his findings to the client—the prognosis, treatment plan—and translate all that into market terms, whether the condition impacts the price and by how much. Recently, a friend asked me to sell the only painting he'd bought in his life, a de Kooning that someone sold him for investment. The condition report supplied by the seller, a dealer, mentioned "a thin line of inpainting," and that the painting was relined. My friend, unaccustomed to reading conservation reports, didn't realize that meant there was a problem. Anyone could see under black light that the line of restoration was at least twelve inches long, the result of a gash. Worse, the relining was so bad that thick paint layers were squashed down, leaving the work flat and lifeless. If the de Kooning owner had had an art advisor look at the painting or explain the report to him, he might not have bought it in the first place. As a result, when he sold it, he didn't get as much as he hoped. Discerning whether a work is a fine example and what is the right price to pay are important. An advisor who has stood in front of dozens of works by the artist you're considering knows the answers. Nonetheless, if you were my client, I'd show you "comps" from auction and private sales. Sure, you can slog through online databases of auction sales for comparisons yourself, but it's easy to get it wrong. You may think "yours" is like one that brought a low price and decide that you shouldn't pay a dime over that price, without realizing that that one was in horrible condition and would have brought more if it was in a better state. Whenever possible, I'd fill you in on back-stories. I'd go through the catalogue raisonné or definitive catalogues with you. Because I notate my CRs, I'd be able to show you which works are in museums, which are in private hands, and how many and which ones might come on to the market. I might even be able to tell you how much various

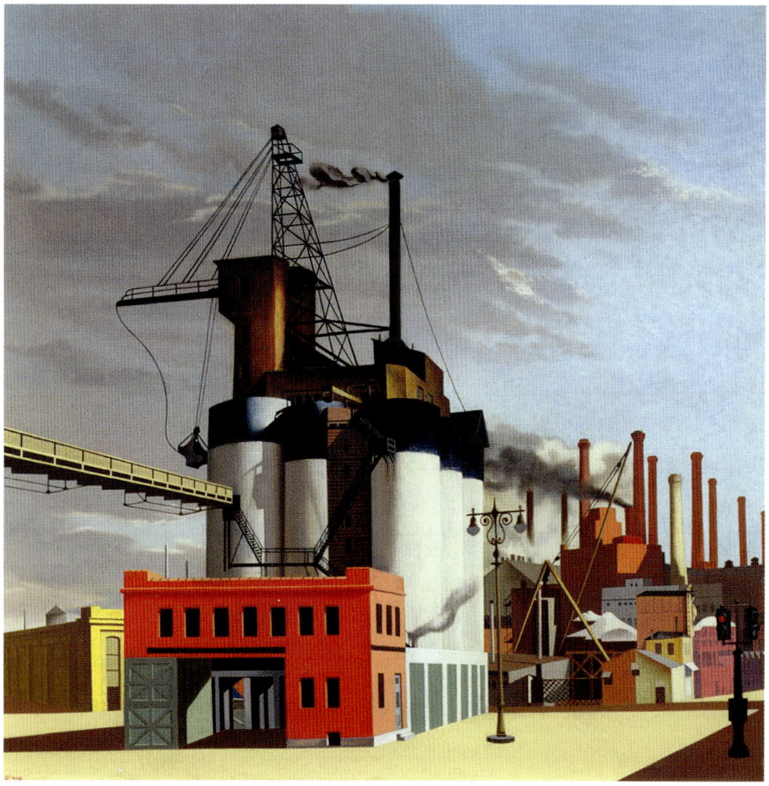

6.
Francis Criss (1901–1973)
New York Waterfront
c. 1944–45
Oil on canvas
30 × 30 in. (76.2 × 76.2 cm)
Signed at lower left: Criss.
Private collection

owners turned down for theirs. Wouldn't you like to know, if you pass up the Rothko you're considering, whether you'll be able to get another? And whether the trajectory for an artist's prices is going up? An advisor answers these questions and others.

If everything checks out, and the "Buy!" button lights up, it's time to negotiate. "Aha!" you say. "No problem. I've negotiated lots of business deals, and I'm great at it." No doubt you have, but your advisor can be an important weapon. If the work is with a dealer he or she has negotiated with before, s/he knows how to read the tea leaves. S/he knows when the dealer is bluffing or can't stretch any more. S/he knows if the dealer is short of cash or if s/he'll take a long payout, and s/he knows whether the dealer will get insulted and blow the deal if you make too low an offer. Since your advisor is a source of clients for the dealer, the dealer has an incentive to keep him/her happy, which is good for you. When the smoke clears, you'll usually get the right painting at the right price.

I laugh when I think of my first outing with Sidney Sheldon, the writer. Because he liked American Impressionism, I visited dealers in advance and picked works for him to see. In the first gallery's viewing room (often called the sting room in the trade), the gallerist brought out the first of four paintings I chose and set it on the easel. Sidney smiled and said, "I'll take it." The dealer brought out the second, and Sidney enthused, "I love it; I'll take that, too." The same with the third. I dragged Sidney into the hall and told him how hard he was making it for me to negotiate, and I begged him to keep a poker face. We returned to the room where the dealer had brought out the fourth work, to which Sidney said, "I guess I'll take them all." I didn't get to negotiate much that day, but Sidney was happy.

At auctions, advisors lead you through, start to finish. When auction season rolls around, and pounds of catalogues arrive on your desk, it could take hours to sift through them and identify promising lots. Advisors do that for you. Then, once you've identified objects you want to pursue, an advisor makes sure you see them early and does the necessary checks, because auction houses can—and do—make mistakes. My partner, Abigail Asher, was once in London viewing a Picasso drawing for a client coming up in a sale. She called from the auction room to tell me she thought it was a print. I heard her call over the expert who told her in his haughty English accent, "Abigail, don't be crazy. It belongs to a fine, fine family." Well, Abigail had a conservator come, take the work out of the frame, and sure enough it was a print. The auction house withdrew it from the sale.

An advisor knows what similar works are or have been on the market and what might become available—all of which is relevant in figuring out how high to bid. And then, of course, if your advisor is well known by the auctioneers, s/he can get "secret" information to execute your bid.

If all that sounds promising, wait until you see your advisor in action at an art fair. It's easy to become paralyzed by the volume of works on view and the hellish need to make quick decisions or go home empty-handed. An advisor finds out in advance what exhibitors are bringing, so you can buy before the opening or put works on reserve until you get to see them. If the latter, your advisor rushes you in as soon as the doors open and takes you to booths where you have works on reserve and where there are things s/he wants you to consider. Your advisor will then walk you through the rest of the fair, giving you an on-the-spot commentary.

Once you've bought a work—in a gallery, at auction, or at an art fair—it's not the end of the journey. While acquiring art is fun, work required by ownership, including conservation, framing, shipping, installation, lighting, lending, record-keeping, etc., can be less interesting. Many collectors use advisors for all that. If you buy an outdoor sculpture, for example, installing it could take a village—from engineers and shippers to conservators and installers. Last summer, I found myself in an empty field in Virginia, in 90-degree weather, supervising the installation of an outdoor bronze. The team sweated it out for hours, literally and figuratively, because the epoxy required to stick the piece to the base wouldn't set in the heat. Meanwhile, an electrical storm moved in, and as the lightning flashed around us, I realized that standing next to a large metal sculpture in an empty field wasn't a great idea. Luckily, our client didn't have to experience this.

Advisors love hanging paintings, and they're good at it. Whenever a collector buys a new work that's joining others, a total re-hang may be necessary to create a meaningful dialogue between works, taking into account color, size, style, and subject matter.

As for collection management, computer programs only go so far. When a loan request comes in, an advisor can save you big headaches. S/he knows whether the museum or gallery asking is a worthwhile venue, and s/he'll take care of the paperwork and lending logistics, including insurance, packing, and shipping. An advisor will also arrange and supervise a conservator to check condition periodically and maintain paintings and outdoor sculptures.

Advisors provide clients with services that have nothing to do with the art itself but everything to do with the collecting experience. If you want to maintain anonymity, your advisor arranges viewings in warehouses or your home. S/he arranges previews of works coming up at auctions after-hours in a private room, and, if you attend the auction, s/he'll arrange for you to bid from a skybox and slip in and out at a side door. For celebrities and the very wealthy, these precautions are not just for personal comfort—they're practical. Your advisor can negotiate better deals if a seller doesn't know you're Mr. Big. One of our clients guards his privacy so fiercely we don't use his real name even when we're alone in our office. On the other hand, if you're interested in making a splash in the art world and want to make a life out of collecting, an advisor can orchestrate that handily. Getting you prominent seats at auctions and invitations to the right openings and dinners at art fairs is an art advisor's métier.

And then there's the end-game—helping you give your art away, trade, or sell it. An advisor can help you choose a museum where your works will have the greatest impact and will not be buried in the basement or sold off. If you're selling, an advisor will determine the price you can expect and the best venue. Looking back at all the things advisors can do, electing to use one seems like a no-brainer. I believe that the small percentage Guggenheim Asher charges makes our services in the long term "free."

But how do you choose the right advisor? When word gets out that you could become a serious player, eager dealers, auction-house experts, museum curators, and even other collectors may try to convince you that you don't need an art advisor, because *they'll* advise you—gratis. It's a nice thought, but it seldom works out. Since you might be tempted, let's quickly look at these options.

Dealers have been advising clients since the dawn of the dealing profession. There's nothing new about that. What is new in recent times is that, as paintings increase in value, more dealers can't afford inventory. That leads them to become dealer/advisors. Some are impeccably honest and are able to switch roles with ease. Others allow their dealer hat to trump their advisor hat. They're so used to making the maximum on every transaction that they'll want you to buy a work from their inventory or one they get from a colleague in which they have an interest. The thought of helping you buy a work that takes you out of the market for a small advisory commission goes against their very fiber, as does their ability to tell you that their competitor has a better, cheaper example. Would Macy's send you to Bloomingdale's? If you think they would, there's a bridge I'd like to sell you.

Dealers will also press hard to make their specialty yours. When a woman banker moved into a new country home, a neighbor, an Old Master dealer, came calling and suggested he act as her art advisor—for free. Flattered, she agreed. One weekend when she was away, he pulled a truck up to her house, unloaded and hung a dozen Old Masters from his inventory. She hated them all and hated the dealer for taking her for granted. She returned the paintings, called us, and bought a houseful of contemporary art. She couldn't wait to invite her dealer/neighbor for dinner.

What about auction-house experts? They're knowledgeable, know the market, and are eager to serve. But they have demanding jobs and don't have the time to scour the world on your behalf and do all the things advisors do. And besides, they have a vested interest in steering you to buy what they're selling.

Museum curators or directors know a lot, and they're not pocketing any money. But they, too, may have an agenda that puts their interests ahead of yours. They may be thinking what's best for the museum and how they can get you to give works or support a program. Or, they like being big man on campus, and squiring you around galleries and art fairs adds to their luster. Most don't have the market acuity and day-to-day knowledge required to make the right decision.

Years ago, a curator of a Western museum, attempting to curry favor with a big supporter of theirs who was also my client, had a landscape by Martin Johnson Heade, a nineteenth-century American painter, flown out from a New York gallery for him to see and buy. When my client called for my opinion, he said that the curator told him that the price was $1.6 million. I explained that I'd seen the painting a month earlier at a private dealer's for $900,000, but I hadn't thought to offer it to him because he had one better. He understood but thought a pair in his entry could be fun. Rather than cut out the intermediary dealer, who likely had it on consignment (and tacked on a $700,000 profit) from the private dealer who'd offered it to me, we decided to make him a generous offer of $1.2 million. The dealer refused, feigning outrage: "I won't accept a penny less than $1.6 million." We instructed the curator to return the painting and bought it from the private dealer the next day for $900,000.

Lastly, other collectors may offer to advise you. They may introduce you to their "hot" dealers, hoping for the payback of being offered something great before anyone else. The moral of the story? Dealers, experts, curators, and other collectors may be knowledgeable, but they're not able to do what's best for you.

What *will* you pay an advisor? It depends. Some advisors work on a retainer, some charge a percentage of the retail or negotiated net price of each object purchased, and others charge a combination of retainer and commission. Art advisors charge differently, and, if collector and advisor agree, any arrangement can work. The one thing advisors shouldn't do is "double dip"—collect commissions from seller and buyer. When I was starting out, a veteran advisor recommended that, if a new client complains about fees, tell them, "Just pay me for the work I do on all objects you *don't* buy."

When you're looking for an art advisor, choose carefully. Since the field has no requirements, it's crawling with self-styled "art advisors" with no credentials and no expertise. Every Park Avenue lady who once called herself an interior designer is now calling herself an art advisor. Look for an advisor or a team with experience, deep knowledge, a good eye, is street smart, and has a sprawling web of connections and access to good material, a solid grasp of the market, an uncompromising attitude about due diligence, negotiating skills, respect and trust of others in the field, diplomacy, and unshakeable honesty.

Since you're going to be spending a fair amount of time together, you should also pick someone you get along with. When Catherine the Great decided that forming a collection might soften her reputation as a ruthless despot, she turned to the famed encyclopedist and art critic Denis Diderot, who favored buying whole collections *en masse*. His astute buys form the nucleus of the Hermitage Museum in St. Petersburg. Despite the fact that Diderot did a fabulous job, however, Catherine fired him in favor of a lesser light, Friedrich Melchior Grimm, whom she felt more comfortable with.

You might ask other collectors or your museum director or curator for recommendations, or get a list from the APAA, the Association of Professional Art Advisors. Below are some questions you might ask candidates:

1. *What's your educational background?* (An advanced degree usually indicates a broader perspective.)

2. *How long have you been an art advisor? Do you have other art-world experience?*

3. *How many people work for you? What do they do?*

4. *How many clients do you work with at a time?* (Too few or too many could signal a problem.)

5. *What do you do if more than one client wants the same painting or the same hard-to-get artist? If you're offered a painting that two clients might like, how do you decide which one to offer it to?*

6. *Do you keep an inventory?*

7. *How do you charge? Is there a minimum?*

8. *How do you charge at auction?*

Bottom line: advisors short-cut the process of building good collections and making it look easy, which, as you'll quickly discover if you go it alone, it isn't. They'll spare you the tedious parts, allowing you to focus on parts you love. They'll save you time and money, prevent terrible mistakes from happening, and get you in front of the right paintings you might never find on your own. Whether you're just starting out and need education and introductions, or you're a sophisticated collector, looking for specific works or to redefine or refine your collection, advisors can make a difference. Collecting is a long journey, and if you work with the right advisor, sit back and let that advisor show you how much fun collecting can be.

The Anatomy of an Auction

Liz Sterling
Senior Vice President, Director of Private Sales, Americas, Sotheby's, New York;
Chairman, American Art, Sotheby's, New York

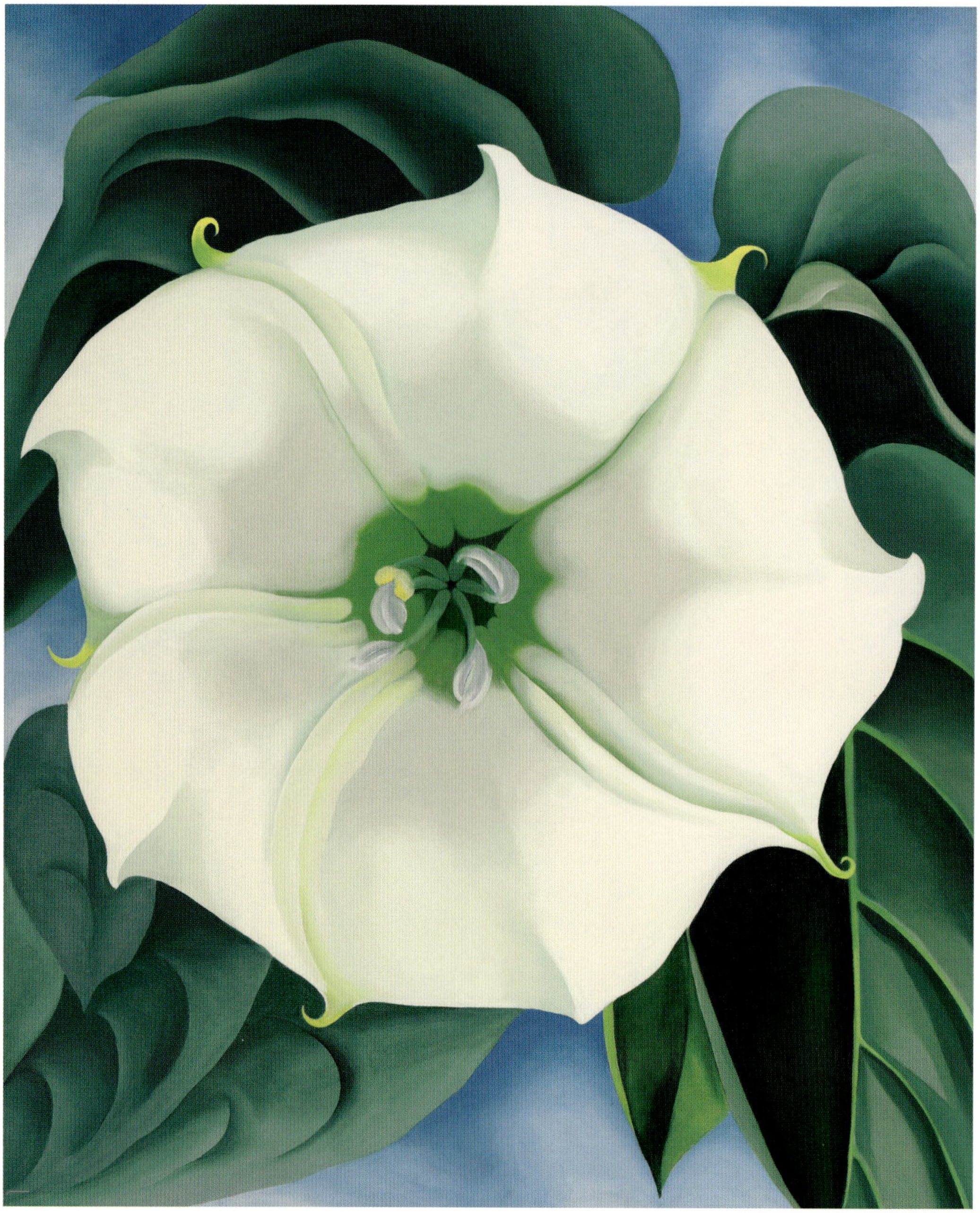

There are a number of factors to take into consideration when assessing and ultimately valuing a work of art. While some might argue it is a fine science—see askART's guiding ideas, "price per square inch option, red paintings sell better than green, horizontal vs. vertical"—it is certainly not a fine science, and understanding these aspects can help to demystify the ultimate price achieved for a piece at auction and explain why there can be such a variance in prices for a single artist. The key factors utilized to evaluate a work of art are subject, medium, date, condition, scale, taste, and provenance. While each is an important factor in its own right, they are not mutually exclusive.

At auction there are two values: the pre-auction estimate, which is often a marketing tool aimed at engaging the largest number of potential bidders so as to create competition in the saleroom; and the final sale price, which is indicative of the true value of a work.

The following pages discuss the aforementioned factors, utilizing specific examples of works sold at auction to illustrate and explicate the role they play in disparities in prices achieved for specific artists. While there are a myriad auction houses throughout the country, the examples chosen were sold at Christie's and Sotheby's as these are the major international auction houses that consistently have the broadest audience and base of buyers. Therefore the prices achieved can be seen as an accurate reflection of the marketplace at the time of sale.

SUBJECT

The first factor taken into consideration when valuing a work of art for auction is the subject. For the majority of artists, there are subjects that are the most coveted by collectors and command premium prices.

When considering how a work's subject matter impacts its monetary value we ask ourselves a series of questions: is this a commercial subject for the market? How will it be received? Does it have broad appeal? Most important, how does it fit into the artist's career?

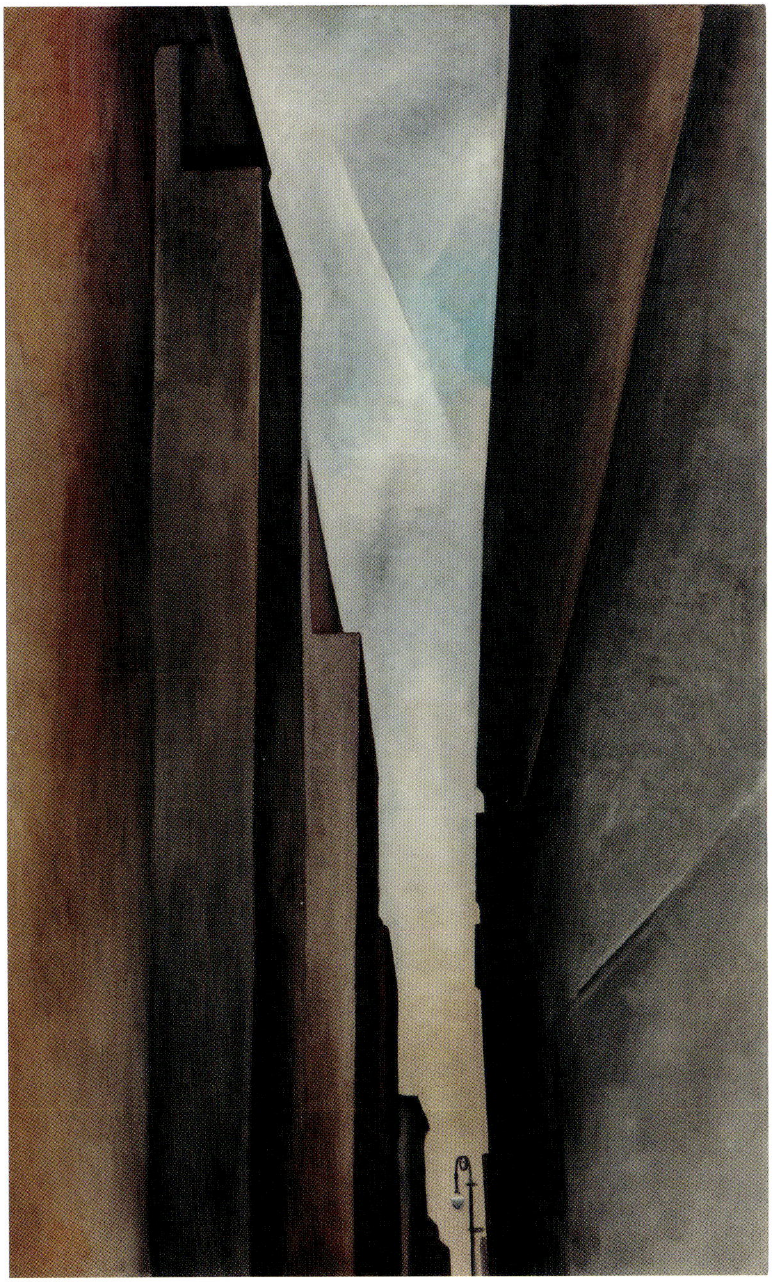

1. *(opposite)*
Georgia O'Keeffe
(1887–1986)
Jimson Weed/White Flower No. 1, 1932
Oil on canvas
48 × 40 in.
(121.9 × 101.6 cm)
Sotheby's NY 11/20/2014,
$44,405,000

2. *(above)*
Georgia O'Keeffe
(1887–1986)
A Street, 1926
Oil on canvas
48 ¼ × 30 in.
(122.6 × 76.2 cm)
Sotheby's NY 11/14/2018,
$13,282,500

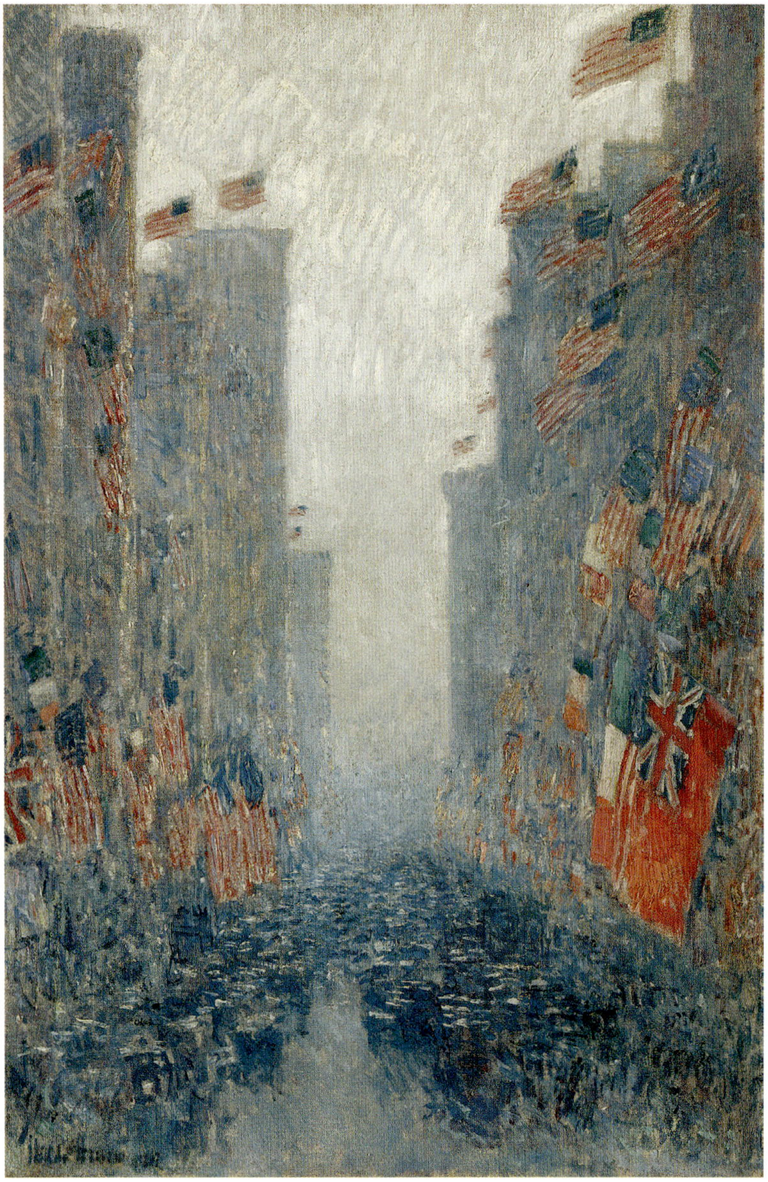

3.
Childe Hassam (1859–1935)
Flags, Afternoon on the Avenue
1917
Oil on canvas
36 x 24 in. (91.5 x 61 cm)
Christie's NY 5/21/1998,
$7,922,500

And finally, how many works of this quality of this subject remain in private hands that could potentially come to market in the near future?

There can be a considerable difference between the prices that collectors are willing to pay for works that are of the most desirable subject matter and other works by an artist that are of similar quality but less popular subject matter. For example, the most desirable subject for works by Georgia O'Keeffe is her flower paintings and the differential between her world record price at auction, $44,405,000 for the iconic 1932 painting *Jimson Weed* (Fig. 1), and the second highest price at auction, $13,282,500 for a striking 1926 cityscape, *A Street* (Fig. 2), which was sold four years later, is notable. The current world auction record for Childe Hassam was set over twenty years ago, in 1998, when *Flags, Afternoon on the Avenue* sold for $7,922,500 (Fig. 3). This painting is one of a series of his most sought-after works, the Flag paintings of 1916 to 1919. Hassam painted less than thirty of these New York City scenes, depicting flag-adorned Fifth Avenue during World War I, and many of them are in museum collections including the National Gallery of Art, Washington, DC, The Metropolitan Museum of Art, New York, and Amon Carter Museum of American Art, Fort Worth, Texas. Their importance, beauty and scarcity make them some of the most coveted works by an American Impressionist and privately Flag paintings have sold for over $20 million. In contrast, the second highest price for the artist at auction was set a decade later, in 2008 for *Spring in Central Park* (see page 48), which sold for $5,641,000. While also a desirable New York subject, *Spring in Central Park* did not command the same price a Flag picture did even ten years before.

For artists who have historically been categorized as American Illustrators (e.g. J.C. Leyendecker, Norman Rockwell, N.C. Wyeth, and others), in addition to the subject, overall quality and narrative character of a work, the ultimate use of the image, such as the book or magazine in which it was illustrated, often impacts value. The paintings by Norman Rockwell that command top prices are those that were used as cover illustrations for *The Saturday Evening Post*, the publication with which the artist is most closely associated.

At times, a work comes to the market that has become so widely representative of an artist's œuvre that it commands a tremendous price. This was the case when Edward Hopper's *Chop Suey* (see page 175), one of the most iconic works by the artist still in private hands, was offered at auction in November 2018. *Chop Suey* has been in every major Hopper exhibition and extensively referenced and illustrated in literature about the artist—it is a widely recognized image internationally even to people who are not art collectors. When the painting came to auction in November 2018 from the collection of Barney Ebsworth it sold for $91,875,000, more than double the existing record for the artist at auction ($40,485,000 for *East Wind Over Weehawken*, sold in 2013).

In contrast, a work that is "rare" or "unusual" for an artist does not necessarily equate to a higher value. These works are often intellectually and academically valuable but lack the commercial appeal of more recognizable imagery. For example, an early student work might have value to a museum or a thoughtful academic collector, but it may not represent the mature style for which an artist is best known. While Clyfford Still's signature abstract paintings from the 1940s sell for prices in excess of $30 million, a rare early work from 1937, when the artist was still painting in a realist fashion, sold for $250,000 in 2016.

MEDIUM

Medium is also an important factor in determining the value of a work of art. Historically oil paintings have been valued more highly than works on paper as collectors perceive oil paintings to be more durable and less susceptible to degradation over time. The sensitivities of works on paper, predominantly toning and fading associated with light exposure as well as vulnerability to the environment, have largely been ameliorated by contemporary conservation methods such as UV protective Plexiglas, acid-free mounts, and modern HVAC systems, yet the bias and price differential continue for the works of a number of artists.

This disparity exists in the market even for some of the most celebrated American watercolorists. The current world auction record for a John Marin oil painting is $1,572,500 (*My-Hell Raising Sea*), November 2018, while the auction record for a watercolor is $724,500 (*New York, 1927*), December 2002. Whereas works on paper by Andrew Wyeth have sold for more than $6 million privately, the world record at auction is $989,000 (*Ice Storm*, Fig.4), May 2015. Both private and auction prices are significantly below the auction record for a tempera on panel, $10,344,000 set in 2007 when *Ericksons* soared above its pre-sale estimate of $4–6 million. Although the top two prices for Winslow Homer at auction are for watercolors (*The Red Canoe*, $4,842,500 in December 1999, and *Where are the Boats?*, $4,572,500 in May 2018), oil paintings have been sold for eight-figure sums privately. John Singer Sargent's auction record for an oil painting is $23,528,000 (*Group with Parasols*, December 2004), while for a work on paper it is $2,696,000 set the same year (*Madame Roger-Jourdain*, May 2004). Finally, the auction record for a work on paper by Edward Hopper is $4,155,750 (*Kelly Jenness House*, May 2013) in comparison to the over $90 million sale price of *Chop Suey*.

4.
Andrew Wyeth (1917–2009)
Ice Storm, 1971
Drybrush, watercolor, and gouache on paper
28 ¾ × 22 ¾ in.
(73 × 57.8 cm)
Christie's NY 5/21/2015, $989,000

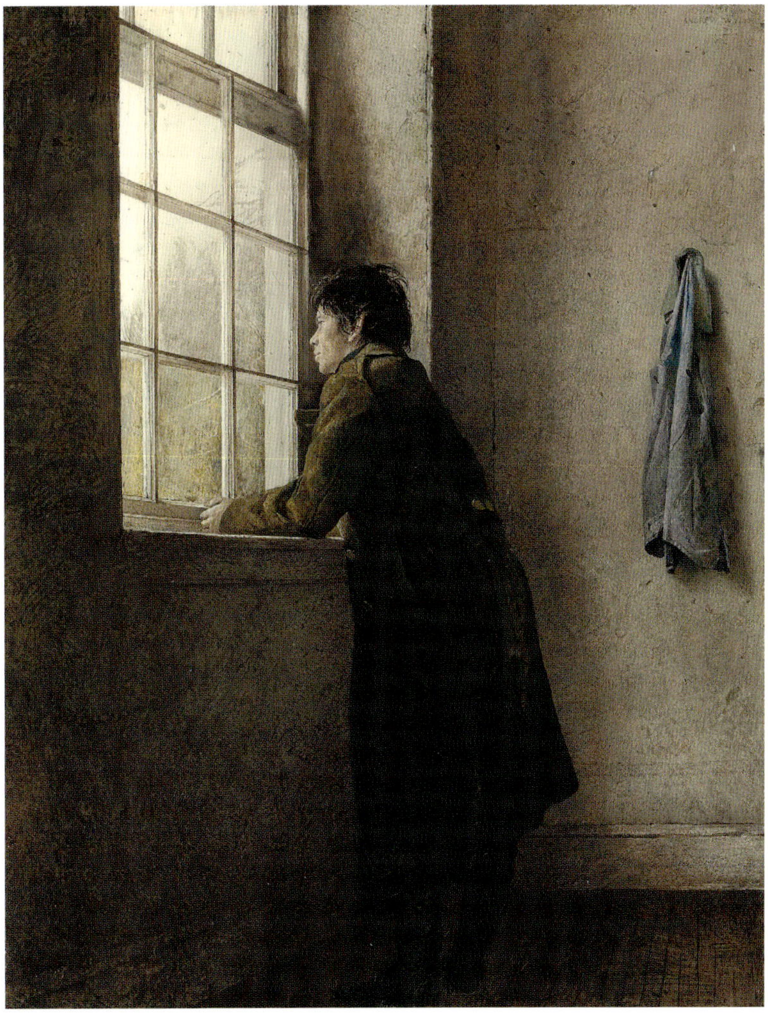

5. *(right)*
Maurice Prendergast
(1858–1924)
The Stony Beach
Watercolor
20 ⅞ × 14 in. (53 × 35.6 cm)
Christie's NY 5/23/2001,
$3,526,000

6. *(below)*
Maurice Prendergast
(1858–1924)
Promenade, 1914–15
Oil on canvas
19 × 42 in. (48.3 × 106.7 cm)
Christie's NY 12/4/2003,
$1,911,500

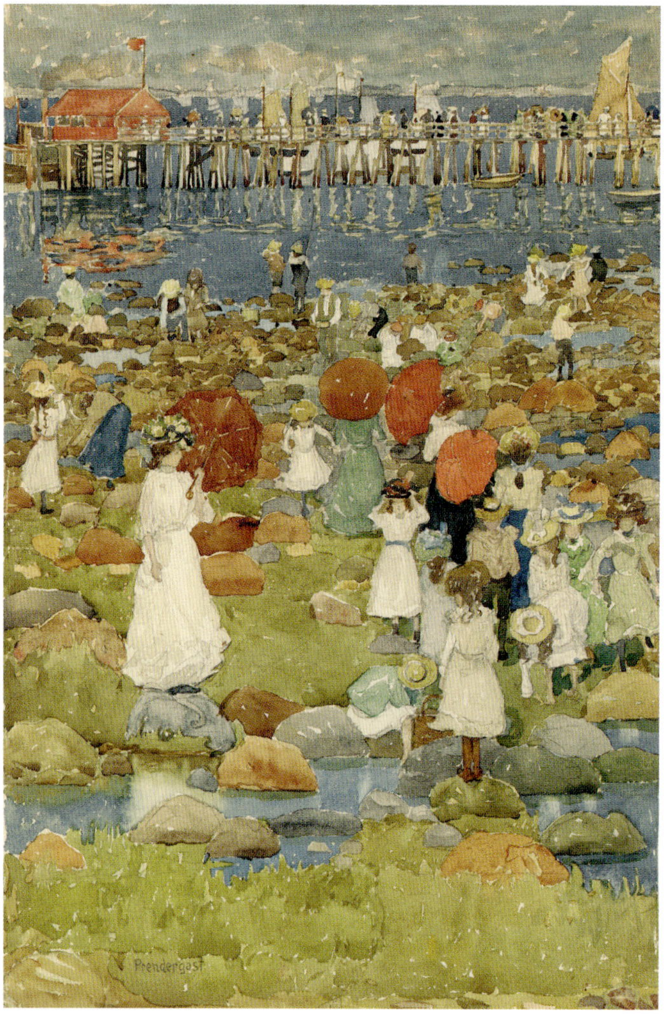

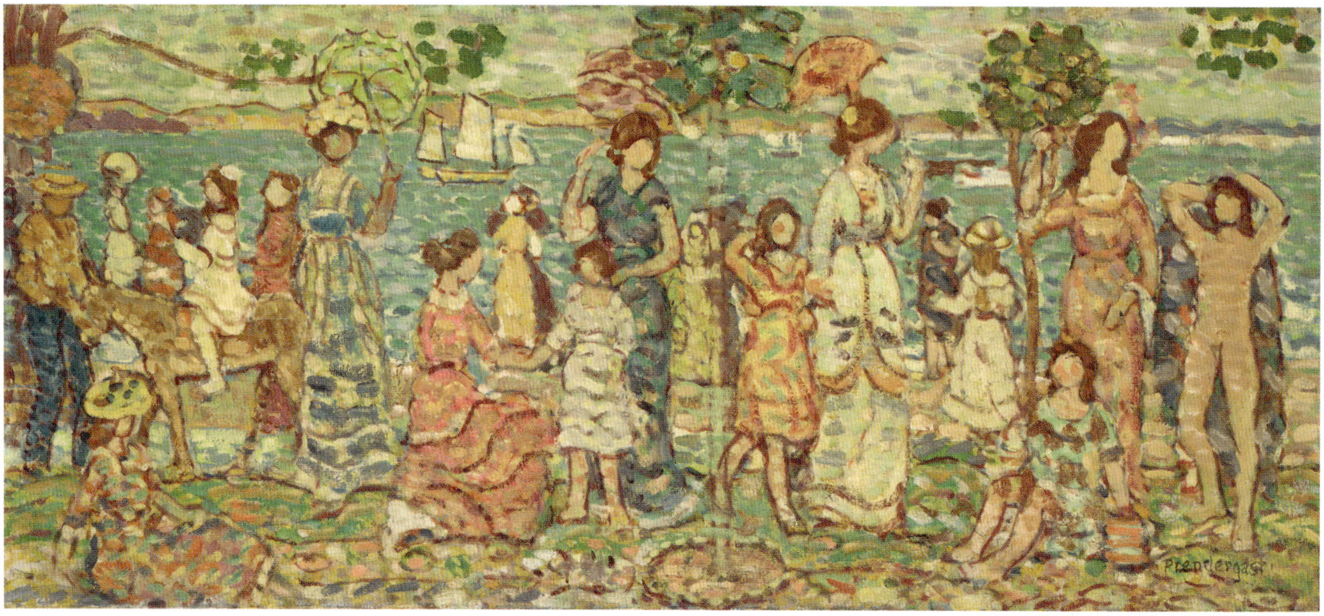

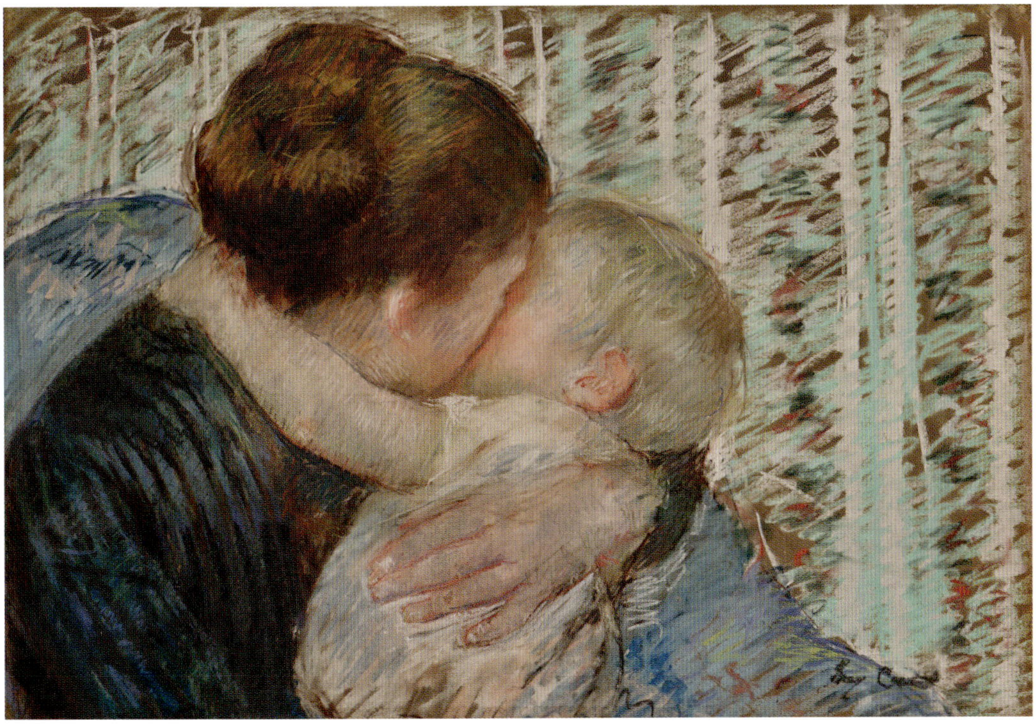

7.
Mary Cassatt (1844–1926)
A Goodnight Hug, 1880
Pastel on brown paper
16 ½ × 24 ¾ in.
(42 × 62.8 cm)
Sotheby's NY 5/14/2018,
$4,518,200

In the art market, there are always exceptions to the "rules" and in the case of medium, Maurice Prendergast is one. The artist's top-quality watercolors are regularly valued above his oil paintings of similar quality. Prendergast's bold and beautiful works on paper are highly coveted by collectors and the top five prices for the artist at auction are all for watercolors, the record price being $3,526,000 for *The Stony Beach* (Fig. 5). The auction record for an oil painting is $1,911,500 (Fig. 6).

At times, truly exceptional works on paper will sell for extraordinary prices. This was the case when Mary Cassatt's pastel on paper, *A Goodnight Hug* (Fig. 7), came to auction in May 2018. Executed in 1880, when the artist was at the height of her association with the French Impressionists, and exhibited alongside their work shortly after it was painted, this boldly modern work was also most likely Cassatt's first depiction of the mother and child subject for which she has become best known. This stunning work on paper soared above its pre-sale estimate of $700,000–1 million to sell for $4,518,200, establishing a new world auction record for a work on paper by the artist and the third highest price at auction overall.

DATE

The date of a work of art can also have a substantial impact on its market value as many artists have periods that are widely considered to be their strongest. For example, Max Weber's works from the late 1900s through the 1910s command a significant premium over his later works. He was one of the earliest American artists to integrate European Modernism and Cubism into his work, and the top price for a work from this period is $1,925,000 (*New York*), May 2016, while the top price for a later work is $79,000 (*The Cellist*), October 2007.

For Ashcan artists such as Robert Henri, Everett Shinn, and John Sloan, the most desirable dates are 1904 to 1910 when these artists were producing innovative depictions of modern urban life and the characters that defined it. Although Shinn continued to depict a number of the same themes throughout his career, including theater scenes, the market places a considerable premium on the works from the early period. A 1906 theater scene, *Stage Scene* (Fig. 8), sold for $7,848,000. In contrast a larger painting, *The Revue* (Fig. 9), that also depicts a single female figure on stage

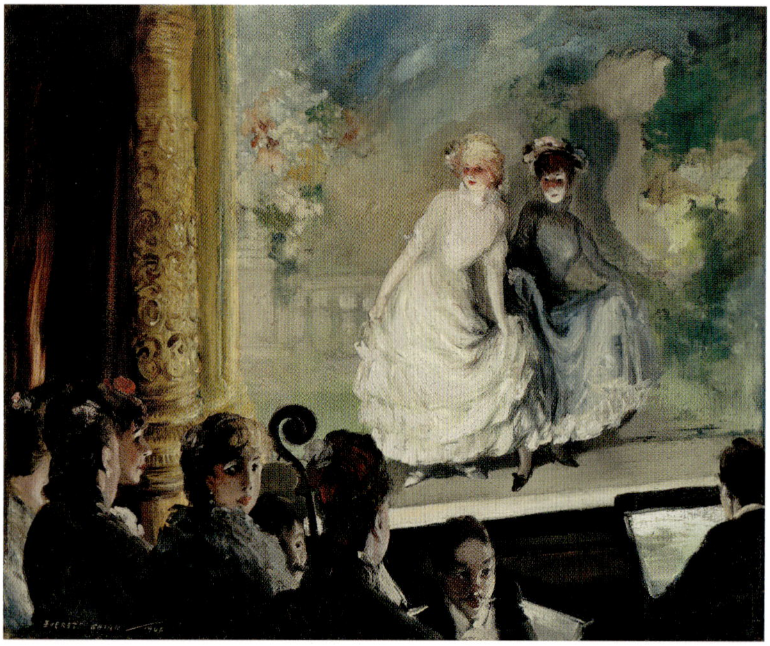

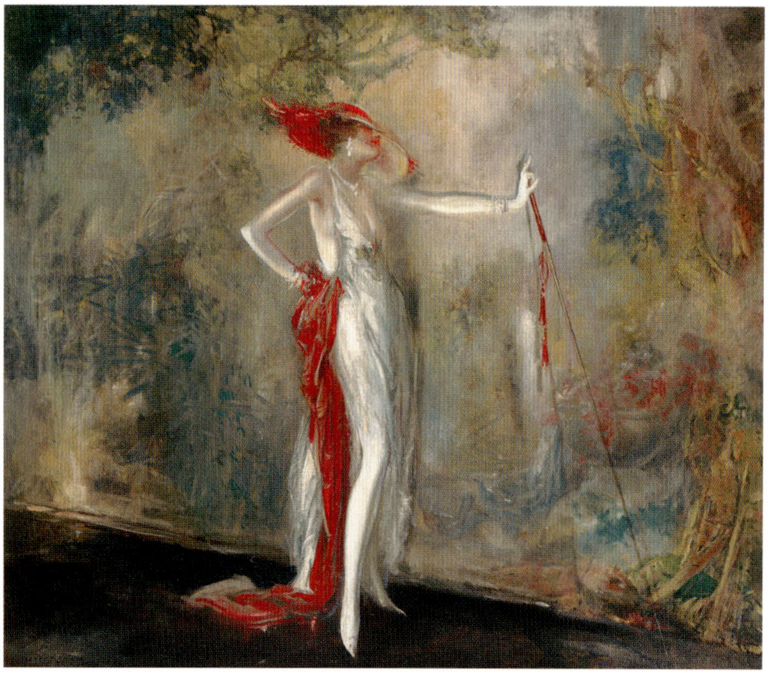

8. *(top)*
Everett Shinn (1876–1953)
Stage Scene, 1906
Oil on canvas
24 × 29 ½ in. (61 × 74.9 cm)
Sotheby's NY 12.1.2004,
$7,848,000

9. *(above)*
Everett Shinn (1876–1953)
The Revue, 1929
Oil on canvas
36 × 42 in. (91.4 × 106.7 cm)
Sotheby's NY 5/21/2003,
$299,200

from 1929, sold the year before for $299,200. For collectors who are not concerned with dates, these later pictures offer a wonderful opportunity to acquire quintessential subjects at much lower price points.

There can also be a shift in taste when the type or period of works that have traditionally been valued highest becomes increasingly scarce, forcing collectors to re-evaluate formerly dismissed areas of an artist's œuvre. Historically the market ascribed a premium to Andrew Wyeth's works from the 1960s and 1970s. As these works became increasingly scarce and following the artist's death in 2009, collectors began to focus on works from the 1980s and to judge works not solely based on date but also on desirability of subject and overall strength of composition, including the degree of detail and use of light. While the top four prices for the artist at auction are for tempera paintings from the 1960s and 1970s, the fifth highest price was achieved in November 2015 when *Flood Plain* (Fig. 10) of 1986 eclipsed its pre-sale estimate of $2–3 million to sell for $5,178,000, a previously unfathomable price for a painting from that date. Collectors responded to the superb quality and subject of *Flood Plain*, rather than focusing solely on its date. The provenance of the work, having been in the collection of Charlton Heston since 1988, was also compelling.

The market for Milton Avery has also experienced a shift in the past decade. Traditionally the paintings that commanded premium prices were from the 1940s. In today's market, while the 1940s works are still desirable, there has been a tremendous growth in demand for the 1950s and early 1960s paintings as collectors of post-war and contemporary art are seeking to add Avery to their collections. These individuals see Avery, who was deeply influential on Mark Rothko and Adolph Gottlieb, as a key artist who bridges American Modernism and post-war art. Now the top three prices for the artist at auction are all 1950 and later.

CONDITION

The condition of a work of art can have tremendous impact on its value. If a work has

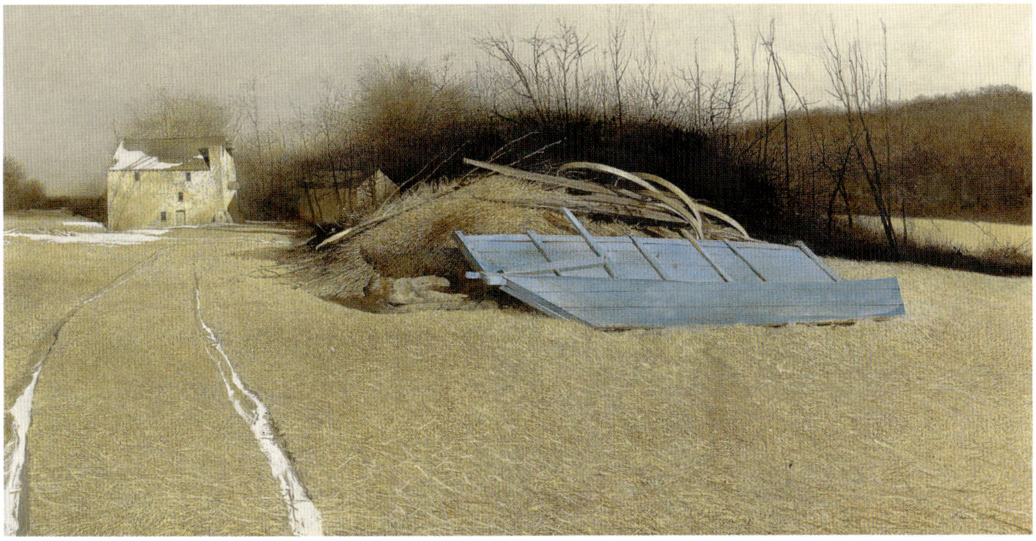

10.
Andrew Wyeth (1917–2009)
Flood Plain, 1986
Tempera on panel
24 ½ × 48 in.
(62.2 × 121.9 cm)
Sotheby's NY 11/18/2015,
$5,178,000

condition issues that have compromised the artist's original intent, it will be reflected in the pre-sale auction estimate as well as the sale price. Some condition issues are more detrimental than others. For example, in a portrait, damage to the subject's face is discounted more severely than damage to the background of the image.

Whenever you are considering buying a work of art, it is important to request a condition report. Any reputable auction house, gallery, or private dealer should be able to provide this. If you are considering a purchase at a high level, it is also advisable to have an outside conservator look at the work for you to ensure you have an accurate understanding of the condition. At times a work of art is so important that the market is willing to overlook condition issues. There are also certain artists whose work consistently has condition issues based on their working methods and choice of materials.

SCALE

This is relatively intuitive. All other characteristics being equal, a larger work will command a higher price than a smaller one. This is true to a certain point, but when a work is too large, the audience is limited, keeping the price down. This was demonstrated when two superb Maxfield Parrish murals came to market—*Sing a Song of Sixpence* and *North Wall Panel*, one of the Whitney murals—and each sold for less than $3 million. Around the same time the artist's *Daybreak*, which is an iconic image though considerably smaller, sold for $5,234,500.

This does not mean that you should always ignore small works in favor of larger ones, as there are some fantastic gems that are small-scale. Despite their size these works have tremendous quality and wall presence and can overpower larger works of lesser quality. It is often better to buy a small work that is of superior quality than a larger work that is not of the same caliber.

TASTE

Taste is constantly evolving in all sectors of the art market and there have been shifts in the American Art market in the past decade. For example, historic landscape depictions by top-tier Hudson River School painters, once highly desirable among collectors, are now less in fashion. This was demonstrated by *Mount Newport on Mount Desert Island* (Fig. 11), which sold for $4,186,000 in 2000 against a pre-sale estimate of $1.5–2.5 million. When re-offered in 2015 with an estimate of $5–7 million, it failed to sell. This result had nothing to do with the quality of the painting—rather it was an indication of changing taste in the marketplace. *Mount Newport on Mount Desert Island* is now in the collection of a significant museum, a testament to its importance.

Similarly, John Singer Sargent's grand portraits were once fashionable and highly

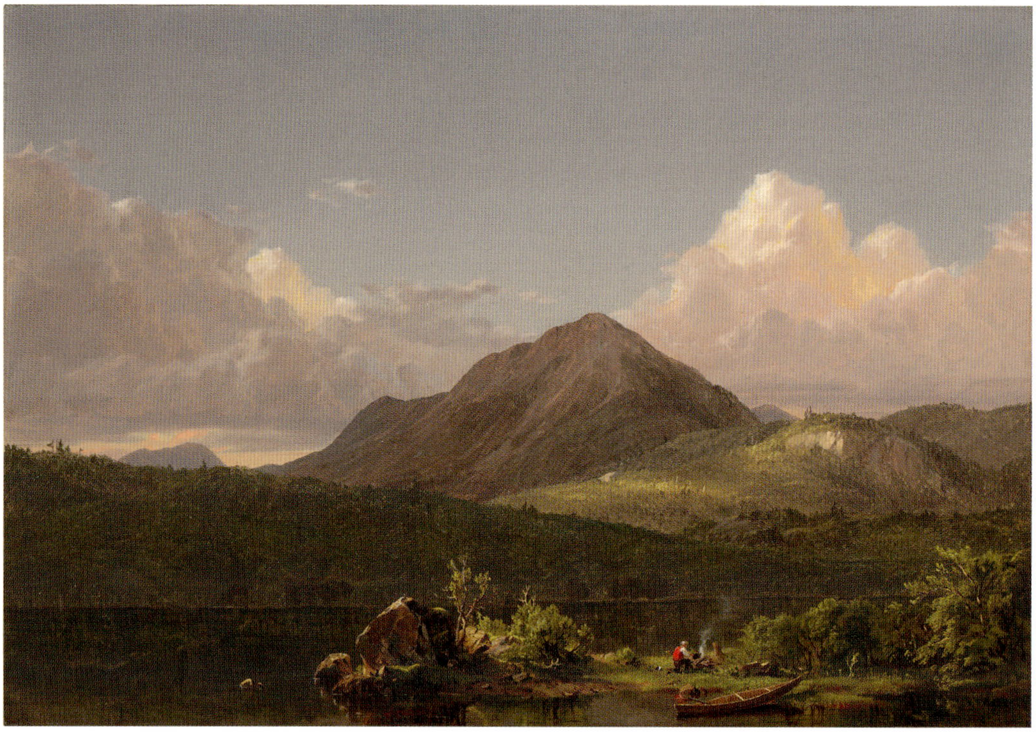

11.
Frederic Edwin Church
(1826–1900)
Mount Newport on Mount Desert Island, 1851–53
Oil on canvas
17 ¼ × 25 in.
(43.8 × 63.5 cm)
Christie's NY 5/25/2000,
$4,186,000

desirable in the marketplace. While the top examples of this portion of the artist's œuvre are still coveted among collectors, there is now a much greater interest in Sargent's work outside his studio. Collectors not only of American Art but also of European Impressionist and Modern art now respond positively to the more spontaneous and modern aspect of this latter group of works. This was demonstrated in 2016 when both *Poppies* (Fig. 12) and *Staircase in Capri* had multiple bidders at auction, driving the prices above the pre-sale estimates and selling for $6,858,000 and $4,058,000 respectively.

The shift in the market for Sargent manifests the general trajectory toward Modernism, as a broader international audience of collectors of European Impressionist and Modern, post-war and contemporary art is showing interest in American art, particularly works by Georgia O'Keeffe, Edward Hopper, Milton Avery and Mary Cassatt.

PROVENANCE AND FRESHNESS TO THE MARKET

The appearance of top-quality works that are fresh to the market consistently creates tremendous excitement among collectors. Competition in the auction room is often generated by works that have long been in private collections or have previously been unknown. Collectors perceive this as a once-in-a-lifetime moment to acquire a specific work. If works are coming from a particularly prestigious collection, this provenance can add considerable value.

In the American field the value of distinguished provenance on ultimate prices achieved at auction has been demonstrated several times in the past two decades when the esteemed collections of Meyer and Vivian Potamkin, Daniel and Rita Fraad, Peggy and David Rockefeller, and Barney Ebsworth have come to market. Each of these renowned collections was formed over years by collectors who were highly regarded for their connoisseurship. When works from these collections came to auction, they created tremendous excitement, breaking existing auction records and setting new benchmarks for specific artists. Some of the many examples are: Theodore Robinson's *Boats at a Landing*, which sold for $2,136,000, over $1 million more than the previous record (Potamkin); John

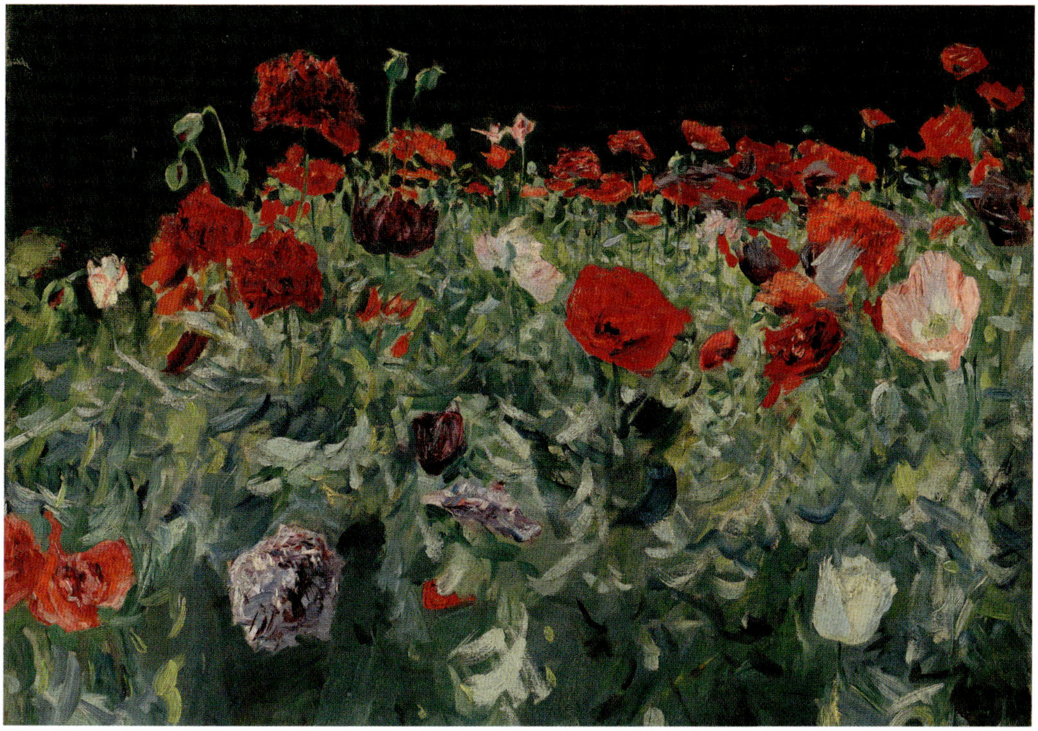

12. *(left)*
John Singer Sargent
(1856–1925)
Poppies (A Study of Poppies for Carnation, Lily, Lily, Rose)
1886
Oil on canvas
24 3/8 × 35 7/8 in.
(61.9 × 91.1 cm)
Sotheby's NY 5/18/2016,
$6,858,000

13. *(below)*
Gilbert Stuart (1755–1828)
George Washington (Vaughan type), 1795
Oil on canvas
29 1/8 × 24 1/8 in.
(74 × 61.3 cm)
Christie's NY 5/9/2018,
$11,562,500

Singer Sargent's *Group with Parasols*, which sold for $23,528,000, more than double the pre-existing auction record (Fraad); Gilbert Stuart's *George Washington* (Fig. 13), which sold for $11,562,500, more than ten times the closest comparable work to sell at auction (Rockefeller); and Edward Hopper's previously discussed *Chop Suey* (Ebsworth).

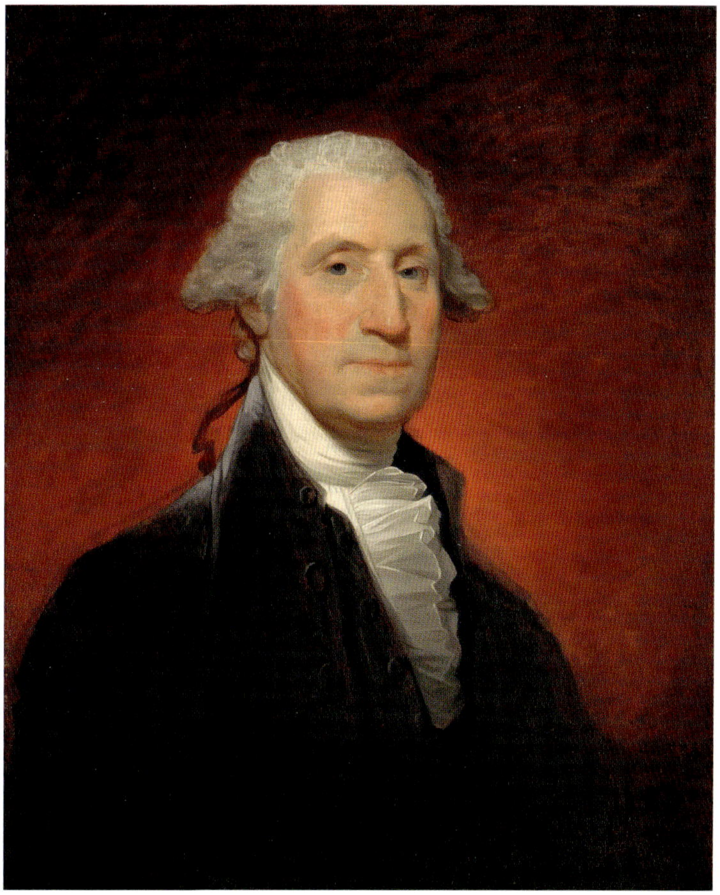

Beware, however, as provenance rarely adds the same value once removed. When Mary Cassatt's *Children Playing with a Dog* was offered in May 2007 from the prestigious Estate of Ellen Mary Cassatt Meigs, a descendant of the artist, it sold for $6.2 million, establishing a new world record price for the artist. The painting was re-offered at auction in November 2018 and sold for $4,812,500.

This chapter has discussed the key factors that professionals and collectors use to assess the value of a work, to demystify aspects of the art market, and to provide a framework for questions that you should ask when considering purchasing a work of art or trying to understand sale prices at auction. Always remember, if an estimate or asking price is too good to be true, it probably is!

Buying Art
Knowing the Law and Using Common Sense

Jo Backer Laird, Esq.
Of Counsel, Patterson Belknap Webb & Tyler, LLP, New York

Most people have purchased art in their lives. We buy posters to decorate our dorm rooms, and paintings that attract us at a street fair.

In a sense, this is the purest way of purchasing art. We buy something because we like it, because it touches our emotions, because it expresses something that has meaning to us. We buy something because we want to buy it.

When one talks about buying and collecting art, however, additional factors come into play. As a collector, we actively engage not only with the experience of looking at the object, but with the object *as* art, with all of its art-historical, cultural, and financial connotations. We thus care who made the work, so we are concerned about authenticity. We want to be sure that we have gotten good title to the work. And, at some point, we may come to care about what rights we have in the work. Do we, for example, own the copyright in the work? (The answer, by the way, is usually no.)

The laws that govern the purchase of art are the same that govern any purchase or sale of goods. This sometimes comes as a surprise to market participants who believe (and act as though) the art market operates in a different sphere and according to its own rules. The art market does have its own rules and customs—and more often than not it works—but as a buyer, you have legal rights, responsibilities, and protections if things go wrong.

This chapter will identify some of the legal pitfalls in collecting art, suggest ways to avoid problems, and discuss what you can (or can't) do when problems occur.

First, let's set the scene. The art market is divided in a number of different ways: there is a primary and a secondary market; and there is a public and a private market.

The primary market is made up of the first sale of any work of art. The sale can be directly from the artist or from a dealer or other intermediary representing the artist. The secondary market is every sale of a work of art that occurs after that. The markets are not physically distinct; a dealer who represents an artist will usually sell new works on behalf of the artist or the artist's estate, as well as works that are being sold by prior owners.

The primary market is almost exclusively part of the private market. The private market is just what its name implies. It is composed of transactions that take place in private. The parties to the sales are not systematically made public; nor are the terms of the sales, including the price. It is like most of the transactions we engage in every day. If I buy a dishwasher or a dining table, the terms of those purchases are not part of a public record.

The public part of the art market is populated by the auction houses. Auction-house sales are public and accessible, at least with respect to the prices achieved, and sometimes with respect to the parties.

One other—and unfortunate—way the art market is divided is between honest and legitimate market participants, and those who seek to exploit the peculiar vulnerabilities of the market to the detriment of buyers.

And what are those vulnerabilities?

- Works of art have no intrinsic value. They are made up of common materials—pigment on canvas, carved stone, digital files. So, prices are purely up to the market. And, since most of the market is private, it is often difficult to find out the simple and critical fact of what other people are willing to pay for a work. You can wind up paying a price that is much higher than other people have paid for similar works.

- The value of a work of art depends in large part on whether it is authentic. Works of art can be forged; that is, they can be created for the purpose of selling them as authentic. If a work of art is a forgery, it has no market value (except, perhaps, as a novelty). A work of art can also be misattributed, so its value can change—up or down—if it is discovered to be by a different artist.

- The provenance of a work of art, i.e., the history of its ownership, can be misrepresented. Provenance has an impact on the value of a work; if the work was owned by an important collector or institution, it receives a kind of imprimatur that matters to the market. If it was owned by a significant historical figure or celebrity, it can take on market value that is extrinsic to its artistic merit.

- Human emotions play more of a role in the purchase of a work of art than in the purchase of most other things. And, emotions can be manipulated. Our love of the work makes us want to believe what we are told about it. Insecurity makes us less willing to ask questions, and more willing to succumb to sales pressure. And greed can be stoked by inflated representations of profitable sales down the line.

A NEW COLLECTOR WALKS INTO A GALLERY...

Let's hypothesize that Sophie Rosen goes to a gallery to see an exhibit of works by Eric Andrus, a contemporary American artist. The gallery represents Andrus in the primary market, but also sells secondary market works. Sophie has seen images of Andrus's work in an art magazine, and is attracted to its style. She spends a while looking at one particular picture—long enough for the owner of the gallery to come over to speak to her. The gallerist talks about the work and the artist. He tells her that Andrus already has an active market—indeed, this particular picture is being sold by a collector who purchased the work ten years before at a significantly lower price. Sophie is told that the work's value will surely double over time, even at its current price of $100,000. She agrees to buy it at that price.

While the gallerist is writing up the invoice, Sophie calls her business partner, and tells him that she found just the right image to use in advertisements for their graphics company. The gallerist overhears the conversation, and tells Sophie that she cannot do that. He explains that she is buying the physical work itself, and not the right to use, reproduce, or publish the image. In other words, she is not buying the copyright in the work, which is a form of intellectual property and is retained by the artist. He offers to ask Andrus if he would agree to give her a license to use the image for this commercial purpose.

Sophie accepts the gallerist's offer, takes the invoice, and walks happily away.

Having purchased the work, what legal protection does Sophie have against having been swindled by the gallery?

AUTHENTICITY

After her purchase, Sophie discovers that Eric Andrus did not create the painting. She wants her money back. Can she get it? It depends.

Warranties

The purchase and sale of goods (including art) in the United States is governed by, among other laws, the Uniform Commercial Code. The Code has been adopted in some form by every state in the Union, and establishes a common set of rules designed to keep commerce moving.

Under the Uniform Commercial Code, any fact stated in an invoice or other documentation of a purchase, where that fact is part of the basis of the bargain, creates an express warranty that the fact is true. In a purchase of a work of art, the attribution of the work to the particular artist is a fundamental basis of the deal. So, if the work that Sophie bought was later proved to be inauthentic, the gallery would have the obligation to refund her money. This is especially true where, as here, Sophie purchased the work from a merchant (the gallery) that sells goods of this particular kind (artwork). In addition to the warranty of authenticity, the Uniform Commercial Code imposes on merchants a warranty of merchantability—that is, that the item purchased will be accepted as what it is purported to be in the market in which it is regularly sold.

That's the good news about warranties. The bad news is that, like any other legal obligation, it is governed by a statute of limitations. In other words, the warranty has a defined shelf life beyond which it offers scant protection. Under the Uniform Commercial Code in New York, the statute of limitations on warranties is four years.

The problem with the limitations period is that a buyer often does not discover that the work is inauthentic until the statute has already run. Then, the buyer has to rely on common law doctrines like fraud to seek relief against the gallery. To allege fraud, you have to allege and prove specific facts that demonstrate that (i) the seller intentionally lied to you (ii) with the purpose of making you rely on the misrepresentation, (iii) you relied on it, and (iv), you were damaged as a result. The statute of limitations on fraud varies from state to state and often includes a period of time after you actually discover the fraud. In New York the statute of limitations for fraud is six years from the date of the fraud, or two years from the date of discovery.

The other bad news about warranties is that they can be limited or waived by contract, as long as the language of the contract (or invoice) makes it clear that the warranty is being affected. If the invoice that Sophie received from the gallery explicitly excluded a warranty of authenticity, a court might decide that she was no longer entitled to return the "Andrus." One New York gallery, in the terms and conditions printed on the back of its invoices, only warrants authenticity for a few weeks—not four years. The "fine print" matters.

Failures or changes in authentication

The art market has no systematic way of determining the authenticity of works of art. The market organically anoints authenticators upon whom it relies—academics, galleries, artists' foundations, and artists' heirs. Those authenticators can change their minds about any given work at any given time. When they die, their successors may not agree with their determinations. And, historical attributions can be confirmed or undermined by advancements in scientific and forensic techniques. As recently as January 31, 2019, the Mauritshuis in The Hague opened an exhibit of the eighteen works in their collection that were acquired as Rembrandts. The exhibit makes the point that five have since been determined not to be by Rembrandt, and two are considered to be questionable and were to be re-examined after the exhibit closed in September. Visitors were encouraged to look carefully to see if they could tell the difference.

Let's assume that, at the time of Sophie's purchase, the recognized market expert had deemed her painting to be authentic. Six years later, the expert reconsiders and changes his opinion—he now believes it to be by a different artist. The statute of limitations on the gallery's warranty has run, and Sophie wants to hold the expert responsible for her loss.

For Sophie, this is likely to be a fruitless quest. While courts will make findings of fact as to authenticity in disputes between, say, a buyer and a seller, they have almost uniformly declined to hold authenticators liable for their opinions, *per se*. A tale of two works by Alexander Calder illustrates this point.

In the first, the buyers of a Calder sculpture titled *Rio Nero* sued the seller in 1993 to rescind the sale, claiming the work was a fake. In order to establish the key fact of the case—i.e., the authenticity of the sculpture—each side offered expert testimony. The buyers offered the testimony of the recognized Calder expert at the time; he had authenticated the work years earlier, but now testified that it was merely a very good copy of the original work. The seller used a different expert, who testified that the work *was* the authentic work. The judge weighed the testimony of the two experts and the examinations by which each had come to their opinion. He determined that the seller's expert was more credible, and found in favor of the seller.

This could have been good news for the buyers—after all, the judge had just ruled that their work was authentic. However, the judge was only doing what judges do—he was resolving a dispute between two parties. His determination that the work was authentic was a "finding of fact" based on a "preponderance of the evidence," the usual standard in a civil case. What that means is that based on the testimony, the judge found that it *was more likely than not* that the work was authentic, and so the buyers could not rescind the sale. The market, however, does not rely on the opinions of federal judges. It relies on its own experts, and the recognized expert had testified that the work was a copy. Twenty-six years after the court's decision, the work remains in storage.

In the second case, in the mid-1970s, theater sets designed by Calder for a 1936 performance of a composition by Erik Satie were reproduced for a new production, allegedly with the artist's permission. In 1997, the owner of the sets sought to have them formally authenticated by the Calder Foundation. The Foundation ultimately declined to respond to the application. The owner sued the Foundation, asking the court to declare that the sets were authentic works by Calder, and to force the Foundation to include them as authentic works in its files. In other words, instead of simply resolving a dispute between two parties, the court was being asked to declare that a work of art was authentic for all purposes.

The court declined, holding that neither the Foundation nor any other authenticator has a legal obligation to render *any* opinion on a work of art, let alone any particular opinion. The court went on to say that it was not competent to declare the authenticity of the sets, and that even if it did, the declaration would have no impact in the market.

Moral rights of artists

Sophie faces one more authenticity risk that is unique to art. Under federal and some state laws, a living artist has the right to disclaim a work of art in certain circumstances. As an example, if you own a Rembrandt and it gets damaged, you have a Rembrandt with a condition issue. If you buy an Andrus and it is damaged, federal and state laws may give Andrus the right to disclaim it. That leaves you with a work of art that the market will not accept as authentic. If Sophie believes that the artist's disclaimer is not permitted by the relevant statutes, she can seek legal relief—and she might win. But the market might remain skittish about a work that the artist himself says is not his.

The bottom line is that there is always *some* risk that a work of art is—or at some point will be deemed to be—inauthentic.

TITLE

Sophie receives a letter from one of the gallery's other clients saying that the Andrus that she bought actually belongs to him. He wants it back. Does Sophie have to return it?

Along with authenticity, good title is fundamental to a purchase of art, and buyers can look to the Uniform Commercial Code to provide several kinds of protection.

First, as with authenticity, the Uniform Commercial Code imposes a warranty of good title on each purchase and sale of goods, including works of art. If, within the warranty period, you discover that you did not get good title, the seller is obliged to take the work back and refund the purchase price.

Secondly, if you buy something in the ordinary course of business from a merchant who deals in goods of that kind, without knowledge of the fact that the sale violates another person's ownership rights or security interest in the work, you get good title to the thing you have purchased. So, if you buy a work of art from an art gallery in the normal course of the gallery's business, you will obtain good title, even if the owner of the work, for example, left it with the gallery to be cleaned but not sold. The owner may be entitled to monetary damages from the gallery, but will not be entitled to get the work back from you. This may seem like a startling result, but, again, the Uniform Commercial Code is meant to keep commerce moving. The same rule seems less startling if you apply it in a more familiar context. If you go into a department store and buy a dress, you get good title to the dress. You are not subject to claims by the manufacturer of the dress that the store never paid them. It is the same with works of art.

When Sophie learns about this rule, she makes a note that if she buys art again in the future, she will ask no questions and do no homework—no matter what. Knowledge can only hurt her. But this kind of "willful ignorance" will not work. Courts look unkindly on claims where information was available to—but disregarded by—a buyer. To be a buyer in the ordinary course, you cannot ignore facts that might give you cause to be concerned.

Just as with authenticity issues, there are unusual concerns about title when dealing with works of art. These tend to arise from ethical, historical, and policy concerns. If, for example, a work of art was stolen from its owners by the Nazis in World War II, the current owners may face title claims from the heirs of the family from whom the work was stolen. Similarly, a nation state may claim that a work of art left its borders unlawfully, and demand the return of the art. The latter is usually an issue with antiquities, but can also occur with more recent art.

PRICE

Sophie purchased the Andrus for $100,000. She later learns that other galleries were offering comparable works for $50,000. She becomes angry that she paid too much, and dubious of the representation the gallerist made about the work doubling in value over time. Is there any way she can get back some of her purchase price?

The short answer is no, unless the gallery *chooses* to give her a rebate.

You only even ask the question because we are talking about art. You wouldn't ask the question if Sophie could have saved money by buying a coat at a department store instead of a chic, high-end boutique, or a toy from Walmart instead of FAO Schwarz. You are expected by the courts to use information that is available to you. And while information is limited in the art market, it is not non-existent. Auction prices are available on various databases. If a recent auction price for a work that is comparable to the one you are purchasing is a fraction of the price you are paying, you are probably paying too much. You can even, to some extent, research private market prices. If Sophie was interested in checking the price of similar Andrus works, she could research and contact other galleries that are selling them. Art fairs offer a particularly good opportunity to compare prices. Multiple galleries may have

Andrus works to show in their booth or on their iPads.

In fact, in a recent case brought by a collector against a gallery that *deliberately* misled her about the prices of works that she was buying or trading with the gallery, the court held that since she did not take advantage of information that was publicly available to her, she could not get damages from the gallery. Again, judges do not reward willful ignorance.

LET'S CHANGE THE HYPOTHESIS

Sophie goes to the gallery and decides that she wants to buy the Andrus painting. She loves the artist. But, her mother is a lawyer and tells Sophie that if she is spending $100,000, she should have a proper contract, not just an invoice. Sophie always follows her mother's advice, but hesitates to ask the dealer for a contract. She fears that if she makes that kind of a fuss, the dealer will decide not to sell her the work.

Sophie's concerns are not unfounded. As a primary market dealer, it is the gallery's job not just to sell the artist's works but to build and nurture the artist's reputation and career. One way a gallery does that is to place the artist's work in important private collections and in museums. For example, if the artist's work is in the collection of The Metropolitan Museum of Art or the Pompidou, it is given the imprimatur of those institutions. It is seen to have passed muster with the people who "know what they are doing"—in the current parlance, the "influencers."

A good primary dealer has made a serious commitment to an artist that involves significantly more than putting the art on the wall and opening the doors. Primary market dealers mount periodic gallery shows of the artist's work. Each show is accompanied by outreach to museums and significant collectors to be sure that they see the work; perhaps the creation of monographs or other publications about the artist; advances to the artist to finance the fabrication of his works; targeted marketing and advertising; and gallery events to highlight the artist—openings, panel discussions, and the like. In addition, primary dealers will seek to encourage museum exhibitions for the artist, or the inclusion of the artist in important international events such as the Venice Biennale, or the Whitney Biennial. And they will encourage and arrange for commissions of works of art by private collectors, museums, cultural institutions, businesses, real estate developers, cities, airports, and others. All of these increase the artist's exposure and are meant to demonstrate their significance.

With all of that investment, a gallery may be loath to sell a work of art to someone who—like Sophie—walks in off the street. Perhaps even less so if that passerby rocks the boat and asks for something more than an invoice.

Nevertheless, a purchase agreement can provide important additional protection.

No matter how solicitous a gallery or auction house may be, when they sell you something, it is an arm's-length transaction. They are either acting as an agent for the owner of the work—either the artist or a consignor—or they are acting on their own behalf. They have no fiduciary obligation to you as the buyer. So it is wise to create contractual obligations, especially where regulatory constraints may not apply.

Moreover, where terms of agreement (or an "understanding") have been reached, but have not been reduced to paper, they may not be enforceable. Every state has what is called a Statute of Frauds, which requires that agreements on matters worth more than, say, $500 must be in writing to be enforceable. A handshake will not be enough.

Among the sorts of provisions that you might think about including in a purchase agreement are:

- An expanded set of warranties (in addition to authenticity and title), including warranties that (i) the seller has given you complete and accurate information about the work, its

Legal Issues for the Collector Selling Art

Thomas C. Danziger, Esq., *and Charles Danziger,* Esq.
*Brothers and Partners in the Law Firm of Danziger,
Danziger & Muro, LLP,* New York

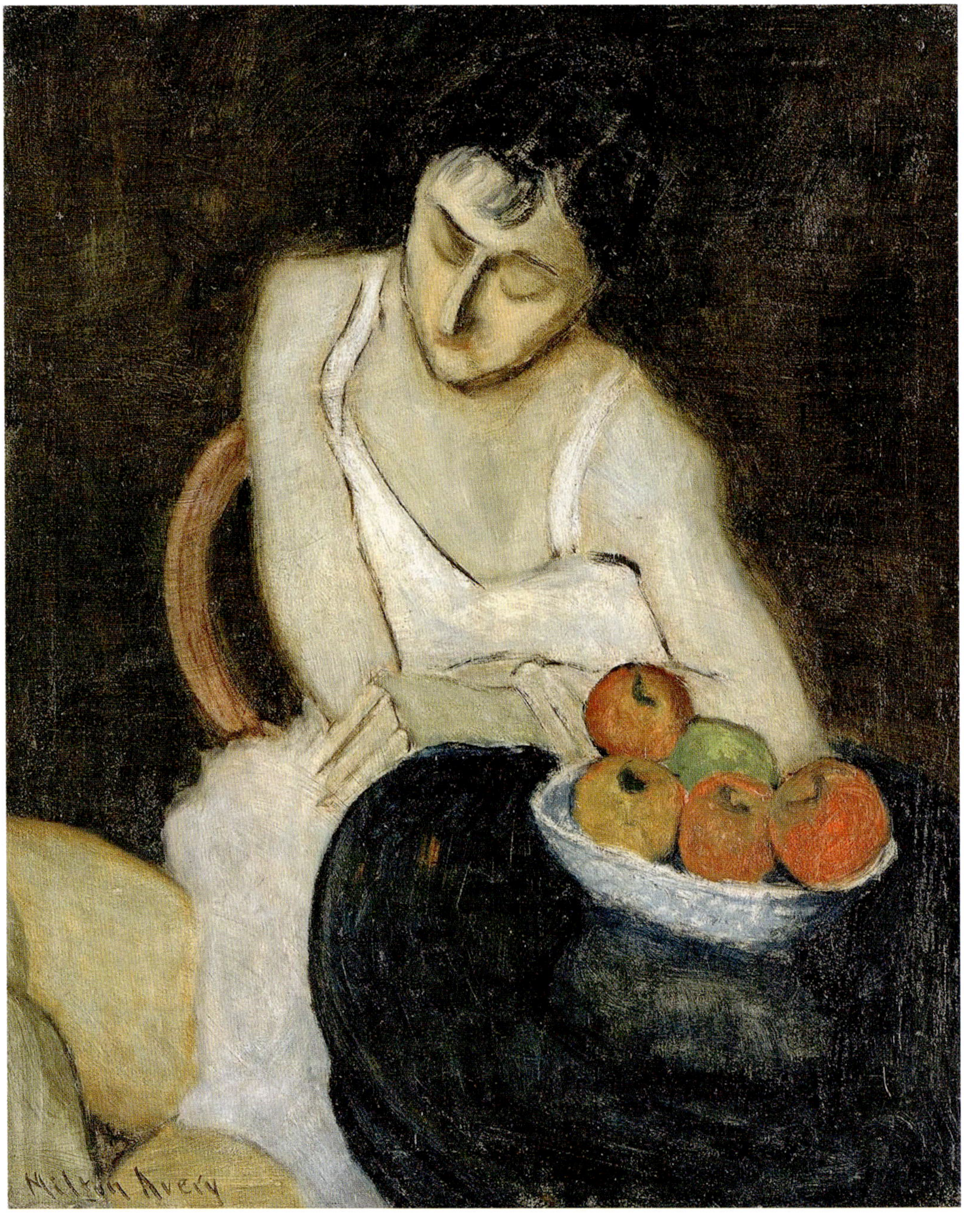

As lawyers, we find that representing a collector selling an American work of art is generally easier than representing a buyer of the work. Unlike buyer's counsel, we usually do not have to worry about whether our client holds good title—meaning unencumbered legal ownership—to the art. We typically do not perform extensive "due diligence" to search for undisclosed liens or other claims on the art. And frequently we even leave the issue of whether the work is actually authentic to the buyer and his attorney. When it comes to selling an artwork, our general view is *caveat emptor*.

Our main concern as seller's counsel is fairly straightforward: to try to make sure that our client is paid the full purchase price in a timely fashion, and if there is a problem with the art after the sale, limit our client's liability as much as possible.

Although this sounds quite simple, over the years representing sellers we have encountered many complex and often hidden legal issues. This chapter will explore a few of the most important issues we address when assisting collectors selling art, whether in private transactions, through a gallery or in public auction-room sales, and will also include a few "tricks of the trade" we use to help our clients.

SELLING PRIVATELY

Although the art world has generally embraced technology as a crucial tool in transacting business—what serious collector today doesn't check the online artnet price database before buying or selling art?—we are constantly surprised by how many otherwise smart collectors still sell or buy even very expensive pieces on a handshake, without putting anything down in writing.

This approach is a bad idea, and for good reason: under the Statute of Frauds as adopted in New York State and other states, an agreement for the sale of goods having a value of over $500 must be in writing in order to be enforceable. Both Federal and State courts have recognized this legal requirement in any number of cases, including the 2010 Federal case *Craig Robins v. Zwirner*, in which the real estate developer Craig Robins sued the well-known art dealer David Zwirner for not honoring his promise to sell Robins paintings by the artist Marlene Dumas. The court noted: "plaintiff has not come forward with any writing signed by Zwirner promising to sell paintings to Robins. Absent a writing signed by Zwirner, enforcement of the oral Gallery Agreement is barred."

So, without a written agreement, a collector selling even a modestly priced artwork has few legal rights if the buyer wants to walk away from the deal. And even a written agreement might not be sufficient: for a contract of sale to be enforceable, it must include all material information on the transaction, including a proper description of the work, precise payment terms, and any other material terms of the agreement.

When we draft contracts for sellers, we are especially careful to limit our client's representations and warranties, especially as to matters beyond the seller's knowledge or control. For instance, buyers often ask for a representation that the work had been legally imported into or exported out of the United States, but we try to limit this representation to the actual knowledge of the seller. After all, how could a collector selling a painting today know whether a former owner of the work had legally imported it into or exported it from the United States, say, twenty years ago?

The question then becomes, what types of representations and warranties is the buyer entitled to receive? We generally advise a seller to stick to the basic facts, and just the facts. The seller should represent that he/she has legal authority to sell the work; upon transfer of title to the buyer, the work will be free from liens and other restrictions; and the seller does not know of any claims which may be threatened or pending, or circumstances which are likely to give rise to any claims.

Depending on the transaction, the seller may also be asked to represent and warrant that the work being sold is authentic, but in this case we try to limit the time period in which the seller will be liable if a work eventually proves not to be "correct." The major auction houses give a five-year warranty of authenticity to buyers in the

1.
Milton Avery (1885–1965)
Sally Avery with Still Life
1926
Oil on cotton
30 × 25 in. (76.2 × 63.5 cm)
Smithsonian American Art Museum, Washington, DC, 1977.43.2

auction room, so not surprisingly that is often the period on which we settle after negotiations with the buyer's counsel—but that is frequently a point we like to trade for a concession from the buyer.

We are also careful to provide in the contract of sale that the seller's representations and warranties are for the benefit of the immediate buyer only, and may not be relied on by third parties, such as someone who later purchases the work from the buyer (or the buyer's buyer). This limitation is a lesson we learned from the circumstances underlying the 2008 case of *Tony Shafrazi Gallery, Inc. v. Christie's, Inc.*, in which the Tony Shafrazi Gallery purchased a painting by Jean-Michel Basquiat from Christie's and then sold it to the collector Guido Orsi. When, fifteen years later, Orsi discovered the work was fake, he and the Tony Shafrazi Gallery sued Christie's in New York State court, and the court allowed the collector's claim of fraud to proceed even though Christie's had sold the work to the gallery, and not directly to the collector. Although Christie's ended up prevailing, the case has provided a cautionary tale to art sellers (and their lawyers) ever since.

The bill of sale is the other legal document we use in connection with the private sale of an artwork and is typically attached as an exhibit to the contract of sale. It is generally very short and lists the seller, buyer, artwork, and purchase price—and not much else. But it is an important legal document because it is the instrument that usually transfers title to the work from the seller to the buyer in a private sale transaction.

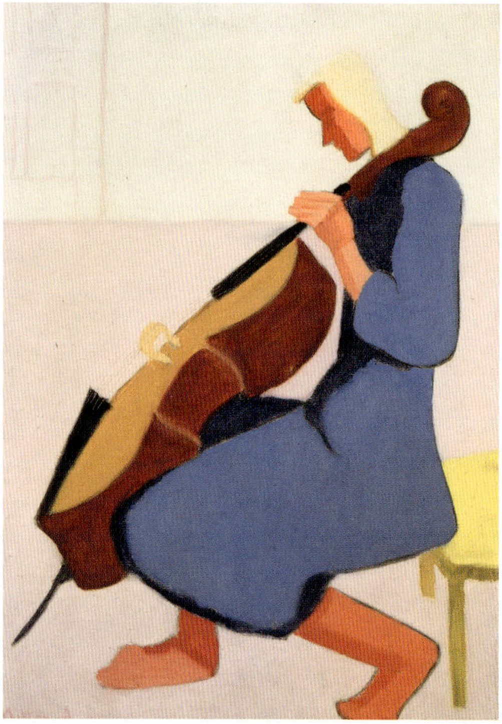

2.
Milton Avery (1885–1965)
Cello Player in Blue, 1944
Oil on canvas
36 × 26 in. (91.4 × 66 cm)
Neuberger Museum of Art, Purchase College, State University of New York, gift of Roy R. Neuberger 1969.01.09

Interesting legal problems—interesting for attorneys, that is—can arise after art is sold and the seller has pocketed the proceeds. For example, what happens if the seller and buyer both believe that a painting is by, say, Milton Avery (Figs. 1 and 2), and only after the sale they discover that the work is by a different artist?

That was the situation in the 2013 federal case *ACA Galleries, Inc. v. Kinney*, in which ACA inspected and agreed to purchase a painting for $200,000 described in the bill of sale as "Milton Avery Oil on Canvas." After the sale was finalized, the work was shown to the Milton & Sally Avery Arts Foundation, which decided it was not authentic. The court held for the seller, ruling that the doctrine of "mutual mistake" in New York "may not be invoked by a party to avoid the consequences of its own negligence," particularly where "the party wishing to invoke the doctrine bears the risk of the mistake because he was aware of his limited knowledge but acted anyway." Again, *caveat emptor*.

What happens if the Gilbert Stuart portrait of George Washington sold decades ago by a collector (Fig. 3) turns out merely to be by a "follower of Gilbert Stuart" based on new findings from the latest expert in the field? May the buyer automatically rescind the sale? In the absence of a specific provision to the contrary in the sale agreement, the answer is usually no, especially when the applicable statute of limitations has expired and the buyer's rights are "time barred." Expert opinions may change, but as a general rule a new expert's opinion does not provide an automatic basis to unwind a sale—though expensive litigation will surely ensue.

SELLING THROUGH AN ART GALLERY

Consigning art for sale through a gallery creates a fundamentally different legal relationship for a collector (in this case called the "consignor") from a direct sale to a buyer because the gallery becomes the consignor's agent and has fiduciary responsibilities to the consignor. In plain English this means that the gallery must act in the consignor's best interests.

What does this mean as a practical matter? To take some very common examples, a gallery may not sell a work for, say, $1000 and tell the consignor that it has sold the work for less, nor may a gallery mislead the consignor about the terms of a sale, or whether the work sold at all. That all sounds obvious enough. However, a number of very well-known art dealers have run foul of these rules and have spent—and some are currently spending—time in prison as a result, including former New York art dealer Ezra Chowaiki, who in late 2018 was sentenced to eighteen months for a host of misdeeds, including selling works he did not own or control, selling artworks consigned to him without the owner's permission, and even pocketing money that clients had given to him to purchase art.

Given the risks, we advise our clients that, prior even to considering consigning a work for sale through an art gallery, they should do basic online "due diligence" on the gallery and its owners to see what turns up. If this simple research doesn't raise red flags, we generally take the due diligence one step further by conducting a Uniform Commercial Code (UCC) lien search in the state where the gallery is located. Many people are not aware that information on filed liens, encumbrances, and even certain loans of artwork is freely available on most states' own websites and may be found by anyone who knows where to look. Delaware and New York, as well as a number of other states, do not even charge a fee for lien searches.

The lien search may show whether a gallery is skating on thin ice (for instance, if it has an unusually high level of recorded debt), which is information that in itself may make a consignor reconsider the deal. The search may also indicate whether other creditors have liens that might take precedence over a client's proposed consignment. This could occur when, say, a bank has taken a lien on "all inventory of the gallery, wherever located"—wording frequently found in filed bank liens today.

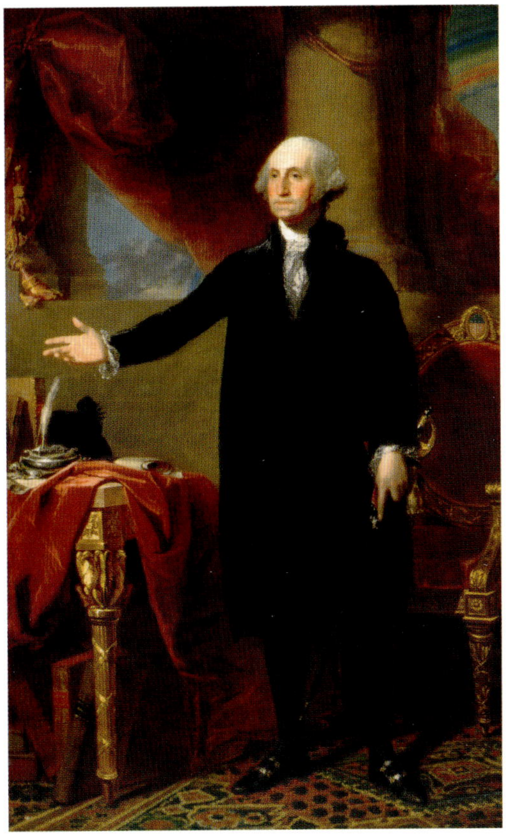

3.
Gilbert Stuart
(1755–1828)
Lansdowne Portrait of George Washington, 1796
Oil on canvas
97½ × 62½ in.
(247.6 × 158.7 cm)
National Portrait Gallery, Washington, DC, Smithsonian Institution, NPG.2001.13

After conducting this lien search, we advise a collector wishing to consign a work to a gallery to file a "UCC-1 financing statement" in the state where the gallery is located, giving notice to the world at large (and, in particular, to the gallery's creditors) that our client is the owner of the consigned work. This filing protects the client against third party creditors of the gallery and is especially important in the unfortunate circumstance where the gallery goes bankrupt while holding the client's property. A consignor with no UCC financing statement protection is typically treated as a "general creditor" (think Con Edison or the phone company) in a gallery bankruptcy, and many collectors have found out the hard way—by actually losing their consigned artworks to other creditors of the gallery—that the few dollars they might have spent filing a financing statement would have proved a good investment indeed.

Filing a financing statement would probably have simplified life for Jerry Ganz, the plaintiff in *Ganz v. Sotheby's Financial Services*, which involved the now-notorious dealer Michel Cohen. Ganz, a collector, gave physical possession of his Chagall painting *Soleil couchant à Saint-Paul* to Cohen, who then transferred the picture to Sotheby's as collateral for a loan. Cohen subsequently defaulted on the loan and fled the country, and litigation ensued between Sotheby's and Ganz over who had a superior interest in the painting.

Unfortunately for Ganz, he had neglected to file a financing statement on the consignment of the work to Cohen, and the New York court observed that Ganz's delivery of the painting to Cohen, even on consignment, did not create a security interest. The upshot was that the court refused to grant summary judgment to any party and instead determined that Ganz bore the burden of proving as a factual matter that Cohen was generally known by his creditors to be substantially engaged in selling the goods of others. The case was settled on a confidential basis prior to trial.

4.
Leonardo da Vinci
(1452–1519)
The Genova Drawing, the Madonna and Child with St. Anne and a Lamb, 1500–01
Venice, Gallerie dell'Accademia

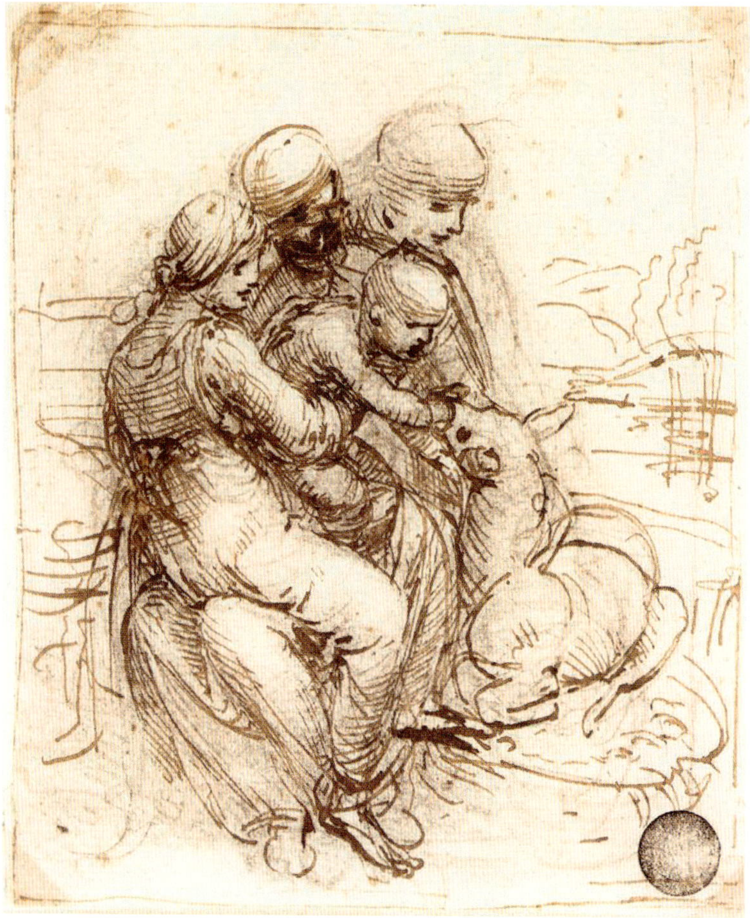

For our collector client considering a consignment, if due diligence on the gallery turns up nothing of concern and our UCC financing statement is ready to be filed, we then get to work on legal documentation—which typically means a written consignment agreement with the gallery. This agreement should clearly state how and when the dealer will be compensated and how and whether the dealer may work with, and compensate, intermediaries in the course of the sale.

The consignor to a gallery should understand that many dealers routinely work with other parties to find buyers for works. Given its fiduciary responsibility to the consignor, a gallery working with undisclosed third-party intermediaries can create unexpected—and expensive—legal problems for everyone. This was the situation in the famous 2010 English case *Accidia Foundation v. Simon C. Dickinson Limited*, where the seller Accidia believed that art dealer Daniella Luxembourg would find a direct buyer for Accidia's Leonardo da Vinci drawing *Madonna and Child with St. Anne and a Lamb* (Fig. 4), but Luxembourg instead made an agreement with gallery Simon C. Dickinson Ltd. to sell the work. The High Court ruled that Dickinson could not keep its commission on the sale since the agreement that it made with the ultimate buyer had not been understood and approved by the seller, and it also could not take a $500,000 commission without the seller's authority.

Fortunately, relatively few sellers of art face legal difficulties with galleries, and there has even been recent legislation in New York to assist some consignors who entrust their works to galleries or private dealers. In the wake of the spectacular bankruptcies of long-established Berry-Hill Galleries and Salander-O'Reilly Galleries, where works consigned by artists and their representatives were caught up and even lost to creditors in bankruptcy proceedings, the New York State legislature in late 2012 strengthened the terms of Article 12 of the New

York Arts & Cultural Affairs Law. The amended statute requires galleries and other art merchants that take works on consignment from artists, their heirs, or personal representatives to hold proceeds of sale in trust for the consignor—with no commingling of these proceeds with other gallery income—and imposes serious criminal and financial penalties on those who violate the law. Note that this statute provides protection only to artists and related parties with respect to their consigned works, but not to collectors.

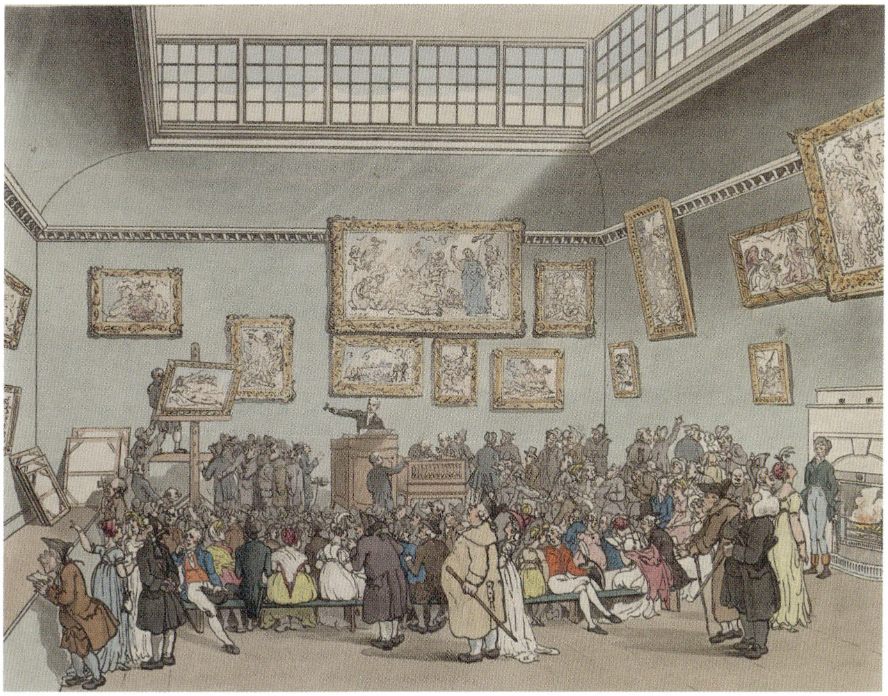

5.
Thomas Rowlandson
(1756–1827)
Microcosm of London, pl. 6: Christie's Auction Room, 1808
Ink on paper
9 ½ × 11 ¹¹⁄₁₆ in.
(24.2 × 29.7 cm)
The Metropolitan Museum of Art, The Elisha Whittelsey Collection, The Elisha Whittelsey Fund, 1959, 59.533.2085

SELLING AT AUCTION (Fig. 5)

As a legal matter, selling art through an auction house is not very different from selling through a gallery or dealer, although auction consignments raise certain practical issues that differ from other types of sales. The very fact that auction houses are—like galleries or dealers—legally the agents of the consignors could come as a surprise to many people bidding at auction, who may mistakenly believe that the auction house is their agent, not the seller's.

This point was made crystal clear (so to speak) in *Cristallina S.A. v. Christie, Manson & Woods*, the famous 1986 New York State appeals court case which specifically held that the auction house is indeed the consignor's agent and, as such, has a fiduciary duty to act in the consignor's best interest. The plaintiffs in the Cristallina case, which was settled out of court during appeal, asserted that Christie's violated various fiduciary duties. These included the duty to provide relevant information, such as the fact that the firm's own experts disagreed about the paintings' marketability; the duty not to attempt the impossible, by trying to sell paintings when the auctioneers knew that the reserves were too high; and the duty to disclose the risks relating to a sale where the auction house's pre-sale estimates were unrealistic.

Although the auction house is deemed to be the agent of the consignor as a matter of law, the consignment agreement signed by the prospective consignor may modify the auction house's fiduciary duties, and as such should be reviewed with care. For example, depending on the terms of the agreement, the auction house may not owe the consignor a duty of undivided loyalty (which is standard for other agency relationships); rather, it may also consider its own interests and the interests of the purchaser.

One 2002 case involving the auction house's modification of fiduciary duty was *Mickle v. Christie's*, in which consignors John and Diana Mickle sued the auction house for rescinding the sale of their painting after the buyer questioned its attribution and refused to pay. The Mickles believed that the painting, known as *Billy Bowlegs*, was by Carl Wimar, an important nineteenth-century American painter known for paintings of Native Americans (Fig. 6).

Although the Mickles argued that Christie's had a fiduciary duty to act in their interest and compel the buyer to complete the purchase, the auction house successfully contended that the following wording in the consignment agreement modified this duty of undivided loyalty: the auction house could "rescind the sale of any lot of Property at any time if Christie's in our sole

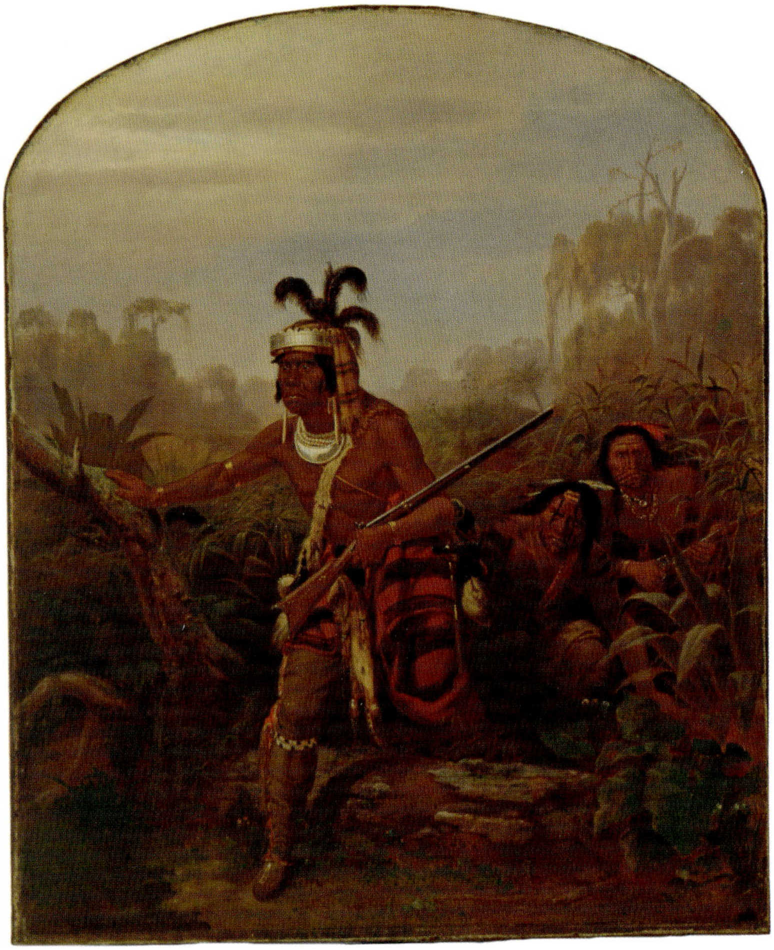

6.
Carl Ferdinand Wimar
(1828–1862)
Billy Bowlegs, 1861
Oil on canvas mounted
on panel
25 ¼ × 30 ¼ in.
(64.1 × 76.8 cm)
St. Louis Art Museum, MO, 9:1938

judgment determines that the offering for sale of any Property has subjected or may subject Christie's and/or Consignor to any liability." This wording still appears in many auction-house consignment agreements we see today and, not surprisingly, we try to delete it whenever we can.

The purchase of art from an auction house is subject to conditions of sale which are customarily printed at the back of the auction catalogue and are also found on most auctioneers' websites. Accordingly, there is often not as much "wriggle room" for the seller at auction as there may be in private sales or gallery consignments. For example, the auction house may be unwilling to modify consignor's representations and warranties on authenticity, title, or liens where the auction house is already committed to giving corresponding representations and warranties to the buyer in the conditions of sale or as a matter of law. That said, every auction-house consignment is different, and especially for very high-value transactions we have found that almost anything is negotiable if the auction house wants a particular consignment badly enough.

Because of the importance of the printed conditions of sale, we advise consignors to familiarize themselves with their terms (fair warning: they do not make for light reading). The conditions of sale are given by the auction house, but since—as the careful reader of this chapter already knows—the auction house is acting as agent for the consignor, the consignor is ultimately responsible for many of the terms set forth in the conditions of sale.

On higher ticket transactions, where we have more leverage with the auction house, we routinely try to modify consignment agreements in a number of ways for the seller. We suggest that the reserve price for the work (the price below which the auction house will not sell the work) be reflected in the agreement, and that any changes to this reserve up to the time of the auction also be agreed to in writing by the consignor. The reserve cannot exceed the low end of the estimate, and we caution sellers not to insist on a low estimate that is too high, which might scare off prospective bidders.

The economics of the auction room are one of the least understood elements of the art world, but they basically boil down to two separate payments made to the auction house: a seller's commission sometimes paid by the consignor and a buyer's premium always paid by the successful bidder at auction.

Every auction house would like to receive a seller's commission (often around 10% of the value of the property) from a consignor, but for higher-value consignments we negotiate to remove this commission. As for the buyer's premium, it can be a substantial percentage of the purchase price, especially for lower-valued property. In the wake of repeated increases over the past few years (which are sure to continue going forward), the buyer's premium at the top auction houses today can equal 25% of the "hammer price"—meaning the sale price of a work announced in the auction room at the bang of the auctioneer's gavel, excluding buyer's premium.

On really high-value consignments we routinely obtain an "enhanced hammer" from the auction house, meaning that the auction house remits to the consignor an agreed—and often hotly negotiated—portion of the buyer's premium that the auction house receives from the winning bidder.

We also pay particular attention to the withdrawal clause found in almost all auction-house consignment agreements. The agreements typically provide that a consignor who pulls a work from a sale after signing an agreement is charged a high fee (often in the range of 20% of the reserve price). This provision does not generally appear in gallery consignment agreements. The fee is intended to deter consignors from changing their minds after agreeing to sell a work at auction or—as may happen—being wooed by a competing auction house after having inked a deal. Depending on the consignor's risk tolerance, we sometimes negotiate a clause permitting withdrawal of a work by the consignor with no payment to the auction house if a specific event occurs, such as terrorism, war, or even steep stock-market decline.

Other issues we negotiate in higher-value auction consignment agreements include lot sequencing (does the consignor really want its painting to be offered last in the sale, after most bidders have left for dinner?), and what happens if a work is damaged or destroyed while in the custody of the auction house. In fact, insurance is one of the most important—and least understood—provisions in any consignment agreement, and this is where some tricks of our trade become especially useful.

For instance, we try to set the insurance valuation of a work at the upper range of the property estimate (generally attached to the consignment agreement as an exhibit) to enable a generous payment if a work is damaged or destroyed prior to auction. We are also careful to provide that the auction-house coverage is (in insurance lingo) "primary and non-contributory," i.e., the consignor will not have to look to its own coverage—with possible resulting premium increases—and there will not be a battle between the auction-house insurer and the consignor's insurer as to who is responsible for payment. And, finally, we drill down on what is excluded from the auction house's standard insurance coverage—meaning what is not insured.

These exclusions may include "inherent defects" in a work (for example, if a heavy sculpture simply falls apart under its own weight), acts of terrorism, and damage done during approved restoration. We are often able to narrow or even omit many exclusions in negotiations with the auction house, thereby providing a broader range of coverage for the consignor. After all, as one of our smarter clients likes to say, "with a good insurance policy, a loss is as good as a sale."

Of course, what is important to one consignor may not matter so much to another. For instance, while all our clients want to obtain the highest price for a work, some are especially interested in how the piece will be presented and sold. This latter situation often occurs with estates, where the consignors may be concerned about the tribute paid to the decedent and want to emphasize that the dearly departed was a great collector. As a result, they focus on how the sale is marketed and titled. All such terms should be reflected in the consignment agreement.

Even we are surprised by the unusual demands sometimes made by our clients—and granted by auction houses—in consignment agreements. For example, in Chinese auction sales consignors sometimes request lots associated with auspicious numbers, such as 8, 88 and 108, while in antiquities sales, lot 69 is often given to a "sexy" piece (can't think why). For us, the most auspicious number is simply the highest possible price paid to our client.

In conclusion, when representing collectors in the sales of art we are often struck by the fascinating legal issues that may arise in these transactions. Even seemingly simple sales can contain hidden traps for unwary collectors. Accordingly, our advice is often not *caveat emptor* but "seller watch out," though this—to use a favorite expression of our mother—is easier said than done.

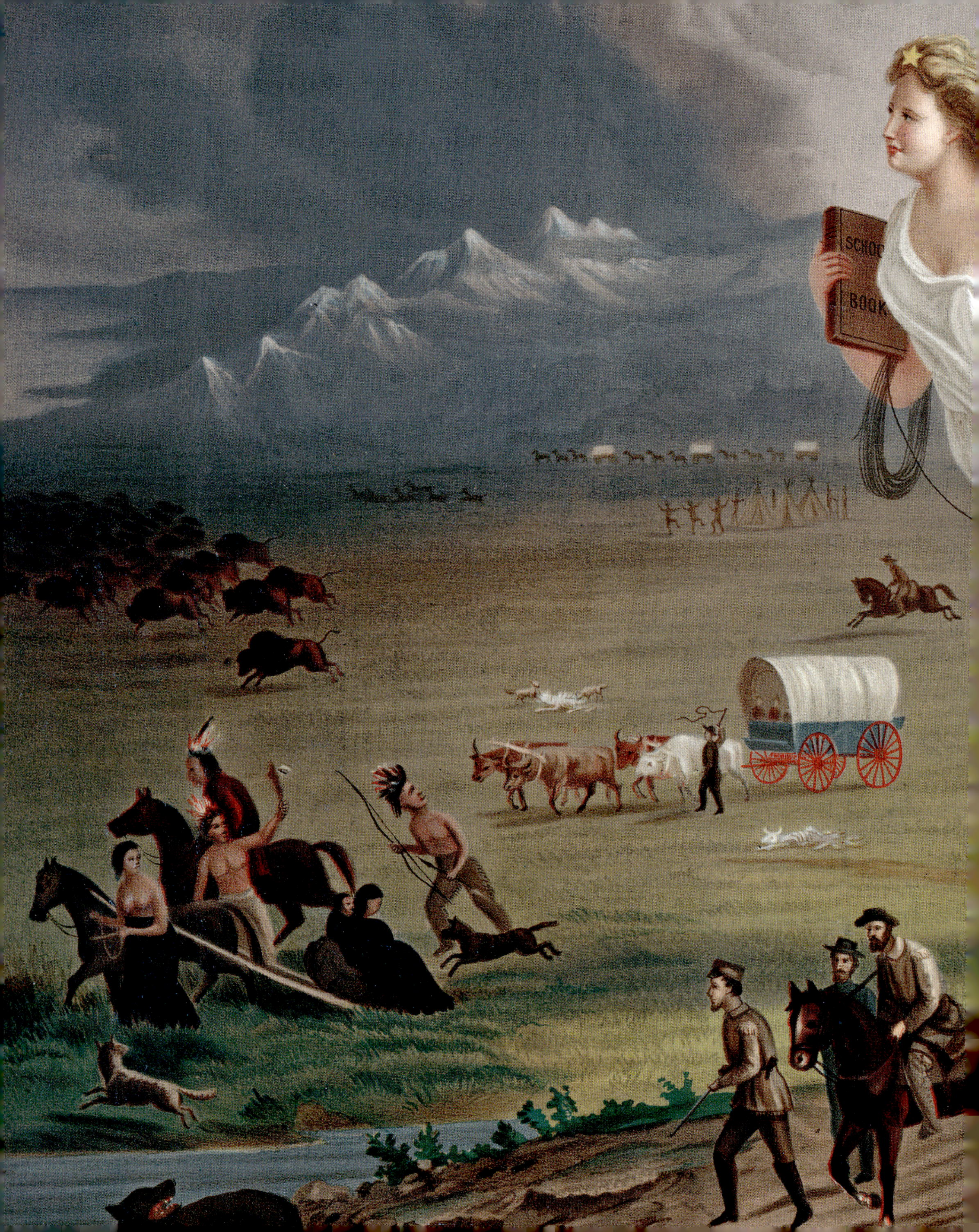
SCHOO
BOOK

III. Changes in the Art Market

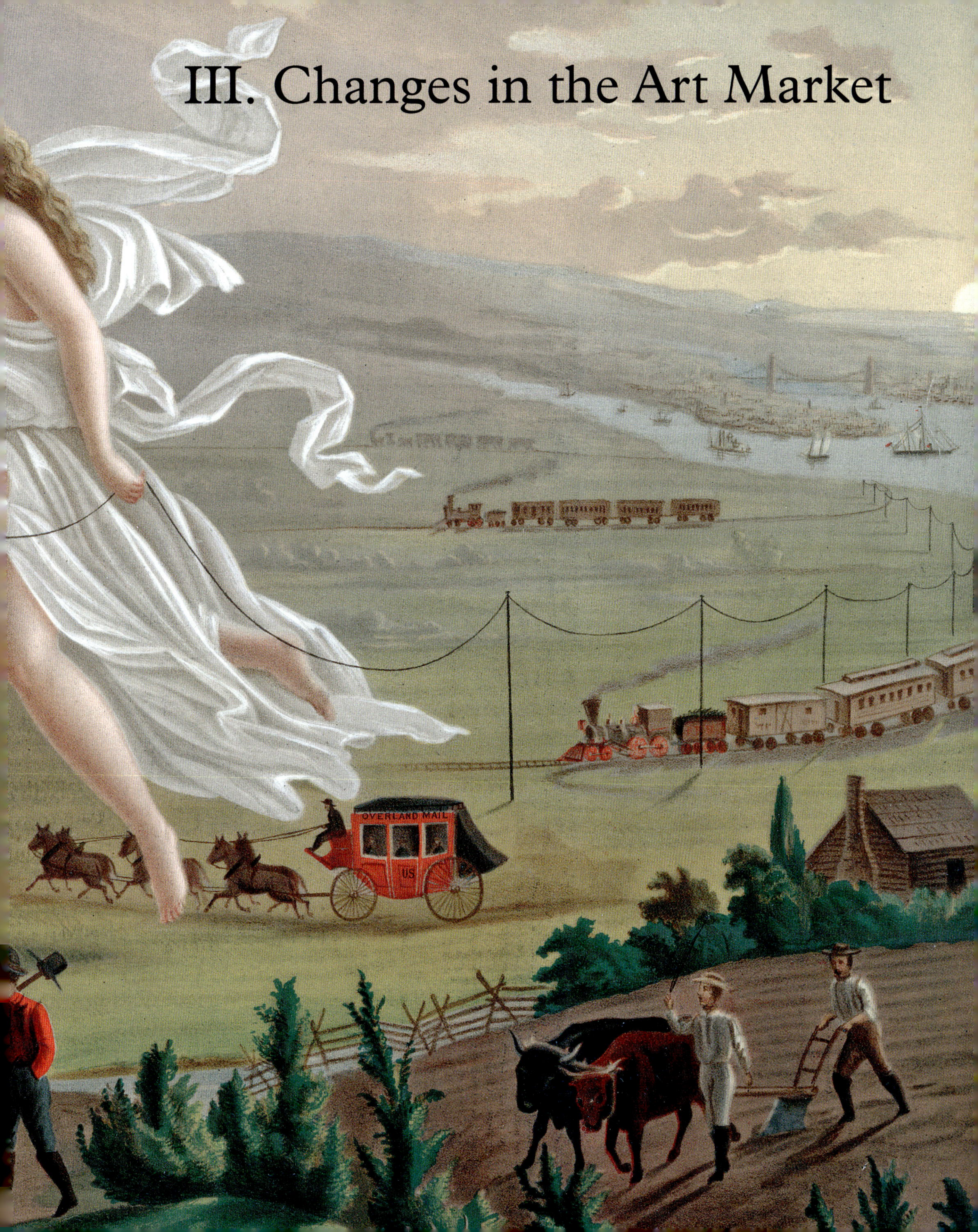

Made in America
A Critical Revisionism to Revive the Canon

Tiffany Elena Washington, PhD, Cleveland, Ohio

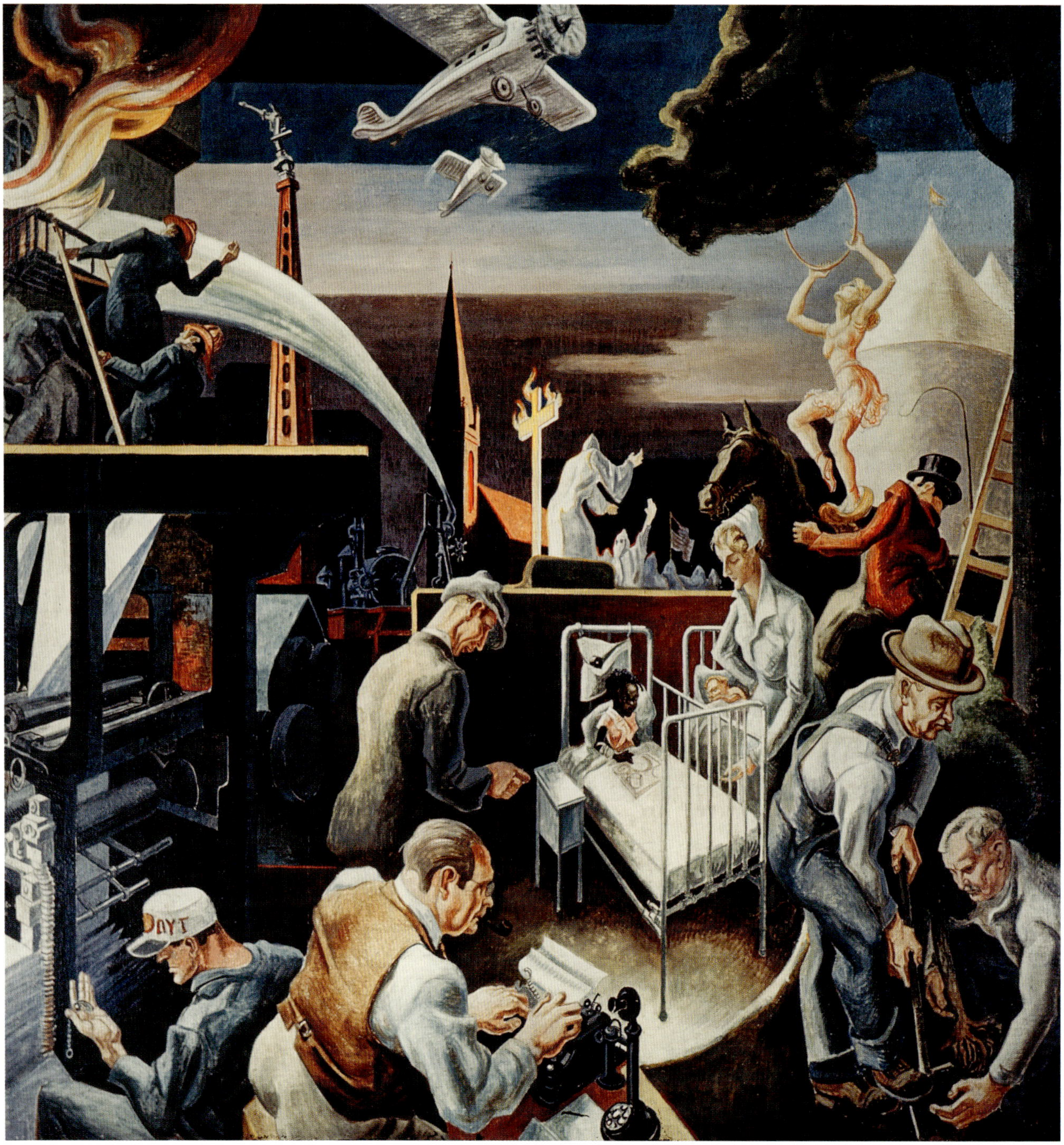

Let the audiences see that old is always new,
if viewed through knowledge
Harold Cotter

The recently renewed crisis over the display of commemorative monuments sheds light on the pressing need for increased knowledge about historical American art and its ongoing relevance. The lack of a coherent public response also points to the need for American art historians to rethink their method of analyzing and writing about canonical American artworks.[1] With society increasingly reliant on fast media, teaching the symbolism and iconography of historical American art—and how it illustrates messages about the nation, democracy, manifest destiny, and race—will help demonstrate the relevance of this art to today's specific issues of nationalism and race, but also the relevance of art in general.

Still relatively young, the field of American art history is presented with a great challenge and a unique opportunity: to interrogate, theorize, and amplify the context of historical American art and then promote it to society as a potential medium for mediation. American historical art reflects the many ills and triumphs of the country's social history, and its interpretation can provide critical insights into how the country can navigate its continually changing identity and cultural history. Today's scholars of American art are tasked with maintaining their study of the objects themselves through all the traditional methodologies of the field, but more enthusiastically taking a revisionist stance alongside those. It is not enough to take one approach on its own as a study of line, color, connoisseurship, and so on, as this doesn't carry enough weight for a less-than-enthusiastic culture of art viewers. Yet viewing the art in a social science context alone ignores its physical and aesthetic merits, which diminishes its other very valid reasons for existence.

We find the United States today in the process of a redefinition. America is reasserting and modifying its identity on the global stage. Notions of cultural identity, the meaning and function of borders and boundaries, and concerns about human impact on the environment bring to light new ways of seeing our nation's priorities and prompt the need for a greater knowledge of our past. An understanding of the relevance, meaning, and definition of historical American art is key to a redefinition of America, its democracy and what both have to do with our culture. Historians of American art have the daunting and critical task of making historical American art timely and relevant again so that it does not fall into obscurity or is misinterpreted, both for the sake of preserving it and for a more complete education of our society. The danger in not doing so is great: without respect for, and understanding of, this art, it will remain alive only within survey classes and museums, and it will be vandalized and petitioned to be removed through lack of understanding or interest in contextual reframing. Additionally, it may easily be misinterpreted and incorrectly categorized, potentially reassigning it as irrelevant and/or harmful, both of which pose major problems for our culture and its future.

The ongoing controversy over the mural Thomas Hart Benton painted for Indiana University is one example of how general ignorance about an artwork can generate such fervor that the artwork, as well as its messages and historical lessons, are threatened with being relegated to obscurity. His 1933 mural, *A Social History of Indiana*, was commissioned by the state of Indiana for the "Century of Progress" exhibition at the World's Fair in Chicago in 1933–34. It was not until 1938 that the university purchased the mural and planned its display. Twelve feet high, its twenty-two panels illustrate topics of culture and industry related to the state. Because of display space constraints, the murals were not all installed together. "Parks, the Circus, the Klan, the Press" was displayed along with "Electric Power, Motorcars, Steel" in Woodburn Hall, with the larger group of panels displayed nearby in the lobby of the university's auditorium.

Unsurprisingly, it is "The Klan" panel (Fig. 1) that has generated heated debate. The

Previous page
John Gast
American Progress, 1872:
detail of Fig. 4, page 247

1.
Thomas Hart Benton
(1889–1975)
A Social History of Indiana
mural, "The Klan" panel
1933
Ht. 12 ft (3.66 m)
Egg tempera
Indiana University, IN, Indiana University Campus Art Collection. THB X Thomas Hart Benton Indiana Murals: Parks, the Circus, the Klan, the Press

KKK imagery in the panel is in the background, with the larger foreground occupied by a nurse caring for both black and white children at the Indianapolis City Hospital and sharing space with a group of journalists, whose prominence and physical arrangement draw the viewer's eyes into the scene. Benton's inclusion of these journalists was to give credit to their reporting on the Ku Klux Klan, specifically referencing the *Indianapolis Times*, whose Pulitzer Prize-winning journalism was directly responsible for uncovering the KKK's influence on, and corruption of, the state government. Above the nurse and children, beyond a half wall, are cloaked members of the KKK, a burning cross, and an American flag. Sharing this space are circus performers and a portrait of Richard Lieber, who was the head of Indiana's park system, shown planting a tree.

Benton was vehemently anti-racist, even learned to speak Gullah, the black dialect of the Sea Islands, and often spoke out against prejudice and racism. His intentions, however, have not mattered to many students and other observers, as the mural has become the subject of controversy since its installment. Recently, members of Indiana University's Black Student Union have called for its removal. The University President issued a statement, and a forum was held to discuss the fate of the mural. It was determined that classes would not be held in the room in which it is displayed. The university has offered lectures about the mural in an attempt to educate the student body, yet complaints still remain that it incites fear in people and is offensive. Unfortunately, many people have not bothered to investigate the artist's reasons for including images of the KKK, among them the intention of highlighting the work of the journalists to bring down the Klan and their evil influence over Indiana's politics. Rather, the very inclusion of the image of the Klansmen has prompted many to demand that the panel be removed.

Intending to provoke reflection and shed light on the traumatic presence of the Klan in Indiana, not to memorialize it, Benton was known for bringing art to the people in a manner many found abrupt. He was without question interested in depicting the truths of his time and throughout history, to spark debate. Covering or removing these panels amounts to censorship. Removing them from view and from conversation because they include sinister figures means we cannot confront these evils and learn from them.

Similarly, the renewed challenge of the confederate monuments, memorializing racist individuals whose actions or beliefs are rightfully offensive to many, has prompted heated public debate. The destruction of these monuments eliminates our opportunities to learn from the mistakes of the past and also to learn about the individuals who commissioned them and the artists who made them. Debates concerning this art allow for a unique opportunity to attack the matter of societal injustices, free speech, and the role of art at their core. Ignorance abounds in the relationship between the modern viewer and historical American art.

Historical American art is rife with signs and symbols that, when viewed in their original context, transmitted powerful messages. Years later, these same artworks need, arguably more than ever, to be decoded for contemporary understanding, as historical American art becomes seemingly less relevant to, and increasingly misunderstood by, those outside the academic realm. Historical American art can be made relevant and understood today if museums and university professors teach the art through a more interrogative lens while underscoring its intrinsic value as a symbol of our culture's evolution.

Historical American art functions simultaneously in several ways: as a mirror to the American past and as a constructed version or a collection of represented facts. Knowledge of these differing realities is key for proper interpretation and understanding of the artwork and, when applicable, its patrons, who are an equally important part of the art's history and representatives of the societal culture of its time. As our nation and its democracy were being formed, artists were called upon to capture visually and preserve its native qualities, the force of man and his influence on its development. Notions of manifest destiny, magisterial gaze, ideas of independence, growth, wealth, and self-improvement were all assigned corresponding visual symbols by the artists and the patrons of this art. Some were allegorical (the image of Columbia, see page 247), some more literal, and some exemplified by representations of actual natural features, such as Niagara Falls, as truly emblematic of the United States. Creating a national art while crafting notions of what was or is "national" is also key to learning about our history. Decoding artists' choices for how to depict art of this country is helpful for understanding early symbolisms of democracy, social behavior, and more. Much of this art acts also as a codex illustrating in paint the viewpoints of early naturalists, expansionists, or sympathizers to land inhabited by Native Americans and then, later, various political ideologies.

One such example of an artwork that is misinterpreted today, without proper context and artist biography accompanying it, is *Buffalo Chase, A Single Death*, 1832–33 by George Catlin (Fig. 2). His series of *Buffalo Chase* paintings is evidence of his interest not only in landscape, but in natural preservation and Native American life. Throughout his career, he visited a total of fifty tribes, visually documenting their lifestyle in his journal and through his collection of artifacts, almost as if categorizing or classifying the information he gathered about the tribes. His efforts, therefore, were somewhat anthropological. Ultimately, he toured much of New England lecturing on this dying race, but his paintings were met with little interest in the United States; he sold more of them in the European market. His view of the Native Americans was uncommonly sympathetic for his time, though he made no efforts to "save" the people he depicted, but denounced their being labeled as savages. But his paintings of them were met with mixed reviews in the United States and, as recently as 2002, Catlin's motive for, and depictions of, the Native Americans has been criticized publicly. Richard West, Director of the Smithsonian's National Museum of the

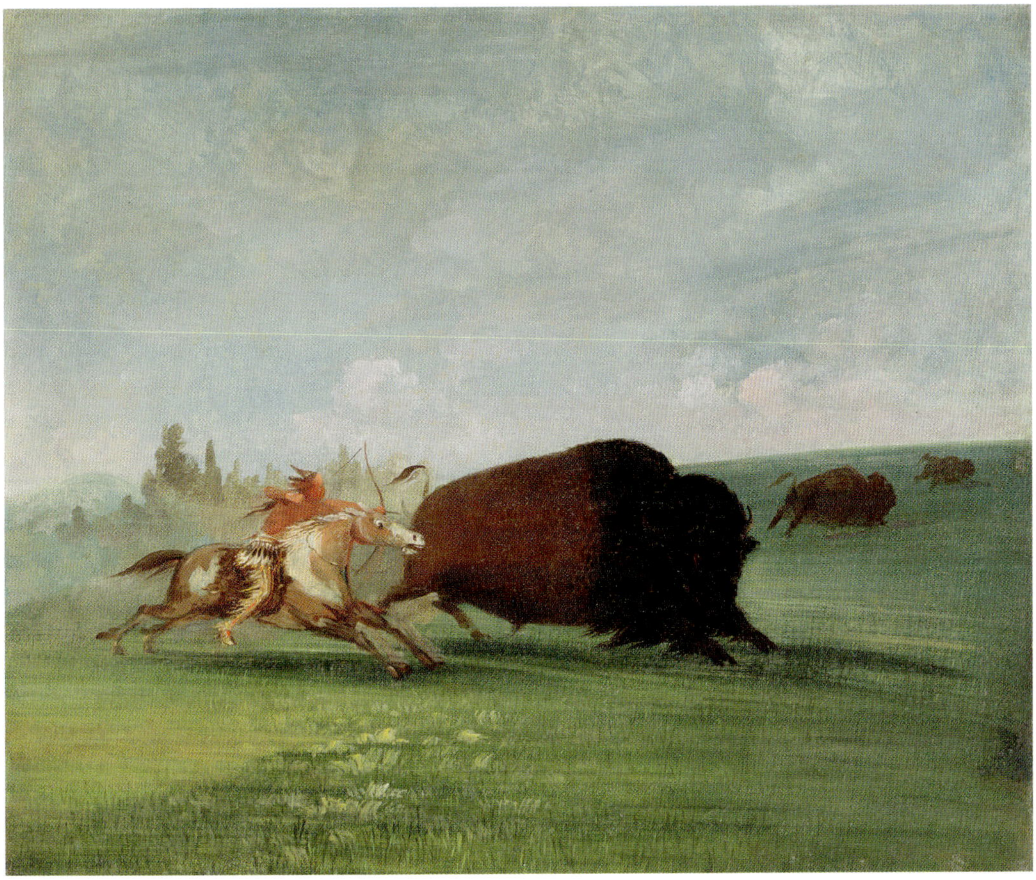

2.
George Catlin (1796–1872)
Buffalo Chase, A Single Death
1832–33
Oil on canvas
24 × 29 in. (60.9 × 73.7 cm)
Smithsonian American Art Museum, Washington, DC
Gift of Mrs. Joseph Harrison, Jr.
1985.66.408

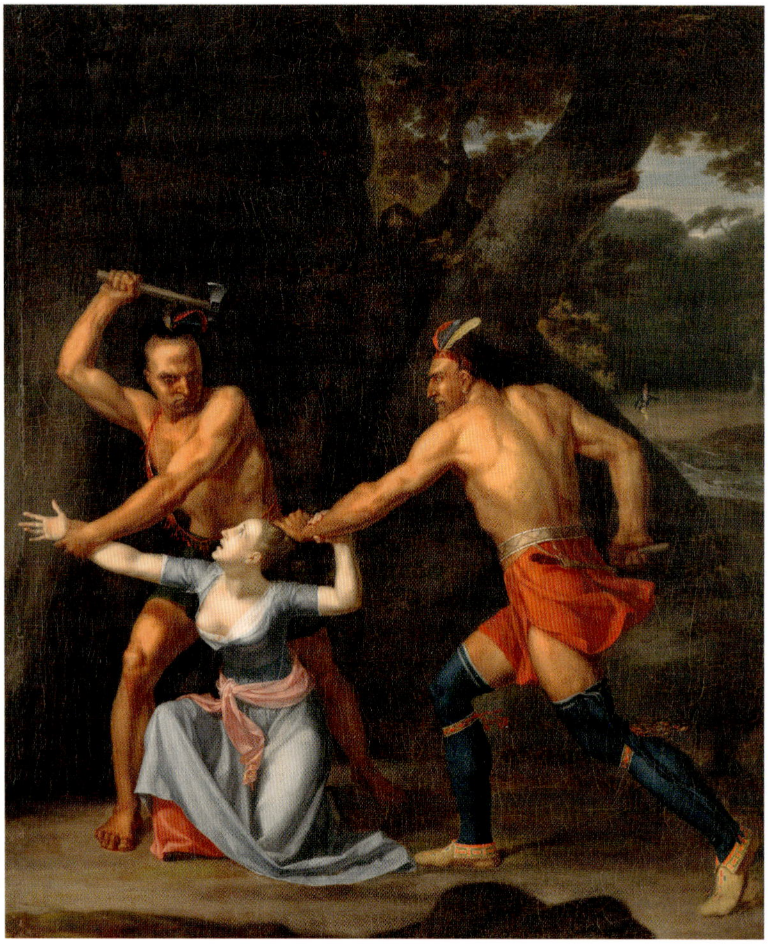

3.
John Vanderlyn (1776–1852)
The Death of Jane McCrea
1804
Oil on canvas
32 ½ × 25 ½ in.
(82.55 × 64.77 cm)
Wadsworth Atheneum Museum of Art, Hartford, CT, 1855.4

American Indian, and a Native American himself, thought Catlin exploited his subjects:

A Native person is challenged, I think, not to feel on some level a profound resentment toward Catlin. His obsession with depicting Indians has an extremely invasive undertone to it. There's no question he was exploiting Indians and the West as a commodity. On the other hand, he was far ahead of his time in his empathy for Indians. Catlin swam against the tide to bring to light information about the Indians that depicts them accurately as worthy human beings and worthy cultures.[2]

In *Buffalo Chase, A Single Death* one may view the image of the Indian, feathered headdress pushed back against the wind, bow ready to strike the massive buffalo and determined horse charging forward, as animalistic and backward. Many may see Catlin's portraits and larger scenes of rituals as offensive, depicting an uncivilized group engaging in what should have been private, undocumented rites of passage that no white man had the right to observe. Yet, taking Catlin's more sympathetic depictions of the Indians and his contemporaries' mockery of the race together, we should contextualize white Americans' historic viewpoints of these tribes, their relationships with them during the early days of our nationhood, and how their actions have affected them and other groups they have marginalized and exterminated as time has gone on. Native Americans are most often featured in today's headlines within the context of natural gas pipelines and their frustration at their land being disrupted by the government. We as a nation should draw from our vast consortium of artwork more often in our educational system in order to give a complete picture of the history of the relationship between Native Americans and the settler colonialists. We can develop a better understanding about this group's stance regarding their land, trespassers, and displacement if we use historical art to bolster our explanation of the reasons for how things came to be. Ideally, both the derogatory and the inoffensive artwork would be shown. Without the visual comparisons we offer an incomplete or falsified view of both our culture's past ills and the efforts made by those sympathetic to the recipients of unjust treatment.

A notable comparison is made with John Vanderlyn's *The Death of Jane McCrea* (Fig. 3), in which the artist used the image of the Native American Indian to stand in for then current political connotations, a practice not unusual for its time. In fact, Vanderlyn belonged to a democratic men's club in New York—the Tammany Society, named after an Indian—in which members dressed as Indians, attempted to speak in Indian code, and used Indian names. This was, in part, an effort to separate themselves from the aristocratic Federalist clubs of the time, as the Tammany Society was generally anti-British and anti-Federalist. Vanderlyn's painting depicts the capture of a young woman, a patriot, by two Iroquois Indians as she was on her way to visit her fiancé, who fought for the British during the American Revolution. Accounts of McCrea's death differ, but the standard account is that she was murdered and then scalped posthumously by the two Indians. The story has been repeated in literature and art and grew more popular, drawing parallels between McCrea and her soldier boyfriend with the colonists under British rule. It is the representation of the Indians whose characterization was a constant: they were brutal murderers.

Once word spread of McCrea's death, local townspeople took up arms against the British. The story had a direct effect on the course of the Revolution, as townspeople helped defeat Burgoyne in Saratoga in the fall of 1777. The story gained fame, and ultimately Vanderlyn put brush to canvas in the creation of his own version. Illuminating the beautiful McCrea and clothing her in blue, posing her figure in a manner loosely resembling something from a classical frieze, Vanderlyn adds drama to the Romantic painting by pulling the Indians out from the dark, savages that they were. This story and the images that ensued promoted the captivity narrative that continued in print, on canvas and, later, in film. The portrayal of the noble savage was again made popular by James Fenimore Cooper in his 1826 novel *The Last of the Mohicans*.

The innocent, civilized, white, and "enlightened" McCrea could not appear more different from the muscular, vicious, ax-wielding, "red-skinned" Indians. Whether it was true or not that she was murdered and scalped by the Indians, the story was used in art to push forward the propaganda that eventually helped underscore the viewpoint of settler privilege over Natives and their land, as well as the narrative of American vs. British during a pivotal moment in the war.

One overlooked, but extremely relevant painting is *American Progress* by John Gast, 1872 (Fig. 4). It bundled together an assortment of ideas that can only be described as propaganda and mythology. Wearing a star of the Empire on her forehead, a classical figure with long blonde hair guides the viewer and the painting's other inhabitants westward. Holding a telegraph wire in one hand and a schoolbook in the other, she is depicted as strongly reminiscent of the Statue of Liberty. In the fore, middle, and background, figures of varying types move in the same direction on foot, in covered wagons, on horseback, in ship, carriage, and steam engine.

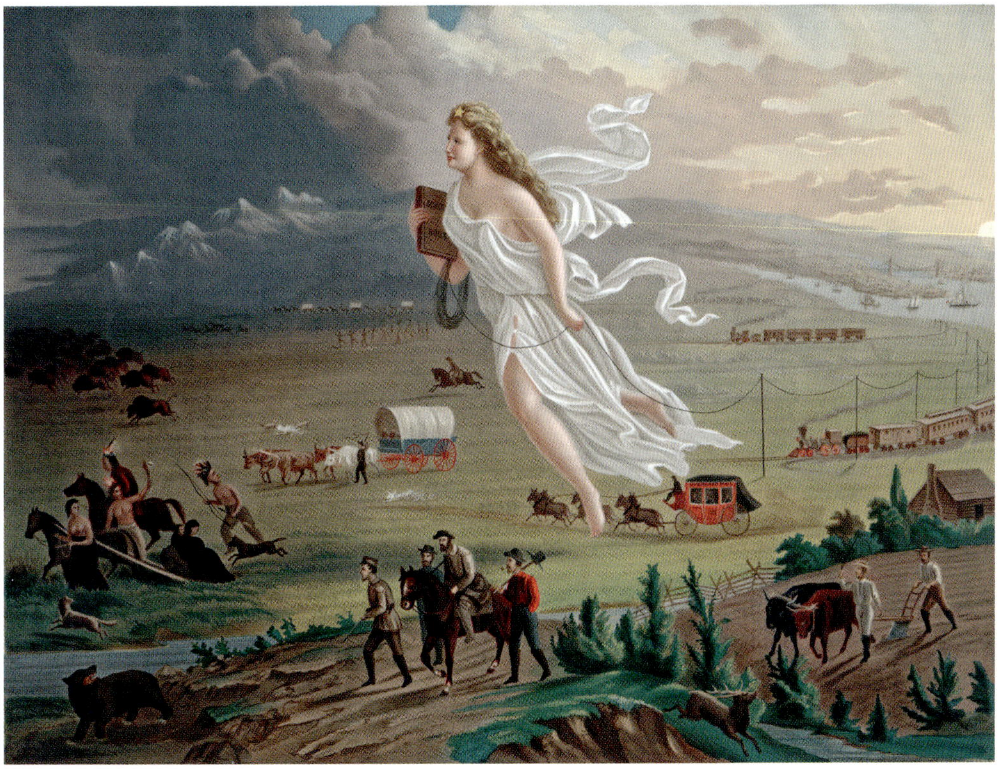

4.
John Gast (1842–1896)
American Progress, 1872
Oil on canvas
11 ½ × 15 ¾ in.
(29.2 × 40 cm)
Autry Museum of the American West, Los Angeles, 92.126.1

Commissioned by the publisher of Western travel guides, George Crofutt, it was reproduced as an engraving and widely published, helping to strengthen the ideas presented within, such as: the rapid expansion westward, fueled by the belief in the concept of *Manifest Destiny*, which resulted in the colonization of land; murder and displacement of indigenous peoples; long-term change to the land and animal habitat; as well as the population of the western half of our country. A connection between higher thinking, progress, expansionism, and technology was understood by contemporary viewers through the propaganda depicted within, i.e., the book representing knowledge and a higher intelligence, the innocent, light-bestowing, angelic figure carrying technology and "improvements" into the uncivilized and savage land whose ownership and taming was the God-given right of the white people, according to the propagandistic view.

The lighter, brighter atmosphere on the right is being carried westward by Columbia into the dark, uncivilized West as the Native Americans appear either to flee from the movement coming toward them or attempt to return to their manner of living while they still have time left. Columbia, a personification of the early nation, was obviously not representative of the whole nation or even of women. In the eighteenth and nineteenth centuries her strength did not translate to a tangible equality given to women in the United States, so her image as a powerful, leading woman is rather misleading. As a national image her strength, whiteness, beauty, and classical form changed little while other figures typecast in art (the Yankee, the farmhand, and the slave) continued to represent imaged versions of their time.

Is John Gast's painting relevant today? Why should young historians or others study and recognize it? What is the general awareness of this painting? Very likely it is not known to most outside the fields of art history or history. Its message is a problematic and offensive one, filled with notions of privilege, racism, superiority, and destruction, with little regard for the past or the environment. Many today might find it insulting and it certainly omits any references to the chief ill of its contemporary American society, namely slavery. It does, however, serve as an excellent example of the post-Civil War mindset and propaganda that perpetuated those beliefs. Learning about and from artworks such as this is only possible in society today by those whose minds are open to a holistic analysis of the artwork. Viewing this on the museum wall or reproduced on the internet or in a book without accompanying details outlining the iconography and what it meant in its time poses a major risk of deaccessioning the artwork or ceasing to reproduce it for purposes of education. Whitewashing such imagery eliminates our opportunity as art historians to educate through the use of artworks as historical tools of education and evidence of past beliefs and their origins. Now, when we see historical American art as an afterthought in the market, ignored by a large segment of our culture, and deemed irrelevant or damaging to those who disagree with its relevance, it is our duty to use these very works as a tool to teach more contemporary concepts and learn from our culture's mistakes.

Can or should images emblematic of a nation be reimaged, recontextualized, or used as tools to explore more contemporary concepts? I argue that they can, but only through both a deep understanding of their initial intended meanings and through serious interrogation. A recontextualization is possible and, today, should be sought for the artworks deemed offensive and/or inappropriate, but also for those that are doomed to be forgotten because they spark no heated debate.

Many of these "neutral" artworks are the landscape paintings. Some are ripe with meaning obvious to those who can read their messages, though most remain misunderstood today, as the signs and symbols of their own visual language were known only to contemporaries. While some American landscape paintings spoke of the destruction of landscape and the evils associated with the hand of man seeking progress, others nodded to its preservation, alluded to man's insignificance compared to the awesome stature of our country's natural features, or even represented various theological underpinnings. They all shaped what became our national identity and are intertwined with our culture's history.

When Congress purchased Thomas Moran's *Chasm of the Colorado*, 1873–74 (see page 18), for $10,000 shortly after its completion and placed it in a small lobby in the Senate wing in the Capitol, one could assume lasting legacy for the piece and its painter. In fact, Congress purchased more than one of Moran's landscapes. The artist's legacy was built both on skill and the influence his artworks had over governmental policy. Moran accompanied geologist Ferdinand Hayden on the first government-sponsored expedition to survey Yellowstone in 1871. His images of the area were the first ever viewed by many people in the eastern United States and were what Hayden used to persuade Congress to preserve it as a National Park and even to create the National Park system in 1872.[3] How much is known today about how Moran's paintings of the awesome natural landscape in the Western area of the United States sparked conservation and preservation efforts? Though not topographically accurate (a fact for which the artist made no apologies), the artist's version of the views he witnessed as he accompanied explorers to these sites offered excitement and promise to citizens and policy-makers in the East. In fact, many of the places Moran painted were eventually designated as national landmarks. Displaying these paintings in the East and reproducing them for distribution in travel guides and advertisements helped solidify the national push to settle and "civilize" the West. Moran chose not to include figures or any sense of a divine element, as did John Gast, and, as a result, he takes a more neutral stance on Manifest Destiny and the supposed endowed right to transform the land and its peoples.

Equally concerned with, or in some cases, less concerned with, formal issues of style and traditional methodologies, many younger-generation historians of American art are now placing more emphasis on economic, political, and social issues, often related to class structure, feminism, and psychology, following in the footsteps of notables such as T.J. Clark, Linda Nochlin, and others. Combining the traditional tenets of the field with a focus on looking at historical American art through lenses that are now more relevant and more riveting to much of today's society seems more appropriate, especially when applicable to the types of art that continue to find themselves in the news headlines.

Thomas Gaehtgens and Heinz Ickstadt noted that "The American people have historically seemed to suffer from a lack of confidence in the intrinsic value of their own art … [while] Europeans have tended to equate the history of art with the evolution of their own culture…."[4] This rings true today more than ever. We need to take a multifaceted view of both the canon and artwork just outside it in order to animate debate about the art itself, what it meant to us as a nation when it was created and what it can mean and teach us now. Not only will this better teach us the origins of American Modernism, it will help us better understand what American art really is, where its borders lie and how art and life need to coexist. Monuments of a fractured union or portraits of early political leaders may celebrate who we don't want to be today, but they are the best reminders of the use of art to shape public opinion and can serve as the strongest examples of whom we should not model ourselves after.

Today's debates about the appropriateness of sports logos, like the Cleveland Indians' Chief Wahoo, or the meaning and function of the Statue of Liberty during a time when the homogeneity of our culture is diffusing, could be made richer if we also discuss figures like Uncle Sam or Columbia and the connections forged between notions of allegory and symbols of the nation. And these symbols can be tolerated, revised, or replaced through knowledge and healthy debate based in a deeper understanding of history.

The relevance of historical American art is endangered. To revive it we need to pitch it, make it fresh, look at it with a very critical lens and tell its truth. Its truth is our own—complicated and flawed—and if we are to do our job as art historians and improve as a culture, we need to appreciate the art of our past, in all its glory, and despite its flaws, as a reflection of the feelings, motivations, and desires of the people it reflected.

Ways of Re-Seeing
Connecting Historical American Art and the Modern World

Lauren Palmor, PhD
Assistant Curator of American Art, Fine Arts Museums of San Francisco, California

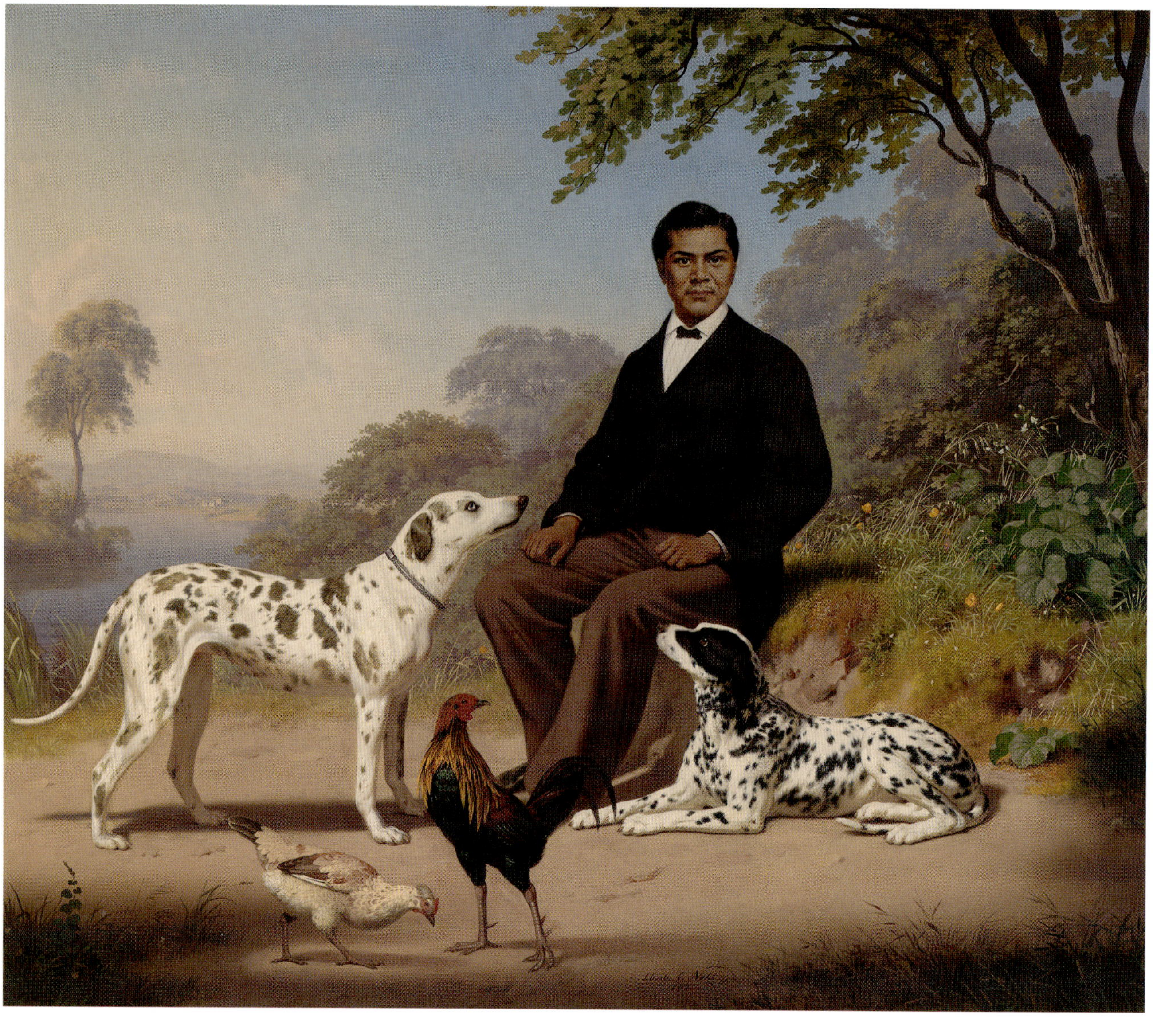

Contemporary museum spaces devoted to American art collections typically pursue a dual responsibility: curators and educators aim to ground objects within a historical chronology while excavating new layers of relevance from works of art. In recent decades, the interpretive spheres around American art have expanded, dissolving the borders between the distinct periods of an object's creation, initial reception, and inevitable—and ongoing—reinterpretation. These practices are employed throughout an increasing number of museums, where objects illustrate the myriad ways in which American art is as bound to history as it is to the present moment.

In 1972, John Berger articulated a truth familiar to contemporary art historians: "The relation between what we see and what we know is never settled."[1] This invitation to subjective and elastic thought is particularly fitting in the field of historical American art, which has long examined our nation's character in tandem with consideration of any physical object. Berger's statement suggests that when we engage with an object, we are also studying our relationship to the past—and when the object is representative of American culture, we are prompted to interrogate the constantly shifting markers of national identity.

It may be this self-conscious examination of our nation's values that sets the field of American art history apart.[2] This flexibility and subjectivity make the study of American art particularly well suited to what David Lubin memorably called "try-what-works art history."[3] "Try-what-works art history," which now permeates institutional collections and installations across the United States, centers the object within a consideration of its myriad historical contexts across time and media. A departure from the connoisseurship of the past, this approach brings to the fore issues of narrative disjunction, political meanings, social behavior, and evidence of cultural preference.[4] Further, when historical objects are inserted into a thoughtful display that exposes the strengths and weaknesses of a collection, viewers enjoy the additional benefit of learning from historical omissions and oversights. This expansive and experimental form of scholarship, which now characterizes the field, keeps historical American art relevant and amenable to the living present.[5]

The American art collection at the de Young museum prominently features masterpieces of painting, sculpture, and decorative arts from the established history of American art alongside recent acquisitions of objects that alternately challenge and call attention to the traditional canon. In his introduction to the most recent handbook of the American collection (2005), Curator-in-Charge Timothy Anglin Burgard notes, "While the paintings in this catalogue are products of their historical contexts, a brief survey of several works reveals that contemporary curatorial considerations have influenced their acquisition by the de Young."[6] The curatorial display strategies deployed in the galleries involve juxtapositions between contemporary art and historical objects, encouraging new ways of seeing and learning. For example, the museum's American still life gallery places *tromp l'œil* paintings by artists such as William Michael Harnett (1848–1892) and John Frederick Peto (1854–1907) in conversation with contemporary *tromp l'œil* sculptures by David Regan (b. 1964), Richard Shaw (b. 1941), and Beth Lipman (b. 1971). Viewed together, the objects in this gallery attest to the enduring power of illusion, symbolism, and closely studied observation. When museum visitors encounter this artistic tradition in both its past and present forms, such a contrast enlivens and makes concrete their experience, making it possible to understand better how these ideas transcend time and place.

In addition to these curatorial display strategies, curators strive to spark creative dialogue through interpretive materials, which intertwine the historical past and contemporary narratives. In the following four case studies drawn from the de Young collection, historical American art is framed by its connection to such critical twenty-first-century issues as identity, labor, justice, and our relationship to nature. These are models of the conversations we try to foster with our audiences, in which the collection is presented as a collection of ideas available for continual reinterpretation.[7]

1.
Charles Christian Nahl
(1818–1878)
Sacramento Indian, 1867
Oil on canvas
42 1/16 × 49 1/4 in.
(106.8 × 125.1 cm)
Fine Arts Museums of San Francisco, Gift of Mrs. Milton S. Latham, 41988

The American art galleries at the de Young museum are replete with patterns of historical inclusion and omission, and cultural competition and alliances.[8] Questions of character and belonging can be used to situate individual objects within the wide spectrum of American identities and national bonds. Works within the galleries are framed by questions about how such identities are bolstered, reinforced, or challenged by the content therein. As Michael Leja has described, "As questions concerning the interactions of cultural forms and artistic traditions within a multiethnic and multiracial population have acquired urgency, the United States has assumed new relevance as a focus of art historical inquiry."[9] This urgency is demonstrated by the contemporary installation and interpretation of Charles Christian Nahl's *Sacramento Indian* (1867), which prominently hangs in the first of the American art galleries (Fig. 1).

Nahl's *Sacramento Indian* is a portrayal of a Native American man circumscribed by the dominant culture of his era. The sitter was originally identified as "Wahla—Chief of Yuba Indian tribe," although "Wahla" may in fact be a generic term for chief among the Southern Maidu people of northern California.[10] "Wahla" is believed to have first received his "Western" education and employment in the household of prominent California businessman Samuel Brannan (1819–1889), and later worked as a coachman for California politician Milton S. Latham (1827–1882).[11] It is said that Latham was so impressed by the young man's training that he commissioned Nahl, California's foremost portraitist, to paint him, producing an image of a model trainee.[12] The artist's representation makes certain assurances that any so-called "natural" or "Native" inclinations have been tamed and transformed by the dominant, "genteel" Western society. Despite the confidence evident in these nineteenth-century assertions, a twenty-first-century encounter with this portrait invites complex questions about identity and acculturation. Today, as identity politics and anti-racist actions increasingly shape conversations in galleries and curatorial offices, Nahl's portrait offers contemporary audiences an opportunity to challenge and correct the prejudice and cultural supremacy of the past.

Dressed in a simple, tidy suit, his dark, glossy hair neatly combed, "Wahla" appears composed and self-aware. He sits within the most unnatural of natural environments, and his new status feels contrived.[13] Notwithstanding his sophisticated demeanor, scholars of a prior era have commented on his comparison with the prized purebred dogs and chickens in the foreground—critic Robert Hughes described his portrayal as that of "one pet among others in his master's household."[14] The coachman represents an ideal domesticated type, though despite his association with the animals, nineteenth-century viewers would have also associated this park-like setting with similar portrait backdrops by Gainsborough and Reynolds, suggesting that "Wahla" has set aside his "Indianness" and has been integrated into Euro-American society (and its visual signifiers).[15, 16]

The sitter's rigid posture may reflect his self-consciousness about being positioned between two worlds, with his acculturation locating him between his heritage and the dominant culture.[17] Conceived in the space between nature and civilization, this image of "Wahla" invites contemporary interrogation of stereotypes, appropriation, and patterns of erasure.[18] Twenty-first-century viewers are sensitized to these issues in new ways, especially as now, more than ever, American conversations about race, racism, and assimilation have moved beyond simple binary formulations of race and culture.[19] As we are always looking at the correspondence between historical objects and our own moment, inevitably, the contemporary viewer will also search Nahl's portrait for shared markers of our national identity.

Recent developments in the study of American identity politics draw new context from *Sacramento Indian*. Scholars have established the myriad ways in which the formation of character is established, moving away from the idea that identity is an expression of our innate nature, but rather a causal explanation of our social position in a world shaped by a hierarchy.[20] The question of social identities in America is fundamentally comparative, and a close reading of Nahl's picture inevitably produces questions about the production of Euro-American identities, ideologies, and institutions in opposition to the sitter's "Indianness."[21] Contemporary museum visitors are better equipped than ever to understand what this portrait reveals about the articulation and erasure of Native American identities.

Wanda Corn has described the historical legacy of American artists' expression of "a perpetual inability to root himself in his land and culture."[22] In a twenty-first-century museum setting, the characteristics of dislocation or alienation in historic American artworks such as Nahl's *Sacramento Indian* are increasingly associated with the production of identity. The field now prioritizes the social, political, and cultural construction of identity as an imperative line of inquiry.

The construction of identities is further enabled by labor practices and production, and contemporary scholarship argues that self-identity is key to understanding the aestheticization of work.[23] Labor has always related to the conditions of contemporary American life, and the social implications of labor are woven throughout American art. Historical American art holds a mirror to labor as an artistic subject, and asks: How does labor look? Do we value workers? How do images of American workers reveal information about the historical status of class, gender, and race?

No object in the de Young museum galleries better exemplifies these charged connections between labor and identity than Thomas Pollock Anshutz's *The Ironworkers' Noontime*, which invites contemporary viewers to engage with the appearance of American labor (Fig. 2). As one of the few fine art images of American industrial

2.
Thomas Pollock Anshutz
(1851–1912)
The Ironworkers' Noontime
1880
Oil on canvas
17 × 23 ⅞ in.
(43.2 × 60.6 cm)
Fine Arts Museums of San Francisco, Gift of Mr. and Mrs. John D. Rockefeller 3rd, 1979.7.4

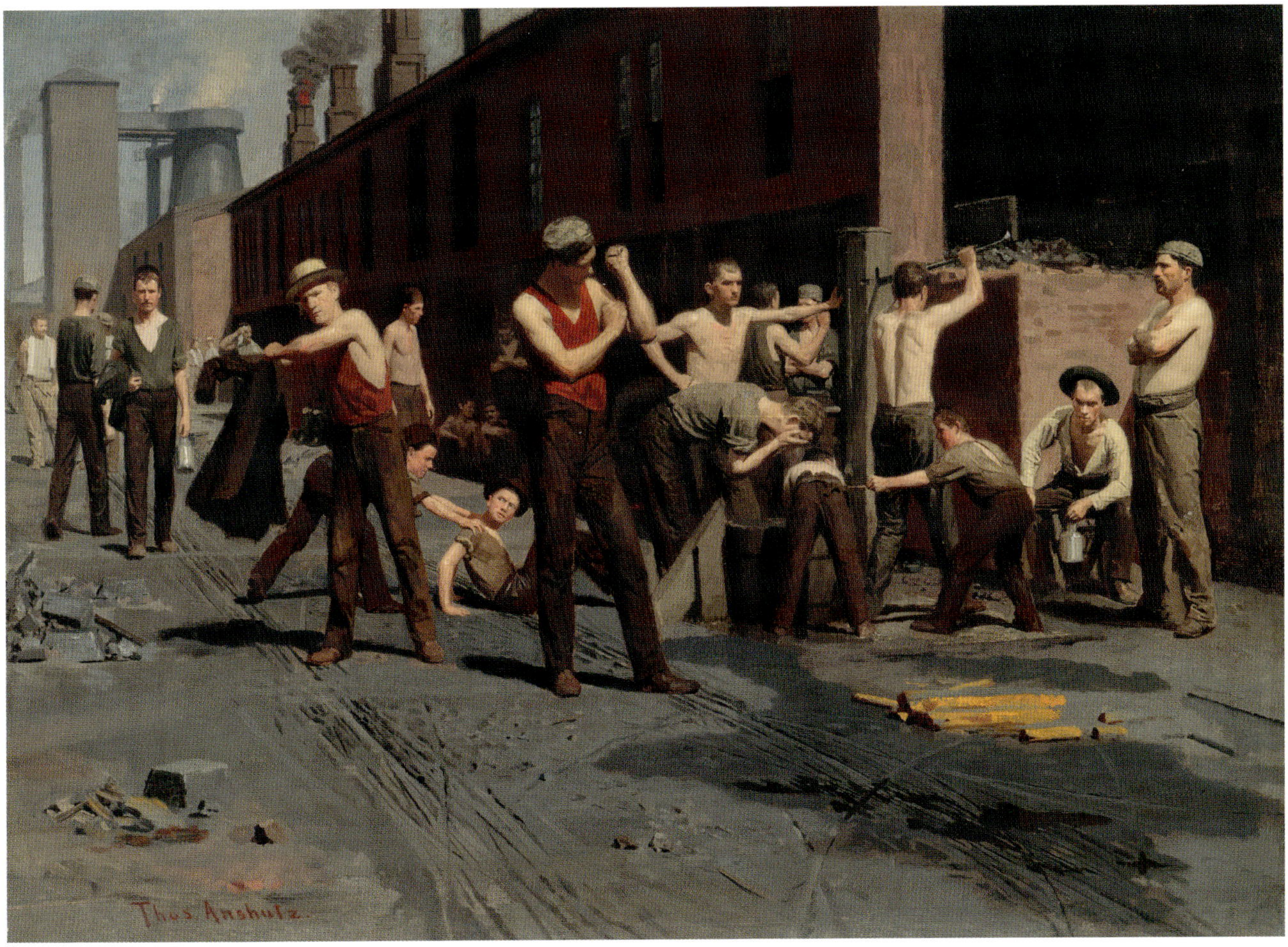

workers dated before 1900, *The Ironworkers' Noontime* evokes the various connotations that can be ascribed to American labor.[24]

Anshutz uses a realist vocabulary to pay tribute to the achievements of a group of workers at the Belmont Nail Works in Wheeling, West Virginia.[25] The men (and boys) are displayed across a shallow foreground, while the colossal foundry stretches back as far as the eye can see. While the laborers embody strength, pride, and autonomy, there is no explicit portrayal of their labor—they are not actually shown at work, but rather on a break.[26] The image is also replete with classicizing references, alluding to the idea that this scene is in part idealized and staged. Although these men likely lead difficult lives, Anshutz's ambiguous portrayal of their resting moment invites the varying interpretations available to a society that ascribes manifold meanings to physical labor.[27]

The Ironworkers' Noontime was developed from preparatory drawings that Anshutz began during one of his annual visits to see family in Wheeling. The laborers he depicts were then being affected by increasing mechanization, which posed a threat to skilled American workers. Anshutz idealized and ennobled the male laborer as a hero of American industry—many contemporary notions of critique or concern produced in the picture's viewers are imposed by the conditions of our own time.[28] As a result of his commitment to realism, Anshutz's enhanced transcription of the Wheeling nail works provides a record of labor history that invites correlation and comparison with our current moment.[29]

In the late nineteenth century, as in the twenty-first, ideas about social mobility and workers' autonomy were being called into question. Americans in Anshutz's time were tasked with reconciling traditional ideas about the dignity of work with the new landscape of labor and manufacturing.[30] *The Ironworkers' Noontime* was painted at a time when the appearance and definition of labor were shifting, and as labor was becoming progressively mechanized, workers began to adapt to serve and assist machines. The fears stoked by this advancement resonate today, as traditional American manufacturing is once again in decline and technological unemployment is forcing workers into new sectors of the labor market.

In the current economic climate, it would be difficult to read *The Ironworkers' Noontime* without considering its resonance with our modern era. The past few decades have been hard on the average American worker, with a growing wealth gap and slipping participation in the labor force. Factors such as improved technology, increasing globalization, and growing competition from foreign workers had made it increasingly difficult for American men and women to find a secure place in the labor market.[31] A masterpiece of American realism, *The Ironworkers' Noontime* spurs contemporary viewers to consider these current social and cultural conditions and their significance expansively. While Anshutz may have intended to capture realistically the strength and autonomy of the nineteenth-century American worker, the painting now appears to eulogize the darker consequences of the worker's decline. Alternatively, the painting might invite contemporary viewers today to consider the historical persistence of labor insecurity.

While Anshutz held a mirror to the potential downfall of the American worker, other historical American artists created images that condemned corruption and a broken justice system. The painter David Gilmour Blythe (1815–1865) was also a severe and willful moralist who critiqued a workforce in decline and the ways in which the American legal system failed the citizenry. His nineteenth-century criticisms ring true with twenty-first-century viewers who are increasingly sensitized to instances of distorted justice and inequality in our legal systems.

In *Justice* (*c.* 1860), a critical view of an urban courtroom, a policeman leads a group of suspects before a magistrate (Fig. 3). They are directed to join the African American man who sits on the bench in the shadows, where he can be interpreted as a symbol of injustice and inequality. The defendants are "Blood Tubs"—members of a Baltimore street gang that supported the restriction of immigration and promoted anti-foreign and anti-Catholic prejudice. The scene is bathed in muddy, gloomy tones, and the prospect of due process takes on a similar murkiness. Despite the painting's title, it does not seem very likely that any of these defendants will receive justice in the end.[32]

Blythe was almost entirely self-taught—he studied popular comic art and political caricature, appropriating images from past and present prints, illustrations, and cartoons.[33] Inspired by the gritty working-class subjects of seventeenth-century Dutch genre painting, he satirized the political and social corruption that he saw in American cities. Blythe chose to depict the absurdities of the justice system more than any other artist of his era, painting the subject at least five times. He saw the faults running through the social and political fabric of America, and he painted the shadows and margins of life in the modern metropolis.[34]

In Blythe's courtrooms, attaining "justice" is as unlikely for the white working-class defendants as it is for African Americans, immigrants, women, and children. Some figures are placed on the margins or in the shadows, illustrating their social isolation and alienation, like the lone African American man in *Justice*, who seems especially prone to the judicial turmoil and inequity that Blythe sought to portray. The painter easily derides the democratic system, undermining the viewer's confidence in any guarantee that truth or justice will prevail.[35]

In a nation that purports to espouse common ideals of liberty, equality, freedom, and justice, Blythe's historic genre pictures remind contemporary viewers that artists have always appraised and evaluated these ideals with a healthy skepticism. Blythe confronted the shifting patterns and inconsistencies of American political life, and a thoughtful evaluation of his pictures can spark a dialogue about the identification, analysis, and eradication of injustices in our world today. The respected criminal justice scholar William J. Stuntz noted, "[i]nequality is a core feature of American criminal justice," and Blythe's *Justice* provides a visual context for appraising this inequality in a justice system that has historically been "hard-wired for punitive racism."[36] The picture similarly illustrates the concepts of "the culture of control" and "governing through crime," David Garland's and Jonathan Simon's terms for the management of the nation's poor through the deployment of criminal punishment.[37]

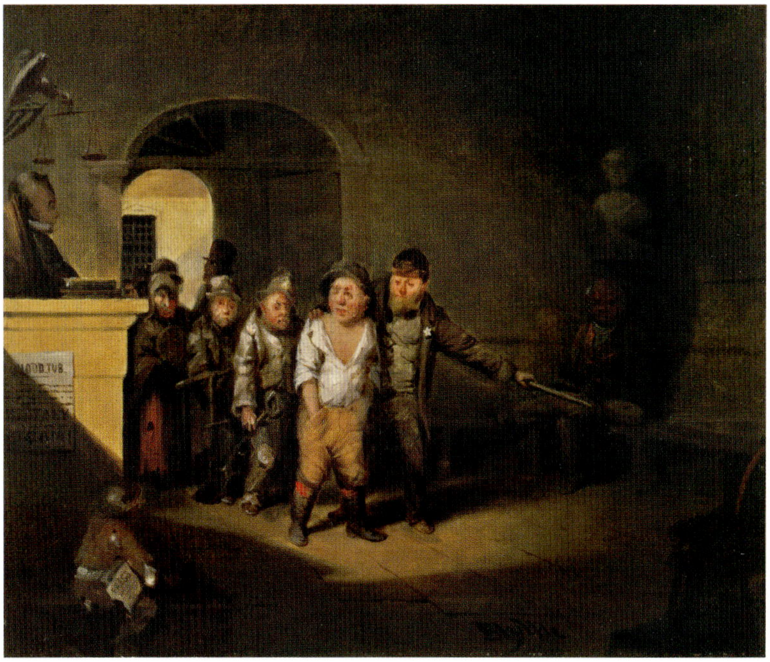

3.
David Gilmour Blythe
(1815–1865)
Justice, *c.* 1860
Oil on canvas
20 ⅛ × 24 ⅛ in.
(51.1 × 61.3 cm)
Fine Arts Museums of San Francisco, Gift of Mr. and Mrs. John D. Rockefeller 3rd, 1979.7.18

Today, the United States routinely receives low scores internationally for providing effective access to civil justice. Current events routinely illustrate the ways in which whole communities have been historically marginalized and have become prone to receiving disparate treatment from the justice system.[38] Blythe's pronounced mistrust of American legal structures can be analyzed and evaluated in tandem with contemporary efforts to correct these imbalances and dismantle social inequality. *Justice* invites twenty-first-century viewers to draw parallels between Blythe's time and our own in order to discover new complexities in our historic visual past.[39]

Blythe's illustration of injustice and inequality resonates deeply today. While the issues of identity, labor, and justice may stir some of the most urgent and divisive political passions, the de Young galleries also tell more anodyne stories about our connection to the land and the ways in which we relate to the environment.

Recreation (1857) by Jerome Thompson (1814–1886) depicts a dreamy picnic gathering near

Mount Mansfield in Vermont (Fig. 4). A group of young men and women have gathered around a tree near the banks of the Winooski River to talk, eat, play music, and flirt. The scene balances the picturesque qualities of the landscape and the activity of the people who engage with the place. The natural environment is welcoming and comfortable—instead of an untamed wilderness, these picnickers have found a place of quiet and peaceful repose. We assume that the group has traveled to this place from a town or city, looking for a refuge from their daily lives. They seek to reconnect to the land, a vital place that city dwellers may too easily forget.

At the time when Thompson painted this scene, rapid urbanization was reshaping America's communities. As more people moved toward centers of industrialization, rural sightseeing and day trips sustained the connection between daily life and the natural world. This desire to maintain a relationship with nature amid rapid urban change reverberates today, as urbanization continues and people increasingly engage with nature in pursuit of feeling grounded and engaged with a deep sense of place.[40]

In our digital era, as people are increasingly drawn to cities for knowledge work, tethered to their desks and devices, nature has again become an important refuge as a place where we share meals, connect with our communities, and strengthen our bonds with the environment. Just as Thompson's picnickers traveled near Mount Mansfield to delight in a nostalgic respite from industrial life, contemporary viewers may relate to *Recreation* (1857) through the popularization of farm dinners, which provide a reprieve from digital devices and encourage connection with people, food, and the environment.[41] New

4.
Jerome Thompson
(1814–1886)
Recreation, 1857
Oil on canvas
40 ½ × 56 in.
(102.9 × 142.2 cm)
Fine Arts Museums of San Francisco, Museum purchase, M.H. de Young Memorial Museum, 47.13

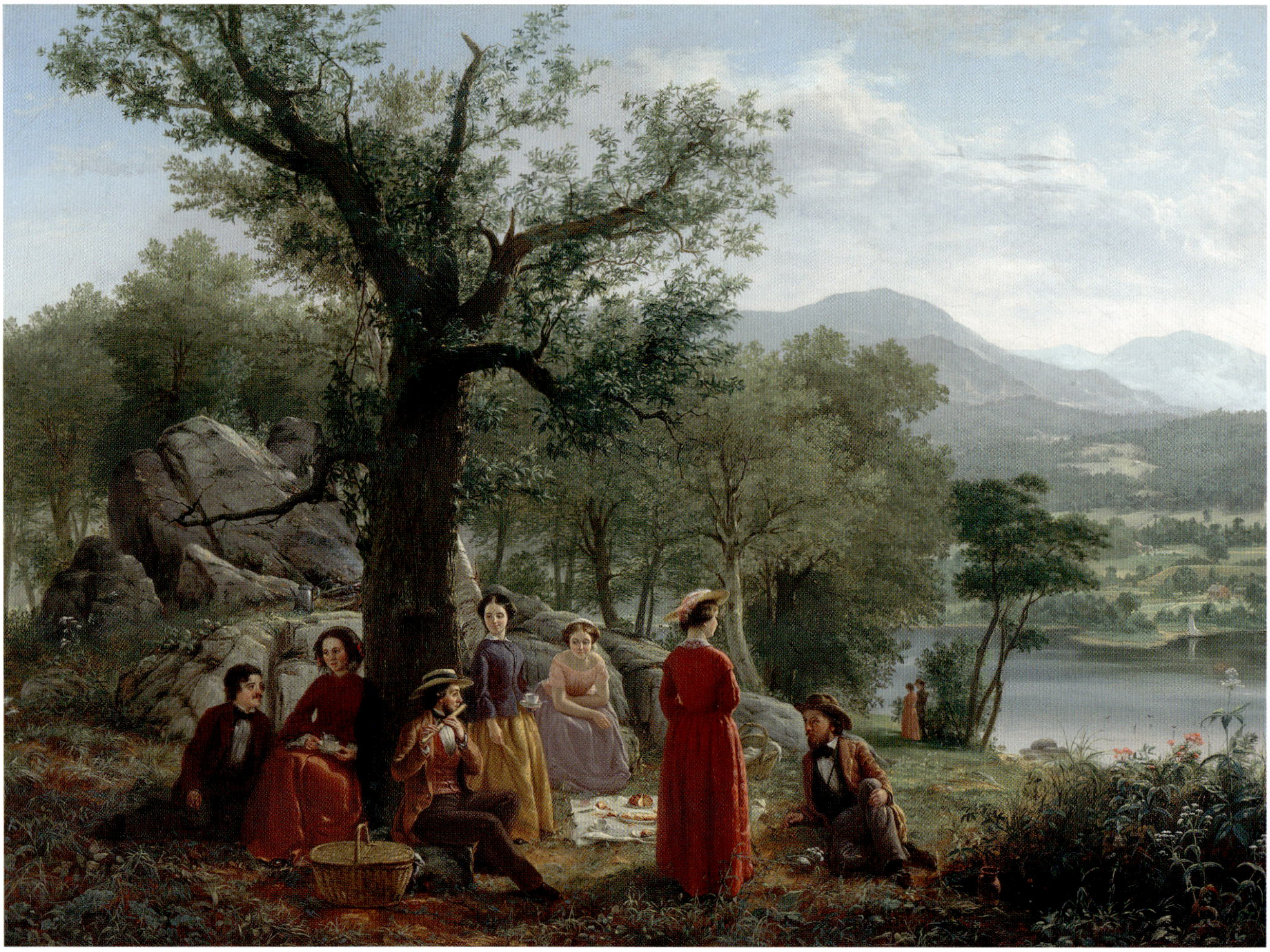

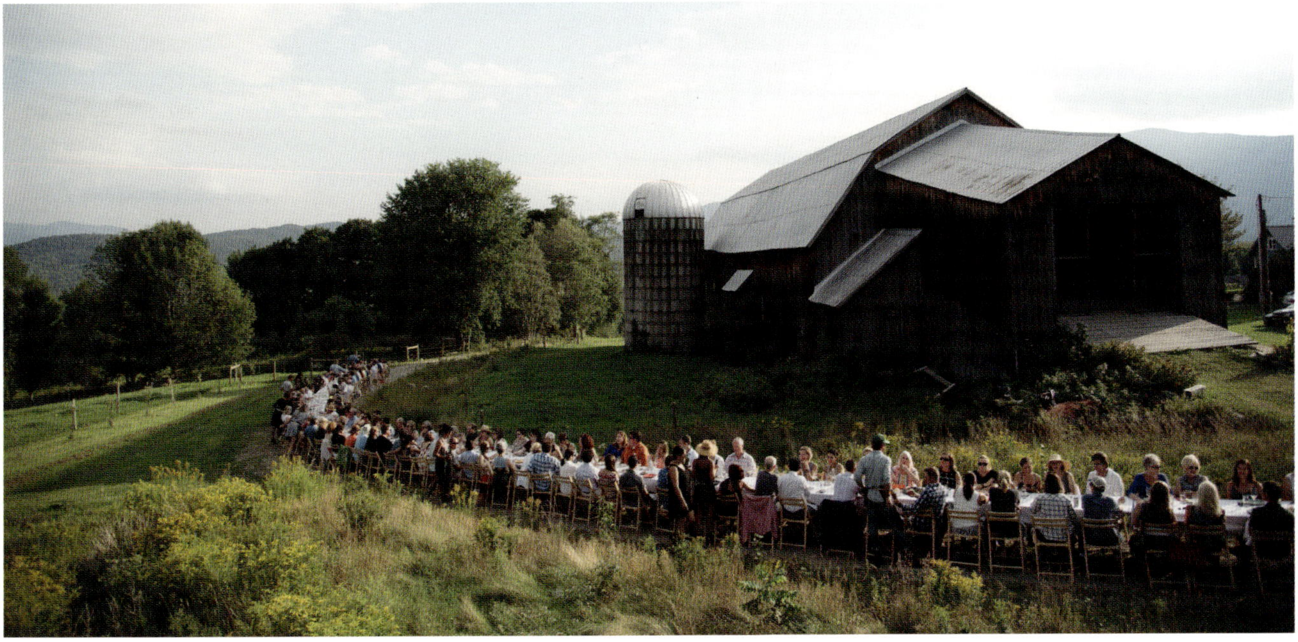

5.
Emmy Hagen, Outstanding in the Field farm dinner at Vermont's Ploughgate Creamery, for *AFAR* magazine, 2018.

trends in "farm-to-table" and "farm-to-fork" eating have contributed to the popularization of farm dinners in which chefs and farmers work together to create a meal that underscores the importance of eating communally in the places where our food is raised or grown. At today's farm dinners, tables are usually set up outdoors in the fields—sometimes the very fields where the ingredients for the meal were harvested (Fig. 5). Such rustic dinners bridge the distance between people and the environment, reconnecting participants with their local farmers and the landscape. Art historian Lee MacCormick Edwards, who wrote extensively about Thompson's life and career, stated, "[his] picnics and pastorals underscore this ethos in their description of an earlier American Eden which, in reality, was undergoing irrevocable physical and social change."[42] As Thompson's *Recreation* depicts a response to urbanization and industrialization, today's farm dinners similarly respond to the physical and social impact incurred by smart phones and digital interconnectivity. In joining together for farm meals across the United States, many now seek the same earlier Eden. Museum visitors standing before Thompson's *Recreation* may find in it "the relation between things and ourselves" and discover a similar desire to reconnect to the land.

Each artwork discussed in this chapter provides visitors with the opportunity to mine new complexities from the historic visual past when coupled with expansive and experimental ways of thinking. The display, study, and appreciation of historical American art will always be coherent and relevant, so long as scholars maintain elasticity in their ability to relate objects to contemporary concerns. As curators increasingly broaden the frames around art objects, more perspectives can be accommodated—everyone benefits when the conversation around an object is expanded to include new information, positions, and texts.[43]

The meaning of an artwork is not merely produced by its composition, content, and style, but also where it is seen, how it is displayed, and how it is framed in relation to our understanding of the present-day world. When Berger issued his invitation to question the affinity "between what we see and what we know," he did so with the understanding that "what we know" is a moveable feast: artworks move with us, constantly incorporating more information in order better to reflect our world. We will always be able to consider America's character in tandem with the physical object, and as long as we remain nonjudgmental and flexible, historical objects will always reflect contemporary American life.

Past, Present, and Future

Why Galleries Matter

Dorsey Waxter
Partner, Van Doren Waxter, New York, and Past President of the Art Dealers Association of America, New York

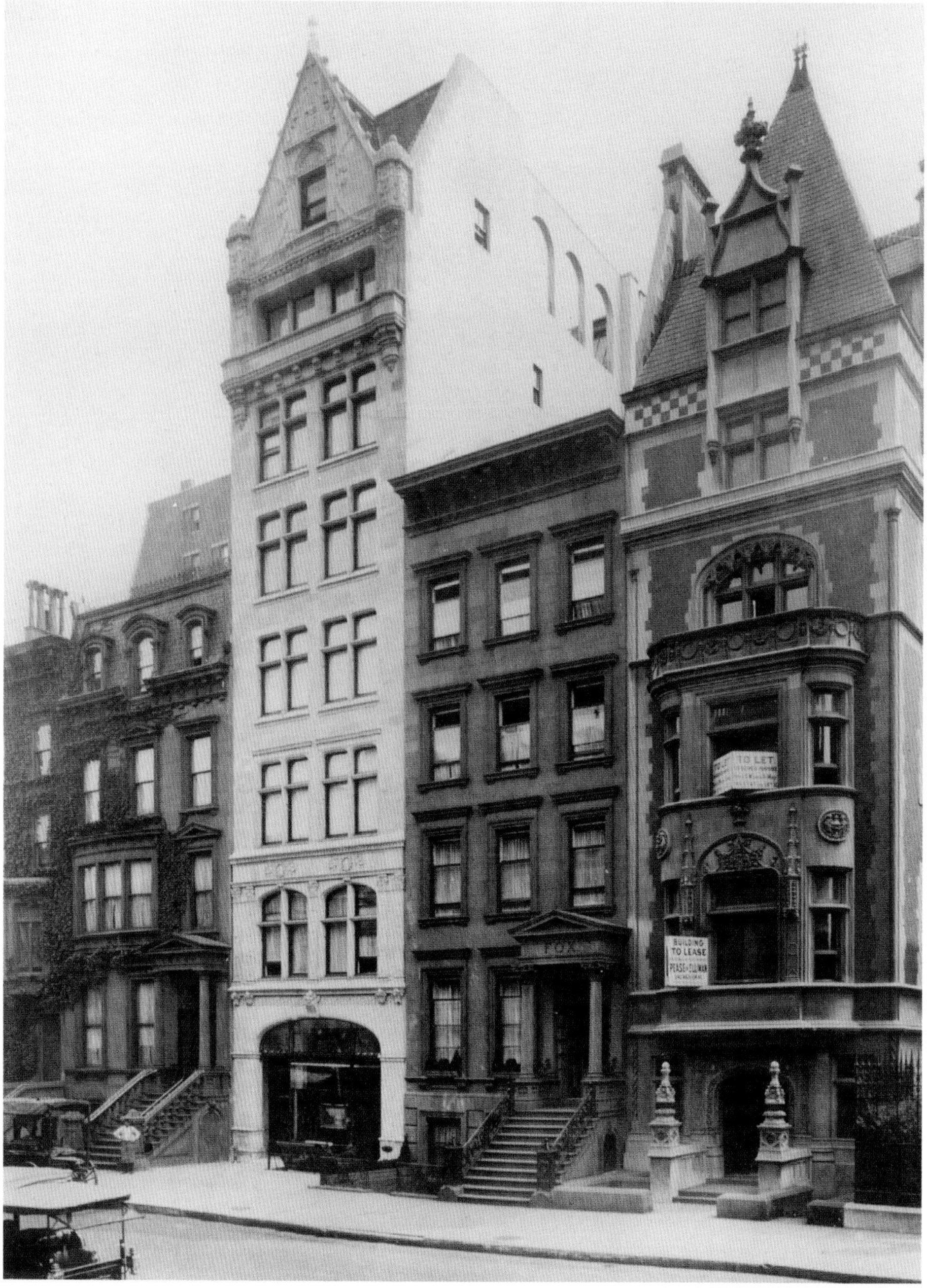

I hear a lot of complaining about the relentless calendar of events in the art world, what with art fairs, auctions, and biennials. This sentiment comes from the myriad people who are the engine of the art world: collectors, gallerists, museum curators and directors, and art writers. There are too many places that we should be visiting to see and/or buy art. As we have become fatigued, both mentally and physically, the thing we ask ourselves is whether the trip was worth the effort. Because of this all-consuming roster of events, galleries have suffered the greatest indignity of all for what remains one of the last free (commercial) cultural experiences available to the public: a scarcity of visitors. This raises the question: why go to galleries at all?

As a past President of the Art Dealers Association of America and as a gallery owner, to me it is an important question. I began to think about the ways in which galleries are vitally significant to the spiritual and economic health of the art world and have some conclusions to share. But before I get to that, I thought it would be interesting to look at the evolution of galleries, specifically in New York City. My disclaimer is that it is not possible to track this history fully here, so I have had to make selections. I am discussing New York in particular because that is where I have the most experience and because it has the largest concentration of galleries in the country—perhaps the world. My guess is that there are no fewer than 500 galleries in the city, and very likely more. That's hundreds of physical spaces and thousands of people.

In the early 1900s, mansion construction in midtown New York was slowing and commerce was moving in. What had been a desirable residential area was becoming rather more downmarket. Around the same time, dealers realized that rather than waiting for the moneyed élite to come to Europe to buy their paintings, tapestries, and porcelains, it was far more lucrative to bring the art to the United States.

Actually, the New York gallery scene started even earlier. Paul Durand-Ruel opened shop in New York in 1887, having had galleries previously in Paris and London (Fig. 1).[1] He built an eight-story building at 12 East 57th Street, with a gallery below and living quarters above.[2] He came with an inventory of 400 Impressionist paintings, which were not finding popularity among European collectors at the time.[3] He had such a big inventory because he supported artists and their studios through stipends. A stipend in this context was money paid to keep the artist solvent in exchange for his or her work. Durand-Ruel also often bought works back from clients, to support the prices he had established for these artists over a period of time. These kinds of market support are rare (and costly) today.

A few years later, the Knoedler family built an art establishment next door, at 14 East 57th Street, but without living quarters. M. Knoedler & Co. was originally a Parisian firm called Goupil & Cie, specializing in the publication and sales of prints. Michael Knoedler, who had emigrated from Paris to New York in 1848, headed up the firm on lower Broadway, which, along with sales of prints, frames, and art materials, restored paintings.[4] Eventually, he bought the firm and moved the business multiple times before bringing it to 57th Street. After his death in 1878, his son Roland took over, expanding it considerably into the areas of Old Masters and British art. It was in 1930, a time when the firm was located in a building on Fifth Avenue, that Knoedler, then owned by Roland's nephew and his partners,[5] engineered Andrew Mellon's purchase of thirty paintings that would form the core of the collection of the National Gallery of Art in Washington, DC. That sale, which many other dealers had been chasing, was made with the cash-strapped Soviet Union.[6]

Another early influential art establishment was that of the Duveen Brothers, who had galleries in Paris, London, and New York. Joseph, who was extroverted and outspoken, aspired to become the most famous Old Masters dealer in New York, and he cultivated relationships with such notable names as Henry Frick, Andrew Mellon, and John D. Rockefeller.[7] Like many other art dealers of the day, he moved his headquarters from downtown to midtown, in 1909, where he leased a space at the corner of Fifth Avenue and 56th Street.[8] Subsequently, there was a physical

1.
Paul Durand-Ruel at 12 East 57th Street, New York.
Gallery Durand-Ruel in New York, 12 East 57th St., 1913–50

2.
Little Galleries of the Photo-Secession. Photo by Alfred Stieglitz from his magazine *Camera Work*, no. 14, 1906.

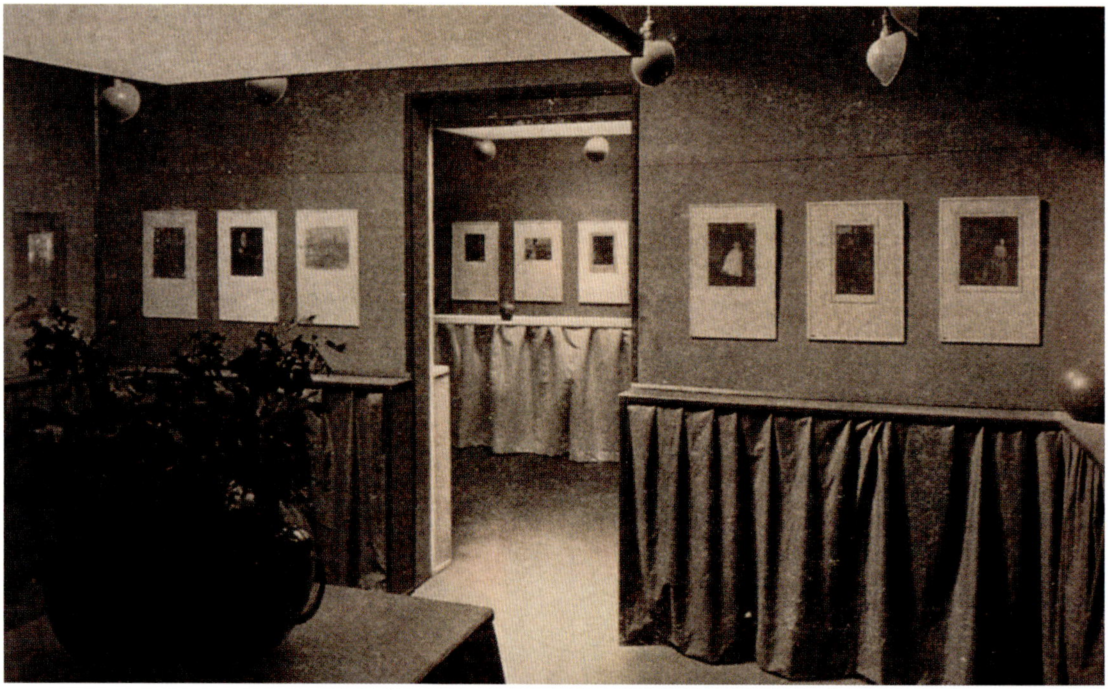

3.
Opening of Andy Warhol exhibition at Stable Gallery, 33 East 74th Street, New York, April 21, 1964.

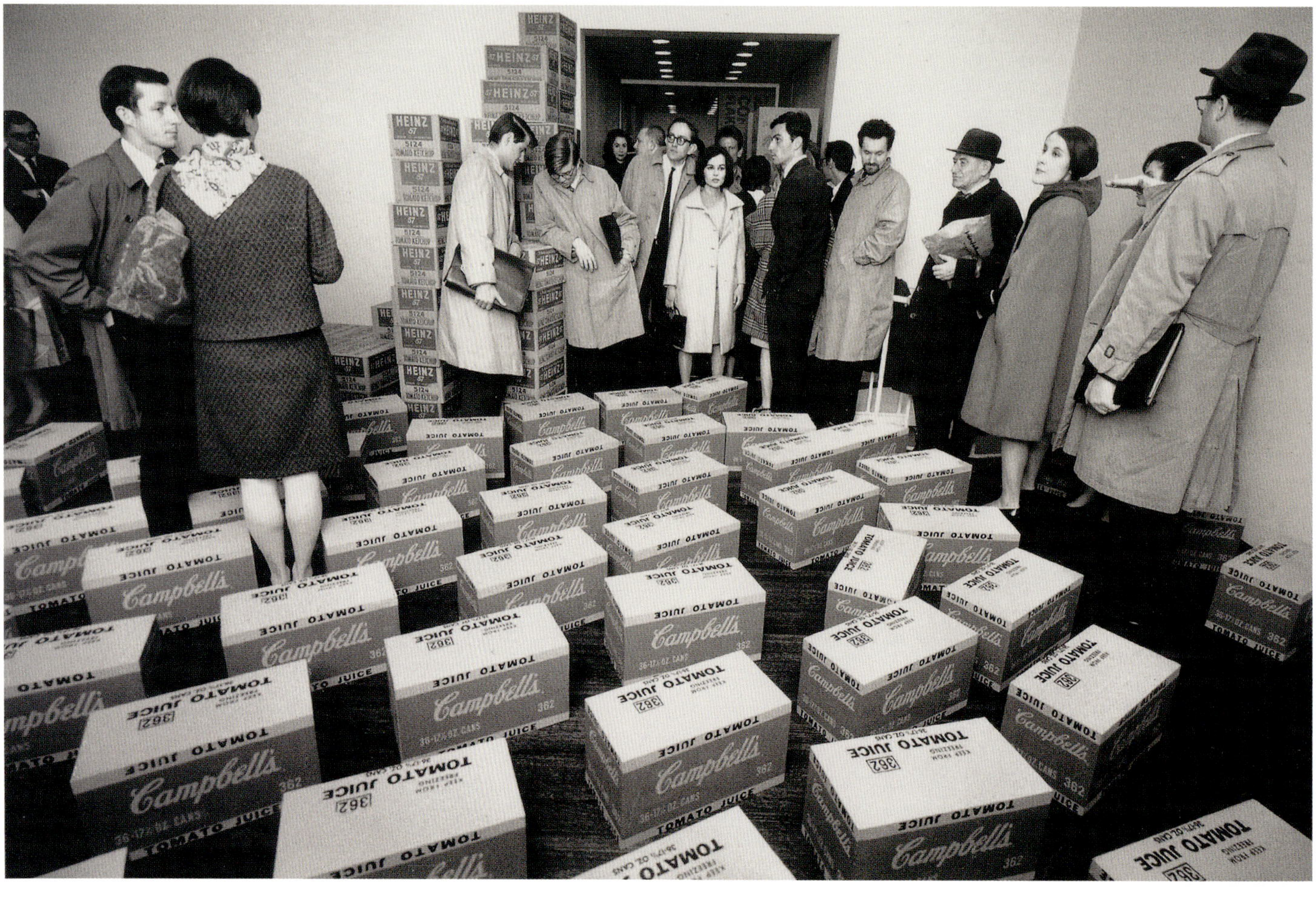

concentration of galleries in this area. As was the practice of many of these galleries, he worked with a French architect to design an elegant limestone façade that recalled the Parisian style. Inside, velvet-lined walls in different colors marked a succession of rooms hung with art that would be swapped around after a client had walked through so that they would appear refreshed upon the person's next visit.[9]

Joseph Duveen was active in New York till his death in 1939, after which the business was moved to East 79th Street.[10] Armand Lowengard, who was Duveen's nephew, and Edward Fowles soon became partners and owners of the firm. The Nazi occupation of Paris forced the closure of their office there, and the one in London closed shortly after the war. The business in New York would gradually lose its luster, and in the years 1963 to 1965, Norton Simon of Pasadena, California, bought the entire stock of important Spanish, French, and Italian eighteenth-century paintings from Fowles, along with the building at 18 East 79th Street, including the library and archive. The purchase netted Simon approximately 800 objects, many of which were subsequently sold off to recoup his investment. Today there are about 130 Duveen objects, primarily paintings, that remain in the Norton Simon Museum.[11] This is another example—after the Knoedler–Mellon transaction—of how one gallery became the source for the large holdings of a museum collection.

But the dealer who broke the prevailing mold of galleries' appearance and what they sold was Alfred Stieglitz. He began his career as a dealer by creating "Little Galleries of the Photo-Secession" (Fig. 2), located at 291 Fifth Avenue from 1905 through 1908.[12] Here he championed photography as a medium worthy of the same status as painting, to be judged on its own merits, not those dictated by the academies or conventional salons. It was an uphill battle, but, importantly, one that bolstered the role of the dealer as advocate for the new. In 1909, Stieglitz reinvigorated his gallery with a name change to simply "291." He showed Europeans and Americans who were making art of the moment, including Matisse, Rodin, Brancusi, Cézanne, and Picasso, along with the Americans Alfred Maurer, John Marin, Max Weber, Arthur Dove, and Marsden Hartley. He did not see the Americans as inheritors of the Europeans but as another group of modern artists unique to this country. His galleries were modest, intimate spaces where the art spoke for itself without a lot of fanfare. By all accounts, Stieglitz was not a shrewd businessman holding out for big sales. If a client was interested in buying a work of art, he would work out a price that was affordable. Stieglitz closed 291 in 1917 but went on to run two more galleries. From 1925 to 1929 he ran the Intimate Gallery, exhibiting the works of Dove and Marin, as well as fellow American Charles Demuth and Stieglitz's then wife Georgia O'Keeffe. From 1929 until his death, in 1946, he ran An American Place, on Madison Avenue, with a comparable roster of artists whom he ardently promoted.[13]

To better characterize the 1950s American art scene, I consulted Joan Washburn, who today owns and operates a gallery on Tenth Avenue in Chelsea and who was on the scene working for the gallery James Graham & Sons in 1955.[14] I asked her what made that era's galleries special. She replied that looking at art back then was the thing to do, that weekends were not for going out of town to a country house but instead going as a couple or an individual to look at art (Fig. 3). She explained that people were hungry for information and curious about collecting. Certainly, there was a lot to see, such as Edith Halpert's Downtown Gallery showing Dove, Jacob Lawrence, and Charles Sheeler; Antoinette Kraushaar, who showed Maurice Prendergast, Gaston Lachaise, and Guy Pène du Bois; and later, Sam Kootz, with Romare Bearden, Robert Motherwell, Adolph Gottlieb, and Hans Hofmann in his stable. Many of these galleries exhibited some combination of American and European artists, not adhering to a particular school of art.

The 1960s and 1970s brought a proliferation of different movements, such as Minimalism, video art, Conceptualism, and Post-painterly Abstraction, that demanded new and different spaces from those on 57th Street. Artists were occupying the area south of Houston Street, a manufacturing district filled with cast-iron buildings whose floors had spans of uninterrupted space. Gradually, galleries sprang up in the ground-floor spaces of these buildings, while the artists lived on the top floors. This new arts district came to be called SoHo, and it marked a forward leap in the evolution of the New York gallery.

Dealers at the forefront of the 1970s and 1980s, such as Leo Castelli, André Emmerich, Ileana Sonnabend, Pace Gallery, and Paula Cooper (Fig. 4), had galleries that were populating not just midtown but SoHo. 57th Street was soon the preserve of the established artists, whereas SoHo was where the young artists were living and exhibiting. The bigger spaces there allowed for shows of monumental works. Larger American homes and more museums accommodated, even demanded, art with scale. Increasing prices for contemporary art meant that dealers were selling the same works not just once but several times. The contemporary market was expanding and deepening in value, a trend that has exploded in the top end of the market today.

The gallery scene now is rooted in the Castelli model: dealers discover and devote time and capital to artists who change the way we look, which is not unlike Stieglitz's approach. But the market and how galleries are perceived in this scene are much more complicated. Galleries are the starting point for the activities that drive so many other entities: art fairs (Fig. 5), auctions, art advisories, e-commerce sites (Fig. 6), and even museums. In the global art world that we are trying to navigate, galleries and the dealers who own and run them are every bit as essential as the historical predecessors just discussed.

For artists, a gallery is the springboard into the world. Artists rely on the gallery to support them in ways that can be essential, such as helping them finance studios or projects that would otherwise be beyond their financial reach. The gallery is often family, seeing artists through times of creative abundance and inspirational drought.

For collectors, both new and established, galleries offer abundant opportunities to look, talk, compare, and absorb. Anyone interested in learning about art or collecting can visit gallery exhibitions, a practice that is essential in gaining the depth of knowledge to become a connoisseur. That growth in knowledge cannot evolve from looking at a computer screen—it happens in front of an artwork, preferably in conversation with an expert.

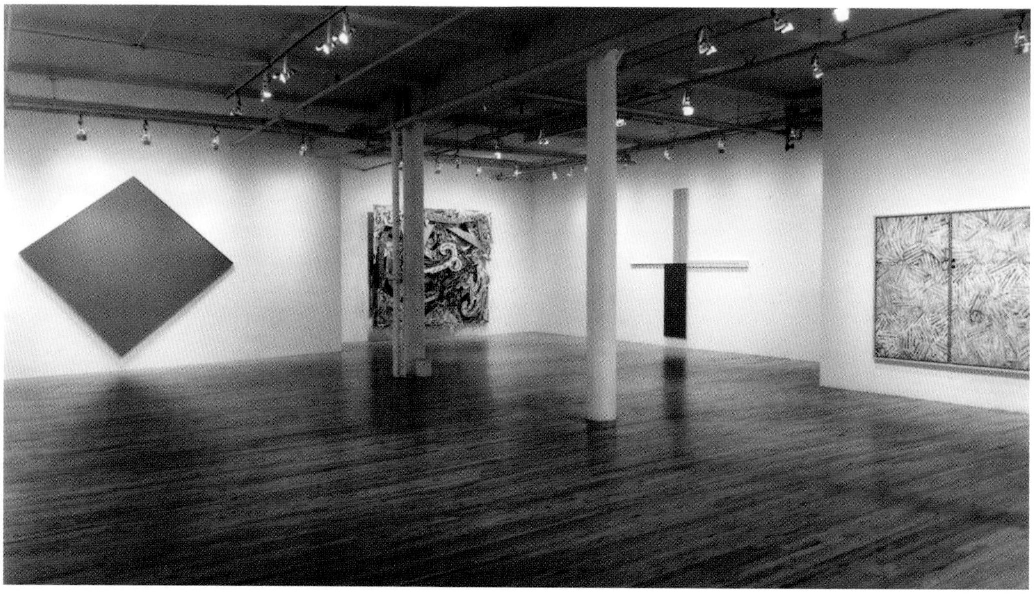

4.
Installation view, *A Painting Exhibition*, Paula Cooper Gallery, 155 Wooster Street, New York, January 18–February 23, 1983. Left to right: Ellsworth Kelly, Frank Stella, Robert Mangold, and Jasper Johns.
Participating artists: Jasper Johns, Ellsworth Kelly, Robert Mangold, Brice Marden, Elizabeth Murray, Susan Rothenberg, Robert Ryman, Frank Stella, Terry Winters.

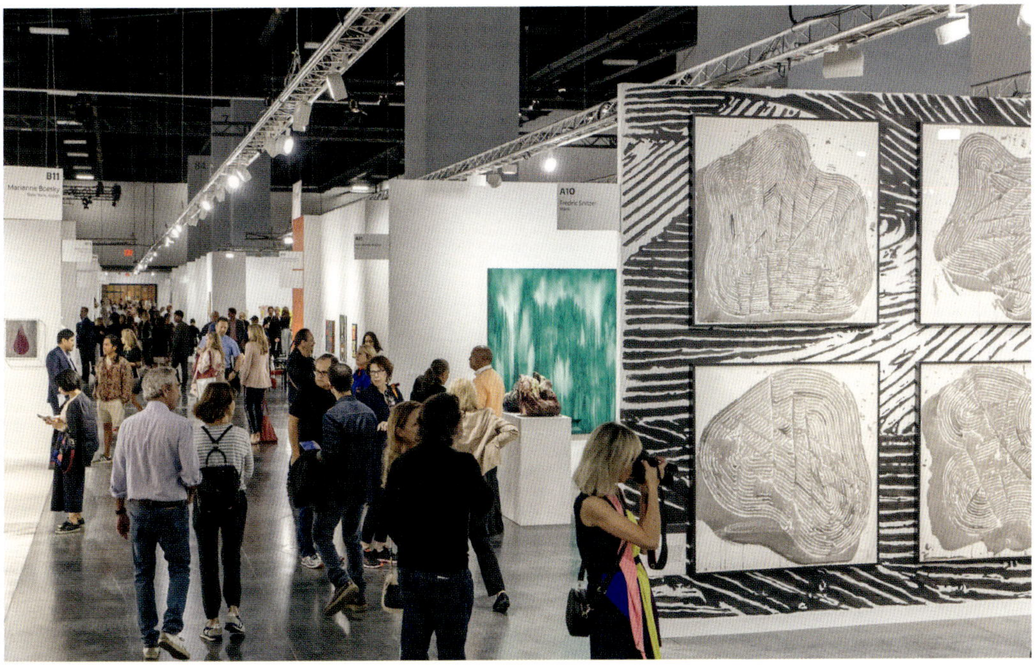

5.
General impression of Art Basel in Miami Beach 2018.
Courtesy of Art Basel

Often the collector's most lasting opinions are formed through discourse with art dealers, who—thanks to their long-term relationships with artists—frequently know more about artworks than curators, auction experts, critics, or advisors.

Because their careers are built on such long-term commitments, dealers are custodians not only of art markets but also of artistic legacies. It would be hard to conceive of a catalogue raisonné—the definitive publication of the entire output of an artist's work, which often takes decades to publish—without the wealth of information provided by a gallery's archive. Galleries are the repository of information such as when a work was exhibited, to whom it was sold or resold, or who wrote about it. Art dealers and their galleries are the support system for the artist, providing services useful to collectors, curators, and auction-house specialists.

The gallery world of 2020 can be divided roughly into three segments: small start-up operations that exhibit artists just beginning their careers, mid-sized galleries that show artists who have been exhibiting for ten years or more, and mega-galleries that show well-established artists, both living and dead. Each of these sectors is connected in a symbiotic way that, in the last decade, has caused a transformation of the marketplace, a process that is still evolving.

Small galleries are often in places that are unexpected but tethered to a location that has potential to draw a new audience. A recent example is the Lower East Side of Manhattan, where the New Museum moved and opened its new building on Bowery in 2007. In anticipation, there were already small storefront galleries populating the neighborhood. Rents were inexpensive, the area was a short walk east from SoHo, and there was an influx of small boutiques

6.
Artsy is the largest global marketplace for fine art, where collectors can explore and purchase works from over 4000 galleries, art fairs, auction houses, and institutions. Galleries partner with Artsy in order to expand their reach and connect with a global audience of millions of users.

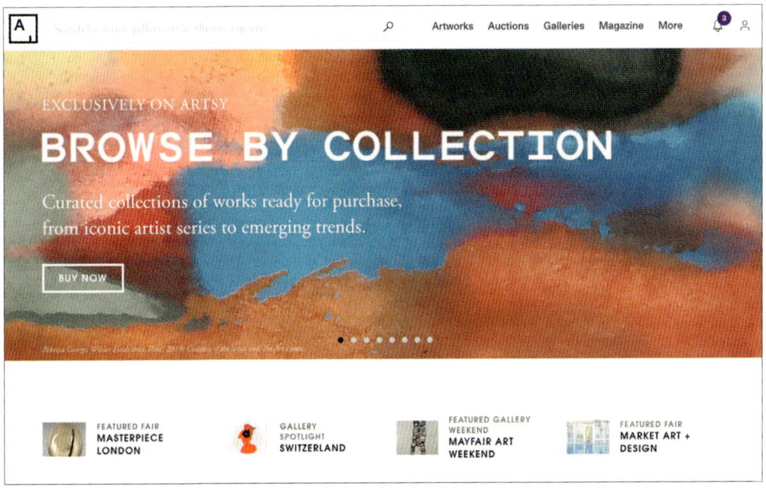

and restaurants. The atmosphere was not unlike that of SoHo in the late 1970s. And just as back then, the draw was to see works by new young artists that were being shown by their peers and sold for prices that were considered easy spending money. If a gallery of this type can hold on to one or more of these artists for a period of a couple of years, it has a chance to make a little money and possibly consider moving into a larger space. The difficulty for small galleries has been undercapitalization and poaching from other bigger galleries that can sense an artist on the rise.

Mid-sized galleries are those that have been in business for ten years or more with a roster of artists in their mid- to late careers. Some but not all mid-sized galleries operate not just in the primary market with living artists or artists' estates but also in the secondary market, defined as the selling of an artwork for a second or more time. In most cases this occurs if an artwork has increased enough in value to cover the cost of the transaction (commissions) and allow the seller to net their cost, plus some profit. These galleries represent artists who have had some measure of career success but who now require a different level of nurturing. The artist's career is not a straight rise; there are highs and lows, meaning these dealers have to be diversified enough in their stable to weather the times when an artist may not be selling well. As such, the gallery must have several artists whose works sell reliably well. Secondary market sales may be works by their own artists or works by others of a particular period or aesthetic for which the dealer has a clientele. Mid-sized galleries occupy the biggest sector of the art market, yet they are under the most pressure to survive, as will be discussed shortly.

At the top of the ladder are the mega-galleries. These entities can represent as many as a hundred artists, have multiple locations within a city or around the world and employ over a hundred people. The dealers are considered a brand unto themselves, just as the auction houses Sotheby's and Christie's have created brands. Their credibility attracts devoted clients who buy on an exclusive basis because the name of the gallery is as important as the artist they are purchasing. Within these galleries, art is often viewed in terms of a high-grade asset because of the strength and power of the gallery. Their business model is so volume-driven that they are in constant need of inventory, but only when an artist is at a particular tipping point in their career. Such an artist is often represented by a mid-sized gallery, having gained credibility within the marketplace, at which point they are vulnerable to being snapped up and moved to a bigger gallery and a higher price point.

Within this three-tiered group, poaching by a larger gallery from a smaller one has become a source of real consternation. What is most troubling here is that the gallery world is largely devoid of contracts between gallery and artist, for fear of incurring large legal expenses that cannot be sustained by either side. As a result, at any given moment an artist is able to change galleries without financial repercussions, and the gallery that has been poached loses a large part of its bottom line. This scenario has caused small and mid-sized galleries to close at an alarming rate. The most common way for larger galleries to swell their ranks continuously with artists is poaching: taking once unknown and/or under-recognized artists from the dealers who have nurtured and grown their careers.

There is another equally difficult transformation happening in the gallery world, which is that collectors no longer go to galleries to see exhibitions, choosing instead to go to art fairs, which have proliferated exponentially. There is one or more art fair somewhere in the world every week, causing galleries to rely increasingly for their revenue on these fairs where they pay to exhibit the very same artists that they show in their home galleries. Collectors are wooed by fair organizers to partake of VIP services, parties, and access to collections, in addition to looking at myriad gallery stands. Often there are between seventy and 250 exhibitors at one fair, allowing collectors a vast selection of works to consider, all concentrated in one place. The fiscal responsibility of supporting a full program of exhibitions at the home gallery along with the expense of going on the road to sell at art fairs has become fatiguing, financially and physically. There's also the negative pressure put on artists, who are expected to produce art for both one-person exhibitions and art fairs.

As long as artists are making art, there will be a need and a demand for galleries to show their work. Social media and websites may make art accessible, but they are no substitute for seeing a whole body of work in a physical space. As for the dual pressures of poaching and art fairs, could there be practical ways to alleviate these concerns and to foster more growth of the galleries in all sectors, not just more consolidation at the top end of the market?

One possible method of alleviating poaching might be to establish a tripartite agreement between the larger gallery, the smaller gallery and the artist, whereby if an artist migrates from a smaller to a larger gallery, a percentage of future sales would be paid to the smaller gallery by the larger one for a period of time. In this way, the smaller gallery is not at risk of losing so much income that it faces fiscal demise.

If collectors travel to art fairs rather than visit individual galleries, as seems to be the case, how can art fairs become more of a partner to the galleries and less of a controlling parent? Booth costs have risen overall, though some relief has been offered by fair organizers to the younger galleries in order to encourage their participation. Art fairs are where a lot of art sales are conducted, but they are also spectacles at which people walk the aisles, savor drinks, and eat good food. Since art sales are typically consummated in the first day or two of a fair, followed by two to three more days of looking by the general public without much sales activity, could a fair organizer offer galleries its "real estate," i.e. booths, at a nominal price with the agreement that the organizer and gallery would divide the profits of art sales based on how well the fair went? Could the galleries participate in a percentage of the gate? This would require a degree of disclosure never tested previously by both the organizers and the galleries, but it could foster a stronger relationship between the two groups. Such a relationship might take the sting out of the most disappointing experience nearly every gallery has had at least once: paying to participate in a fair and having no sales to show for the investment.

There are very likely other ideas worth exploring that would help galleries cope with the transformative state they find themselves in. And though I've tried to imagine a world without art dealers or galleries, and what that would be like, fortunately, I cannot. All sectors of the art world are tied to one another, though, it seems to me, galleries matter most. Their impact on artists, their influence in the arts community and body of knowledge are irreplaceable. Galleries are where the excitement of art really begins.

Shifting Tastes in American Art

Debra J. Force
President, Debra Force Fine Art, New York, and Board Member,
The Archives of American Art, Washington, DC

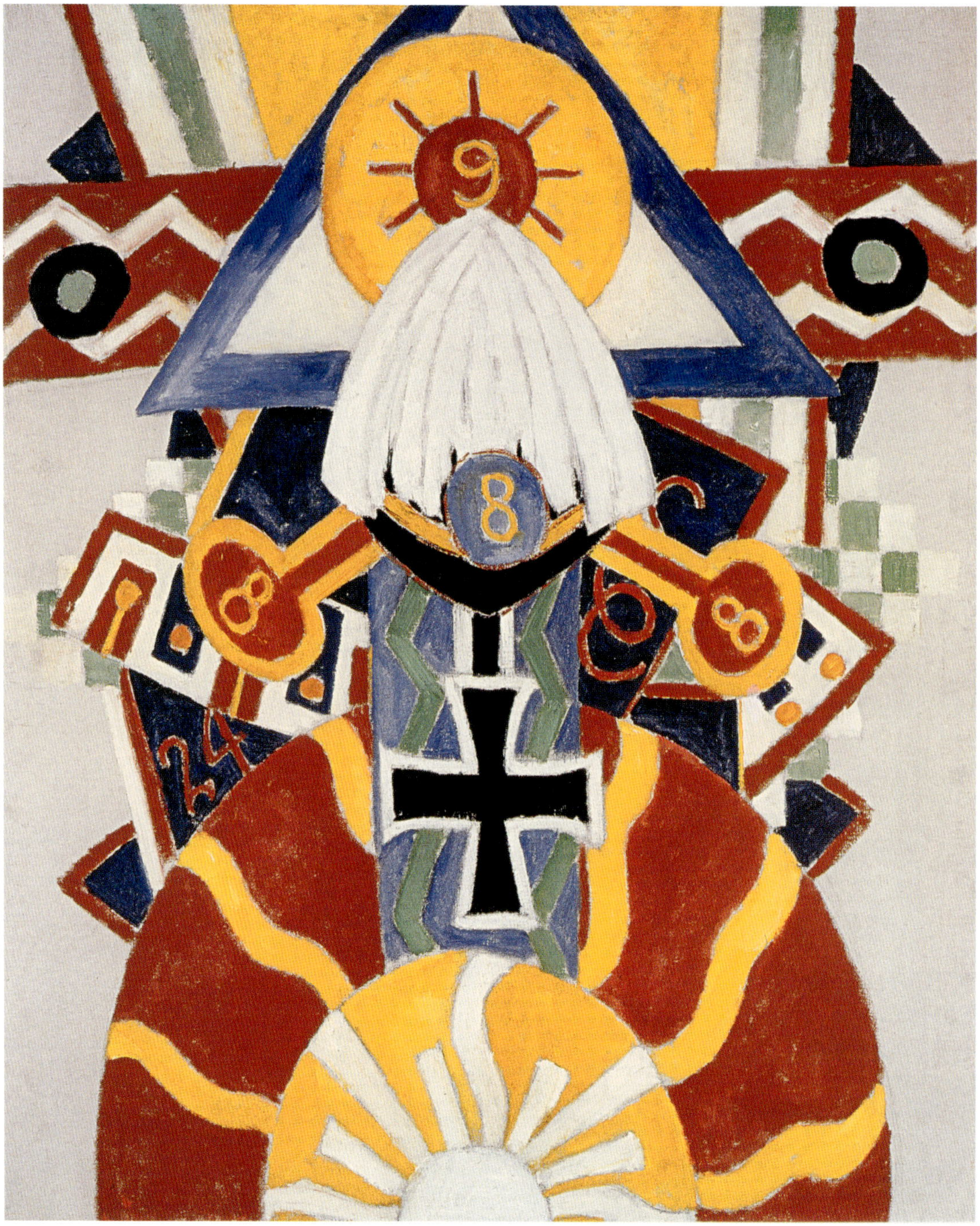

The history of collecting in America from its inception to the present resonates through the eyes of collectors and their legacies. Since the emergence of American artists in 1750, collectors have acquired the contemporary art of each period, while eventually developing an appreciation for the art of the past. Throughout, collectors have had a commonality among them: focus, motivation, passion, and nostalgia for American art. Some were artists' patrons, some collected wholly on their own, and others used mentors and advisors. Many have had the foresight and generosity to share their collections with the public through gifts to institutions or by establishing their own museums. This chapter addresses those special collectors who have had a significant impact on the evolution of American art.

In pre-Revolutionary and early America, the initial acquirers of American art were generally the élite families of Boston, Philadelphia, and Charleston, who commissioned the premier portraitists of the day to paint themselves and their children. Sitters presented themselves in all their riches from their elaborate clothing to the lush appointments of their settings in order to demonstrate their success. Patriotic fervor after the American Revolution led to multiple commissions of important historical figures such as George Washington and other Founding Fathers. From the earliest American portrait painters, Robert Feke and Jeremiah Theus, to the itinerants who traveled distances to find their sitters, to the widely popular John Singleton Copley, Gilbert Stuart, Charles Willson Peale, and Thomas Sully, American art was primarily limited to portraiture until the nineteenth century.

Developing from the European tradition, however, history painting became popular in the late eighteenth century. Much of the subject matter was religious or was copied after the Old Masters. However, American artists began painting annals of their own history. Benjamin West immortalized *Penn's Treaty with the Indians* in 1771–72 (Pennsylvania Academy of the Fine Arts), while Copley captured the daring rescue of a boy in *Watson and the Shark* from 1778 (National Gallery of Art) and John Trumbull painted his commemorative *tour de force*, *The Death of General Warren at the Battle of Bunker's Hill* in 1786 (Wadsworth Atheneum).

During this period, given the dearth of American art, most of the gentry were collecting Old Masters or contemporary European art. Thomas Jefferson, for example, was an avid collector who primarily embraced the fine art of France as well as Native American artifacts, although he did own portraits by C.W. Peale and Stuart. Others held to the notion that it was more cultured to collect European art, an overall trend that would continue into the nineteenth century and beyond, often stunting the growth of desire for America's own.

America's first original or native art was that of the Hudson River School painters. Thomas Cole, although born in England, is considered the father of the group, which included Asher B. Durand, Sanford Gifford, John F. Kensett, and Frederic Church, among others. Primarily landscape painters, these artists communed with nature and depicted the rugged, uncharted, and newly discovered views of America's wilderness.

One of the first serious patrons of American Art and the Hudson River School was Luman Reed, a prominent New York merchant who commissioned works from Cole and Durand and whose extensive collection became a large contribution to the New-York Historical Society's holdings in 1858. One of his most renowned acquisitions is one of America's masterpieces, a five-part series by Cole titled *The Course of Empire*, tracing the development of the savage wilderness through tranquility and prosperity and, ultimately, destruction (Fig. 2; see also page 171). Reed was an avid collector of genre painting, also becoming a patron of William Sidney Mount, acquiring *Bargaining for a Horse*, 1835 (New-York Historical Society). Others such as Robert Gilmor, a Baltimore merchant and shipowner, and the wealthy Daniel Wadsworth of Hartford, amateur artist and architect, were major patrons of Cole in particular; Wadsworth's collection formed the basis of the Wadsworth Atheneum, which he founded in 1842. William Wilson Corcoran, a prominent Washington, DC, banker, real estate

1.
Marsden Hartley
(1877–1943)
Painting Number 49, Berlin
1914–15
Oil on canvas
47 × 39 ½ in.
(119.4 × 100.3 cm)
Seattle Art Museum, Seattle, Gift of Barney A. Ebsworth, 2001.1067

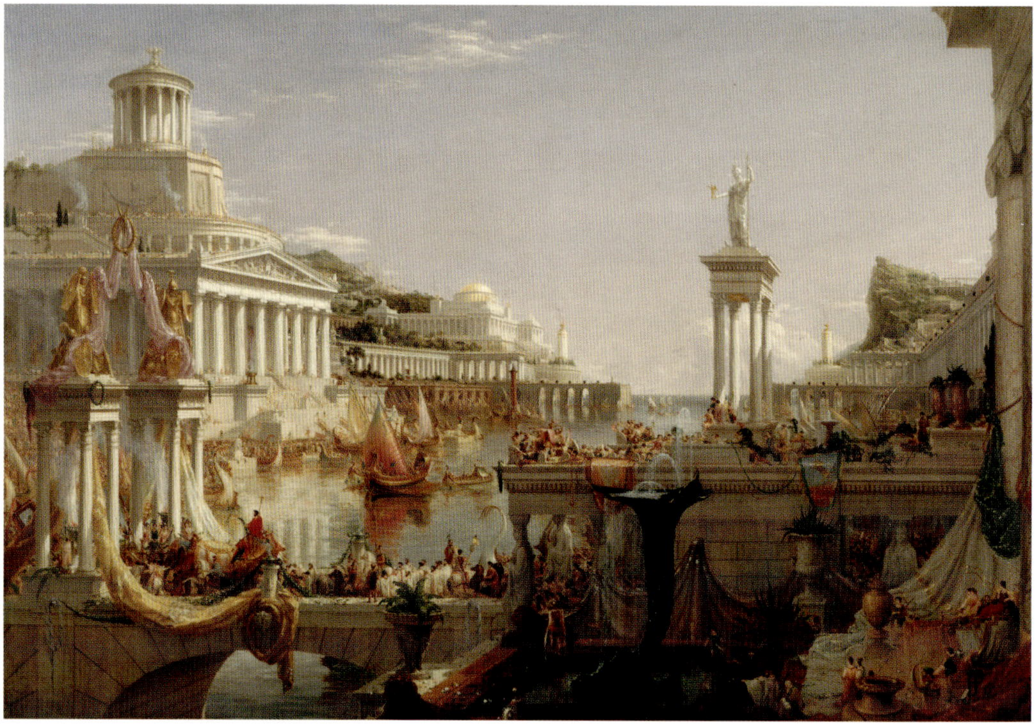

2.
Thomas Cole (1801–1848)
The Course of Empire: The Consummation of Empire
1835–36
Oil on canvas
51 ¼ × 76 in.
(130.2 × 193 cm)
New-York Historical Society Museum & Library, New York, Gift of The New-York Gallery of the Fine Arts, 1858.3

investor, and philanthropist, embraced the monumental landscapes of Frederic Church and what were then the exotic Sioux subjects of Seth Eastman, ultimately bestowing the Corcoran Gallery of Art to his native city in 1874.[1]

Up to the 1830s, collectors acted as patrons and acquired art directly from the artists and their studios, since galleries and auction houses had not yet come into being. In 1838, however, businessman James Herring opened the Apollo Gallery in New York City to provide a place for American artists to exhibit and sell their art. It was the first gallery to open at night; its hours were from 9 am and "every fair evening until nine o'clock" with the use of gas lamps.[2] It transitioned into the Apollo Association for the Promotion of the Fine Arts in the United States, eventually becoming the American Art Union, a subscription-based organization, whereby members paid an annual fee to gain admission to the gallery, a monthly subscription to a bulletin, access to a lottery for winning works of art, and the receipt of an engraving or sculpture made by a famous American artist. The most popular subjects in painting were genre-related, often sentimental and idealistic, or scenes showing conflict among the classes, patriotism, or conquest of the continent.[3] The American Art Union provided the resource for American artists to thrive and sell their works, which previously had been difficult for them on their own.

The first semblance of a traditional American art gallery materialized in 1852, when John Snedecor founded Babcock Galleries, also in New York, selling the contemporary art of the day. By the 1860s, Vose Galleries in Boston followed; both remain extant. In terms of public sales, although auction houses had existed in Europe (Sweden) since the seventeenth century and in the United Kingdom since the eighteenth century, Freeman's in Philadelphia, although regional, was the earliest and primary such venue in the United States, having been organized in 1805. Buying American fine art at auction was therefore limited until 1883, when the American Art Association was founded in New York to promote American art in a highly visible and cosmopolitan auction venue.[4]

In some cases, collectors became advisors or private dealers. Thomas B. Clarke, a New Yorker in the linen and lace business in the 1870s, was a leading patron of the Hudson River School; two of his most highly revered artists were Albert

Bierstadt and George Inness. In 1888, he retired to become a full-time dealer as well as the art advisor to J.P. Morgan. Like another New Yorker, Samuel P. Avery, he used his connoisseurship in his own collecting as well as to inspire others.

Collectors who were world travelers brought an even more expansive scope to their art holdings. Originally from New York and later Detroit, Charles Lang Freer, an industrialist with pursuits in railroad and automobile concerns, made a more notable contribution as an art collector and patron. His collecting interests were Asian, Middle Eastern, and American, and he was particularly enamored of Asian culture and its influence in James McNeill Whistler's works. The two met in London around 1890, became friends and engaged in riveting correspondence during their lifetimes. Freer embraced the artist's aesthetics, purchasing the Peacock Room from the estate of Frederick Leyland, a wealthy shipowner from Liverpool and Whistler's English patron, who had originally installed it in his London home to display his Chinese blue and white porcelain (Fig. 3).

Freer also offered patronage to several other artists of the time, including Thomas Wilmer Dewing, Abbott Handerson Thayer, and Dwight Tryon, ultimately owning over forty of Dewing's works. Freer's collecting philosophy was clear: "… a masterpiece required neither explanation nor cultural context to communicate its message: its importance lay in its aesthetic integrity, not in the evidence it might incidentally provide about religious, social, political, or economic issues."[5] His vision was secured when he donated his entire collection of 5000 objects to the United States in 1906 and provided funding for the building, now the Freer Gallery of Art in Washington, DC.

In early twentieth-century New York, Gertrude Vanderbilt Whitney, an accomplished sculptor in her own right, became a major patron of the arts, supporting the contemporary art of the time by funding exhibitions, the Armory Show of 1913, and shows in her own studio on West 8th Street in Greenwich Village (Fig. 4). She became a champion of The Eight, acquiring their art and encouraging camaraderie

3.
James McNeill Whistler
(1834–1903)
The Princess from the Land of Porcelain, 1863–65
Oil on canvas
78 ¾ × 45 ¾ in.
(201.5 × 116.1 cm)
In The Peacock Room
Freer Gallery of Art, Smithsonian Institution, Washington, DC, Gift of Charles Lang Freer, F1903.91a-b, Item #2

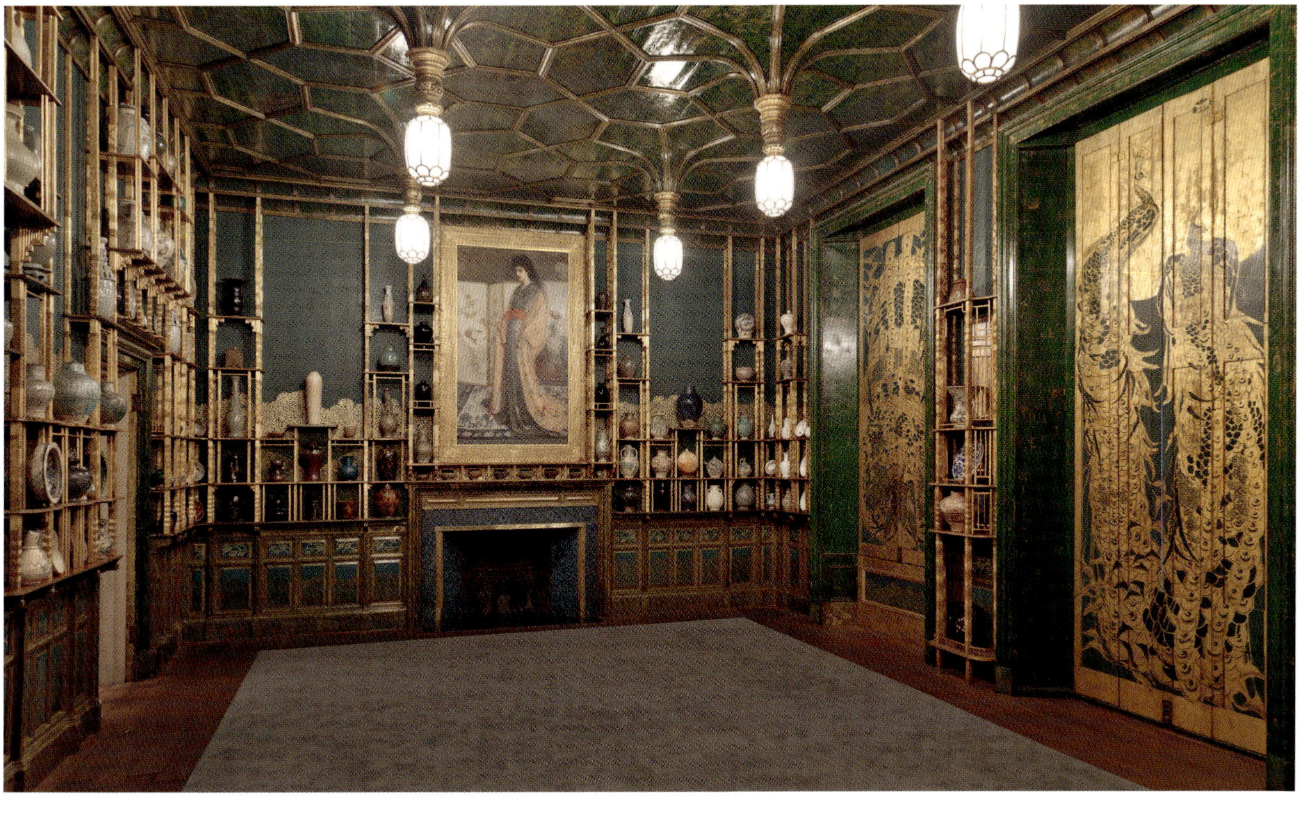

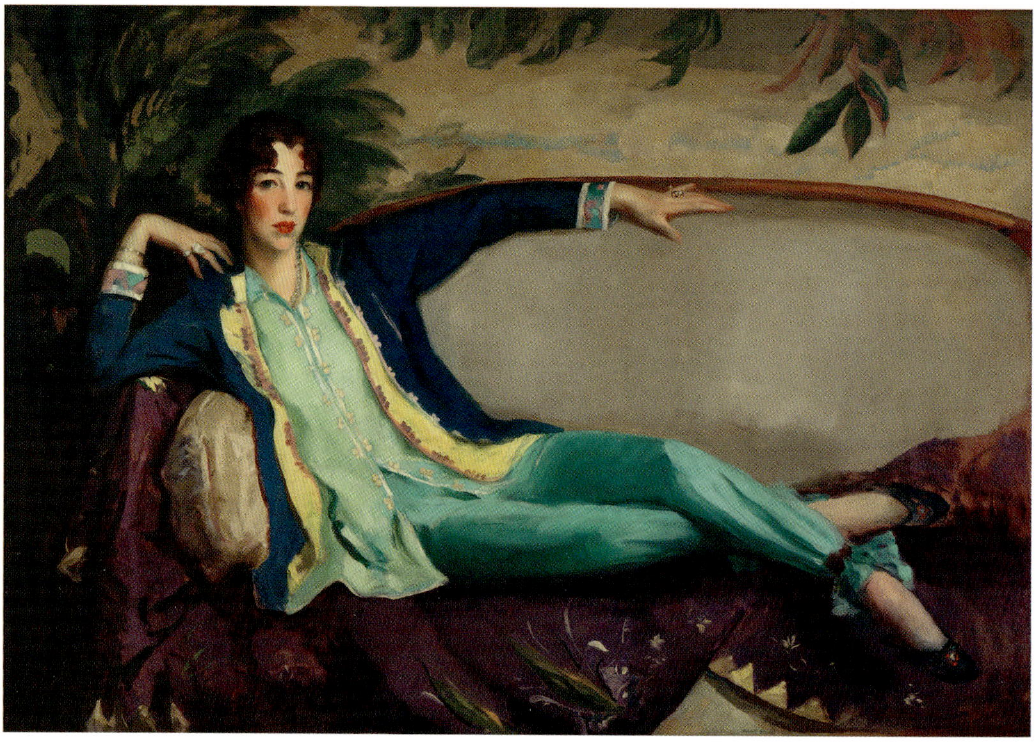

4.
Robert Henri (1865–1929)
Gertrude Vanderbilt Whitney
1916
Oil on canvas
49 15/16 × 72 in.
(126.8 × 182.9 cm)
Whitney Museum of American Art, New York, Gift of Flora Whitney Miller, 86.70.3

and artistic interaction among them. Her legacy is the Whitney Museum of American Art, which she formed in 1931, when The Metropolitan Museum of Art refused to accept the donation of her twenty-five-year-old collection of over 500 modern works.[6] The snobbishness against and lack of regard for the contemporary American art of the time was almost universal in the 1930s, unlike the embracing of such art today. European art remained the bill of fare among the culturally élite.

Likewise, Dr. Albert Barnes of Philadelphia faced a similar dilemma. Having grown up in the slums, he propelled himself to become a prominent doctor, chemist, businessman, collector, and educator. After he made considerable wealth from the manufacture of Argyrol, he began collecting art and enlisted his high-school classmate, the artist William Glackens, to help him.[7]

In 1912, Barnes sent Glackens to Paris with around $20,000 to buy art and ultimately acquired major works by Auguste Renoir, Henri Matisse, Pablo Picasso, and Paul Cézanne.[8] Both Leo and Gertrude Stein and the dealer Paul Guillaume were also helpful to Barnes. Widening his vision beyond the European masters, he embraced American art, ultimately collecting works by Glackens, Charles Demuth, Horace Pippin, and Maurice Prendergast. In 1923, Barnes exhibited some of his collection at the Pennsylvania Academy of the Fine Arts but found it ill-received as being too avant-garde for local public taste. As a result, when faced with the placement of his collection, as neither the Academy nor the Philadelphia Museum of Art was an option, he established the Barnes Foundation.

Duncan Phillips, the Washington, DC, collector and art critic from a wealthy Pittsburgh family, is distinguished for introducing Modern Art to America and for building his collection for a museum from the outset. He began acquiring European masters to serve as a reference point for the young, contemporary artists that he was supporting by buying their art. His patronage gave them the means to pursue their art and among his favorites were John Marin and Arthur Dove. As with Dr. Barnes in Philadelphia, Phillips faced similar obstacles in Washington. During the 1920s, America was critical of modern art, which was viewed as a break from the achievements of the past, but Phillips sought to change that notion by displaying more traditional work along with Modernism. His vision was to bring together "congenial spirits among artists;" the Phillips Collection opened in 1921 and follows this tenet today.[9]

By the 1920s, galleries handling contemporary American art became available for collectors. Kraushaar Galleries, established in 1885, focused upon Urban Realism and Modernism and represented Glackens, George Luks, and John Sloan. Alfred Stieglitz formed the Intimate Gallery in 1925 and later, An American Place, featuring the works of his wife Georgia O'Keeffe, Dove, Marsden Hartley, and Marin. Women gallerists were also influential; Edith Halpert founded the Downtown Gallery in Greenwich Village in 1926, focusing upon American Modernists.[10]

While Whitney, Barnes, and Phillips were supporting living artists, a patriotic movement, nostalgia for America's past, and interest in collecting eighteenth- and nineteenth-century American fine and decorative art emerged in the 1920s and 1930s as well as the establishment of historic restorations such as Greenfield Village, Sturbridge Village, and Colonial Williamsburg. Henry Francis du Pont, a member of Delaware's prominent industrialist family, embraced this mission wholeheartedly. He had inherited the family home, Winterthur, built in 1837, expanding it in 1928–32 to house his superb collection of furnishings enhanced by paintings to fit the décor of his period rooms. Similarly, Ima Hogg, a Houston philanthropist, began collecting for her 1928 home, later opened to the public as Bayou Bend in 1966.

During this period, one of the more colorful collectors who wholeheartedly embraced his newly found country was Maxim Karolik, a Russian-born opera singer who met heiress Martha Codman while performing at her home in Newport, Rhode Island. From one of Boston's wealthiest families, she was so enamored of Karolik that she invited him to join her on a trip to Europe to buy art for the Museum of Fine Arts, Boston. Karolik was thirty-five years her junior, but they ended marrying and amassing one of the largest and finest collections of nineteenth-century American art in the United States.

Rather than bestowing patronage upon living artists, the Karoliks' mission was to form an historic collection to enable the MFA to become a national museum, as opposed to a provincially recognized institution focusing on Boston artists. Between 1938 and 1964, the Karoliks gave over 2000 objects, including works by Bierstadt, Cole, Martin Johnson Heade, Thomas Moran, and John Frederick Peto, to the museum (Fig. 5).[11] In his collecting, Maxim Karolik sought advice from curators and dealers, and in his pursuit was motivated by quality over the renown of an artist.

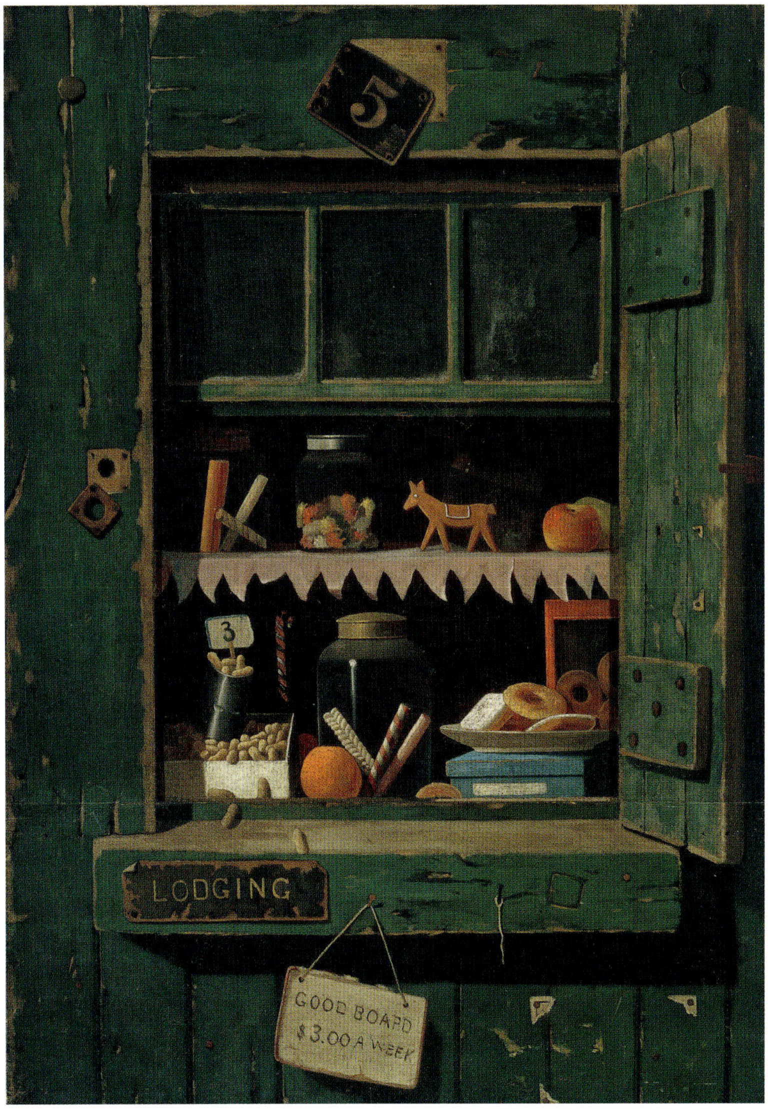

5.
John Frederick Peto
(1854–1907)
The Poor Man's Store, 1885
Oil on canvas and panel
35 ½ × 25 ⅝ in.
(90.17 × 65.09 cm)
Museum of Fine Arts, Boston, Gift of Maxim Karolik for the M. and M. Karolik Collection of American Paintings, 1815–1865, 62.278

His motto was: "Tell me whether the painting is good, and I will not care who the painter is."[12]

From the 1950s to the 1970s, a handful of collectors began to address American Impressionism, an area neglected primarily because of the bias toward its European counterpart. In addition, given the eruption of post-war Abstraction, American Impressionists were no longer considered in vogue, even though they had been collectible during their lifetimes. These collectors were of more modest means than those discussed previously and, given the price accessibility of such art, found that they could afford to form small, choice collections within their budgets. They generally bought from galleries, since at that period auctions were havens for the trade and not frequented by private collectors.

Many were couples who worked as teams in their collecting and they indeed became role models for the collectors who followed in the later twentieth century. Margaret and Raymond Horowitz from New York would walk up and down Madison Avenue on Saturdays, visiting American art galleries and buying only what both liked. Given the reasonableness of the market, they were able to acquire many museum-quality examples by Impressionists such as William Merritt Chase, Childe Hassam, and Theodore Robinson. Their collection was shown at the National Gallery of Art in 1999, and upon their deaths, The Mr. and Mrs. Raymond J. Horowitz Foundation for the Arts, Inc., was formed for funding American art exhibitions and projects.

Rita and Daniel Fraad from Scarsdale, New York, were friends with Mr. and Mrs. Horowitz, and their camaraderie encouraged both couples to learn more about the field; in turn, they influenced one another. At one point, the two couples were looking at the Sargent painting *Group with Parasols (A Siesta)*, 1905, at Hirschl & Adler Galleries, and according to Mr. Horowitz, he and his wife would have bought it in an instant if they could have afforded it at the time. Mrs. Fraad adored the work's lyric and painterly quality; however, her husband did not really care for it as he gravitated toward more vigorous paintings. Mrs. Fraad and the Horowitzes succeeded in convincing Mr. Fraad to buy it and the painting became one of their most revered pieces. When their collection was sold at Sotheby's in 2004, *Group with Parasols* graced the cover of the auction catalogue and realized a record price for the artist at $23,528,000.[13]

The Fraad collection was widely exhibited and included works by Winslow Homer, George Bellows, and The Eight. Others such as Vivian and Meyer Potamkin of Philadelphia collected similarly and much of their collection graces the walls of the Pennsylvania Academy of the Fine Arts and Philadelphia Museum of Art. New York collectors Joy and Erving Wolf took a somewhat different tack in acquiring American paintings, sculpture, and furniture and over the years have made generous donations to The Metropolitan Museum of Art.

Somewhat later, Arthur Altschul, a New York collector of American Impressionism and The Eight, JoAnn and Julian Ganz, Los Angeles collectors of major nineteenth-century American paintings, and Marie and Hugh Halff, San Antonio collectors of American Impressionism and Modernism, likewise embraced the field. Sandy and Robert London, Atlanta, used a more unusual approach by acquiring American artists specifically represented in the Barnes Collection and by following the radical installation method conceived by Dr. Barnes. Paula and Peter Lunder have kept much of their collection of Western art, Whistlers, and major nineteenth- and twentieth-century works intact by generously gifting over 1000 works to the Colby College Museum of Art in Maine and by establishing the Lunder Institute for American Art in 2017.[14]

Another collector who was able to take advantage of reasonable values for traditional American art was Dr. John J. McDonough, a gynecologist from Youngstown, Ohio. McDonough developed a more textbook collecting approach, buying everything from early portraiture through The Eight. An avid and passionate collector, he acquired many museum-quality works, such as *Breakfast in Bed*, by his favorite artist Mary Cassatt (Fig. 6). Sadly, after a divorce, he was forced to sell his collection at auction in 1978. His sale witnessed the first time

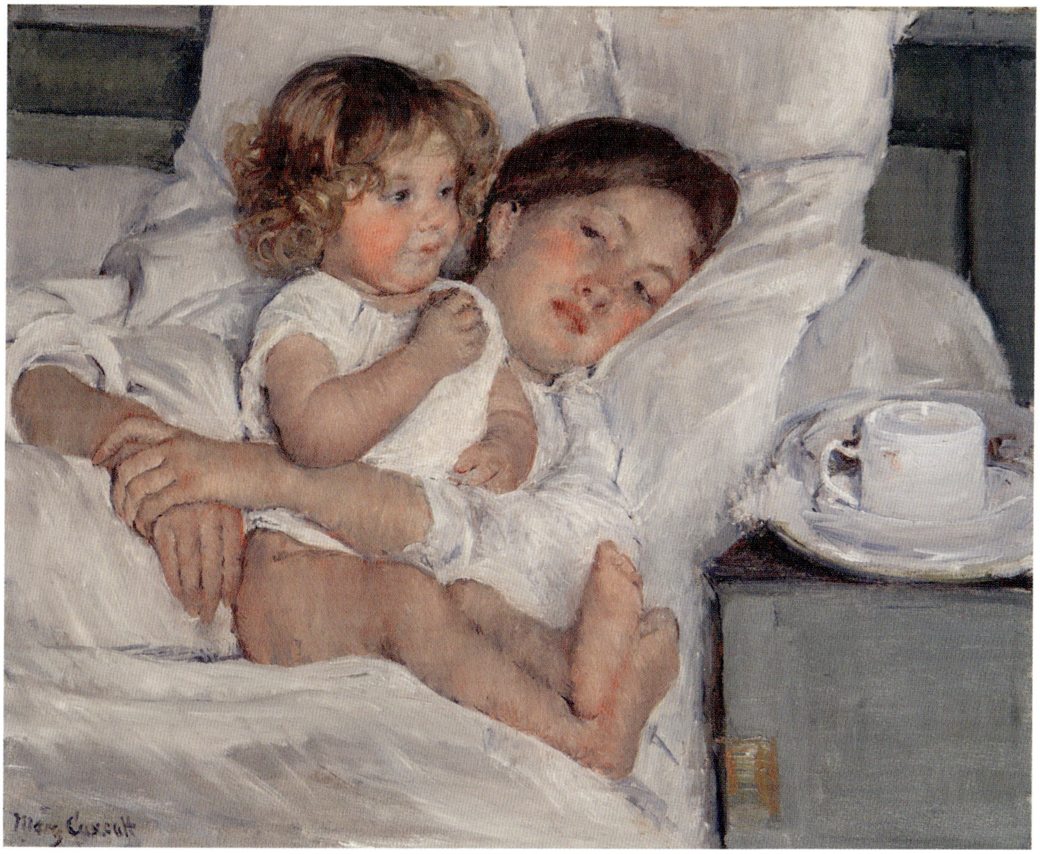

6.
Mary Cassatt (1844–1926)
Breakfast in Bed, 1897
Oil on canvas
23 × 29 in. (58.4 × 73.7 cm)
The Huntington Library, Art Collections, and Botanical Gardens, San Marino, CA, Gift of the Virginia Steele Scott Foundation, 83.8.6

that American art sold for meaningful prices at auction, thereafter encouraging the participation of private collectors, rather than merely the trade. Driven by his passion, Dr. McDonough did not let the sale slow him down and he began a second collection, which, given new price levels in the market, precluded him from buying the quality that he had had previously.

Impressionism and Modernism were not the only movements that were popular from the mid-twentieth century onward. A group of collectors mostly west of the Mississippi were infatuated with Western art, both landscape and genre subjects. One such aficionado was Amon Carter of Fort Worth, Texas, whose collection of Frederic Remington and Charles Marion Russell is immortalized in the Amon Carter Museum of American Art, founded in 1961. The real thrust for collecting Western art, however, emerged in the 1970s with the oil boom and included two of the most fervent and influential collectors: cattleman William Foxley, who focused upon the art of the West from 1832 to 1940 and established his own museum in Denver (1983–98), and oil man and entrepreneur Philip Anschutz whose collection of Western landscapes by Bierstadt and Moran along with historical cowboy, Taos, and Modernist Western art has traveled internationally and is now housed in the American Museum of Western Art in Denver. Collectors of this genre have always been competitive and yet have nurtured special fraternal relationships that set them apart from those collecting in other areas. Over the years, they have frequented specialized galleries, such as Rosenstock in Denver, Forrest Fenn in Santa Fe, or Bartfield in New York, and today at a smattering of resources in Montana, Phoenix, Santa Fe, and Texas, as well as at auctions such as Coeur d'Alene's.

In the late 1970s and the 1980s, two rivals who were often on the hunt for the same material emerged, Richard Manoogian and Daniel Terra. In the days before the internet and email were in universal use, who won the prize was dependent upon which one received the phone call first. Richard Manoogian from Detroit, the head of Masco Corporation, was a major player in the field for decades and largely relied on specific gallerists, American art experts, and auction-house specialists for guidance to amass his collection of nineteenth- and early twentieth-century American art. His collection has traveled worldwide and in the twenty-first century he sold much of it to prominent entities such as Crystal Bridges Museum of American Art and major collectors in Pennsylvania, Seattle, and Virginia, among others. His generosity has placed works at the Detroit Institute of Arts and at the National Gallery of Art, which received the iconographic George Caleb Bingham's *The Jolly Flatboatmen*, 1846. Mr. Manoogian also enjoyed the asset quality of the works he was buying and, as Raymond Horowitz commented, "... we knew that everything was for sale at one time or another."[15]

Daniel Terra from Pennsylvania made his fortune from Lawter Chemicals, which in turn allowed him to collect. His collecting interests were insatiable. Terra bought primarily from one gallery, at auction, directly from collectors, and acquired many iconographic American nineteenth-century, Impressionist, and early twentieth-century works, such as Samuel F.B. Morse's *Gallery of the Louvre*, 1831–33 (see page 183). He established a museum, first in Evanston, Illinois, and later in Chicago, and had a museum near Monet's property in Giverny. Ultimately, his philanthropy led to the establishment of the Terra Foundation for American Art, which funds worldwide projects devoted to the promotion of American art.

Barney Ebsworth, a luxury travel business entrepreneur from St. Louis and later, Seattle, began collecting Dutch seventeenth-century painting and Japanese prints in the mid-1960s and moved on to American Modernism in the 1970s, followed by post-war art. He had the distinction of being one of the few collectors who became friends with Georgia O'Keeffe. From her he bought *Music—Pink and Blue, No.1* from 1918, which he gifted to the Seattle Art Museum, along with Marsden Hartley's *Painting Number 49, Berlin* (Fig. 1). When Mr. Ebsworth's collection was sold in 2018, his well-known Edward Hopper painting *Chop Suey*, 1929 (location unknown—see page 175), sold for $91,875,000, a record price for any American artwork made before 1945.

Myron Kunin from Minneapolis founded Regis Corporation and began collecting American Modernism in his quiet, unassuming fashion in the 1970s. He was fastidious in his endeavor to collect in depth, often acquiring several examples by a given artist in order to exhibit their full impact. He had eclectic interests in other fields such as Old Masters, African, and nineteenth-century and Impressionist American art, and acted when he saw an opportunity. His expert eye led him to acquire, and later sell for record prices, Bierstadt's *The Last of the Buffalo*, 1888, and Cassatt's *The Conversation*, 1896, both sold at Christie's in 1988.[16]

However, Kunin's passion was truly for Modernism including the works of Ralston Crawford, Stuart Davis, Dove, Hartley, the rare Gerald Murphy, and Charles Sheeler. His motto was: "I like a painting that reaches in and grabs your heart and stomps on it."[17] He loved to discuss art with dealers and others in the field, but generally was his own man when it came to an acquisition. After his death, much of his collection was placed on view at the Minneapolis Institute of Art, while during his lifetime, some works were sold to the Amon Carter Museum and the Crystal Bridges Museum of American Art. Mr. Kunin enjoyed both the hunt for the right picture and the challenge of selling.

A bigger than life personality, Jack Warner was an impassioned collector who loved tracing American history through his art collection, beginning with early portraiture and moving to Modernism. He collected personally as well as corporately through Gulf States Paper Corporation in Tuscaloosa, Alabama, his family's business. Two of his best-known works were Cole's *Falls of the Kaaterskill* (private collection) and Daniel Garber's *Tanis*

(Philadelphia Museum of Art). Mr. Warner used the "shoot from the hip" method of collecting; that is, he never asked anyone for advice, but did it all on his own. He bought from both dealers and at auction and often sat in the saleroom of the latter, holding his paddle high and continuously until he was the successful bidder.

Another constituency that has produced significant collectors is the entertainment industry. Although many such as Edward G. Robinson, Billy Wilder, and Anne and Kirk Douglas focused upon European art, others such as Frank Sinatra found American paintings to their liking. Mr. Sinatra particularly admired the work of Hassam and owned *The Fourth of July, 1916* (The New-York Historical Society), one of the artist's celebrated Flag paintings from World War I. Cole Porter was instrumental in garnering interest among his celebrity friends for Grandma Moses, whose works appear in many Hollywood and New York collections. In more recent times, Steve Martin, Barbra Streisand, and Oprah Winfrey have been active participants in the American art market. Mr. Martin began collecting more traditional American paintings and later moved into more post-war and contemporary art; however, his Hopper, *Captain Upton's House*, 1927, remains one of his signature pieces. Ms. Streisand collected and later sold her Arts and Crafts and Art Deco furniture, although she still collects female figurative paintings and Modernism, while Ms. Winfrey collects African American artists as well as the work of Thomas Hart Benton. Although frequenting New York galleries, many Hollywood collectors relied upon the expert eye of Terry DeLapp, a Los Angeles-based dealer, active from the 1960s to 1990s.

Numerous collectors have been reliant on mentors, whether in the trade or museums. Several influential galleries such as Hirschl & Adler (still extant), Knoedler, and Spanierman have enriched the collections of many. Imparting its infectious belief in the validity of American art, Kennedy Galleries (founded in 1874) in New York was responsible for building numerous collections throughout the United States over a period of decades.[18] Thomas Gilcrease's outstanding collection of Western art (now the Gilcrease Museum in Tulsa) grew primarily from his relationship with the gallery. Likewise, Harold Hochschild who put together the Adirondack Museum, Harrison Eiteljorg of Indianapolis in his quest for major Western art and sculpture, and members of the Havemeyer and Rockefeller families were all Kennedy devotees.[19]

Winton ("Red") Blount was a later disciple whose mission was to acquire a chronological collection with representative examples from each period of art from Copley to Hopper. Kennedy's expansive inventory enabled the acquisition of outstanding works, including three Hoppers, which later became the core of the Montgomery Museum of Fine Arts. Others who were guided similarly include Alvin and Jean Snowiss of Lock Haven, Pennsylvania, with a comprehensive survey of American art and eventual gifting of major works to the Palmer Museum of Art at Penn State University, and Arthur and Holly Magill from Spartanburg, South Carolina, with major Modernist works, including those by Charles Burchfield, Marin, and Andrew Wyeth, many of which were donated to the Greenville County Museum of Art.

Likewise, museum curators and directors have left their mark on significant collections of American Art. One example is Michael Quick, former curator of American Art at the Los Angeles County Museum of Art, who fostered encouragement for collecting in his region and specifically influenced the taste of many collectors in California. Guided by his eye, Willard and Libby Clark and John and Gail Liebes embraced American aestheticism, acquiring works by Dennis Miller Bunker, Dewing, John LaFarge, Sargent, and Whistler. Museum directors and curators including Dr. Graham Boettcher, Director of the Birmingham Museum of Art, John Coffey, Deputy Director of the North Carolina Museum of Art, and Dr. Linda Ferber, Museum Director Emerita, New-York Historical Society, have more recently been instrumental in building collections among their patrons, many of whom will gift their holdings to museums for posterity.

Others who have influenced the development of collecting American art include art historians such as Dr. Barbara Novak, Dr. William Gerdts, and Dr. Theodore Stebbins, who have not only written tomes in the field and organized important exhibitions bringing American art to the forefront, but who have also offered their expertise to many collectors. The camaraderie of collectors themselves has also served to spark the zest for collecting. Over past decades, many regional groups have formed to explore American art through the development of friendships, exchange of ideas and knowledge, and organization of educational programs and trips nationwide to view art. The cities and museums of Atlanta, Birmingham, Louisville, Los Angeles, New York, Orlando, and Washington, DC, have all fostered such groups.

The collectors of traditional American art in the twenty-first century are those who have a passion for and acquire art for the pure sake of collecting, with or without a determined thematic goal. Some still collect with philanthropy in mind, have nationalistic pride, or wish to preserve their predecessors' legacies. Others have a mission to seek art for decorative purposes to enhance their environments. However, there are fewer collectors, except in the Contemporary art arena, who buy for prestige or investment.

Alice Walton has made great strides in establishing a textbook collection of American art in her landmark Crystal Bridges Museum of American Art established in 2011 and making Bentonville, Arkansas, a visual art cultural center for the region. She has acquired many masterpieces including Durand's *Kindred Spirits*, 1849, and O'Keeffe's *Jimson Weed*, 1932. Ms. Walton has been creative in her quest to find the best, particularly in her partnership with Fisk University to secure the Alfred Stieglitz Collection.

George Lucas and Steven Spielberg have brought the art of American Illustration to the forefront with their outstanding collections of Norman Rockwells and have been instrumental in the recognition of such as a legitimate art form. Mr. Lucas's penchant for storytelling will have even more impact with the opening of the Lucas Museum of Narrative Art in Los Angeles in the decade of the 2020s. Others like Jim and Fran McGlothlin, Heywood and Cynthia Fralin, and James and Ann Goodnight have enriched the collections of the Virginia Museum of Fine Arts, The Fralin Museum of Art at the University of Virginia, and the North Carolina Museum of Art, respectively, with their generous donations.

Traditionally, American art had a national market base, not an international one. Exceptions include the acknowledgment of certain expatriate Impressionists such as Cassatt, Sargent, and Whistler as well as the influx of German and English collectors of Western scenes in the nineteenth century. In the 1980s, Japanese collectors sought works by Andrew Wyeth and Yasuo Kuniyoshi. American art, however, garnered major international notoriety in the 1970s and 1980s when Baron Hans Heinrich Thyssen Bornemisza, a Dutch-born Swiss industrialist and world-renowned collector, met New York gallerist Andrew Crispo, who encouraged the Baron to acquire significant American art including works by Copley, Homer, Hopper, and Sargent, now on display at the Thyssen-Bornemisza Museum in Madrid. Other international collectors include Gregory Callimanopulos, the Greek shipping magnate, who became enamored of and acquired *A Bedouin Arab* by Sargent at Christie's in 1984, and Swiss collectors Rolf and Margit Weinberg who collected 1930s and 1940s American Modernism along with their European masterpieces.

This century has witnessed the recognition of American art abroad, with interest in Nicolai Fechin among Russian buyers as well as in iconographic paintings by artists such as Bellows, evidenced by the purchase of *Men of the Docks*, 1912, by the National Gallery, London, in 2014.[20] Other artists such as Hopper and Rockwell, who are recognized for their truly American aesthetic, have been of note to both Europeans and Asians. Additionally, artists such as Georgia O'Keeffe and Milton Avery are now in the purview of contemporary buyers who see examples popping up in evening auction sales, along with other blue-chip works from the second half of the twentieth and the twenty-first centuries. Such exposure promises to drive up prices, as foreign money and contemporary buyers are more conversant with paying millions for important works.

In the twenty-first century, the market for traditional American art faces complicated challenges, given present-day collecting tastes, evolving demographics of collectors, supply and demand for such art, and the extreme price points that have emerged, where many works are worth half what they once were, and others are setting records in the multi-millions of dollars. As existing collectors age and younger collectors embrace contemporary art, this genre has been diminishing in popularity since 2008, particularly regarding eighteenth- and nineteenth-century works, a factor that has in turn created the price fluctuations. This downturn is even more significant for average or mediocre examples and for works by lesser or more decorative artists. The exceptions to this trend are monumental works, which hold their value regardless of the market, twentieth-century art, including American Modernism, Regionalism, Magic Realism, and Surrealism, and works by women and African American artists.

As the third decade of the twenty-first century opens, the present market affords greater acquisition opportunities for collectors and especially for museums. The hope for the future of collecting traditional American art is through education and exposure. Museums, auction houses, galleries, and higher education institutions must do more to promote it so that future generations will understand and revere its merits and carry on the legacy of those who have laid the groundwork.

Notes

Salerno *(pp.14–22)*

1 William Cullen Bryant, "Thomas Cole. A Funeral Oration, Delivered Before the National Academy of Design, New York, May 4, 1848," in *Orations and Addresses by William Cullen Bryant*, New York (G.P. Putnam's Sons), 1873, pp. 12–13.
2 Kevin J. Avery, "A Historiography of the Hudson River School," in *American Paradise: The World of the Hudson River School*, introduction by John K. Howat, New York (Metropolitan Museum of Art), 1987, pp. 3–4.
3 Asher B. Durand, "Letters on Landscape Painting. Letter 1," in *Crayon* 1, January 3, 1855, p. 2.
4 See Oswaldo Rodriguez Roque, "The Exaltation of American Landscape Painting," in Howat, intro., *American Paradise*, *op. cit.*, pp. 21–48.
5 Thomas Cole to Robert Gilmor, December 25, 1826, quoted in Roque, *op. cit.*, p. 25.
6 Asher B. Durand, "Letters on Landscape Painting. No. VIII," in *Crayon* 1, June 6, 1855, p. 354.
7 James Thomas Flexner, *That Wilder Image: The Paintings of America's Native School from Thomas Cole to Winslow Homer*, New York (Bonanza Books), 1962, p. 5.
8 *Ibid.*, p. 20.
9 See David P. Grey, "Doughty to Cole—A Discovered Link," in *Thomas Cole National Historic Society Newsletter* (Fall 2015), pp. 5–7.
10 Flexner, *op. cit.*, p. 74.
11 *Ibid.*, p. 75.
12 See Linda S. Ferber, "Albert Bierstadt: The History of a Reputation," in Nancy K. Anderson and Linda S. Ferber, *Albert Bierstadt: Art & Enterprise*, New York (Hudson Hill Press), 1990, pp. 27–31.
13 Ralph Waldo Emerson, *Nature*, Boston (James Munroe & Company), 1849, p. 8.
14 See Jervis McEntee papers, 1796, 1848–1905, Archives of American Art, Smithsonian Institution.
15 A catalogue raisonné of William Hart's paintings by Gary Stiles is currently in production, and will no doubt shed light on the importance and lasting influence of this underappreciated American artist.

Hopkins *(pp.23–31)*

1 William H. Goetzmann and William N. Goetzmann, *The West of the Imagination*, New York (W.W. Norton), 1986, pp. 6–7.
2 Robert Hughes, *American Visions: The Epic History of Art in America*, New York (Alfred A. Knopf, Inc.), 1997, pp. 177–80.
3 Goetzmann, *op. cit.*, pp. 54–62.
4 J. Gray Sweeney, *Masterpieces of Western American Art*, New York/Avenel, NJ (Crescent Books), 1996, p. 170.
5 Hughes, *op. cit.*, pp. 388–89.
6 Dean A. Porter *et al.*, *Taos Artists and Their Patrons, 1898–1950*, Notre Dame, South Bend, IN (Snite Museum of Art), 1999, pp. 305–08.
7 www.santafe.org, official travel website, accessed 1/19/19.
8 Patricia Janis Broder, *The American West: The Modern Vision*, Boston (Little, Brown and Company), 1974, pp. 261–68.
9 Don Hedgpeth, *New Western Images: The Hillin Collection of the Cowboy Artists of America*, Flagstaff, AZ (Northland Press), 1978, pp 3–5.
10 Broder, *op. cit.*, p. 326.
11 Bob Brown in *Timeless Treasures, 50 Favorites from the Whitney Gallery of Western Art*, Cody, WY (Buffalo Bill Historical Center), 2008, pp.104–05.

Boettcher *(pp.32–39)*

1 Henry T. Tuckerman, *Artist-Life: or, Sketches of American Painters*, New York (D. Appleton & Company), 2nd edn, 1849, p. 49.
2 Benjamin West to John Singleton Copley, in Guernsey Jones, ed., *Letters and Papers of John Singleton Copley and Henry Pelham, 1739–1776*, 71, Boston (Massachusetts Historical Society), 1914, p. 194. Also quoted in Jules David Prown, "Benjamin West and the Use of Antiquity," *American Art*, 1, no. 2, summer 1996, p. 29.
3 Crawford Alexander Mann III, "Pilgrims of Beauty: Art and Inspiration in 19th-Century Italy," *Exhibition Notes*, no. 38, spring 2012, February 3– July 8, 2012, Providence (Museum of Art, Rhode Island School of Design), n.p.
4 *Daily Cincinnati Gazette*, May 30, 1861, p. 3, quoted in Joseph D. Ketner, *The Emergence of the African-American Artist: Robert S. Duncanson, 1821–1872*, Columbia (U. of Missouri Press), 1993, p. 84.
5 *Myth and Reality: Elihu Vedder and American Painters in Italy*, exh. cat., essay by Graham C. Boettcher, New York (Questroyal Fine Art, LLC), 2010, n.p.
6 Elihu Vedder, *The Digressions of V*, Boston (Houghton Mifflin Company), 1910, p. 139.
7 *Ibid.*, pp. 373–74.
8 I am grateful to provenance researcher James R. Wooten for his superb investigation of the painting (on file at the Birmingham Museum of Art), and for making this connection. For a reproduction of Vedder's *The Gate, Volterra*, see *ibid.*, 299.
9 *Ibid.*, p. 437.
10 Nancy K. Anderson, *Thomas Moran*, exh. cat., Washington (National Gallery of Art), 1997, p. 123.
11 Amy O. Bassford and Fritiof M. Fryxell (eds.), *Home-Thoughts, from Afar: Letters of Thomas Moran to Mary Nimmo Moran*, East Hampton, 1967, 77, quoted in Anderson, 1997, p. 122.
12 Anderson, 1997, p. 122.
13 Margaretta M. Lovell, *Venice: The American View, 1860–1920*, San Francisco (The Greenwood Press), 1984, p. 66.
14 Letter to Christian Klackner, 1888, quoted in pamphlet *"The Gate of Venice" Etched by Thomas Moran, N. A.* (located in the Print Room, New York Public Library). Quoted in *op. cit.* pp. 66–67, fn. 1.
15 Helmut von Erffa and Allen Staley, *The Paintings of Benjamin West*, New Haven, CT (Yale U. Press), 1986, pp. 23, 127–30, 145.
16 Ketner, 1993, p. 72.
17 Anderson, 1997, pp. 192–93.
18 Clive Holland, "Lady Art Students' Life in Paris," *The Studio*, XXX, 1904, p. 225. Quoted, but not cited, in Kathleen Adler, "'We'll Always Have Paris': Paris as Training Ground and Proving Ground" in *Americans in Paris, 1860-1900*, exh. cat., London (National Gallery), 2006, p. 11.
19 Adler, 2006, p. 11.
20 Richard J. Boyle, "Willard Metcalf: Genesis of an American Artist" in *Willard Metcalf (1858–1925): Yankee Impressionist*, exh. cat., New York (Spanierman Gallery, LLC), 2003, pp. 11–12.
21 *Ibid.*, p. 12.
22 *Ibid.*
23 William H. Gerdts, "Three Themes," in *Childe Hassam, Impressionist*, by Warren Adelson, Jay

E. Cantor, and William H. Gerdts, New York (Abbeville), 1999, p. 159.
24 Bruce W. Chambers, "Willard L. Metcalf: 'A Partial History of the Renaissance,'" in *Willard Metcalf (1858–1925): Yankee Impressionist*, 2003, p. 41.
25 For more on Butler's relationship with Monet's stepdaughters, see Ch. 11, "Theodore and Suzanne," in Richard H. Love, *Theodore Earl Butler: Emergence from Monet's Shadow*, Chicago (Haase-Mumm Publishing Company), 1985, pp. 102–16.
26 *Ibid.*, pp. 362–64.
27 *Ibid.*, pp. 369–75.
28 *Ibid.*, pp. 393–98.
29 For more on Chapman, see John F. McGuigan and Mary K. McGuigan, *John Gadsby Chapman: America's First Artist-Etcher. With a Catalogue of His Italian Etchings*, Harpswell, ME (Arcady Editions), 2015.
30 Robert Henri, *The Art Spirit*, Philadelphia (J.B. Lippincott Company), 1923, pp. 7–8.

Peters *(pp. 40–49)*

1 John I.H. Baur, *Leaders of American Impressionism*, exh. cat., New York (Brooklyn Museum), 1937, p. 3.
2 *Ibid.*, p. 3.
3 John I.H. Baur, *Theodore Robinson, 1852–1896*, New York (Brooklyn Museum), 1946, p. 52.
4 Lewis Mumford, *The Brown Decades: A Study of the Arts in America, 1865–1895*, New York (Harcourt, Brace and Company, Inc.), 1931.
5 *Ibid.*, pp. 8 and 197.
6 *Ibid.*, p. 197.
7 *Ibid.*, pp. 209–10.
8 James Thomas Flexner, *History of American Painting, Volume 3: That Wilder Image—The Native School from Thomas Cole to Winslow Homer*, New York (Little, Brown and Company), 1962, p. 306.
9 John McCoubrey, *American Tradition in Painting*, Philadelphia (U. of Pennsylvania Press), 1963, p. 26.
10 "Jackson Pollock: Is he the greatest living painter in the United States?" *Life Magazine* 27, August 8, 1949, pp. 42–45. The article is not credited, but is believed to have been written by Clement Greenberg.
11 Robert Rosenblum, "The Primal American Scene," in *The Natural Paradise: Painting in America, 1800–1950*, New York (Museum of Modern Art), 1976, p. 18.
12 Author's conversation with Ira Spanierman, December 2016.
13 Raymond Horowitz, "Reminiscences and Reflections on Collecting," in *American Impressionism and Realism: The Margaret and Raymond Horowitz Collection*, exh. cat., Washington, DC (National Gallery of Art), 1999, p. 16.
14 Hal Opperman, "The Thinking Eye, the Mind that Sees: The Art Historian as Connoisseur," *Artibus et Historiae* 11, 1990, p. 11.
15 The shift to globalism and the "omnipresentness of reception" are discussed in Richard Brilliant, "'Not the Art History I Used to Know,'" *Notes in the History of Art* 35, Fall 2015/Winter 2016, pp. 194–98. Brilliant argues for an evaluation of the relationship between creation and reception.
16 For example, see "The Museum and Art History," prepared by Lorenz Eitner, in Andrew C. Ritchie, ed., *The Visual Arts in Higher Education*, New Haven, CT (Yale U. Press for the College Art Association of America), 1966.
17 Horowitz, p. 18.
18 Horowitz, p. 17.
19 Jay E. Cantor, "The Eyes Have It," *American Fine Art Magazine*, November–December 2014, p. 42.
20 Donelson Hoopes, *The American Impressionists*, New York (Watson-Guptill Publications), 1972; Richard J. Boyle, *American Impressionism*, Boston (New York Graphic Society), 1974.
21 William H. Gerdts, *American Impressionism*, exh. cat., Seattle (Henry Art Gallery, U. of Washington), 1980.
22 William H. Gerdts, *American Impressionism*, New York (Abbeville), 1984.
23 Among many additional books by William H. Gerdts on American Impressionism are *Monet's Giverny: An Impressionist Colony*, New York (Abbeville), 1993, and *Impressionist New York*, New York (Abbeville), 1994.
24 Wanda M. Corn, "Coming of Age: Historical Scholarship in American Art," *The Art Bulletin*, Vol. 70, No. 2, June 1988, pp. 188–207.
25 *Ibid.*, p. 193.
26 *Ibid.*, p. 205.
27 The exhibition was held at The Metropolitan Museum of Art (May 10–July 24, 1994), the Amon Carter Museum of American Art, Fort Worth, Texas (August 21–October 30, 1994), The Denver Art Museum (December 3, 1994–February 5, 1995), and the Los Angeles County Museum of Art (March 12–May 14, 1995).
28 H. Barbara Weinberg, Doreen Bolger, and David Park Curry, *American Impressionism and Realism: The Painting of Modern Life, 1885–1915*, exh. cat., New York (The Metropolitan Museum of Art), 1994.
29 *Ibid.*, p. 3.
30 Robert L. Herbert, *Impressionism: Art, Leisure, and Parisian Society*, New Haven, CT (Yale U. Press), 1988, pb 1991.
31 Trevor Fairbrother, "Review of *American Impressionism and Realism: The Painting of Modern Life, 1885–1915*," *Archives of American Art Journal* 33, 1993, pp. 15–21; Michael Kimmelman, "Two Schools of Painting at the Met," *New York Times*, May 13, 1994; John Updike, "Beyond the Picturesque," *New York Review of Books*, June 23, 1994; Eric Gibson, "Exhibition Notes," *The New Criterion*, June 1994; "American Impressionism and Realism—Fort Worth," *The Burlington Magazine* 136, November 1994, pp. 786–87; Douglas Tallack, "American Impressionism and Realism: The Painting of Modern Life," *Journal of American Studies* 29, December 1995, pp. 453–59.
32 Weinberg, Bolger, and Curry, p. 8.
33 Hilton Kramer, "Nutty Wall Texts Besmirch Met's Lyric American Show," *New York Observer*, May 30, 1994.
34 "American Impressionism and Realism—Fort Worth," p. 787.
35 Fairbrother, p. 16.
36 *Ibid.*, p. 17.
37 Herbert, p. xiv.
38 James Hall, "Is it Time to Pull the Plug?" *The Guardian*, July 14, 1994, p. 10.
39 Two recent examples are *Like Breath on Glass: Whistler, Inness, and the Art of Painting Softly* (2008), organized by the Sterling and Francine Clark Art Institute, Williamstown, MA, and *Thomas Cole's Journey: Atlantic Crossings* (2018), organized by The Metropolitan Museum of Art.

Coyle *(pp. 50–59)*

1 *New York Realists*, exh. cat., New York (Whitney Museum of American Art), 1937, pp. 5–6.
2 "New York's Art War and the Eight Rebels Who Dared to Paint Pictures of New York Life (instead of Europe) and are Holding Their Rebellious Exhibition All by Themselves," *New York World*, February 2, 1908.
3 Joseph Edgar Chamberlin, "Two Significant Exhibitions," *Evening Mail*, February 4, 1908.
4 *New York Realists*, p. 5.
5 Letter, Juliana Force to Everett Shinn, March 12, 1937, Everett Shinn Papers, Delaware Art Museum, box 4, folder 5.
6 "'The Eight' Reunited Thirty Years Later," *Art Digest* 12, January 1938, p. 6.
7 "Brooklyn Revives Memories of 'The Eight,'" *Art Digest*, December 1943, p. 12.
8 Walter Pach, "The Eight Then and Now," *Art News* 42, January 1–14, 1944, p. 31.
9 In 1937, The Metropolitan Museum of Art acquired *The Green Car*, 1910, by William Glackens. The following year, Glackens's *Girl in Black and White*, 1914, went to the Whitney. In 1940, the Brooklyn Museum acquired *Hester Street*, 1905, by George Luks. The next year, his painting *The Butcher Cart*, 1901, was purchased for the Art Institute of Chicago by the Friends of American Art. Also, in 1941 the Whitney purchased Sloan's *The Picnic Grounds*, 1906–07, and the Brooklyn Museum bought Glackens's *East River Park*, *c.* 1902. The following year, Brooklyn purchased *Keith's Union Square*, 1902–06, by Shinn. In 1945, the Museum of Fine Arts, Boston, bought *The Wrestlers*, 1905, by Luks. Before his death in 1951, Sloan's early paintings were placed in major public museums in Boston, Chicago, Cleveland, Columbus, Detroit, Minneapolis, Newark, Philadelphia, Rochester, and Washington, DC. By the time of his death in 1953, Shinn had works in the Addison Gallery of American Art, Andover, MA, the Albright-Knox in Buffalo, the Art Institute of Chicago, the Newark Museum, the New Britain Museum, and the Detroit Institute of Arts, as well as the Whitney, the Brooklyn Museum, and The Metropolitan Museum of Art in New York.
10 There are a variety of reasons for Sloan's drift from painting New York: in 1914 he began to spend summers away from New York, first in Gloucester, Massachusetts, and later in Santa Fe, and he developed an interest in landscape painting. Sloan also changed studios, obtaining a space separate from his home for the first time in 1912, where he could more comfortably paint from nude models. And he began teaching at the Art Students League in 1916, where teaching with live models reinforced his interest in figure painting and portraiture.
11 Sloan's only completed New York painting between 1919 and 1921 is *Cornelia Street*, 1920, private collection.
12 On *New York by Night*, see Rebecca Zurier, *Picturing the City: Urban Vision and the Ashcan School* (U. of California Press), 2006, pp.170–178.
13 The scope of Shinn's early exhibition and illustration work can be gleaned from his two account books dating from 1898 to 1912, in the Everett Shinn Collection, Archives of American Art, Smithsonian Institution, Washington, DC. In these he tracked illustration commissions, private sales, decorative commissions, gallery consignments, museum loans, and submissions to juried shows. Between 1900 and 1905, he showed with Boussod-Valadon, Durand-Ruel, Knoedler, Kraushaar, and Gimpel and Wildenstein in New York City, as well as dealers in Philadelphia and Boston.
14 Shinn showed at invitational exhibitions at the New York School of Art and the MacDowell Club. His work was accepted regularly to the annual juried shows at the Pennsylvania Academy of the Fine Arts, the Boston Art Club, the Art Institute of Chicago, and the Cincinnati Museum Association, but he submitted to the National Academy of Design only once early in his career, in 1907 when Henri was on the jury, and he was rejected.
15 I have found only a few traces of Shinn's practice in the 1920s: Knoedler hosted a show in 1920, and his scrapbooks at the Archives of American Art memorialize a scandal over a nude exhibited at the YMCA in Westport, Connecticut, in 1928.
16 Shinn's prickly correspondence with Price is in Everett Shinn Papers, Delaware Art Museum, box 5, folders 4a and 4b.
17 These observations are based on my attempts to rectify Shinn's various lists of work for *New York by Night* and my examination of the annotated exhibition records in the Everett Shinn Papers, Delaware Art Museum, boxes 4 and 5.
18 To provide just one example: The work shown as *Owl Eating House, New York* and dated 1904 in Shinn's exhibition at the American British Art Center in 1945 is likely the same as the pastel *Lunch Wagon, Madison Square*, dated 1900 in the exhibition of James Graham & Sons in 1958 (and later in the Altschul collection).
19 Some of Shinn's drawings, such as the Delaware Art Museum's *Backstage Scene* (1900), feature two legible signatures and dates.
20 Reproduced in *Everett Shinn, 1873–1953*, exh. cat., Trenton, NJ (New Jersey State Museum), 1973, p. 52.
21 A typescript of Shinn's story about Luks, "Plush and Cut Glass," is in Everett Shinn Collection, Archives of American Art, box 1, folder 81. Drafts of his autobiography are in Everett Shinn Papers, Delaware Art Museum, boxes 7 and 8. I have repeatedly failed to confirm Shinn's autobiographical stories about his newspaper years.
22 Shinn, "Recollections of The Eight," *The Eight*, exh. cat., New York (Brooklyn Museum), 1943, pp. 11, 12.

Ward *(pp. 60–66)*

1 Also on the list were Max Weber, Yasuo Kuniyoshi, Stuart Davis, Ben Shahn, Edward Hopper, George Grosz, and Charles Burchfield.
2 Quoted in Ruth E. Fine, *John Marin*, Washington, DC (National Gallery of Art), 1990, p. 9.
3 John Marin to Alfred Stieglitz, August 7, 1914, in Herbert J. Seligmann, ed., *Letters of John Marin*, New York, 1931, n.p.
4 Marin to Stieglitz, September 16, 1914, *ibid.*
5 Marin to Stieglitz, August 14, 1923, *ibid.*
6 Louis Finkelstein, "Marin and de Kooning," *Magazine of Art*, 43, October 1950, pp. 202–06.

Broun *(pp. 67–73)*

1 Sketch of Picasso's *The Architect's Table*, ink on paper in letter to Alfred Stieglitz, received July 12, 1912, Beinecke Library, Yale University; reproduced in Jonathan Weinberg, *Speaking for Vice: Homosexuality in the Art of Charles Demuth, Marsden Hartley, and the First American Avant-Garde*, New Haven, CT (Yale U. Press), 1993, p. 160, fig. 54.
2 MH to Alfred Stieglitz, October 31, 1913, Berlin, in *My Dear Stieglitz: Letters of Marsden Hartley and Alfred Stieglitz 1912–1915*, ed. James Timothy Voorhies, Columbia, SC (U. of South Carolina Press), 2002, pp. 104–05.
3 *Somehow a Past: The Autobiography of Marsden Hartley*, ed. Susan Elizabeth Ryan, Cambridge, MA (The MIT Press), 1997, pp. 50–52.
4 Hartley evokes the blue of the Virgin Mary's traditional robe in a poem called "Soldier on his Knees in the Snow," where he addresses "Mary Mother" while looking at the sky, writing "I saw the hem of your gracious dress through every branch…." *The Collected Poems of Marsden Hartley 1904–1943*, ed. Gail R. Scott, Black Sparrow, 1987, p. 161.
5 *Ibid.*, p. 50. "Sang magnificats and epiphanies" is from Hartley's poem, "Lewiston is a Pleasant Place," *ibid.*, p. 254.
6 MH to AS, early October 1913, Berlin, *My Dear Stieglitz*, *op. cit.*, p. 104.
7 Hartley to Richard Tweedy, May 27, 1900, Yale, copy at the Archives of American Art; quoted in Barbara Haskell, *Marsden Hartley*, New York (Whitney Museum of American Art), 1980, p. 11.
8 *Ibid.*, p. 27.
9 Paul Rosenfeld, "American Painting," *The Dial*, 71, December 1921, p. 658, quoted in Haskell, *ibid.*, p. 56.
10 Rosenfeld, "The Paintings of Marsden Hartley: Characteristics of the Work of One of the Very Great Talents Among Present Day American Artists," *Vanity Fair*, 18, August 1922, pp. 47, 96.
11 Brooklyn Museum website, https://www.brooklynmuseum.org/opencollection/objects/2091
12 Rosenfeld, *Vanity Fair*, *op. cit.*, p. 96.

Bianco *(pp.74–81)*

1 Bernice Kert, in *Abby Aldrich Rockefeller: The Woman in the Family*, New York (Random House), 1993, pp. 279–80.
2 The Farnsworth Art Museum, Rockland, Maine, showed the Rockefeller family portrait with paintings and textiles by Marguerite Zorach in a retrospective exhibition, June 2017–January 2018. See Jane Bianco, Betsy Fahlman, and Cynthia Fowler, *Marguerite Zorach: An Art-Filled Life*, catalogue published on the occasion of the exhibition.
3 Zorach's Aunt Harriet Adelaide Harris introduced her to friends, collectors Leo and Gertrude Stein and their circle, which included the artists Henri Matisse and Pablo Picasso. Marguerite Zorach portrayed Leo Stein in a Matisse-like painting she called *The Collector*, currently privately owned.
4 William Murrell Fisher, "Sculpture at the Exhibition," in *Arts & Decoration*, Vol. 3, No. 5, March 1913, p. 168.
5 Zorach's later rug, *Eden*, was an early textile version of this and a painted mural depicting Adam and Eve entwined, a collaborative embellishment painted by the couple in their West 10th Street home in New York. The tender depiction of Adam and Eve may reflect the Zorachs' own closeness as newlyweds. The program of wall decorations in their Maine residence and the family units that both artists were to render in the years to follow derive from this early piece. See also Mildred Cole Péladeau, *Rug Hooking in Maine, 1838–1940*, Atglen, PA (Schiffer Publishing), 2008, pp. 133–40.
6 Art historian Cynthia Fowler suggests that "With its long history related to the fine arts tradition, the female nude comes to symbolize art itself," in her essay in Bianco, Fahlman, and Fowler, *op. cit.*, p. 49.
7 *New York Sun*, February 15, 1930, no au. cited; see Downtown Gallery Records, Archives of American Art, Smithsonian Institution (Reel 5556, frame 965).
8 Cynthia Fowler likens *The Family Supper* to Leonardo da Vinci's *Last Supper*. See her essay in Bianco, Fahlman, and Fowler, *op. cit.*, p. 51.
9 "... for she has chosen those subjects which are close to her daily life, the people of New England, her family, and the Maine landscape as seen under the cold northern light. Her pictures of 'the vanishing Americans' of an older New England have about them a feeling of unspoken tragedy, of 'the quiet desperation' that Thoreau found in the lives of most people. They are gentle and melancholy portrayals, lighted occasionally with a gleam of quiet humor." Edith Halpert press release in *The Art Digest*, November 1, 1934.
10 *The New York Times*, February 23, 1930, Downtown Gallery Records, Archives of American Art, Smithsonian Institution (Reel 5556, frame 966).
11 October 17, 1934, press release from The Downtown Gallery, 113 West 13th St, New York, Downtown Gallery Records, Archives of American Art, Smithsonian Institution (Reel 5556, frame 997).
12 First established as Sieur de Monts National Monument in July 1916 by President Woodrow Wilson and finally named Acadia National Park in 1929, it was the first national park east of the Mississippi. It was established partly to prevent over-development of the island and to maintain a sense of its wildness for future generations. John D. Rockefeller, Jr., played a critical role by building the system of roads for passage of horse-drawn carriages, and by donating over 11,000 acres of land for the park.
13 This portrait graced Rockefeller family homes and was also shown in exhibitions in New York, Chicago, Boston, and Dallas from the 1930s until 1966, when it was part of the exhibition *Three Hundred Years of New York City Families* at Wildenstein & Company, a New York art gallery—fifty years before coming to the Farnsworth Art Museum for the 2017 Zorach exhibition.
14 The Mount Desert Land & Garden Preserve, founded by David and Peggy Rockefeller, manages 1165 acres of historic gardens, lands and trails for the public.
15 The latter is shown in the upper left of the composition in the guise of Mr. Rockefeller, Sr., as a tiny figure swinging a golf club on the lawn below the church and parallel to a couple of ESSO gas pumps in town. Marguerite Zorach may be the figure lounging on the lawn of the Abby Aldrich Rockefeller garden, in the same pose adapted in the Halpert portrait discussed above.

Caldwell *(pp.82–89)*

1 Donald Judd, *Complete Writings 1959–1975*, New York (Judd Foundation), 1975, pp. 55–56.
2 For more thoughts on color see Robert Morris, "Notes on Sculpture," ArtForum, February 1966, "The more neutral hues which do not call attention to themselves allow for the maximum focus on those essential physical decisions which inform sculptural works."
3 Stuart Davis Papers, 1967.79, Harvard Art Museums/Fogg Museum, Gift of Mrs. Stuart Davis.
4 By mid-century it was important to Davis that "Art [does] not rob the square of its everyday meanings, it enlarges the scope of its usefulness in enriching our experience with common things." Diane Kelder, *Stuart Davis*, New York (Praeger), 1971, p. 104.
5 Also illustrates Morris's belief that one iteration of a work should not be privileged over another, as noted by Andrew Chesher, "Desublimating the Gestalt: Towards an Archaeology of Robert Morris' Anti-Form," in "Sublimation: Mind, Matter", Concept in Art After Modernism," December 14–16, 2017, Johannes Gutenberg-Universität Mainz.
6 Lowery Stokes Sims, with contributions by William C. Agee, Robert Hunter, Lewis Kachur, Diane Kelder, John R. Lane, Lisa Servon, and Karen Wilkin, *Stuart Davis: American Painter*, New York (Metropolitan Museum of Art), 1991, p. 18.
7 Kelder, *op. cit.*, p. 100.
8 *Ibid.*, p. 11.
9 Bruce Glaser, *Questions to Stella and Judd*, interview, edited by Lucy R. Lippard, *Art News*, September 1966, p. 6, as reprinted in *Minimal Art: A Critical Anthology*, ed. Gregory Battcock, U. of California Press, 1995.
10 As defined by Harry Cooper in his essay for the exhibition catalogue *Stuart Davis: In Full Swing*, Whitney Museum of American Art, New York (Prestel Publishing), 2016, p. 25.
11 *Ibid.*, p. 24.
12 Barbara Haskell, *Donald Judd*, New York (Whitney Museum of American Art), 1988, p. 17.
13 Quoted in letter from Thomas Nonn to Donald Judd, April 21, 1965, *Donald Judd, Complete Writings 1959–1975*, New York (Judd Foundation), 1975, p. 171.

Wilkin *(pp.90–99)*

1 Dorothy Dehner, foreword to John Graham, *System and Dialectics of Art*, annotated from unpublished writings with a critical introduction by Marcia Epstein Allentuck, Baltimore (Johns Hopkins Press), 1971, p. xiii.
2 For an accurate chronology see Alicia G. Longwell with Michael Pinto and Michelle Fikrig, "John D. Graham: a Chronicle of Life and Work," in Alicia G. Longwell, William C. Agee, Sophie Egly, Karen Wilkin, and Terrie Sultan, *John Graham: Maverick Modernist*, exh. cat., New York, London, and Munich (Parrish Art Museum, Delmonico Books, and Prestel), 2017, pp. 144–67.
3 Graham, *System and Dialectics of Art*, *op. cit.*, p. 111.
4 *Ibid.*, p. 94.
5 *Ibid.*
6 *Ibid.*, p. 102.
7 *Ibid.*, p. 101.
8 Graham to Duncan Phillips, April 2, 1928, quoted by Longwell, *John Graham and the Quest for an American Art in the 1920s and 1930s*, unpublished dissertation, City University of New York, 2007, p. 46.
9 Dehner recalled Graham's telling her that "Graham" written in English looked like his mother's name written in Cyrillic (foreword Allentuck, *op. cit.*, p. xvi.) This seems doubtful, since his mother's name was Brezinska—according to a translation of 1891 baptismal records in the John D. Graham records, Archives of American Art, cited by Longwell, p. 24. A more likely explanation is that he adapted his patronymic "Gratianovitch," since the first syllable of his father's name "Gratian," when written in Cyrillic script, resembles "Gram," written in English.
10 The chronology in William S. Lieberman, ed., *Art of the Twenties*, exh. cat., New York (Museum of Modern Art), 1979, and the chronology by Julia May Boddewyn in Michael Fitzgerald, *Picasso and American Art*, exh. cat., New York, New Haven, and London (Whitney Museum of American Art and Yale U. Press), 2006, are particularly informative.

11 Dehner, foreword Allentuck, *op. cit.*, p. xiii.
12 Dehner, p. xiii. *Cahiers d'Art*, founded by Christian Zervos in 1926, was a relatively new publication in 1930.
13 James T. Valliere, "De Kooning on Pollock," *Partisan Review*, Fall 1967, p. 603.
14 De Kooning, interview with Harold Rosenberg, in Harold Rosenberg, *De Kooning*, New York (Abrams), 1974, p. 38.
15 Stuart Davis, "Autobiography," from *Stuart Davis*, New York (American Artists Group), 1945, reprinted in Diane Kelder, *Stuart Davis*, New York (Praeger), 1971, p. 27.
16 Stuart Davis Papers, Harvard University Art Museums, on deposit at Houghton Rare Book Library, Harvard University. Reel numbers refer to microfilm copies of the papers; there are no frame numbers; some pages are dated. Reel 4, January 8, 1942.
17 Davis Papers, Reel 1, December 30, 1922.
18 Davis Papers, Reel 7, October 29, 1943.
19 Graham, *op. cit.*, p. 131.
20 Graham, *op. cit.*, p. 106.
21 Graham, *op. cit.*, p. 119.
22 Graham, *op. cit.*, p. 94.
23 Graham to Duncan Phillips, December 28, 1930, in Eleanor Green, *John Graham: Artist and Avatar*, exh. cat., Washington, DC (The Phillips Collection), 1987, p. 139. Green adds: "This group never coalesced," an observation contradicted by the evidence of fruitful exchange in the three artists' work during the 1930s and by de Kooning's characterization of them as "The Three Musketeers."
24 Stuart Davis, "Arshile Gorky in the 1930s: A Personal Recollection," *Magazine of Art*, February 1951, reprinted in Kelder, *op. cit.*, p. 182.
25 Dehner, foreword Allentuck, *op. cit.*, p. xv.
26 Arshile Gorky, "Stuart Davis," *Creative Art*, September 1931, reprinted in Kelder, *op. cit.*, p. 192.
27 Davis, "Arshile Gorky in the 1930s: A Personal Recollection," in Kelder, *op. cit.*, pp. 178–83.
28 Mark Stevens and Annalyn Swan, *De Kooning: An American Master*, New York (Alfred A. Knopf), 2004, p. 97.
29 *Ibid.*
30 *Ibid.*, p. 105.
31 Graham, *op. cit.*, p. 93.
32 Graham, *op. cit.*, p. 118.
33 Graham, *op. cit.*, p. 117.
34 Graham, *op. cit.*, p. 153.
35 Graham, *op. cit.*, p. 154. He later eliminated this list when he edited *System and Dialectics* for an unpublished second edition.
36 David Smith, "Atmosphere of the Early Thirties," in Cleve Gray, ed., *David Smith by David Smith*, New York, Chicago, San Francisco (Holt, Rinehart and Winston), 1972, p. 35.
37 Davis, "Arshile Gorky," in Kelder, *op. cit.*, p. 18.
38 The Graham scholar Alicia Longwell surmises that Graham made the connection with McMillen, Inc. through Frank Crowninshield.
39 Unsigned, "Congenial Company," *The Art Digest*, January 15, 1942, p. 18.

Fahlman *(pp. 100–106)*

1 For more on Gertrude Vanderbilt Whitney, see Ellen E. Roberts, *Gertrude Vanderbilt Whitney: Sculpture*, West Palm Beach, FL (Norton Museum of Art), 2018; Cynthia Kaye Fischer, "Memorializing Chivalry: Gertrude Vanderbilt Whitney's Titanic Memorial," *Woman's Art Journal* 32, no. 2, Fall/Winter 2011, pp. 30–37; Alexis L. Boylan, "Dressing Up: Robert Henri's Portrait of Gertrude Vanderbilt Whitney," in *Searching for America: Essays on Art and Architecture*, ed. Robert Sheardy, Jr., Newcastle, UK (Cambridge Scholars Press), 2006, pp. 59–71, 188–89; Janet Wolff, "Women at the Whitney, 1910–1930: Feminism, Sociology, Aesthetics," in *AngloModern: Painting and Modernity in Britain and the United States*, Ithaca (Cornell U. Press), 2003, pp. 15–40; Kennedy Fraser, "Love and Struggle: Gertrude Vanderbilt Whitney," in Beth Venn and Adam D. Weinberg (eds.), *Frames of Reference: Looking at American Art 1900–1950, Works from the Whitney Museum of American Art*, New York (Whitney Museum of American Art), 1999, pp. 18–57; Avis Berman, *Rebels on Eighth Street: Juliana Force and the Whitney Museum of American Art*, New York (Atheneum), 1990; Patricia Hills and Roberta K. Tarbell, *The Figurative Tradition and the Whitney Museum of American Art*, New York (Whitney Museum of American Art), 1980; *The Whitney Studio Club and American Art 1900–1932*, New York (Whitney Museum of American Art), 1975; B.H. Friedman, *Gertrude Vanderbilt Whitney*, Garden City, NY (Doubleday & Company), 1978; and Hermon More and Lloyd Goodrich, *Juliana Force and American Art*, New York (Whitney Museum of American Art), 1949.
2 Henry McBride, "Hale and Farewell," *New York Sun*, April 24, 1942, quoted in Roberta K. Tarbell, "Gertrude Vanderbilt Whitney as Patron," in Hills and Tarbell, *op. cit.*, p. 11.
3 Anna Hyatt Huntington (1876–1973) was a very successful public sculptor during this period. Her statue of Joan of Arc (dedicated 1915) in New York represented a variety of "firsts": the first public sculpture in New York by a woman as well as the first to honor a woman.
4 The Club was named variously the Whitney Studio (1914), the Whitney Studio Club (1918–28), and finally the Whitney Studio Galleries (1928–30). These activities culminated in the 1930 founding of the Whitney Museum of American Art, which opened in 1931. See Peter Hastings Falk, ed., *The Annual & Biennial Exhibition Record of the Whitney Museum of American Art, 1918–1989*, Madison, CT (Sound View Press), 1991.
5 Adam D. Weinberg, "Introduction," in Venn & Weinberg, p. 10.
6 For more on Guy Pène du Bois, see three publications by the author: "Complicating the Modern Woman: Guy Pène du Bois in France," *The Magazine Antiques* 181, no. 3, May–June 2014, pp. 98–103; *Guy Pène du Bois: Painter of Modern Life*, New York (James Graham and Sons), 2004; and *Guy Pène du Bois: Artist About Town*, Washington, DC (Corcoran Gallery of Art), 1980.
7 Thirty came to the institution the year it opened; thirteen were gifts from Whitney, and the other seventeen were purchased with funds provided by Whitney. Seventeen more came in 2014 from Flora Miller Biddle, Whitney's granddaughter. She was the daughter of Flora Payne Whitney Miller (1897–1986), the first of Gertrude Vanderbilt Whitney's three children. It is the seventeen Biddle watercolors that are the subject of this chapter.
8 More and Goodrich, *op. cit.*, p. 13.
9 Forbes Watson in More and Goodrich, *op. cit.*, p. 57.
10 *Juliana Force at the Whitney Studio Club* (1921) is in the collection of the Whitney Museum of American Art. There is a second series of three watercolors by Guy Pène du Bois in a similar style that were inspired by events in connection with the dedication of Whitney's monument to the American Expeditionary Forces in St-Nazaire, France, on June 26, 1926. They are *Saint Nazaire Buglers Announcing the Public Kiss*; *Saint Nazaire The Banquet; the Officer's Mess, the Speaker's Table and, Because of the Size of this Paper only a Few of the People Present*; and *Saint Nazaire Repopulated by the Youth Who Went to War on the Occasion of the Dedication of the American Monument June Twenty-Sixth 1926*. Formerly in the collection of Whitney's daughter, Flora Payne Whitney Miller, they are now owned by Flora Miller Biddle's daughter Fiona and her husband Mark Donovan. The three are reproduced in Roberts, *op. cit.*, pp. 82–83.
11 Guy Pène du Bois diary, July 15, 1921, Guy Pène du Bois papers, Archives of American Art, Smithsonian Institution, Washington, DC.
12 Kennedy Fraser in Venn & Weinberg, p. 19.
13 Kennedy Fraser in Venn & Weinberg, p. 19.
14 Friedman, *Gertrude Vanderbilt Whitney*, p. 400.
15 "Mrs. Whitney's New Idea," *American Art News* 16, February 9, 1918, p. 6.
16 James Britton, "Paint Orgy a la Whitney," *American Art News* 16, February 16, 1918, p. 2.
17 "20 Sculptors Show Work of Three Days: Paul Manship Carries off Laurels in Humoresque in Exhibit at Mrs. H.P. Whitney's Studio," *New York Times*, March 12, 1918. James Earle Fraser's *Storm Driven* depicted a pair of horses; Mahonri Young contributed *Sailor*, Edward McCartan *Acrobat*, Laura Gardin Fraser was inspired by a pair of wrestlers, while Hunt Diederich fashioned *Death on Horseback*. Paul Manship finished two works: *The War Waif* and *Fallen Angel*. Whitney also made a small piece. Jo Davidson contributed a portrait head.
18 See Peter Pennoyer and Anne Walker, *The Architecture of Delano & Aldrich*, New York (W.W. Norton), 2003.
19 For more on Chanler see Gina Wouters and Andrea Gollin, eds., *Robert Winthrop Chanler: Discovering the Fantastic*, Miami (Vizcaya Museum and Gardens) and New York (Monacelli Press), 2016.
20 Jo Davidson, *Between Sittings*, New York (The Dial Press), 1951, p. 148.
21 Guy Pène du Bois, *Artists Say the Silliest Things*, New York (American Artists Group), 1940, p. 86.
22 *Ibid.*, p. 190.

Amaki *(pp.107–117)*

1 James A. Porter, *Modern Negro Art*, New York (Arno Press), 1969, p. 51.
2 Sharon F. Patton, *African-American Art*, New York (Oxford U. Press),1998, p. 73.
3 Johnston's portraits were sold in an Americana Folk and Decorative Arts auction that included fine furniture, decorative arts, folk art, silver, etc., unlike those of white contemporaries whose works are listed in American Portrait or American Fine Art auctions.
4 Patton, p. 79.
5 See www.taftmuseum.org/art/duncanson-murals/ or Taft Museum brochure.
6 Bannister is quoted in several sources stating: "...when the awards committee realized I was the person who won the award, an explosion could not have created more of a sensation in that room." The painting sold a few years later for $1500 to a Boston collector.
7 The statement appeared in a vignette on his travels in *Knickerbocker* Magazine where Tuckerman was a regular writer.
8 W.E.B. DuBois articulated his point of view in the well-known and widely read 1926 essay "The Criteria of Negro Art," with a preference for figurative, representational art.
9 Alaine Locke's views on an ancestral art legacy are usually interpreted as a call for abstract art, differing from the position of DuBois.
10 Harlem being the main stage for the Renaissance made Van Der Zee's photographs of national importance; but there were important New Negro photographers in various locations: Addison Scurlock in Washington, DC; Paul Poole in Atlanta; Elise Harleston in Charleston, SC; Charles "Teenie" Harris in Pittsburgh; Prentice Polk in Tuskegee, AL; and, Allen E. Cole in Cleveland, among others.
11 For detailed accounts of the impact of the AU Annual see *The All-Black Exhibition in America, 1863–1976*, unpublished dissertation by this author, for Emory University, 1994.
12 Robert Goodnough, ed., *Artists' Sessions at Studio 35*, Chicago (Soberscove Press), 2011.

Rosenkranz *(pp.120–129)*

1 Richard P. Wunder, *Hiram Powers, Vermont Sculptor, 1805–1873, Volume II Catalogue of Works*, Newark (U. of Delaware Press), 1991, pp. 188–202.
2 Dolly Sherwood, *Harriet Hosmer, American Sculptor 1830–1908*, Columbia, MO (U. of Missouri Press), 1991, pp. 218–23.
3 Henry James, *William Wetmore Story and His Friends* (1903), reprinted New York (Kennedy Galleries & Da Capo Press), 1969, p. 257.
4 Thayer Tolles, "The Puritan as Statuette," in *In Homage to Worthy Ancestors: The Puritan, The Pilgrim*, ed. Henry Duffy, Cornish, NH (The Saint-Gaudens Memorial), 2011, p. 70.
5 *Famous Small Bronzes: A Representative Exhibit Selected from the Works of Noted Contemporary Sculptors*, New York (Gorham Company), 1928.
6 Founded in the last quarter of the nineteenth century, the Alexis Rudier Foundry continued under the same family ownership until the early 1950s. Then it was taken over by a relative, Georges Rudier, and was no longer the same guarantor of quality.
7 One exception was Cecil Howard, who limited his editions to four bronze casts and often did not produce even that many.
8 John Flannagan, "The Image in the Rock," reprinted in Dorothy C. Miller, *The Sculpture of John B. Flannagan*, New York (Museum of Modern Art), 1942, p. 7.

Gill and Lagodich *(pp.130–145)*

1 Eight paintings by George Inness, Art Institute of Chicago, in chronological order: *Crossing the Ford*, 1848, oil on canvas, 22 ½ × 24 ½ in. (57.2 × 62.2 cm), Gift of Mrs. Edith Kepke MacDonald, 1977.487; and seven paintings, Edward B. Butler Collection: *Summer in the Catskills*, 1867, oil on canvas, 20 × 30 ½ in. (50.8 × 77.5 cm), 1912.1837; *Catskill Mountains*, 1870, oil on canvas, 48 ¾ × 72 ⅝ in. (123.8 × 184.5 cm), 1912.1623; *A Marine*, 1874–75, oil on canvas, 30 ¼ × 45 ¼ in. (76.8 × 114.9 cm), 1913.90; *The Mill Pond*, 1889, oil on canvas, 37 ¾ × 29 ¾ in. (95.9 × 75.6 cm), 1911.30; *Early Morning, Tarpon Springs*, 1892, oil on canvas, 42 3/16 × 32 ⅜ in. (107.2 × 82.2 cm), 1911.32; *The Home of the Heron*, 1893, oil on canvas, 30 × 45 in. (76.2 × 114.3 cm), 1911.31; *After a Summer Shower*, 1894, oil on canvas, 32 ¼ × 42 ⅜ in. (81.9 × 107.6 cm), 1911.29.
2 Details of Hassam's framing preferences can be found in Susan G. Larkin, "How Hassam Framed Hassams," in *Childe Hassam, American Impressionist*, H. Barbara Weinberg, New York (The Metropolitan Museum of Art), 2004, pp. 325–42.
3 Technical definitions of the gilding and related processes, including gold and metal leaf, bole, composition ornament, etc. throughout this chapter are adapted from *Origin to Originality* glossary, pp. 50–52 (ref. note 5 below).
4 Collection of the Birmingham Museum of Art: George Ferdinand Of, Jr, *Frame*, 1917, gesso and paint on wood, 23 ⅛ × 19 ⅞ × ⅜ in. (58.7 × 50.5 × 1 cm), Gift of Tracy Gill and Simeon Lagodich in memory of Franklin Riehlman, 2017.60; original to John Marin, *The Tree*, 1917, watercolor and graphite on paper, 19 ¼ × 16 in. (48.9 × 40.6 cm), Museum purchase with funds provided by the Altec-Styslinger Foundation, 1999.46.
5 *One Hundred Years on the Edge: The Frame in America 1820 to 1920*, exh. cat., Tracy Gill, Santa Monica, CA (Tatistcheff/Rogers), 1996. *Frames of Reference: From Object to Subject*, exh. cat., Nina Felshin and Tracy Gill, Middletown, CT (Wesleyan University), 2000. *The American Frame: From Origin to Originality*, exh. cat., Tracy Gill, New York (Gill & Lagodich Fine Period Frames), 2003. *Beaux Arts & Crafts: Masterpieces of American Frame Design 1890–1920 from the collection of Edgar O. Smith*, exh. cat., Tracy Gill, New York (Gill & Lagodich Fine Period Frames), 2011.
6 *Beaux Arts & Crafts: Masterpieces of American Frame Design 1890–1920 from the collection of Edgar O. Smith*, premiered at the High Museum of Art, Atlanta, GA, from September 25 to November 27, 2011. Four frames from this collection were also exhibited at the Hood Museum of Art, Hanover, NH, June 11 to September 4, 2011. All frames were included as part of a larger frame exhibition, *A Change of Taste: From the Gilded Age to the Craftsman Aesthetic, Featuring Beaux Arts and Arts & Crafts frames from the Edgar Smith Collection*, Julius Lowy Frame & Restoring Company, New York, January 24 to April 15, 2011. Selected empty frames in the collection were exhibited previously in the following venues: *The Regilded Age*, Newark Museum, NJ, 1991; *The American Frame: From Origin to Originality*, Hamilton College, Clinton, NY, and New York School of Interior Design, New York, 2003; *Framed in America*, Savannah College of Art & Design, GA, 2004; *The Secret Lives of Frames: One Hundred Years of Art and Artistry*, Chrysler Museum of Art, Norfolk, VA, and The Butler Institute of American Art, Youngstown, OH, 2007.
7 Edgar Smith in *Beaux Arts & Crafts*, *op. cit.*, p. 6.
8 "An interesting series of frames was produced by Henry Heydenryk, Jr. (1905–1994) in the 1940s and 50s; the carved 'wormy chestnut' frame style is sometimes referred to as 'driftwood.' Heydenryk's innovative design was inspired by the availability of unusual wood resulting from a chestnut tree blight in the 1920s and 30s. These frames were not gilded, and were finished instead with a pickled or painted patina that enhanced the unusual texture of the wood. Wormy chestnut frames are a popular choice for framing American Modernist works of art." *The American Frame*, *op. cit.*, p. 46.
9 Gertrude Stein, *Picasso*, New York (Dover Publications), 1984, p. 32 (reprint. Originally published London, B.T. Batsford, 1938).

Stoner *(pp.160–167)*

1 Personal correspondence by email by the author with Marc Simpson, September 5, 2018, and Kristin Hoermann, "A Hand Formed to Use the Brush," in *Winslow Homer: Paintings of the Civil War*, The Fine Arts Museums of San Francisco (Bedford Arts, Publishers), 1988, pp. 103–19.
2 Eleanor Quandt, "Technical Examination of Eighteenth-Century Paintings," in *American Painting to 1776: A Reappraisal*, ed. Ian M.G. Quimby, Charlottesville (U. Press of Virginia for the Henry Francis du Pont Winterthur Museum), 1971, pp. 345–70. Abigail Quandt, the daughter of Russell and Eleanor Quandt, is now the esteemed Senior Conservator of Manuscripts and Rare Books at the Walters Art Museum, Baltimore, MD, and has carried out a sophisticated technical study of the Archimedes Palimpsest.
3 The author published an article in 2012: Joyce Hill Stoner, "Turning Points in Technical Art History in American Art," *American Art*, 26, No. 1, Spring 2012, pp. 2–9, listing many published collaborative technical studies in

American art. Some of those are reiterated here, but the present article emphasizes collaboration toward connoisseurship, especially more recently.

Here follow some earlier landmark studies. See, for instance, John Paul Driscoll and John K. Howat, *John Frederick Kensett: An American Master*, New York (W.W. Norton in association with Worcester Art Museum), 1985; *The Voyage of Life by Thomas Cole: Paintings, Drawings, and Prints*, Utica, NY (Museum of Art, Munson-Williams-Proctor Institute), 1985; Elizabeth Broun, *Albert Pinkham Ryder*, Washington, DC (Smithsonian Institution Press), 1989; Elizabeth Mankin Kornhauser, *Ralph Earl: The Face of the Young Republic*, New Haven, CT (Yale U. Press for the Wadsworth Atheneum), 1991; Doreen Bolger, Marc Simpson, and John Wilmerding, eds., *William M. Harnett*, New York (Metropolitan Museum of Art), Fort Worth, TX (Amon Carter Museum), 1992; Elizabeth Hutton Turner, ed., *Jacob Lawrence: The Migration Series*, Washington, DC (Rappahannock Press in association with Phillips Collection), 1993; Judith E. Stein, ed., *I Tell My Heart: The Art of Horace Pippin*, New York (Universe Publishing), Philadelphia (Pennsylvania Academy of the Fine Arts), 1993; Sarah Cash with Claire M. Barry, *Ominous Hush: The Thunderstorm Paintings of Martin Johnson Heade*, Fort Worth, TX (Amon Carter Museum), 1994; Brady M. Roberts *et al.*, *Grant Wood: An American Master Revealed*, Davenport, IA (Davenport Museum of Art), San Francisco (Pomegranate Artbooks), 1995; Stephen Hackney, "Colour and Tone in Whistler's 'Nocturnes' and 'Harmonies,' 1871–72," *Burlington Magazine* 136, no. 1099, October 1994, pp. 695–99; Joyce Townsend, "Whistler's Oil Painting Materials," *Burlington Magazine* 136, no. 1099, October 1994, pp. 690–95; René Paul Barilleaux and Sarah Whitaker Peters, *Georgia O'Keeffe: Color and Conservation*, Jackson, MS (Mississippi Museum of Art in association with Penn State U. Press), 2006; Judy Dion, "A Technical Comparison of Two Paintings from Inness's First Italian Trip," *George Inness in Italy*, in *Philadelphia Museum of Art Bulletin*, no. 2, 2011, pp. 45–60.

4 Personal correspondence by email between the author, Shelley Svoboda and Laura Pass Barry, August 29, 2018.
5 Continued studies by Anna Marley and Amber Kerr appeared in 2012 in Anna O. Marley, ed., *Henry Ossawa Tanner: Modern Spirit*, Berkeley (U. of California Press), Philadelphia (Pennsylvania Academy of the Fine Arts), 2012.
6 Dorothy Mahon, "Thomas Cole's *The Oxbow* and *The Consummation of Empire*: A technical comparison," in Elizabeth Mankin Kornhauser and Tim Barringer, *Thomas Cole's Journey: Atlantic Crossings*, New Haven, CT, and London (Yale U. Press), 2018, pp. 106–15.
7 See Fig. 4, page 164.
8 Personal correspondence by email between the author and Kathleen Foster, September 17, 2018.
9 Mark S. Tucker, "Framing *The Gross Clinic*: Conservators and Exhibitions," *American Art*, Vol. 26, No. 1, 2012, pp. 10–13.
10 Personal correspondence by email between the author and Jeffrey Weiss, September 10, 2018.
11 Maurice J. Cotter and E.V. Sayre, "Neutron Activation Analysis of Oil Paintings by Ralph A. Blakelock," *Bulletin of the American Group. International Institute for Conservation of Historic and Artistic Works*, Vol. 11, No. 2, April 1971, pp. 91–99, 101–06.
12 Anna Krez, Mark D. Mitchell, and Anikó Bezur, "Art of Darkness: Ralph Blakelock's *Moonlight*," *Yale University Art Gallery Bulletin*, 2017, pp. 42–48.
13 Susan Hobbs, Yu-tarng Cheng, and Jacqueline S. Olin, "Thomas Wilmer Dewing: A Look beneath the Surface," *Smithsonian Studies in American Art*, Vol. 4, Nos. 3, 4, Summer–Autumn 1990, pp. 62–85.
14 Maryan Wynn Ainsworth *et al.*, *Art and Autoradiography: Insights into the Genesis of Paintings by Rembrandt, Van Dyck, and Vermeer*, New York (Metropolitan Museum of Art), 1982.
15 E. Carl Grimm, "A Study of Authenticity in Paintings Attributed to Albert Pinkham Ryder," PhD diss., U. of Delaware, 1999.
16 Sadakichi Hartmann, "The Story of an American Painter," cited by Sheldon Keck, "Albert Ryder: His Technical Procedures," in William Innes Homer and Lloyd Goodrich, *Albert Pinkham Ryder: Painter of Dreams*, New York (Harry N. Abrams, Inc.), 1989, pp. 179–80.
17 Homer and Goodrich, *op. cit.*, p. 117.

Reist *(pp. 194–202)*

1 See Luhrs (ed.), *op.cit.*, pp.57–58, on page 195, caption to Fig. 1.
2 The study mount in the Frick Art Reference Library cites multiple unpublished sources to trace the provenance. Primary among them are communications with the owners, Mrs. Arkell, Mrs. Campbell, and Mrs. Wilson, in 1951, 1971, and 1976, respectively.
3 Frederic Fairchild Sherman, 'Gilbert Stuart's First Portrait of Washington from Life: The Vaughan Picture Painted in 1795', *Art in America*, Vol. 11, no. 1, December 1922, p. 44. For the complete provenance of the work see https://www.nga.gov/collection/art-object-page.1121.html#provenance. At one time the Gallery version was considered the original portrait by Stuart that was said to have been purchased by the artist William Winstanley, but it has since been recognized as an autograph replica, as is explained in Carrie Rebora Barratt and Ellen G. Miles, eds., *Gilbert Stuart*, exh. cat., New York (Metropolitan Museum of Art) and New Haven, CT (Yale U. Press), 2004, pp. 136–37.
4 John Hill Morgan and Mantle Fielding, *The Life Portraits of Washington and their Replicas*, Philadelphia, 1931, pp. 229–35, 250; Lawrence Park, *Gilbert Stuart: An Illustrated Descriptive List of His Works*, 4 vols., New York (W.E. Rudge), 1926, Vol. 2, pp. 845–46. See also the earlier publication that identifies fourteen versions: Mantle Fielding, *Gilbert Stuart's Portraits of George Washington*, Philadelphia, 1923, pp. 113–28.
5 See Fig. 3, page 198.
6 Barratt and Miles, *op. cit.*, pp. 141–46.
7 Adelyn Dohme Breeskin, *Mary Cassatt: A Catalogue Raisonné of the Oils, Pastels, Watercolors, and Drawings*, Washington, DC (Smithsonian Institution Press), 1970, p. 125, no. 268. Sotheby's, New York, American Paintings, May 20, 1998. Carter B. Horsley, *The City Review*, http://www.thecityreview.com/amptsp98.html.
8 *First Exhibition: Watercolors by Andrew Wyeth*, exh. cat., New York, Macbeth Gallery, October 19–November 1, 1937. The checklist is viewable online at http://www.libmma.org/digital_files/macbeth/B16372062.PDF#view=Fit.

Washington *(pp. 242–249)*

1 Confusion remains, among the general public and civic officials, about the difference between monuments and memorials. This confusion is, in part, responsible for the cultural iconoclasm that has led to the vandalism and destruction of monuments to Robert E. Lee and others and requests to eliminate monuments, memorials, and even street and school names honoring figures such as George Washington. In some cases, such as in Baltimore, problematic sculptures were removed until determination for either a recontextualization or less public display is planned. In other cases, such artworks were destroyed by riotous crowds in rebellion of the ideals or motivations for which the memorialized figure stood.
2 https://www.smithsonianmag.com/arts-culture/george-catlins-obsession-72840046/ Accessed January 19, 2019.
3 Richard A. Grusin, *Culture, Technology, and the Creation of America's National Parks*, Cambridge, UK (Cambridge U. Press), 2004, p. 102.
4 Thomas W. Gaehtgens and Heinz Ickstadt (eds.), *American Icons: Transatlantic Perspectives on Eighteenth- and Nineteenth-Century American Art*, Santa Monica, CA (Getty Center for the History of Art and the Humanities), 1992, p. 1.

Palmor *(pp. 250–257)*

1 John Berger, *Ways of Seeing*, BBC broadcast, London (Penguin), 1977, p. 7.
2 Frances K. Pohl, "Framing America: A Social History of American Art," *American Art*, 4th ed., vol. 1, New York (Thames & Hudson), 2017, p. 12.
3 David Lubin, *Picturing a Nation: Art and Social Change in Nineteenth-Century America*, New Haven, CT (Yale U. Press), 1994, unpaged preface.
4 See Wanda M. Corn, "Coming of Age: Historical Scholarship in American Art," *The Art Bulletin*, Vol. 70, No. 2, June 1988, p. 202.
5 *Ibid.*, p. 203.
6 Timothy Anglin Burgard, "The Evolving Collection," in *Masterworks of American Painting at the De Young*, Timothy Anglin Burgard, ed., San Francisco (Fine Arts Museums of San Francisco), 2005, p. xi.

7 Introductory text from the de Young American galleries, Timothy Anglin Burgard, Curator-in-Charge.
8 Pohl, *op. cit.*, Vol. 16, No. 2, Summer 2002, p. 12.
9 Michael Leja, "American Art's Shifting Boundaries," *American Art*, Vol. 11, No. 2, Summer 1997, p. 48.
10 De Young museum ledger book entry, 1916.
11 Claire Perry, *Pacific Arcadia: Images of California, 1600–1915*, New York (Oxford U. Press), 1999, p. 84. While undocumented tradition maintains that Latham arranged for the education of the sitter (the painting came into the collection with a note in the ledger, "Educated by Milton S. Latham/1827–1882," the precise nature of the sitter's association with Latham is still unknown. A reference to "Wahla's" employment by Brannan can be found in the caption to the illustration entitled "California Indians," illustration no. 13 on page 52 in *The Annals of San Francisco* by Frank Soulé, John H. Gihon, and James Nisbet, New York (D. Appleton), 1855. Latham was California's governor in 1860 and a United States senator from 1860 to 1863.
12 Perry, *op. cit.*, p. 85.
13 Julie Schimmel, "Settlement and Development: Claiming the West," in William H. Truettner, *The West as America: Reinterpreting Images of the Frontier, 1820–1920*, Washington, DC (Smithsonian Institution Press), 1991, p. 182.
14 Robert Hughes, "How the West Was Spun," *TIME*, May 13, 1991, p. 80.
15 Perry, *op. cit.*, p. 85.
16 Schimmel, *op. cit.*, p. 182.
17 Eugenio M. Rothe, M.D., Dan Tzuang, M.D., and Andres J. Pumariega, M.D., "Acculturation, Development, and Adaptation," *Child and Adolescent Psychiatric Clinics of North America* 19, Issue 4, October 2010, p. 684. Also see Sally Mills, catalogue entry in *The American Canvas: Paintings from the Collection of the Fine Arts Museums of San Francisco*, New York (Hudson Hills Press in Association with the Museums), 1989, p. 88.
18 See Henry Nash Smith's description of Western types "conceived in terms of antithesis between nature and civilization, between freedom and law, that has governed most American interpretations of the westward movement," Henry Nash Smith, *Virgin Land: The American West as Symbol and Myth*, Cambridge, MA (Harvard U. Press), 1950, p. 60. Also see C. Richard King, *Unsettling America: The Uses of Indianness in the 21st Century*, Lanham, MD (Rowman & Littlefield), 2013, p. xvi.
19 King, *op. cit.*, p. xvi.
20 Linda Martín Alcoff and Satya P. Mohanty, "Reconsidering Identity Politics: An Introduction," in *Identity Politics Reconsidered*, New York (Palgrave Macmillan), 2015, p. 6.
21 King, *op. cit.*, p. xvi.
22 Corn, *op. cit.*, p. 196.
23 Lisa Adkins and Celia Lury, "The Labour of Identity: Performing Identities, Performing Economies," *Economy and Society* 28, no. 4, 1999, p. 598.
24 Rachel Schreiber, *Gender and Activism in a Little Magazine: The Modern Figures of the Masses*, Burlington, VT (Ashgate), 2011, pp. 39, 41.
25 Daniell Cornell, *American Accents: Visual Culture as History*, San Francisco (Fine Arts Museums of San Francisco), 2002, p. 43.
26 John Gladstone, "Social Realism in American Art: The Generation of 1876," *The Journal of Decorative and Propaganda Arts*, Vol. 20, 1994, p. 128.
27 Schreiber, *op. cit.*, p. 41.
28 Erika Doss, "Toward an Iconography of American Labor: Work, Workers, and the Work Ethic in American Art, 1930–1945," *Design Issues*, Vol. 13, No. 1, "Designing the Modern Experience, 1885–1945," Spring 1997, p. 60.
29 Thomas H. Pauly, "American Art and Labor: The Case of Anshutz's *The Ironworkers' Noontime*," *American Quarterly*, Vol. 40, No. 3, September 1988, p. 336.
30 Randall C. Griffin, "Thomas Anshutz's 'The Ironworkers' Noontime': Remythologizing the Industrial Worker," *Smithsonian Studies in American Art*, Vol. 4, Nos. 3/4, Summer–Autumn 1990, p. 133.
31 Katharine G. Abraham, "The Pendulum Will Swing Back," US Bureau of Labor Statistics, *Monthly Labor Review*, August 2015, unpaged.
32 Michael G. Kammen, *In the Past Lane: Historical Perspectives on American Culture*, New York (Oxford U. Press), 1999, p. 119.
33 Sarah Burns, *Painting the Dark Side: Art and the Gothic Imagination in Nineteenth-Century America*, Berkeley, CA (U. of California Press), 2004, p. 46.
34 Bruce W. Chambers, "David Gilmour Blythe's Pittsburgh: 1850–65," *Carnegie Magazine* 55, no. 5, May 1981, p. 19.
35 Marjorie B. Searl, *Seeing America: Painting and Sculpture from the Collection of the Memorial Art Gallery of the University of Rochester*, Rochester, NY (U. of Rochester Press), 2006, p. 80.
36 William J. Stuntz, *Unequal Justice*, Harvard Law Review, Vol. 121, no. 8, June 2008, pp. 1970–71.
37 *Ibid.*, pp. 1972–73.
38 See Elizabeth Hinton, LeShae Henderson, and Cindy Reed, "An Unjust Burden: The Disparate Treatment of Black Americans in the Criminal Justice System," New York (Vera Institute of Justice), 2018, and Bruce Western, *Punishment and Inequality in America*, New York (Russell Sage Foundation), 2006.
39 Roderic B. Mathews and Juan Carlos Botero, "Access to Justice in the United States: Findings from the Newly Released Rule of Law Index of the World Justice Project," *Virginia Lawyer*, Vol. 59, December 2010, p. 25.
40 Beau Dure, "Millennials Continue Urbanization of America, Leaving Small Towns," *NPR*, October 21, 2014, https://www.npr.org/2014/10/21/357723069/millennials-continue-urbanization-of-america-leaving-small-towns, accessed December 27, 2018.
41 Mary Ellen W. Hern, "Picnicking in the Northeastern United States, 1840–1900," *Winterthur Portfolio*, Vol. 24, Nos. 2/3, Summer–Autumn 1989, p. 142.
42 Lee M. Edwards, "The Life and Career of Jerome Thompson," *The American Art Journal*, Vol. 14, No. 4, Autumn 1982, p. 11.
43 Leja, *op. cit.*, p. 49.

Waxter *(pp. 258–265)*

1 Christopher Gray, "Set in Flight by Gouache and Oil," *The New York Times*, August 29, 2014, RE6.
2 *Ibid.*
3 *Ibid.*
4 Sam Hunter, *The Rise of the Art World in America: Knoedler at 150*, New York (Knoedler & Co.), 1996.
5 *Ibid.*
6 *Ibid.*
7 Christopher Gray, "Where Old Masters Flew Off the Walls," *The New York Times*, December 5, 2014, RE8.
8 *Ibid.*
9 *Ibid.*
10 *Ibid.*
11 Suzanne Muchnic, "Norton Simon: A Look at the Art Purchase That Transformed the Collector," *Los Angeles Times*, October 17, 2014.
12 Robert Doty, *Photo-Secession: Photography as a Fine Art*, Rochester, NY (George Eastman House), 1960, p. 43.
13 Sarah Greenough, *Modern Art and America: Alfred Stieglitz and his New York Galleries*, New York & London (National Gallery of Art, Bulfinch Press), 2000, pp. 26–53.
14 Joan Washburn, Interview with Dorsey Waxter, New York, December 11, 2011.

Force *(pp. 266–277)*

1 The Corcoran Gallery of Art was absorbed by the National Gallery of Art in 2014.
2 Charles E. Baker, "The American Art-Union" in Mary Bartlett Cowdrey, ed., *American Academy of Fine Arts and American Art-Union, 1816–1852*, Vol. 1, New York (New-York Historical Society), 1953, p. 98.
3 *Ibid.*, pp. 232–36; pp. 138–39. The American Art Union existed until 1852, while other such entities including the Western Art Union in Cincinnati were active from 1847 to 1850.
4 In 1929, the American Art Association merged with Anderson Auction Company to form American Art Association-Anderson Galleries, Inc. In 1938, they were taken over by Parke-Bernet Galleries, the largest auction company in the United States, and by 1964, they had been absorbed by Sotheby's in the UK.
5 Thomas Lawton and Linda Merrill, *Freer: A Legacy of Art*, Washington, DC (Freer Gallery of Art, Smithsonian Institution, in association with H.N. Abrams), 1993, p. 9.
6 *History of the Whitney*, Whitney Museum of American Art, accessed on 3/27/2019: https://whitney.org/about/history.
7 Argyrol is a silver nitrate antiseptic to prevent blindness in newborns.
8 *American Paintings and Works on Paper in the Barnes Foundation*, exh. cat., Richard J. Wattenmaker and Derek Gillman, Merion, PA; New Haven, CT (The Barnes Foundation in association with Yale U. Press), 2010, pp. 17–20.
9 *INTERSECTIONS @ 5: Contemporary Art Projects at the Phillips*, exh. cat., Vesela

Sretenović, Washington, DC (The Phillips Collection), 2015, p. 12.

10 Lindsay Pollock, *The Girl with the Gallery: Edith Gregor Halpert and the Making of the Modern Art Market*, New York (Public Affairs), 2006, pp. 381–85. When Halpert's collection was sold at Sotheby's in 1973, it brought the sale of American Modernism to new heights.

11 Gerard C. Wertkin (ed.), *Encyclopedia of American Folk Art*, New York (Routledge), 2004, p. 317.

12 Quoted in *American paintings, 1815–1865: one hundred and thirty-six paintings from the M. and M. Karolik collection in the Museum of Fine Arts, Boston, together with fourteen paintings from the private collection of Maxim Karolik*, exh. cat., Museum of Fine Arts, Boston, 1957–59, p. 10.

13 Oral history interview with Raymond J. Horowitz, Oct. 20–Nov. 5, 2004. Archives of American Art, Smithsonian Institution. Raymond Horowitz was a corporate lawyer and founding partner of Graubard Miller in New York and Mr. Fraad was chairman of Ogden Allied Maintenance Corporation.

14 *Major Gift to Colby Establishes Lunder Institute For American Art*, Colby University, accessed 3/27/2019, http://www.colby.edu/news/2017/02/03/major-gift-to-colby-establishes-lunder-institute-for-american-art/.

15 Oral history interview with Raymond J. Horowitz, Oct. 20–Nov. 5, 2004. Archives of American Art, Smithsonian Institution.

16 The Bierstadt sold for $1,870,000 and the Cassatt for $4,100,000. All auction records include buyer's premium.

17 "MIA Welcomes Long-Term Loan of Myron Kunin Collection," Minneapolis Institute of Art, accessed 3/24/2019: https://new.artsmia.org/press/mia-welcomes-long-term-loan-of-myron-kunin-collection/.

18 Kennedy Galleries was founded as H. Wunderlich & Co.

19 The Eiteljorg Museum of American Indians and Western Art was founded in 1989 and is one of only two museums east of the Mississippi that features both Western art and Native American art and artifacts.

20 George Bellows's *Men of the Docks* was purchased by the National Gallery for $25,500,000.

Author Biographies

AMALIA K. AMAKI is an artist, art historian, curator, and writer. She received a BA in Journalism from Georgia State University, BA in Photography from the University of New Mexico, and an MA and PhD in Modern American Art and Culture from Emory University's Institute of Liberal Arts, where she was a Foreign Study Fellow in France. Dr. Amaki taught at Spelman College, University of North Georgia, University of Delaware, and University of Alabama, and was visiting scholar at Student Art Centers International (SACI) in Florence, Italy. Her publications include *A Century of African American Art: The Paul R. Jones Collection*; *Hale Woodruff, Nancy Elizabeth Prophet, and the Academy*, and several anthology essays on art topics. Her thirty solo shows include a retrospective at the National Museum for Women in the Arts and the Spelman College Museum of Fine Art. She received an NEA photography fellowship, and has had commissions from Hartsfield-Jackson Atlanta International Airport, Valdosta State University, the 1996 Olympics, and several public agencies and private corporations.

JANE BIANCO, with a BFA from Boston University and an MA from the University of Wisconsin-Madison, has a background in art-historical research, collections management, exhibitions organization, teaching, conservation assistance, painting, and illustration. Since joining the Farnsworth Art Museum, she has curated exhibitions of paintings, drawings and prints, textiles, sculpture, decorative arts, and architectural concentrations featuring eighteenth- through early twenty-first-century works. Recently, she mounted a retrospective on Modernist painter Marguerite Zorach, securing sixty works of art on loan, including paintings and large-scale textiles, from public institutions and private collectors nationwide. In 2018 she organized the first in-depth examination of Maine's role in the New Deal-era art project, the Index of American Design, borrowing twenty-four watercolor renderings from the National Gallery of Art in Washington, DC, as well as historic photographic files, reuniting them with artifacts from local institutions. She is currently working on future exhibitions of a twentieth-century textile artist, an amateur nineteenth-century photographer, the arts and crafts movement in Maine, and photographer Eliot Porter.

GRAHAM C. BOETTCHER is the R. Hugh Daniel Director of the Birmingham Museum of Art, Birmingham, Alabama. Arriving in 2006, he served variously as a postdoctoral fellow, curator of American art, chief curator, and deputy director prior to his appointment as director in 2017. Boettcher has held fellowships at the Yale University Art Gallery, Amon Carter Museum of American Art, and Terra Foundation Summer Residency in Giverny. His exhibitions include *The Look of Love: Eye Miniatures from the Skier Collection*, named by *Architectural Digest* in "The Season's Best Museum Shows" (2012). Boettcher's publications include *The Look of Love*, and contributions to *American Sublime: Landscape Painting in the United States, 1820–1880* (Tate Britain, 2002) and *Life, Liberty, and the Pursuit of Happiness: American Art from the Yale University Art Gallery* (2008). Boettcher received his BA and PhD from Yale University, and an MA from the University of Washington.

ELIZABETH BROUN is Director Emerita of the Smithsonian American Art Museum and its branch museum, the Renwick Gallery, which she led from 1989 through 2016. During her tenure, the Museum was consistently a leader in distance learning and digital media; the traveling exhibition program served more than 200 museums; and the resident fellowship program became the largest in the American art field. In addition, the peer-reviewed journal of new scholarship called *American Art* was enhanced and a half-million electronic records were published online, including a database of all outdoor sculptures in the country.

Dr. Broun led comprehensive renovations of the museum's two National Historic Landmark buildings. Enhancements to the Old Patent Office Building include a visible conservation center and public art storage facility, and a courtyard canopy designed by Norman Foster. Renovation of the Renwick Gallery transformed the nineteenth-century structure into a twenty-first-century destination. Attendance at the two museums quadrupled post-renovation, to 1.8 million visitors.

Currently Dr. Broun serves on the Board of Directors of the Henry Luce Foundation and The Olana Partnership. She is Visual Art Advisor to the Kennedy Center for its expansion project, called The Reach.

PRISCILLA VAIL CALDWELL has been an art dealer, curator, and advisor for over twenty years and currently serves as advisor to the Estate of Stuart Davis. She works with a select group of private collectors building significant collections and is an independent curator. Recent well-received and -reviewed exhibitions include in 2017 *The Enormity of the Possible* and in 2018 *Lines Thicken: Stuart Davis in Black and White*, both held at Kasmin Gallery in Chelsea. She graduated from Northwestern University with a BA in art history and went on to complete graduate studies in art history at Williams College. She is currently an active member of the board of SculptureCenter in Long Island City and serves as a member of the Advisory Committee at Northwestern University's Block Museum of Art. She has juried numerous shows, taught art history, participated in panels, and is a recipient of a Kress Foundation Grant.

HEATHER CAMPBELL COYLE is Chief Curator and Curator of American Art at the Delaware Art Museum. She is the editor and lead author of *Howard Pyle: American Master Rediscovered* (2011), *Fashion, Circus, Spectacle: Photographs by Scott Heiser* (2014), and *An American Journey: The Art of John Sloan* (2017), and co-editor and co-author of *John Sloan's New York* (2007). She has also published essays and curated exhibitions on Leonard Baskin, William Glackens, Robert Henri, Gertrude Käsebier, and the Society of Independent Artists. Dr. Coyle lectures and researches primarily on photography and American art from the late nineteenth and early twentieth centuries.

THOMAS C. AND CHARLES DANZIGER are brothers and partners in the New York City law firm of Danziger, Danziger & Muro, LLP, which specializes in advising both buyers and sellers of works of art. Thomas graduated with Honors in General Scholarship from Wesleyan University, and The New York University School of Law. Before founding Danziger, Danziger & Muro, LLP, he practiced law with the firm of Shearman & Sterling in New York. Charles Danziger is a *Magna Cum Laude* graduate of Yale University, and also graduated from The New York University School of Law. Before joining Danziger, Danziger, & Muro, LLP, he practiced law at Milbank, Tweed, Hadley & McCloy in New York and Nagashima & Ohno in Tokyo, and was Assistant General Counsel at The Museum of Modern Art. He is fluent in Japanese, French, and German. The brothers have been listed by artnet and *Art +Auction* magazine as among the world's top art lawyers.

BETSY FAHLMAN is a Professor of Art History at Arizona State University, where she has taught since 1988. She is also Adjunct Curator of American Art at the Phoenix Art Museum. Her specialties include American Modernism, the New Deal, industrial archeology, and women artists. Her books include *Kraushaar Galleries: Celebrating 125 Years* (2010), *New Deal Art in Arizona* (2009), *James Graham & Sons: A Century and a Half in the Art Business* (2007), *Chimneys and Towers: Charles Demuth's Late Paintings of Lancaster* (2007), and *Guy Pène du Bois: Painter of Modern Life* (2004). Essays include "Marguerite Zorach: The Thirties and Beyond," in *Marguerite Zorach: An Art-Filled Life* (Farnsworth Art Museum, 2018), "Robert Winthrop Chanler: Reclaiming an American Modernist," in *Robert Winthrop Chanler: Discovering the Fantastic* (Vizcaya Museum and Gardens, 2016), "Pennsylvania Precisionism: Regionalism and Modernity," in *Rural Modern: American Art Beyond the City* (Brandywine River Museum of Art, 2016), and "Tumult and Triumph: Taking the Pulse of Western American Art in the 1930s," in *Western Passages: Decades: An Expanded Context for Western American Art, 1900–1940* (Denver Art Museum, 2013).

DEBRA J. FORCE holds a BA from Ohio Wesleyan University and an MA from and post-graduate work at the University of Pennsylvania. She is the President of Debra Force Fine Art in New York, a gallery established in 1999, offering American paintings, works on paper, and sculpture of the eighteenth to twentieth centuries as well as consulting and appraisal services. Previously, she has held positions as Curator and Director of the CIGNA Museum and Art Collection in Philadelphia, and as Senior Vice President and Head of the American Paintings Department at Christie's, Director of American Paintings at Hirschl & Adler Galleries, and Director of Beacon Hill Fine Art, all in New York. She is a member of the Art Dealers Association of America and presently serves on the board of The Archives of American Art, a division of the Smithsonian Institution, Washington, DC. Since 1999, she has appeared as a specialist appraiser on the PBS series *Antiques Roadshow*.

TRACY GILL and SIMEON LAGODICH are frame scholars, consultants, and co-founders of Gill & Lagodich Fine Period Frames, New York (est. 1991), pre-eminent framers of American paintings for museums. The firm's period and custom-made replica frames are displayed in museums and noteworthy private collections internationally.

Tracy Gill is a New York City native. She earned a BA in English and Fine Art from Hamilton College. Co-curator of four period frame exhibitions, she authored the accompanying catalogues, has written numerous magazine articles on period frames and decorative arts history, and lectures on the history of frames. Previously she held positions as senior editor and corporate promotion director, Hearst Magazines Division, New York. She researched and wrote *Wedding Nightmares: As Told to the Editors of Bride's Magazine* (Condé Nast/Penguin Books, 1993), and authored *Forget-Me-Nots: A Victorian Book of Love* (Workman Publishing, 1990).

Simeon Lagodich is the primary frame buyer for Gill & Lagodich, and co-curator of four period frame exhibitions. He is a hands-on expert in frame restoration and historical fabrication. An authority in his field, Lagodich serves annually on the Frame Vetting Committee for the world-renowned East Side House Settlement Winter Antiques Show, New York. A native of Kenosha, Wisconsin, Lagodich is an American realist painter and frame designer. He attended the University of Wisconsin, Milwaukee, and earned a Max Beckmann scholarship to complete post-graduate studies at the Brooklyn Museum Art School. Lagodich oil paintings, watercolors, prints, and frames hang in major corporate and private collections; and his artwork has been reproduced in a number of books featuring American realist painters.

BARBARA GUGGENHEIM is an art advisor. She has a doctorate in Art History from Columbia University, has taught on the college level, and has worked at Sotheby's and Christie's. She and her partner at Guggenheim Asher Associates have built collections for several corporations, such as Sony and Coca-Cola, and individuals such as Tom Cruise and Steven Spielberg.

She has written numerous articles and several books on the art business, including *Art World: The New Rules of the Game*. In addition, she lectures widely on art as an investment, all aspects of art collecting, and nineteenth- and twentieth-century art. As well, she is a humorist, with published essays in *W*, *Elle*, and *Harper's Bazaar*.

She is married to an attorney, lives in Malibu, commutes between offices in Beverly Hills and New York, and travels all over the world finding works for her clients.

SETH HOPKINS is the Executive Director of the Booth Western Art Museum in Cartersville, Georgia, a position he has held since 2000. The Booth Museum houses the largest permanent exhibition space for Western American art in the world. He is also the Executive Director of Georgia Museums, Inc., which operates the Booth Museum, Bartow History Museum, Tellus Science Museum, and, opening in 2020, the Savoy Automobile Museum. He has served as the President of Museums West Consortium, an association of fourteen museums organized for the advancement of Western American art, history, and culture. He holds an undergraduate degree in journalism from Syracuse University and a graduate degree in liberal arts from the University of Oklahoma with concentrations in Western history, Museum studies, and Western American art history.

BETTY KRULIK has over forty years of experience in the handling of American and European nineteenth- and twentieth-century art; she has sold to and on behalf of major collectors and museums around the nation. She has acted as appraiser for corporate and institutional collections as well as private collectors.

She is a Certified Member of the Appraisers Association of America, and currently serves on its board as a past president. She is on the Personal Property Resource Panel of the Appraisal Foundation in Washington, DC. Currently she serves on the board of the American Friends of Masterworks Museum of Bermuda Art. She has appeared as an appraiser on *Antiques Roadshow*, and has lectured at universities and museum groups around the nation. She serves on the Scholars Lecture committee of the Frick Art Reference Library. She is a member of the Private Art Dealers Association.

JO BACKER LAIRD is Of Counsel at Patterson Belknap Webb & Tyler, LLP. Her practice includes all aspects of art law, working with artists, private collectors, museums, art organizations, tax-exempt organizations, galleries, dealers, advisors, and financial institutions. Prior to joining Patterson Belknap in 2008, Ms. Laird served for ten years as Senior Vice President and General Counsel of Christie's, Inc., where she was responsible for all legal issues relating to the company's business in North and South America. She has extensive knowledge and experience in the full range of transactions and litigation issues related to works of art and the art market, including auction and private sale agreements, consignments, financing arrangements using art as collateral, commissions of art, authenticity and title disputes, artists' rights and intellectual property, and issues relating to World War II restitution and cultural property cases. Ms. Laird also co-teaches a seminar on art law at the Columbia University School of Law.

LAUREN PALMOR received an MA with Merit in the History of Art from the Courtauld Institute of Art (2009), and a PhD in Art History from the University of Washington (2016), where her dissertation research addressed questions of ageism in the study of nineteenth-century genre painting. She has held fellowships at Winterthur and the Philadelphia Museum of Art, and has worked for a number of institutions, including the Brooklyn Museum, The Metropolitan Museum of Art, the Seattle Art Museum, and the Frye Art Museum. She has contributed to a number of exhibition catalogues, including *Revelations: Art from the African American South* (2017) and *Cult of the Machine: Precisionism and American Art* (2018). She frequently supports institutional digital partnerships, working collaboratively to design new ways of sharing and experiencing American art with museum audiences.

LISA N. PETERS received her PhD from the Graduate Center, City University of New York, in 1995, completing a dissertation on the art of John Henry Twachtman (1853–1902). She is currently an independent art historian, teaching at Pratt Institute (Brooklyn) and St. Joseph's College (Brooklyn). Her publications include *The Portrait Collection of New-York–Presbyterian—Weill Cornell Medical Center* (2015); "'All the Paintable Things in Europe': Edgar Payne's European Art and Travels, 1922–24, 1928" (Pasadena Museum of California Art, 2012); "'An Atmosphere of Youthful Enthusiasm under a Hospitable Sky': The American Artists' Colony in Polling, Bavaria, 1872–1881" (*American Art Journal*, 2000); *John Henry Twachtman: An American Impressionist* (High Museum of Art, 1999); *Visions of Home: American Impressionist Images of Suburban Leisure and Country Comfort* (Dickinson College, 1997); and *American Impressionist Masterpieces* (Hugh Lauter Levin, 1991). She was research and publications director at Spanierman Gallery, New York (1986–2012). Dr. Peters is the author of the forthcoming online complete catalogue of Twachtman's work, to be published on the website of the Greenwich Historical Society, Cos Cob, Connecticut.

INGE REIST is the Director Emerita of the Center for the History of Collecting, which she established at The Frick Collection and Frick Art Reference Library in 2007. Prior to that, she was the Chief of Research Collections and Programs and Head of the Photo Archive at the Frick. In 2013, she was the founding president of PHAROS – The International Consortium of Photo Archives. Holding a PhD in Art History from Columbia University, specializing in

Italian Renaissance and Baroque art, she has published widely in major journals including *The Art Bulletin*, *Gazette des Beaux-Arts*, and in the *Blackwell Companion to Renaissance and Baroque Art*. She has edited many books and published numerous articles on the history of collecting, among them *Provenance: An Alternate History of Art*. From 2005 to 2011 she was Chairman of the Association of Research Institutes in Art History. Since retiring after thirty-seven years at the Frick, she remains active in the field, having recently presented at conferences at Brandeis University, the New Orleans Museum of Art, and the Gulbenkian Foundation in Lisbon, as well as The Frick Collection.

JOEL ROSENKRANZ with emerita partner Janis Conner founded Conner • Rosenkranz, LLC, in 1980 as a private gallery focusing on American sculpture of the late nineteenth and early twentieth centuries. Together they co-wrote *Rediscoveries in American Sculpture: Studio Works, 1893–1939*, published in 1989 by the University of Texas Press. The gallery has produced numerous catalogues highlighting outstanding examples of American sculpture in the inventory. In 2018 the gallery published a new catalogue titled *The Art of Display*, an original study of American pedestals of the nineteenth century. Other areas of strong interest are African American artists, early twentieth-century garden sculpture, and American works on paper, particularly from artists of the Woodstock (NY) artist colony.

He is a former board member of the Art Dealers Association of America and a supporter of the Friends of the American Wing at The Metropolitan Museum of Art and of the Noguchi Museum. He has a BA, an MA, and a PhD in English literature from New York University and came to the art world sideways in 1980—a detour he has never regretted.

RICHARD ROSSELLO was born and raised on Cape Cod. He received his BA from Colgate University and his MBA from Wharton at the University of Pennsylvania. After a stint working for CBS, Inc., he spent the next twenty-five years of his business career developing and operating more than a dozen restaurants in Pennsylvania and Delaware. In 2001, at the age of forty-eight and after a brief illness, he made the decision to switch careers in order to pursue his true passion—American art. During the last two decades, his Avery Galleries has had the good fortune to assist in building some of the country's most important collections and has forged relationships with many major museums around the nation. Richard lives near the gallery on Philadelphia's Main Line with his wife Bonnie. They have two grown children and a grandson.

LOUIS M. SALERNO is the owner of Questroyal Fine Art, LLC, New York, an established gallery specializing in quality American paintings from the nineteenth and twentieth centuries. Once a successful seller of thoroughbred breeding stock, he discovered his interest in American art in the 1970s. Driven by his entrepreneurial spirit and creativity, he later became a prominent art dealer, establishing Questroyal in the mid-1990s. Disenchanted by his experiences with other galleries, he vowed to differentiate Questroyal by treating all clients equally, regardless of their wealth or position. Together with his partner and son, co-owner Brent L. Salerno, he actively and persistently acquires quality American paintings, fueled by his confidence in and passion for American art. Hudson River School paintings remain at the core of Questroyal's constantly changing inventory, and every March the gallery mounts a highly anticipated exhibition and sale of more than one hundred Hudson River School paintings.

LIZ STERLING worked at Christie's for a decade, most recently as Head of American Art where she played a critical role in bringing in major business and growing both auction and private sales, as well as developing institutional relationships. During her tenure, the department set a number of auction records including $40,485,000 for Edward Hopper's *East Wind Over Weehawken*. Having worked with clients in a variety of collecting categories, Ms. Sterling left Christie's in December 2014 to become a curator for a prominent collector of Post-War and Contemporary Art. She received a BA in Art History from Williams, and spent time studying for an MA at Hunter College. She began her career as an associate at Linda Hyman Fine Arts. Now at Sotheby's, where she is a Senior Vice President, she has played an instrumental role in bringing in a wide variety of important and diverse consignments, most recently earning herself the title of Director of Private Sales.

JOYCE HILL STONER has taught for the Winterthur/University of Delaware Program in Art Conservation since 1976; she received her conservation certificate and MA from the Institute of Fine Arts of New York University, a PhD in Art History from UD, and has been a Visiting Scholar at the Metropolitan Museum and the Getty Museum. Both an art historian and a practicing paintings conservator, she has authored more than 120 book chapters and articles, and over the last two decades has been studying and treating the paintings of the Wyeth family. Andrew Wyeth painted her portrait in 1999. She is the founder and coordinator of the Foundation of the American Institute for Conservation oral history project; she is Edward F. and Elizabeth Goodman Rosenberg Professor of Material Culture Studies; Director, Preservation Studies Doctoral Program, UD. She has served on the board of the College Art Association and hopes to connect conservators and art historians whenever possible.

CAROL STRONE, founder of Carol Strone Advisory, Inc. in New York, provides comprehensive art and philanthropy advisory services to collectors and philanthropists nationwide. She holds a BA in History from Stanford University, a JD of Law from the University of Virginia School of Law, and an MA in the History of Decorative Arts, Design History and Material Culture from the Bard Graduate Center. After becoming a Senior Attorney at Shearman & Sterling in New York, she pursued a second career at The Metropolitan Museum of Art, where she worked for nearly a decade as a curatorial researcher in the American Wing. Thereafter, she became Director of Vance Jordan Fine Art before founding her own firm in 2004. Her multi-disciplinary background equips her to collaborate with mission-driven philanthropists in stewarding their art collecting and their charitable giving across multiple areas of expertise to achieve maximum well-being of people, place, and planet.

MEREDITH WARD is President of Meredith Ward Fine Art, a New York City gallery specializing in American art of the nineteenth and twentieth centuries with a particular focus on American Modernism. She received a BA in Art History from Tufts University and an MA in Art History from Columbia University. She is a member of the Art Dealers Association of America and is Vice President of The Private Art Dealers Association. She is the author of several essays for museum exhibitions, including "'The Life of a Great City': John Marin and the Brooklyn Bridge" for *Icon of Modernism: Representing the Brooklyn Bridge, 1883–1950* at The Georgia Museum of Art, University of Georgia, Athens (2016); and "'With Startling Conviction': The John Marin Collection at The Arkansas Arts Center" for *Becoming John Marin: Modernist at Work* at The Arkansas Arts Center, Little Rock (2018).

TIFFANY ELENA WASHINGTON, PhD, is an independent scholar specializing in the primary market for prints in the United States, Regionalist art, and the corporate and government patronage of art between 1934 and 1945. She has lectured on the art market, art and civic engagement, multiples, the distribution of art among the middle class, and Associated American Artists. She has taught at the University of Akron, Youngstown State University, and Cuyahoga Community College. She has written articles on Regionalist prints, Imperial Byzantine mosaics, Associated American Artists, the marketing and sales of art, and has contributed articles to the *Encyclopedia of Design* and the *Art Market Dictionary*. Recently she has been involved in community education surrounding the crises of problematic public monuments, helping to bring together art historians in conversation about how to recontextualize these monuments and handle their nuanced situations in ways that can benefit both art historians and the general public.

DORSEY WAXTER is a Partner at Van Doren Waxter, New York City. She is a past President of the Art Dealers Association of America (ADAA), 2012–2015. Her career began as a gallery assistant at Nancy Hoffman Gallery in 1974. In 1977 she began work at the André Emmerich Gallery, and rose to Director, contributing to the gallery's specialization in New York Color Field and post-World War II Abstraction. In 1991, she established Dorsey Waxter Fine Art, Inc., advising clients primarily in the secondary market and representing prominent estates. She then became Director of Greenberg Van Doren Gallery in 1998—which became Van Doren Waxter in 2013. The gallery's roster of estates and artists includes some of the most influential artists of the twentieth and twenty-first centuries such as James Brooks, Richard Diebenkorn, Moira Dryer, Ellsworth Kelly, John McLaughlin, Harvey Quaytman, Alan Shields, Frank Stella, Hedda Sterne, and Dorothea Rockburne.

ERIC WIDING, Deputy Chairman, Christie's Americas, is a recognized authority on American art and sculpture. He has worked at Christie's for over twenty years, twelve of them as head of the American Paintings Department. In 2018, the Collection of David and Peggy Rockefeller was among the major collections managed by Mr. Widing and the Christie's team. For its American art alone, the Rockefeller sale achieved $114,000,000, a record immediately overtaken by the sale of the Barney A. Ebsworth Collection, which achieved over $323,000,000 for its American paintings and sculpture, becoming the most valuable collection ever offered in the category. Among the Ebsworth highlights was Hopper's *Chop Suey*, which fetched almost $92,000,000, becoming the most expensive pre-war American artwork ever sold at auction. Prior to joining Christie's, Mr. Widing was an owner of Widing & Peck Fine Art, and before that he was director of the Richard York Gallery. His responsibilities as Deputy Chairman focus primarily on the market-leading American Paintings department, and he also works closely with colleagues across Christie's business categories.

KAREN WILKIN is a New York-based curator and critic specializing in twentieth-century Modernism. The author of monographs on Stuart Davis, David Smith, Anthony Caro, Kenneth Noland, Helen Frankenthaler, Isaac Witkin, Giorgio Morandi, Georges Braque, Hans Hofmann, and Edward Gorey, she has organized exhibitions of the work of these artists internationally. She was a juror for the American Pavilion of the 2009 Venice Biennale. Ms. Wilkin was a contributing editor of the Stuart Davis and Hans Hofmann Paintings Catalogues Raisonnés. She was co-curator of *American Vanguards: Graham, Davis, Gorky, de Kooning, and their Circle, 1927–1942* for the Addison Gallery of American Art (named best exhibition of 2012 by *The Boston Globe*) and *John Graham: Maverick Modernist* for the Parrish Art Museum. The Contributing Editor for Art for *The Hudson Review* and a regular contributor to *The New Criterion* and *The Wall Street Journal*, Ms. Wilkin teaches in the New York Studio School's MFA program.

Index

Page numbers in *italic* refer to the illustrations

Picture Credits

Jacket front: Fine Arts Museums of San Francisco, Gift of Mr. and Mrs. John D. Rockefeller 3rd, 1979.7.4

Jacket back: © 2019. Digital image Whitney Museum of American Art/Licensed by Scala

Endpapers: Frames designed by Stanford White, Gill & Lagodich Fine Period Frames, New York. © Gill & Lagodich, 2019. Photo credit: Simon Cherry

6. © Estate of Stuart Davis/VAGA at ARS, NY and DACS, London 2020. Photo: Collection of Stephen and Linda Sessler, Atlanta, Georgia
12–13. Collection of the Birmingham Museum of Art, Alabama; Gift of the Birmingham Public Library. Photo: Sean Pathasema
14. CC0 1.0 Courtesy of the RISD Museum, Providence, RI
17. CC0 1.0 Courtesy The Metropolitan Museum of Art, New York
18. Art Heritage/Alamy Stock Photo
19. CC0 1.0 Courtesy The Metropolitan Museum of Art, New York
20. Courtesy Questroyal Fine Art. Collection of J. Jeffrey and Ann Marie Fox
21. Courtesy Questroyal Fine Art
23. Historic Images/Alamy Stock Photo
25. Collection of the Birmingham Museum of Art, Alabama; Gift of the Birmingham Public Library. Photo: Sean Pathasema
26. Historic Collection/Alamy Stock Photo
27t. Collection of the Birmingham Museum of Art, Alabama; Gift of Dr. and Mrs. Harold E. Simon. Photo: Sean Pathasema
27b. Montana Historical Society, Mackay Collection, X1952.01.06
29. Photograph courtesy The Coeur d'Alene Art Auction
32. Collection of the Birmingham Museum of Art, Alabama; Museum purchase with funds provided by Mr. and Mrs. Houston Blount, Mr. and Mrs. Michael Bodnar, John Bohorfoush, Mr. and Mrs. Percy W. Brower, Jr., Mr. and Mrs. Thomas N. Carruthers, Jr., Catherine Collins, Mr. and Mrs. Henry C. Goodrich, Mr. and Mrs. Hugh Kaul, Harold and Regina Simon Fund, Mr. and Mrs. William M. Spencer III, Mr. and Mrs. Lee Styslinger, and other donors, 1987.4. Photo: Sean Pathasema
34. Collection of the Art Fund, Inc. at the Birmingham Museum of Art, Alabama. Photo: Sean Pathasema

35. The Birmingham Museum of Art, Alabama; Promised gift of Dr. and Mrs. Frederick Baekeland in honor of Margaret Livingston. Photo: Sean Pathasema
36. Collection of the Art Fund, Inc. at the Birmingham Museum of Art, Alabama; Bequest of Virginia Bissell Spencer. Photo: Sean Pathasema
37. Collection of the Art Fund, Inc. at the Birmingham Museum of Art, Alabama; Partial and promised gift of Mr. and Mrs. Donald L. Cook. Photo: Sean Pathasema
38. Collection of the Art Fund, Inc. at the Birmingham Museum of Art, Alabama; Gift of Marlene and Crawford Taylor in honor of Margaret G. Livingston, Thomas N. Carruthers, Jr., and William M. Spencer, III for their long years of service to this Museum, our community at large, and for their personal examples of servant leadership at its best. Photo: Sean Pathasema
40. CC0 1.0 Courtesy The Metropolitan Museum of Art, New York
43. Courtesy of the Pennsylvania Academy of the Fine Arts, Philadelphia. The Vivian O. and Meyer P. Potamkin Collection, Bequest of Vivian O. Potamkin
44l. Courtesy Abbeville Press
44r. CC0 1.0 Courtesy The Metropolitan Museum of Art, New York
47t. Art Heritage/Alamy Stock Photo
47b. Photography ©Terra Foundation for American Art, Chicago
48t. The Picture Art Collection/Alamy Stock Photo
48b. Historic Collection/Alamy Stock Photo
50. © Estate of John Sloan. ARS, NY/DACS, London 2020/John Sloan Manuscript Collection, Helen Farr Sloan Library & Archives, Delaware Art Museum
51. Everett Shinn Papers, Helen Farr Sloan Library and Archives, Delaware Art Museum
53. © Estate of John Sloan. ARS, NY/DACS, London 2020/Universal Images Group North America LLC/Alamy Stock Photo
54. © Estate of John Sloan. ARS, NY/DACS, London 2020/Photo courtesy National Gallery of Art, Washington, DC
56. Courtesy of The Huber Family Collection
57. Digital image Whitney Museum of American Art/Licensed by Scala
60. © ARS, NY and DACS, London 2020/Photo courtesy National Gallery of Art, Washington, DC
61. Photo courtesy Meredith Ward Fine Art, New York
62. © ARS, NY and DACS, London 2020/Photo © 2019. The Art Institute of Chicago/Art Resource, NY/Scala, Florence
63. © ARS, NY and DACS, London 2020/Photo: Private collection, courtesy Meredith Ward Fine Art, New York.
64. © ARS, NY and DACS, London 2020/Photo © 2019. The Art Institute of Chicago/Art Resource, NY/Scala, Florence
65. © ARS, NY and DACS, London 2020/Photo courtesy National Gallery of Art, Washington, DC
67. Private Collection/Photo © Christie's Images/ Bridgeman Images
68. Photograph Courtesy of Sotheby's, Inc. © 2019
71t. Photograph Courtesy of Sotheby's, Inc. © 2019
71b. Photograph Courtesy of Sotheby's, Inc. © 2019
72. Photograph Courtesy of Sotheby's, Inc. © 2019
74. Photograph by Ben Asen, Courtesy Private Collection. © The Zorach Collection, LLC
77t. Photo © Christie's Images/Bridgeman Images/© The Zorach Collection, LLC
77b. Photo © 2019. Christie's Images, London/ Scala, Florence/© The Zorach Collection, LLC
79. Collection of the Farnsworth Art Museum, Rockland, Maine; Museum purchase, 1991.17/© The Zorach Collection, LLC
81t. © The Zorach Collection, LLC
81b. Photo Digital Imageworks in Waterville, ME/© The Zorach Collection, LLC
82. © Estate of Stuart Davis/VAGA at ARS, NY and DACS, London 2020. Image Courtesy of Kasmin Gallery. Photo: Diego Flores
83. © Estate of Stuart Davis/VAGA at ARS, NY and DACS, London 2020. Image Courtesy Priscilla Caldwell
84t. © Estate of Stuart Davis/VAGA at ARS, NY and DACS, London 2020/Image Courtesy of Kasmin Gallery. Photo: Christopher Stach
84b. © Estate of Stuart Davis/VAGA at ARS, NY and DACS, London 2020. Photo: Peter Horree/Alamy Stock Photo
85t. © Estate of Stuart Davis/VAGA at ARS, NY and DACS, London 2020. Image Courtesy Priscilla Caldwell
85b. © Estate of Stuart Davis/VAGA at ARS, NY and DACS, London 2020. Image Courtesy of Kasmin Gallery. Photo: Diego Flores
86tl. Archive PL/Alamy Stock Photo
86tr. © Frank Stella. ARS, NY and DACS, London 2020/Photo © 2019. Digital image, The Museum of Modern Art, New York/Scala, Florence
86b. © Estate of Stuart Davis/VAGA at ARS, NY and DACS, London 2020. Image Courtesy of Kasmin Gallery. Photo: Diego Flores
87t. © The Estate of Robert Morris/Artists Rights Society (ARS), New York/DACS, London 2020/Photo © Tate
87b. © Judd Foundation/ARS, NY and DACS, London 2020/Photo: Christie's Images, London/Scala, Florence
88. © Estate of Stuart Davis/VAGA at ARS, NY and DACS, London 2020. Photograph Courtesy of Sotheby's, Inc. © 2019
89. © Judd Foundation/ARS, NY and DACS, London 2020
90. The Collection of Tommy and Gill LiPuma. Photo courtesy the Parrish Art Museum, Water Mill, NY
92. © Estate of David Smith/VAGA at ARS, NY and DACS, London 2020/Image courtesy of the Weatherspoon Art Museum at UNC Greensboro
95. © 2019. Digital image Whitney Museum of American Art/Licensed by Scala
96. © The Willem de Kooning Foundation/Artists Rights Society (ARS), New York and DACS, London 2020/Photo courtesy The Forum Gallery
97. © Estate of Stuart Davis/VAGA at ARS, NY and DACS, London 2020. Photo © 2019. Digital image Whitney Museum of American Art/Licensed by Scala
99. Collection of Anthony F. Bultman IV and Family. Photo courtesy the Parrish Art Museum, Water Mill, NY
102t. ©Estate of Yvonne Pène du Bois McKenney/© 2019. Digital image Whitney Museum of American Art/Licensed by Scala
102b. ©Estate of Yvonne Pène du Bois McKenney/© 2019. Digital image Whitney Museum of American Art/Licensed by Scala
103t. ©Estate of Yvonne Pène du Bois McKenney/© 2019. Digital image Whitney Museum of American Art/Licensed by Scala
103b. ©Estate of Yvonne Pène du Bois McKenney/© 2019. Digital image Whitney Museum of American Art/Licensed by Scala
104. ©Estate of Yvonne Pène du Bois McKenney/© 2019. Digital image Whitney Museum of American Art/Licensed by Scala
105t. ©Estate of Yvonne Pène du Bois McKenney/© 2019. Digital image Whitney Museum of American Art/Licensed by Scala
105b. ©Estate of Yvonne Pène du Bois McKenney/© 2019. Digital image Whitney Museum of American Art/Licensed by Scala
106. ©Estate of Yvonne Pène du Bois McKenney/© 2019. Digital image Whitney Museum of American Art/Licensed by Scala
109. The Artchives/Alamy Stock Photo
111. 'Photography: Patrick Young, The University of Michigan-School of Art & Design.' © Estate of Meta Vaux Warrick Fuller
112t, 112ct, 112cb. © Heirs of Aaron Douglas/VAGA at ARS, NY and DACS, London 2020/Everett Collection Inc./Alamy Stock Photo
112b. © Heirs of Aaron Douglas/VAGA at ARS, NY and DACS, London 2020/Everett Collection Historical/Alamy Stock Photo
114. © Donna Mussenden Van Der Zee, Courtesy Howard Greenberg Gallery, New York
116. © Estate of Norman Lewis; Courtesy of Michael Rosenfeld Gallery LLC, New York. Photo courtesy National Gallery of Art, Washington, DC
117. Atlanta University Center, Robert W. Woodruff Library
118–119. Allen Family Collection
120. Photo Mark Ostrander, courtesy of Conner • Rosenkranz, NY
122. Photo Mark Ostrander, courtesy of Conner • Rosenkranz, NY
123. Photo Mark Ostrander, courtesy of Conner • Rosenkranz, NY
124. Adam and Eve, 2020. © Estate of Paul Manship. Photo Mark Ostrander, courtesy of Conner • Rosenkranz, NY
125. Photo Mark Ostrander, courtesy of Conner • Rosenkranz, NY
129. Photo Mark Ostrander, courtesy of Conner • Rosenkranz, NY
130. © Gill & Lagodich, 2019. Photo credit: Simon Cherry
135. © Gill & Lagodich, 2019. Photo credit: Simon Cherry
138. © Gill & Lagodich, 2011. Photo credit: Eric M. Tollefson
141. © Gill & Lagodich, 2019. Photo credit: Simon Cherry

143. © Gill & Lagodich, 2019. Photo credit: Simon Cherry
144. © Gill & Lagodich, 2019. Photo credit: Simon Cherry
145. © Gill & Lagodich, 2019. Photo credit: Simon Cherry
146. The Picture Art Collection/Alamy Stock Photo
149. Courtesy Barnard College Archives
152. Avery Galleries, Bryn Mawr, Pennsylvania
155. Avery Galleries, Bryn Mawr, Pennsylvania
158. Richard Rossello, Haverford, Pennsylvania
159. Avery Galleries, Bryn Mawr, Pennsylvania
162t. Courtesy Colonial Williamsburg Foundation
162bl. Courtesy Colonial Williamsburg Foundation
162br. Courtesy Colonial Williamsburg Foundation
164. Conservation Division, Philadelphia Museum of Art
166. Copyright 1999 Carl Grimm
167. Courtesy Longevity Art Preservation
168–169. Allen Family Collection
171. Heritage Image Partnership Ltd/Alamy Stock Photo
173. Courtesy of the Pennsylvania Academy of the Fine Arts, Philadelphia. Gift of Mrs. Sarah Harrison (The Joseph Harrison, Jr. Collection)
175. © Heirs of Josephine Hopper/Licensed by Artists Rights Society (ARS) NY/DACS, London 2020/Private Collection/Photo © Christie's Images/Bridgeman Images
177. CC0 1.0 Courtesy The Metropolitan Museum of Art, New York
179t. Isabella Stewart Gardner Museum, Boston. Photo: Sean Dungan
179b. Photo © 2019 The Barnes Foundation
182. Art Collection 3/Alamy Stock Photo
183. Photography ©Terra Foundation for American Art, Chicago
185. Printed by permission of the Norman Rockwell Family Agency/Copyright ©1962 (The Connoisseur), the Norman Rockwell Family Entities/Art Connoisseur image provided by Curtis Licensing
186. Hirschl & Adler Galleries, New York; photograph by Eric W. Baumgartner
187. Photo courtesy of Questroyal Gallery, New York
188. © 2019. Image copyright The Metropolitan Museum of Art, New York/Art Resource/Scala, Florence
189. Photo courtesy Michael Altman Fine Art and Advisory Services, LLC
195t. CC0 1.0 Courtesy The Metropolitan Museum of Art, New York
195b. © 2019. Image copyright The Metropolitan Museum of Art, New York/Art Resource/Scala, Florence
197. Courtesy of The Frick Collection/Frick Art Reference Library Archives
198. Courtesy of The Frick Collection/Frick Art Reference Library Archives
199. © Heirs of Josephine Hopper/Licensed by Artists Rights Society (ARS) NY/DACS, London 2020/Courtesy of The Frick Collection/Frick Art Reference Library Archives
201. Art Heritage/Alamy Stock Photo
202. © Andrew Wyeth/ARS, NY and DACS, London 2020/Courtesy of The Frick Collection/Frick Art Reference Library Archives
203. © Estate of Joan Mitchell/ Photograph Courtesy of Guggenheim, Asher Associates
205. © Helen Frankenthaler Foundation, Inc./ARS, NY and DACS, London 2020/Photograph Courtesy of Guggenheim, Asher Associates
206. Historic Collection/Alamy Stock Photo
207. Artepics/Alamy Stock Photo
208. Printed by permission of the Norman Rockwell Family Agency/Copyright © 1945 (Back to Civvies) the Norman Rockwell Family Entities/Photograph Courtesy of Sotheby's, Inc. © 2019
209. Photograph Courtesy of Guggenheim, Asher Associates
214. © Georgia O'Keeffe Museum/DACS 2020/ Photograph Courtesy of Sotheby's, Inc. © 2019
215. © Georgia O'Keeffe Museum/DACS 2020/ Photograph Courtesy of Sotheby's, Inc. © 2019
216. Private Collection/Photo © Christie's Images / Bridgeman Images
217. © Andrew Wyeth/ARS, NY and DACS, London 2020/Photo: © 2020 Andrew Wyeth/ Art Resource NY
218t. Private Collection/Photo © Christie's Images/ Bridgeman Images
218b. Private Collection/Photo © Christie's Images/ Bridgeman Images
219. Photograph Courtesy of Sotheby's, Inc. © 2019
220t. Photograph Courtesy of Sotheby's, Inc. © 2019
220b. Photograph Courtesy of Sotheby's, Inc. © 2019
221. © Andrew Wyeth/ARS, NY and DACS, London 2020/Photograph Courtesy of Sotheby's, Inc. © 2019
222. Private Collection/Photo © Christie's Images/ Bridgeman Images
223t. Photograph Courtesy of Sotheby's, Inc. © 2019
223b. Private Collection/Photo © Christie's Images/ Bridgeman Images
232. © Milton Avery Trust/Artists Rights Society (ARS), New York and DACS, London 2020/ Photo: Artepics/Alamy Stock Photo
234. © Milton Avery Trust/Artists Rights Society (ARS), New York and DACS, London 2019/ Photo: Neuberger Museum of Art, Purchase College, State University of New York, gift of Roy R. Neuberger © Jim Frank
235. RTRO/Alamy Stock Photo
236. The Picture Art Collection/Alamy Stock Photo
237. CC0 1.0 via The Metropolitan Museum of Art, New York
238. Public Domain via The St. Louis Art Museum
240–241. The Picture Art Collection/Alamy Stock Photo
242. © Benton Testamentary Trusts/UMB Bank Trustee/VAGA at ARS, NY and DACS, London 2020/THB X Thomas Hart Benton Indiana Murals: Parks, the Circus, the Klan, the Press. Photograph by: Michael Cavanagh and Kevin Montague, Eskenazi Museum of Art at Indiana University
245. © 2019. Photo Smithsonian American Art Museum/Art Resource/Scala, Florence
246. Niday Picture Library/Alamy Stock Photo
247. The Picture Art Collection/Alamy Stock Photo
250. Fine Arts Museums of San Francisco, Gift of Mrs. Milton S. Latham, 41988
253. Fine Arts Museums of San Francisco, Gift of Mr. and Mrs. John D. Rockefeller 3rd, 1979.7.4
255. Fine Arts Museums of San Francisco, Gift of Mr. and Mrs. John D. Rockefeller 3rd, 1979.7.18
256. Fine Arts Museums of San Francisco, Museum purchase, M.H. de Young Memorial Museum, 47.13
257. © Emily Hagen
258. Photo Archives Durand-Ruel © Durand-Ruel & Cie, all rights reserved
260t. CC0 (Via Wikimedia)
260b. © 2020 The Andy Warhol Foundation for the Visual Arts, Inc./Licensed by DACS, London. 2020/ Photo © Ken Heyman
262. © ARS, NY and DACS, London 2020/© Jasper Johns/VAGA at ARS, NY and DACS, London 2020/© Frank Stella. ARS, NY and DACS, London 2020/Photo: Geoffrey Clements. Courtesy Paula Cooper Gallery, New York, © Estate of Ellsworth Kelly 2020
263t. Courtesy Art Basel
263b. Courtesy Artsy
266. Seattle Art Museum/Gift of Barney A. Ebsworth/Photo Susan Cole
268. Heritage Image Partnership Ltd/Alamy Stock Photo
269. CC BY-SA 2.0 Smithsonian's Freer and Sackler Galleries via flickr
270. © 2019. Digital image Whitney Museum of American Art/Licensed by Scala
271. © 2019. Museum of Fine Arts, Boston. All rights reserved/Scala, Florence
273. Private Collection/Photo © Christie's Images/Bridgeman Images

The publishers have made every effort to trace and contact copyright holders of the illustrations reproduced in this book; they will be happy to correct in subsequent editions any errors or omissions that are brought to their attention.

Sponsors

Our warmest thanks go to our many benefactors, patrons, sponsors, and supporters for their great generosity in the publication of this book.

Principal Benefactor

The Mr. and Mrs. Raymond J. Horowitz Foundation for the Arts, Inc., New York, New York

Principal Patrons

Brenda A. Thompson and Larry D. Thompson, Sea Island, Georgia

Mr. and Mrs. Merritt P. Dyke, Atlanta, Georgia

Patrons

Marcia and Marvin Gilliam, Bristol, Virginia

MONTAG Wealth Management, Atlanta, Georgia

D. Wigmore Fine Art, Inc., New York, New York

Questroyal Fine Art, LLC, New York, New York

Sally and Allen McDaniel, Atlanta, Georgia

Menconi + Schoelkopf, New York, New York

Liz Sterling, New York, New York

Lou and Carol Moelchert, Richmond, Virginia

Michael and Jean Antonello, Minneapolis, Minnesota

Avery Galleries, Bryn Mawr, Pennsylvania

Jeanne Levie Berry, Atlanta, Georgia

Anonymous, Atlanta, Georgia

Principal Sponsors

Jack and Russell Huber, Atlanta, Georgia

Bill and Lyn Reed, Somerville, Tennessee

Joyce and Henry Schwob, Atlanta, Georgia

Cynthia and Thomas Sculco, New York, New York

The Daniel P. and Kathelen V. Amos Fund, Columbus, Georgia

Leon and Joy Borchers, Atlanta, Georgia

Sara and Keith Chambless, Columbus, Georgia

Anna-Louise and Keith Glover, Atlanta, Georgia

Homrich Berg Wealth Management, Atlanta, Georgia

Lacey and Bill Jordan, Atlanta, Georgia

Martha and Jack Pietri, Atlanta, Georgia

Roberta Zeck Foley, Atlanta, Georgia

Sponsors

Anonymous, Atlanta, Georgia

Mrs. William Bowen Astrop, Atlanta, Georgia

Ann and John Beach, Atlanta, Georgia

Howard and Helen Elkins, Atlanta, Georgia

Bob and Sandy London, Atlanta, Georgia

Hollis Taggart, New York, New York

The Woodcrest Foundation, Cathy and Bob Fisher, Trustees, Atlanta, Georgia

Supporters

Carey and Doug Benham, Atlanta, Georgia

Michael D. Horowitz, Lebanon, Georgia

Marian and Carl Mullis, Atlanta, Georgia

Jeb and Eleanor Stewart, Atlanta, Georgia

George Gregory Barnard, Atlanta, Georgia

Jonathan Boos Gallery, New York, New York

Heritage Auctions, New York, New York

Matt and Sue Kendall, Atlanta, Georgia

Dr. Elaine L. Levin, Atlanta, Georgia

Elizabeth Morgan Spiegel, Atlanta, Georgia

Dr. and Mrs. Stuart J. Toporoff, Atlanta, Georgia

Dr. Barbara A. Wolanin, Bethesda, Maryland

First published 2020 by Merrell Publishers Limited,
London and New York
Merrell Publishers Limited
70 Cowcross Street
London EC1M 6EJ

merrellpublishers.com

A catalogue record for this book is available from the Library of Congress and from the British Library

ISBN 978-1-8589-4682-5

Produced by Merrell Publishers Limited
Designed by Nicola Bailey
Edited by Elisabeth Ingles
Picture research by Nick Wheldon
Proofread by Barbara Roby
Indexed by Hilary Bird

Printed and bound in China

Jacket front:
Thomas Pollock Anshutz, The Ironworkers' Noontime
(detail), 1880 (see page 253)

Jacket back:
Arshile Gorky, *Painting*, 1936–37 (see page 95)

Endpapers:
Frames designed by Stanford White, Gill & Lagodich
Fine Period Frames, New York

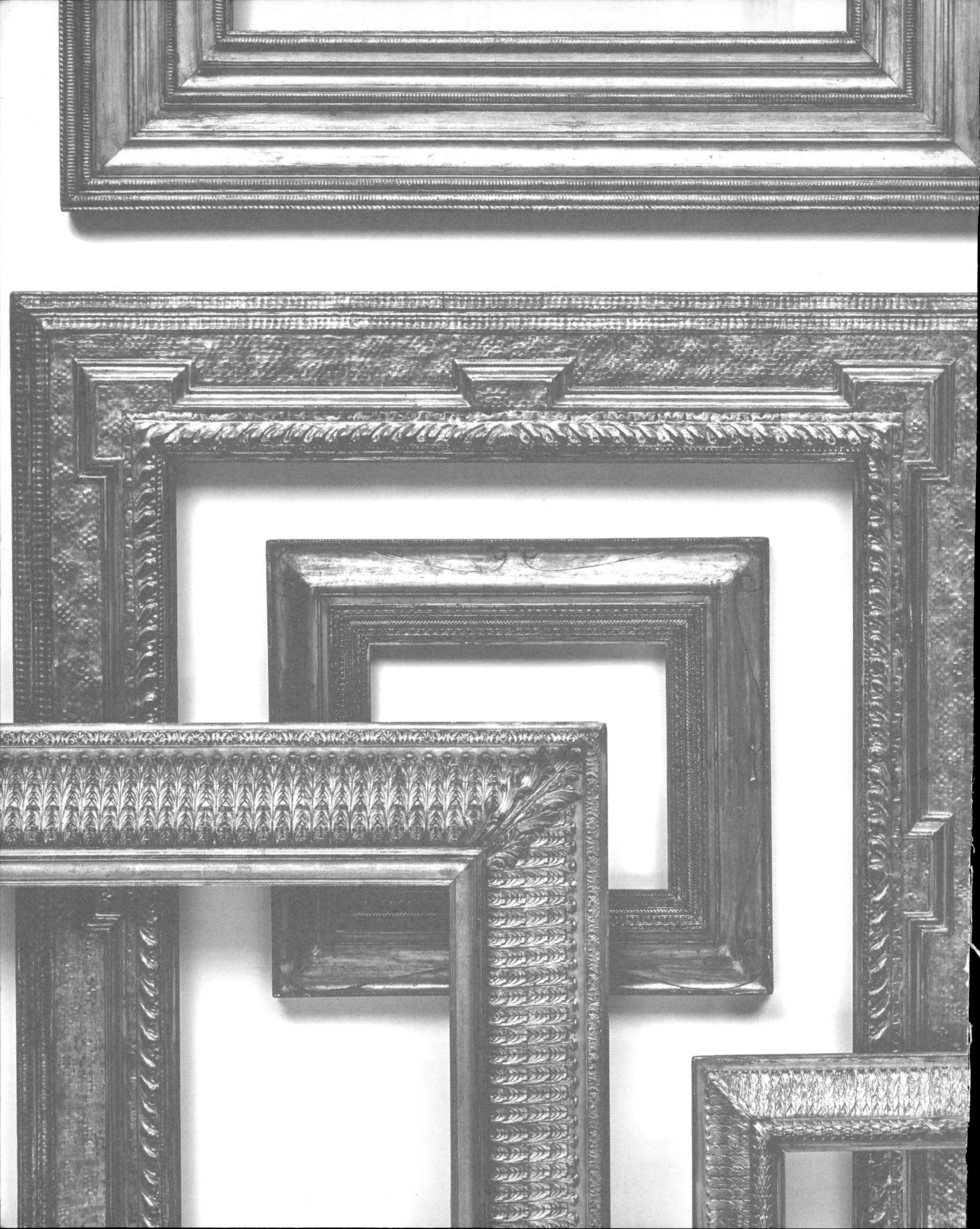